THE CIVIL RIGHTS MOVEMENT IN TENNESSEE

THE
CIVIL RIGHTS MOVEMENT IN TENNESSEE
A NARRATIVE HISTORY

BOBBY L. LOVETT

THE UNIVERSITY OF TENNESSEE PRESS / KNOXVILLE

Copyright © 2005 by The University of Tennessee Press / Knoxville.
All Rights Reserved. Manufactured in the United States of America.
First Edition.

This book is printed on acid-free paper.

Library of Congress Cataloging-in-Publication Data

Lovett, Bobby L.
The civil rights movement in Tennessee : a narrative history / Bobby L. Lovett.
    p. cm.
Includes bibliographical references and index.
ISBN 1-57233-443-6 (hardcover : alk. paper)
1. African Americans—Civil rights—Tennessee—History—20th century.
2. Civil rights movements—Tennessee—History—20th century.
3. African Americans—Segregation—Tennessee—History—20th century.
4. Tennessee—Race relations—History—20th century.
I. Title.

E185.93.T3L68 2005

323'.09768—dc22   2005011647

CONTENTS

ILLUSTRATIONS

DEDICATION

This book is dedicated to the principles of American freedom. The following civil rights leaders are hereby acknowledged: Sterlin N. Adams, Benjamin F. Bell, Curry P. Bond, Robert R. Church, Jr., Jack Civil, Carl A. Cowan, James F. Estes, Lt. George W. Lee, Z. A. Looby, Clarence B. Robinson, Kelly Miller Smith Sr., J. E. Walker, Avon N. Williams, Jr., and A. W. Willis Jr. Additionally, the book is dedicated to Emmett Ballard, Robert J. Booker, Bruce C. Boynton, Henri Brooks, H. C. Bunton, Catherine Burks, Bobby L. Cain, Will E. Campbell, R. H. Craig, W. T. Crutcher, Lois M. DeBerry, Gene M. Gray, Frank Gray Jr., D. S. Cunningham, Charles L. Dinkins, O. Z. Evers, Rita Sanders-Geier, Alexander Gladney, William Harbour, Benjamin L. Hooks, Charles Hamilton Houston, the Howard High School sit-in demonstrators, Billy Kyle, Dwight V. Kyle, Paul LaPrad, James M. Lawson, Jr., John Lewis, George A. Long, H. T. Lockard, Roy C. Love, James Mapp, Thurgood Marshall, J. D. Martin, Tarlease Matthews, John and Viola McFerrin, Willa McWilliams, J. Allen McSwain, Joseph M. Michael, Milton L. Minyard, Ira Murphy, James C. Napier, R. W. Norsworthy, Diane Nash, S. A. Owens, Leon A. Ransom, William B. Redmond, Raymond Richardson, Avon Rollins, Glenn Smiley, Vasco and Maxine A. Smith, A. Philip Randolph, Walter C. Robinson, Theotis Robinson Jr., Cordell H. Sloan, Eliehu Stanback, Russell B. Sugarmon Jr., Alphonso Sumner, the Tennessee Caucus of Black State Legislators, Andrew P. Torrence, Jessie H. Turner Sr., C. T. Vivian, J. E. Walker, Maurice C. Weaver, Ida B. Wells, W. F. Yardley, and Jim Zwerg. This dedication also recognizes the eleven students who integrated Clinton High School, the officials of the Oak Ridge school system, the governors of Tennessee, the many plaintiffs of civil rights court cases, the NAACP, the NCLC, the Freedom Movement in Memphis, and all other civil rights leaders, organizations, men and women regardless of color, who gave their time and talents and even risked their safety and lives in order that the civil rights movement could move forward in Tennessee.

I also respectfully dedicate this book to my parents, the late Edward K. and Frances M. Lovett, who endured the effects of Jim Crow all their lives. Until I researched this book, I had not realized and appreciated their will to survive and produce offspring in a society so offensive, oppressive, and brutal to the aspirations of Negroes. They migrated from rural Mississippi and rural West Tennessee, respectively, with their families during the Great Depression, and met and married in Memphis. Edward served as a staff sergeant in the U.S. Army from World War II until his death in 1961. Frances worked in a World War II furniture factory and later as a domestic in homes in Memphis until her death in August 1960. They barely lived forty years—just long enough to see the rising sun of desegregation and the beginning sunset of Jim Crow. Their tenacity and endurance—despite relatively short lives—overcame the ravaging disease of American racism and the educational and occupational constraints placed on their future possibilities. Their hopes and aspirations remained in me and the other three children (Louis William, Julian, and Katherine Ann). Except for my sister, who died in 1993 at age forty-six from lupus, we children have survived, achieved middle-class status, and prospered in spite of being born within a brutal and merciless Jim Crow system. And now we endure Jim Crow's persistent offspring—a continuing racially divided American society ruled by *de facto* racial discrimination and the designation of racial categories.

Nevertheless, the lives of Edward and Frances Lovett account for this book being made possible through one of their children. Their more than twenty-two grandchildren and more than fifteen great-grandchildren yet benefit from their sacrifices and from the contributions of the civil rights leaders within this book. I hope that many other citizens within and without Tennessee shall benefit from the telling of this American-Tennessee story, *The Civil Rights Movement in Tennessee: A Narrative History.*

PREFACE

In as much as many have taken in hand to set in order a narrative of those things which have been fulfilled among us, just as those who from the beginning were eyewitnesses and ministers of the word delivered them to us, it seemed good to me also, having had perfect understanding of all things from the very first, to write to you an orderly account, most excellent Theophilus, that you may know the certainty of those things in which you were instructed.

LUKE 1:1–4

I was fortunate to study the papers of the late Senator Avon N. Williams Jr., which are stored at Tennessee State University. I appreciate the encouragement I received from Senator Williams, his wife, Joan, his daughter, Wendy, and his son, Avon III, to write something biographical about Avon Williams's fruitful career. However, the process of exploring a possible biography only led me to the conclusion that more research was needed to know how far back in Tennessee history the civil rights movement extended and how all state divisions and other persons in Tennessee were affected by this movement. Avon Williams was Tennessee's foremost civil rights attorney; however, the movement in Tennessee included thousands of participants and dozens of lawyers and civil rights leaders. Even more, the Tennessee civil rights movement preceded and extended beyond the careers of most civil rights attorneys.

Therefore, I soon learned through my early research that hardly any of us Tennesseans, including historians, knew the whole story and the complexity of the civil rights movement in Tennessee, which affected and still affects all our lives. Although many people say they were involved in the movement, perhaps 90 percent or more of us lived during the 1950s and 1960s without being active in the demonstrations. Except for being occasional participants or observers of a march, mass meeting, or public demonstration, most of us saw these developments through the eyes of others. And persons who fought against the movement (black or white) mostly have remained quiet until now. The story of the civil rights movement reveals Negro and white leaders in the fight for justice and equality in Tennessee—a story not yet closed on either side. More than fifty years have passed since *Brown v. Board of Education Topeka* (1954); moreover, many memories have faded to no more than a recounting of news reports; and more important, the current generation of students have barely heard about the Tennessee movement from their teachers, who really have had no comprehensive resource to explain the details.

Yet, there are many books, including ones just now appearing, on the civil rights movement, but their focus is usually on great men and women, their memoirs, general movements across the South, and the popularly remembered events of the 1950s and 1960s. There is not much about Tennessee's civil rights story. The most recent textbooks on Tennessee history include general information about the movement, and the *Tennessee Historical Quarterly* has published a few articles, such as "Few Black Voices Heard: The Black Community and the 1956 Desegregation Crisis in Clinton" by June N. Adamson, "Darwin School and Black Public Education: Cookeville in the Decade of the Brown Decision" by Wali R. Kharif, "White Lunch Counters and Black Consciousness: the Story of the Knoxville Sit-ins" by Cynthia G. Fleming, and "The Struggle of African Americans in Fayette County: To Fulfill the Unfulfilled Right of the Franchise" by Linda T. Wynn. The book *Vanderbilt Divinity School: Education, Contest, and Change* (2001), edited by Dale A. Johnson, includes essays on Nashville civil rights leaders Kelly Miller Smith Sr. and James M. Lawson Jr., but such grassroots personalities often are missing from the bigger story. David Halberstam's *The Children* (1998) is the best detailed account of the movement in Nashville but does not cover events elsewhere in Tennessee.

Therefore, the work I had begun, which originally focused solely on the life of Avon N. Williams Jr., eventually led me to research a larger and more complex history, that of Tennessee's civil rights movement. Among Tennessee's civil rights lawyers, nevertheless, Williams shines the brightest. He handled many court cases and much state legislation to effect change in the state, and in dealing with civil rights cases and related legislation, his career undoubtedly was the longest—forty-two years. Other Negro leaders—especially in Memphis—directed the movement in the streets, worried the federal district courts, and defended jailed demonstrators in county and city courtrooms. Particularly in Memphis we must recognize a host of civil rights lawyers and political and civic leaders, including those mentioned in this book's dedication and many more. I have talked to some of them or their survivors, had conversations with persons close to them, used their papers and letters, or drew on newspaper accounts found in local libraries.

I have consulted many books, articles, and papers to find information about the movement and the politics of the time. These publications are listed in the brief bibliography as suggested sources and references for the general reader and especially for teachers and their students. I have also included a bibliographic essay to specify my sources in more detail. Newspapers, Negro and white, served as the eyes and ears of the civil rights movement, and, therefore newspapers from across the state are appropriately noted throughout the book. My regular visits to the Tennessee State Library and Archives (TSLA) in Nashville made this chore convenient, because the TSLA staff files the microfilmed newspaper copies by counties and cities. Reading hundreds of newspapers is a lonely, tedious task for a scholar without graduate assistants and hired help. Over time I consulted other sources and even visited some of the towns and cities to corroborate news accounts, because I found that reporters sometimes made mistakes when writing stories about Negroes—often using police information rather than consulting the people themselves.

Newspaper photographs are so numerous that I could include no more than a few symbolic ones to provide visual reminders of the civil rights movement and its participants. The Metropolitan Nashville–Davidson County Archives afforded me the excellent file of photographs given to them by the former *Nashville Banner* newspaper, and the archives staff and members of the Friends of the Metro Archives have always been gracious about my research interests. The main facilities of the Nashville Public Library in downtown has a "Banner Room" with files from this longtime daily, which ceased publishing in 1998. At the main public libraries in both Chattanooga and Nashville, I saved a lot of time by using their folders of newspaper clippings on civil rights and related topics. These folders are extremely helpful to a lone researcher. Most of the large city libraries had audio tapes of interviews. The downtown public library in Nashville recently opened a Civil Rights Collection—thanks to philanthropists Bill and Wilma King of Nashville. Other sources used here include census data, city directories, local and county histories, some county records at the TSLA, records and papers of state agencies, and the papers of the governors of Tennessee. I was particularly interested in getting as close as possible to the hearts and heads of the governors to really ascertain how they felt about their minority citizens and the civil rights movement. In the case of the papers of Governor Buford Ellington, the files and letters for 1959–62 are missing. Apparently, someone removed the papers, or else these files (i.e., the ones referring to Tennessee State University) were never included in the collection. And yet these letters would reveal the most conservative side of Governor Ellington in regard to the sit-in demonstrations, the Freedom Rides, and the turmoil at Tennessee State University and how he related to Negro citizens. I had to consult alternative sources—letters between Ellington and neighboring governors, particularly in Alabama, Arkansas, and Georgia, as well as the papers and correspondence of various departments of the Tennessee government, including the Senate and House journals, messages of the governors of Tennessee, records of the commissioner of education, State Department of Education records, and the *Biographical Directory of the Tennessee General Assembly* in the State Archives.

I used the papers of Avon N. Williams Jr., Walter C. Robinson, and Clarence B. Robinson—all housed in the Special Collections of Tennessee State University, where staff members treated me dearly and like another member of the staff. I reviewed the list of Robert R. Church Jr.'s papers, articles and papers on Maxine Smith, and the Kelly Miller Smith papers. The few papers on Z. A. Looby and James C. Napier are housed at Fisk University Library's Special Collections, and there, as usual, Beth Howse, the director, accommodated my every request. I was fortunate to spend several days at the Memphis–Shelby County Room of the new Memphis Public Library on Poplar Avenue and to be served by the gracious staff. For several days, the staff at Special Collections, Vanderbilt University Libraries, also provided me access to the Kelly Miller Smith Papers and the James G. Stahlman Papers.

On March 6, 2002, while in the Memphis–Shelby County Room, a gentleman who had been watching me came to my table and asked if he knew me. Ironically, on that day of several spent in the Memphis library, I was working with the Maxine Smith Papers, which the facility had recently received. The meeting turned into a conversation with none other than Dr. Vasco Smith, Maxine Smith's husband and a leader in the Memphis movement. I reminded him that he had been my dentist when I was in the seventh grade at Porter Junior High School in Memphis. I took the opportunity to get several perspectives from him about certain people, including Avon Williams and George W. Lee, and to hear his opinions on the civil rights movement. I also had the opportunity to use the George W. Lee Papers and the extensive photographs file at the Memphis Library's Memphis–Shelby County Room. While there for my second trip in May 2004, staff member Wayne Dowdy, who has published several articles on E. H. Crump, was gracious enough to afford me time to discuss some historical interpretations and perspectives about this former political boss.

I saved conversations for the last part of my research process, taking only written notes, and I made these encounters quite informal and conversational as a method of corroborating specific incidents and adding personal accounts. I avoided making the story another set of interviews and "oral history of the Civil Rights Movement"—which may please some and displease others, but at any rate will, hopefully, forestall too many telephone calls telling me that "you left so-and-so out, and he or she definitely should be included in this book." I am grateful for the conversations with many other persons, including Julian Blackshear, Calvin Calhoun, Richard Dinkins, Renard Hirsch, Milton Kennerly, Dwight V. Kyle (whom I reached in California via telephone), Dwight Lewis, Kwame Lillard, Elizabeth McClain, Joy Sims, Jamye Coleman, and McDonald Williams. I also attended recent civil rights commemoration events to see and hear James Bevel, Bernard Lafayette, James Lawson, Diane Nash, and C. T. Vivian.

On May 27, 2004, I motored to Memphis to hear an ACLU panel on *Brown*, which featured Mayor Willie Herenton, Judge Otis Higgs, the new black editor of the *Memphis Commercial Appeal*, and others, including the hosting staff of the National Civil Rights Museum. I was intrigued to hear Judge Higgs proclaim emphatically that "Memphis will never be integrated!" I also took photographs and talked to Jacqueline Smith, who continues to sit on a sofa across the street from the National Civil Rights Museum to protest being forced to move from her home in the Lorraine Motel in order to make way for the museum. She also was protesting the commercialization of "Dr. King's image." We must be careful about placing the civil rights movement in vaults and confining the movement to narrow timeframes and places. America's civil rights movement is far from being over.

Through one of my former secretaries, Latoya Gibson, I found Bobby L. Cain—one of the first Negroes to graduate, in 1957, from the integrated Clinton High School; he now lives just north of Tennessee State University in a black Nashville suburb. He was gracious about allowing a conversation in his home and reading a section of the manuscript. And then, while putting the finishing touches on another book, *A Touch of Greatness: History of Tennessee State University, 1909–2003*, I discovered a photograph of Cain in the *Meter*, taken when he enrolled at TSU for the 1957–58 academic year. In *Life* magazine I discovered a beautiful picture of him and nine other African American students walking from the Negro community to Clinton High School during those turbulent days in September 1956. Cain traveled to his hometown of Clinton in May 2004 to commemorate the fiftieth anniversary of the *Brown* decision with the town's people.

I especially appreciate the staff at the Metropolitan Archives in Nashville, the Nashville Room in the downtown public library, the Tennessee State University Library's Special Collections, Fisk University Library, the Tennessee State Library and Archives, libraries in Memphis, Chattanooga, Knoxville, Oberlin College, Wilberforce University, Howard University, and the National Archives and Records Administration. I also thank the staff at the Vanderbilt University Law School for guiding me to information in the law library and the Federal Judicial Center Web site, among other sources. I am grateful to Susan Chappell, line editor, who was referred to me by John Egerton after he read the rough manuscript. After having lunch with Egerton and the late Sam Smith (at the time, my colleague and a retired history professor at Tennessee State University), I was even more encouraged to finish this writing project. I regret that Sam Smith has passed away, because being a European American (like Egerton) did not deter him (or Egerton) at all from embracing and promoting his friends, whatever their color of skin. I also appreciate Wali R. Kharif, professor of history at Tennessee Technological University, and Robert Belton, professor of law at Vanderbilt University, for careful review of the manuscript and for making critical remarks that led to improvements and corrections. I also thank the University of Tennessee Press editors for their comments and suggestions for the improvement of the structure and accuracy of this manuscript. I give credit to all the articles, authors, books, collections, and libraries listed in the bibliography and others that contributed to my knowledge about the history of Tennessee and the civil rights movement. This project truly has been a great reading, study, research, and writing program for me. I have learned a lot.

Bobby L. Lovett
January 21, 2005

A NOTE ON TERMINOLOGY

The persistent and evolving uses of racial terminology can be confusing to both writers and readers. However, American historians—and particularly African American historians—must continue to use such terms so long as the artificial concept of "race" matters to Americans, who otherwise may not understand historical explanations without such descriptive terms. Therefore, in this book, I use *Negro, black, Colored,* and *African American* to label persons of African descent who descended from American slaves. The reason I use different terms rather than one term throughout the book is to avoid historical anachronism; that is, I try to avoid using terms *not* used by the people of a particular historical period. The terms *Negro, mulatto,* and *Colored* (but seldom *black* and never *African American*) were used often during the antebellum period (i.e., before the Civil War). *Colored, Negro* more often, and sometimes *Afro-American* (but seldom *black*) were used thereafter. *Afro-American* and *Colored* were preferred by late-nineteenth-century and early-nineteenth-century light-skinned, elite-class Negroes, who were often first- or second-generation mulattoes (having a mixture of white, black, Indian, and other non-African blood) and who argued that they were "neither black nor white." This made for a heated ethnic debate, and in 1959 an *Ebony* magazine survey concluded that blacks preferred *Negro* to *Colored* and that the word *Negro* "has official status and is legally binding." However, *Colored* and *Negro* (the latter "a member of the black race," says *Webster's Dictionary*) became offensive, especially to young activists during the mid-1960s, when the more militant and defiant term *black* was popularized. *Black* was spelled with both a capital B, as demanded by militants who argued for "respect" of Americans of African descent, and a small *b*, as used by writers in an adjectival sense. *Black* was used almost solely until non-blacks within American society gave the term negative meanings along the lines of "militant, dirty, soiled, and dark-skinned." And there were also negative terms like *blackball,* meaning "to exclude socially." Since the 1980s, the term *African American* became more appropriate—although still used interchangeably with the term *black*. *African American* discarded the notion of race and denoted cultural and geographical origin, describing those of African descent who descended directly from people enslaved in Colonial America and the United States from 1619 through 1865. Thus, *African American* set them apart from immigrants who settled in the United States from the West Indies, South America, Africa, and other places within the huge African Diaspora.

INTRODUCTION

THE HISTORICAL BACKGROUND

As soon as they arrived in 1779 to help build Fort Nashborough on the Cumberland River, slaves, free Negroes, and others resisted oppression and discrimination in Tennessee. They fought for equal rights and full human freedom. In 1780, when the daily use of the terms *white* and *black* was not so widespread, free Negroes, including Jack Civil among the original settlers, protested when the other settlers discriminated against them in the allocation of land grants. Civil left Nashville and resettled in a place later called "Nickajack Cave" in Middle Tennessee. Elihu Embree, a Quaker living in Jonesborough, published two of America's earliest abolitionist newspapers, the *Manumission Intelligencer* (1819) and the *Emancipator* (1820). Robert Renfro, a slave and the owner of "Black Bob's Tavern," successfully sued his absentee owner for freedom before his death in 1822. Some Negro and white leaders helped Tennessee slaves escape to the North. Alphonso M. Sumner was the first native Negro brave enough to organize a freedom movement in Tennessee. A free Negro barber, Sumner opened Nashville's first Negro school in 1833 and allegedly wrote passes for runaway slaves until he was caught, whipped and exiled in 1837 to Cincinnati. There he edited the newspaper *Disenfranchised American*.

Racial conservatives successfully moved to disenfranchise Tennessee's free Negro citizens through constitutional changes in 1835, although free Negroes protested and submitted petitions to prevent these changes. During the Great Revival of the 1830s and 1840s, urban Negroes demanded their own churches, and because of the need for the South to show a more human face of slavery, some white churches granted Negro members the freedom to operate quasi-independent congregations in Columbia, Edgefield, Knoxville, Memphis, and Nashville. Negro churches would serve as educational centers and gathering places throughout the civil rights movement.

When working-class citizens and European immigrants in Nashville thought that the Negroes offered too much socioeconomic competition, they started a small race riot in December 1856, forcing some free Negro entrepreneurs to flee town. Also, in late 1856, whites reacted to rumors of rebellions by the ten thousand slaves who worked the iron-producing plantations in Tennessee; consequently, in various parts of Tennessee, whites abused suspected slaves and hanged some of them. Recalling those times for the *Nashville Tennessean* in 1933, James C. Napier told how, as free Negroes, he, his mother, and siblings fled from Nashville to Cincinnati aboard the steamboat *Wenoah*. The Fugitive Slave Law, enacted in 1850, had made it difficult for the Underground Railroad to operate, and the U.S. Supreme Court in 1857 issued the *Dred Scott v. Sanford* decision, which interpreted Negroes as non-citizens. Nevertheless, a change was on the horizon.

That change came decisively with the eruption of the Civil War—the result of the longstanding sectional conflict over slavery and, more immediately, the November 1860 election, in which Abraham Lincoln, who opposed expanding slavery into the territories, became president. When Tennessee joined the Confederacy in June 1861, many urban Negroes, both enslaved and free, hid rather than allow themselves to be taken off to fight for the rebellion. When testifying before the U.S. Southern Claims Commission (1877), William C. Napier (James C. Napier's father) said, "I was on the side of the Union from the time the first gun was fired to today." He believed that the secession movement would destroy the Union and "the condition of a free man of color [would] be made intolerable and induced to slavery." Indeed the freedmen and their descendants would be among the most loyal citizens to sustain the Fourth of July celebration throughout the former Confederate South. Negroes often preceded these celebrations with a parade, including signs with civil rights messages.

When Union troops entered Nashville in February 1862, it became the first Confederate state capital to fall. Military Governor Andrew Johnson, upon his arrival in March 1862, committed himself to reconstructing Tennessee. In September, Daniel Wadkins and other Negroes opened the first freedmen's schools. Northern missionaries, both Negro and white, helped the freedmen establish hospitals, schools, churches, and colleges. Some 20,133 United States Colored Troops served in the victorious Union Army of Tennessee.

The organization of the Negro's civil rights movement began in earnest in 1864 and continued through 1880. The objectives included (1) the ending of economic slavery through the constitutional process, (2) gaining equal rights and suffrage, and (3) obtaining due process and equal protection of laws.

The leaders of this movement used the following tactics: forming schools to educate the Negro people; recruiting Negroes for the Union army; forming associations to achieve social, economic, and political goals; and forming an alliance with the Republicans.

To achieve their goals and objectives, Tennessee's Negro leaders organized freedom rallies, petitioned Johnson in October 1864 to declare slavery dead, formed the Tennessee Chapter of the Equal Rights League in November 1864 to push for the right to vote and hold office, and developed the State Colored Men's Convention (1865–84) to unite the Tennessee freedmen and articulate black Reconstruction issues without the Republican Party forums. The State Colored Men's Convention met annually in late summer in Nashville, usually in St. John AME Church or in Liberty Hall (the Freedman's Bank Building), drawing delegates from across Tennessee. In March 1865, Tennessee citizens approved amending the state constitution to abolish slavery. In December of that year, slavery was abolished across the nation with the enactment of the Thirteenth Amendment to the U.S. Constitution. Congress granted citizenship, due process of laws, and equal protection of the laws to freedmen in the Civil Rights Act of 1866, and this act became the Fourteenth Amendment to the Constitution (1868). The Tennessee General Assembly granted Negro suffrage in February 1867, and the Fifteenth Amendment to the Constitution (1870) gave freedmen the right to vote in all elections.

With their increased numbers as a result of migration into the towns and cities during Union occupation, Negro men began to use their new political power. After the war, in 1866, when a private Nashville streetcar company tried to segregate its cars, Negroes staged their first "freedom rides" by boarding the cars, paying the fare, and refusing to sit in the "colored section." In 1867, black Republican leaders demanded that transportation to the biracial Fourth of July celebration be integrated. White Republicans agreed, and for the next forty years there was no "colored section" on Nashville's streetcars. In Memphis the Negroes became a majority by 1869. They constituted 37 percent of Nashville's population by 1867 and 40 percent of the city's people by the 1880s. Negroes became a majority in Fayette County and Haywood County and made up nearly half of the citizens in Tipton County—all in West Tennessee. In the late 1880s, ten Negroes were elected to the state legislature: three from Fayette County, two from Hamilton County, two from Haywood County, one from Robertson County, and two from Shelby County.

The nadir of Reconstruction in Tennessee began when former Confederates and neo-Confederates gained power in the Conservative and Democratic parties. These "Redeemers" took over the state government from the

Republicans, wrote a new constitution in 1870, instituted a poll tax, and allowed a reign of terror. Congress offered Negro citizens some assistance by passing the Civil Rights Acts of 1870 and 1871 to punish those who used terror and violence to interfere with other citizens' rights. Congress then approved the 1875 Civil Rights Act to guarantee equal access to public accommodations. In March of that year, Nashville Negroes tested the act with sit-in demonstrations.

By 1881, the civil rights movement had entered a second phase with four major objectives: (1) to regain the right to vote and full political participation, (2) to eliminate discrimination in public accommodations, (3) to remove all Jim Crow practices, and (4) to further promote equal protection of the law through federal and state governments.

Negro citizens resisted the new racial oppression, although whites used the courts, the state legislature, newspapers, local police, anarchy, and terrorism (including lynching) to enforce their new racial order of Jim Crow against Negro citizens. In spring 1881, a group of Negroes marched on a Nashville railroad depot with first-class tickets in hand to conduct another "freedom ride" and protest the state's new Jim Crow railroad law. In 1884, Ida B. Wells, a feisty Negro schoolteacher in Memphis, sued a railroad company for refusing to honor her first-class ticket to travel to the nearby Woodstock community. The local court awarded damages to Wells; however, the Tennessee Supreme Court upheld the company's appeal in April 1887. In 1891, the Memphis school board fired Wells. In 1892, when three Negro businessmen were lynched by a white mob, Wells published a stinging newspaper indictment against white women and their false claims of rape by Negro men. White reaction forced Wells and hundreds of Negro citizens to flee Memphis.

The second phase of the civil rights movement, 1881–1935, came to include a fifth objective—the building of a Negro political economy. The Negro elite especially wanted to avoid the humiliating Jim Crow practices in white-controlled business institutions. Soon after Booker T. Washington and others formed the National Negro Business League in 1900, J. C. Napier formed a Nashville chapter, and chaired the executive committee on the national level. Some of the Tennessee chapters continued into the 1940s. Largely because of the Business League, Negroes in Tennessee formed four banks, two insurance companies, publishing companies, other industries, and local business associations. For instance, to oppose the state's 1905 Jim Crow streetcar law, Negro leaders organized streetcar boycotts in Nashville, Chattanooga, and Memphis, and they formed several streetcar companies.

National authorities struck the Negro's post-emancipation civil rights movement with some severe blows. President Rutherford B. Hayes, a Republican, began the end of Reconstruction with the "Compromise of 1877"—an agreement to cease military occupation of the South and allow the states to deal locally with Negro problems in return for electoral votes in the disputed election of 1876. In other words, the federal government agreed not to interfere in race relations and would let the defeated South alone. In 1883, the U.S. Supreme Court ruled that the 1875 Civil Rights Act was unconstitutional, declaring it an infringement on states' rights. Frederick Douglass called the court's decision "a damnable outrage." The 1890 Morrill Land Grant Act allowed southern states to gain federal funds even if they established separate land-grant colleges for Negroes. Months after Douglass's death in February 1895, seven of the nine justices decided in *Plessy v. Ferguson* (1896) that "separate but equal" facilities for Negro citizens were not unconstitutional and did no injury to them. This beginning of the white solidarity movement was affirmed soon after troops from the North and the South participated side-by-side in the Spanish American War (1898–99). American Negroes also fought in this war, but most of the states in the South (including Tennessee) forbade armed Negro troop involvement. Even Theodore Roosevelt ridiculed the Negro's contribution to that American victory, and as president he backed away from initiating any racial reforms in the United States.

The unbridled drive for wealth and an appetite for imperialism that Roosevelt supported led whites to push full steam ahead toward building an uncharacteristic twentieth-century society—one that was racially separate, unfair, unequal, undemocratic, and justified by spurious social theories such as "survival of the fittest," white supremacy, and the biological inferiority of Negroes and people of color. Race riots, white anarchy, lynching, and social disorder plagued the country. Madison Grant of New York, a Nordic advocate, would intellectualize the white solidarity movement in his book *The Passing of the Great Race* (1916), giving European Americans more justification to maintain "white" as a racial classification and to classify citizens of African descent as "blacks."

The Negro's response was to form civil rights organizations: the Afro-American League in 1890, the Niagara Movement in 1905, the National Association for the Advancement for Colored People (NAACP) in 1909, and the National Urban League in 1910, among others. Ida B. Wells and Mary Church-Terrell met a biracial group in New York City to form the NAACP. In June 1917, Robert R. Church Jr., Mary Church-Terrell's younger brother, and fifty-two other Negroes opened the Memphis chapter of the NAACP. J. C. Napier and others opened the Nashville chapter of the NAACP in January 1919 with ninety-two charter members and soon led two thousand people to the governor's office to protest lynching.

When Negroes and rural whites continued to crowd into the towns, the urban areas became places of conflict, lynching, and racial riots; Knoxville, for example, became the scene of such violence in 1919. Between 1920 and 1950, Tennessee's urban population, as a portion of the total, increased from 26 to 44 percent, with Negroes comprising significant percentages in seventy-one urban areas. Also, according to the U.S. Census, the collapse of the old plantation system between 1890 and 1910 sent more Negroes into the towns, including many who joined the Great Migration. Some five million Negroes and three million impoverished whites would move to the North by 1960. From a high of 26 percent in 1860, Tennessee's Negro population declined to 15.8 percent by 1970. Particularly in West Tennessee, where 70 percent of Negro citizens lived, Tennessee society became more racially oppressive. In Memphis, the regional capital of the Mississippi Delta, socioeconomic decay, political corruption, and archaic social practices imposed by the white majority contributed to the near collapse of democracy. White supremacists in Alabama, Georgia, and Mississippi increasingly entered anti–civil rights campaigns in Tennessee to ensure that regional racism remained intact.

Partly as a result of urbanization, a sense of cultural consciousness among Negroes of all colors and classes emboldened some. In 1924, Nettie Langston-Napier served as president of the Frederick Douglass Historical and Memorial Association to restore and maintain the old civil rights warrior's home in Washington, D.C. By the 1930s, students and faculty at Negro colleges in Tennessee were regularly singing James Weldon Johnson's "Lift Every Voice and Sing"—the "Negro National Anthem"—in various public programs. After the appearance of Howard University professor Alain Locke's book *The New Negro* (1925), there was much talk about the Negro's intent to demand equality in American society. Tennessee was even affected by Marcus Garvey's Universal Negro Improvement Association (UNIA), a movement that expressed black culture, Negro pride, self-help, self-protection and the right to bear arms, separatism, and efforts to establish trade and political connections with Africa. The UNIA had chapters in Alcoa, Chattanooga, Franklin, Henry County, Knoxville, Memphis, Nashville, and other Tennessee communities.

On the night of August 4, 1927, forty-eight Chattanooga policemen invaded the UNIA meeting at the Steele Orphanage ("Liberty Hall"), claiming they were there on a disturbance call. When two armed and uniformed

UNIA men confronted the police about a warrant, the police captain kicked the hallway lamp out, and the shooting began. Three Negroes and one policeman were wounded; women, children, and other UNIA participants were scattered into the streets; and several UNIA officers were arrested. Policemen armed with machine guns entered Negro homes in the area without search warrants, seizing local UNIA records, and disarming the entire Negro community, disregarding the "right to bear arms" provision of the U.S. Constitution. Milton L. Minyard, the head of the Chattanooga UNIA Division, said that the trouble had begun weeks earlier when the city denied the UNIA a parade permit. The *Chattanooga News* (Aug. 5, 1927) congratulated the police "on the firmness they displayed on Thursday night in coping with the belligerent Negro radicals whose nest they raided." The *Negro World*, a UNIA publication, reported the raid on August 20, 1927, while on August 13, the *Baltimore Afro-American* said, "The Chattanooga riot represents the typical Southern white reaction to colored organizations provided with military uniforms and weapons." The UNIA developed a defense fund to defend arrested leaders, including Emery Bailey, James Johnson, Ira Johnson, and Louis Moody. Minyard, who had arrived from Chicago to establish the chapter in 1925, managed to escape to the North. Minerva Alexander served as reporter for the Chattanooga UNIA. Members moved the meetings to northern Georgia. The Federal Bureau of Investigation arrested Marcus Garvey in 1923. A federal court sent him to federal prison in the Deep South. On November 18, 1927, President Calvin Coolidge pardoned Garvey, and the Immigration Service deported him to Jamaica. Garvey continued to run the UNIA until his death in 1940.

Negro protests at both the state and national levels continued. A. Philip Randolph and his Brotherhood of Sleeping Car Porters were demanding rights for Negro workers by 1929. These workers distributed urban newspapers to rural Negro communities along the routes of the trains; some local leaders would often stand by the tracks, waiting for copies of the *Pittsburgh Courier, Chicago Defender, Baltimore Afro-American, Memphis World, Nashville Globe,* and other newspapers to be thrown from the windows of the speeding trains. Carter G. Woodson and other Negro historians had started the Association for the Study of Negro Life and History, Inc. (ASNLH), in 1915, publishing the *Journal of Negro History* by 1916 and directing Negro History Week by 1926. ASNLH workers like Lorenzo Greene visited Tennessee A&I State College before moving on to other places in Tennessee, while selling Negro history materials and urging pride in Negro culture. A chapter of the ASNLH was formed at Tennessee A&I by 1927, and the school began its first Negro history course in 1928, the same year that Fisk University in Nashville began the slave narratives project to record the recollections of local former slaves.

Negroes in Tennessee and the South continued their protests. On July 24, 1931, the Southern Commission on the Study of Lynching met in Chattanooga to present data to Congress for an anti-lynching bill. Negro sociologist Charles S. Johnson of Fisk University and one of the officials from the Southern Baptist Convention in Nashville were present at the meeting. The National Baptist Convention, centered in Nashville, was urging its membership of Negro pastors to preach sermons against the Amos 'n Andy radio show, "which caricatures and degrades the Negro people." In September 1931, the Negro delegates at the state American Legion Convention in Nashville refused to be segregated to the balcony of Ryman Auditorium, taking chairs to the main floor or sitting on the windowsills in acts of defiance and protest. At that meeting, Negro Legionnaires also got R. Q. Venson of Memphis elected as a delegate to the organization's national convention, a first for them. Around the same time, the *Memphis World* was informing its Negro readers that the legislature had forced Michigan State University to admit Negro students into the dormitories, and W. E. B. DuBois was declaring, "Until Negroes are assured a permanent place in the industry of America, the real emancipation of this race will not be accomplished."

In his "Down on Beale" column in the *Memphis World,* beginning in 1931, Nat D. Williams kept alive issues of race. On the surface, Williams's essays seemed simply to be reports on general happenings and gossip on Beale Street—the main business and entertainment thoroughfare in downtown Memphis, which was frequented by huge crowds of Negroes, dominated by Jewish-owned businesses, and patrolled by white policemen. Williams's column occasionally used local, rural Negro dialect in a comical way to criticize blacks for being "loud enough to wake the dead" and using manners on the streets that embarrassed other Negroes in front of whites. (It was estimated in the 1930 census that 402,368 Negroes had left Mississippi and that half of them had come to Memphis.) But Williams's columns contained cleverly disguised messages for his Negro readership—messages that criticized Jim Crow practices and racial discrimination against blacks. Over the years, Williams became increasingly, perhaps unconsciously, bold in his criticisms of local race relations. On May 10, 1932, he wrote, "The Memphis Negroes practically are defenseless, that a black man's life isn't worth a dime. . . . And not a single Negro organization . . . would dare lift its voice in public protest." He was speaking of a recent murder of a Negro man by a white man, which the white justice system had done nothing about. (In that same issue of the *World,* editor Lewis O. Swingler also protested official inaction in the case.) A month later, on June 17, Williams made another bold declaration on the racial situation: "Now, it is one thing most white men don't like, it's the sight of Ham's sons in any kind of position of authority or privilege." Increasingly, the Memphis political machine headed by Edward H. Crump would not tolerate such criticism, especially after 1936, when a stern warning from local police caused Williams to leave the city for a period. Crump disliked what he called "racial agitation" and the various groups—such as the Fellowship of Reconciliation (FOR) and the Commission on Interracial Cooperation (CIC)—which he saw as promoting such activity.

Indeed, groups such as FOR did try to better organize Memphis Negroes against the racial discrimination that prevailed under Crump. In the spring of 1932, the FOR sent Howard A. Kester, its southern organizer, to Memphis, where a new chapter was formed with Ira H. Latimer, a sociology professor at LeMoyne College, as chairman; a pair of white ministers, John C. Petrie and R. L. Owenly, assisted in the organizational effort. Less effective at the time was the local NAACP branch. Although its youth chapter at LeMoyne College attempted to protest police brutality and the sorry state of race relations in Memphis, local NAACP heads refused to allow the organization to upset Boss Crump. Meanwhile, the Memphis chapter of the Urban League also stayed out of Crump's way until the 1940s, when a new director tried to stir things up in the Delta capital.

In spite of the generally oppressive atmosphere in Memphis, the city did see some civil rights success stories. For example, the Tennessee American Legion held its conference in Memphis in August 1933, and R. Q. Venson and Post No. 27, located at 391 Beale Street, recruited white veterans to join a protest against the segregation of blacks in the balcony of the city's downtown Ellis Auditorium. A new chairman was elected as a result. Venson and Post No. 27 became active in the local vanguard against Jim Crow. Indeed, in the mid-1930s, as one era of the Negro's battle for equal rights was ending, a new civil rights movement was already underway in Tennessee and the South.

CHAPTER 1

THE STRANGE CAREER OF JIM CROW

THE EARLY CIVIL RIGHTS MOVEMENT IN TENNESSEE, 1935–1950

Negroes began to initiate a new civil rights movement, slowly and uneventfully—but definitively—during the mid-1930s, with the advent of President Franklin D. Roosevelt's New Deal. At that time, the NAACP developed new strategies against racial discrimination. The chief lawyer in these efforts was Charles Hamilton Houston, a graduate of the Harvard University Law School. Most recently, Houston had rebuilt the law school at Howard University in Washington, D.C., where he engaged his students in researching and debating issues being considered by the nearby U.S. Supreme Court. In 1935, the NAACP hired Houston to head a campaign to attack Jim Crow in the courts. One of Houston's students, who subsequently became deeply involved in the civil rights movement, was the Baltimore native and future Supreme Court justice Thurgood Marshall.

Marshall's mother, Norma, was the sister of Avon N. Williams Sr. (1875–1949), who married Carrie Belle Erskine (1884–1930), the daughter of Charles Cole, a Virginia-born laborer living in Baltimore. Partly because she felt neglected and partly because of her husband's heavy drinking, Carrie left Baltimore in 1918 with the couple's three children, Haydn (b. 1899), Ravine (b. 1900), and Velaine (b. 1902), to live with her sixty-one-year-old widowed grandfather, Frank Erskine, at 1204 East Vine Avenue in Knoxville, Tennessee. The family in Baltimore forced Avon to join his family. He settled down, cut down on drinking, and worked in local restaurants as a waiter. He and Carrie had two more children, Lee Livingston (b. 1919) and Avon Jr. (b. 1921). Avon Jr. would complete Johnson C. Smith College in North Carolina in 1940. Years later, he remembered how, while on his way to college, he would be forced to sit in the back half of a Jim Crow baggage car to which black people were assigned.

Meanwhile, Thurgood Marshall, Avon Jr.'s first cousin, had graduated from the segregated Negro high school in Baltimore in 1925, completed Lincoln University, and entered Howard's law school in 1930. Marshall recalled that he and a group of college mates would meet in the campus library and talk about "What we'd do to the Southern states when we got out [of college]." Upon graduation in 1933 he opened a law practice in Baltimore, "the southern gateway to the North." There, he became involved with the NAACP and filed a suit that successfully forced the University of Maryland to admit Donald Murray, a Negro graduate of Amherst College, to its law school. Charles Hamilton Houston guided Marshall in the case.

Working for the NAACP, Houston developed a strategy that was designed to attack Jim Crow where southern authorities had tried to cut Negroes off at their knees: denying them and their children access to equal and quality education. In the "Tentative Statement Concerning Policy of NAACP in its Program of Attacks on Educational Discrimination" (July 12, 1935), Houston wrote, "The graduate and professional study [program] was selected for attack because a large portion of the leadership of the race should come from Negroes who have had access to graduate and professional schools. The whites are educating their own children for public leadership through graduate and professional study out of taxes in which Negroes contribute, while Negro students are cut off with under-graduate training. In other words, the white system of education is designed to perpetuate the inferior status of Negroes." Houston continued, "Finally, the National Office of the NAACP deems its function in this program to be that of (1) exposing the inequalities and discriminations and (2) wherever requested by the local populace, to render such assistance as it can through its branches and its own staff in making an attack on these evils." In addition to attacking Jim Crow over the issue of admitting Negroes to graduate and professional schools, Houston focused on the issue of public school teacher salaries. He believed that salary cases could persuade Negro teachers to support the NAACP, help finance the movement at the grassroots level, improve Negro schools, and render Jim Crow too expensive for impoverished states to maintain, with its requirements for two of everything—one set of institutions and facilities for whites and one set for Negroes. Thurgood

Marshall would join Houston at the NAACP in October 1936. Houston sent letters to Negro lawyers, asking for their help.

[*]

Among those willing to respond to Houston's call to initiate suits against Jim Crow was one of Tennessee's first civil rights lawyers, Carl A. Cowan of Knoxville. A graduate of the Harvard Law School, Cowan lived at 1412 College Street and began practicing law in 1931 in a one-room office at 100.5 East Vine Avenue. J. Reuben Sheeler, a high school teacher in Athens, Tennessee, seemed willing at first to allow Cowan to file a suit on his behalf against the University of Tennessee law school. But Sheeler backed out for fear of losing his job. In January 1936 William B. Redmond, a recent graduate of Tennessee Agricultural and Industrial State College and a resident of Franklin, contacted Houston about his application for admission to the UT School of Pharmacy, which was being held up by school officials. While Redmond studied chemistry at Fisk University, Cowan and Z. Alexander Looby filed a case of race discrimination against UT.

Born in the West Indies, Z. A. Looby earned a bachelor of law degree from Columbia University and a doctorate in law from New York University before coming to Nashville in 1928. For a while he practiced law in Memphis but found that the local political machine was too oppressive for a progressive Negro to advance there. He returned to Nashville in 1933 but was appalled that Nashville had just four "real good" Negro lawyers. Besides teaching a course at Tennessee A&I, Looby announced the opening on September 25, 1933, of the Kent College of Law, "incorporated under the laws of Tennessee, and of University quality." More than ninety students would study at Kent, and 37 percent of them would pass the bar exam by 1947. The school, however, became a victim of wartime shortages and conscriptions. With so many potential students in military service, it had to close before the end of World War II.

In response to criticism about its new legal strategies, the NAACP declared on March 13, 1937: "We simply stand ready to assist any eligible candidate who exhausts the ordinary means of entering these schools in the event he wishes to go forward with a court fight." The Tennessee trial judge in the Redmond case said that the NAACP, "a New York group," had urged Redmond to commit this mischief. According to the judge, Redmond had not exhausted local remedies before going to court and had not given UT time to respond to his application; furthermore, the Negro public college, Tennessee

A&I, was available to him. Memphis Chancery Court dismissed the case *State of Tennessee ex rel. William B. Redmond, II v. O. W. Hyman, et al.* on April 16, 1937. NAACP officials in New York were disappointed at this outcome because funds were too limited to lose a case. "This [Redmond] case means nothing in 1937," Houston said. "But in 2000 A.D. somebody will look back on the record and wonder why the South spent so much money in keeping [equal] rights from Negroes rather than granting them." After dropping out of the graduate program at Fisk University, Redmond operated several businesses in Franklin, Tennessee, where he eventually ended his career.

[*]

Tennessee continued to abide by its Jim Crow statutes. A 1901 Tennessee law stated, "It shall be unlawful for any school, academy, college, or other place of learning to allow white and colored persons to attend the same school, academy, college, or other place of learning." However, in 1937 Tennessee joined Kentucky, Maryland, Missouri, Oklahoma, Virginia, and West Virginia in providing out-of-state fellowships for its Negro graduate students. According to a Tennessee law enacted that year:

> The State Board of Education (SBOE) is authorized to establish scholarships for colored students, payable out of the state appropriations made for the Agricultural and Industrial College for Negroes. Such scholarships shall be granted to take professional courses not offered in said A&I State College for Negroes, or other state-maintained institutions for Negroes, but which are offered for white students at the University of Tennessee. Such scholarships shall be in an amount sufficient to give the recipient thereof education facilities equal to those provided by the UT, without cost to the recipient in excess of the cost, which would be required to attend the University of Tennessee.

In 1938, the NAACP won its appeal in the case of *Missouri ex rel. Lloyd Gaines v. Canada, Registrar of the University, et al.* This decision, overturning a Missouri state court ruling, required the state to establish a Negro law school; Missouri had previously tried to force Negro law student Lloyd Gaines to use an out-of-state scholarship. Hoping that *Plessy* would protect them from further integration, some states opened graduate and professional schools exclusively for Negroes, although Arkansas, Maryland, and West Virginia, which were unable to bear the extra expense of providing separate programs for a handful of Negro students, admitted them to existing professional schools.

The white colleges and universities had graduated only 7.4 percent of the two thousand Negro college graduates, and the public Negro colleges—90 percent of which were in the South—had no graduate-degree programs by 1937.

Tennessee A&I State Teachers College attempted to start some graduate courses in 1935, with twenty-five school teachers enrolled in the classes. But the state commissioner of education stopped the program within months and ordered a self-study for accreditation. The 1936 study found, among other things, a lack of doctorate-holders on the faculty, low salaries, and the need to hire more faculty members to lower teaching loads. After reflecting on NAACP lawsuits in Kentucky, Maryland, Missouri, Virginia, and West Virginia, the dean at Tennessee A&I wondered aloud when graduate work would be started there. His frustration was shared by the executive committee of the Tennessee State Association of Teachers in Colored Schools, which "waited upon the Commissioner of Education and several members of the State Board of Education" to take action. "Promises were made, but to date there has been no definitive action," observed the editor of the *Broadcaster*, the Tennessee Negro Teachers' Association newsletter, in 1937.

Incidentally, the Southern Association of Colleges and Schools (SACS) had only just begun to recognize historically black colleges and universities (HBCUs) in 1930. During 1930–39, SACS approved seventeen HBCUs, including Fisk University (1930) and Lemoyne College (1932), for a collegiate status, "A" rating; most of the approved institutions, including Fisk and LeMoyne, had white presidents. Tennessee A&I would gain SACS approval during the 1942–49 period, when public HBCUs, all with Negro presidents, gained political ground in the accreditation process.

[*]

President Franklin D. Roosevelt and the liberal wing of the Democratic Party were quietly trying to nudge the South into changing its archaic socioeconomic system. However, behind the "Cotton Curtain," southern leaders perpetuated a corrupt political system that protected them from outside meddling. Liberals hoped that the embarrassment of recent research findings by scholars or the naked power of the federal government might help bring about progressive changes. In 1937, the National Emergency Council, which was started under the New Deal, issued the "Report on the Economic Conditions in the South," which provided conclusive proof of dire economic conditions in that region. Because of Jim Crow practices, the report said, the South did not effectively employ nearly a third of its citizens.

Liberal southern New Dealers convened the Southern Conference for Human Welfare (SCHW) in Birmingham on November 20–23, 1938. They would try to do what the president could not do politically and that was to convince the southern leadership to change its ways. Birmingham was a large industrial town with many downtrodden workers of both races. Mary McLeod Bethune, Benjamin Mays, Charles S. Johnson, James A. Dombrowski, and Myles F. Horton (the latter two from the Highlander Folk School in Tennessee) were present at the Birmingham meeting, which included about twelve hundred delegates in all. On the second day of the meeting, the city commissioner, Theophilus Eugene "Bull" Connor, ordered segregated seating for the meeting, but Eleanor Roosevelt protested by sitting on the Negro side and then taking a seat in the aisle. In his book *Eleanor Roosevelt: First Lady* (1999), James T. Baker notes that after seeing the poor southern whites, unpainted houses, dilapidated cars, and children without shoes and clothes, Mrs. Roosevelt argued that the right to work should know no color lines.

During the following year, 1939, there was an especially important development: the NAACP created the Legal Defense and Educational Fund (LDF) as a separate tax-exempt, public-interest legal organization; it would become the legal arm of the civil rights movement. Along with the NAACP, the LDF would raise money, fight court cases, and strive to help make racial equality a reality in America. With the LDF's assistance, Looby and Cowan once more filed suit against the University of Tennessee in November 1939, using several local qualified Negro candidates for admission to UT's graduate programs—including Joseph M. Michael, L. E. Hardy, Clinton Marsh, Homer L. Saunders, P. L. Smith, and Ezra Totten—as plaintiffs in the case, which was filed in state court in Knoxville. For this lawsuit, *State et rel. Michael et al v. Witham et al.*, the NAACP added Leon A. Ransom, a 1927 graduate of the Ohio State Law School, to the legal defense team. He was Houston's point man for approving the Cowan-Lobby candidates for plaintiffs. Ransom recalled that poorly educated locals acted as if they had never seen Negro lawyers in suits and ties "talking to the judge like they were white people." A police officer was so upset about this bizarre social phenomenon that he struck Ransom, but the judge did nothing about it.

[*]

As a new decade began—and despite the lingering effects of the Great Depression—the civil rights struggle continued on various fronts, both in Tennessee and in other parts of the South. In January 1940, Joseph E. Walker of Memphis, the newly elected president of the National Negro Business League, spoke in Nashville and advised Negroes to gain "religion, education, and money" to uplift themselves, and as the black-owned *Nashville Globe* reported on January 20 and 26, 1940, Negro and white sharecroppers appeared in Washington, D.C., to tell federal officials "stories of unbelievable cruelty, unjust treatment, and hardships" in the South. Tenant farmers wanted settlements at the end of each harvest, fair interest rates instead of the 25–100 percent charged by landowners, and a dollar for each ten-hour workday, plus fifteen cents per hour for overtime. Landowners had been evicting tenant protesters for some time, as reported by Knoxville's Negro newspaper, the *East Tennessee News* on March 31, 1936. In February 1940 the *Globe* reported that Nashville's NAACP, Agora Assembly, Interdenominational Ministers' Alliance, and Negro Board of Trade wrote to city officials, protesting the inordinate unemployment and police brutality affecting Negro citizens.

The Southern Conference on Human Welfare (SCHW) convened its second meeting in Chattanooga on April 14–16, 1940, with more than a thousand delegates attending the meetings in the Memorial Auditorium. Chattanooga was a strong union town, and the Tennessee Valley Authority (TVA), whose goals included the alleviation of regional poverty, was headquartered there. A director of the TVA, David E. Lilienthal, cosponsored the SCHW meeting, and Robert C. Weaver, the Negro assistant secretary in the Department of the Interior, was among the attendees. (Months later, Weaver would be threatening to quit the Roosevelt administration in protest of how Negroes were treated in New Deal agencies.) Among the organizations represented were the NAACP and its Nashville branch, the National Negro Congress, the Highlander Folk School, the National Youth Administration, the Chattanooga Teachers' Union, the Council of Young Southerners, the Congress of Industrial Organizations, the Tennessee League of Women Voters, the Atlanta School of Social Work, the United Mine Workers of America, and the Southern Tenant Farmers' Association. The presidents of several Negro Colleges, including W. J. Hale of Tennessee A&I, were also there.

When Eleanor Roosevelt arrived on Eastern Airlines, a biracial welcoming committee, including the president of Atlanta University and local Negro school children, met her at the Chattanooga Airport. She would speak on "Children in the South" that evening in the Memorial Auditorium. The Howard High School choir provided the music that night. The director of TVA impressed the First Lady and the audience by reporting that the federal agency was attacking poverty and serving 375,000 customers in the valley. However, what he did not say was that after the TVA was established, the NAACP sent Houston and Marshall to investigate the conditions of the Negro workers it employed and that they reported that Negroes had the most menial jobs. Until 1950 only two Negro professionals worked for TVA. Maury Maverick, the mayor of San Antonio, Texas, addressed the meeting, saying, "Civil rights for everybody and poll taxes for none. Let us free our minds from prejudice, let us see to it that the Negro gets full economic opportunity, equal pay for equal work, political justice, protection of civil rights, and education." He urged southerners not to be satisfied as an isolated minority. The delegates concluded that conditions in the South had really worsened in the last two years, according to reports in the *Chattanooga Evening Tribune* (Apr. 15–18, 1940). After the unions had trouble with race vigilantes who opposed integrated meetings, the SCHW decided to move both its next biennial meeting and its headquarters from Chattanooga to Nashville. Pressure against the poll tax—which restricted participation by poor people (especially Negroes) in the electoral process by, in effect, charging them for the right to vote—could be applied better in the state capital, it was thought. On April 26, 1940, the *Nashville Globe* announced that Negroes were welcome to attend the anti–poll tax rally at the War Memorial Building in Nashville on May 19.

In June 1940, large crowds and representatives of the Knoxville NAACP chapter entered the Knoxville Chancery Court to hear Looby, Ransom, and Cowan argue the *Michael* case against the University of Tennessee. State Attorney General Roy Beeler was present to represent Tennessee. Cowan sought a writ of mandamus to force the officials to admit Michael and the other Negro students named in the suit to graduate and law programs. However, the judge dismissed the case, declaring that the plaintiffs' lawyers should have sued the UT trustees as a corporate body. The decision to file the case in a state court, rather than federal district court, had proved to be a mistake, and it was one that the NAACP lawyers would learn from as they pursued later cases.

That same month, for the annual NAACP meeting in New York, President Roosevelt did not show up to speak, but he at least sent greetings: "Organizations like yours are necessary safeguards in a democracy. You remind us constantly of our principles by calling our attention to our weaknesses and our deficiencies. This service of your organization to strengthen Democracy is needed now more than ever." His message was appreciated, although some Negro leaders felt that Roosevelt was not doing much to help the civil rights movement.

At the time, the union organizer A. Philip Randolph was protesting openly about racial discrimination in war industries. In Europe, the Nazis were imposing on Jewish populations an oppressive racial system that already existed for Negroes in America. The Nazis, of course, went even further and developed a program to commit genocide against their minority citizens. Comparisons of Hitler's Germany to the racially oppressive socioeconomic system in the American South would bring endless embarrassment to FDR and northern industrialists. In September 1940, Randolph, Walter White of the NAACP, and others presented Roosevelt with a list of seven points for improvement of racial conditions, including appointment of Negroes as military officers, federal administrators, and draft board members. On October 16, 1940, Roosevelt appointed Benjamin O. Davis Sr. (1877–1970) as the nation's first Negro general in the U.S. Army. W. E. B. DuBois and Atlanta University started *Phylon, A Journal of Race and Culture* to report on Negro progress and civil rights–related events.

The LDF and the NAACP had begun addressing the matter of states paying Negro public school teachers less than what white teachers were paid. In *The NAACP's Legal Strategy against Segregated Education* (1987), Mark V. Tushnet said salary differentials by race ranged from $25 to $55 per month for teachers and reached $150 per month for school principals. On January 4, 1935, Houston had written to Looby and two other Negro lawyers, asking, "Is there any agitation in Nashville on the part of the schoolteachers for equal salaries? If so, what procedure would you suggest in raising the question? Are there any teachers available for test plaintiffs? Would any of you or other lawyers in Nashville be interested in handling such a case?" The first salary case was filed on December 8, 1936, in Maryland, and in August 1939 authorities there agreed to equalize salaries. This victory encouraged Looby to send a petition about the pay issue to members of the Nashville City Council and the mayor, who acknowledged the need for equal pay. The members of the Nashville Board of Education, however, refused to deal either with the matter itself or with any Negro lawyer.

In Chattanooga, Clarence B. Robinson encouraged Negro teachers to start agitating for equal pay. A Chattanooga native who completed Howard High School in 1929 and received a bachelor's degree from Tennessee A&I in 1934, Robinson had become a teacher in 1937 and was soon involved with the Chattanooga Trades Labor Council. He became founding president of the Mountain City Teachers Association (Union Local 428, affiliated with the American Federation of Teachers) and remained head of that local for twenty years. When the Chattanooga school system published the 1938–39 teachers' salary schedule, it showed that a Negro teacher, after fifteen years, could earn only about 75 percent of what a white teacher earned—$1,745 compared to $2,332 for a white teacher.

The Tennessee cases were helped by successful NAACP suits elsewhere. On June 18, 1940, the U.S. Circuit Court of Appeals reversed a negative lower court decision in *Alston v. School Board of City of Norfolk, Virginia,* and said that lower pay for Negro teachers "is as clear a discrimination on the ground of race as could well be imagined and falls squarely within the inhibition of both the due process and the equal protection clauses of the 14th Amendment." The U.S. Supreme Court refused to hear an appeal of the lower court's decision on October 28, 1940.

[*]

In January 1941, A. Philip Randolph became impatient with FDR's slow pace in dismantling Jim Crow. Out of more than one hundred thousand workers in the defense aircraft industries, less than three hundred were Negroes. Randolph threatened to organize one hundred thousand citizens to march on Washington and demand that Negroes be employed in the war industries on a non-discriminatory basis. His "Call to the March on Washington" appeared in the *Black Worker* in May 1941: "This is the hour of crisis. It is a crisis of democracy. It is a crisis of minority groups. It is a crisis of Negro Americans. . . . The federal government cannot with clear conscience call upon private industry and labor unions to abolish discrimination based upon race and color as long as it practices discrimination itself against Negro Americans." After conferences with Eleanor and Franklin Roosevelt and others, Randolph was persuaded to call the march off. On June 25, 1941, Roosevelt issued Executive Order 8802, which established a Committee on Fair Employment Practice and declared "that there shall be no discrimination in the employment of workers in defense industries or government because of race, creed, color, or national origin. . . ." Even so, Randolph continued to pressure the Roosevelt administration, because some department heads continued de facto social discrimination in federal employment.

In Chattanooga, meanwhile, the unions were pushing for equalization of salaries between county and city teachers. This development encouraged C. B. Robinson, on January 9, 1941, to send a letter to the Chattanooga school board, asking for "equalization of Negro schools with white schools, both city and county" in light of the proposed consolidation of Chattanooga and Hamilton County schools. His petition did not threaten the system of racial segregation but only asked for what the *Plessy* decision seemed to grant to Negroes—"separate but equal" education. Robinson sent another non-threatening petition in April. Then, in June 1941, the NAACP, Robinson, and his Mountain City Teachers Association filed *Clarence B. Robinson and the Chattanooga Teachers Association v. the Board of the City of Chattanooga, Tennessee* in the federal court, District of East Tennessee. The suit charged that the Chattanooga Board of Education had violated the Fourteenth Amendment and failed to provide equal protection of the laws. The plaintiffs argued that Negro teachers were required to meet the same requirements for teacher certification as white teachers and thus should be given equal pay. "Such discrimination is being practiced against the plaintiffs and all other Negro teachers and principals in Chattanooga, Tennessee, and is based solely upon their race or color," said NAACP lawyers. Chattanooga asked for dismissal on the grounds it had not been sued by its proper name: "The Board of Education of the City of Chattanooga."

However, for the June 10, 1941, trial in Chattanooga, a formidable defense team was assembled, consisting of Leon Ransom, Thurgood Marshall, and William H. Hastie. Hastie had been born in Chattanooga in 1904, completed high school in Washington, D.C., graduated from Amherst College and Harvard University Law School, and succeeded Houston as dean of Howard University Law School. Describing potential plaintiffs in civil rights cases, Hastie said that the desirable candidate should be "of outstanding scholarship . . . neat, personable, and unmistakably a Negro. . . . Every time a branch of the NAACP can combine a demand of disadvantaged Negroes with a demand of disadvantaged whites . . . that branch will have done something . . . significant."

To support the teacher pay equity cases, NAACP researchers in 1941 produced a report entitled "Teachers' Salaries in Black and White," which estimated an annual loss of $25 million by Negro teachers as a result of salary discrimination. Southern schools, the report said, spent "an average of $38.87 on each white pupil and only $13.09 on each Negro pupil." Negro teachers in Tennessee earned only 69 percent of the salaries paid to white teachers, while in Mississippi, the statistics were even worse and stunned the federal judges. According to the report, "Court action as a remedy for social ills has its limitations, but its use as an effective device to crystallize public opinion against injustices is well justified. When the NAACP started its campaign of employing the courts as an opening wedge in its fight against educational inequalities and discriminations, many dire predictions were made as to the effect of such action upon race relations. To date, little or no race frictions [have] resulted, but important gains have been made."

An important gain was made that same year on a different civil rights front in Tennessee—the implementation of graduate programs at Tennessee A&I. The General Assembly enacted a law that read in part:

> The State Board of Education and the Commissioner of Educa-
> tion are hereby authorized and directed to provide educational
> training and instruction for Negro citizens of Tennessee equiva-
> lent to that provided at the University of Tennessee by the State
> of Tennessee for white citizens of Tennessee. The facilities of
> the Agricultural and Industrial State College may be used when
> deemed advisable by the State Board of Education and the Com-
> missioner of Education, insofar as the facilities . . . are adequate.
> The cost of providing such facilities shall be paid out of appro-
> priations made to the State Board of Education or from other
> available funds.

Meanwhile, in Chattanooga, the teacher salary case was retired on Sep-tember 20, 1941, without going to trial. The local school board had offered to allocate 62 percent of money for salary increases to the Negro teachers and gradually eliminate any differences in salaries based on racial categories. Although Thurgood Marshall advised the plaintiffs not to accept the promise, C. B. Robinson decided to work with white leaders for the sake of "good race relations." In December 1941, Robinson and the MCTA sent letters to politi-cal candidates to ask how they stood on issues dear to the Negro, including equal salaries, equal textbook distribution, and public housing. Some candi-dates answered affirmatively.

[*]

With the Japanese attack on Pearl Harbor on December 7, 1941, America entered World War II. The New Deal and the Great Depression were effec-tively over, and with the country's new wartime preoccupations, the Negro's push for civil rights would be slowed down in some ways. Nevertheless, activ-ists kept certain key battles going in the courtrooms and elsewhere.

In Nashville, for example, beginning in April 1942, Looby argued a case involving teacher pay inequity—*Harold E. Thomas v. Louis H. Hibbits et al.*— in the federal district court of Middle Tennessee. Thomas, a teacher at Pearl Elementary School, had a master's degree in biology from Fisk University but received twenty-five dollars less per month than his white counterparts. Judge Elmer D. Davies stunned the defendants by asking: "Where can a Negro teacher buy a bottle of milk cheaper than a white teacher?" On July 28, 1942, Judge Davies—a Vanderbilt University law graduate and practicing attorney who had been appointed to the federal bench by FDR—ordered Nashville to equalize the pay of Negro teachers. Thomas and Looby were later honored in a dinner sponsored by the local NAACP. Unfortunately, Thomas's teaching contract was not renewed by Nashville, and he opened a business to support himself.

In Chattanooga, C. B. Robinson asked his Mountain City Teachers Association members to send money to help with the legal fees in equity pay cases: "We are happy to have gained another step in our fight for equalization of salaries. As gratifying as this is, our fight is not over. It will be reached only if we remain united, vigilant and financially prepared." The Chattanooga–Hamilton County Teachers Association declared that it had no opposition to funding allocations that would bring salaries of Negro teachers up to more equitable levels, and even the Hamilton County League of Women Voters and the Chattanooga Council PTA supported adding $203,000 to the city budget to honor the promise made to Negro teachers. On October 24, 1942, Robinson sent a letter to the superintendent, reminding him that equal pay adjustments should be implemented within a year.

Elsewhere in the South, Louisville and Little Rock were successfully added to a "snowball" effect (as Thurgood Marshall called it) of equalizing teachers' salaries. However, as Donald G. Nieman has noted, many states developed "rating" measures that allowed school administrators to maintain racially discriminatory pay scales, with some school systems raising the requirements. Chattanooga set up a new uniform "Teachers Salary Schedule," whereby to receive "Class I" top salary, a teacher had to have five years' experience and a master's degree by the next three years. Tennessee A&I would grant master's degrees by 1944. C. B. Robinson would receive his master's degree at nearby Atlanta University.

The SCHW convened its third biennial meeting in Nashville's War Memorial Auditorium in April 1942. About five hundred delegates issued the "Statement of Principles of Action" and authorized the publication of the *Southern Patriot* newsletter. The distinguished Negro actor and singer Paul Robeson gave a memorable concert, while Eleanor Roosevelt was again a featured speaker. Another attendee, Mary Bethune, spoke to students at Tennessee A&I on April 19.

[*]

During this era, America's progressive leaders were worried about violence, southern poverty spawned partly by Jim Crow, and America's racist image abroad. In 1937, Frederick P. Keppel, president of the Carnegie Corporation, New York, had invited visiting Swedish scholar Gunnar Myrdal to direct "a comprehensive study of race relations in the United States, to be undertaken in a wholly objective and dispassionate way as a social phenomenon." Myrdal began the study in September 1938 by conducting a two-month tour of the South. After the trip "to see things with my own eyes," he said, "I was shocked and scared . . . by all the evils I saw, and by the serious implications of the problem." He conferred with many scholars, including sociologist Charles S. Johnson at Fisk University and officers at the NAACP. And to lessen their opposition to a white foreigner heading such a study, Myrdal gave research contracts to America's most notable white and Negro scholars. Myrdal returned to Sweden in 1940 after Germany invaded adjacent countries, leaving the study to others until his return. Collaborating scholars completed several books based on the Myrdal research materials.

Charles S. Johnson, for one, used the Myrdal materials to complete *Patterns of Negro Segregation* (1943). Since coming to Fisk University in 1929 to head its department of social research, Johnson, known as "the midwife of the Harlem Renaissance," had written several notable books on Negro tenancy and its collapse in the South, including *Shadow of the Plantation* (1934), *Growing up in the Black Belt* (1941), and, in the same year that *Patterns of Negro Segregation* appeared, *This Tide: A Survey of Racial Tension Areas in the United States*. He was responsible for bringing to Fisk University James Weldon Johnson, who published *Negro Americans, What Now?* (1934), which included observations on Nashville's Negro community. C. S. Johnson played the vital role of building bridges between the races, working behind the scenes, conducting research on race relations, using the results to influence public policy, gaining philanthropic support, and stimulating peaceful activism in the Negro community. In 1944, he convinced the American Missionary Association to help sponsor the Institutes of Race Relations at Fisk University. However, some local whites criticized the annual institutes as a plot to undermine current race relations and bring in "outside agitators." James G. Stahlman, publisher of the *Nashville Banner*, reportedly pressured the Fisk president to stop the interracial meetings on campus. Moreover, Fisk had some children of white faculty members from Fisk and Meharry Medical College (a privately funded school for Negroes) in its classes, and this was a violation of Tennessee's 1901 Jim Crow law. Fisk administrators decided to stop the annual conferences but then backed down, allowing the 1945 meeting to be held. In 1946,

Charles S. Johnson would become the first Negro president at Fisk University. His inauguration, held at the downtown Ryman Auditorium before an integrated audience, was itself a statement on civil rights.

Myrdal's main findings resulted in his book *An American Dilemma: The Negro Problem and Modern Democracy* (1944), in which he stated: "The author fully realizes, and hopes the reader will remember, that he has never been subject to the strains involved in living in a black-white society and never has become adjusted to such a situation—and that this condition was the very reason why he was asked to undertake the work. He was requested to seek things as a stranger." Noting how the South shut the Negro out of politics, Myrdal wrote, "Most Northerners seem also to be convinced of the mental and moral inferiority of the Negroes, even if their racial beliefs are not so certain, so extreme and so intense as the southerners. But, the Negro's right to political participation as voters is actually seldom questioned [in the North]." He argued that the New Deal had "not succeeded in stamping out discrimination against Negroes in the agencies in the South [e.g., the TVA], but it has brought discrimination within some limits, and it has given Negroes a new type of contact with public authority." But, he added, "The fact that the administration of justice is dependent on the local voters [who elect the judges] is likely to imply discrimination against an unpopular minority group, particularly when this group is disfranchised as Negroes are in the South. The elected judge knows that sooner or later he must come back to the polls, and that a decision running counter to local opinion may cost him his position." Myrdal concluded:

> To this should be added that Negro lawyers are scarce in the South. In some places, Negro lawyers are not allowed to appear in courts, and even where they are allowed they tend to stay away. Most of them seem to be engaged in settling matters outside of court or working in real estate or insurance offices or giving legal advice. Their white business is mainly restricted to debt collection among Negroes. In lawsuits they may work with white lawyers but do not appear much before the courts themselves. Negro clients know that a Negro lawyer is not much use in a Southern courtroom. They have not had the experience of handling important cases; they cannot specialize.

Myrdal found that race had become a caste system in America and that Negroes could only break out of the barrier through "passing"—becoming a white person. Only light-skin Negroes with no Negro features had the opportunity of passing, but, concluded Myrdal, "To whites, passing is an insult and a social and racial danger." He also noted, "Most whites have heard about passing, but, for natural reasons, do not know any specific cases." Of course, Negroes could name many cases with ease. Myrdal argued, "The American nation will not have peace with its conscience until inequality is stamped out, and the principle of public education is realized universally." *An American Dilemma* opened a critical dialogue in America, and Myrdal's study would set a standard for later studies, including the massive research to be done for the *Brown v. Board of Education* case. Myrdal's data about what was going on behind the Cotton Curtain influenced both political parties to include race relations in their post–World War II platforms. It was a study long overdue— one that governments should have financed and conducted immediately after slavery.

[∗]

Negroes continued the attack on Jim Crow and *Plessy*, while white newspapers such as the *Chattanooga Free Press* (Apr. 16, 1942) needled them about their impotent status as "black boys" and inhabitants of "dark town." In September, Randolph told the press: "When this war ends, the people want something more than the dispersal of equality and power among individual citizens in a liberal, political democratic system. We want the full works of citizenship with no reservations. We will accept nothing less." And in response to the NAACP's continuing attacks on the failure of *Plessy v. Ferguson*, in September 1943 the commissioner of education told Tennessee A&I State College's newly appointed president to build the Negro institution into one "equivalent to UT [the University of Tennessee] for white students."

The Southern Conference on Human Welfare remained an active force in the civil rights struggle. Its executive committee created the Southern Conference Education Fund to focus on fundraising and education, while the SCHW would focus on abolition of the poll tax and electoral issues. Mary McLeod Bethune, an SCHW board member, was selected to conduct an eight-state tour, beginning in Tennessee in January 1946, to raise funds for the movement. She arrived in Nashville from Washington, D.C., by Capitol Airlines and stayed at the home of J. Frankie Pierce, head of the State Federation of Colored Women's Clubs. Bethune began the SCHW tour at the Spruce Street Baptist Church on Thursday night, January 17, 1946. Pierce's pastor at First Colored Baptist, R. W. Riley, helped Henry A. Boyd, editor of the *Nashville Globe*, play host to Bethune, who urged Negroes to help get rid of the poll tax and strive for their civil rights.

The SCHW would hold its biennial meeting in November 1946 in New Orleans. In September, Director James Dombrowski and the SCHW executive committee had decided to move the conference from Nashville's War Memorial Auditorium because the janitors were opposed to an integrated SCHW meeting. Governor Jim McCord reportedly supported this segregationist policy, despite mild lectures from the *Globe* (Jan. 11, 1946) about the need for a non-discriminatory society. According to a July 5, 1946, letter now contained in the governor's papers, McCord actually believed that the SCHW was Communist-inspired, a feeling shared by the *Nashville Banner,* which expressed this criticism in a July 9, 1946, editorial. A total of 269 delegates, 40 percent of whom were Negroes, registered for the New Orleans meeting. Absent, however, was Eleanor Roosevelt, although she sent a message by telephone. The meeting agenda included condemnation of discrimination in employment and wages, housing, transportation, education, and government and private industries. The SCHW also decided to hire its first Negro staff members.

In the years after World War II, the Communist label attached to the SCHW would become a popular refrain among those opposed to the civil rights movement. American segregationists increasingly claimed that this or that manifestation of the movement was "Communist-inspired," particularly after the rise of the Soviet Union as a superpower. The American Communist Party was one of the first non-black organizations to decide that race was no more than a bourgeois concept designed to oppress human beings for the benefit of elite whites and "white chauvinism." "Communists may have taken the lead on the race question among predominantly white organizations," noted Matthew Frye Jacobson in *Whiteness of a Different Color* (1998). The segregationists and economic conservatives even perceived American labor unions and the Communist movement in Eastern Europe as equally contributing to Negro unrest at home. American labor union leaders argued that the plutocracy was using race to keep workers divided and oppressed. American conservatives rejected this argument as Marxist, liberal, radical, and divisive, as a form of class warfare that encouraged Negroes to think they were equal to white people. On July 21, 1935, the *New York Times* reported that the AFL, CIO, and one hundred other labor unions had decided to fight to remove racism from their ranks. Ten years later, after the beginning of the Cold War, anyone associated with socialism became branded as "Reds," "Commies," and enemies of the American nation. Negro leaders Paul Robeson and W. E. B. DuBois were restricted from travel abroad for fear they would lay bare the lie about America being a democracy for all citizens. The seventy-eight-year-old

DuBois spoke at an NAACP meeting on July 4, 1947, and said that Negroes "must not be scared or intimidated by the fear of being called Communists." The federal government placed him under relentless attack for his socialist views. He renounced his citizenship and moved to Ghana in 1961.

[*]

In another strategy to defeat Jim Crow, the NAACP gave legal assistance to local Negroes in highly publicized criminal court cases. The organization hoped to gain visibility, support, and better community organization among the common Negro masses. Gunnar Myrdal also identified the southern penal system as a particular evil and a key obstacle to racial equality. With the absence of Negro lawyers in most rural areas in the South, a problem compounded by the prejudices of elected local judges and all-white juries, many innocent Negroes went to prisons and often to death row. Alabama, Arkansas, Louisiana, and Mississippi had, on average, less than eight Negro lawyers each. Tennessee had a much larger number, but these attorneys resided mostly in Chattanooga, Knoxville, Memphis, and Nashville. Negroes made up the bulk of the workers who fed a corrupt peonage system that supplied massive amounts of free and cheap labor to large planters, small farmers, factories, and mining companies. Negro legislators had fought this system in Reconstruction Tennessee and yet the South's Jim Crow criminal justice system abused Negro men, women, and children. Z. A. Looby wrote a letter about a Nashville juvenile court judge who had two Negro children brought into court in handcuffs. "I did not know nor did I expect that children were treated in a way similar to dangerous criminals," said Looby. The judge sheepishly replied that they "were big boys," but new procedures would prevent handcuffs, he promised.

Just after World War II had ended, Looby, Marshall, and other NAACP-LDF lawyers became involved in the murder trials that followed a race riot in the Middle Tennessee town of Columbia, where Negro men had defended their community against attacks by white mobs. In earlier years—1925, 1927, and 1933—Negroes had been lynched in Maury County (of which Columbia is the county seat), but none of the murderers were charged. The latest trouble in Columbia had started on February 25, 1946, when James Stephenson, a World War II veteran, accompanied his mother, Gladys Stephenson, to return a radio to a local repair shop, demanding that either the radio be properly repaired or the money returned. After a heated argument, both Negroes were attacked by twenty-eight-year-old white man. The skilled veteran beat the attacker badly, knocking him through a plate glass window. Other whites came across the street to gang up on Stephenson and arrest him for "stabbing" the man, who had in fact been cut by the shattering plate glass. The two Negroes were arrested, charged with assault, and released after paying a fifty-dollar fine. Authorities decided to arrest them again for attempted murder. A Negro businessman bailed the mother and son out of jail.

Local policemen headed into Mink Slide, "the Bottom" where the Negroes lived. Negro men had posted armed lookouts on the roofs. They remembered Maury County during the 1930s when lynch mobs had murdered two young Negroes, Henry Choate and Cordie Cheek, accusing them of "raping white women." But this time Negroes, who made up 28 percent of the populace, would not submit so easily to local custom. They fired their guns, killing and wounding four policemen.

The county sheriff asked Governor McCord to send help to subdue the Negroes. But the sheriff disapproved of the seventy-five state patrolmen, who proceeded to arm some of the mob as "deputies." Later, on February 26, about eight hundred members of the Tennessee National Guard arrived in Columbia. Some patrolmen led mob attacks on Negro property, destroying a doctor's office and an insurance company across the street and leaving every Negro business damaged. Two unarmed Negro men were killed in jail in what the *Columbia Daily Herald* (Mar. 1, 1946) called "an exchange of gunfire." The Reverend Calvin Lockridge of the Mount Ararat Baptist Church was indicted for "having firearms" simply because he spoke out about the lawlessness of local authorities. The *Nashville Globe* (Mar. 15, 1946), however, blamed the state troopers and Governor McCord for alleging a "Negro threat against law and order."

The NAACP called a white labor attorney, Maurice Weaver, from Chattanooga to help Looby file writs of habeas corpus for thirty-four jailed Negroes. Seventy-five-year-old Julius Blair, his two sons, and James Morton, the leading local Negro undertaker, gained bond and fled to the safety of Nashville. Someone had ransacked Morton's Funeral Home and marked the caskets in white paint with the letters "KKK." The Negro Civil Rights Congress sent $250 from New York to post bond for Lockridge. Hastie and Ransom joined the NAACP defense team. Walter White, arriving on the scene from NAACP headquarters in New York, was quoted in the March 8, 1946, *Nashville Globe* as saying: "This is no ordinary case. Unless they receive outside aid, unless the country is aroused to condemn the kind of thing that took place in Columbia, Negro citizens of small communities throughout the nation will be helpless. The NAACP intends to give the defendants complete and uncompromising legal defense. We appeal for contributions."

The Colored Interdenominational Ministers Alliance of Chattanooga petitioned Governor McCord, protesting the behavior of the patrolmen and asking for strict law enforcement. They called for a federal grand jury to investigate the Tennessee patrolmen and for the Columbia matter to be removed from McCord's hands. On May 14, McCord addressed the Tennessee Historical Society, saying, "Let us endeavor to counterbalance the fevered extremists of whatever race or nationality by citing the precious legacy inherited from our fathers, a legacy that breathed forth a deep desire that domestic righteousness and universal fraternity might and should prevail." The governor said that the left-wing element was trying to create discord in Tennessee over the race riot.

Thurgood Marshall arrived in Maury County on May 30, and helped the NAACP legal team, including Looby and Ransom, to challenge the local practice of excluding Negro jurors. This attempt failed, but the attorneys persuaded the judge to move the trial to Lawrenceburg in Lawrence County. The NAACP added Robert Carter to the legal team after the trial in August seemed to be going against the defendants. Marshall was suffering from pneumonia and had to leave the trial to Looby and the others. McCord again opposed outsiders interfering in southern affairs. "It is a fight to the finish against the reactionaries," said the *National Baptist Union-Review* on June 15, 1946.

Lawrenceburg citizens resented having to deal with a matter that had occurred in Columbia. On October 4, 1946, the jury convicted two defendants and acquitted the remaining twenty-three. Indictments against others were dismissed. Two Negro men were tried on November 18, two days after Marshall returned to the legal team. One was acquitted, while the other received a commuted sentence of one year. The local prosecutor was so angry that he challenged Looby to a common fistfight. The *Globe* reported on November 23 that Looby angered the man by saying calmly, "We came to Columbia to have a contest of brains not brawn." Meanwhile, some observers in the courtroom had grown to dislike Marshall, whom they saw as an arrogant "yellow boy."

The NAACP legal team found itself the target of racist police harassment. The lawyers had to travel to and from Nashville each evening. After the sentencing on November 18, at about 7:00 P.M., Marshall, Looby, and Weaver headed back to Nashville, but daylight soon turned into darkness. A car full of policemen stopped the lawyers' car on the pretext of searching it "for illegal whiskey," but the police inexplicably decided to leave the scene. However, the lawyers' car was soon stopped again, with the police claiming that Marshall was drunk. They placed him in the back seat of the police car, with guns drawn on each side of him, and started down a rural road toward the Duck River. Looby and Weaver insisted on following them, although the policemen stopped and told them to return to the main highway. When they refused, the policemen traveled instead to a nearby justice of the peace. Marshall was told to approach the house, but he refused to budge unless the policemen walked beside him. Looby and some local Negroes stood across the street to watch in case the whites tried to shoot Marshall on a pretense that he was escaping. After the justice of peace was asked to check Marshall's breath, the man dismissed the charge. Marshall rejoined the other lawyers. A local man, James T. "Popeye" Bellanfant, drove them to Nashville in his car, while other local Negroes returned Looby's black sedan to Nashville the next day. The NAACP lawyers reported the incident to the U.S. attorney general.

The NAACP and national civil rights groups exposed the racist, corrupt, and oppressive nature of the South's criminal justice system. They pressured the Harry S. Truman administration to send Department of Justice officials into Tennessee to investigate whether federal civil rights had been violated. When a local grand jury decided that there were no violations, McCord praised the decision and repeated his resentment of federal interference in the South's affairs. Yet, despite such criticism of the federal government when it came to civil rights for Negroes, the Tennessee government was trying at the same time to shift the burden of its antiquated Confederate pensions bill (1906) for white widows to be paid through the federal Social Security program.

The SCHW and several other associations formed the "National Committee for Justice in Columbia, Tennessee," using the incident to raise money for the LDF. The National Alliance of Postal Employees sent financial support from Chicago. The SCHW distributed two hundred thousand pamphlets entitled "The Truth about Columbia" to the national media and also had twenty thousand protest notes sent to McCord. Petitioning Truman, the Civil Rights Congress declared that "Columbia is a deep stain on our national honor and a threat to our democracy. This whitewash [meaning the court trial] places in even greater jeopardy the [Negro] men and women who are being tried on trumped up charges. It encourages terror against the Negroes, particularly in the South. Not only is the Klan riding again—but also, time and again, police are fulfilling the role of the Klan in assaults on the rights of Negroes." An SCHW brochure asked, "Will America White Wash This?"

On October 10, the public welfare committee of the Interdenominational Ministerial Alliance of Chattanooga sent a letter to Looby: "To get 23 acquittals out of 25 was a clean and clear victory for you. We are justly proud of you as American citizens who have not only saved the lives of innocent men; but you have given hope and encouragement to the Negro race as well." On October 30, Houston wrote a letter to the NAACP, nominating Looby for the famed Spingarn Medal. Marshall received the 1946 award instead. In Nashville, five hundred persons attended a dinner in honor of Looby. The *Globe* (Dec. 20, 1946) said, "The colored lawyer has a definite part to play in making democracy real in the United States, and the place to begin is right here in the South."

Five years later, journalist Carl T. Rowan headed to his old hometown of McMinnville to begin a tour of the South and write his book *South of Freedom*. He then went to nearby Columbia where the riots had occurred, interviewing Negroes to determine what had happened and whether things had changed since then. "No, there will be no more trouble," said Henry Harlan, one of those he interviewed. "That's the one thing I learned from 1946. They know now that Negroes have guts. They were the first Columbia Negroes ever to stand up like men. Blood was shed, but it paid off. I dare as to say times have changed. A Colored man used to not have the chance of a sheep-killing dog. But 1946 changed that."

[*]

The years 1946 and 1947 were active ones for the civil rights movement. Recent Negro law school graduates pressured Marshall and the NAACP to launch a wider attack on Jim Crow. Marshall held a conference in Atlanta in April 1946. The conferees, including war veterans and Looby, agreed on public school desegregation cases to be filed in five southern states. Randolph transformed his threat of a "March on Washington" into postwar civil rights objectives: (1) demands for an end to Jim Crow in education, housing, transportation, and every other social, economic, and political privilege; (2) full enforcement of the Fourteenth and Fifteenth Amendments; (3) abolition of all suffrage restrictions and limitations; (4) abolition of private and government discrimination in employment; and (5) expansion of the role of Negro advisors in all administrative agencies. On June 27, 1946, at the NAACP's national convention, Walter P. Reuther, president of the United Auto Workers, was scheduled to speak and reaffirm union support for civil rights. Fisk announced the third annual Race Relations Institute for two weeks in July 1946, including discussions on federal policy and practices on racial minorities, returning Negro veterans, housing, health, and education. Houston was there, representing the LDF and the American Council on Race Relations. On December 5, President Truman issued Executive Order 9808, which created the President's Committee on Civil Rights to investigate and make recommendations for improvement. William H. Hastie, Benjamin E. Mays (president of Morehouse College), and boxing champion "Sugar" Ray Robinson, among others, held a "Freedom Rally" in New York City. The theme was "Democracy Is on Trial." The Congress for Racial Equality (CORE) placed Jim Crow under severe siege with sit-ins and public demonstrations in Washington, D.C. On October 29, 1947, President Truman's committee issued "To Secure These Rights," a report that called for elimination of racial discrimination, especially in higher education.

Henry Allen Boyd, the head of the National Baptist Publishing Board (NBPB), was doing all he could to promote the movement in the *National Baptist Union-Review* and his *Nashville Globe*. Boyd, a Republican, criticized Truman and the Democrats for not doing enough for civil rights. On June 3 and 7, 1947, the *Union-Review* reported that the local NAACP's goal of 5,000 members in the latest drive had netted 2,827 members; the editor declared, "Do we need another Columbia case . . . to wake us up? You who have not joined the NAACP for 1947 can answer that question." At A&I, the campus *Bulletin* (1947) announced a local white college professor as the inaugural speaker for the W. S. Davis Lecture Series on February 2; the title of his speech was "Background of Race Relations in the South." In the *Chattanooga Observer*, for Negro History Week in February 1947, P. A. Stephens, head of Carver Hospital for Negroes and president of the local NAACP, spoke to a race relations class at the University of Chattanooga, outlining NAACP goals. Posing the question "What can whites do to help?" he said that they could pressure their congressmen to support proposals for a fair employment practices commission, anti-lynching legislation, and anti–poll tax bills.

Under Truman, the federal government was abandoning the Compromise of 1877 that had left the South to its own devices in areas such as race relations. In *Shelley v. Kraemer* (1948) the U.S. Supreme Court prohibited housing discrimination based on race-restrictive covenants. The decision attacked a 1911 covenant that prohibited "the occupancy as owners or tenants of any portion of said property for resident or other purpose by people of the Negro or Mongolian Race." Reversing decisions by the Missouri and Michigan Supreme Courts, the U.S. Supreme Court declared: "The Constitution confers upon no individual the right to demand action by the State which results in the denial of equal protection of the laws to other individuals. State action erects no shield against merely private conduct, however discriminatory or wrongful." The federal courts forced the University of Oklahoma to admit Ada Lois Sipuel even though the state had established a separate law school just for her. In protest, hundreds of students burned a copy of the Fourteenth Amendment, placed the remains in an envelope, and mailed the package to Truman. On July 26, 1948, Truman issued Executive Order No. 9981, which declared "equality of treatment and opportunity for all persons in the armed forces without regard to race, color, religion, or national origin."

Avon N. Williams Jr. soon would join Cowan and Looby as part of the NAACP-affiliated civil rights legal team. After serving in World War II, Williams entered Boston University, completing the bachelor's and master's degrees in law by 1948. After being admitted to the Massachusetts bar, he apprenticed under Looby because of the latter's notoriety from the Columbia case. In 1949, Williams returned to Knoxville to practice law and live with his siblings in the old house on Vine Street. Cowan's law office was at 101 Vine Street, while Williams set up office at 511 Vine Street. Soon, he paired with Cowan and filed *Gene M. Gray v. University of Tennessee* (1949) on behalf of four black students who wished to be admitted for graduate study at UT. They took the issue to federal court this time and argued that placing a few graduate-degree programs at Tennessee A&I had not given the Negro sufficient access to graduate education. The Negro state college had no schools of pharmacy, medicine, law, or graduate degree programs in science. One of the plaintiffs wished to study law, and Gray and others wanted to gain master's degrees in chemistry and science. The possibility of establishing a law school at Tennessee A&I State College had been considered in 1942, but the state chose to grant scholarships to out-of-state schools instead. Meanwhile, between 1939 and 1951, the states of Louisiana, North Carolina, Texas, and Florida established law schools at their publicly funded Negro colleges.

Charles Hamilton Houston died in April 1950 just before Heman Sweatt entered the University of Texas Law School and before *Gray* could be decided. "End of Jim Crow in Sight," said the *Baltimore Afro-American* (June 17, 1950). Looby acknowledged Houston as the best civil rights lawyer he had worked with, adding that "Marshall is what he is because of Houston."

Tennessee Attorney General Roy H. Beeler issued an opinion that UT should at least admit Negro students for programs not offered at Tennessee A&I State College. Beeler, who had held his position since 1932, pointed out, however, that the Negro college had a $3 million plant and an adequate annual appropriation; in addition, the state had paid $14,858 for out-of-state scholarships and another $22,969 to Meharry Medical College for its arrangement with the Southern Regional Education Board, an organization established in 1948 to contract with certain graduate and professional schools, including Meharry, to enroll Negro students at state expense and thus help keep them out of all-white schools in the southern states. Of these expenditures, Beeler said, "Thus it will be seen that the state is not engaged in an idle gesture in an effort to escape its responsibility to members of the Negro race but is endeavoring to provide a first-class education institution at Nashville for the race." He tried to assure UT officials that most Negroes were "satisfied with their access to higher education," and would not apply in great numbers to attend UT. Beeler quoted Fisk University's first Negro president, Charles S. Johnson, who said that most Negroes certainly would not prefer UT's graduate program to the [superior] graduate programs of northern universities. Johnson was talking in code about how Jim Crow had forced southern authorities to be content with poor-quality higher education as long as the Negro was held behind. Beeler said, "It is contended that from here on out, our colored people should quit looking to Washington [Truman] and to the allegedly 'wise men' from up North [the NAACP and the unions] to furnish guidance in solving the South's so-called 'race problem.' Colored and white Southerners can work out mutually satisfactory solutions of their 'problem' better if they are not interfered with by outside kibitzers." Beeler felt that the outsiders, "who do not reside in Tennessee," were trying to "make political capital out of it." The *Nashville Sun* (Oct. 7, 1950) reported, "Three Colored Students Will Enter UT Soon." By January 27, 1951, UT had twenty days to answer the suit by Gray, Lincoln A. Blakeney, Joseph H. Patterson, Jack Alexander, and others, including Audrey L. Totten. The Supreme Court was to hear the Tennessee case in January 1952; however, in light of Beeler's opinion and because of similar cases won by the NAACP, UT admitted the students.

[*]

From the 1930s onward, a number of Negro newspapers, books, and magazines kept black communities informed about developments in the civil rights movement. The newspapers were especially important, and among these was the *Nashville Commentator* (1948–71), published by Leonard B. Robinson and others. Meredith W. Day, J. F. McClelland, and L. D. Williams started the *Nashville Independent* in the 1930s, but it soon merged with Henry A. Boyd's *Nashville Globe* (1906–60). For a while in the 1930s, the Reverend E. D. W. Isaac edited the *Nashville Clarion*. Since the late 1890s, the National Baptist Publishing Board in Nashville had published the *National Baptist Union-Review*. The *Nashville World*, *Memphis World*, and *Chattanooga World* were published by the W. A. Scott Newspaper Syndicate based in Atlanta. The *Atlanta World* had begun in 1927 and developed into a chain by 1929. The *World* entered the Tennessee market around 1931 and was edited by Lewis O. Swingler at 546 Beale Street. The *Memphis World* lasted through the 1970s. Robert Sengstacke founded the *Chicago Defender* in May 1905 and syndicated the paper in several cities before his death in 1940. An affiliate, the *Nashville Defender,* began in May 1938 and quickly died. The *Memphis Tri-State Defender* began publication in November 1951 with the intent of serving Delta residents in parts of Arkansas, Mississippi, and Tennessee. The paper would be published through 2003 by the Sengstacke family. In Knoxville, the *East Tennessee News* began around 1907 and was published through the 1940s. It was succeeded by minor papers, including William J. Robinson's *Knoxville Monitor,* in the 1950s. Marion Barry, while a graduate student at UT in 1963, published the *Crusader.* From the 1940s through the 1960s, Walter C. Robinson published his weekly *Chattanooga Observer.* Still other papers that started in support of the civil rights movement included the *Nashville City Examiner* and the *Nashville News-Star.* The latter paper was published by civil rights leaders C. T. Vivian and Andrew White, among others. The Nashville Christian Leadership Council (NCLC) and the Student Nonviolent Coordination Committee (SNCC) published newsletters at various times. The Reverend F. D. Colman and others of the AME Church started the *Nashville Sun* in the 1950s, while the *Clarksville Sun* also was published by the Southern Publishing Company on Jefferson Street in Nashville. Such papers proved to be a vital presence in black communities through every phase of the civil rights struggle.

CHAPTER 2
WE ARE NOT AFRAID!

BROWN AND JIM CROW SCHOOLS
IN TENNESSEE

America designed a Jim Crow system of education to deny access to quality education to Negroes. This ill-fated legacy of anti-intellectualism reached back to slavery times and was enforced upon minority citizens of color by racial violence, by law, and through deeply ingrained Negrophobia among those who labeled themselves as whites. As a consequence of the Europeans' desire to limit competition in exploiting America's vast resources and wealth, Negroes were denied equal access to real economic and educational opportunity in the South and the North.

Tennessee traditionally was a state with a lower literacy rate than most other American states. The minority slavocracy was a class of slave owners that owned nearly 60 percent of cultivable and valuable lands in Tennessee. This class of slave owners constituted less than 20 percent of families, but they continued to defeat attempts to provide a tax base sufficient for a public education system. The position of state superintendent of schools was abolished. More than half of free Tennesseans could not read and write by 1860. The state's common school law was passed in 1867, but most counties provided little tax revenue for schools. By 1900, 15 percent of white children and nearly a quarter of white adults were illiterate.

Even in the face of opposition, free Negroes operated clandestine schools in Nashville from 1833 to 1856 until vigilantes closed them down. Soon after Union army occupation began in 1862, Negroes reestablished schools, often in church buildings. The Union army and northern missionaries, both Negroes and whites, joined the effort in 1863–65, and the Freedmen's Bureau (1865–74) gave support.

However, in a postwar biracial state, Tennessee authorities began to erect a Jim Crow system to favor themselves and their ethnic descendants by devising a more exact definition of "race" and using violence to enforce racial restrictions. Freedmen's schools were raided by some native Tennessee Union Army regiments, and they were also burned by Klansmen and other terrorists. In 1866, Tennessee law declared that people "having any African blood in their veins shall be known as persons of color or Negroes." During the Memphis race riot of May 1866, whites burned every Negro school in the city. In the 1867 common school law, officials were required to segregate black and white children. In 1870 whites refined the racial statutes so that Article 11, Section 12 read: "No school established or aided under this section shall allow white and Negro children to be received as scholars together in the same school." Section 11 of the same article said, "The intermarriage of white persons with Negroes, mulattos, or persons of mixed blood, descended from a Negro to the third generation, inclusive of their living together as man and wife, in this State, is prohibited."

The Jim Crow education system rested on a complex political and philosophical base that was constrained by widespread anti-intellectualism. Even most southerners did not understand it, but they adhered to it by practice and tradition. Both the legacy of slavery and the postwar movement to put an end to the widespread antebellum practice of miscegenation helped to advance the southern tradition of segregated schools. Whites understood that mob violence was necessary to keep "traditions forever." These illogical practices were so ingrained in the region's psyche that the idea of schoolhouses equally accessible to all citizens, regardless of skin color, was impractical. Historian Grace E. Hale has suggested that the construction of a culture of segregation enabled southern European Americans to identify their place in an American nation that was fast becoming modern. To hold the Negroes to a lower status was to help lift white southerners, with their regional inferiority complexes, to a false level of equality with northern white brethren. Segregation (or Jim Crow) allowed southerners to identify a place for the former slaves within the region's post–Civil War society: if Negro workers could no longer be completely controlled after slavery, at least they could be separated and manipulated through the hegemony of race relations. Jim Crow would homogenize southern civic culture and elevate the idea of "white." It accommodated the presence of large numbers of "blacks" while excluding them from the larger society and from equal access to wealth.

Elite southerners made it clear that they were against the idea of educating Negroes at all. On the Belle Meade plantation in Davidson County, for example, the owner refused to allow the Freedman's Bureau to establish a school for freedmen on his vast property. Throughout that Civil District (no. 11) in Davidson County, where Belle Meade and other large former slave farms existed, there were only two one-room freedmen schools by 1880. William Edmondson (1874–1951), who would gain fame as a sculptor, grew up with former slave parents on the W. H. Compton plantation in Civil District 11 and never attended school. In West Tennessee, where slavery had been heaviest in the state, freedmen would find it even harder to get a public education. Had the schools been separate but equal, southern black children would have experienced school more frequently and achieved higher literacy rates earlier.

Indubitably, because of its cultural and economic backwardness, the South was a drag on an aspiring young American nation. Northern whites—who harbored their own prejudices against people of color—were not too busy accumulating mountains of dollars earned from the Industrial Revolution to be completely unconcerned about the high degree of illiteracy and cultural degradation in the South. Some northerners argued that southern resources could be properly developed with northern capital and know-how if the southern masses were better educated and that improving the education of the southern population would help the region bear its fair share of federal taxes.

As a new century began, northern foundations and wealthy philanthropists began efforts to reform education in the South just as northern missionaries had attempted to do before the failure of Reconstruction. John D. Rockefeller established the General Education Board around 1902 to assist education in the South for all citizens, regardless of color. His donation of $53 million to the GEB included money to upgrade Tennessee A&I State Teachers College for Negroes. Other funds were established by Anna T. Jeanes (whose board included a black Tennessean, J. C. Napier of Nashville), Caroline Phelps-Stokes, and Julius Rosenwald of Sears Roebuck Company in Chicago. The Rosenwald Fund, which stationed its Tennessee Negro agent, Robert E. Clay, at Tennessee A&I, built thousands of schoolhouses in the South. It also commissioned a report that, in 1936, underscored the neglect of Negro public education in the South with its finding that 198 counties in southern states had no schools for Negroes as late as 1928.

Tennessee laws ensured the delivery of inferior education to its Negro citizens. State law required county boards of education to "designate the schools which the children shall attend; provided that separate schools shall be established and maintained for white and Negro children." County taxes supported eight months of public school, but state officials provided fewer months of schooling for Negro children. Like surrounding states, Tennessee created a Division of Negro Education, but the directorship remained in the hands of white men whose attitudes about "progress for the Negro people" were paternalistic at best. "Many white Tennesseans," noted the authors of one recent history of the state, "believed that education past basic literacy— enough to read the Bible and 'cipher,' or do simple arithmetic—was a waste of time for farmers and their wives, and outright dangerous for blacks, who might get ideas about their [social] stations."

Under Jim Crow, for Negroes to equal or exceed white socioeconomic progress generally was not permitted. For example, as late as 1945, no bus was provided in Williamson County so that rural Negro children could attend school; the Reverend J. T. Patton, a local Negro minister, had to spearhead an effort to raise $2,760 in private funds to buy a bus. Even by 1950, thirty of Tennessee's ninety-five counties offered no high school education for Negro citizens. Many of them were forced to send their children to segregated, inferior schools in nearby counties and even across the state line into Virginia. Public school teacher Helen Work recalled how she became fed up and barged into the superintendent's office to demand some textbooks for her students in Nashville. He was so startled that he complied with her demand. In Chattanooga, the Negro teachers' union forced the equal distribution of textbooks.

In his *Scars of Segregation: An Autobiography* (1974), Arthur V. Haynes remembered being a school principal in 1941 at the Goodlettsville Colored Elementary School near Nashville:

> On the first day of school, I got a let down when I approached the building where I was to spend the next nine months. There were two large rooms and a smaller room on the back next to a small porch. The interior was depressing. There was a photograph of Abraham Lincoln hanging on the wall of one room and one of George Washington on the wall of another room. There were spider webs attached to each picture as they silhouetted against the unpainted wall. A teacher's desk in my room where upper grades were to be taught was in disrepair. A leg was almost gone from the chair I was to sit in. The décor of both rooms was enough to destroy any ambition of an educator's love for the community. I knew that before I could do any constructive teaching there would have to be some physical changes made throughout the building. A trip was made to the maintenance and supply building for the [Davidson] county schools to seek paint and new furniture. The supply superintendent told me that none of these things were available for colored schools. I was given a box of

chalk and ushered out of the building. I reasoned that we could turn to the [Negro] community for some of our needs. There were two beautiful large brick buildings on the highway a few blocks from our school where the white students attended school. These buildings were fitted with the latest equipment. I went down to the white high school one day and introduced myself to the principal. I was given a tour through the beautiful school.

Haynes, who had attended Tennessee A&I State College, had to raise money from local businesses, Negro citizens, and a New Deal agency to get furniture, paint, and food for his school. From Virginia and South Carolina to Texas, a new generation of Negro high school students had begun in 1949 to protest such conditions.

[*]

On December 5, 1950, the first Tennessee public school desegregation court case was filed in Anderson County. The county seat, Clinton, had a population of 4,000 people, 5 percent of whom were Negro citizens. They, like the whites, worked in mining and farming. Negroes there had always thirsted for education. In 1868, John C. Tate and other Negro Methodist leaders chartered the Colored Institute of Anderson County, but terrorists burned the Negro church and school in 1869. By 1900, five of the fifty-eight segregated public schools in Anderson County served Negroes. By 1950, about 220 Negroes lived two blocks north of Clinton High School (CHS), and a few more were mixed into the residential areas. There was a Negro elementary school and two Negro churches. When they reached high school age, Negro children could not, of course, attend the nearby white school but were sent to a "Grade D" school twenty-four miles to the north. This school served several counties and cost $30 per year in tuition. In 1950, some Negro parents and their children sought admission to CHS but were turned away when they tried to meet with authorities. Anderson County responded to the protest by transferring all the Negro high school students to Knoxville's Austin High School, a "Grade A" facility eighteen miles to the south, which cost $190. The Negro youngsters had to leave home by 6:30 A.M. to walk about a mile down a hill, past Clinton High School, to catch the bus, which then picked up Negro children in other towns and arrived in Knoxville two hours later.

The federal courts had by this time decreed that Jim Crow states could not use scholarships to force Negro citizens to attend school outside their communities. Thus, on December 5, 1950, NAACP-affiliated lawyers Avon

Williams, Z. A. Looby, and C. A. Cowan filed *J. McSwain et al. v. Board of Education of Anderson County, Tennessee* in the federal district court in Knoxville. The plaintiffs were J. Allen McSwain and his son Joseph H. McSwain; Clifford Duke and his children James and William; and O. W. Willis and his children Lillian and Shirley. Sidney Davis, John T. Gilbertson, and W. B. Lewallen served as attorneys for the defendants. According to the plaintiffs' argument, the students' rights under the Fourteenth Amendment were being violated because they were forced out of Anderson County while white students attended local schools. For their part, the defendants argued that, while the number of blacks in Anderson County was too small to provide a high school solely for Negroes, they had nevertheless provided equal access to education by contracting with a school in another county and thus satisfied the "separate but equal" requirement of *Plessy*. On April 26, 1952, Judge Robert Love Taylor, a Yale law graduate who had served on the federal bench for two years, ruled against the plaintiffs. Plaintiffs' lawyers appealed to the Sixth Circuit Court in Cincinnati. The U.S. Supreme Court had recently decided to study five state school desegregation cases as a package, especially *Brown* in Kansas and *Briggs v. Elliott* (1952) in South Carolina, and in 1953 the Sixth Circuit decided to delay the Tennessee case because of the pending *Brown* decision.

Also in 1953, Avon Williams decided to leave his native Knoxville and move to Tennessee's political center—the city of Nashville. When he arrived there, Williams found that Negroes had two representatives on the city council and a string of businesses in the downtown area along Charlotte Avenue. There was also a thriving business district on Jefferson Street in suburban north Nashville under the shadow of Fisk University, Meharry Medical College, and Tennessee A&I State University. The city's seven Negro neighborhoods included two business colleges and the American Baptist Theological Seminary, three religious publishing houses, and three weekly Negro newspapers. Nashville was changing in the 1950s when the city began clearing away Negro slum neighborhoods like "Hell's Half Acre" and "Black Bottom" in the downtown area. Segregation was still the unspoken law of the city, and the elite Negroes—doctors, lawyers, teachers, college professors, and businessmen—also lived on the black side of town, although they had their exclusive social scene, including the Agora Assembly (an elite men's club), Chi Boulé (an elite fraternity), personal automobiles, and much nicer homes than the average Negro in the neighborhood. However, when elite Negro men and women ventured downtown to shop, they received the same Jim Crow treatment that a Negro of the working class would receive. Z. A. Looby, who also resented this horrid scene when he had arrived in Nashville in 1928, would be Avon Williams's law partner.

[*]

On May 11, 1954, the *Memphis World,* reporting on Thurgood Marshall's appearance at the Regional NAACP meeting in Mississippi, quoted him as saying that he had "news for those 'peanut politicians.' Come hell or high water, we will be free by '63." That would be the one hundredth anniversary of the Emancipation Proclamation. Marshall, the LDF, the NAACP and others were still waiting anxiously for the *Brown* decision. The NAACP-LDF had employed sociologists and psychologists, as well as historians at Howard University such as John Hope Franklin (a Fisk graduate), to help with the research for the case.

At last, on Monday, May 17, 1954, the U.S. Supreme Court issued its opinion in the case of *Brown v. Board of Education of Topeka, Kansas.* Negroes, reporters, and the normal run of tourists had packed the chambers of the Supreme Court on a daily basis, and others had crowded the steps outside the building in Washington, D.C., waiting for the court's decision. Officials from the Highlander Folk School in Monteagle, Tennessee, were in the audience. After reading the decisions in other cases, Chief Justice Earl Warren said at 12:52 P.M.: "I have for announcement the judgment and opinion of the Court in No. 1—*Oliver Brown et al. v. Board of Education of Topeka.*"

"A shiver ran through the room and spectators shifted to the front of their seats," historian and author Lerone Bennett Jr. wrote. Negroes and others had been packing the courtroom on a daily basis, expecting the ruling at any time. Chief Justice Earl Warren proceeded to deliver the Supreme Court's historic opinion:

> These cases come to us from the States of Kansas, South Carolina, Virginia, and Delaware. They are premised on different facts and different local conditions, but a common legal question justifies their consideration together in this consolidated opinion. In each of the cases, minors of the Negro race, through their legal representatives, seek the aid of the courts in obtaining admission to the public schools of their community basis. In each instance, they had been denied admission to schools attended by white children under laws requiring or permitting segregation according to race. This segregation was alleged to deprive the plaintiffs of the equal protection of the laws under the Fourteenth Amendment. In each

of the cases other than the Delaware case, a three-judge federal district court denied relief to the plaintiffs on the so-called "separate but equal" doctrine announced by this Court in *Plessy v. Ferguson*, 163 U.S. 537. . . . The plaintiffs contend that segregated public schools are not "equal" and cannot be made "equal," and that hence they are deprived of the equal protection of the laws. We come then to the question presented: Does segregation of children in public schools solely on the basis of race, even though the physical facilities and other "tangible" factors may be equal, deprive the children of the minority group of equal educational opportunities? We believe that it does. . . . We conclude that in the field of public education the doctrine of "separate but equal" has no place. Separate educational facilities are inherently unequal. Therefore, we hold that the plaintiffs and others similarly situated for whom the actions have been brought are, by reason of the segregation complained of, deprived of the equal protection of the laws guaranteed by the Fourteenth Amendment. . . .

Thurgood Marshall leaned toward an aide and said, "We hit the jackpot!" Spectators began embracing one another and shaking hands in a daze. A reporter for the *Chicago Defender*, according to Lerone Bennett, left the courtroom so excited that she felt "drunk." Newsmen rushed from the court and flashed the news to all corners of the world. At a party that night, Marshall said, "You fools go ahead and have your fun, but we haven't begun to work yet." Newspapers around the globe, including ones in the Soviet Union, England, and Switzerland, carried the news about *Brown*. Author James T. Patterson said, "*Brown* called for changes that the Court by itself could not enforce. In time, however, some of these changes came to pass, even in schools, those most highly sensitive of institutions. And it was the courts, aided by civil rights activists, civil rights acts, and federal officials, that stepped forward to give these changes constitutional standing."

Many southern newspapers spewed the venom of defiance, and many white southerners became as united as the men who had volunteered to serve the Confederate army in 1861. Hardcore segregationists called for a legal war based on the Civil War issue of "states' rights." They raised Confederate flags over the state capitols of Alabama, Georgia, South Carolina, and Mississippi. Huge billboards and Confederate emblems confronted motorists with the slogan "Impeach Earl Warren." The *Knoxville Journal* declared the justices unfit to sit on the Supreme Court. Northern dailies rushed reporters into the post-*Brown* South to see how southerners would react. Carl T. Rowan, a native of McMinnville, Tennessee, who had attended Tennessee A&I State College and was now a reporter for the *Minneapolis Tribune,* toured the South and gauged its pulse. In his book *Go South to Sorrow* (1957), he described people "still living in the shadow of the Civil War," adding, "One newspaperman told me, 'We are a sick and miserable people, we southerners. We are in America, but not of it. We can see justice and recognize it at a distance, but we cannot embrace it. We are super-sensitive, overly defensive. We are a miserable bunch of bastards—nice bastards, but without guts, or whatever it takes, to get off our backs the burdens and sins of our grandpappies.'"

When asked about *Brown,* Nashville mayor Ben West said that he was sworn to uphold the law. Governor Frank G. Clement of Tennessee was contacted on vacation, and he refused to use *Brown* as a campaign issue in the 1954 elections. Senator Estes Kefauver, campaigning for reelection, cleverly told reporters, "I will fight for fair treatment for all segments of American economic life." Moderates believed that the court would order the equalization of education facilities instead of social integration. Some southern authorities hoped compliance with *Plessy* could save them. For a story headlined "Supreme Court Outlaws Segregation in Schools," the chairman of the Chattanooga school board told a reporter for the *Chattanooga News-Free Press* (May 18, 1954): "We had a segregation ruling in mind when construction was launched on the Chickamauga and Summit Schools." The city recently built a new $2.5 million Howard High School for Negroes. The head of the Chattanooga NAACP said that *Brown* was "The most momentous ruling which has occurred in eighty or ninety years."

Hardcore segregationists applauded the "Declaration of Constitutional Principles," a declaration of war on *Brown* issued by a group of southern congressmen. This "Southern Manifesto" denounced the court's historic ruling. Tennessee congressmen Albert Gore Sr., Estes Kefauver, and J. Percy Priest refused to sign the document, although they, too, did not publicly support *Brown.* The *Grundy County Herald* (June 3, 1954) reported gubernatorial candidate Gordon W. Browning's remarks: "I have always favored segregation of the races in America, as a condition of bringing the best possible relations. All the whites and 95 percent of the Negroes much prefer it to a mixture. It will be my aim as governor to appeal to the good common sense of both races to keep what we have by consent, and prevent any sort of friction. It must be recognized that many of the colored teachers, who are doing a good job, would be placed in keener competition, and their positions jeopardized if this change is made."

In the heart of the Delta, the *Memphis Press-Scimitar* (May 17, 1954) announced: "Court Bans Segregation." The mayor and the Memphis school superintendent took a wait-and-see attitude, contending that the local public Negro schools were already equal to the white public schools, "except for a couple of bad cases." At any rate, neighborhood racial patterns would prevent forced integration in Memphis, the city officials believed. Little was heard from Edward Hull Crump, the city's longtime Democratic political boss, who was seriously ill and would die just five months after the *Brown* decision. However, one of his apologists later said, "Mr. Crump was a Southern white man, but he certainly was no enemy to Negroes as such." A moderate white in Memphis, Lucius E. Burch, wrote in his diary on May 18, 1954: "The country is still shaken by the Supreme Court's ruling on segregation, but most of the country has accepted it as a sensible way and as a requirement it is for the best." The *Memphis Tri-State Defender* (May 22, 1954) devoted a whole page to *Brown*, including pictures of Marshall, the entire Supreme Court, and the Supreme Court building. Levi Watkins of the S. A. Owen Junior College spoke for the Negro community, saying, "The decision offers new hope for accelerated progress toward a more completely democratic society." The *World* (May 18, 1954) carried large photographs of Warren and Marshall. The Reverend S. A. Owen and his Metropolitan Baptist Church sponsored a panel discussion on integration.

Elsewhere in Tennessee, the *Columbia Daily Herald* (May 17, 1954) printed a huge headline, "Segregation Ruled Unconstitutional," and reported that the school superintendent in Maury County had no comment. Some southerners sadly proclaimed, "Segregation is gone." In Middle Tennessee, the *Clarksville Leaf-Chronicle* (May 18, 1954) called *Brown* a "momentous Supreme Court edict" but added that "an actual end to segregation still is months and perhaps years away." With 1,056 Negroes among their 3,601 public school students, school officials in Clarksville, including George W. Brooks, principal of the Burt High School for Negroes, said that they would abide by state Department of Education directives. The *Leaf-Chronicle* also reported that some segregationist leaders had anticipated *Brown* and were planning Christian academies and private schools for the white children with state vouchers, while improving Negro public schools.

Farther east, the *Bristol Herald* (May 18, 1954) declared, "School Desegregation Outlawed." This newspaper, which served citizens on the Tennessee and Virginia sides of the town, said the U.S. Supreme Court had dealt the South its hardest blow since the Civil War but added: "Progress begets progress. There will be the troublemakers in the North as well as the South—an expression of bigotry based on ignorance." Negro citizens made up less than 7 percent of the total population in Bristol and the surrounding counties.

Through a contract with Tennessee, Frederick Douglass High School on the Virginia side served the ninety Negro students in Washington County, Tennessee. The monthly Interracial Council of Bristol offered assistance to the school board for peaceful desegregation of the schools.

The Supreme Court refrained from issuing implementation guidelines for *Brown*. It was best to let the smoke clear after they had fired the first shot. Chief Justice Warren had agreed with his colleagues to withhold any language about implementation until state attorneys general could submit briefs for a September 15 hearing.

A week after *Brown*, Roy Wilkins, Walter White, Thurgood Marshall, and other NAACP officials issued the "Atlanta Declaration," urging all branches to petition local school boards for an immediate end to Jim Crow schools. On May 25, 1954, in Nashville, thirteen civil rights groups, including the Colored Parents and Teachers Association and the League of Women Voters, met to "respond to the challenge" of *Brown*. The participants decided to wait for "*Brown II*" and allow the local school board to do the right thing. They advised school associations to begin some biracial meetings. Among the speakers were Charles S. Johnson and George Mitchell, the executive director of the Southern Regional Council. Paul R. Christopher, a Knoxville labor leader, and Alfred Mynders, editor of the *Chattanooga Times*, were charter members of the SRC, which came under attack in Atlanta. "No matter what any court may rule," Governor Marvin Griffin declared, there would be no end to racial segregation in Georgia.

Charles S. Johnson called *Brown* "the most important national mandate in civil rights since the Emancipation Proclamation." He, like others, thought *Brown* meant the end of *all* segregation. In July, Johnson invited Thurgood Marshall to be the principal speaker at the Eleventh Annual Race Relations Institute at Fisk University. Marshall advised the South to cooperate, recognize *Brown*, and make integration painless. Two white professors at Fisk University tried without success to enroll their children in a nearby Negro public school.

The civil rights offensive would be slowed by massive southern resistance. On July 11, 1954, a segregationist group called the White Citizens' Council—a sort of "uptown" version of the Ku Klux Klan—was formed in Mississippi to maintain the status quo. Senator James Eastland of Mississippi took the floor of the U.S. Senate, armed with files obtained from J. Edgar Hoover's Federal Bureau of Investigation, to declare that Communists were behind the *Brown* decision. Eastland later spoke to a convention of White Citizens' Council chapters in Mississippi, urging them to take the offensive.

The citizens' councils movement spread into adjacent Tennessee, and the sentiments expressed by the reactionary forces on the borders encouraged segregationist activists in the Volunteer State. Segregationists in Chattanooga, encouraged by border-crossers from Georgia, headed a group "to maintain segregation." A professor at Vanderbilt University organized the Tennessee Federation for Constitutional Government (TFCG) to oppose school desegregation. The TFCG brochure read, "Our organization is composed of members of upstanding character," adding that it had "the will to defend our rights—peacefully and legally."

School systems that sought to move ahead and desegregate as quickly as possible hesitated for fear of coming into conflict with militant white segregationists. Although Governor Clement made a smart decision not to lead a fight to oppose *Brown,* he did say that local school boards had power under Tennessee law to make decisions about school desegregation. Some conservatives in the Tennessee Department of Education argued that Tennessee was *not* included in *Brown,* and Quill E. Cope, Tennessee State Board of Education commissioner, told school officials that segregation remained in place until further notice. Roy A. Beeler, the state attorney general, said, "As we see it now, the question of whether there will be segregation was settled in the decision last May. We see no point in arguing that point. Instead we will present our ideas [to the U.S. Supreme Court] about how the ending of segregation can be carried out with a minimum of disturbance in the school system." On August 18, Beeler submitted a proposal for one-grade-at-a-time school desegregation. The *Nashville Globe* praised Beeler's decision to move forward.

[*]

The first city in Tennessee to voluntarily comply with *Brown* would be Oak Ridge in Anderson County. This community had been created by the federal government in 1942 to help develop, under a veil of enormous secrecy, the atomic bomb. Federal recruiters brought hundreds of Negroes from Alabama, Georgia, Mississippi, and Tennessee to work at Oak Ridge. Thousands of white workers from those states and others were also recruited. Although President Roosevelt's Executive Order No. 8802 (1941) forbade discrimination in war industries, officials did not immediately comply in the Oak Ridge settlement. Negro workers received menial, low-paying jobs and a segregated section of town in which to live.

On May 17, 1954, under the headline "Supreme Court Bans Segregation," the *Oak Ridger* newspaper reported the response of the local school superintendent, Hilary D. Parker, to the historic decision: "I have felt for a long time that segregation is a dead issue, and has been for years, and that it now is a matter of how to work it out in a way that will be least disrupting to the local schools." The Oak Ridge Town Council had already discussed desegregation of the schools in light of a position taken by President Dwight D. Eisenhower on May 25, 1953—that no segregation should exist on U.S. military bases—which reaffirmed President Truman's desegregation of the military in 1948. The council interpreted Eisenhower's position to include Oak Ridge because of its huge government jim research and uranium production facilities, and on December 21, 1953, it approved a resolution to request that the Atomic Energy Commission (AEC), which oversaw the Oak Ridge facilities, desegregate the schools. A copy was sent to Eisenhower. Superintendent Parker and Mrs. Robert Officer, the Negro principal of the Scarboro School in Oak Ridge, began discussions on how to implement the desegregation plan for fall 1954. The several dozen Negro students in high school and junior high would be the first to be sent to white schools.

Gubernatorial hopeful Gordon W. Browning claimed that Governor Clement was pushing desegregation because "he wants to run for the Democratic vice president nomination" and called Clement "a coward" for not taking a public stand on *Brown*. Voters in Oak Ridge voted two to one for Clement in the Democratic primary.

A local citizens' panel, which had been appointed on February 3, 1954, to study the Oak Ridge Town Council's December 1953 resolution, asked the council to wait until the Tennessee General Assembly convened in January, and in the meantime to try some visitations by students and teachers between the Negro and white schools. The members of the panel claimed that a survey showed that most local citizens were opposed to desegregating the schools, and on August 16, the *Oak Ridger* reported that some members of the citizens' panel argued that Eisenhower had in fact made no school desegregation order for Oak Ridge. "If President Eisenhower has such convictions, he has not expressed them," they said. On August 23, at a packed meeting, the Town Council voted 4–1 to withdraw the desegregation resolution from the AEC. Two council members were absent and did not vote. The only Negro councilman, Albert C. Stewart, voted no and reminded the crowd that the nation's capital was already desegregating its schools. He said that 40 Negro students could not possibly disrupt the high school football schedule—a response to claims by desegregation opponents that other schools would not play against an integrated Oak Ridge team. "I cannot vote for it [Jim Crow] to continue for *one* more day," said Stewart. The *Oak Ridger* (Sept. 14, 1954) reminded everyone that Governor Clement had said the public schools would remain segregated until the *Brown II* decree. On June 3, 1954, 272 whites and 9 Negroes graduated from the segregated Oak Ridge high schools. A total of 7,840 public school students were enrolled in Oak Ridge for the 1954–55 academic year.

On January 6, 1955, AEC members and Fred W. Ford, the director of community affairs for the AEC, directed the Town Council and the school superintendent to implement school integration for fall 1955. They argued that there was no reason for the United States to embarrass itself before the whole world by not voluntarily complying with *Brown*. Segregationists countered by saying that Oak Ridge schools were part of Anderson County schools, even though the AEC paid money for the county to operate the schools in Oak Ridge. Clement and other government officials gave no public opposition to the AEC decision. On January 11, 1955, an *Oak Ridger* headline read, "Local Schools Integrate Next Fall." The superintendent told the parents' advisory council that the administrators and teachers had discussed potential problems and that all would go well in the fall. The juniors and seniors at Scarboro would transfer to Oak Ridge High School and Robertson Junior High School. "Athletes would be treated equally, but we do not propose to force anything [integration] on other teams," he said. The hard part was to have Negroes teaching white children in a segregated southern society. The principal said that the appointment of teachers would be based on merit and that the eleven Negro teachers would be given "proper consideration for jobs." Desegregation was expected to save fifteen thousand dollars a year.

[*]

On January 21–22, 1955, the Inter-Organizational Conference on Establishing Democratic Patterns in Human Relations, which encompassed states across the South, convened at the Race Relations Institute. Nearly ninety delegates arrived in response to the invitation. The organizations included representation from the NAACP, the African Methodist Episcopal Church, the Christian Methodist Episcopal Church, the National Negro Business League, Tennessee A&I State University, the AFL-CIO and other labor unions, Phi Delta Kappa, the Christian Life Commission of the Southern Baptist Convention, the Anti-Defamation League of B'nai B'rith, LeMoyne College, the Southern Reporting Service, the Methodist Church, Fellowship House of Knoxville, United Church Women, and local Baptist ministers. Charles L. Dinkins of First Baptist Church in east Nashville represented the local NAACP. The regional director of the NAACP said there was a fund to help leaders who suffer economic retaliation.

On May 31, 1955—just thirteen days after the civil rights champion Mary McLeod Bethune, whom Eleanor Roosevelt called "my best friend," passed away—the U.S. Supreme Court issued its *Brown II* decision on school desegregation. The input for implementation had included a few reasonable suggestions—from Tennessee, among other states—while many responses had been negative and defiant. The court still refused to set any deadlines but simply ordered school desegregation to proceed with "all deliberate speed."

President Eisenhower told worried southern congressmen that he would not push for "all deliberate speed" but he refused to say that the federal government would *not* use its authority to enforce court decisions. Eisenhower obviously was disappointed in his nomination of Earl Warren, the former Republican governor of California, to head the court. While the president continued to avoid direct reference to the school desegregation issue, he made a mild statement about race relations: "We [Republicans] believe in the equal dignity of all our people, whatever their racial origin or background may be; in their equal right to freedom and opportunity and the benefits of our common citizenship." Eisenhower's statement was intended perhaps to counter anticipated criticism from the Soviet Union's major newspaper.

[*]

That fall, according to the principal of Oak Ridge High School, all went "as smooth as silk" when Negroes were integrated with the other 1,540 students. Some 45 Negro students, including Jimmy Lewis, Archie Lee, and C. H. Shannon, integrated the Robertson Junior High School. More than 200 elementary students remained at Scarboro for the time being. On September 5 and 6, 1955, a group calling itself "Oak Ridge for Segregation" was out front with pickets and handbills, urging parents to boycott the schools. The Anderson County chapter of the Tennessee Federation for Constitutional Government (TFCG) accepted the Oak Ridge segregation group for membership.

The Oak Ridge elections for Town Council took place in the midst of this initial school integration. On September 13, 1955, some thirty-five candidates vied for the seven at-large council seats. The issues included schools, disposal of nuclear waste, a push for self-government, and proposed election of a school board by districts. Albert Stewart, the lone Negro on the council, was one of the first people to announce for reelection and was placed second on the ballot. A Ph.D. from St. Louis University, he was a dark brown–skinned man, a member of the Town Council since January 1952, a senior inorganic chemist for the Oak Ridge National Laboratories, and an occasional professor of chemistry at nearby Knoxville College. Stewart was reelected in September 1955, placing fourth among the top seven candidates. The Negro precinct of Scarboro gave him 92 of its 127 votes, despite the fact that the Scarboro voting machine was the only one "inoperable" on the morning of election day. The school desegregation issue died quietly after the elections, and "Oak Ridge for Segregation" and the TFCG rescinded their appeal for parents to keep their children at home.

Z. A. Looby told Nashville reporters that Clinton, just a few miles from Oak Ridge, would now serve as the test case the attorney general had been looking for and that all Tennessee schools would be desegregated. In June 1954, the federal appeals court had directed Judge Robert L. Taylor to initiate further proceedings, but Taylor would stall for two more years.

In July 1954, in Knoxville, some Negro leaders approached the school board about instituting *voluntary* desegregation, but their appeal was refused. The board members argued that to voluntarily integrate Negro students into the public schools would be a violation of Tennessee law. The school board's attorney advised that *Brown* was "an opinion, and not yet law." They and Taylor would stall the Knoxville issue for six years.

In the state capital, the school board was confident that *Brown* was not a threat—that the Negroes had good schools. However, in June 1955, the NAACP headquarters recommended to its branches to "file at once petitions with each school board, calling attention to the May 31 decision." Looby, Williams, and the NAACP filed *Robert W. Kelly, et al. v. Nashville Board of Education* (1955). The plaintiff, Alfred Z. Kelly, was a barber in East Nashville. His son Robert was not allowed to attend East High School near their home; instead, he had to ride the bus across the river to the Negro high school two blocks south of Fisk University.

[*]

Segregationist forces had decided to make their stand in Clinton. In August 1955, the TFCG circulated an open letter addressed to "Dear Fellow Tennesseans," which declared, "The vast majority of people in this state, we believe, want to maintain separate schools for whites and Negroes, as required by our state Constitution. . . ." They offered free legal service to all "mothers and fathers who desire to keep their children in schools with their own [white] cultural group."

One of the Anderson County commissioners reportedly opposed compliance with *Brown*. The commissioners tossed the desegregation decision back to the school board members, who merely wanted to proceed to integrate the twelve or so Negro students in Clinton. David J. Brittain, the principal of Clinton High School, had begun a progressive program to improve instruction and increase the number of students who would go on to college. The teachers had bought into this improvement program and seemed little bothered by pending desegregation. In 1956, there were only sixty-seven Negro students in the Clinton public schools, and CHS had eight hundred students. Twenty-one percent of local parents had not completed elementary school, while only 21 percent had graduated from high school, and only 6 percent had finished college. School board members had decided to wait on Judge Taylor's opinion, asking him in September 1955 to allow them to integrate the schools "with no time limits." For their part, NAACP lawyers asked the judge for desegregation according to *Brown II*, that is, with "all deliberate speed."

On January 4, 1956, Taylor finally ruled that court-ordered desegregation was to proceed at Clinton High School on August 23, 1956. The Anderson County school board agreed to comply with Taylor's order, because most local residents respected "the rule of law." An exuberant Looby declared that he intended to file a suit to desegregate the parks and golf courses throughout Tennessee.

On January 20, 1956, Governor Clement refused "to permit the problem of desegregation to become a political issue." He answered hundreds of angry letter writers and repeatedly said, "It is hard to stand up for your convictions." He thanked dozens of writers who gave him their support. On January 23, he said, "I do not think the public display of profanity and the admitted use of. pressure tactics represent the will of the people of Tennessee. We have had no trouble here; only in Anderson County has a school been desegregated and that was on a Federal reservation. I do not intend to interfere with the rights of local authorities. I hope all Tennesseans will help us as we endeavor to promote the welfare of our people. It is easy to give in to the clamor of the crowd; it is hard to stand for your convictions [to do what is right]." The *Globe* reported that Negro leaders praised Clement for not joining the segregationist governors in opposing *Brown*. Yet, they warned Clement: "It cannot be believed that the Tennessee counties down on the Mississippi border are prepared to obey the Constitution any more faithfully than the counties in Mississippi itself. It is going to be much easier to get Nashville and . . . D.C. authorities to carry out the edict of the Supreme Court than other counties and the State of Tennessee."

In Clinton, Principal David J. Brittain dutifully prepared his high school for desegregation after the responsibility was placed on his shoulders. His bira-cial committee, including members of the Negro PTA, discussed potential problems and solutions. Brittain also engaged discussions about race relations with his students and faculty members. He invited nearby Negro elementary students to visit CHS classes. By May 1956, students, parents, and teachers were prepared for desegregation. But regional segregationists continued to assemble their forces in Clinton: the North Alabama Citizens Council joined the mob, and the TFCG recruited segregationists from across Tennessee.

Fredrick John Kasper was the most active of the segregationist leaders. He had been born and educated in the North, but he hated Jews and Negroes, even though it was reported that he had a Negro girlfriend. He had reportedly gained notoriety by opposing liberal issues in Washington, D.C., and heading the Seaboard White Citizens' Council. The *Clinton Courier-News* identified Kasper as the "self-styled executive secretary of the White Citizens' Council" and claimed that the TFCG had connections to Kasper's organization. Both groups, the TFCG and the White Citizens' Council, represented white people and segregationists just as the NAACP represented Negroes and integration-ists. Neo-Confederates considered them southern patriots in a new battle for the moral soul of the South.

The *Clinton Courier-News* was urging compliance with *Brown* and avoid-ance of any further pain for the community. The editor, Horace V. Wells Jr., supported the school board's efforts to do right and move into the future. To counter the *Courier-News*, Leo Ely started the *East Tennessee Reporter* in Feb-ruary 1957. The *Reporter* quoted a preacher from Columbia who claimed Christian justification for the anti-desegregation movement. This white min-ister said that the Negroes and the NAACP were being led by "UN-godless Communists"; he wanted an investigation of the NAACP and suggested that desegregation be left to local biracial leaders who would "work out their own problems." Neither of the Clinton newspapers paid attention to the Negro community. "The controversy here was between whites about blacks," Horace Wells later said. "The Negroes were on the sidelines, even though they were the cause. People assume blacks were involved, but they stayed home."

The Negro children and their parents approached Clinton High School on Monday, August 27, 1956, the first day of classes. Regina Turner, one of the students, said, "I didn't want to go to Clinton High School in the first place, but I knew I had a right to be there and I wasn't afraid." As planned, the chil-dren were accepted by the principal and most of the 732 students in atten-dance. Many Negro and white children lived near each other and played together. The Negro high school students were, in addition to Turner, Jo Ann Allen, Bobby Cain, Theresa Caswell, Minnie Ann Dickey, Gail Ann Epps, Ronnie Hayden, Alva J. McSwain, Edward Lee Soles, Maurice Soles, Alfred Williams, and Charles Williams. Five or so pickets showed up on the first day, but after television coverage of the event was aired, the number grew to about fifteen the following day.

John Kasper, who seemed to have the support of the TFCG, had come to Clinton, and by Monday night, he had organized night and morning demonstrations that included some young protesters carrying signs that read, "We Wont [sic] Go to School with Negroes." Because Kasper's protesters lined the street to the school, the twelve Negro children did not attend classes on Tuesday. The *Courier-News* (Aug. 30, 1956) published photographs that showed hundreds listening to Kasper's segregationist speeches on Tuesday night. The TFCG and chairman Donald Davidson, a Vanderbilt University professor, sought an injunction from the state Chancery Court—and, ultimately, a Tennessee Supreme Court panel in Knoxville—to prevent public funds from being used to operate an integrated school, which they argued was against state Jim Crow laws. If granted, the injunction would close CHS. The disease of racism had blinded Donaldson and his supporters about the effect that closing the schools would have on the future of a generation of young people.

Negro students were back in school on Wednesday. One of them, Bobby L. Cain, had to be placed in temporary police protection after responding to an attacker who had confronted him as he returned to school following the lunch break. Principal David Brittain closed the school early and sent all children home for safety reasons. He surveyed parents, who voted to keep the school open and integrated. Superintendent of Schools Frank E. Irwin, School Board Chairman Chester E. Hicks, and Mayor W. E. Lewallen urged citizens to "obey the law." For the most part, the people of Clinton did so.

School officials and town leaders conferred with Judge Taylor in Knoxville for further injunction against interference at CHS. Kasper was arrested and placed in jail. (He would eventually be sentenced to a year in federal prison for violating a federal court order.) Five others were arrested with Kasper but released with stern warnings.

The head of the Alabama White Citizens Council, meanwhile, took Kasper's place in front of the crowd, declaring that integrated schools would lead to a mongrel white race through miscegenation. Kasper was back in town after posting bond for his appeal. On Friday night, CHS played an old rival in football, which attracted more people into the town. On Saturday, September 1, more than four thousand people, including persons from outside the county and even from outside Tennessee, gathered around the courthouse, shouting that they wanted Kasper to speak. The crowd rocked cars, destroyed property, and surrounded a visiting Knoxville Negro in a U.S. Navy uniform until the police rescued him. There were threats to burn the mayor's house down. The disturbances prompted Clinton's six-man police department to call for state troopers. Kasper was again arrested by the sheriff for inciting riots and sedition.

At the urging of Mayor Lewallen and the Anderson County sheriff Glad Woodward, who had taken a chartered plane to Nashville, Governor Clement tried to control the explosive situation. He ordered highway state patrol cars and 110 state troopers with riot guns, submachine guns, and sirens shrieking to the scene. "I cannot sit back as governor and allow a lawless element to take over [Tennessee]," Clement said. On Sunday, September 2, he sent 633 battle-ready Tennessee National Guardsmen with M-41 tanks and armored personnel carriers to Clinton. The governor was angry that his intent to keep Tennessee peaceful was being upset by outside agitators. Clement said, "I am trying to do this [only] to promote law and order." Many Negroes were in church services when the troops arrived. State troopers blockaded the narrow, two-lane highways to control access to Clinton. The guardsmen would stay until September 13.

Meanwhile, rumors continued to spread that all area schools would be subjected to immediate desegregation, while members of the tiny Negro community remained mortified of bombings and harassment from their neighbors. In nearby Oliver Springs, guard units rushed to the scene after two Negro men in a car fired their pistol and shotgun into the ground to force a white mob back. The rioters had heard that the school in Oliver Springs was about to accept some Negroes. Unknown persons set off dynamite on the Negro side of town and threatened a news photographer. The National Guard commander in Oliver Springs told his troops, "I'll be damned if I will let some country bastards push me around." Fifteen whites and two Negroes were arrested. In Knoxville, some students at Rule High School planted a tombstone out front, daring any Negro to integrate their school. Two shots were fired at the home of Steve Williams, father of one of the Negro students in Clinton. School windows were smashed with bricks, and Principal Brittain was harassed by telephone calls.

Things calmed down after the stay by the National Guard. However, the *Courier-News* (Sept. 27, 1956) reported a bomb explosion in the Negro area near the home of Ronald Hayden, but it did no damage. Kasper was arrested for the third time by Sheriff Glad Woodward; this time, he resisted arrest and had to be tackled and subdued after hitting a deputy. On September 27, the local grand jury indicted Kasper on charges that could bring him a year in jail, but Kasper said he had fought because there was no warrant for his arrest—a violation of his rights. The segregationists soon received more bad news that further inflamed their anger: on September 28, 1956, a panel of the Tennessee Supreme Court met in Knoxville and answered the TFCG petition by ruling that *Brown* had nullified the school segregation laws in the Tennessee constitution (Sec. 12, Art. XI). On Saturday, October 13, Ku Klux Klansmen, robed but without their hoods, boldly entertained hundreds in the Clinton town square, according to the *Courier-News* (Oct. 4, 18, 1956). In nearby Oak Ridge, Tennessee's moderate U.S. senator, Albert Gore Sr., was heckled by a crowd. There had been speculation that Harry Truman would campaign for the Democrats during the November 1956 presidential election; however, the former president reportedly said that he would not visit the Clinton–Oak Ridge area because his pro–civil rights stance had angered southern Democrats in 1948 and that a visit to the area now would only open old wounds.

Free on bail, Kasper led a delegation of segregationists to confront Principal Brittain. Kasper told him to resign or get the Negroes out of the school. "I am going to obey the court and the law," Brittain replied. The principal could count the Auxiliary Police, the *Courier-News*, most of the faculty, the student council, the PTA, various religious groups, and most public officials on the side for desegregation. The school board offered the Negro parents the option of having their children sent as usual by bus to Knoxville's Austin High School. One parent, Herbert Allen, left for California with his daughter Jo Ann because he wanted her to "get a good education" after the trouble had caused her to miss numerous days of school. Another family, after receiving threatening telephone calls late at night, sent their child to the segregated school in Knoxville.

After Kasper, who still faced federal charges, was acquitted on local charges by an Anderson County jury on November 17, the harassment of the Negro students became intolerable. On Wednesday and Thursday, November 28–29, following intimidation by white students, the ten Negro students stayed home. The Anderson County School Board met and offered transportation to Austin High School in Knoxville, but the students, parents, plaintiffs, and lawyers refused the offer. The Negro students stayed home again on Friday, and on Monday, December 3, the school board criticized the federal government for not doing more to help in the situation.

December 4 became the most violent day in Clinton since the harassment had resumed. The Reverend Paul Turner, pastor of the First Baptist

Church, went to the Negro neighborhood to escort six children who wished to return to school. Sidney Davis, a local attorney, and Leo Burnett, a mill worker, also helped protect the children. But then the Reverend Turner, while walking to his church office, was attacked by a mob of men and women and severely beaten. Brittain closed the school at 11:30 A.M. That same day, local voters rejected the segregationists' candidate for mayor. *Life* magazine published pictures from Clinton for national consumption.

Meanwhile, NAACP lawyers and others were pressuring the Eisenhower administration to do more to enforce the *Brown* decision, but the president seemed to be afraid of making any strong public statements lest his "southern strategy" for the Republican Party be upset. He wanted to hold blacks in their traditional place within the Republican Party, but he also wanted to bring southern whites—who were disgruntled with the Democratic Party since Truman's civil rights thrust of 1948—into the party. Behind the scenes, President Eisenhower was walking a dangerous tightrope and trying to protect three political interests. He wanted (1) to help extend and protect black citizens' civil rights, (2) to not interfere with southern states' rights, and (3) to insure respect for the constitutional authority of the federal government. The pro-Republican *Nashville Globe* (Nov. 26, 1956), a Negro paper, was mildly critical of the GOP's stance on civil rights and yet remained loyal to the party. To demonstrate Ike's commitment to the black readership, the *Globe* reported that U.S. attorney general Herbert Brownell Jr. had recently called a conference of local U.S. attorneys to discuss how they might help the courts enforce the federal court orders. Brownell, who served in 1953–57, decided to file the first desegregation suits in compliance with *Brown*.

On Tuesday, December 4, at a meeting in Knoxville, Anderson County–Clinton school officials apprised Judge Taylor of the difficulties. Surprisingly, perhaps because of Brownell's decision that the federal government would enforce its laws and court decisions, local U.S. attorney John C. Crawford attended the meeting and became actively involved in the discussions about what to do about the Clinton situation. The local school officials argued that the federal government should enforce its own decision. Crawford said that he had no problem with that, but that Governor Clement wanted state control over law and order. Therefore, Crawford said, the local officials should perhaps confer with Clement. But meanwhile, he added, Uncle Sam would enforce federal court orders.

On the next day, eight U.S. marshals, assisted by Clinton police and Anderson County sheriff's deputies, divided into pairs and rounded up fifteen persons for violating court orders, including W. H. Till, the alleged head of the

Anderson County White Citizens Council. They were taken to Taylor's court-room. This action and the possibility of a federal sentence still hanging over Kasper's head seemed to calm things down once more, according to the *Clinton Courier-News* (Dec. 6, 1956).

In the meantime, there were mixed feelings about *Brown* and how its implications would play out. The *Nashville Globe* (May 11, 1956) believed that integration in Nashville would be smooth. But several months earlier, the *Globe* (Sept. 22, 1955) had reported on lectures by Fisk University president Charles S. Johnson, who foresaw difficult times ahead. As he told a gathering in New York: "State governments in the South are dominated by rural legisla-tors, whose overall attitude is anti-labor, anti-capital, anti-race, anti-liberal, anti–civil rights, anti-education, anti-intellectual, anti-technology, and anti–federal government. World opinion and intervention of the federal govern-ment wrought most changes in the South. This is a tragic pity that while the rest of the world is giving attention and respect to basic human rights, every device from subversion of law to violence is being employed to defeat the Court [in the South]." A typical segregationist view came from a letter writer to the *Memphis Press-Scimitar* (Nov. 6, 1956), who opined, "Millions of non-Southerners will support quickly the South's position on public school inte-gration when they realize that integration in the South would transform America into a nation of mixed people." For its part, the *Memphis Commercial Appeal* (Nov. 28) maintained a position of caution. Three days later, the *Tri-State Defender*, also in Memphis, said that many Negroes expected Clement "to throw a rock, and hide his hand" in not doing more about the unrest.

In January 1957, a crew from the CBS television network arrived in Ten-nessee to film a documentary on the school crisis in Clinton and get local reaction to *Brown*. In the view of many southerners, the northern press feasted on sensationalism and images of backward southern whites and ignorant Negroes in that place beyond the Ohio River—the South—and therefore, some local citizens were suspicious, believing that the CBS crew would try to make the South and Tennessee look like the only villains in this business of American racism. The January 6 telecast, "Clinton and the Law," would be one of Edward R. Murrow's renowned *See It Now* programs, and it proved to be balanced—even sympathetic—toward the residents of Clinton, who said they were "trying hard to adjust to a Supreme Court decision they were not crazy about." The Negro students who were interviewed recalled that Murrow was morally concerned about the unfairness of Jim Crow. The telecast pre-sented Clinton as an example of how to accept the Supreme Court ruling. Letters arrived in praise of the Reverend Paul Turner and Principal David J.

Brittain. However, a few members of Turner's church charged him with violating their rights to hold segregationist views.

Segregationist forces started to pressure Governor Clement. An Alabama segregationist named C. W. Walker wrote Clement on January 16, 1957, to suggest: "Blackball him [the Negro] from all jobs in the South, and let 'Old Man Hungry' get after him." A man from Shreveport wrote Clement on January 27: "A group here has been Praying God strikes Governor Clement down for sending shoulders [sic] to a school to see some old Black, Black Buck Negro on the seat with some poor little white girl. We all praid [sic] God Allmightly [sic] to kill you ded [sic] the very nest [sic] time Governor Clement tries."

On the night of February 14, 1957, dynamite blasts ripped through the Negro section of Clinton known as Foley Hill. More than eight explosions, including one near the home of the editor of the *Courier-News*, came under investigation. Violence had taken place in Anderson and Knox counties since the Oak Ridge desegregation, indicating the great frustration felt by segregationists, who still feared federal power. Shots were fired into many homes, and fights were provoked in Clinton High School. Some CHS teachers found their cars vandalized. The school board expelled Alfred Williams for fighting with a white student. Negro parents continued to be harassed on their jobs and by late-night telephone calls. Only seven of the original twelve Negro students remained by February 21, 1957. Bobby Cain decided at one point to quit school but changed his mind.

[*]

Carloads of segregationists traveled to Nashville on February 11, 1957, to pressure the General Assembly to pass anti–school integration laws. On March 22, 1957, the *East Tennessee Reporter* named state representative Thurman Thompson of Lewisburg as the sponsor of a bill to allow the governor to shut down the schools, but no such law was ever passed in Tennessee. On March 17, 1957, Clement received a letter from the Reverend C. A. Davis of Seymour, who said, "Perhaps you know but did you know COMMUNISTS are working in Tennessee Schools?" He named the Highlander Folk School and its activist director, James Dombrowski, along with Martin Luther King Jr. and the NAACP, and declared, "My God, Govener [sic]—Ther [sic] will be anarchy if this continues."

Earlier, in January, Clement had addressed the joint General Assembly and declared:

The words I speak to you today represent a decision I must live with the rest of my days on this earth and through all Eternity. Human that I am I would have gladly let the cup pass from me. However, I am perfectly willing to accept both Divine and human judgment of my words and deeds on this occasion. I come before you to speak the truth. I come to suggest that course of which, under prevailing circumstances, I honestly believe to be in the best interest of all of you in general—and Tennessee's children in particular. I am not so concerned with what extremists on either side think of what I shall say here today—nor those out-of-staters [sic] of both races who come into our midst stirring up trouble and strife where none existed in order to further their own gains. I shall not attempt to please them. But I am greatly concerned about what our God-fearing law abiding citizens think—the farm families who put their children on school buses in the early dawn not to see them again until dark; the thousands of factory workers trying to educate their children, trusting them to the care of our good teachers; the doctors, lawyers, merchants—yes, all of our good citizens. I am tremendously concerned with your thinking and your problems and it is to you, our loyal, peace-loving, God-fearing citizens—through your representatives whom you have sent here to Capitol Hill, that I address my message.

Clement's address presented the history of the race problem as the greatest one faced by Tennesseans. He continued:

We could render no greater service to our State, to our Nation and to posterity than to show that we as Tennesseans, as southerners, as Americans, white and Negro can adjust our problems and work and live in peace and harmony.

After recounting some history from slavery through Reconstruction, Clement said:

But in our recognition of the existence of different backgrounds for white and Negro, we must not overlook the fact that the Negro is equal to the white in the eyes of the law and in the sight of God.

Clement said that the Negro was an American citizen who paid taxes and served in the armed forces and that "he is entitled to equality of opportunity." Clement then tried to reduce the fear of *Brown* among Tennesseans by saying:

The court held that statutes COMPELLING segregation in the public schools on the basis of race were unconstitutional. It held that
no state could in the operation of its public schools discriminate
against persons on account of their race. The court did not purport to take over the administration of . . . schools. It expressly
left that administration where it has always been, in the hands
of the local . . . officials. It did not purport to require the states to
mix arbitrarily persons of different races in the schools. It did not
deprive individual parents and children of their rights of voluntarily choosing the schools they wish to attend.

Clement said that he respected *Brown* and over the last two years had
"given this matter my constant attention," as well as ordered studies by lawyers, the commissioner of education, and executive staff members. "I did not
then think it proper, and I do not now think it proper, to fan this problem into
a raging conflagration," he said. He proposed (1) providing adequate educational opportunities for all Tennessee children, (2) preserving and promoting
peaceful and harmonious relations between the races, (3) giving people the
opportunity of choosing without force or compulsion the course which best
suits their needs and desires, (4) not attempting to impose an inflexible system
throughout the state, (5) giving local officials the fullest powers to cope effectively with their problems, and (6) yet providing checks and balances essential
to the prevention of arbitrary action harmful to the protection of the rights
and privileges of all of Tennessee's people. He asked the legislature to grant
new powers to the school systems to create separate schools for white and
Negro children whose parents so desire, assign and transfer students, deal with
transportation of children, and consolidate school systems if needed for different local circumstances.

The Clinton school board sent a letter to Clement, saying his proposal
would do nothing to forestall desegregation. The school boards already had
power to segregate students except for the federal court orders, the letter noted,
but as long as Negroes insisted on attending integrated schools, it could do
nothing.

The southern states rushed into the battle, and enacted more than 450
laws and resolutions to prevent or limit school desegregation. By 1956, the
South had desegregated only 665 of 3,700 school districts, and the number of
school districts diminished as consolidations took place. Hundreds of Negro
professionals were fired or demoted. Just below Chattanooga, the Georgia legislature prepared a resolution to urge Congress to impeach the justices. Georgia governor Marvin Griffin even traveled to Little Rock, Arkansas, to address

a White Citizens' Council rally. The disease of Georgia racism was infectious. The legislative delegation from Hamilton County, where Chattanooga is located, was supposedly elected on a straight anti-desegregation ticket in 1956. Conservatives in the Tennessee General Assembly also tried to follow the lead of Alabama and Georgia by passing bills to denounce *Brown* and place the NAACP under rules of scrutiny for subversive activities, but no effective bill passed. Another bill proposed to allow school boards to establish separate schools for boys and girls—an apparent effort to allay white fears about miscegenation.

[*]

The *Clinton Courier-News* (April 11, 1957) continued to report on trouble at Clinton High School. Racial attacks on black students persisted, but Brittain handled the incidents as disciplinary problems. A cross was burned on the lawn of a teacher who had sent letters to parents about the failing grades of students who stayed home. As the school year ended, some students proclaimed that they had made it through the year "in fellowship." However, several teachers decided not to return the following year; the school superintendent said he would resign; and Brittain announced that he would accept a graduate fellowship at New York University. The *Nashville Globe* (May 17, 1957), which had criticized Clement and Eisenhower in January, praised Brittain's decision, noting that nine faculty members at Tennessee A&I State University held degrees from NYU. On the third anniversary of *Brown*, the Ku Klux Klan staged a parade in Clinton, where the speakers spoke against Governor Clement, Catholicism, Jews, and the U.S. Supreme Court before ending the program with a cross-burning on the edge of town. But the *Courier–News* (May 23, 1957) reported that graduation at CHS went smoothly except for when one student dumped water in the face of the editor of the *East Tennessee Reporter,* who had peered in a window to take a picture of Bobby L. Cain, the school's first Negro graduate.

On May 26, the NAACP presented Cain with a freedom award; baseball star Jackie Robinson made the presentation during a ceremony in New York City. Cain received private and institutional money to attend Tennessee A&I, from which he graduated in 1961. He was drafted into the U.S. Army during the Vietnam War and later came back to work in Oak Ridge. He subsequently moved to Nashville, where he retired in 2001 as a counselor with the State of Tennessee. In the spring of 1958, Gail Ann Epps became the first female Negro student to graduate from CHS, and like Cain she attended

Tennessee A&I. Among those first involved in the Clinton desegregation effort, Theresa Caswell, Minnie A. Dickey, and Alva McSwain would later graduate from CHS.

In Nashville, the state capital, hundreds of citizens held meetings in early 1957 at Belmont Methodist Church, near Vanderbilt University, to discuss ways to improve race relations and integrate the schools. But the local school board gained approval from the court for a gradual desegregation plan—one grade per year. The defendants argued that keeping the children together would continue a cohesive group to peaceably integrate the schools each year. Coyness Ennix, the only Negro on the local school board (and the first since 1867), voted against the plan, partly because the school board had gerrymandered the districts to minimize the number of Negro children eligible to attend white schools. Although he approved the gradualism plan, Federal Judge William E. Miller asked for a full plan by December 31, 1957. Williams and Looby appealed to the Sixth Circuit and argued that a better climate for change would be produced by a less protracted process of desegregation. But the court would uphold gradualism in 1959.

The *East Tennessee Reporter,* among many other conservative southern papers, predicted desegregation would be defeated. But A. Philip Randolph, the "dean of civil rights leaders," and his Brotherhood of Sleeping Car Porters union kept up national pressure for school desegregation. Such labor leaders believed that the same people who opposed civil rights were against unionism. BSCP members were asked to contribute an hour's wages to support the implementation of *Brown* and over the years sent thousands of dollars to the NAACP. At the same time, the Brotherhood was contributing to the purchase of station wagons for the ongoing Montgomery bus boycott. In New York City on April 24, 1956, the BSCP held a "State of the Race" conference to encourage all leaders to support *Brown.* On May 17, 1957, they carried out a "Prayer Pilgrimage for Freedom" at the Lincoln Memorial in Washington and organized two racially integrated marches to support school desegregation. Student marchers carried signs, including some that read, "It's Time for Every State to Integrate."

During the spring of 1957, as he awaited trial in Judge Taylor's court, John Kasper tried to persuade Knoxville school board members to resign rather than comply with *Brown.* At the time, the local racial climate seemed to favor desegregation, although Knoxville newspapers did carry stories about the June 3 birthday of slaveholder and Confederate president Jefferson Davis, which was proclaimed a holiday for public employees. On July 23, a federal district court jury found Kasper, Lawrence T. Branley, William Brakebill,

Alonzo Bullock, Clyde Cook, May N. Currier, and W. H. Till guilty of violating Judge Taylor's injunction. Taylor sentenced Kasper to a year in federal prison, but he appealed the verdict, was released on bond, and continued his movement against *Brown*.

After speaking against *Brown* in North Carolina, Kasper struck out west, heading to Nashville in August. The *Nashville Globe* had been following Kasper's escapades and already branded him a troublemaker. On August 6, it announced his arrival: "Lawbreaker Comes to Nashville." The *Globe* also claimed that Kasper was feuding with local attorney Jack Kershaw, the vice chairman of the TFCG, about Kasper's hogging the anti-desegregation spotlight. The TFCG had reportedly assisted Kasper with his legal problems. The *Globe* (June 14, 1957) was still critical of Eisenhower because only 18 percent of thirty-seven hundred southern school districts, mostly in the border states, had desegregated. The *Globe* also urged the Nashville school board to ignore Kasper, Kershaw's TFCG, and other segregationists, and to proceed with desegregation of local schools.

Nashville Mayor Ben West opposed Kasper and his allies. Kasper was denied a permit to hold a rally in Centennial Park and was arrested three times for illegal parking and other violations. But Kasper made bail, held his rallies, and on September 8, 1957, proclaimed, "When they put the niggers in school with your kids in September, load your shotgun to defend your wife and home—be prepared for the worst: race riots, hanging, anything."

The public schools in Nashville opened on September 9, 1957, under the school board's gradualism plan, which Judge Miller had approved. But a mere 19 of 115 eligible Negro first-graders entered seven previously all-white schools. Mortified Negro parents had helped the segregationists by taking the board's offer to transfer their children back to all-black schools. The Reverend Kelly Miller Smith, pastor of First Colored Baptist Church, and his wife, Alice, a biology instructor at Tennessee A&I, allowed their daughter Joy to be the first child to enroll in the integrated schools when classes began. "Before we allowed our daughter to be the first Negro child to enter a white school, my wife and I searched ourselves wondering if we had a right to submit her to such a task," Reverend Smith said. "The dangers of accepting the humiliation were worse than pioneering in a worthy cause."

In March 1956, the Reverend Smith, along with Mr. and Mrs. R. B. J. Campbelle, longtime employees at Tennessee A&I and parents of the first Negro graduate of the UT law school, had been elected as chief officers of the Nashville branch NAACP. They were pictured in the *Globe* on March 23. In May 1956, Reverend Smith, the local NAACP officers, the National Council of Negro Women, the National Association of Colored Women's Clubs, and other Negro groups had thrown their support behind A. Philip Randolph's proposed "Prayer Pilgrimage for Freedom" to flood Washington, D.C., with thousands of civil rights marchers in respect of *Brown*. And while the Nashville school desegregation crisis was underway, Fisk University held its fall convocation, with Stephen J. Wright, the institution's seventh president and its second black president, presiding. Wright, like his predecessor, Charles S. Johnson, would firmly support the civil rights movement.

Photographs in the *Nashville Banner* showed angry crowds in front of the schools on September 9. Earlier that morning, just after midnight, someone had bombed Hattie Cotton Elementary School. Even the *Banner*, no great friend to desegregation, said, "There is no room in Nashville for kindred elements of malicious mischief." The newspaper offered a one-thousand-dollar reward for the arrest and conviction of the terrorists. Eventually, five white men were charged in connection with the incident. Kasper, meanwhile, left town rather than suffer more arrests. The *Globe* (Sept. 13, 1957) praised his departure and noted, "Desegregation in Little Rock [Arkansas] to Start Soon." Kasper, like the Ku Klux Klan, had accused Jews of encouraging Negro protests, and the Jewish Community Center in Nashville was bombed months later. The FBI was keeping tabs on local terrorists, but under J. Edgar Hoover's rules, the agency stayed out of local law enforcement affairs.

[*]

In Blount County in East Tennessee, not far from Knoxville, the *Maryville-Alcoa Daily Times* had announced *Brown* on May 18, 1954, in this way: "Actual End to Segregation Months Away despite Court Ruling." Negroes had lived in the area since before the Civil War, and by the late 1910s many were working in the metal industry in the "company town" of Alcoa, established by the Aluminum Corporation of America. The first local Negro school, the Freedman's Institute, was established in 1867. In addition to support from the Freedmen's Bureau and the Methodist Church, direct support to teachers of Negroes came from members of the Quakers (Society of Friends), who lived in nearby Friendsville. There were ten Negro schools in Blount County by 1910, but only three of them existed by 1954, when twenty-four Negroes graduated from Hall High School, established in 1932. In September 1957, thirty-six Negro students and ten adults showed up at the whites-only Bassel School in Alcoa. However, they were ordered to return to the school for Negroes and told that Alcoa would not integrate until the city government said so. Hall's Negro principal was forced to reprimand the students. The Colored Parents Teachers Association protested by claiming that Hall School was a fire hazard. Of the more than sixteen hundred pupils in the Alcoa Public Schools, nearly six hundred were Negroes.

As local newspapers also reported that same month, some bold Negroes were denied admission to the white high school in nearby Maryville. The city maintained the William J. Hale School for Negroes, whose name honored the former president of Tennessee A&I State College—a native of the area and a product of Maryville College. In the year that *Brown* was announced, only five students graduated from Hale School. No one would admit as to where the pro-integration activity among the Negro students of Maryville had originated in September 1957. However, members of the county school board were prepared to discuss the matter at its September 13 meeting after it had received a letter from the Blount County Improvement Association (BCIA), a local organization, led by Leroy Porter, that was dedicated to better race relations. However, BCIA members declined to attend the meeting after the *Maryville-Alcoa Daily Times* highly publicized the fact that discussion of integration would be part of the agenda. Indeed, hundreds of whites packed the meeting. Later, the BCIA said its goal was to improve race relations and the economic, educational, and civic conditions in the county—not to start a race riot. The BCIA asked the board to quietly appoint an advisory committee to plan for implementation of *Brown*. The school board voted to develop a plan by which area schools would be gradually integrated by 1960.

Meanwhile, Tennesseans and other southerners were paying close attention to newspaper reports of the unfolding events in Little Rock, Arkansas. Tennessee's neighbor to the west, Arkansas, offered a violent example of the response to the desegregation of public schools. The federal court ordered Little Rock public schools to desegregate by the fall of 1957, but Governor Orval Faubus called National Guard units to block the students entering Central High School. Riots broke out, and President Eisenhower had to order federal troops from the Tennessee-Kentucky Fort Campbell base to Little Rock. Frank Clement and several other southern governors pressured Eisenhower to withdraw the troops and compromise with Faubus. Clement also criticized the North for its hypocrisy about the integration issue, and he labeled John Kasper "a rascal" for interfering in Tennessee school desegregation. But the *Globe* called Clement "a reactionary for opposing federal troops escorting nine youngsters to school." Clement described himself as a law-abiding segregationist, which was doubtless how many white southerners saw themselves. However, a national Gallup Poll showed that 64 percent of Americans approved of Eisenhower's actions. The federal court blocked a law to turn Little Rock public schools over to a private school company. As the *Oak Ridger* put it, "Thus Little Rock has clarified the issue." In *Cooper v. Aaron* (1959), the U.S. Supreme Court ruled that state laws could not nullify a citizen's right to attend public schools. Little Rock's nine Negro students and Daisy Bates, the NAACP activist who advised them, became national celebrities. In the preface to Bates's book, *The Long Shadow of Little Rock* (1962), Eleanor Roosevelt wrote, "I hope that before long the people of my race in my country will wake up to the fact that they are endangering the peace of the world. The world is made up of people of many races and many colors. They must be accepted as people and treated with the same dignity and respect wherever they are."

Neither the students who integrated Clinton High School nor their lawyers received the kind of fame given to Daisy Bates and the Little Rock Nine, although events in Clinton were certainly as dramatic. Tensions remained as the 1957 school year got underway. On October 16, 1957, the *Oak Ridger* reported the circulation of secret leaflets that said, "We are in sympathy with Little Rock. We too have faced bayonets! Walk out—Stay out. Please pass this on." Some twenty-nine students left Clinton High School, but parents returned many of them to classes. The school principal confiscated the leaflets, but after receiving criticism from the segregationists, he told the news media: "I am not making any difference in people here."

In 1958–59, Clinton High School had an overflow of more than eight hundred students, including seven Negro students. Five of the Negroes walked to school, and the other two children rode the school bus with the white children. Negro parents remained under relentless pressure to send their children to the Negro high school in Knoxville. This pressure came from some local whites who claimed to be moderates and "friends to your people."

On October 5, 1958, three explosions destroyed the high school building in Clinton. John Kasper called the bombing "a great victory for the white people of Tennessee." The Oak Ridge school district offered space for the displaced students, and Anderson County furnished buses to transport them. On November 8, two men were jailed for plotting to blow up CHS. A new facility would be built, while CHS classes continued in a borrowed school building seven miles away.

[*]

In Nashville, students and parents were allowed to openly harass Negro children inside and outside the schools. When it became too much for some

Negro parents to withstand, many of them transferred their children to other schools. Approximately 115 of 1,400 Negro first-graders and 55 of 2,000 white first-graders lived in zones previously restricted to the opposite racial group. All the 55 whites assigned to Negro schools transferred out because the board allowed various exceptions. Only 10 of the 115 Negro students dared to continue attending white schools. In June of 1958, only 9 Negro first-graders had completed the school year at integrated Nashville schools. In January 1959, Buford Ellington, formerly the commissioner of agriculture, became the new governor of Tennessee. During the Clinton crisis, according to the *Memphis Press-Scimitar* of November 17, 1956, Ellington had said, "I want to be quoted. I think integration in Tennessee now would be harmful to both races." Ellington did, however, refrain from supporting extremist efforts to fly Confederate flags over the state capitol of Tennessee, as had been done in his native Mississippi.

In March 1959, the U.S. Civil Rights Commission met in Nashville to assess the last five years of desegregation of public schools. School superintendents from thirteen states and Washington, D.C., testified that school boards, city officials, and police must support the superintendents if desegregation was to work. By the fall of 1959, nine years since Avon Williams, Z. A. Looby, and Carl A. Cowan filed the Anderson County case, only four Tennessee school districts had been integrated, and just 169 Negro children were attending integrated schools.

Resistance to *Brown* was worse elsewhere. Rather than implement the federal court order in the fall of 1959, officials in Prince Edward County, Virginia, closed all public schools. A private school system was set up for the 1,400 white students, with aid coming from across the South. The 1,700 Negro children in Prince Edward County had no schools except for a few "freedom schools." Many children stayed home and played in the dirt, while some Negro parents sent their children to relatives in adjacent counties and North Carolina to attend public schools.

In September 1959, thirty Negro airmen at Steward Air Force Base in Rutherford County, Tennessee, filed a complaint in federal district court in Nashville. The men argued that their children were bused past the public schools in nearby Smyrna and sent fourteen miles to Murfreesboro to attend Bradley School for Negroes. This two-story brick structure was formerly Bradley Academy and was hardly big enough to provide a quality school for so many children. Judge William E. Miller ordered a desegregation plan by September 15. He reasoned that if the U.S. Air Force base was integrated, the children should also go to integrated schools and that Oak Ridge had set a precedent for integrated schools serving federal installations. Sixteen Negro children, aged six through twelve, whose parents were affiliated personnel at the air base, entered grades three through eight at Coleman Elementary School in Smyrna. On opening day, while three law enforcement officers stood nearby, the principal met the Negro students and their parents at the front door and politely led them to the cafeteria to complete the necessary paperwork. "I want to thank you," he said, "for your cooperation this morning and assure you that your children will be treated just the same as all other children in the school." Rutherford County filed a motion to dismiss the case, but the judge ordered the county to submit a plan to desegregate all schools.

Rutherford County authorities would delay full school desegregation until forced to do so by the Civil Rights Act of 1964. They continued to maintain some segregated schools for the benefit of white children for several years more. When the Rutherford County schools were fully integrated in 1965, one high school, one city school, and six county elementary schools were operating for African Americans: Holloway High School, Bradley School, Shiloh, Bethel, Smyrna Rosenwald, Locke's, Cedar Grove, and 231 School. The latter school was erected at the late date of 1962, because the authorities still hoped to continue limited segregation. Three of the former Negro schools became integrated schools in the system for a while. By 1968, Holloway, Bethel, and Cedar Grove were closed, as whites apparently objected to attending inferior facilities they previously approved for blacks only.

In Knoxville, Negro parents sued for desegregated schools on January 7, 1957. Including some 4,000 Negro children, Knoxville had 21,500 schoolchildren. Knox County public schools included another 300 Negro children. The suit was dismissed by Taylor because three of the five school board members named in the suit had been replaced. Attorney Carl A. Cowan was frustrated because a new suit would delay a hearing for up to two years. The Knoxville Area Human Relations Council members published a booklet entitled *There's Nothing New about Being Fair* (1958), and said no discrimination existed. "In the present emotion-charged atmosphere," the group contended, "it is helpful to remember that the issue at stake is fairness and equality, and though its application has been spotty, the principle of fairness has been accepted by people in the Knoxville area." The council claimed that there had been 150 Negro graduate students at the University of Tennessee, Knoxville, since 1952 and also pointed to Negroes enrolled at Maryville College, whites enrolled at the historically black Knoxville College since 1957, the desegregation of the Oak Ridge public schools, and some integrated churches. Also noted were the integration of bus lines in 1956, of the public library since 1950, of public parks in 1956, and of the airport restaurant in July 1955. Negro policemen, the council said, had been included on Knoxville's force since 1908.

After conferring with Thurgood Marshall, Avon Williams, and the parents of Josephine Goss, Cowan filed *Goss v. Board of Education of Knoxville* (1959). Even though he had handled the case since 1957, Judge Robert Taylor granted the school board a year of delay, which the board had requested to "prevent the kind of violence that occurred in Little Rock." In November 1959, parents representing twelve Negro students filed a petition with the Knoxville school board, asking for a reversal of the decision to delay school integration. The board members refused the request. The Board of Education acknowledged that school integration was inevitable, given all that was going on nearby and across the South, but it also argued, "Most Negroes do not want to integrate." After heated remarks from both sides, Taylor ordered the school board to submit a desegregation plan, which it presented on April 8, 1960. Taylor approved the grade-a-year plan to begin in the fall of 1960–61. About twenty-eight Negro children enrolled in eight previously all-white elementary schools.

[*]

Memphis was sitting nervously on the sidelines of the school desegregation battle. So far, the first schools to desegregate were in East Tennessee and Middle Tennessee, including Oak Ridge (1955), Clinton (1956), Nashville (1957), Smyrna (1959), and Alcoa, Maryville, and Knoxville (1960). However, six years after *Brown*, in West Tennessee, where more than two-thirds of Tennessee's Negro citizens lived, no public school system had been desegregated. The pace of school desegregation in Memphis was affected by local politics, the financial condition of the NAACP and the Legal Defense Fund, and conservative federal district judges on the West Tennessee bench. Indeed, these judges were more conservative than Taylor and much more obstructionist.

Memphis seemed to adhere to *Plessy v. Ferguson*. The city built new Negro schools as fast as needed in order to prevent any discussion about racial inequality. The city began supporting its second Negro high school by 1931 and had several Negro high schools, not including a Catholic high school for Negroes, in the 1950s. Memphis Negroes seemed to be content with their schools, parks, and swimming pools. Besides, neighborhood segregation was so rigid in Memphis that integration of black and white schools would require massive busing, which by the early 1960s the federal courts would not even entertain. The *Brown* plaintiffs, after all, had asked for *desegregation* and only reluctantly for *integration*.

NAACP officers hoped to avoid a court suit because the national head-quarters had exhausted its legal fund in the lengthening battle of *Brown*. On December 10, 1959, the NAACP branch sent a request to the Memphis Board of Education to voluntarily desegregate city schools. One hundred parents—joined by J. H. Turner, the local NAACP president; R. B. Sugarmon and H. T. Lockard, attorneys; D. S. Cunningham, an NAACP officer; and Vasco Smith, the head of the NAACP branch's education committee—signed the petition. "This committee is interested in complete compliance with the law of the land," said Smith, adding, "I cannot understand why school boards do not take some action on their own initiative instead of waiting for Negroes to bring lawsuits against them." The committee petitioned the school board on February 8, 1960, but the board still refused to discuss the issue. According to the *Memphis World* (Feb. 13, 1960), the school board president, Walter P. Armstrong, defended Jim Crow, saying that he would comply with "custom" and state law.

At the rally for the Freedom Fund—a drive to raise money in the war on Jim Crow—the crowd gave support for the NAACP to employ B. L. Hooks, A. W. Willis, H. T. Lockard, and R. B. Sugarmon to file a school desegregation suit. Eighteen students and their parents became plaintiffs in *T. W. Northcross v. Memphis City Schools* in March 1960. The NAACP-LDF joined the suit. When the federal judge, Marion S. Boyd, finally held the trial for the case in April 1961, half the Negroes who packed the courtroom walked out in disgust because Boyd approved a grade-at-a-time plan and upheld the Tennessee Pupil Assignment Law, which allowed schools to deny a child's enrollment in a particular school because of IQ and the school's pupil load. The NAACP opposed the gradualist plans and the Pupil Assignment Law. As reported in the *World* on June 8, the NAACP was pushing for "all-out school desegrega-tion." The plaintiffs appealed the case, but the plan went into effect in the fall of 1961.

In September, thirteen Negro children, out of fifty who applied, were approved by a three-member panel of the Memphis Board of Education to attend all-white elementary schools: Bruce (three students), Rozelle (four), Springdale (two), and Gordon (four). Knowing that the plan by the board and the judge was designed to discourage school integration in Memphis, the Memphis branch NAACP canvassed the parents and urged them to appeal the school assignments given the children. The local NAACP also recruited volunteers to transport the thirteen children to the four schools, watch over them, and meet them at the end of the day. Maxine Smith, the executive secretary of the local NAACP, escorted children to Springdale, while Sugarmon, Turner, and Willis acted as escorts to Gordon, Rozelle, and Bruce, respectively. Smith recalled that one racist man drove up from Mississippi to protest the desegregation but noted, "No unfavorable incidents have been reported." The police kept watch and things went smoothly on October 3, 1961.

On March 23, 1962, the Sixth Circuit Court of Appeals in Cincinnati ruled that the Tennessee Pupil Assignment Law was unacceptable and had no place in a legal plan for school desegregation. Boyd was forced to order the Memphis school board to submit a final plan. The city appealed to the final tribunal in the land, but on June 25, 1962, the U.S. Supreme Court let stand the circuit court's ruling against the assignment law. Memphis schools were integrated up to the third grade, involving fifty-three Negro students in twelve schools. Boyd rejected the NAACP's request to integrate all grades over the next three years, and he allowed the school board to permit students to transfer out of an integrated school even though the Supreme Court had recently struck down such a provision in the *Goss v. Knoxville* case.

It seemed that many Negroes cared little about school integration in Memphis, and this complacency perhaps slowed the process. Nevertheless, it was proudly reported by the *World* (June 3, 1961) that the Negro high schools in Memphis and Shelby County had graduated a record 1,758 students. Moreover, the county school board appointed Blair T. Hunt, the first Negro member, to the board in May 1961, and mass meetings in Memphis gave the NAACP and local civil rights leaders the support they needed to continue forward.

Another appeal was registered for the Memphis case. On May 22–23, 1963, Boyd heard the plaintiffs' arguments, but he upheld the school board's gradual plan. In June, the plaintiffs' lawyers filed another suit. In February 1964, at last, Boyd's court approved a plan to desegregate all twelve grades, but he rejected the NAACP's plan for specific racial balances in each school. Boyd's move precluded busing and other measures to address racial imbalances in specific schools. When Maxine Smith made her 1965 local NAACP report, four thousand Negro children were attending twenty elementary and thirteen junior high schools that were previously all white. By then, the city school system was 50 percent black. The local NACCP chapter sent a letter to the U.S. Department of Housing, Education, and Welfare to protest "continuing discrimination practices" by the local school board and the school administration.

In rural Shelby County in 1962, 307 parents of 884 children signed petitions to "request immediate desegregation" of the county schools. In September 1963, the Shelby County Public Schools admitted six Negro children to one school. Negroes constituted 32 percent of the children in the county system. On April 3, 1967, the education committee of the Memphis NAACP would send a letter titled "Segregation and Discrimination in Shelby County Schools" to the Shelby County government. The report claimed that there were no black administrators, that students were bused past the closest school, that black teachers were labeled and treated as inferior, that racially biased textbooks were being used, and that the superintendent continued to meet with black and white teachers separately.

[∗]

In Chattanooga, where U.S. Colored Troops had garrisoned and kept the city secure from the Confederates during the Civil War, the city denied jobs to Negro teachers from 1867 through 1881. This changed after Negro Republicans gained some power during Reconstruction. William C. Hodge, a Republican councilman (1878–87) and a state representative (1885–87), also sat on the Board of Education. The first Negro student graduated from high school in Chattanooga in 1886. In 1890, Chattanooga had two two-story brick schools for Negroes: Gilmer Street Elementary School and Howard High School, which were combined in one building, and the Montgomery Avenue School in another building. There were four white schools, including a high school. Howard High School graduated 6 of its 31 Negro students on May 19, 1893; Gilmer School had 741 pupils, with a 93 percent attendance rate; and Montgomery School had 1,085 students, with an average daily attendance of about 765. School board members were elected for each ward, including the heavily black Sixth Ward. When Jim Crow became entrenched, however, Negro political representation disappeared, although Negroes made up nearly a third of Chattanooga's people.

In July 1955, the Chattanooga school board tried to begin voluntary school desegregation. Chattanooga had 22,633 students and forty-four schools, including six Negro schools and no Negro board members. The school board appointed twenty-eight whites and twelve Negroes (30 percent) to an interracial advisory commission in November 1955. One of the city commissioners opposed the decision to voluntarily desegregate schools. The school board said it stood by the July decision and warned local officials: "But once the court decides we are not acting in good faith, the court will tell us what to do." If the students were assigned to the nearest school, thirty-one public schools would be integrated. At an anti-desegregation rally in Chattanooga, featured speakers included Arthur A. Canada of the Tennessee Society to Maintain Segregation; R. Carter Pittman, an attorney from Dalton, Georgia; and Florence Dean of Newman, Georgia, a former president of the Daughters of the American Revolution. They bitterly attacked *Brown* and said the South should turn to the right to bear arms as a way of solving the problem of federal interference. Canada accused Governor Frank Clement and Senator Estes Kefauver of selling out "to the integrating radicals of the North and East."

After trying for years to work something out with the white leaders, not until 1960 did local Negroes file for desegregation of the public schools in Chattanooga. The plaintiffs included parents of four children: James J. Mapp, president of the Chattanooga branch NAACP; Josephine Maxey-Derricks; and the Reverend H. H. Kirnon, pastor of Clegg's Chapel AME Church. The plaintiffs were represented by Negro attorney R. H. Craig of Chattanooga, Avon N. Williams, and Constance Baker Motley of the Legal Defense Fund. James Mapp and the others had decided to file suit after attending a statewide NAACP meeting at Nashville's Pleasant Green Baptist Church in September 1959. "I learned how to file a school desegregation suit," Mapp recalled, "and returned to Chattanooga to get others to help file it."

James Mapp had arrived in Chattanooga from Mayfield, Georgia, in 1937 at the age of ten, after his grandfather's horse and farm were taken by a local white power broker. "Down in Georgia, at that time, they took black folks' land when ever they felt like it; in fact, my grandfather had bought the land that probably had been taken from a previous Negro farmer," Mapp recalled. This white man owned land, the general store, and the saw mill, and Negroes had no lawyers to whom to turn. Mapp attended public schools, including Howard High School, from which he graduated in 1947, and briefly attended Tennessee A&I State College to study business administration. Responding to talks by his junior high school teacher, he joined the NAACP's youth council in 1942, and in remembrance of what had happened to his grandfather, young James decided to dedicate his life to fighting for human justice. By 1944, he was president of the NAACP youth council. He served as secretary of the local NAACP from 1953 to 1959 and became its president in 1959, serving for twenty-six years. He also would serve as state and regional NAACP president for several years.

In early 1960, Mapp, Maxey-Derricks, and Kirnon formed a group to register their children at a nearby white school that had vacant rooms and plenty of space for neighborhood children. After being refused, they and their attorney, Craig, contacted the NAACP-LDF, which assigned Constance

Baker Motley to the case. Motley in turn contacted Avon N. Williams Jr. in Nashville for help. The case was filed on April 6, 1960. Mapp said the authorities promised a Negro on the school board if the suit was withdrawn, and strangely, officials of the relatively new Southern Christian Leadership Conference (SCLC) threatened that if the deal was turned down, the Chattanooga NAACP chapter would be destroyed. The SCLC was headquartered just two hours away in Atlanta. But Mapp was a stubborn man, and he refused to give in as his grandfather had done in Georgia. Maxey and Kirnon left Chattanooga because of marriage and church transfer, leaving Mapp and two of his eight children, Debra and James J., as plaintiffs in the case, which would be heard by Judge Leslie R. Darr, a native of Jasper, Tennessee, and a former practicing attorney and circuit court judge whom FDR had named to the federal bench in 1939.

The NAACP wanted the lawsuit to include the issue of teacher assignments by race, but the school board's attorney asked Judge Darr to exclude this issue, arguing that the assignment of Negro teachers to white schools "does not affect the rights of the Negro plaintiffs herein." And indeed, for the time being, federal district courts were avoiding the teacher-placement issue. On October 21, 1960, Darr ruled in favor of the plaintiffs and ordered the school board to submit a desegregation plan by December 20. It was a summary judgment, which dismisses a case without a trial on its merits. Darr set a hearing on the desegregation plan for January 9, 1961. In the meantime, however, attorney R. H. Craig died of cancer, and Bruce C. Boynton, a graduate of Fisk University and Howard University Law School, established a practice in Chattanooga and took up the *Mapp* case. The board submitted a grade-a-year plan, including liberal transfer (freedom of choice). The plan would desegregate three grades in a few schools but leave other schools segregated to satisfy potentially violent race radicals. "Getting the people ready is not the plan of integration," Judge Darr said. "The plan is to expedite the constitutional rights of Negro students." On January 27, he declared the plan unacceptable. Chattanooga's Negro population by then was 32.4 percent of the total. A new plan was submitted to integrate the first grade in September 1961. However, Judge Darr retired.

Judge Frank L. Wilson assumed the case. He was a University of Tennessee Law School graduate who was practicing law in Knoxville when President John F. Kennedy nominated him to the bench on May 24, 1961. Mapp recalled that "Wilson was a good man, but he delayed the local case to see what would happen in another Tennessee case." Wilson allowed "reasonable" transfer plans, but Avon Williams threatened an appeal. Constance Baker Motley also threatened an appeal unless teachers were included in the plan. It was a grade-a-year plan, which would desegregate the high schools by 1967. Walter C. Robinson, the Negro Republican Party leader, argued in his *Chattanooga Observer* on November 3, 1961: "As long as there is housing area segregation, whether by law, custom, or tradition, there will be school segregation."

Hamilton County school officials chose to voluntarily desegregate rather than endure an expensive court suit. On August 29–30, 1962, sixty-two Negro children registered at six city schools and two Hamilton County schools. Representatives of the news media were kept across the street from the schools. Although no whites were enrolled in previously all-black schools, some white parents boycotted them anyway. Negroes would briefly launch a boycott of their own when the city closed two Negro school buildings. In 1963, Mapp, Williams, and Boynton asked for desegregation of the city's technical schools. Judge Wilson ordered a plan. Avon Williams read the recent Sixth Circuit Court appeals decision and argued that "an order should be made ending the assignment of teachers and principals on the basis of race or color." Four hundred twenty-nine Negroes attended nine white schools, and six whites enrolled in two Negro schools, and for 1963–64, ten of thirty-three elementary schools were peacefully desegregated. In January 1964, the Chattanooga SCLC chapter called a meeting of five hundred people at the Olivet Baptist Church and demanded that school desegregation be speeded up.

Meanwhile, in rural Davidson County outside Nashville, six Negro students and their parents had requested transfer to the Bordeaux Elementary School and Glencliff High School on September 8, 1960. The board members voted to deny the requests, claiming that the petition had arrived after school began and that the Negro schools were "as equal in every respect to the white schools." Avon Williams angrily said, "We can go over to Rome to the Olympics, but we cannot go to school here." The federal district court ordered county schools to begin desegregation in 1961.

[*]

Politicians in Tennessee and the South responded to *Brown* as a call to arms for whites to protect their exclusive society based on race "purity" and racial supremacy. *Brown* only called for desegregation—the dismantlement of segregation by law and the end of racial discrimination based on law. But whites—and soon almost everyone else (including Negroes)—translated *desegregation* into *integration*. Especially in the culturally isolated South, where many considered themselves to be the nation's guardians of white supremacy, they took

Brown to be an attack on their exclusiveness and ethnic monopoly of power and wealth. In the U.S. Senate, where the 1960 civil rights bill was being debated, there was an attempt to delete the provision that supported the *Brown* decision. Segregationist senators, particularly from southern states, believed that school integration would lead to intermarriage, and intermarriage with people of color would wipe out the "white race." Senator John McClellan of Arkansas told his fellow congressmen: "The time will come when you will weep about it [race mixing]." Tennessee senators Estes Kefauver and Albert Gore Sr. refused to participate in a southern filibuster to kill the 1960 civil rights legislation, but they did vote to cut the *Brown* provision. Some congressmen argued that *Brown* was the cause of the "racial disturbances in the South and now spreading to the North." The Tennessee legislature passed a mild anti-NAACP bill in 1957 but not to the extent of outlawing the organization as Alabama did. Governor Clement successfully vetoed the bill.

＊

CHAPTER 3

HELL NO, WE WON'T INTEGRATE

CONTINUING SCHOOL DESEGREGATION
IN TENNESSEE

Brown had not proven to be a substantial threat to southern segregation by 1963. In rural areas, Negroes had little access to local lawyers who would take civil rights cases. Many rural Negro leaders simply "let well enough alone," and others were in perpetual fear of violent white segregationist forces representing all classes of whites. Although poor, working-class, and lower-middle-class whites led the fiercest opposition to *Brown*, perhaps 15 to 30 percent of affluent whites were involved directly and indirectly in opposing it. Elite and very wealthy whites never worried about *Brown's* forcing their children to integrate by class or race because they continued to support exclusive schools whose tuition and fees were out of reach even for most middle-class whites. These practices led to continued racial separatism and white ethnic supremacy in all aspects of American life—in the North and in the South. By 1964, only 6 percent of 3 million southern Negro school children attended integrated schools.

The federal government continued to wrestle with different approaches to the desegregation of the schools, hoping to evolve an effective policy to speed up the process. In *McNeese v. Board of Education* (1963), the U.S. Supreme Court decided to allow civil rights plaintiffs to bypass state and local administrative remedies, if necessary, and bring suit directly in federal district courts. In *Griffin v. County Board of Education* (1964), the Supreme Court ruled that the schools in Prince Edward County, Virginia, had to be reopened. On March 20–21, 1963, the U.S. Supreme Court heard arguments in *Goss et al. v. Board of Education of Knoxville, Tennessee et al.*, in which the plaintiffs contended that minority-to-majority transfer provisions—which allowed white and black students to transfer from schools in which they were in the minority to ones in which they would be among the majority—constituted a tactic of avoiding further desegregation of schools. The boards of education in Chattanooga and Memphis entered the *Goss* case as amicus curiae, or friends of the court, arguing for retention of the pupil-transfer plan because the Sixth Circuit Court had affirmed *Maxwell v. County Board of Education of Davidson County, Tennessee.* Cowan, Looby, and Williams argued that Knoxville had rezoned school districts without reference to race but had included a transfer provision based on race. Ruling on June 3, 1963, the court agreed that such transfer plans were based on racial factors that would lead toward resegregation.

In the urban areas, it would take U.S. Supreme Court approval of the NAACP's recommendation for massive busing to attempt to further desegregate the school systems. In the rural areas, busing over long distances was common and generally accepted. However, the submission of desegregation plans in rural Tennessee generally occurred ten years after *Brown.*

The integration of the public schools in the Upper Cumberland was quite slow but smooth and uneventful. Jim Crow schools served the small Negro populations in Clay, DeKalb, Jackson, Overton, Putnam, and White counties. The largest Negro school was located in the largest town, Cookeville, in Putnam County, which contracted with the surrounding counties to educate their small groups of Negro children. Darwin, the Negro public school in Cookeville, began in 1928 and became a high school in 1936, graduating its first high school student two years later. When *Brown* was announced in 1954, Cookeville had just over a hundred students through the twelfth grade, with nearly a third of them bused from surrounding counties. Some of these counties had had up to 10 percent Negro population after the Civil War, but that percentage declined to less than 5 percent after Negroes migrated to the cities. Negroes made up only 2 percent of the Cookeville population, which numbered about eight thousand citizens in the 1960s. For the most part, graduates of Tennessee A&I State University and Knoxville College made up the teaching staff at Darwin, and about 30 percent of the eight or nine annual high school graduates attended A&I. Although there were plans to renovate or build a new Negro school, by 1963 the local school boards were feeling the

71

pressure of demands for desegregation. In April 1963, the *Putnam County Herald* announced plans to integrate Negro students into the white schools. After the students were assigned to the white schools, the school administrators instituted some rules, including separate cafeteria tables, to maintain peace and a little segregation.

[*]

In West Tennessee's Fayette County, where Negroes outnumbered whites, the battle for school desegregation was brutal. Fayette County had always been resistant to public education, with its rural legislators usually voting against measures to support schools. In 1890, Fayette County had 2,897 white and 8,829 Negro children, with fifty-four schools for whites and forty-five schools for Negroes. Help from the Rosenwald Fund and New Deal money changed that imbalance by 1937. There were twenty-three white schools and seventy Negro schools, with 69 white teachers and 103 Negro teachers teaching 1,800 white and 4,000 Negro students. There was 1 white teacher for every 26 children and 1 black teacher for every 39 children. By 1960, 99 percent of the children attended public schools. Only the passage of the comprehensive Civil Rights Act of 1964 helped to speed up the desegregation of schools in rural areas. The U.S. Department of Health, Education, and Welfare developed federal guidelines on school desegregation in April 1965 and strengthened them a year later, providing for withholding of federal funds. The Supreme Court upheld the guidelines.

On September 3, 1965, the Justice Department agreed to intervene in *McFerrin v. Fayette County Board of Education*, renaming it *McFerrin et al. and the U.S. of America v. Board of Education of Fayette County*. Avon Williams cooperated with attorney Louis Lucas of Memphis while trying that case. They learned that it was difficult to provide an equitable distribution of the races when 75 percent of the children were Negro. As the result of a consent decree on June 21, 1966, the school board developed a plan to integrate grades one and eight in 1965, grades nine and twelve by 1967, and all grades by 1969. The plan included freedom of choice. In June 1968, *McFerrin* plaintiffs asked the court for further relief because the plan identified black schools, assigned all-black faculty to those schools, and told black students they could no longer attend integrated schools in the county's largest town, Somerville. Judge Robert McRae approved a new plan on June 9, 1969, saying, "The court finds nothing in the record which would justify a continuation of freedom of choice, in view of its previous ineffectiveness in Fayette County." The county was divided into nine school zones, with only the high school zone given freedom of choice. Negroes outnumbered whites in every zone but one, in which there were nineteen Negro and seventy-seven white students. The freedom-of-choice option for high schools was similar to minority-to-majority transfer, allowing white students and parents to avoid schools with predominantly black enrollments. Moreover, many whites feared miscegenation among older students—a fear that partly explains why freedom of choice was allowed at the high school level.

In the fall of 1961, Negro citizens began boycotts and Saturday marches in downtown Somerville. Jessie Epps, a union leader and civil rights activist from Memphis, and others brought buses and cars from Memphis filled with demonstrators. Judge McRae prohibited the county officers from stopping the marches and ordered the release of Epps and other civil rights leaders—James Bevel, Viola McFerrin, James Mock, and B. Bryant—who had been jailed for their activities. On Monday, September 8, when schools opened, Negro students at Ware High School marched around the courthouse and then to the white Fayette County High School before being forced back to their campus. White citizens began boycotting classes at public schools, McFerrin's store was firebombed, and fire destroyed a building at Ware High School. McRae ordered revisions to the plan, and prohibited public transportation for children living outside the county.

On December 31, 1969, McRae ordered a new desegregation plan for January 26, 1970, and rejected the school board's suggestion of separate schools for boys and girls. All schools would have integrated teaching staffs. However, whites retained the top administrative jobs, and forty-two Negro teachers were fired until the federal court ordered their reinstatement. The black principal at Ware was sent to an elementary school to be "co-principal" with a white man, who was placed "in charge of instruction." The county placed grades nine and ten at Ware (called "the south campus") and grades eleven and twelve at FCHS (called "the north campus"), with a maximum of 60 percent blacks. Black students were suspended for the least offense, and black complainants said that several white teachers lived outside the county and sent their children to private schools.

Between 1960 and 1970, Fayette County's population declined from 24,577 to 22,086. During that period, three blacks won election to the school board, and Warren Dickerson became the county's first black school superintendent. But nearly half the whites had left the school system by 1980.

Not far from Fayette County, in the city of Jackson in Madison County, another school desegregation drama unfolded. The case was handled by

Avon N. Williams Jr., the NAACP-LDF, and local civil rights attorney Emmett Ballard. In Jackson, the Tigrett Junior High School had admitted two Negro students in January 1962 but then turned around and sent them back to the Negro school. After Williams and the NAACP filed suit in federal court in January 1963, the Jackson school system opened on September 3, 1963, under a definitive desegregation order. The gradualism plan called for forty Negroes to integrate grades one through three in 1963, grades four through six in 1964, and two grades a year thereafter. Williams and Ballard returned to court to argue that the Jackson school board had gerrymandered the zones to force Negro students back to the Negro school while keeping white students from attending such schools. There were no whites in Negro schools, and only thirty-eight Negroes in white schools. The city argued that the motion should be denied, claiming that the Negro parents did not exhaust appeal procedures, that Negro transfers would create turmoil in the schools, and that *Brown* had ordered *desegregation,* not *integration.* Judge Bailey Brown denied Williams's motion on September 20. One of the plaintiffs, Frank Walker, insisted that his children could receive a better education at the better-equipped white schools. Williams threatened to examine seventy-four hundred pupil registration cards to prove that school zoning was rigged to prevent integration. The local Negro citizens organized a protest whereby 95 percent of the black students were reported absent on Mondays. On September 23, Brown said, "I made a mistake and have changed my mind." He ordered the Jackson school board to send four Negro students back to the white schools.

Below the southern border of Tennessee, the Deep South states were trying to outflank *Brown.* In Alabama, Governor George Wallace ignored the history lesson from Little Rock and sent state troops to block the school doors, backing down only when President John F. Kennedy took control of the state's National Guard. Members of the National States' Right Party, which Wallace headed, paraded defiantly in their cars with Confederate flags waving. As Carl T. Rowan observed in his 1993 book, *Dream Makers, Dream Breakers: The World of Thurgood Marshall:* "Wallace . . . taught some ugly political lessons that would be used in later years by Richard Nixon, Ronald Reagan, and George Bush." In Alabama's neighbor to the west, the Mississippi State Sovereignty Commission, a state agency, received an anonymous gift of $100,000 through the Morgan Guaranty Trust Company in New York City to organize the Coordinating Committee for Fundamental American Freedoms as a lobbying organization with a staff in Washington, D.C. The Puritan Fund, operating out of Mississippi, and the conservative political Pioneer Fund also participated in funding the anti–civil rights campaign. Clerical personnel were planted as spies in the offices of various civil rights organizations, and ghost-written editorials were sent to hundreds of daily newspapers. The fund hired lawyers and distributed more than a million pamphlets and thousands of letters to influence Congress to oppose school desegregation. In the 1964 presidential election, Republican candidate Barry Goldwater made the Supreme Court and school desegregation a campaign issue when he said, "The Supreme Court is threatening our system by its lack of restraint." Though defeated decisively by Lyndon Johnson, Goldwater did carry five states in the Deep South.

[*]

Franklin County, located in the extreme southern part of Middle Tennessee, was a notable example of how *Brown* was disregarded in some school districts. Franklin County's Negro population was quite small, and for a long while, the vulnerable Negro community did not even push the desegregation issue or sue the county. Franklin is on the Cumberland Plateau, fifty miles west of Chattanooga and an hour's drive from Nashville. Negroes had been slaves there during the antebellum era, working in lumbering and mining and on small farms. By 1860, about 25 percent of the white population owned the county's 3,551 slaves. Railroads ran through the Franklin County towns of Decherd and Cowan and aided the Union Army's control of the county through the end of the Civil War. U.S. Colored Troops and freedmen laborers had helped to maintain those military railroads, thus bringing more Negroes into the county. After the Civil War, freedmen migrated elsewhere seeking a better life. By the 1950s, only a few hundred Negroes lived in Franklin County, mostly in Decherd, Cowan, and Winchester.

Within Franklin County's borders was the University of the South in Sewanee, where faculty members tried to stay attuned to the changing world around them. In Sewanee, many Negro families lived within the ten thousand acres of the University of the South, where they worked in non-professional and mostly service jobs. In 1952, this school, which was supported by the Episcopal Church, grappled with the moral issue of racial segregation. Eight divinity professors resigned in protest of the school's discriminatory practices, believing that the University of the South should provide leadership for desegregation and justice on the Cumberland Plateau—or at least in Sewanee. The dissenting faculty members were persuaded to remain in their jobs while plans were made to desegregate the university by 1959. Around 1962, the small Negro Episcopal congregation was discontinued and integrated into the main Episcopal church in Sewanee.

In anticipation of *Brown* having "adverse social effects" on Franklin County, public school officials hurriedly repaired the dilapidated Negro schoolhouses. The one in Sewanee, the Kennerly School (run by a family of that name), was just five years old in 1954, but it was only a cinderblock building no larger than a small house; it was situated in a hollow and hardly equal to the beautiful brick school building for white youngsters. The school had one teacher at first and then just two teachers. Milton Kennerly recalled attending the stucco school when it opened in 1949 and living on the grounds of the University of the South before heading to Tennessee A&I State University in 1959. His mother cooked and delivered the meals for the Kennerly School.

When some Negro and white parents approached the school board about school desegregation in Franklin County in 1963, the superintendent agreed that the best place to begin was in the more tolerant town of Sewanee. However, he said that the school building could not hold any more students. The local PTA raised fifty thousand dollars to build an addition to the Sewanee School. After the construction was finished, the superintendent flatly refused to desegregate. A biracial delegation traveled from Franklin County to Nashville to hire Avon N. Williams Jr., having heard of his reputation as a courageous and skilled civil rights attorney with connections to the NAACP. A suit was filed in federal court in Chattanooga, with three Negroes and three whites as plaintiffs. The federal judge ordered a gradual desegregation plan for the county, beginning with Sewanee schools. In 1964, the superintendent sent the twenty-four students from the Kennerly School to the white school, but he ordered the two teachers to report to the empty Negro school, where they sat each day with nothing to do. They wrote a protest letter to the superintendent, who ignored them, undoubtedly with the intention of firing them at the end of the school year. The nearly thirty Negro teachers in Franklin County met and decided to aid the stranded teachers. Another delegation headed to Williams's office, asking for NAACP intervention. Williams exclaimed, "This is 1964, not 1864!" The teachers felt they were being blamed for not having demanded desegregation earlier.

Williams filed another federal court suit, and several faculty members at the University of the South pledged their support. The superintendent was ordered to place the Negro teachers at the integrated school in Sewanee. The board gerrymandered the Cowan school zones to prevent white students from going to Negro schools, and no contracts came forth for Negro teachers in Franklin County. The Franklin County delegation returned to Williams's office in Nashville and also visited the state superintendent of public schools, who ordered teaching positions for the Negro teachers in the integrated schools. The Franklin County superintendent placed all of them in isolated mountain schools. Milton Kennerly recalled that upon graduating from Tennessee State in 1965, he was offered a teaching position in Sherwood, which required driving on curving roads and down into a deep valley. He refused to take the job and began teaching in Nashville. Interestingly, Ely Green, a mulatto born in 1893 and one of Kennerly's relatives, related stories of living among whites on the ridges and in the dense hollows of Franklin County in his autobiographical book *Too Black, Too White* (1970). Green spoke frankly of incest and miscegenation, as well as racial prejudice, among the mountain dwellers. White teachers often avoided such places, which is why black teachers were assigned to these one-room schools. The NAACP and the state intervened, forcing the county to find suitable, "protective places" for displaced Negro teachers. The county superintendent fired one of the teachers, saying she was not qualified. Of twenty-six Negro teachers in the county, twenty-one of them held bachelor's degrees and two of them had graduate degrees. In 1965, the county closed black elementary schools and the Negro high school.

[*]

In Kingsport, in the northeastern corner of Tennessee, desegregation of the schools was also slowly paced. According to historian Margaret Ripley Wolfe, "During the 1960s, Kingsport's relatively small black community became restive. For them and their counterparts across the United States, as well as for some whites, equality of opportunity for the [blacks] . . . was an idea whose time had arrived. In 1960, when per capita income in Kingsport stood at $5,900 dollars, only 55 percent of the city's black families reportedly had incomes that exceeded $3,000." Kingsport was an industrial town where the average income for local families was higher than in most places in Tennessee, yet the town was not socially progressive. The city began with a plan to integrate one grade at a time in 1961. Three Negro first-graders entered Lincoln School, and four enrolled at Lee School. In December 1966, because of federal mandates, Kingston had to integrate all grades. Fights and name-calling by students drew protests from black leaders. One racially motivated fight in the school cafeteria threatened to cause even more discord. On May 2, 1969, the *Kingsport Times* blamed the trouble on "punks—mostly white who seemed deliberately to try to cause trouble" at the newly integrated high school. The newspaper also spread the blame to prejudiced parents, who intentionally and even unconsciously taught their children to hate and shun people of color.

The school board endorsed a plan to form biracial student committees to talk to other students in the schools and calm things down.

Shelbyville was a small town in Bedford County in southern Middle Tennessee. By 1960 its population numbered 10,466 citizens. The largest local annual events were "Mule Day" and the "Tennessee Walking Horse Association Show." The AME Church had opened the first Negro school in Shelbyville several years after emancipation. Not until May 1890 did the first Negro class graduate from a Shelbyville public school. Early Negro leaders included the Reverend J. H. Turner, Thomas Talley, R. P. Purdy, and AME preacher Moses B. Salters. Twenty-seven schools for Negroes (mostly one-teacher schools) existed in Bedford County by the end of the nineteenth century, and it was not until 1923 that John McAdams High School, the public school for Negroes in Shelbyville, expanded from tenth grade to twelfth grade. Arithmetic, geography, grammar, reading, and vocational subjects dominated the limited curriculum. This school later became the Bedford County Training School for Negroes, with Sidney W. Harris heading it from 1935 to 1965.

The nearly seven hundred Negro students in Shelbyville–Bedford County remained in segregated East Bedford School and the Bedford County Training School. Negro attorney Robert E. Lillard from Nashville was the speaker for the 1961 graduation of thirty-five students. Negro leaders R. L. Suggs, the Reverend H. L. Parks of the AME Church, Edward Finley, Marion Clayborn, Roy Campbell, and others worked with local white leaders to "maintain racial harmony." Federal funds were used to build a housing project for Negroes and a swimming pool at the high school campus. In August 1960, the *Shelbyville Times-Gazette* was carrying news about the regional civil rights movement, occasionally including pictures of local Negro teachers and students and even outlining progress on the 1960 voter rights bill in Congress. John F. Kennedy beat Richard Nixon by 4,457 to 2,633 votes there in November 1960. Yet, only after passage of the Civil Rights Act of 1964 did Bedford County begin to allow Negroes (11 percent) into the white schools. Eight students—Camille Alexander, Mabel Bailey, James Claiborne, Donald Cleveland, Thomas P. Johnson Jr., James Marable, Bonnie Price, and Fred Sparrow—went to Central High School. In 1967, Harris High School for Negroes was merged into Central High School.

In nearby Pulaski, located in Giles County on the Alabama border, school integration did not take place until after the eleventh anniversary of *Brown*. Negroes constituted nearly a third of the population in Giles County and had begun their schools in 1864 in the Union army contraband camps. The Ku Klux Klan was born in the Pulaski area in 1866. The Freedmen's

Bureau assisted the schools, helping to pay teachers' salaries and construct buildings. The county took over the freedmen schools under Tennessee's Common School Law in 1867–68. Pulaski High School for Negroes began in 1899, and by 1920 Giles County had thirty Negro schools—most of them in church buildings and one-room facilities. Thanks in part to the New Deal, the modern Bridgeforth High School in Pulaski was built. After the county's Negro population continued to decline to less than half its original percentage, some one-room Negro schools had to be closed by 1953. There remained nine one-teacher schools and four two-teacher schools. The county school board decided to schedule desegregation discussions for September 1955, but such talks were put off the board's agenda for ten years. The Negro teachers remained dedicated despite receiving second-hand books and damaged equipment, and they believed that "The [Negro] youth needed every advantage to succeed in a racially divided society."

The Giles County School Board voted unanimously on May 1, 1965, to desegregate the schools that fall. The *Pulaski Citizen*, on May 5, 1965, carried the headline "Complete School Mixing is Planned for Fall Term." The authorities took pride in the fact that they were beginning desegregation, although they had until 1967, according to HEW guidelines. On May 12, the *Giles County Free Press* declared, "It is our hope that all stand ready to abide by the board's decision." Four Negro schools would be closed because of "low enrollments." On *Brown's* eleventh birthday, May 17, 1965, the last class of seniors graduated from Bridgeforth High School, but many were outraged to the point of tears that the school was to be closed, the trophies and history to be discarded, and the building to be turned into a junior high school. The black teachers would be integrated into all the schools, and the principal at Bridgeforth would resign and then become "coordinator for desegregation problems." On August 4, the *Giles County Free Press* announced, "Giles' Integrated Rural Schools to Open Monday." One official angered blacks when he said that before transforming the Bridgeforth building into an integrated junior high school, the facility should "be cleaned up, painted, and decontaminated."

The school board's rules allowed parents to transport children to a school other than the assigned school. Those rules notwithstanding, on May 26, 1965, a white citizens' group calling itself the Citizens for Better Education Council met to establish a stock corporation to begin a private school. Several people offered to donate land upon which to build the school named for a Confederate hero. The council sent representatives into Alabama to view a similar academy.

In far northwest Tennessee, Obion County had developed an expensive way of maintaining Jim Crow in the public schools. When five Negro children completed the eighth grade, a plan was developed in September 1950 to bring them to Union City to attend a consolidated Negro high school. Although many counties used this approach to gather up small pockets of Negro students, it would obviously have been cheaper to allow a handful of black children (as in Clinton) to attend school with their neighbors. But racial prejudice and continuing respect for state Jim Crow laws trumped the economic advantages. This arrangement was still unquestioned when the *Union City Daily Messenger* (May 17, 1954) announced *Brown* to the residents, under the headline "School Segregation Is Held as Unconstitutional." The article made it clear that for the time being there was little for whites to worry about; indeed, it would be twelve years after *Brown* before school desegregation reached Union City. Here, in this land noted for nightriders, the Negro community was small and had no newspaper of its own, while the local white-owned paper carried neither news nor pictures of Negroes except when crimes occurred. In September 1955, the school board entered discussions about *Brown II* and school desegregation, but nothing was done about it at the time. As late as 1958, the county would not even allow Negro children, except those in high school, to ride the county school buses into Union City to attend the better schools. Finally, parents in South Fulton, a community about fifteen miles northeast of Union City, engaged Williams and Looby to sue the county school system. On December 16, 1961, Judge Bailey Brown ordered desegregation of schools in Obion County, effective September 1962. Things went peacefully.

[∗]

In 1967, the Tennessee Commission on Human Rights issued a report entitled *School Desegregation in Tennessee, 1965–1966*, which summarized the state's progress, or the relative lack of it. According to the report, Tennessee had 2,167 schools with 679,700 white and 174,416 Negro students (20.4 percent of the total). Some 126 of the 152 school systems had integrated student bodies, but 1,100 schools had all-white student bodies, while 358 schools were all-Negro. Only 8.1 percent of the 5,735 Negro teachers worked within integrated faculties.

In addition to summarizing the statewide statistics, the report took note of various individual school systems. It pointed out, for example, that Coffee County in Middle Tennessee had implemented a plan approved by the U.S. Department of Health, Education, and Welfare (HEW) in August 1965 and had begun integration of public school faculty in 1966. "Giles County, McMinnville, and Johnson City had fully integrated school systems," the report observed, while also noting that Brownsville in Haywood County still had two one-race schools, as did Morristown, Newport, Huntingdon, Lexington, and Trimble. For several years after *Brown*, the Morristown Normal and Industrial College for Negroes in Hamblen County administered the high school program for the small Negro population in Hamblen, Grainger, Union, Claiborne, and Hancock counties in far northeast Tennessee. Crockett, Lake, and Lauderdale counties, all in West Tennessee, had significant Negro populations but no black students in classrooms with whites. Nashville, meanwhile, had ended gradual desegregation and integrated all twelve grades; however, just 12.59 percent of southern Negro children attended integrated classes. In Memphis, only 30,000 of the 122,000 students were in integrated classrooms. The Committee of the Judiciary, U.S. House of Representatives, published *Guidelines for School Desegregation* as a result of the hearings before the Special Subcommittee on Civil Rights, on December 14–15, 1966. The most important guideline specified that federal funds could be cut off from any school system maintaining any vestiges of segregation, and southern governments relied heavily on federal funds to operate public schools.

In January 1967, Jessie H. Turner, head of the Memphis branch NAACP, called for an end to all discrimination and for appointment of some black school administrators in the local school system. James M. Lawson Jr., a Methodist minister who had earlier been involved in civil rights activism in Nashville (see chapter 4), announced his candidacy for the school board but because of the at-large system, he lost his race in 1967. In a September 8 letter to the board, the local NAACP lamented the situation: "We feel that the Memphis Board of Education has failed this community. Negroes constitute more than half of the public school population in Memphis, but they are crowded into 40 percent of the buildings. Special education programs are segregated, Freedom-of-Choice is destroying the intent of desegregation, there are no top black administrators, integration so far is window dressing, and this will not do."

In 1968, the Supreme Court began outright to suggest methods of desegregation and deny gradual plans. Federal judges began refusing to dismiss the suits after a mere plan had been submitted, and they monitored implementation of the plans over the years. The federal courts also allowed the plaintiffs to return to court if they were not satisfied with the progress of local school desegregation. All school districts were told to integrate at once, with no more delays. And the justices became hostile toward freedom-of-choice guidelines. They began to demand "working" plans, including the concept of busing. However, busing—the transportation of students from one part of town to another to achieve racial balance—became a key factor in causing greater numbers of white families to flee from public schools to private schools.

The Whitehaven community south of Memphis—whose best-known resident was rock-and-roll star Elvis Presley—offered an important example of "white flight." For years, Whitehaven residents feared the future implications of racial integration, busing, and higher property taxes and thus resisted annexation by the city of Memphis. Under the old Crump regime, Memphis had accepted limited federal housing funds for fear of federal interference in the city's racial practices, and therefore, the city had less than seven thousand public housing units. This situation forced working- and middle-class Negroes to seek single-family houses for shelter. For a while, the new Interstate 240 and the nearby Memphis International Airport provided artificial barriers to the rapid expansion of heavily black south Memphis toward Whitehaven. However, by 1963, Negro suburbanites had rapidly moved farther south into ranch-style houses along Alcy Road, pressing Whitehaven on its northern and western borders. The new Horizon Town and Country Club complex closed down, finding the streets to its entrance on Alcy Road filled with Negro working- and middle-class families. The unincorporated Whitehaven area, south of Alcy Road, the city limit, and stretching to the Mississippi state line, favored Congressman Ray Blanton, who represented twenty-three West Tennessee counties and that southern portion of Memphis. Blanton began working with his fellow congressman from neighboring Mississippi to place a rider on the HEW appropriations bill to prohibit busing for school desegregation. Out of the other side of his mouth, he called for a reconciliation of the races and rejection of the "rabble rousers, both white and black, who divide us." White families increasingly resorted to white flight into East Memphis and even south over the Mississippi state line, creating Southhaven, Mississippi. Whitehaven would become heavily black by the 1990s.

About an hour's drive northeast of Memphis, the plaintiffs' lawyers were able to reverse the decisions in the case of *Monroe v. Board of Commissioners of the City of Jackson, Tennessee* (1968). On August 13, 1968, federal judge Robert M. McCrae ordered a new plan for Jackson and the Madison County schools "upon the basis of a unitary school system of non-racial geographic attendance zones or a plan of consolidation of grades or schools, or both."

In Middle and East Tennessee, there were sometimes open racial clashes. Nashville blacks became upset when the school board suspended black Cameron High School from interscholastic athletics after thirty or forty black students fought students at white Stratford High School during a 1968 basketball game. Some whites wanted to hold on to the neighborhood public schools and run the Negroes away, using such tactics as calling out "Nigger," singing "Dixie," and waving Confederate flags. Ironically, Cameron eventually became a well-integrated middle school, while Stratford became mostly black as whites with children fled the east Nashville neighborhoods. Meanwhile, nineteen black students and one white student in Chattanooga were arrested for a fight at a basketball game in 1968. The NAACP and the American Civil Liberties Union had to resort to the courts and hire Avon Williams when six students were expelled for walking out of a pep rally in which Confederate flags were waved. The federal court ordered the students reinstated. Chattanooga's black youngsters then began to call for representation on the cheerleading squad, better treatment from white teachers, and hiring of more black teachers.

[∗]

While the case of *Mapp et al. v. Board of Education of the City of Chattanooga* had resulted in a desegregation order by the federal district court judge in March 1962 (followed by an order to desegregate the city's technical schools in 1963), plaintiffs remained dissatisfied. James Mapp and other local NAACP members presented a resolution in early 1966 to the Board of Education that declared: "The Negro child has persistently been given inferior education. The time has come for the Negro children to be given the same opportunity at quality education to qualify for today's opportunities as white children." By the fall, twenty-seven schools were integrated, but seven all-white and ten all-black schools still existed. The local NAACP called for "full desegregation" without delay. The Sixth Circuit Court of Appeals ordered the district court to rehear the case, and Chattanooga high schools desegregated further in 1967. Mapp and others served on a city committee to review schools desegregation in 1969, when Central High School had twelve hundred students, including two hundred blacks. Members of the Downtown Interracial Dialogue Group protested against the Board of Education's "Freedom of Choice" plan, but the Parents Determine Quality Education group demanded it: "We cannot see that eliminating freedom of choice will do anything but deteriorate race relations and lower the quality of education we now have. It would be unfair to any student, Negro or white, to be unable to select the schools he or she wishes to attend." As a result of freedom of choice and white flight, Howard and Riverside high schools remained practically all-black. C. B. Robinson and others also pressured the school board to do something about the underrepresentation of black professionals in the Chattanooga schools' administration. In 1970, the public school board finally gave in on the teacher desegregation issue, and set quotas of 43 percent black teachers, 57 percent white teachers, and 18 percent black principals. And finally, the court gave the school board an order to implement all desegregation plans by 1973.

Despite such rulings, white flight eventually re-created a dual system of education in Chattanooga. The city's total population declined by eleven thousand inhabitants, while the number of black citizens (36 percent in the 1970 U.S. Census) and their children had increased since 1960. Blacks would increase to about 50 percent of local public students by the mid-1980s. After the death of Judge Wilson in September 1982, H. Ted Milburn was selected to replace him in June 1983. But Milburn was elevated to the Sixth Circuit Court of Appeals in October 1984, and thus for months there was no federal judge on the Chattanooga bench.

Judge R. Allan Edgar became Milburn's replacement on February 26, 1985, and began hearings on the nearly twenty-five-year-old Chattanooga school desegregation case. Plaintiffs objected to the 1979 magnet school at Brainerd High School and moved to stop the closing of black Riverside High School. (A "magnet school" was designed with a special curriculum [business, science, health, performing arts, etc.], high admission and academic standards, and a higher-quality teaching staff to attract whites to a hard-to-integrate inner-city or predominantly black school.) In October 1985, defendants asked the court to grant full compliance with the implementation order and relieve the school system from final judgments. School officials argued that they had done all that was asked of them and had done nothing to foster resegregation. The NAACP threatened appeal if Edgar dismissed the case—which the judge, according to Mapp, said he would do if the schools achieved a 60-40 black-white ratio of teachers. But a black deputy school superintendent argued that black teachers were hard to find, adding, "It's getting to be a desperate situation." The Chattanooga case did not really end until 1985.

Yet, in the early 1990s, Mapp and the local NAACP would try to involve the U.S. Department of Education's Civil Rights Division in the Chattanooga situation, mainly because the board had been building new schools in the white areas, while neglecting the black ones. And although there was a black superintendent by 1987, the Board of Education closed sixteen schools—because of "the condition of the buildings," said the mayor—and let fourteen black principals go. The almost all-white East Brainerd School was kept open. "Magnet school concepts sapped the higher-quality students from the black schools," said James Mapp, who noted that Signal Mountain had had two new schools and that white students from other counties were allowed there. Although there were two blacks among nine people on the school board in

Chattanooga, they seemed to go along with the plans, he felt. The *Chatta-nooga Times* of January 1, 1998, reported, "Three decades after the vestiges of legal segregation were stripped away in Chattanooga, black and white Chattanoogans still work, worship, study, and play in separate worlds."

Some study groups were trying to bridge the gap and find ways to solve the racial divide. But the legacy of white supremacy and reactionary racial attitudes among many of the citizens in Chattanooga and nearby northern Georgia was much to overcome. In 1998, local newspapers recalled how John P. Hooper, president of the Citizens Council of Chattanooga, was arrested while waving his Confederate flag and protesting in front of integrated Brainerd High School in the 1960s. The East Ridge Tri-State Citizens Council also had opposed school desegregation. Such groups had the support of some prominent Tennesseans, including former governor Prentice Cooper. "We looked at them [White Citizens Councils] as being un-American, not violent like the Klan," Mapp said, "but we didn't know what these people were doing behind the scenes." Mapp, whose home was bombed in 1971, believed that resegregation of local schools had occurred by 2003, adding that he was "getting ready to write the officials about building new schools in the black areas." He suggested a study by the NAACP to precede a reparations suit to recover what was lost by blacks during the civil rights movement.

In nearby Franklin County, the racial climate and limitations on economic opportunity had helped to induce "black flight," whereby young blacks migrated to Chattanooga. Others joined the Great Migration (1896–1970) up the Ohio Valley to Cleveland, Ohio, and other industrial centers in the North, while some went south to nearby Atlanta. By 1970, when the Great Migration had mostly ended, blacks in Franklin County numbered about twenty-one hundred citizens, with just one school administrator, two teachers, less than one hundred students, one Negro doctor, and four churches. In 1972, when asked by an interviewer if they would remain in Franklin County after graduation, only six of the thirty-five black high school students said yes. They complained about the lack of black teachers and said that white teachers were unwilling to really educate blacks.

[*]

In Tennessee's largest city, Memphis, the battle was far from over by the late 1960s. Since 1965, some 70 percent of new teachers hired in Memphis were whites. The percentage of black teachers was on the decline. In Memphis, the school board finally began token integration of faculty in fall 1969. At White Station High School, a higher percentage of the eight black teachers had master's degrees than the white teachers there. Ezekiel Bell, president of the local NAACP, demanded even more Negro administrators and teachers. The NAACP demanded discussions with the board and were refused. Then, when some four hundred teachers tried to attend a Board of Education meeting to ask why board members had refused to meet with the NAACP, as suggested earlier by the Chamber of Commerce, city policemen blocked their entry. The local NAACP began nightly mass meetings and asked school principals to allow NAACP officers to speak to the teachers in 1968.

NAACP leaders demanded representation for the black citizens of Memphis on the Board of Education and thus a change from at-large-districts to election of school board members by districts, based on *Baker v. Carr* (1962), the U.S. Supreme Court ruling that affirmed the "one-man, one-vote" principle. On September 24, 1969, Maxine Smith and the NAACP devised the "Black Monday" protest, which had been used in Jackson, Tennessee, on a limited basis. On Black Monday, October 20, 1969, some 67,000 students and 774 teachers were absent. On October 27, 46,000 students stayed away from the schools, and on the fourth Black Monday, 68,000 students were absent. Smith, along with other NAACP leaders and Ralph Abernathy of the Southern Christian Leadership Conference, led a march of 5,000 people on City Hall on November 10. Among the 53 leaders arrested were Abernathy, Maxine and Vasco Smith, Alvin M. King, Ezekiel Bell, A. W. Willis Jr., Cornelia Crenshaw, and members of the American Federation of State, County, and Municipal Employees Union. The Black Monday protest threatened to bankrupt the Memphis city schools because Tennessee appropriated public school funds based on local per-pupil daily attendance. In November, board members sued the leaders of the Black Monday movement for $10 million. A few city councilmen berated the board for not moving faster on desegregation.

The Black Monday movement caused division within black leadership ranks. Jessie H. Turner, then a member of the Shelby County Quarterly Court, was forced to deny that he had "sold out" and was not supporting the Black Monday tactic. In a heated executive board meeting, Ezekiel Bell resigned as president and member of the NAACP's board. He announced his new role as president of the soon-to-be chartered SCLC chapter in Memphis. On November 13, 1969, the local NAACP suspended Black Mondays. In December, warrants were issued for the arrest of Bell, Epps, Maxine Smith, James Lawson,

Ralph Abernathy, and others. On December 20, 1969, the *Tri-State Defender* observed, "There seems to be a national attempt to suppress and harass the poor and the black community. Here in Memphis the issuing of fugitive warrants and arresting of black leaders in the community is only one method of suppression." Abernathy sent word from Atlanta that he was coming to Memphis to turn himself in and would march from Clayborn Temple to the jail if anyone cared to join him. "Memphis," he said, "is still trying to isolate itself in a shell and withdraw into its own dark desolate world where it can oppress people who are concerned about truth and justice." He believed that the nation's law enforcement agencies had launched an attack on black leadership. The leaders refused to pay the one-dollar bail and stayed in jail through Christmas. Coretta Scott King, whose husband, Martin Luther King Jr., had been assassinated in Memphis the previous year, brought her children to the city to march in symbolic protest.

Memphis city policemen increased their physical attacks on black citizens. Under the headline "Police Continue Assaults on Citizens," the *Tri-State Defender* reported on March 14, 1970, that one black citizen was stopped, cursed, and then beaten for "driving a Cadillac, better than our police car." The police jailed the man, after giving his car keys to another Negro. Soon after the man's release and protest, the two policemen and some fellow white officers showed up at his door, cursed his wife, beat the man for "resisting arrest," and took him to jail again. Black teachers were also arrested on trumped-up traffic violations. The Memphis NAACP created an ad hoc committee to investigate the police—an action that drew the ire of the police chief, who declared it outrageous and against police authority.

The local NAACP voted to suspend Black Mondays tactics indefinitely after the Memphis Board of Education agreed to include two blacks as advisors to the board, appoint blacks to the next two vacancies on the board, develop a plan to restructure the board to give blacks a chance to be elected, hire a black assistant superintendent, drop suits against the protest leaders, and not penalize students, parents, and teachers who had participated in Black Mondays. The General Assembly changed the system of voting for Memphis school board members to the district method as a result of a bill submitted by State Representative Alvin M. King and the Memphis delegation in 1970. The act allowed nine district members, retained two at-large positions, and assured the black community of at least three seats. The charges against black leaders were dismissed in June 1972.

[*]

CONTINUING SCHOOL DESEGREGATION

In his 1971 autobiography, *Born to Rebel,* Morehouse College president Benjamin E. Mays said that the Negro would never go back to segregation. In a 1970 speech, he also said, "Every scheme that can be thought of is coming to the front in an effort to avoid desegregation in elementary and secondary schools. Running to the suburbia is widely practiced throughout the country. Another way to avoid desegregation on the part of whites is to establish private schools. It all shows the gulf that separates black and white is wide."

Whites devoted to the concept of ethnic supremacy were determined to maintain control of public education's teaching, administrative positions, and funding sources. They objected to white children being sent to flimsy Negro school buildings and opposed the dismissal of surplus white teachers in desegregated schools. Many whites detested the idea of blacks teaching white children. Negro school professionals might be subjected to dismissal when Negro schools were closed. Black teachers and the black middle class were often thought to be prime supporters of the NAACP, which many whites considered a subversive organization. In rural areas where racial pressure was more direct and life-threatening, some black teachers felt the urge to leave town while others would suffer in silence, quit their jobs, or go to the nearest city to get help from civil rights lawyers. Most black communities had no representation on local school boards. From 1968 to 1970, the number of black teachers in the South declined by 8.5 percent. Forty black teachers were lost in Tennessee during this period, but in Alabama, Mississippi, and South Carolina, the losses were much higher—533, 469, and 948, respectively. In Tennessee, civil rights lawyers fought a dozen cases on behalf of teachers who were unfairly discharged. After Avon Williams filed a suit, a federal court ordered the reinstatement of 12 black teachers who had been dismissed by the Fayette County school board because of "expected loss of [white] enrollment in 1970–1971." Williams filed seven such lawsuits in Tennessee. Within thirty years, America's percentage of black teachers was expected to decline dramatically, perhaps by two-thirds. The situation often left the masses of black children at the mercy of other races within an American society that was still defined along the color line.

American conservatives began pushing for "quality-education" reform movements during the 1980s and early 1990s, including raising standards for teacher education, tests, certification, and licensure, although most of their children no longer subscribed to public schools. Some national education associations, including the College Board, tried to temper such racially coded movements with a theme of "Quality and Access," a principle that forced many school districts and teacher-education colleges both to upgrade their programs and to make earnest efforts to increase the number of minority students in the late 1980s. The teacher-education accrediting body, the National Council for Accreditation of Teacher Education (NCATE), made faculty and staff diversity a criterion by 1990. These moves by NCATE and other professional associations would help slow the demise of black teachers. By 2003, the Southern Education Fund in Atlanta would publish *Unintended Consequences: Perspectives on Teacher Testing and Historically Black Colleges and Universities* to call attention to the nation's need to invest in such colleges and universities to help increase the supply of African American teachers. Through state desegregation programs, including minority scholarships, Tennessee began to increase the number of African American students in teacher education programs by 2003, showing a 127 percent increase in black teachers in the last ten years, according to annual reports by the Tennessee Higher Education Commission.

[*]

During his years as governor of Tennessee (1959–63, 1967–71), Buford Ellington came under pressure from the South's most outspoken segregationists to have Tennessee join regional resistance to *Brown*. Ellington received segregationist tracts, including *The Pending Tragedy in the South* (1959) by a segregationist Presbyterian minister from Selma, Alabama. Fred McCoy of Pine Bluff, Arkansas, wrote Ellington on August 19, 1959: "To Southern States Governors who have not been brain washed. Interposition can whip this Nigger question." After attending an interdenominational church meeting in Tennessee on September 3, 1962, John C. Pritchett Jr. of Alabama complained to Ellington that he had "slept in the same room with Negro boys. I would like to know if a meeting of this type is legal in your state."

Although his record on desegregation was often not exemplary, Ellington resisted such pressures to some extent. In an August 8, 1969, letter to Governor Lester Maddox of Georgia, Ellington declined to attend a meeting to discuss ways of defying federal authority. "We have, with very few exceptions," he told Maddox, "dealt with our education problems in Tennessee in a manner which benefits all of our citizens and it is our intention to continue to do so." In a letter dated February 25, Maddox again contacted Ellington, saying, "On February 23, 1970, I signed into law an act which makes it illegal to transfer students or teachers, or to change school districts, so as to require forced racial segregation or forced racial integration." According to the bill, no teacher would be forced to work at a school to achieve a certain ratio for teachers by race. Maddox was an avowed racist who in 1964 had prevented African Americans from entering his restaurant by carrying a pistol and enlisting supporters who wielded ax handles. He attached a copy of the Georgia bill to his letter to Ellington. Tennessee, however, did not pass such laws.

Meanwhile, on January 5, 1970, U.S. Senator Sam J. Ervin Jr. of North Carolina sent Ellington a copy of a bill to prevent the Department of Housing, Education, and Welfare, the Supreme Court, and other federal agencies from using busing and transfers to achieve school desegregation. He asked Ellington to contact the congressional delegation for their support. On January 15, Ellington replied, "We frankly, at this time, do not plan to take an active part in this legislation."

On January 26, 1970, Governor Albert P. Brewer of Alabama asked Ellington to join in a Supreme Court case to sue John N. Mitchell, the U.S. attorney general, and Robert Finch, the secretary of HEW, for discriminating against southern states in imposing unfair and inconsistent school desegregation guidelines. Brewer attached the court papers, which included these facts and figures: there were all-Negro schools in California (49 percent), Colorado (45 percent), Illinois (72 percent), Indiana (43 percent), and Ohio (43 percent), as well as all-Negro schools in Los Angeles, Chicago, Washington, D.C., Dayton, Ohio, and many places outside the Deep South. Chicago had 208 all-Negro schools. Brewer believed that the busing controversy was hurting Alabama's ability to attract outside industry and business "for the economic support and wellbeing of the people." Ellington told Brewer on February 6 that Tennessee probably would not join in the suit, "although I am entirely opposed to some of the practices required in this area by the federal courts."

[*]

The election of conservative U.S. presidents further hindered efforts by the U.S. Supreme Court to truly desegregate America's public schools and society in general. Interrupted only by the one-term Carter administration following the 1976 election, the Republican Party enjoyed a conservative reign of some two decades, pushing Congress for tax-supported vouchers, packing the courts with conservative judges, and issuing messages for the courts to go slow on integration and affirmative action. The Nixon administration discouraged the courts from using racial quotas to assign teachers to schools, partly because this would supposedly discriminate against qualified whites and cause the hiring of blacks solely because of race. The Supreme Court, meanwhile, ruled in favor of countywide busing in *Swann v. Charlotte-Mecklenburg Board of Education* (1971), a case that had originated in North Carolina.

On May 28, 1971, a little over a month after the *Swann* decision, Maxine Smith reiterated the NAACP's support for busing in a presentation before the Memphis Board of Education:

> The NACCP wants it understood that we are wholeheartedly behind busing. Whites have barred us legally and illegally from certain residential areas by restrictive zoning, by outright exclusion, by violence, and by pricing us out of certain housing markets because of discrimination in employment. Such practices have precluded the possibility of integrated neighborhoods and therefore any concept of the neighborhood school which would be acceptable. Therefore busing white children into black areas and black children into white areas is the only means by which black children can receive quality education. . . . Neighborhood schools have not been accepted in the South, where children have been bused past a nearby school to maintain Jim Crow.

Smith blasted the segregationists, white supremacists, and hypocrites who continued to defy *Brown* and had even attempted to nullify the Tennessee compulsory school attendance law. These "outstanding 'blue-bloodied' citizens," she contended, had no more regard for the law than the murderer, the rapist, and the robber. She said:

> To set the record straight, we could care less about your children going to school with our children. But as long as you control the public tax dollars, as long as you control the schools; as long as you control the legislature, the judicial and business processes in the state, your past actions indicate that you will short-change us and our children, and the only way we can share in this American Dream is to require and insist that black and white children go to school together regardless of the cost.

In August 1971, the federal district court at first accepted the Memphis desegregation plan, but the NAACP appealed the ruling. The judge found de jure segregation still existed, and in November 1971, he directed the U.S. Department of Heath, Education, and Welfare to draw up a plan with minimum busing. No school was to have less than a 30 percent minority. According to the plan, the system had to bus 13,006 students to achieve such racial balance by January 22, 1973. Still, eighty one-race schools remained in a system that was 52 percent black. These were to be done away with in 1973–74. In the teacher-exchange program, black teachers took their assignments diligently at other-race schools, but most white teachers responded indifferently, grading their papers, writing letters, and even studying Sunday school lessons when they had to visit other schools. Local private schools increased from forty in 1971 to eighty-five in 1974.

Parents were still concerned about miscegenation and increasing crime in Memphis. Maxine Smith and two other black citizens were elected to the Memphis Board of Education and took their seats in January 1972. According to Smith's NAACP report, 37 percent of local blacks lived below the poverty level, thirty thousand families (95 percent of them black) lived in substandard housing, 30 percent of blacks remained segregated in all-black schools, and the justice and police systems continued to terrorize black citizens. Blacks held only 25 percent of the administrative positions in the school system; charges of grading discrimination and physical abuse of black students persisted; there was white pressure to rename some formerly all-black schools; and several black teachers in Memphis were dismissed for "poor evaluations." At Lester Junior High School, in the middle of a black enclave in northeast Memphis, a white principal was appointed in the fall of 1974 to stop white flight. He found 450 broken windows and a yard filled with trash, but he got parents and students to clean it up. He managed to raise white enrollment by 3 percent (434 blacks and 189 whites) when integrated schools in the east Memphis cluster had lost white enrollment by 4 to 8 percent. In the 1974 annual report for the Memphis NAACP, Maxine Smith wrote:

> In retrospect, the year 1974 has been in some ways paradoxical in the area of the Black Man's quest for his rightful share of America; a year of painfully won gains, though far too minimal in some areas of the struggle; a year of desperation and deprivation particularly for the poor, which in disproportionate instances, is synonymous with the Black of our land; and a year, the revelations of which, could and should bring us to a brighter tomorrow in 1975 if America indeed has any belief in her creeds that supposedly form the moral fiber of this nation; if America has any remorse for her sins that have amplified around the globe; and if Black men and women, hand-in-hand with all other Americans who truly believe in and seek the promises of our Constitution that were made to all citizens; yes if determined Blacks will rekindle that fervent desire for freedom left over 350 years ago by our fore-parents shackled in bondage, a burning desire eluded by the chronicles of time, yet a raging desire for those of us of our

generation that was kindled in the decades of the fifties and
sixties—yes if America can be found to believe in America,
there is hope for 1975 and the years to come.

The community honored Maxine Smith on March 8, 1974, at a banquet
attended by eighteen hundred people at the Holiday Inn. She had served seventeen years in the movement and twelve years as executive secretary of the
local NAACP.

In June 1974, the local NAACP sent a letter of protest to the Shelby
County Board of Education because four whites were approved for administrative positions and no black professionals held such jobs. The county did not
appoint black principals at any integrated school. The NAACP marked the
county school desegregation plan unsatisfactory and asked that the district
judge be dismissed from the case.

The U.S. Supreme Court let stand Memphis's plan that left 30 percent
of the blacks in one-race schools. The student population of the Memphis
school system was already 71 percent black since the busing order. Maxine
Smith asked the board to pass a policy to fire school personnel who withdrew
their children from the public schools to avoid integration. In her 1976
NAACP report, she wrote, "Racism and vindictiveness on the part of those
who disfavor change as expressed through the political process, over the years
have resulted in a community indifference to public apathy." She would make
113 speeches and appearances at churches, radio and television stations, newspapers, and wherever anyone would listen to the NAACP's vision in 1975.
When the school system became blacker, she noted, "By-and-large the same
people who resisted any form of [school] desegregation still serve in top administrative positions." She observed, "The fight for dignity and decency is not an
easy one and was not intended for the faint at heart. The toil in the field is for
the most part laborious, but the yield of the crop is scant. Our community and
our nation remain resistant to change as regards the upward movement of the
status of Blacks in America."

The Memphis school system soon increased to 73 percent black students,
causing Maxine Smith to say in her 1978 report to the Memphis NAACP
meeting:

> We must completely convince America that nearly 25 years is
> too long to wait for implementation of that momentous 1954
> decision; that 14 years is far too long to live with the decree of
> the Civil Rights Act of 1964; that 13 years is too long to tolerate
> the lingering hypocrisy of the Voting Rights Act of 1965; that we

cannot continue to accept the deteriorating housing conditions for poor and Black Americans despite the passage of the Fair Housing Act a decade ago. Our country has produced many great decisions, edicts, proclamations, declarations, and orders, yet it seems the *Dred Scott* decision of 1857, which states that a black man has no rights that white America must respect, is the one to which she holds most tenaciously. This we must realize is not the democracy we purport ourselves to be.

An unexpected change in the Memphis case came in 1978 when the school board had to select a new superintendent of Memphis City Schools. Reportedly, the white majority met secretly, which was thought to be typical of integrated boards and commissions in the South at that time, and decided on a candidate. But Smith, the NAACP, parents, and others "launched a vigorous protest, including picketing, petitions, appearances before the board, a law suit charging violation of the Tennessee Sunshine Law, threats of recall, political action, legal action against the constitutionality of at-large positions, and school boycotts," according to the local NAACP's annual reports. The board's preferred candidate withdrew, and on December 6, 1978, the next candidate on the list, W. Willie Herenton, an African American, was selected as the superintendent. Some whites angrily charged reverse racial discrimination. Only 26.4 percent of the students in the Memphis Public Schools were classified as whites, and less than 3 percent of all students were bused to achieve racial balance. Herenton led efforts to improve school attendance and program quality, and he instituted magnet schools to regain some whites. Some blacks criticized Herenton for compromising with the whites, but he had no choice except to lose even more of the white parents and students.

In 1984, the twenty-two-year-old *Northcross v. Memphis Schools* case (as the NAACP's desegregation lawsuit was known) was settled by consent decree. Later, a judge initially awarded the NAACP lawyers a mere $50,000 instead of over $1 million for fees. This mutual agreement eliminated "nonproductive busing, instituted a special studies program for the twenty-five inner-city all black schools which were never involved in the desegregation plan; created a position of Housing Monitor to determine areas to be eliminated from the transportation plan once the neighborhood has become sufficiently desegregated to assure similar racial makeup in the area school." In the NAACP Annual Report (1989), Smith wrote, "As we enter 1990, the need for creative and progressive change in our educational delivery becomes more and more persistent." The Memphis City Schools had resegregated to 83 percent black. White flight was causing a declining tax base and a corroding city infrastructure. The schools did not have enough resources, dedicated teachers, involved parents, and quality programs for most students to be academically ready for college. And most of them failed the state-mandated algebra test in 2000.

[∗]

In Davidson County, 12 Negro children and their parents had forced the integration of schools in rural areas, but little else had happened to improve the situation since 1960. The consolidation of the county government with that of the City of Nashville in 1962 would dilute the city's 43-percent Negro population bloc to about 24 percent, giving whites even more countywide political power. The schools integrated all twelve grades, but inner-city schools, those within the Briley Parkway, remained mostly black. By 1963, only 773 Negro children attended Nashville's integrated schools.

Williamson County, on the southern border of Davidson County, had done nothing about desegregating schools thirteen years after *Brown* and even by the time Congress had passed the 1964 Civil Rights Act. Williamson County had been one of Middle Tennessee's heaviest slaveholding counties. When the old plantation system began to disintegrate during the period from 1880 to 1910, the Negroes crowded mostly into Nashville but with little share of the profits from the land. The old slaveholding families had passed that wealth on to subsequent generations of whites, who quietly transformed wealth from slaves, land, and Negro tenant farmers into profits from new farm products and real estate sales. The county seat of Franklin retained its nineteenth-century feel long after World War II.

The population growth of Nashville, followed by the white flight attending its desegregation battles, benefited Williamson County with its huge availability of open land. In post-*Brown* decades, subdivisions mushroomed south of Nashville's city boundaries on the Williamson County side. There, old money derived partly from land once worked by slaves and freedmen tenants was melded with entrepreneurial money when a service industry developed to cater to the new arrivals, providing them with schools, stores, and other services. Some companies and businesses followed the money to the suburbs, building hotels, office buildings, restaurants, car dealerships, and shopping centers. The "yuppie" middle class had good jobs, plenty of mortgages, debts, and the appearance of having money, but those poorer native whites who could not afford more expensive housing fled east into cheaper suburban housing, mainly apartments and smaller homes in Wilson, Sumner, and Rutherford counties, which also absorbed part of Nashville's white flight. These demographic trends did nothing to loosen conservative racial attitudes in Middle Tennessee and ease resistance to *Brown* and busing. Nashville, however, continued to attract new residents—whites, blacks, and immigrants—although these new arrivals were not always as affluent as the taxpayers who fled town.

In 1964, ten years after *Brown*, the Williamson County NAACP leaders organized Citizens for Human Dignity to push for school desegregation in this county where so little had been done. The public schools had no choice but to accept desegregation or face punitive federal measures. In 1967, the black Natchez High School was closed and later converted into a community center. Williamson County's population had been more than 40 percent Negro in slavery times, but by 2003 its schools included only 4.2 percent blacks, and the Franklin City Public Schools had only 15.1 percent blacks.

The ongoing schools-desegregation case in Nashville was a key factor in the white flight into surrounding counties. In early 1970, Avon Williams and the plaintiffs renewed hearings in the Nashville case. They called for county-wide busing as a further relief remedy. After extensive court hearings, Federal District Judge William E. Miller held that the school desegregation plan had been ineffective, and he ordered preparation of a new plan. Later, Miller met the parties at a neutral site and advised the group that he was withdrawing his injunctive order and staying the implementation for another year. Avon Williams, by now a state senator from Nashville, appealed Miller's decision to the Sixth Circuit Court, which remanded the case for an effective plan. In September 1970, President Nixon nominated Miller to the Sixth Circuit Court, and the Nashville case was assumed in October by Miller's replacement, Leland McClure Morton, a University of Tennessee law graduate who would go on to serve as chief judge of the district from 1977 to 1984.

Williams and plaintiffs prepared expert briefs for the court presentations. Young intellectuals in the recently integrated Sevier Park neighborhood, including Gina Carter and Kitty Smith, introduced their own plan. Williams invited Smith and other neighborhood activists to discuss the school case in his office, where he convinced them to give assistance to the academic desegregation experts whom he and the school board had hired. Williams used the experts to develop a workable plan that would place all children into integrated schools, using the school board's ideal ratio of 15 to 35 percent black children.

In 1971, a mob of protesters from the suburbs outside the Briley Parkway thronged the outer court corridors at the Federal Courthouse in Nashville. Casey Jenkins, an antibusing activist, led the unruly crowd. Judge Morton ordered U.S. marshals to escort Williams and the plaintiffs through the side doors to avoid the crowd, which spilled into the streets. Jenkins, who attracted thousands to his rallies, challenged incumbent Beverly Briley in the mayoral elections of 1971, but Briley won reelection and declared that local citizens would have to abide by the court's decision on busing. Many citizens preferred freedom of choice, with "convenient busing"—that is, the privilege of having a child transported by bus from home to school but not for the purpose of desegregation. The Metro school board's desegregation plan had simply tinkered with the existing system here and there to avoid angering the segregationists and the business community. Williams argued that this do-nothing posture warranted a busing plan. But the Chamber of Commerce feared that a city school system where busing and Negroes predominated would hurt Nashville's ability to attract national corporations, especially at a time when out-of-county suburbs were attracting families from the city. Judge Morton asked the Department of Health, Education, and Welfare to prepare a plan that minimized busing in the inner city and *excluded* busing in the far ends of the county. Still, the crowd at the courthouse shouted racist slogans.

Morton's plan was ultimately a failure. Whites fled to the far ends of Davidson County where there was no busing, and as the population in those areas increased, the schools there became overcrowded. This phenomenon also swelled Nashville–Davidson County's private schools and fueled the creation of new ones called "Christian academies." Pearl High School became nearly all black. White parents in suburban Davidson County pressured the school board to expand suburban schools and relieve overcrowding. Commenting on the situation, Vanderbilt professors Richard A. Pride and J. D. Woodard wrote:

> Busing was not popular with white citizens, parents, or teachers. Whites believed that busing was harmful to children's educational development. Yet this belief does not square with the facts. Both our own research and the bulk of research done elsewhere shows the educational achievement of white children was not adversely affected by busing. On the other hand, the surveys showed that whites believed that busing did not improve race relations, and this sentiment seems accurate.

On October 19, 1973, another judge in the desegregation case, former Franklin mayor Frank Gray Jr., was advised by the Metro Board of Education through legal counsel that the "need to begin the proposed construction [of new school buildings] is urgent." Nearly 50 percent of the school buildings had been constructed before 1940. In 1974, the school board prepared the *Comprehensive School Plan for Metro Nashville Public Schools*, which proposed the expansion or building of three high schools in suburban areas. The plan excluded inner-city Pearl High School, which was a predominantly black school dating back to 1898, with current buildings dating as far back as 1937, and these facilities had been expanded many times since then. Williams was able to get the court to stop the increase of portable classrooms for suburban schools. Williams and the plaintiffs argued that, instead of using portables to handle the overflow, the school system should bus suburban students to the many empty inner-city classrooms. White flight had resegregated the inner-city schools, and the building of more schools and the use of portable classrooms in the suburbs were keeping Davidson County from both using its school space effectively and maintaining adequate integration of all schools in the system. But whites seemed to prefer to close underutilized schools in black neighborhoods and bus the black children to the suburbs to integrate the expanded, predominantly white facilities. They believed that such plans would satisfy the courts' mandates to desegregate. On December 27, 1976, the plaintiffs filed objections and asked for contempt citations against the defendants and further relief to the board's 1972 plan.

Meanwhile, at the national level, the busing debate remained tense. In 1973 officials in Prince Edward County, Virginia, decided to sue the federal government "for the cost of busing." In 1975 the U.S. Senate approved a money bill with a provision that HEW could not order school districts to use busing as a remedy for desegregating schools. Senator Robert C. Byrd, a Democrat from West Virginia, offered $300 million for improvement of inner-city schools, but the only black U.S. senator at the time, Edward Brooke, a Republican from Massachusetts, declared, "In effect, this amounts to a separate but equal [*Plessy*] amendment. Anyone who would vote for this would only be voting for it to appease their conscience." Byrd countered, "Nobody controls my conscience!" Byrd's plan was approved. In this heated climate, twenty federal district judges met behind closed doors in Washington, D.C., to "discuss civil rights [school] litigation."

The Nashville school desegregation underwent another change in federal judges. Upon Judge Gray's retirement, President Jimmy Carter agreed with Tennessee Democrats to nominate Thomas A. Wiseman to the federal bench in 1977. He was a law school graduate of Vanderbilt University, a former state representative, state treasurer, and an unsuccessful candidate for the Democratic nomination for governor. Avon Williams and plaintiffs decided to return to court in 1979 even though a July 19, 1979, report from the Metro

Planning Commission to the Metro Board of Education argued that white migration to suburban areas was attributed to natural growth. On August 27, 1979, the court ordered "a unitary school plan" to minimize the number of schools with more than 41 percent black enrollment. The school board's staff was directed on December 24, 1979, to develop specific mechanisms, as far as was possible, to create and maintain equity in curriculum, facilities, staff, materials, and extracurricular opportunities. Isaiah Creswell, Delores J. Wilkinson, and Barbara Mann represented the black community on the nine-member Nashville–Davidson County school board appointed by the mayor. Creswell had been the only black on the board in 1971, but after liberal Democratic congressman Richard Fulton became mayor, blacks gained two more seats. Creswell, the treasurer of Fisk University, became chairman of the school board by 1979. Wilkinson was a former teacher and a leader of the "social action committee" at First Baptist Church, Capitol Hill. Mann was a civic leader. Black children constituted nearly 40 percent of public school pupils in the county at the time.

The Nashville–Davidson County Board of Education decided to involve local citizens and hold public hearings for the development of this so-called unitary school plan. Each board member was to select one citizen to sit with the board during the hearings and the development of the plan. In October 1979, the black board members chose the Reverend William C. Dobbins, pastor of Clark Memorial United Methodist Church, a member of the Board of Trustees at Meharry Medical College, and a former civil rights leader in Florida; the Reverend Kelly Miller Smith Sr.; and this author, a history professor at Tennessee State University, parent, and chairman of the Alex Green Elementary School's Citizens Advisory Committee. Other school board members chose white citizens: Joseph J. Cunningham, Dorothy Thompson, Charles R. Dorrier, Mackie Rice, Bill Manning, and Phillip Burnett. By November 19, neighborhood groups and Citizen Advisory Councils presented proposals and petitions to the board, calling for this plan or that plan and for keeping their favorite schools open and unchanged. Most parents said in a survey that they believed a unitary school district should "provide for educational needs of all children in Davidson County regardless of race, economic or social status." A Hillwood Parents-Teachers Association leader said at the November 6, 1979, hearing: "I was told in my youth that I was the future hope of our nation—personally, I am ashamed of what's happening to my nation. Our priorities seem to be terribly confused. Let us return to the concern of quality education for *all* youth."

Inner-city groups expressed the concern that "teachers should be limited in their freedom of transfer ability if that transfer should be to concentrate experience and expertise in just a few schools." Blacks proposed that teachers should live in Metro–Davidson County; that Board of Education members' children should attend public schools; that school staff should reflect the racial makeup of the student body of a particular school; that attention should be given to the suspension policy relative to race; and that no inner-city schools be closed. On January 29, 1980, the black members submitted a motion to "request the Court to approve the building of an inner-city comprehensive high school to be named Pearl." No new schools had been built in the inner city since the 1957 court order. All but two white board members supported the Pearl proposal, which would clear the way for whites to build badly needed schools in outer parts of Nashville–Davidson County. However, one citizens' group said, "As we see it, if Pearl High School remains open, the only way we can support it is if it becomes a 'magnet school' totally devoted to a unique curriculum, such as the performing and fine arts, science and mathematics, or other special area of study." The black members of the panel wanted to reject the magnet school concept because admission requirements to such schools usually favored the whites from across the city over the neighborhood children from historically disadvantaged black families. The black leaders wanted countywide desegregation—even if it meant several two-grade schools.

The Nashville board was under pressure to vote on a desegregation plan by February 4, 1980. At the January 19, 1980, meeting, a citizen panelist said, "It is obvious the [board's] plan is 'stacked' against African American children." As the *Nashville Banner* reported, the objection was that the board's plan continued to place the burden of busing on minority parents and their children, including closing some schools in black neighborhoods, sending large numbers of black children into white areas, while busing few white children into inner-city schools. However, the majority of the school board members and the Chamber of Commerce continued to believe that extensive busing would cause more white flight from the county. A white citizens' group said, "Our children are being moved [bused] around like checkers on a board in order to make one man's [Martin Luther King Jr.'s] dream become a reality." The Citizens Advisory Committee at suburban Percy Priest School asked "that we be excluded from the new desegregation plan due to the apparent impracticality of including us in it." One couple said, "We are supporters of public education, but we do not feel we can allow our young children to be bused to some distant location. Please give your most careful consideration to leaving the zone lines as they are now in Bellevue." And another person declared, "My generation has spent our adult lives trying to change the system and ourselves. I sincerely believe that the vast majority of Nashvillians want to go forward, and they want to improve educational opportunities for all children. . . . While we cannot go back to the old system, community pride and community resources must be weighed in forging a new plan."

Things were also happening on the state level. In May 1981, state legislation imposed a moratorium on creating additional school districts except for consolidation purposes until a comprehensive study of special school districts and city districts could be completed. Black state legislators sponsored a bill that established in-school suspensions and night school for suspended students. With the stroke of a pen, another piece of state legislation established a high school proficiency test even though desegregation of schools was still being delayed and black citizens were still suffering the lingering effects of Tennessee's one-hundred-year-old Jim Crow education system. However, with input from the dean of education at Tennessee State University, black state legislators sponsored an appropriation bill to establish remedial and tutorial programs to lower the minority failure rate on such tests. On March 12, 1982, the State Board of Education passed a resolution against busing: "That the policy of forcing students to be transported out of their community school to other community schools solely to achieve racial balance is damaging both to the social and educational development of the student." The board members asked the Tennessee congressional delegation "to support any reasonable legislation that will effectively diminish and terminate the practice of forced busing in Tennessee." The lone black member of the SBOE hurriedly sent this information to the black state legislators, who quickly passed a resolution to have the SBOE resolution rescinded and for the governor's office to condemn the antibusing resolution rather than return public education to the "pernicious practice of racial segregation in education."

Judge Wiseman decided to reject the plan submitted by the Metro School Board on May 20, 1980. He rejected the plan by the plaintiffs and then directed the school board to revise its plan, which he later approved. The plaintiffs complained that the defendants ended up administering and monitoring a desegregation plan that only satisfied them: it embodied a neighborhood school concept, elimination of busing for most white children, closing Pearl High School, a generous allowance for majority race schools, and disproportionate busing for black children in the middle grades.

Williams appealed Wiseman's decision to the federal appeals court on May 31, 1981, and on a breezy night later that summer, he assembled the principal black panelists and plaintiffs in his four-story office building at 203 Second Avenue, North, to work out the details of a possible new plan. The school board members met next door in their attorney's offices, and a courier carried messages back and forth so as not to violate Tennessee's open-meetings law. The black negotiators demanded that a new high school be built in the inner city near Tennessee State University, that the burden of busing be shared, that inner-city schools be treated equitably in allocation of resources, and that Pearl be preserved as a magnet program. Minority representation at any school could vary 15 percent from the system's average; thus, a school's student population could range from 50 to 17 percent blacks.

Two days before the Metro Public Schools were to open, the Sixth U.S. Circuit Court of Appeals acted on Williams's appeal and ordered a stay of Wiseman's order. This caused the local schools to open three weeks late in September 1981, and angry whites blamed Williams for the delay. The appeals court ordered Nashville to develop a plan that involved all public schools. The court took the board's appeal under advisement on December 11, 1981, but denied relief on July 27, 1982. Wiseman ordered the school to prepare a new plan by April 1983.

Wiseman would not allow the school system to build a new Antioch High School in 1984 unless the suburban zone reached a minimum of 18 percent black students. Citizens pulled together and were able to meet the goal after more families moved into Antioch, allowing the new school to be built. In its "Integration Report, 1986–1987," the Metro schools reported that 49.1 percent of the special education students were non-white and that 38.3 percent of first-graders were blacks. And, as the dropout rate increased after the ninth grade, only 31 percent of twelfth graders were blacks. However, between 1986 and 1989, the number of black high school graduates increased from 960 to 1,160. The total graduates in Metro schools increased from 2,986 to 3,395. White enrollment went down, and black enrollment rose to 42 percent.

Metro children were spared extensive busing for desegregation in grades K–4, but busing was heavy for grades 5–8, and it slacked off for grades 9–12. Many working- and middle-class white parents placed their children in private schools for grades 5–8 and tried to enter the choice public magnet schools lottery for grades 9–12, while trying to save money for the children's college education. Since there were not enough magnet schools to accommodate this pattern, many families with children moved out of Davidson County. According to the 1990 U.S. Census, nearly half of the one million citizens in the Nashville Metropolitan Statistical Area lived outside the city limits. This exodus left many Metro schools mostly non-white and impoverished, and the city with a lower tax base. When city taxes were steadily raised, even more middle-class families took flight into suburban counties where government officials and builders accommodated them with plenty of reasonably priced housing, lower taxes, and more commuter highway lanes. About 47 percent of the children in Nashville public schools lived below the poverty level fifty years after *Brown*. Some schools, like Ross Elementary School, had a "100 percent poverty rate." Even for the whites remaining in the Metro public schools, 45 percent lived below the poverty level and in single-parent homes. Nine percent of students originated from other minority and immigrant groups, who required expensive special services. By 2003, other-race minorities (Hispanic, Asian, Native American, and Pacific Islander) had grown to 11.4 percent, and the black and white school population dropped to 45.7 percent and 42.8 percent, respectively.

Nashville's schools and the plaintiffs reached a consent decree in 1998. The agreement essentially embraced neighborhood schools, with a minimum of busing, a huge increase in magnet schools, enhanced option and practice schools in inner-city neighborhoods, and extra resources for schools with high incidences of poverty. There was one predominantly black public high school in the 1982 Nashville–Davidson County desegregation plan, but there were four mostly black high schools by 2003. And all four of these schools had low achievement test scores, declining graduation rates for black males, and social problems that overwhelmed the teachers. Yet, the parties had agreed to monitor and adjust the plan, making major changes where needed.

Just north of Nashville, in Robertson and Montgomery counties, blacks essentially went along with school desegregation plans composed by the mostly white school boards. Jackson was in the hunt for a consent decree. But many people would look the other way as America's schools resegregated on an increasing scale.

[*]

In Knoxville, despite the rulings in *Goss v. Board of Education of City of Knoxville* (1957, 1963), the city had managed to continue mostly racially separate schools. The plaintiffs objected to the twelve-year gradualism plan and got the Sixth Circuit Court to order a new plan. *Goss* was back in court in 1967, when plaintiffs objected to the 1964–65 plan approved by district court. Avon Williams pointed out overcrowding in all-white schools, empty classrooms in all-black schools, construction of new schools to accommodate white flight, and gerrymandering of school zones to perpetuate segregation. In *Goss* (1972),

Judge Robert L. Taylor declared that Knoxville had achieved a "unitary system" and that residential segregation patterns were not the fault of the school board. The case ended in 1974, when the Supreme Court refused to hear the plaintiffs' petition. Realtors redlined residential areas, busing was not used, and white transfers continued to be allowed. Highly credentialed black teachers were sent to integrate the city's predominantly white schools.

The NAACP filed a complaint about the Knoxville situation with the Office of Civil Rights, U.S. Department of Justice, in 1989. The federal agency found the school board in violation of Title VI guidelines of the 1964 Civil Rights Act. Knoxville agreed to correct violations and began renovating neglected inner-city schools to counterbalance expansion of schools in outlying areas. Sarah M. Greene, chairman of the Knoxville NAACP's education committee, argued that the system still discriminated in hiring and placement of teachers. The school director denied wrongdoing. A community task force began developing new guidelines for school desegregation in order to satisfy requirements of the Office of Civil Rights. In 1990, the federal agency even sent some of its personnel to Knoxville to help with the plan. After the magnet school concept was incorporated into the plan, the school board had to sue the Knox County Commission for funding the six magnets, causing the plan to linger through 1993. By 1996, $39 million was approved for the desegregation plan. The federal agency declared the case closed, but Dewey Roberts and Sarah M. Greene of the NAACP asked the Office of Civil Rights to reopen the case. After a visit from the federal agency, the NAACP and the school board came to an agreement in 1997.

A University of Tennessee doctoral student, Ruby J. A. Hassan, noted in her 1999 dissertation on desegregation in Knoxville: "Despite the time, energy, and resources invested in the desegregation effort, the racial balance between predominantly white and black schools has not altered to any significant degree." Hassan found low participation in the magnet programs, which "are at best a partial solution to segregation." One African American leader objected to renovating predominantly black Austin-East High School and turning it into a magnet, because it was no more than a "hand-me-down," an old high school that had previously been all white. The leader believed that such schools should have been closed and the students sent to integrated, modern facilities. But many of the black leaders wanted to hold onto "history and culture" and keep neighborhood school buildings open and staffed with mostly black teachers. The lone black board member was caught in the crossfire, because many whites also wanted their own neighborhood schools, no busing, and minimal racial integration. In the new staffing plan, many white teachers resented inner-city school assignments. Their indignant attitudes showed, and this friction caused student discipline problems to escalate. Principals and teachers at predominantly white schools often rejected black students by imposing higher punishments, failures, school transfers, and suspensions (19.4 percent by 2003) on them.

[*]

In 2003, the Tennessee school systems with the largest percentage of black student populations were Memphis (86.3), Fayette County (65.8), Haywood County (64.4), Jackson–Madison County (53.4), Nashville–Davidson County (45.7), Union City (41.9), Hamilton County (33.1), Shelby County (23.0), and Murfreesboro (21.3). As in Knoxville, black students in these districts suffered a higher percentage of suspensions than other groups of students.

Judicial scholar J. Harvie Wilkinson, in his *From Brown to Bakke: The Supreme Court and School Integration 1954-1978* (1979), has perhaps best explained the evolution of the school desegregation efforts in the nation. Wilkinson pointed out that *Brown* made racism a southern problem though it should have declared racism a national problem that required a national solution. *Brown* launched an attack on the defiant South but hardly touched the cloaked discrimination in the North. It was not until 1972 that the U.S. Supreme Court, in *Bradley v. Milliken*, turned a flank to the North and the West to deal with segregated schools. Wilkerson outlined the stages of development for the post-*Brown* civil rights movement: (1) there was absolute defiance from 1954 to 1959; (2) there was only token compliance from 1960 to 1964; (3) modest integration took place from 1964 to 1968 mainly because of the 1964 Civil Rights Act; and (4) massive school integration occurred after the case of *Green v. County School Board* (1968).

Finally, there was resegregation of many American schools, North and South, by 2004. Beverly Daniel Tatum, in *"Why Are All the Black Kids Sitting Together in the Cafeteria?"* (2003), points out the tendency of America's ethnic groups to resort to resegregation. Whites became the most segregated group in the nation's public and private schools. The proportion of black students in majority-white schools decreased by 13 percent—a level lower than any year since 1968. And despite segregation proving to be a failed education policy, American apartheid-like schools educated one-sixth of the nation's African American students. Jack M. Balkin, in *What Brown v. Board of Education Should Have Said: The Nation's Top Legal Experts Rewrite America's Landmark Civil Rights Decision* (2000), pointed out that several government decisions would become obstacles to desegregation and reverse the momentum of desegregation in the South where the movement had by far achieved its greatest success.

The increased involvement of middle-class whites in the school desegregation controversy likely led to increased attention by politicians to better funding of education. In 1953, Tennessee spent $68.3 million on education but increased the expenditure to $117,271,900 by fiscal year 1958–59. In 1965, Tennessee spent $276 million on public education. The high school graduation rate for Americans was 86.5 percent in 2000, and the graduation rate in Tennessee (1998–2000) was 89 percent. Nationally, blacks had an 83.7 percent graduation rate for high school, and the rate in Tennessee was nearly the same. The Tennessee General Assembly eventually approved $1 billion dollars in new state money for education, and, under Governor Lamar Alexander, began a master teacher plan to improve schools. However, economic disparities by race and class remained a fundamental problem in American society and within its public schools. Some 10 percent of the poorest children dropped out of school compared to 1.6 percent of the wealthiest children.

Still, the hope spawned by *Brown* did not end despite the furious war of massive resistance. One example of hope was exhibited by First Baptist Church, Capitol Hill, in Nashville, on Sunday, April 14, 2002, when this civil-rights-conscious congregation chose to read II Corinthians 4:8–9 as part of its service: "We are hard pressed on every side, yet not crushed; we are perplexed, but not in despair; persecuted but not forsaken; struck down, but not destroyed." *Brown* was not dead.

CHAPTER 4
KEEP MEMPHIS DOWN IN DIXIE
SIT-IN DEMONSTRATIONS AND DESEGREGATION
OF PUBLIC FACILITIES

In late December 1955—just six months after the announcement of *Brown*—Tennesseans received news of the boycott of Jim Crow buses in Montgomery, Alabama. Edgar D. Nixon, a railroad porter, and Jo Ann Robinson, head of the Negro Women's Political Club and a professor at Alabama State University, were among the principal leaders of the movement. Robinson enlisted some students to print and distribute protest flyers at the bus stops. "Boycott, Stay off the Buses," they proclaimed. Nixon and a white lawyer bailed Rosa Parks out of jail after she refused to give up her seat for a white bus rider and hired a Negro attorney to help convince Parks to allow her case to be used to challenge Jim Crow. Nixon enlisted Martin Luther King Jr., the new pastor of Dexter Avenue Baptist Church, to serve as the articulate spokesperson for the newly created Montgomery Improvement Association (MIA). The MIA achieved integration of the transportation facilities through the U.S. Supreme Court decision *Gayle et al. v. Browser,* delivered on November 13, 1956. However, in Nashville and Memphis, Negroes failed to get immediate desegregation of city buses.

In Memphis, Tennessee's largest city, history most certainly framed the local problems in race relations. From the first quarter of the twentieth century through the 1950s, Edward H. Crump and his well-oiled political machine dominated the city's government and maintained tight control on local Negroes. Crump considered himself a friend of the Negro; yet, he once threatened the editor of one large Negro newspaper with these words:

> You have a bunch of niggers teaching social equality, stirring up
> social hatred. I am not going to stand for it. I've dealt with nig-
> gers all my life, and I know how to treat them. That darn paper is
> using communistic propaganda—we are not going to put up with
> Pittsburgh [*Courier*] stuff here. This is Memphis. We will deal
> with them in no uncertain terms and it won't be in the dark. You
> be sure to tell them I said so. We are *not* going to tolerate a bunch
> of niggers spreading racial hatred and running things their way.
> Tell them Mr. Crump said so. You understand me?

Memphis maintained a policy not to hire Negroes as bus drivers, mechanics, managers, and clerical personnel. Bus drivers were allowed to treat Negro riders with disdain and abuse. In January 1954, a driver stopped the bus and made a Negro woman leave her seat and move to the back to accommodate more white riders, while exclaiming, "There is *still* segregation in Tennessee." On the sixteenth, another bus driver pulled a pistol on a Negro woman and said, "A [nigger] on my bus gets off at the back door!" Labor leader James T. Walker and schoolteacher Willa McWilliams of the Bluff City and Shelby County Council of Civic Clubs began protests. Crump was old and quite sick at the time, but the Memphis mayor, Frank Tobey, who had been handpicked by Crump, promised to look into the bus matter "in order to maintain good relations between white and Negro passengers." Why was Memphis such a tough nut to crack?

Memphis's political machine had encouraged indefensible black poverty through racial employment discrimination and a contrived surplus of Negro labor—that is, Negroes entered the city faster than employment could rise and the city did nothing to create jobs for them. Negroes were confined to menial jobs and kept at the bottom of the socioeconomic chain—as it was in Crump's native Mississippi, where whites had managed to retain labor practices held over from slavery days. A Negro woman wrote to President Roosevelt in January 1943, complaining that the Memphis authorities had relegated Negroes to domestic work but had not given them jobs in defense industries as federal guidelines required. Negro welders had completed their Works Progress Administration training and passed the tests, but whites assigned them to jobs as busboys and truck drivers. The local economy was dominated by retail, agricultural marketing, and light industrial firms.

Since the 1930s, area land owners had been evicting white and black tenants who dared to unionize, and this movement produced even more surplus labor for Memphis. Negroes comprised 121,003 citizens (57,133 males and 63,870 females) in the 1940 census, but they grew to 125,965 (41 percent) of the city's 305,000 citizens in 1943. About a million Negroes lived in the Memphis-Delta area, and this population exploded after World War II. Although Negroes threatened to outnumber whites in Memphis, the labor surplus was tolerated to keep wages low, keep whites enriched, and provide seasonal farm workers for "King Cotton." This chief product of the Delta was grown and harvested in surrounding counties in Mississippi, Arkansas, and West Tennessee and brought to the auction houses in Memphis. Acres of cotton bales could be seen on the banks of the Mississippi near Front Street waiting to be hoisted aboard the riverboats for transport to faraway markets.

The Crump machine pressured thousands of Negroes to work for low wages, or else go to the jails and prisons on trumped-up charges, including vagrancy. Some chose to leave town, perhaps joining the Great Migration to the North. Thousands of surplus Negro workers in Memphis were bused daily, before sunup, to the nearby cotton fields during the summer and fall months to chop weeds and pick the crops, often for fifty cents, a dollar, two dollars, or three dollars a day—depending on how many hundreds of pounds of cotton the person could pick and how desperately the planters needed them. Often they were taken to Arkansas and Mississippi to help break strikes by the Southern Tenant Farmers' Union. When the sun set over the Mississippi River, dropping into the orange-lit horizon formed by the adjacent plains of Arkansas, the old buses and open-bed trucks of many colors would unload their weary workers at the street corners in Negro neighborhoods. Despite a long, hard day in the mosquito-infested cotton-growing areas, the Negro workers laughed and joked with one another as they began their slow, painful walks to their houses. At least they had a little money for their families.

For the remainder of the year, Memphis's surplus Negro workers did "day work"—some of them standing on specified street corners early in the morning while the chill was still in the air and the fog was just lifting from the Mississippi River. There they would wait for some contractor, freight truck driver, local warehouse supervisor, or homeowner to stop and hire them for the day. Employers picked and chose the Negroes they wanted and decided on the spot the cheap wages they would receive. Above the streets where the Negroes stood, large billboards ironically advertised gleaming new automobiles and a smiling, well-dressed white family of four under the heading, "This is The American Way." Grown Negro men crowded the corners near the warehouses along the Mississippi River, especially near E. H. Crump Boulevard, waiting each morning to be selected to unload boxcars, trucks, and river barges and earn a few dollars—being careful to pronounce "yes, sir" or "no, sir" with a heavy southern drawl. Sometimes they took their teenage sons along to "learn the ropes" and earn extra money unloading boxcars. Negro women could get domestic work in white women's homes for two to three dollars a day and carfare. Over 80 percent of Negro female workers were domestics. But Negro families hesitated to send their young daughters into white homes where men could "have their way"—that is, rape them—as had happened in slavery. Young boys sold newspapers, and delivered groceries and goods on bicycles. Memphis Negroes learned to do whatever was needed to earn a few dollars for survival. When times were really tough, many Negro families depended on relatives who remained on nearby farms—"out in the country," as they put it—for cured pork meat, wild game, fish, chicken, beef, eggs, sorghum, wild grapes made into wine, corn whiskey for the men, fresh ears of corn, watermelons, other vegetables, and jars of fruit preserves.

There were no social security and health benefits for most Negro workers in Memphis in those years. A third of them were regularly unemployed. Some 25 percent of the rest seldom worked a full forty-hour week. The Negro median family income was 47 percent of that for white families, forcing a third of Negro families below the poverty level. A Negro in Memphis could not buy a loaf of bread and a bottle of milk any cheaper than a white person could. Yet, a white man, even if equally uneducated, earned more than the average black man. In 1954 in Memphis, five pounds of flour cost twenty-nine cents, ham thirty-five cents per pound, eggs thirty-nine cents a dozen, and sugar nineteen cents for five pounds with a newspaper coupon. A television cost ninety-three dollars, and a topcoat could be bought for thirty-nine dollars. Many adult Negro men were earning three to five dollars a day. The "Great Society" programs of the Lyndon Johnson administration—food stamps, breakfast and lunch programs in the schools—had not been invented yet.

The profits generated from the surplus black labor seemed to produce a good, comfortable life for a vast number of whites, who could afford Negro laborers to clean their houses, cook meals, care for children, mow lawns, and do common labor at a moment's notice. Previously impoverished and working-class whites, who had migrated primarily from surrounding Delta counties with little education and hardly any marketable skills—but with a deep hatred of Negroes—benefited immensely from this Jim Crow system. Many of these rural migrants lived near Negro areas or in rental units and low-income housing, but they received wages slightly higher than those given Negroes. By and large, whites were careful not to violate racial mores by openly socializing with Negro neighbors.

On Walnut Street, for instance, some poor whites lived in frame rental houses next door to Negroes, but mostly they crowded into what the Negro residents called the "nice" two-story brick apartment houses on the west side of Walnut and the corner of Tate Street. The white children sometimes played with their Negro neighbors' children until they reached early teenage years. The white parents worked in the nearby factories and warehouses, and their children attended all-white schools on the other side of Lamar Avenue, on the northeastern edge of this peculiar southern neighborhood, Walnut Street. Boss Crump and other leading whites lived in huge houses just north of Lamar Avenue, not far from the Central High School for whites, and farther east. Middle-class and elite whites did not associate socially with poor whites, although their children sometimes went to the same public schools, and they sometimes worked for the same employer. Yet, however "dirt poor" and inadequately educated some whites might be, they were at least "white" and thus might rise out of poverty in the next generation—an opportunity that their Negro neighbors were generally denied. Negroes, not "whites," were stuck in a racial caste system. And it was into this oppressive system and racial milieu that the civil rights movement had to enter Memphis.

[∗]

On October 16, 1954, E. H. Crump finally succumbed to his illness and died—one day shy of the five-month anniversary of the *Brown* decision. Black teachers, who depended on their annual appointments through some protective politician or a pro–Crump machine Negro preacher, were always reminded to pay respect to "Mr." Crump. And so it was that the teachers marched the school children from the Alonzo Locke Elementary School (grades 1–6) on St. Paul Avenue a couple of miles to the burial site. The Negro students looked through the fence at Crump's elaborate funeral exercises in Elmwood Cemetery as if a king were being laid to rest.

Ironically, Crump's grave in one of the city's oldest cemeteries was near the border of a large Negro federal housing project—the LeMoyne Gardens— which had been built in the 1940s. LeMoyne College, founded in 1871 for Negro students, was across the street on Walker Avenue. Unlike the LeMoyne area, the Walnut Street neighborhood to which the elementary school students returned after Crump's funeral consisted of working-class duplex shotguns and frame houses and graduated to middle-class brick houses and even large brick houses owned by elite-class Negroes in the St. Paul and Tate Avenue area. Negro doctors, lawyers, teachers, and businessmen lived within this Jim Crow confinement. Some of the two-story brick houses had been divided into one- and two-room apartments, with large numbers of Negroes packed into them, including some of those on the waiting list for the LeMoyne Gardens and Foote Homes low-income public housing projects. A few public school teachers lived in the "nice" housing projects.

Several blocks to the west of the cemetery, some Negro men strutted down Walnut Street near St. Paul Avenue, and they seemed to be saying "Crump is dead!" to their head-nodding fellows sitting on the front porches. On that evening in October 1954, locals crowded into the neighborhood's little cinderblock café (still standing on Walnut Street), which was owned and operated by a "good looking brown-skin woman," who may well have concealed a pistol under her clean, white apron. In this "joint" with no air conditioning (just a huge, roaring electric fan), the door was open to the sidewalk. Out poured the sounds of blues from the jukebox, as well as the mouthwatering smells of barbecue cooked out back; catfish and buffalo fish sandwiches, with plenty of free Louisiana hot sauce; thick-sauced spaghetti, with huge meatballs; and "cold, cold beer." Inside the café, there was a loud celebration—as if the cruel master of a nearby slave plantation had died. Children managed to venture inside the smoky place every now and then to "buy a sour pickle or pickled pig feet," except when white policemen cruised menacingly by the door.

Although 58 percent of Memphis's Negroes lived in poverty or thereabouts, 42 percent did not. Memphis's Negro community had its educated cadre and professional corps. Memphis had a chapter of the prestigious and secretive Boulé long before Nashville had a chapter. There were few lawyers. Attorney A. A. Latting had the largest Negro practice, and in 1943 he led the fight with the city commission to get slums cleared and the LeMoyne Gardens federal housing project built near the college. By 1952, Memphis had twenty-one Negro public schools, including five high schools. There was also a Catholic elementary and high school for Negroes who could afford the private tuition. Memphis had thirty-one physicians and surgeons, including five with offices on Beale Street. Jim Crow confined Negro doctors and teachers to the same neighborhoods as other members of the black community. The many funeral homes boosted several Negro owners and their families into the Negro elite. There was a viable City Federation of Colored Women's Clubs like the one in Nashville. Henderson Business College and LeMoyne College constituted the Negro institutions of higher education. But Miriam DeCosta-Willis recalled that when she moved to Memphis in 1956, downtown street banners read, "Keep Memphis Down in Dixie." She and her husband, Russell B. Sugarmon Jr., as well as other northern-educated Negroes, were called "the young Turks," and they became determined to push harder for changes in Jim Crow Memphis.

In reality, the movement for this change had already started in 1951–52, when the Tennessee poll tax was being phased out. Roy Love, G. W. Lee, and J. E. Walker had formed the Non-Partisan Voters [registration] Committee. They won no public offices. (Walker once ran for the school board as the only candidate to oppose the Crump machine; he received less than eight thousand votes, even though some twenty thousand Negroes were registered to vote.) Love, Lee, and Walker broadened the movement by involving the churches and forming the Ministers and Citizens League. The Reverend Roy Love's Mt. Nebo Baptist Church would serve as one of the meeting places. It was on Vance and Lauderdale, four or five blocks west of Walnut Street and about two blocks from Beale Street. The federal low-income housing projects Clayborn Homes and Foote Homes, with their well-tended playgrounds and "spray pools," dominated the Mt. Nebo area. Booker T. Washington High School and Porter Junior High School were located up the street on Lauderdale. The people from the Walnut Street neighborhood and Alonzo Locke School, among others, fed into these two schools and housing projects. Several doors down Vance, not far from Mt. Nebo Church, Vasco Smith, "a young Turk," would establish a dental office.

Besides Mt. Nebo in South Memphis, there was the Collins Chapel CME, the Pentecostal Temple, Clayborn Temple AME Church, and the Mason Temple Church of God in Christ (COGIC). These became major auditoriums for mass civil rights meetings. The beautiful Clayborn Temple at Hernando and Pontotoc was formerly the Second Presbyterian Church until it was bought by the AME Church, dedicated on November 27, 1949, and named for the Reverend Henry Clayborn. Mason Temple on Fourth Avenue, a building on the National Register of Historic Places, was the headquarters for the COGIC. Henry C. Bunton, a Colored Methodist Episcopal Church (CME) minister was presiding over the Ministers and Citizens League by 1955, when Walker and Lee headed mass meetings at the Pentecostal Temple (COGIC) on Wellington Street, around the corner from Beale Street Baptist Church and Beale Street Park and in sight of Walker's insurance company. The League's mass meetings helped to organize more than forty-six thousand Negro voters.

In September, Mayor Frank Tobey, a remnant of the Crump machine, unexpectedly died in office and was succeeded by Edmund Orgill, a progressive businessman. Orgill defeated S. Watkins Overton in what the *Press-Scimitar* called the "first really free" election for mayor since Crump died.

These historic events, plus the Montgomery bus boycott in December 1955, inspired Negro leaders in Memphis to move further with their civil rights movement. On April 20, 1956, the *Nashville Globe* reported that Memphis Negroes—James T. Walker, Maceo Walker, Hollis Price, Blair T. Hunt, S. A. Owens, and Julian Simpkins Jr.—had formed an interracial committee on race relation but the whites had their own committee, one that was dedicated "neither to integration nor segregation." The *Globe* further noted, "Nashville Negroes appeared to cast more votes on Election Day than the [black] Memphians who had little or nothing tangible to show for their prowess. It seems, however, the [black] Memphians may come into their own under [the leadership of] Mr. Edmund Orgill."

On April 26, 1956, on the edge of East Memphis, at Bellevue and Lamar Streets, O. Z. Evers, a World War II veteran, and a friend boarded a city bus and sat on the front seat. From that point on, the buses usually picked up white passengers. The bus company was trying to increase white riders and had even promised a group of concerned white women that better service would be provided for the Negro maids who depended on the buses to get to work on time. After Evers and his friend took their seats, the driver stopped the bus and called the police, who told the two men they had to leave the bus or sit in back with the other Negroes. Evers and his companion left the bus and later filed suit in federal district court. Attorney H. T. Lockard took the case and asked Judge Marion S. Boyd for a summary judgment because of the recent Montgomery episode. Boyd refused and denied a motion for a three-judge panel to hear the case, but this was overturned on appeal. Boyd, joined by William Earnest Miller of the district court in Nashville and John D. Martin of the Sixth Circuit, heard the Evers case in January 1958, which they dismissed. In an action similar to what the Tennessee court had done in the Ida B. Wells case in 1887, the Boyd panel applied the "troublemaker" judicial principle to Evers, declaring that he was not a "regular rider" and that he had only boarded the bus to start a lawsuit. However, the full Sixth Circuit Court of Appeals concluded that Evers had a right to test any restrictions on his constitutional rights, forcing the issue back to Memphis on February 27, 1959. But, as the *Tri-State Defender* reported on February 28, Boyd stalled relief for the plaintiff until Memphis officials could work out their own plans to address this local threat to Jim Crow.

Judge Boyd was a key to the slow pace of dismantling Jim Crow in Memphis. He was born in 1900 in nearby Covington, received his law degree from the University of Tennessee, Knoxville, in 1921, was elected to the General Assembly, and became assistant state attorney general for Shelby County.

Among other offices, Boyd became state attorney general for Shelby County before being nominated to the federal bench by President Roosevelt in September 1940. In 1962 Boyd was mentioned as a replacement on the Sixth Circuit Court of Appeals. However, the Memphis NAACP branch sent telegrams to President John F. Kennedy, Senators Estes Kefauver and Albert Gore Sr., and newspapers to successfully block the nomination. Boyd remained on the Memphis bench and served until his death on January 9, 1988. He would sit on the Evers case for four years.

The Evers case was not the only civil rights lawsuit testing Jim Crow's limits in Memphis. In late 1957, Jessie H. Turner and the NAACP sued the city in state court for ejecting Turner from a "whites-only" public library. Turner was vice president of the local Tri-State Bank, an officer of the Memphis NAACP, and a native of Longview, Mississippi. He had arrived in Memphis in 1931 to attend LeMoyne College and later received a master's degree in business administration from the University of Chicago.

Housing discrimination was still another problem facing Negroes in Jim Crow Memphis. It was hard for Negroes to rent or buy a decent place to live. Although the U.S. Supreme Court had ruled against such discrimination in the 1940s, some citizens still placed racial restrictions on the deed covenants to prevent selling property to Negroes. Memphis, like other cities in Tennessee, had no residential segregation ordinances, but the city was de facto segregated in residential patterns that mirrored those of most southern towns. Poor whites usually had to tolerate Negroes moving into housing on adjacent streets (short of resorting to mob violence), but middle- and upper-class whites had no tolerance for integration in their neighborhoods, *Brown* or no *Brown*. In the lower-middle-class Glenview neighborhood, the residents campaigned to remove a Negro pastor and his family from a home they had somehow managed to purchase in 1956. These residents created an organization to keep Negroes from moving into Glenview and had the Negro pastor arrested on trumped-up charges. The Negro family did not move into the house until early 1958 because of threats and cross burnings. White residents confronted city politicians about upholding residential segregation, and the officials in turn felt obligated to protect white interests.

Also off-limits to Negroes were the Memphis city zoo, auditorium, art galleries, and parks and swimming pools, except on certain days or at segregated facilities. Indeed, back in 1911, the city commissioners debated about whether to allow even Negro public school students to visit the city zoo at all. They finally agreed that youngsters and their teachers could enter the park— but only on Tuesdays from eight until one o'clock.

On October 13, 1958, Tarlease Matthews and her friend Anna Williams had been ejected from the Overton Park Zoo for being there on a day when Negroes were not allowed. After an hour passed, fifteen police cars rushed to the scene to eject the women, who were rudely asked, "Do you gals have any white children with you?" Negro maids could enter the park on any day, so long as they accompanied their white employers and the white children they cared for. Matthews and Williams were members of the Binghamton Civic League in North Memphis, presided over by O. Z. Evers, who advised the city "to sit down right now and work out a program of desegregation of all facilities in the city." He continued, "I am sure that they have been reading about what is going on in other sections of the country regarding segregation, and they know that white supremacy is legally dead." City officials cited estates, wills, and deeds that restricted some park land to whites only, and argued that opening the parks on all days to Negroes would require additional expense for police to keep down increased crime. On January 5, 1959, Matthews and attorney H. T. Lockard filed a desegregation suit in federal court.

Policemen harassed Negro citizens, homes were illegally entered, and Negroes were publicly beaten, sometimes shot, arrested, and fined for frivolous and false charges including "staring at an officer," talking too loudly, disorderly conduct, and traffic violations. Roy Love and his wife were stopped for "reckless driving," verbally abused, arrested, and taken to jail, and because Mrs. Love continued to protest and stare at the policemen, one officer took the seat next to her in the car and shouted, "Nigger, shut up!" The officers declared in court that the Loves must have been drinking, because no Negroes would dare to talk back to white policemen.

That spring, Negro leaders in Memphis urged a boycott of the city fairgrounds with its "Negroes, Thursday Only" signs and spoke out on civil rights in various venues. LeMoyne College announced its statewide Race Relations Conference for Saturday, April 4, 1959. Kelly Miller Smith, a trustee of Memphis's S. A. Owen Junior College, would be the speaker at St. John Baptist Church on Vance Avenue. Upon his return from India, Martin Luther King Jr., along with another activist, Fred Shuttlesworth, was engaged to speak at the National Baptist Sunday School and Training Union Congress scheduled for June in the Ellis Auditorium downtown. In May 1959, at the Fifth Anniversary Program for *Brown*, the speaker was Charles C. Diggs, a Negro congressman from Michigan and former Fisk University student. Addressing the 2,709 attendees at Mason Temple, Diggs noted that only Clinton High School and Nashville's public schools, among 141 school districts in Tennessee, had desegregation plans underway, and he reminded the audience that the one hundredth anniversary of the 1863 Emancipation Proclamation was fast approaching. America, he said, was "still not getting ready for it."

In April, Evers, T. R. Fugh, and Eliehu Stanback petitioned the president of the Greyhound Bus Company in Atlanta about the signs for "Colored" and "White" rooms still posted in Memphis bus stations. All three of these Negro men were officers of the Binghamton Civic League. The Jim Crow signs remained at the Greyhound and Continental bus stations because city officials had told the station managers that segregation was still the law in Memphis and that the police commissioner had ordered policemen to evict and arrest any violators. In June 1959, Evers, Stanback, and the Binghamton Civic League appeared in federal district court to ask for an injunction against the city's tax collection in the Negro community so long as the city refused equal access to facilities and did not give equal services to Negro citizens. The judge ignored the request. The matter of segregated bus stations, meanwhile, was referred to the Interstate Commerce Commission. The bus station managers soon complied with the law of the land after the bus companies ordered them to do so. In October 1959, O. Z. Evers received news from Greyhound company officials that the signs had been removed at the Memphis station. Policemen, however, continued to harass Negro customers at the bus terminals, insisting that racial segregation remained local law.

Claiming nearly seven thousand members, the Memphis NAACP was the organization's largest chapter in the South, and in June 1959, it sent a delegation consisting of Maxine and Vasco Smith, the Reverend David S. Cunningham (local branch president and pastor of Collins Chapel CME Church), S. A. Owen (pastor of Metropolitan Baptist Church), and H. T. Lockard and his wife to the NAACP annual national meeting in the North. Lockard used the convention's expert workshops on legal training and school desegregation plans to further prepare for local civil rights battles. The NAACP held its Tennessee Conference in Memphis on September 25–27, 1959, at the Mount Pisgah CME Church on Park Avenue in the community of Orange Mound. Chapters from Chattanooga, Clarksville, Jackson, Knoxville, Memphis, Nashville, and Oak Ridge, along with college chapters from Fisk University, LeMoyne College, Knoxville College, and Lane College in Jackson, were represented at the conference. They discussed the events and developments of the civil rights movement, the successes of the NAACP court cases, and how to better organize and speed up desegregation in their communities. The Memphis division of the Brotherhood of Sleeping Car Porters, under the leadership of C. J. Jackson, Harry Fletcher, Floyd L. Newman, and David Tillman remained supportive of the NAACP.

A key factor in the Memphis civil rights movement was Maxine A. Smith—the counterweight to Judge Marion S. Boyd. She was one of the new, bold leaders who rose in Memphis in the late 1950s. She was born Georgia Maxine Atkins in 1929. Her father, thanks to a federal job as a postman, had not had to kowtow to the Crump machine and local racists as many of his contemporaries were forced to do. Maxine attended the public schools at Lincoln Elementary, Porter Junior High, and Booker T. Washington High School. She completed Spelman College in Atlanta and received her master's degree at the integrated Middlebury College in Vermont, using one of Tennessee's Jim Crow out-of-state scholarships. She and dentist Vasco Smith married in 1953, spent two years in Illinois, and returned home, where she taught at LeMoyne College. She and another Negro woman, Laura Willis, became involved in the movement when they were not allowed to register as graduate students at Memphis State University. From 1957 through the next three decades, Smith served the local NAACP as membership chairman, director of voter education, coordinator of sit-in demonstrations, and executive secretary. She was to Memphis what Daisy Bates was to Little Rock and more. A *Memphis Commercial Appeal* reporter described her this way: "[Maxine Smith's] thunder has inflamed rivals and inspired supporters. It has made her the most loved and the most despised woman in Memphis. She has been spat on and bowed to, cursed and applauded, called everything from crusader to fiend."

In early October 1959, civil rights leaders approached Memphis Police Commissioner Claude Armour about widespread, excessive police brutality in Negro neighborhoods. The Bluff City and Shelby County Civic Clubs, which claimed twenty thousand Negro members, helped lead this effort, and under the leadership of the Reverend Alexander Gladney, they hired attorney R. B. Sugarmon as their legal representative. Armour pretended that police brutality did not exist but agreed to meet with Sugarmon to discuss the evidence and petitions. In October, at a rally at Clayborn Temple, Sugarmon said, "We as Negroes ought to humbly recognize the fact that history seemingly has selected us as destiny's children. The Negro in Memphis is faced with a challenge." Armour agreed to "investigate the matter." To the newspapers, Sugarmon said, "Unfortunately, the truth is that the personnel of the Memphis Police Department [are] drawn from an area [Mississippi], which conditions its inhabitants to accept the doctrine of white supremacy. Today, that doctrine has been destroyed [legally]. Those who persist in this belief can sustain the doctrine of white supremacy only on emotional grounds." The police, however, continued the reign of terror.

Memphis desegregation cases involving its library and parks were stalled in federal district court. Judge Boyd flatly told Sugarmon and Lockard that he would not even hear motions for summary judgments. The Reverend Cunningham and attorney Ira Murphy brought up the fact that no Negroes had served on juries in Memphis since 1940. Local Negroes also suffered bias in the application of automobile insurance rates, and the police gave Negro drivers—especially anyone caught driving a new car—enough tickets to make their insurance rates rise even higher.

[*]

About 210 miles east, in Nashville, an Upper South city in which the Negro community had an active NAACP chapter, a group of competent lawyers, two weekly newspapers, four colleges, and a large middle and professional class, Negro leaders began thinking of new ways to push the civil rights movement to another phase. From 1955 to 1957, they had focused their efforts on school desegregation. However, *Brown* did not lead to voluntary desegregation of public facilities, and that became a new objective. In 1958, speaking at the First Baptist Church East Nashville, at the invitation of Harriet H. Davidson and the Women's Day Committee, the Little Rock civil rights leader Daisy Bates told a crowd of about five hundred: "I am with you. . . . The NAACP is all we have got, and it is the only organization in America today fighting for the civil liberties of all the people." But as it would turn out, Nashville civil rights activists would not rely so heavily on the NAACP as on a newer organization to advance their goals.

The formation of the Southern Christian Leadership Conference (SCLC) in 1957 by Dr. Martin Luther King Jr. and fellow preachers encouraged formation of a chapter in Nashville, an effort in which Kelly Miller Smith, the pastor of the First Colored Baptist Church (FCBC), later named the First Baptist Church, Capitol Hill, was instrumental. Smith's church lay in the heart of downtown Nashville. The state capitol building looked down upon this historic edifice, which stood next door to the old church building (Spruce Street Baptist Church) where Frederick Douglass had graced the pulpit in May 1892 when invited to speak against racial lynching. The membership was well represented by professors and administrators from Meharry Medical College, American Baptist Theological Seminary, Fisk University, and Tennessee A&I State University (including its president, Walter S. Davis), as well as by lawyers, doctors, dentists, businessmen, schoolteachers, principals, and others.

The Reverend Smith (1920–1984) was formerly a student at Tennessee A&I and now the dean of its chapel. Having earned his bachelor's degree in religion at Morehouse College, he arrived from his native Mound Bayou,

Mississippi, in March 1951 to pastor FCBC. At the American Baptist Theological Seminary, where John Lewis, James Bevel, Bernard Lafayette, and other inquisitive students studied religion, Smith taught an occasional course on Howard Thurman and the philosophy of social activism of the Negro church. Smith was viewed by church members as "a man who has exemplified before us the Christian qualities of patience, humility, faith, and love. Slow to anger, governed by prayer, a genuine friend of all mankind." He corresponded with King as early as 1955, and as a charter member of the SCLC (along with two other Tennesseans, Henry C. Bunton of Memphis and Reverend W. A. Dennis of Chattanooga), Smith served on the SCLC's national board. He also served as president of the NAACP Nashville branch from 1956 to 1958 and was a charter member and a trustee of the reorganized Nashville chapter of the National Urban League. Smith was one of the featured speakers at the SCLC's meeting held at New Zion Baptist Church in New Orleans on February 14, 1957, and he supported King's letter to President Eisenhower protesting Ike's silence on the escalating racial violence in the South. (Eisenhower would have his aide reply on March 13, and he would meet with King and other civil rights leaders over a year later.)

On January 18, 1958, Smith and others founded the local chapter of the SCLC, the Nashville Christian Leadership Council (NCLC), after convening at Gordon Memorial Christian Methodist Episcopal Church. Officers of the SCLC arrived in town to help with the meeting. At first, the NCLC was a typical male-dominated preachers' organization like the SCLC, but Smith was less of a chauvinist than some. He was careful to recruit lay female church leaders into the new organization. The first NCLC objective was to register more Negro voters. This was an old tactic for the local NAACP, and it had been adopted in the SCLC's recent Voters' Crusade. The monthly NCLC meetings alternated at churches, including an April 4 meeting at New Hope Baptist Church, which drew a total of eight people. At the April 26 meeting at Friendship Baptist Church, the small crowd decided to support the "Youth March for Integrated Schools." This national project was led by the NAACP and A. Philip Randolph's labor union office. The NCLC's executive committee met regularly at Smith's church office, where they agreed to focus on the SCLC's objective to create the "beloved community" and "a city without a color line." Smith would espouse this objective at an SCLC rally at Holt Street Baptist Church in Montgomery on February 25, 1958.

NCLC had neither a method nor a strategy to achieve its objective and attract large numbers of participants until the Reverend James M. Lawson Jr., a Vanderbilt student, and Glenn Smiley, field secretary of the Fellowship of

Reconciliation (FOR), offered to teach workshops on nonviolence and Christian social action discipline. Smiley was a white liberal and a firm believer in nonviolence. He had toiled throughout the South for decades promoting chapters of FOR; he had been involved in the pacifist movement during World War II; and he instructed others in Gandhian principles of nonviolence. FOR had organized a chapter in Memphis in the 1930s, but it went nowhere in Boss Crump's town.

James Morris Lawson Jr. was the son of a militant church minister and Jamaican mother. His father had carried a pistol when preaching and organizing NAACP chapters in the South. Lawson was a Methodist preacher, a disciple of King's nonviolent civil-disobedience movement, and an admirer of A. Philip Randolph. But Lawson also reverently adhered to the nonviolent activism of Mahatma Gandhi of India. He decided to leave Ohio and come south after hearing King speak during the 1956–57 year at Oberlin College. King told Lawson that "we really need you" in the South. Lawson left the Oberlin College Divinity School and arrived in Nashville by bus in January 1958. Smiley, who had agreed to hire the young man to work in the FOR office, met him there. Lawson settled in Nashville, enrolled in Vanderbilt University's Divinity School, and married a local woman. He became an NCLC board member and projects committee chairman.

One Sunday, Smith announced to his congregation that the Reverend Lawson would hold a workshop on the evenings of March 26–28, 1958, beginning at Bethel AME Church. Lawson had contacted Smith for his help in this endeavor. Lawson, Smiley, and Anna Holden, a member of the FOR, led the first local "workshop on Christian non-violence and love." Smiley, Lawson, and Ralph Abernathy frequently held workshops at Negro colleges, using a comic book entitled *Martin Luther King and the Montgomery Story and the Power of Nonviolence* by Richard B. Gregg. For his own part, King summarized his philosophy of nonviolence in his 1958 book, *Stride Toward Freedom*: "Nonviolence is not cowardice; it is active resistance to violence. It is designed not to humiliate the opponent, but to 'awaken a sense of moral shame in the opponent.' The nonviolent attack is directed against forces of evil rather than against persons who happen to be doing evil." The nonviolent protestor, according to King, should be willing to accept suffering without retaliation and to exchange love for hate of the opponent. Central to this philosophy, King further explained, is the ethic of *agape* love—loving a neighbor for his own sake and not on account of that person's friendliness. *Agape* "means a recognition that all life is interrelated," King wrote, adding that "the universe is on the side of justice" and that "nonviolence has deep faith in the future."

In the same vein, Lawson wrote, "Nonviolence strips the segregationist power structure of its major weapon: the manipulation of law or law enforcement to keep the Negro in his place."

Workshops, as Lawson recalled, were sponsored by Kelly Miller Smith's church. Among the eight college students who attended the meetings was eighteen-year-old John R. Lewis, then a sophomore at American Baptist Theological Seminary and now a U.S. congressman from Georgia. "Even before he began speaking," Lewis said of Lawson, "I could see that there was something special about this man. He just had a way about him, an aura of inner peace and wisdom that you could sense immediately upon seeing him. He was tall, bespectacled, and about to turn thirty." Lawson told the students that he came into the South to join in "indicting the people of the South who are mistreating us and visiting violence upon us and trying in every desperate and despicable way to deny us the dignity and the rights that belong to every human being . . . Our governmental system is on trial. Is this the land of the free, or only the land of the white free?"

Lawson's group held two or three workshops at Bethel to "settle on an issue, to examine the situation, and to decide where we wanted to focus." They moved the workshops to the basement of the Clark Memorial Methodist Church near Jefferson Street to better accommodate college students at nearby Fisk University and Tennessee State. They then organized workshops on Monday nights of about three hours each. At Clark Memorial, which was pastored by the Reverend Alexander Anderson, the Lawson group decided to focus on desegregation of downtown eateries. Ten students, including Lewis, faithfully attended the lessons on theology, the Bible, and nonviolent traditions. Bernard Lafayette, a student from Florida attending American Baptist Seminary, soon joined the group. In October 1959, they became the "Nashville Student Movement" (NSM) and rotated the leadership jobs. The team taught workshop participants not to strike back or curse if abused, not to laugh out loud, not to hold conversations with floor workers, not to leave one's seat until the leader gave permission to do so, and not to block entrances to stores or the aisles inside the stores. They told the trainees to be friendly and courteous at all times, to always sit straight and face the counter, to report all serious incidents to the leader, to refer information seekers to the leader in a polite manner, and to maintain eye contact with any assailant. They were told to always remember the teachings of Jesus Christ, Gandhi, and Martin Luther King Jr. Then, with the words "May God bless each of you," the trainees were called to prayer. Word spread about the meetings, and aboard came Fisk students Marion Barry, Diane Nash, Angeline Butler, and Peggy Alexander.

The students were eager to transform their studies into some "test protest demonstrations." They even wanted to move against visiting white evangelists who were holding a segregated-seating event downtown, but Lawson and Smith demanded patience and discipline. Smith wanted to make something happen before the students lost interest or struck out on their own; however, to take any semblance of militancy from the movement, Smith and others approached the downtown merchants, asking them to voluntarily desegregate their facilities. The merchants refused. At the November 17 NCLC executive board meeting, Lawson suggested that talks be continued with Harvey's Department Store because the management seemed reasonable. When NCLC officers discussed their new role and how the NCLC was "different from the NAACP," both Lawson and Smith concluded, "The Christian faith should dictate the things we do." The NCLC officers voted to make Smith co-chairman of the projects committee with Lawson the strategist. The time had come for the students to make use of their training.

On Saturday morning, November 28, 1959, twelve students met Smith, Lawson, and a few other NCLC leaders at the First Colored Baptist Church. Three church members drove the cars, taking the students to Harvey's Department Store a few blocks away. This store had many Negro customers, and its clerks were usually polite to all customers; yet, they followed the management's directives to prohibit Negro customers from sitting at the lunch counters. The students purchased some small items, went to the lunch counter, and asked to be served. The manager said no, and not even two white students from Fisk would be served. Diane Nash, now the NSM leader, nodded, and the group left the store. Nash was afraid and trembled inside during this first episode, but as her courage grew, she would become the boldest leader among the students. After reporting back to FCBC, the students resumed their nightly meetings and prepared for the next test.

"In the fall of 1959," Lawson recalled, "we did some testing of the places downtown in November, a couple of weeks of experimental testing. This was to allow people to test themselves, but also for us to find out who was responsible for the decision regarding desegregation and to see how the protesters were treated—and, if possible, to talk to a manager or a policy maker in each of the places. . . . We sent them in teams of four to six people." On Saturday, December 5, 1959, a group of eight students quietly staged the second test at the Cain-Sloan Department Store's lunch counter. The manager turned them away by reciting the policy of not serving Negroes. The students were polite as they turned away and returned to FCBC for debriefing and lessons on Christian nonviolence. Lawson remembered: "We shared our information and our experiences with each other, and then we waited until after Christmas to start back up again—and with exams at Fisk and Vanderbilt, that got delayed some more."

While the movement was gathering steam in Memphis and Nashville, four students from North Carolina A&T State College—Ezell Blair, Frank McCain, Joe McNeil, and David Richmond—held a spontaneous sit-in demonstration at the segregated lunch counter of Woolworth's stores in Greensboro, North Carolina, on February 1, 1960. In the following days, the number of students continued to grow as the word spread on the Negro college campus and to other North Carolina cities. The Greensboro sit-ins, therefore, were the first to draw national media attention, but the lack of training, mature leadership, and organization among the participants threatened to make the North Carolina movement no more than a passing student fad. Fearful that the North Carolina movement might die quickly, one leader, the Reverend Douglas Moore of Durham, decided to contact his friend Jim Lawson.

Lawson got the phone call from Moore on February 10, 1960. Upon hearing about the Greensboro demonstrations, Lawson remembered, his group had immediately called meetings "and we talked about what we would do and when." About seventy-five to a hundred students showed up in the evening in Fisk's chemistry auditorium, where Lawson announced to a crowd of students that the sit-in demonstrations were to begin in Nashville. "We planned it for, as I remember, February 13," said Lawson.

"The idea for the sit down strike . . . spread . . . like a snow ball rolling," said a student leader, Carl May. Hundreds of students showed up at First Colored Baptist on the evening of February 12, 1960. Lawson and Smith worried about there being so many untrained participants. Lawson, Smith, the NCLC, and the NSM had to be careful not to send an undisciplined mob to cause disorder and violence, which would galvanize whites behind the segregationist radicals. The solution they arrived at was to send the students in waves, replacing those arrested while teaching nonviolent training to the reserves waiting in First Colored Baptist Church.

Nine students, including a white exchange student at Fisk, were sent downtown to count seats and check out the lunch counters. Smith was still reluctant to proceed because the NCLC did not have enough money to bail so many people out of jail. Only a few dollars had been collected at each NCLC executive and mass meeting, and no one knew how the rest of the Negro community would respond to requests for bail money. They decided that it was too late to worry about such things—they would pray, and the Lord would provide all needs.

The participants now came not just from the relatively small campuses of American Baptist Seminary and Fisk University but also from the huge student body at Tennessee State. Lawson gave the group a short course in nonviolence and told them to dress neatly, to bring books to read, and to go to the bathroom only when other students could take their seats. They prayed, and the group went home to sleep and gain strength for the next day, February 13.

On that weekend, there was deep snow on the ground, bringing a sense of peace and quiet to Nashville. More than a hundred students marched from First Colored Baptist to Fifth Avenue North to make small purchases and sit at various lunch counters. The women at the church made sandwiches for the marchers, served hot drinks, and raised money. Lawson recalled:

> It went very well. The police were orderly, the managers kept people from congregating without shopping, and the police did the same thing. There were plainclothes detectives, so for those two weeks the demonstrations went on with complete smoothness, well organized and without a hitch. We had observers in the streets. Will Campbell [a white civil rights activist] had put together a number of other white observers to be present every time we sat in, in case we needed witnesses—so we had that organized. Others of us walked from place to place and kept our eyes on things.

By February 18, approximately two hundred students became directly involved. On February 20, more students marched downtown, but some stores removed the seats and others closed the counters.

Since 1854, Nashville's merchants had seen themselves as guardians of the city's white-dominated power structure. Therefore, more than a hundred years later, no single business, especially John Sloan and his Cain-Sloan Department Store, would voluntarily announce desegregation of its restrooms and restaurants. Also, such a move would make them vulnerable to the loss of a large number of white customers. "We also were staying in touch with the pulse of the community and with the official city government, police especially, and we were staying in touch with managers and merchants," Lawson remembered. "We had uncovered by this time a number of friends in the merchant community downtown. We discovered that Harvey's Department Store was owned by a group in Chicago and . . . they were interested in making changes that could be made." (The Cain-Sloan store, by contrast, was locally owned.) Downtown merchants continued to pressure the city to enforce the laws about disorderly conduct and obstructive interference with commerce.

On February 20, 1960, the *Tri-State Defender* in Memphis reported, "Nashville students have 'Sit-in Fever'—Z. A. Looby said he had nothing to do with it." Nashville's civil rights lawyers, including Looby and Avon Williams, were involved in the continuing *Kelly v. Nashville* school desegregation case, but they and other local lawyers did not become involved in the downtown public demonstrations against Jim Crow until a crisis developed over the mass arrests of student demonstrators.

Those arrests occurred on February 27. As the first wave of demonstrators that day occupied the lunch counters, about four hundred students waited in the basement of First Colored Baptist Church, ready to go downtown in subsequent waves as word of arrests got back to the church. The idea was to keep the lunch counter seats occupied and the jail full. The mayor apparently had promised the merchants that some arrests would be allowed. Nearly two hundred arrests took place, and female and male students were crowded into the same cells, with standing room only.

The mass arrests started discussions in black barber shops, beauty shops, churches, and even in the Negro women's bridge-playing clubs. As a result, the Negro community began to feel guilty for having so long been passive about the oppressions of Jim Crow, and it was ready to attack those injustices and stand behind the students. The homes of most Negro faculty members and black professionals were located on the streets around Fisk, Meharry, and A&I—the institutions from which most of the arrested students originated—and many of these homeowners put up their property to help raise the fifty thousand dollars needed for bail money. Z. A. Looby, with the assistance of the Fisk University treasurer, I. T. Creswell, would handle this process.

Mayor Ben West met with a group of Negro leaders and citizens at FCBC on February 29. Thousands of college students and civil rights supporters had marched and assembled in front of police headquarters singing freedom songs. White reporters insulted the Negro leaders, including Cordell Tindell Vivian, student Luther Harris, and others, by asking whether the local movement had a national network, as if local Negroes surely would not do this on their own. Vivian had arrived in Nashville in 1955 to attend American Baptist Theological Seminary after having already been involved in some public protests in the North, and his demonstrative refusal to ride the "Colored Section" of a Nashville bus helped lead to the desegregation of the city's bus system in January 1957. Meanwhile, for the upcoming trial of the students, the Negro lawyers—Looby, Williams, Coyness L. Ennix, and Robert E. Lillard—wanted a judge appointed who would be free of racial prejudice, but the mayor could not change judges.

On March 1, hundreds of students and two thousand supporters marched six blocks east from First Colored Baptist to the Davidson County Courthouse to face the judge. Citizens, defendants, news media representatives, and lawyers filled the courtroom, while hundreds of Negroes waited outside on both sides of the street. The president of Tennessee A&I was not there, but Robert Murrell, an A&I dean highly respected by students, was present. The judge found all the demonstrators guilty of obstructing commerce. The mayor and the police really wanted these students and the bad publicity for the city off their hands. The judge reduced the fine for each demonstrator from one hundred dollars to five dollars. Diane Nash argued in front of the judge that to pay the fines would contribute to the injustices already heaped on Negro citizens. Attorneys Williams and Looby waited at the jailhouse, taking names, addresses, and asking students if they wished to make bail. Eighty-one students refused to pay the fines and stayed in jail. Elizabeth Harbour (now McClain), a frightened A&I student and now an assistant professor of history at Tennessee State University, was comforted by the male students who held her hand through the adjacent bars.

Around 11:00 P.M., the students were booked and released after spending about six hours in jail. They and two hundred other cheering student supporters left the jail singing freedom songs. On the next morning, they headed to the Fisk University Memorial Chapel. A bomb scare was telephoned to Fisk. President Stephen Wright, who assumed custody of the released students, addressed the audience and also told news reporters that he would not expel any sit-in demonstrators from Fisk, contending that they were exercising their constitutional rights. In his memoir, *Walking with the Wind* (1989), John Lewis said, "Dr. Wright announced that morning that he and many others in Nashville's established black community were with us. He was the first black college president in the country to take such a stand. We were euphoric." The presidents at American Baptist and Meharry would not expel any of their sit-in demonstrators, but administrators at Tennessee A&I State University, which was subject to decisions made by the governor and other state officials, could not make such a statement. Joseph A. Payne, vice president for student affairs, spoke for Tennessee State, saying, "The school is not involved in any way and the school has no intention of becoming involved [in the sit-ins]. The students are acting as individuals." Governor Ellington's staff reportedly conferred with

President Davis and said the governor might act if the A&I students continued to break the law. Vanderbilt University would take drastic action against James Lawson.

News about the events in Nashville spread across Tennessee, drawing an especially interested response in the western section where two-thirds of the state's Negro population lived. The *Memphis Tri-State Defender,* which sent a reporter-photographer to Nashville, described the details on March 5, 1960. On March 2, 1960, the *Memphis World* called the Nashville sit-ins "the largest such movement to be staged by students."

Speaking at Fisk University weeks later, Thurgood Marshall admonished the students for refusing to allow lawyers to bail them out of jail. Of that appearance, Lewis recalled in his memoir: "It was clear to me that evening that Thurgood Marshall, along with so many of his generation, just did not understand the essence of what we, the younger generation of blacks . . . were doing." Marshall and the NAACP did not support the tactics of Dr. King's SCLC and other civil rights groups whose demonstrations led to arrests and sometimes violence. Marshall and his colleagues believed that such acts of public disobedience diverted attention from the NAACP-LDF's legal methods and might lose support for the Negro's civil rights movement among moderate and liberal whites. James Lawson, Lewis, and others thus became critical of the NAACP, believing its tactics moved too slow to dismantle Jim Crow in 1959–60. By late 1960, however, largely because of the sit-ins that spread across the region (especially in cities like Memphis and Chattanooga, which had long-established NAACP chapters), the national NAACP would unofficially embrace public protest methods to complement legal methods by late 1960.

The city's evening daily, the *Nashville Banner,* played its role as guardian of southern racial customs well. The paper's publisher was James G. Stahlman, who was born in 1893 and inherited the *Banner* from his grandfather in 1931. (He remained publisher until the Gannett Corporation bought the paper in 1972.) He hired a Negro reporter, Robert Churchwell, but would not allow him to cover civil rights activities. The *Banner* at first required Churchwell to file his regular stories, along with Negro church news, from his home. After being admitted to the *Banner* newsroom, the Negro reporter was given a desk in the back. Even there he often overheard other reporters using the racist word "niggers." The *Banner* tried for the most part to ignore the students, except to depict their demonstrations in photographs as civil disorder and Communist-inspired agitation. Stahlman ordered his reporters to print no stories on these activities. Some local businessmen urged Stahlman, a member of the Vanderbilt Board of Trustees, to investigate James Lawson for "a bloodcurdling attack made on the South, the vilest kind imaginable, and of a promise to go south." The *Banner* sent a reporter to Ohio to check out Lawson's background. They uncovered a copy of an Ohio court record showing that Lawson had once been convicted as a conscientious objector to the military draft. He had been sentenced to three years in prison and fined, but released on probation after serving about a year in jail. A Quaker agency then sent Lawson as a missionary to India where he studied Gandhi's nonviolent philosophy. A *Banner* editorial declared: "He [Lawson] was sent here deliberately to create trouble and was planted in the Divinity School at Vanderbilt as a sanctuary behind which he could pursue his nefarious enterprises with the least suspicion and subsequent penalty. He is a fraud of the first magnitude. There is no place in Nashville for flannel-mouth agitators, white or colored."

On May 3, 1960, Mayor West appointed a biracial committee. George E. Barrett, a local white attorney who often represented labor unions, supported this effort to bridge the communication gap between the Negro and white communities. Such support was indicative of the stands the unions had been taking since the 1930s against Jim Crow and its negative effects on all workers, regardless of race. Eight more college students, including three whites—Barbara Bigger, Carol A. Anderson, and Paul LaPrad—were jailed on the same day the committee was appointed for demonstrating at a local bus station's segregated lunch counter. Thomas W. McNair, a twenty-three-old white bookstore clerk, also went to jail, along with Bernard Lafayette of American Baptist Theological Seminary and John B. Stallworth Jr. and Richard A. Robertson of Tennessee A&I State University. The judge would threaten Looby with contempt for advising the students to invoke their federal constitutional rights.

Meanwhile, a faction within the Vanderbilt University Board of Trustees was pressuring Chancellor Harvie Branscomb to expel Lawson. Considerable discussion took place on March 2 among the executive committee of the board. On March 3, Branscomb surprised the Divinity School faculty by informing them that Lawson was being expelled for his participation in civil disobedience. The next day, the *Banner* opined that "Vanderbilt did its duty." The chancellor appeared afraid not to do what trustees Stahlman and John Sloan, the department store owner, wanted him to do against Lawson. Branscomb had pressured the dean of the Divinity School to visit Lawson at his home on several occasions in an effort to persuade him to sign a letter of withdrawal from Vanderbilt. On the advice of local civil rights leaders, including Will Campbell, Lawson refused. "I did not anticipate being expelled from Vanderbilt," he later said, "but when it happened, against my will and wish, nevertheless, I went on with my life." Reflecting his nonviolent philosophy, he declared, "I held no ill will toward Branscomb as a consequence of my expulsion."

On March 4, 1960, word reached Lawson that city policemen had a warrant for his arrest. Lawson headed to First Colored Baptist Church, deciding that they would have to arrest him there. A group of policemen was sent to FCBC to arrest Lawson on charges of conspiracy to obstruct trade and commerce. The white policemen (including one known for brutality against blacks) entered the church, bound Lawson, and dragged him toward the waiting police vehicle. A crowd of Lawson supporters followed the scene outside the church in order to make sure that the whites did not "accidentally shoot Lawson." Nashville's white dailies did their part to promote the idea of Negro lawlessness by publishing a photograph of four police sergeants bringing Lawson down the steps. Were not churches sanctuaries in the South? The police chief answered by saying that the meeting was a political gathering and not a religious one. One photograph showed the sign in front of the FCBC that read, "Father, Forgive them." The same slogan had been emblazoned on cloth crosses and worn on the lapels of protesters during the Montgomery boycott.

Harvie Branscomb had taken charge of Vanderbilt in October 1946. He worked hard to bring this regional university up to par with the great universities of the North. Branscomb feared bad publicity for Vanderbilt if it maintained a militant stance for segregation. Paradoxically, he also feared that widespread integration would negatively affect the quality of the student body. As a native of Alabama, Branscomb abhorred racial mixing and held deep suspicions about miscegenation and the innate abilities of Negroes. He was part of the elite Belle Meade Country Club crowd that openly used terms like "the Negras" when referring to black citizens. The chancellor and the trustees were mortified that northern foundations would stop giving money to Vanderbilt if it did not desegregate. The Vanderbilt divinity faculty quietly admitted the first Negro graduate student in 1953, Joseph A. Johnson, now president of Lane College in Jackson, Tennessee. The Vanderbilt School of Law admitted two Negroes ("two boys," they were called) in 1956 for fear of losing its accreditation. The athletic teams already had encountered Negro players when competing against northern universities. Indeed, for Vanderbilt and desegregation, the handwriting was on the wall.

Many faculty members, including some in science, drama, philosophy, and medicine, as well as some students, supported racial justice. On March 10, 1960, dozens of engineering and English faculty members backed Branscomb for expelling Lawson. The student senate tried to pass a resolution to support the National Student Association's condemnation of Jim Crow, but the measure was defeated, 14–13. There were meetings on the campus and in the homes of faculty members, including Charles Roos of the Physics Department. The teachers had to decide about whether they should resign or to stay and help determine whether Vanderbilt "was going to be a university and not a southern finishing school." Roos said, "The question was what each of us was going to do." Lawson said, "To emerge from being a Southern finishing school to become a . . . viable university . . . was the course . . . it had to take."

As Vanderbilt faculty members were contemplating their options, racial conservatives in Nashville placed pressure on the presidents of the Negro colleges whose students were participating in the demonstrations. There was a bomb scare at Fisk, but Wright supported the students: "As president of the university, I approve the ends our students are seeking by these demonstrations. From all I have been able to learn, they have broken no law by the means they have employed so far, and they have not only conducted themselves peaceably, but with poise and dignity, and as long as this is true, I have no present intentions of instructing them to discontinue their efforts." Wright suggested that the city should start to solve the sit-in problem by "desegregating the airport." President Walter S. Davis at Tennessee A&I was not sure what to say about the demonstrations and referred the reporters to Joseph A. Payne, dean of student affairs. "The students are acting as individuals," Payne told the press.

Around March 4, the demonstrations halted while Mayor West and the race relations committee struggled to come to a solution. The mayor's committee took three weeks to prepare a report. When the patience of the demonstrators grew thin, the NCLC held a meeting at the First Colored Baptist Church to allow the students to report their findings on recent sit-in demonstrations. The local media were barred from the meeting, but a film crew from CBS in New York was already inside the church. This infuriated local newspaper editors and reinforced the "outside agitators" theory. It should be noted that local Negroes had no radio station, television station, or daily newspaper of their own. If any local black news was leaked to a national audience, usually it was carried by the *Tri-State Defender* based in Memphis and Chicago and the *Pittsburgh Courier*. The weekly *Nashville Globe* ceased publication by 1960. Another Negro weekly, the *Commentator*, continued to be published through 1970, but it carried only tidbits on the national civil rights scene. Local Negro readers had to choose between the two local dailies for reportage that rarely reflected their interests.

Some local reporters did manage to force their way into the meeting at FCBC. Arrogantly proclaiming the right of freedom of press while apparently denying that Negroes had any constitutional right to freedom of association, they were met by a militant student who told them that "the meeting is closed!" They sat down anyway. To prevent an altercation that might give authorities another excuse to invade the church, the uninvited reporters were allowed to remain inside. Reverend Smith said that "Our goal is total desegregation of the community," while noting that the mayor had had ample time to resolve the crisis. "The demonstrations are resuming," Smith said. Some students left the church to picket a store, and a New York film crew went tagging along after it. However, the store's manager was forewarned, perhaps by local media, to lock the doors. After telephoning the secretary, the students returned to FCBC. The local media verbally attacked commentator Harry Reasoner of CBS, claiming that he had asked the Negroes to stage a sit-in for northern consumption. Two members of the NCLC executive committee, including physician C. J. Walker, walked out of the church rather than answer insulting and racist questions about conspiracy against the southern media. After all, as they well knew, the southern white press—even in Nashville—had discriminated against Negroes and refused to hire them in meaningful jobs. Smith persuaded NCLC members to come back inside rather than allow these whites to destroy the group's unity. As NCLC flyers proclaimed, "We were called of God to continue this resistance."

On March 14, the NCLC executive committee met in Smith's pastoral office to privately discuss the situation. Lawson suggested holding prayers in front of churches to force white Christians to support the movement. C. T. Vivian, labeled by some "the most dangerous man in the movement," suggested going inside the white churches to hold prayer. The police chief appointed two Negro detectives to work "on the sit-in case." At the March 25 executive committee meeting, NCLC suggested donating some money to help Lawson, who reminded them that any such money should be deposited under his employer, the Fellowship of Reconciliation.

The CBS affair was not over. The resurrected issue of Negro cooperation with "Yankees" galled many local whites, who saw such cooperation as an echo of what had happened during the Civil War. Some of the local media continued to feel jilted and, perhaps, treated as inferiors when the northern media aired their stories on national television. Psychologically, many white southerners were "still fighting the Civil War" and still had a sense of inferiority in the shadow of northerners. Governor Buford Ellington sent a stinging telegram to the president of CBS, claiming a conspiracy to instigate a sit-in demonstration and perhaps to provoke violence for the television cameras. The president of CBS replied to Ellington on March 26, 1960: "Since these unsupported charges strike at the very integrity of CBS News, we believe the situation calls for retraction and apology from you." Ellington shot back the next day, saying no apology would be forthcoming. The Tennessee Council on Human Relations and the Nashville Community Relations Conference at Belmont Methodist Church responded to Ellington with its own statement: "We are shocked and disturbed by the [Governor's] attacks on freedom of the press in this community over the past few days."

The demonstrations resumed after the college spring break. On April 3, 1960, more arrests were made, but some whites who seemed to support desegregation sat at the counters and requested service, too. The stores again used the tactic of closing the counters. The mayor's committee finally made a report, including a recommendation that by the following month, the lunch counters would include "sections for blacks *and* whites." This Jim Crow practice was already used in the downtown theaters in other Tennessee cities. The NSM rejected the committee's proposal, and when moderate leaders asked Ennix and Looby to do something, they declared that they had "no control over student actions." At FCBC, the students ignored new pleas from the Reverend Will D. Campbell to hold up the marches for fear of violence breaking out.

A white activist in the civil rights movement, Campbell had arrived in Nashville in 1956 to work as the field director for the Southern Project in the National Council of Churches. Campbell was born in Mississippi in 1924 to a poor family, attended a Southern Baptist college, served as a medic in World War II, and completed Wake Forest and Yale University's divinity schools. In his 1999 book, *But Now I See: The White Southern Racial Conversion Narrative,* Fred Hobson wrote of Campbell:

> Sociologically speaking, one could hardly imagine a less promising
> beginning for one who would become a staunch advocate of racial
> justice—dirt poor, fundamentalist, born and raised in the state
> [of Mississippi] at the bottom of nearly all the nation's social and
> cultural indexes, and into a family near the bottom of even that
> state's white social scale, a family with no tradition of higher
> education, social outreach, general enlightenment, or noblesse
> oblige. But that, as Campbell saw it, was precisely the answer; he
> understood the oppressed, both black and white, because he had
> been oppressed himself.

Campbell wrote several books: *Race and the Renewal of the Church* (1962), *Brother to a Dragonfly* (1977), and *Forty Acres and a Goat* (1986). "The civil rights movement may be over for black people," he wrote in *Forty Acres and a Goat.* "It is far from over for whites." Campbell worked alone but cooperated with other local civil rights leaders. He joined the local NAACP and Reverend Smith's church and persuaded Smith to serve as president of the Committee of Southern Churchmen, which funneled money to the NCLC.

Notwithstanding the segregationists' theory of "outside agitators," many of Nashville's civil rights leaders, including Smith and Campbell, had deep southern roots. The student leaders in the sit-in movement had similar roots. Marion Barry was born in 1936 in Mississippi. His mother moved the family to nearby Memphis, took a job in the World War II plants, and sent Barry to Booker T. Washington High School and then LeMoyne College. The *World* (Feb. 7, 1959) viewed Barry as a promising young man who had been president of the LeMoyne College youth chapter of the NAACP in 1958. Barry had made some "troublesome statements" about racism in Memphis, where, he said, "nobody went anywhere except reform school or jail." He would earn a master's degree from Fisk in 1960, enter graduate school at the University of Kansas, leave for the University of Tennessee a year later, drop out of the UT doctoral program, and re-enter the movement as chairman of the Student Nonviolent Coordinating Committee. He eventually became mayor of Washington, D.C. Diane Nash was born in Chicago into a lower-middle-class family and raised in the Catholic faith. Though born in the North, she was well-acquainted with southern customs through her stepfather, a product of the Great Migration from the South who became a waiter on railcars. He had warned her about segregation and racial violence. As he made clear to her, once a Negro left the confines of Chicago and headed south, his or her freedom, body, and life were in danger. Nash attended Howard University in Washington, D.C., before entering Fisk University. While attending the Tennessee State Fair, she and others encountered crudely made posters designating restrooms for "Whites" and "Colored." And so, responding to such injustices, Nash joined Lawson's workshops and served as head of the NSM because she wanted to do something to positively change Jim Crow Nashville.

[*]

In East Tennessee, another proponent of the civil rights movement had emerged. The Highlander Folk School was a predominantly white institution whose principal founder, Myles F. Horton, was born in the Hardin County town of Savannah on the Tennessee River. He graduated from Cumberland University in Lebanon, Tennessee, in 1928, and worked for the YMCA before attending Union Theological Seminary in New York City in 1929. After spending some time in Denmark, he returned to the United States and settled in Grundy County in 1932 to develop workers' education programs for the neglected mountain people. Lillian Johnson of Memphis, a member of a wealthy banking family and a graduate of Wellesley College and Cornell University, gave an indefinite lease of her land in Grundy County to the Highlander School. Ava Taylor of Nashville and Albert Barnett at Scarritt College helped Horton with relief efforts for the poor.

The Highlander program fostered unionism, individual growth, social change, attacks on southern poverty, the value of complete personal liberty, thoughtful citizenship in community, brotherhood and racial equality, and the full enjoyment of life. Local residents began to accept biracial meetings at Highlander and visited the place for its singing sessions, occasional dances, dramatic plays, and other entertainments in a community where few radios and other amusements were available. In 1952, the board of directors decided that race relations would also be a focus of Highlander. After *Brown,* Highlander held workshops on the Supreme Court and public schools and printed a guide entitled "Working toward Integrated Public Schools in Your Own Community." Many participants left the workshops with encouragement to start desegregation movements in their states. The FBI office in Knoxville began an extensive file on Highlander, although the FBI director, J. Edgar Hoover, claimed that no investigation was officially underway.

In 1959, the Highlander Folk School was targeted by the FBI and Tennessee authorities, perhaps as part of a regional crackdown on supposedly subversive organizations. Bruce Bennett, attorney general of Arkansas, led the regional attack, even testifying against Highlander before the Tennessee General Assembly's investigating committee in 1959. U.S. Senator James O. Eastland of Mississippi urged the FBI to send agents to Highlander. Horton was interviewed by the FBI, and the reports on Highlander were sent to the Knoxville FBI office. The state attorney general claimed that Highlander had violated state laws by selling whiskey in dry Grundy County. The complaint was amended to include violation of state segregation laws for holding racially integrated parties. The *Chattanooga News–Free Press* published anti-Highlander editorials. An insurance company cancelled the school's policy "for fear of bombings." On July 31, 1959, the authorities called the school "a public nuisance" and sent sheriff's deputies and twenty highway patrolmen to raid the workshops and arrest the participants on charges of possessing illegal whiskey. George E. Barrett and Cecil F. Branstetter of Nashville served as defense attorneys for *State of Tennessee v. Highlander* (1959). A Tennessee court ordered Highlander to close in September 1959. On January 2, 1960, a state judge declared "the segregation laws of the state . . . are constitutional and valid." While Highlander appealed the case, the institution's educational workshops director, Septima Clark, the only Negro officer there, announced that the programs would continue into the summer, including workshops entitled "Community Services and Segregation" and "Voting and Registration."

On April 5, 1961, the State Supreme Court ignored the lower court's proclamation about the constitutionality of Tennessee's segregation laws, and instead ruled that Horton had used the property for his personal gain and violated state law by selling whiskey on the property. Eleanor Roosevelt and others signed appeals and held a fund-raiser in Washington, D.C., to save Highlander. Claiming no federal rights were violated, on October 9, 1961, the U.S. Supreme Court refused to overturn the Tennessee court decision. The state revoked Highlander's charter and on November 7, 1961, confiscated $136,000 in properties and auctioned them off on December 16. The Highlander program soon acquired new property in Knoxville and reopened under the name Highlander Research and Educational Center. An October 25, 1962, FBI memorandum accused Highlander of supporting agitation "by a few Negroes in stirring up racial trouble by sit-in" demonstrations and involving students from Maryville College, the University of Tennessee, and Knoxville College to meet at the Negro Presbyterian Church in Knoxville. Highlander would celebrate its fiftieth anniversary in 1982 in a widely publicized week of programs, while focusing on the institution's original mission.

[*]

In Nashville, when hundreds of citizens held a mass rally at Pleasant Green Missionary Baptist Church on April 5, 1960, Vivian Henderson, a Fisk University economist, called for an economic boycott. His report showed that Negroes held only 12 percent of local wealth. Such impoverished conditions had caused many southern Negroes to join the Great Migration to the North. In Tennessee the Negro population would decline from 26 percent in 1860 to 15.8 percent by 1970, and in Nashville, the black population would drop from 38.19 percent in 1890 to 19.12 percent by 1970. Yet, those Negroes who remained in the Tennessee capital constituted a significant portion of local consumers, despite their limited financial means. As Henderson's report showed, they made up a quarter of the customers for the downtown stores, contributing about $7 million annually to those businesses. A boycott could well prove to be a formidable weapon.

Meanwhile, in 1960, white leaders were building a "better Nashville" of the whites, by the whites, and for the whites. The Chamber of Commerce expected a "business boom in the city," but the Negro sit-ins and boycotts disrupted those plans. Some businessmen expressed anger because the chamber seemed to be doing nothing when "we were having economic hell being beat out of the downtown area." Although whites had already systematically beaten the economic hell out of the black community since slavery, the chamber (whose constitution at the time barred Negro membership) sent a committee to meet with the mayor and discuss a permanent biracial committee. Chamber leaders also approached the editors of the major newspapers, hoping to decrease coverage of the downtown protests, but soon backed off after some members argued that the "question is more a sociological problem than it is a business problem" and noted that the downtown merchants' committee was engaged in discussions with the NCLC. Cordell T. Vivian observed, "It is radical evil that rules this town, and it will take radical good to break it up."

On April 1–3, 1960, the Highlander Folk School held its Annual College Workshop, which some seventy-five people, including fifty Negroes and a few Nashville Student Movement leaders, attended. But Septima Clark wanted Highlander to make an even bigger impact on the student movement, so she sent a letter on April 9, 1960, to Ella Baker, activities coordinator at the SCLC, asking Baker to "serve with me on an educational committee for Highlander [which] has always been an educational institution working for the development of leaders in an interracial residential setting . . . I need your help in planning bigger and more vitalizing workshops for the entire South." Baker agreed on April 14 but said, "I am about to terminate my present stay with the SCLC." She was upset at the male chauvinism in the SCLC and the slow pace at which the organization dared to embrace the students and their tactics. There was concern that students would not adhere to the nonviolent philosophy and could alienate white moderates and "white friends."

Kelly Miller Smith received a letter from Ella Baker that a Youth Leadership Conference would be held at Shaw University in Raleigh, North Carolina, on Easter break weekend, April 15–17, 1960. She asked the NCLC to help finance five seasoned sit-in rights demonstrators from Nashville colleges. Baker said the meeting was "to provide an opportunity for youth leaders from the area of recent sit-in demonstrations to exchange and share experiences, to evaluate efforts, and look into the future." Glenn Smiley was in Durham, and he conferred with Baker about the plans. The Reverend Douglas Moore—a member of the SCLC executive board and an advisor to the early sit-in demonstrators in North Carolina—worked closely with Baker in planning the meeting. Baker believed that the students could help the SCLC launch "A Crusade for Freedom," like the NAACP. Lawson, whom the students trusted as "the young people's Martin Luther King," drafted the meeting's declaration of purpose using the students' ideals. Lawson criticized the NAACP for being timid and proclaimed the student protests a judgment upon middle-class, conventional, halfway efforts to deal with a radical social evil. "Finally," he said, "the issue is not integration . . . If progress has not been at a genuine pace, it is often because the major groups seeking equal rights tactically made desegregation the end and not the means." He used Nashville to make his point. King viewed the sit-in demonstrations as moving away from the NAACP tactic he thought was suitable merely for gradual and long-term change. The historic Raleigh meeting resulted in the formation of the Student Nonviolent Coordinating Committee (SNCC). Members of the Nashville Student Movement held leadership positions. Diane Nash became head of protest activities and chairman of the coordinating committee between students and adults. A SNCC office would be established in Atlanta.

Roy Wilkins viewed the remarks at the SNCC organizational meeting as attacks on the NAACP. He sent a protest message to King, arguing that the NAACP could not control the courts' slow pace; the race problem was more varied and complex than the SCLC supposed. Only a strong organization like the NAACP could survive the wear that went on year after year. "We also know," said Wilkins on June 7, 1961, "that solid, basic legal moves are necessary if there is to be foundation for other action . . . the Freedom Riders did not run into violence until they entered a state where there was no NAACP . . . The lesson here is that all methods should be used and that history and experience should not be ignored."

The Reverend Smith and NCLC brought Martin Luther King Jr. to Nashville to speak at a mass meeting on April 18, where the civil rights leader addressed thousands in the Fisk gymnasium, calling Nashville's student protesters "the best organized and the most disciplined in the Southland."

In the early morning on the day after King spoke, a bomb exploded at the home of Z. A. Looby, destroying 85 percent of the house and shattering 147 windows at Meharry Medical College across the street—a few blocks east of Tennessee A&I State University. Amazingly, although shaken from bed and facing a gaping hole in their walls, the Looby family escaped unhurt. The incident would make news across the world, with pictures of the house and a dazed sixty-one-year-old Looby. On the same day as the bombing, approximately five thousand people quickly gathered at the A&I campus, merged with another group near the Looby house, and marched two abreast on the sidewalks to City Hall. (In its story on the event, the *Tennessean* lowballed its estimate of the number of marchers, reporting it as only two thousand.) The spokesmen demanded that the mayor speak about his position on segregation. On the outside steps of City Hall, Mayor West was so shaken that he responded publicly to a bold question by Diane Nash: "Mr. Mayor, do you believe that segregation is wrong?" The mayor responded that he thought racial discrimination and segregation were wrong, that he was against such practices, and that integration should take place. The crowd cheered this moral victory. However, the mayor reminded the crowd that he could not force a businessman to operate his business in a certain way. When recalling his answer to Nash for a television reporter, West said, "I felt outraged with them [the bombers]. . . . I do not think someone should serve Negroes their merchandise and then not serve them [at the lunch counter]. I received considerable criticism [from whites] for it, but if I had to answer the moral question again, I would answer it the same . . . as a man and not a politician."

The white news media dubbed Looby "the leader of the Nashville movement." He received letters and telegrams from dozens of persons. The rector of the local Christ Episcopal Church, Raymond T. Farris, sent a letter: "Our community is indeed in a sad condition to have such things going on such as this." Another letter, from civil rights leader Walter N. Vernon said, "Many of us who are white are ashamed and outraged at the dastardly attack on your house, and presumably attempted against your life. Many of our prominent southerners are simply unaware that the world has changed, and that the march of progress has passed many of them by. Justice and civil rights are inevitably coming, and it is tragic that so many today think they can prevent it by sprinkling sand on the tracks—or even by dropping a bomb." NAACP headquarters sent a letter of support to Looby. He also received a telegram from the Civic Interest Group that sponsored the student demonstration in Baltimore, informing him that the insult he had suffered in a Baltimore restaurant in 1958 had been avenged: "Bickford's now serves all people—good luck in your demonstrations in Nashville." At least two letters arrived from Nigeria and Rhodesia, where Africans were struggling for freedom from European colonialism. Francis G. Brown of the Philadelphia Yearly Monthly Meeting of the Religious Society of Friends (Quakers) visited Nashville and expressed support for "the Negroes nonviolent efforts to obtain full citizenship. We attended the mass meeting that evening and were glad to hear Mr. [Avon] Williams speak. This was a particularly impressive meeting and I could feel the power and determination of which underlies this movement. If the situation develops that the Quakers in our area can be of assistance we want you to feel free to get in touch with us." A. Robert Nelson, the dean of Vanderbilt's Divinity School, wrote, "Also, I wish to say that I am in accord with the goal of racial equality in our time, and I appreciate your persistent, wise, and courageous leadership." White conservatives blamed the whole situation on Communist infiltration, but Diane Nash said, "I think segregation is an evil that is really holding America back in this international struggle."

City leaders decided to work out something to initiate desegregation. On May 10, 1960, a small group of demonstrators calmly walked up to selected lunch counters, sat down, and ate an afternoon snack. Peggy Alexander, Stanley Hemphill, Diane Nash, and Mathew Walker had lunch at the Greyhound bus terminal. Nashville became the first southern city to merely begin downtown desegregation.

The accolades continued to pour in for Looby, and he accepted them. A judge in Philadelphia wrote Looby on May 10, 1960, saying, "Your courageous and forceful support of the Negro in all his many trials and tribulations not only in your own state of Tennessee but throughout the South, which problems you have so fearlessly and consistently fought for several decades stamps you as one of the distinguished leaders in a triumphant march of the Negro in America for full freedom and 100 percent citizenship to which he is entitled by our Constitution as his American birthright." Looby responded to the judge on May 20: "This is to acknowledge receipt and thank you sincerely for your letter which was consoling and comforting. They have torn down the balance of my house and are now removing the debris. In the meantime, plans have been drawn and I am now receiving bids for the erection of another target for cowards who work in the darkness of night." Tennessee A&I faculty, staff, and students raised money to help rebuild Looby's house, and the NCLC raised four thousand dollars for the same purpose.

Late in May 1960, Looby accepted an invitation to speak at the West Side YMCA and later at a Baptist church in Atlanta. There he spoke about his bombing ordeal and the situation in Nashville. With tears and a trembling voice, Looby told the audience that a white reporter had even asked him if he would resign from the city council. Looby said the answer was no. He declared that the students in Nashville were justified in their actions. When the students were arrested, Looby said, it was not known where the bond money would come from, but within hours some ten thousand dollars arrived at his offices. The downtown merchants could not stand the pressure, so they gave in, said Looby. As an NAACP man, Looby had to admit that he was not the leader of the public demonstrations, but he wanted the young people to recognize that "older people have laid the foundation" for the civil rights movement since 1935. "This is not a Negro fight. It is the fight of all right-thinking people," Looby said. He encouraged the audience to continue to fight for justice. Massive demonstrations broke out in Atlanta, and Dr. Martin Luther King Jr. and eighty other persons were arrested in that city.

Banner publisher James "Jimmy" Stahlman found himself under questioning from a *New York Herald Tribune* reporter in May 1960 about how he may have abused the freedom of the press in attempts to silence the local civil rights movement. Perhaps motivated in his questioning by the bombing of Looby's home, the reporter suspected Stahlman of cutting the northern press off from the local sit-in news, possibly working with the *Tennessean* and downtown merchants to keep any bad publicity from leaking to outsiders. Stahlman claimed that he was not prejudiced against Negroes. He noted that he had attended classes with them at the University of Chicago in 1916, and as a member of the Board of Trustees at Vanderbilt University, he had, on May 1, 1953, authored the resolution to admit the first Negro graduate student. "Mr. Lawson's race had nothing to do with his dismissal," Stahlman argued. "I would have voted to dismiss my own brother or son under the same conditions." He went on to say that he had a full-time Negro reporter on staff and had used Negro reporters, including A&I historian Merle R. Eppse, before the full-time man, Robert Churchwell, was hired. The *Banner*, Stahlman said, helped Tennessee A&I State College gain university status in 1951, pushed for Negro police in the city, and gave an air-conditioning unit to Hadley Park, the city's park for Negroes. "When Meharry Medical College was literally on the rocks and was in a state of prospective total suspension, right after the war [1948]," said Stahlman, "I personally started the campaign and made the first contribution to a fund to keep Meharry open long [enough] to enable it to get on its feet again financially." He claimed that he was not trying to black out news about the sit-ins but believed that the two sides would have followed recommendations of the mayor's biracial committee until CBS fostered the "reenactment on the part of the students, and this threw the whole thing wide open again and left it in an unwholesome state until this past two weeks." Stahlman continued:

> I felt for the sake of the community that it made sense for us to pay as little attention as possible to the reopening of this [sit-in] situation. For years, we have had a very happy and cordial relationship until the Supreme Court decision of May 17, 1954, and I think we could have adjusted all of our problems satisfactorily had it not been for the Kaspers, the NAACP, and a lot of these people from the outside who have been deliberately sent here to

disturb this situation. . . . There are times when prospective crises arise that might endanger the public welfare, endanger public safety, which would indicate that certainly the welfare of the community generally transcends any idealistic concept of a free flow of the news.

These words revealed that Stahlman, despite his protests of having no racial prejudice, was in fact voicing the undemocratic feelings of some trustees at Vanderbilt, downtown businessmen, and the country club crowd who saw their exclusive world threatened by agitation from Negro "troublemakers," "outsiders," and those "Yankee" amendments to the U.S. Constitution that came after the Civil War.

During a rally at John Wesley Methodist Church, a black congregation in south Nashville, in late June, the Reverend C. T. Vivian said, "We cannot stop now. Nashville must be washed and washed and washed, until she is clean, and then she must be put in the wringer and squeezed and squeezed until every drop of segregation, malice, and hatred is pressed from her." The speaker urged the possession of the land politically and economically. Maryann Morgan, an A&I student, pleaded, "Don't let Nashville down, and above all, remember that God is in your corner and you cannot let Him down." And to make a point, a former Nashville resident, living in Delaware, sent a letter to Looby (July 13, 1960), saying, "The first thing I want to say is that you have been the moving spirit in Nashville during my generation. You have inspired a generation, changed a city's (both white and Negro) attitude in part and practice in general."

Some local whites became more pronounced in their criticism of Jim Crow. Attorney George E. Barrett, head of the Nashville Council on Human Relations (NCHR), told an NCLC mass meeting, "It is deplorable that the conditions exist in our city and state that make these meetings necessary." Barrett and a few others had formed the NCHR in 1956 and expanded it to include three hundred participants who would meet at the Methodist Publishing House offices. This organization would encourage moderate and liberal white support behind the scenes. Everett Tilson, a Vanderbilt professor, friend of James Lawson, and author of *Segregation and the Bible* (1960), told one NCLC gathering:

> Segregation breaches the first commandment: 'You shall have no other God before me.' Jim Crow substitutes race for God as the organizing center of life. And this, as we all know, is worse than immoral; it is idolatrous. Segregation breaches the eighth com-

mandment: 'You shall not steal.' It robs him [the Negro] of equal access to public facilities, of a typical work week, of favorable working conditions, access to adequate hospital facilities, and respect and dignity due him as a human being.

That summer, James Lawson enrolled in the divinity program at Boston University. Stahlman and another member of the Vanderbilt Board of Trustees, O. H. Ingram, drew up a set of resolutions on June 13, 1960, to close the Lawson affair. They instructed Chancellor Branscomb to accept immediately all faculty resignations in the Divinity School, keep the school open, and not to award Lawson a degree in absentia. Branscomb supported the proposal but was willing to give faculty members a grace period to rescind their resignations. Philosophy professor John Compton recalled: "There was a desire to support the Divinity faculty, a deep regret of Branscomb's actions, but also a sense of being in the middle of a situation that we had no serious control over, and at once hoping it would go away and not wanting to be called to any ultimate action, like resignation—living in a kind of ambiguous hope." Branscomb was pressured to select another acting dean, William C. Finch, and to send a statement to the entire faculty: "Vanderbilt University stands on the principle that racial progress in the South must be based on obedience to law." Several faculty members refused to take the job as dean unless Lawson was readmitted. Gene L. Davenport, one faculty member, said, "I feel very strongly that Harvie Branscomb made a major error in his life. It was in contradiction to his books, his own temperament, and his whole work. . . . He made an error in judgment; he obviously did not have enough people around him to help him get through in a fashion that could have reduced the tension in the University." Stahlman was constantly using his private line and new speakerphone to bring other members of the Vanderbilt Board of Trustees into line with his position; he claimed the support of trustees John C. Sloan and Sam Fleming, a bank president, both past presidents of the Vanderbilt Alumni Association.

Forty years later, Lawson had no bitterness, saying, "Branscomb was not free to charge ahead; he had to work within constraints that some of us liberals did not think should be there." Lawson said that many schools, unlike Vanderbilt, did nothing about admitting Negro students until "the Civil Rights Act of 1964 gave the cowards the courage of the crowd." Branscomb retired in 1962. In 1994, four years before Branscomb's death, the two men met for reconciliation. "Dr. Lawson," Branscomb said, "I want you to know that I now regret the decision I made in 1960, and I think it was a mistake. I want you to know that, and I should like your forgiveness for any harm that came to you as a result of that decision." Lawson said he had long since forgiven him.

[*]

By late 1960, Negro leaders finally began to relate the various parts of the civil rights movement across Tennessee into a statewide picture. In September, the NCLC hosted a statewide meeting at First Colored Baptist Church to organize a Tennessee-wide branch of the Southern Christian Leadership Conference. Wyatt T. Walker, director of SCLC, attended this meeting, and he and Smith wanted Tennessee affiliates to be formed in order to focus on the "Christian concept." The Reverends Benjamin L. Hooks, H. C. Bunton, and Charles L. Dinkins represented Memphis. They detailed the "Freedom Movement" unfolding there, identifying the Memphis NAACP as the able leader of that movement, and said that they intended to ride at the front of buses, persuade outsiders to boycott Memphis, sponsor a mass bus ride by local students, turn in all charge cards and boycott downtown stores, and raise six thousand dollars. They saw no urgent need for the SCLC in Memphis. The group met again at FCBC on November 3, 1960, and discussed the need to "spread nonviolence statewide and to improve relations between the students and the adults." But the NAACP had the civil rights lawyers, a better treasury, and a longer history.

Several significant developments occurred in the latter half of 1960 and early part of 1961. In August, James Lawson was assigned by the Methodist Church to be pastor of the Scott Memorial Methodist Church in Shelbyville. Although this town was fifty miles south of Nashville, Lawson maintained his home in the capital city and stayed on the NCLC board. In late 1960, the NCLC and NSM protesters restarted demonstrations against the most resistant of the segregated businesses: Morrison's Cafeteria, Cross Keys Restaurant, and Krystal's Hamburgers. Thugs pulled a Fisk student from his seat and whipped him. One storeowner ordered the students out of the building at gunpoint, but they returned the next day. The police continued to arrest students and send them to jail at the request of the business owners. The students next launched demonstrations at the movie theaters just two blocks from FCBC. Fred Leonard and other students were injured by policemen. In February 1961, Smith called a meeting at First Colored Baptist and argued for a cooling-off period, but John Lewis insisted that he and the other students

were going to continue the marches. About twenty businesses agreed to desegregate their seating. Kroger Stores hired an A&I student as a clerk.

In 1961, Looby received a consent order to have the sit-in cases dismissed,
and the bond money was refunded. With the help of Fisk's Isaiah T. Creswell
he was able to determine how much money was due each person who had
helped make bond and arrange for reimbursements. This action saved a number of property owners from possibly losing their homes. For transportation to
a Highlander conference held from February 23 to 26, the NCLC supplied a
car for members of the Student Nonviolent Coordinating Committee and the
Nashville Student Movement. In April, the NCLC hired a coordinating secretary to be housed at Smith's church, and it also helped SNCC establish an
office at 1905 Jefferson Street, for which the owner of nearby Otey's Grocery
Store paid the first four months of rent. Avon Williams, meanwhile, was working on an official state charter for the SCLC. By this time, NCLC leaders and
SNCC members, as well as some civil rights leaders from Memphis, were making trips back and forth to rural West Tennessee, trying to help the Negroes
in Haywood and Fayette counties with their struggle for voting rights.

[*]

In East Tennessee, Knoxville leaders had begun agitating for Negro rights by
1957, when a group of professors and students from the historically black
Knoxville College mounted a drive to register black voters. The city's Negro
population numbered about twenty-three thousand, with nine thousand eligible to vote. The registration effort pushed the registered voter total to forty-
five hundred. The Knoxville Monitor, the local Negro newspaper published by
William J. Robinson, was also pushing civil rights issues.

Knoxville College students and staff members planned protest marches
and sit-in demonstrations in downtown Knoxville for February 15, 1960. However, a stormy meeting at the college resulted in students rejecting the argument by older Negro leaders that public demonstrations would destroy good
race relations with moderate whites. Such arguments led many local young
people to conclude that the older generation, who believed in old-style negotiated settlements, did not fully understand the real intent of the civil rights
movement. In their view, this was no halfway movement that would leave part
of Jim Crow standing. Knoxville College president James A. Colston persuaded
the students to at least wait until he and twenty-one other men could talk
with the mayor, who really wanted racial peace. They contended that the

mayor would perhaps negotiate with downtown businessmen to spare the city any violence. The merchants at first agreed to begin desegregating lunch counters, but then some of them changed their minds, preferring to wait until absentee storeowners also gave approval.

Mayor John Duncan, two student representatives, and Knoxville Chamber of Commerce representatives went to New York to speak to department store chain owners about desegregating the major downtown stores, but the businessmen refused to have a meeting that included the college students. Without student participation, however, there was no agreement. Back in Knoxville, the students decided on a single-file march through the downtown area to make a point of their persistence and express frustration at the breakdown of negotiations. Merrill Proudfoot, a white Presbyterian clergyman on the Knoxville College faculty, had agreed to join the students if they first tried to negotiate a desegregation settlement, and when the negotiations failed, he kept his promise and became prominent in the Knoxville movement. The *Knoxville News-Sentinel* opposed the demonstrations, as did the *Knoxville Journal*, which declared on March 2, 1960: "Lunch counter assaults serve only to create annoyance, and lend nothing to the solution of the problem." The *Journal* editor restated the familiar complaint of "outside agitators," blaming that "organization [the NAACP] in New York" for the brewing unrest. The students staged a few sit-in demonstrations and distributed "Stay Away from Downtown" leaflets that promoted a boycott of downtown stores. The *Journal* advised Knoxville's Negro community to focus on school integration and voting rights. The standoff lasted until the college students took summer vacation.

To keep the movement peaceful and organized, some adults in the local Negro community formed the Knoxville Associated Council for Full Citizenship and held mass meetings on Sunday nights in local churches. Demonstrators, both students and adults, were trained for nonviolent tactics during some meetings in the Mt. Olive Baptist Church. On June 6, 1960, they resumed their sit-in demonstrations and picketing of downtown stores. One of the picket signs in front of Rich's Department Store said, "Khrushchev Could Eat. We Can't!!"—a reference to a 1959 visit to the United States by the Soviet premier. The mayor ordered the police to protect the students and other citizens. Among the demonstrators were students Theotis Robinson, Ann Robinson, Robert J. Booker, Avon Rollins, and Jerry Pate, as well as Professor Robert Harvey, all affiliated with Knoxville College. On July 12, 1960, the merchants agreed to desegregate Knoxville's downtown facilities rather than continue to suffer monetary losses. The Reverend W. T. Crutcher of Knoxville spoke at the NCLC statewide meeting at Nashville's St. John AME Church on August 8, 1960, where he said, "It challenges us to join hands with Knoxville, Nashville, Memphis, Somerville, Brownsville, Chattanooga, and hammer out a program for the entire state." He reported that his group would "attempt to enter a Negro undergraduate student into the University of Tennessee–Knoxville within a few days, and picket the grocery stores." Crutcher reminded the audience that the United Church Women, a white group, had helped the movement in Knoxville, adding, "They did not have to do it, but they felt a kindred spirit with us." Crutcher concluded, "We have tasted something that is good. We are not alone; we have [white] friends." (White women's groups, incidentally, would help smooth desegregation elsewhere in Tennessee.) Demonstrations and arrests continued in downtown Knoxville through 1963. John Bell, the Knoxville College dean of men, checked on the students in jail. By 1967, when J. Harvey Kerns prepared a report for the National Urban League, "Social and Economic Conditions in Knoxville, Tennessee, As They Affect the Negro," he concluded that Knoxville was a more open city.

[*]

Chattanooga, with its 130,009 citizens, had a long history of racial accommodationism—that is, local black and white leaders usually worked out compromises in order to maintain the racial order and peace. The NAACP's successful 1942 teacher-pay-equity court case had helped to broaden the Negro middle class there. To determine where the Negro community in Chattanooga stood with its peers, in 1947 C. B. Robinson, businessman Joe Howard, and H. E. White, branch manager for the Universal Life Insurance Co., convinced the National Urban League in New York to complete "a study on the life of the Negro in the mainstream of American and Chattanooga life." That study, conducted between April 23 and May 14, 1947, focused on "Employment, Industrial Relations and Education" in Chattanooga. Consultant Richard R. Jefferson's report noted that Afro-Chattanooga included four Negro branch insurance companies, the only Negro-owned five-and-dime store in Tennessee, and dozens of beauty and barber shops, as well as dentists, druggists, doctors, a few lawyers, funeral directors, building contractors, school principals, postmen, schoolteachers, caseworker and public health nurses, a few clerical workers, and mostly semiskilled and unskilled laborers in the work force. The report made strong recommendations that Negro auxiliary policemen be appointed and that the public library be opened to Negroes—both of which were implemented. And, on another front on June 17, 1947, after Chattanooga's nine Negro physicians and their Mountain City Medical Society pushed the city to improve health care for its black citizens, the city bought two buildings of a former hospital and converted it into the fifty-bed Carver Memorial Hospital for Negroes, one of the first such city-supported hospitals for blacks in the country. This health care initiative won the support of many whites who feared the spread of tuberculosis by Negroes during the 1940s.

Perry A. Stephens, a physician and the founding chief of the local NAACP branch, had been fighting Jim Crow all his life, but in heading Carver Hospital, he, too, learned to restrain his criticism of local race relations. In 1952, he said, "With our fight just beginning and the winning of many friends among the white race, the filibuster rampant in Congress against yours and my right to be an American citizen, can we afford to lag?" Stephens toured local schools, colleges, and union meetings to inform whites about "what the Negro wants": equality, freedom, and justice. To advertise NAACP membership drives and communicate more radical messages to the Negro masses, Stephens had to rely heavily on the *Pittsburgh Courier*, instead of solely on the local *Chattanooga Observer*, edited by the conservative black Republican leader W. C. Robinson. The *Courier*, like the *Chicago Defender*, was often militant and read nationally by Negroes. Copies of these papers were frequently distributed to southern rural communities from the windows of fast-moving trains by the members of A. Philip Randolph's Brotherhood of Sleeping Car Porters union.

Among the things that Chattanooga's African American community wanted was better housing—a concern that the city began to address in 1954 when, as one local Negro publication, *Sephia* magazine, reported on April 1, construction of modern housing projects for Negroes was undertaken. Still other needs were outlined in a letter that local leader C. B. Robinson sent to Governor Frank Clement on the day after the *Brown* decision. "May I take the opportunity," Robinson wrote, "to transmit some of the things that the Negro of Hamilton County and Tennessee want?" He then listed paved roads, improvements at Booker T. Washington State Park, a school for mentally retarded children, and more Negro state employees. Chattanooga's black citizens obviously considered it an outrage that even the State of Tennessee's local employment office had hired no Negroes and maintained a "Colored Waiting Room."

"Since the Court has made the decision, it becomes a law of the land," Walter C. Robinson noted soon after the *Brown* decision, while adding a note of caution: "We are a minority group and we must take a position of favoring law and order." Robinson would not be for marches, sit-ins, and public protests; instead, he worked closely with the local establishment, following the accommodationist approach that Booker T. Washington had used. Some progress was made, as when the Southern Coach Lines removed its Jim Crow signs on the buses in early 1957, but the threat of white violence was still evident when police took down a dummy hanging from a bridge, with a sign that served as a warning to "All NAACP bus-riding Niggers." In January 1960, Emancipation Day speaker Daisy Bates told Chattanooga Negroes to fight and pay for their freedom through NAACP memberships. C. B. Robinson, meanwhile, urged teachers to "head the NAACP membership campaign in your school." Things were about to change.

On February 19, 1960, after debating each other in their third-period mathematics class while reading about the Nashville sit-ins in the newspaper, some thirty students from Howard High School headed to downtown Chattanooga stores. They staged a sit-in demonstration at the lunch counter of the McLellan's Store at 713 Market Street. After they were refused service and the counter was closed, they sang freedom songs and prayed for about thirty minutes before leaving. The traditional Negro leadership was not trained in such nonviolent tactics, and the support the demonstrators needed from the *Chattanooga Observer* did not arrive. "Economic Security is the Way Out for Negroes," editor Walter Robinson told his readers, later claiming that he had received "many letters from white people for this sensible editorial" in which he spoke against the sit-in. Young Negroes demonstrated downtown again on February 22 and 23. After a fight broke out between Negroes and segregationists on the second day of the renewed protests, the city administration took steps to prevent further public violence. Six whites were arrested and charged with assault. Claude C. Bond, the principal at Howard, and his teachers were sent downtown to make sure that the students did not tarry as they transferred between city buses. Lingering on the streets during these tense times, it was feared, might make them vulnerable to assaults by whites. "They feel they have made their point," Bond said, hoping to prevent any further violence. However, the students were not accommodationists, and they soon tried to force the integration of Warner Park. But whites saw them coming and closed the concessions and rides. The police forced the Negro youngsters to leave the park.

Local preachers became involved in the Chattanooga movement, and through April 1960 there were periodic downtown demonstrations. Seven Negro ministers, including Dogan Williams and Horace Tyler, stood in the median of Market Street near the Ninth Street intersection and held prayers for Jim Crow to end: "We pray for our city in Christian love. Stop Jim Crow." As in Memphis, most of Chattanooga's white ministers stayed out of sight during this moral battle. Student pickets marched outside S. H. Kress and Company, and for the first time since February, Howard High School students demonstrated at several lunch counters, including those at W. T. Grant and Woolworth's. After the store manager at Woolworth's asked that arrests be made, around May 13 about fifty students, twenty-two of them female, were arrested and marched into a police van as they sang "Battle Hymn of the Republic" and "Onward Christian Soldiers." Six of the students refused the one-hundred-dollar bond and release to civil rights attorney R. H. Craig. But Kress management, which wanted no more bad publicity, refused to prosecute James Gaines, Rudolph Graham, Frankie Hartsfield, Shirley Jones, Imogene Leslie, Marvin Nicholson, Betty Raines, Edna Sanders, Wanda Wells, and others.

Negroes marched around the jail in protest of the arrests. The NAACP and the Council for Cooperative Action met with the mayor and others the next morning "to counter racial trouble here." C. B. Robinson, who was a member of this biracial delegation, said, "Whites were aware that if blacks were to be satisfied, they would have to be shown that negotiations between the leaderships were effective. I have always had good relationships with whites in my part of town. They know I am not a racist or obstructionist." Four white youths were placed on probation for assaults on demonstrators. Desegregation began in August 1960, when seven lunch counters served Negro customers. A *Chattanooga Times* editorial (Aug. 6, 1960) said, "The plan was the result of excellent work by the ministers' group."

In August 1960, two Negro homes were bombed, injuring two Negro children. Mayor Gene Roberts offered a two-thousand-dollar reward to bring about the arrest of the perpetrators. It was the fifth blast in Chattanooga since the demonstrations began, prompting an FBI investigation.

By the end of the year, Chattanooga's Negro ministers considered themselves a chapter of the SCLC, and several of them—including Dogan W. Williams of Wiley Memorial Methodist Church, M. J. Jones of Stanley Methodist Church, and William A. Dennis of Orchard Knob Baptist Church—arranged to have Martin Luther King Jr. speak in Chattanooga's Municipal Auditorium. Branded a radical by local whites, King had been denied the right to speak in a local Negro school auditorium. At the Emancipation Proclamation observance in January 1961, King talked not only about the Chattanooga movement but also about the terrible situation in Fayette and Haywood counties in West Tennessee. Referring to the newly elected U.S. president, King

said, "We must remind Mr. Kennedy we helped him get into the White House
[last November] and that we expect him to use the full weight of his office to
remove the burden of segregation from our shoulders." Calling for a rejection
of "gradualism" and "tokenism," King urged the audience to register to vote
and work for an immediate end to segregation. The crowd took up a collection
to help in the movement.

On February 17, 1961, the first anniversary of local sit-in demonstrations,
young Negroes began "stand-in" demonstrations outside the downtown movie
houses. They were also denied service at a Krystal restaurant. In March, the
Interdenominational Ministerial Alliance asked citizens to boycott segregated
events at the auditorium, after a February 24 meeting with the facility's board
had produced no results. Racist thugs attacked some of the pickets. James
Mapp, the local NAACP head, called on the mayor to denounce violence
against peaceful demonstrators. When a juvenile court judge declared twelve
of the demonstrators as delinquents, attorney Bruce C. Boynton, replacing the
late R. H. Craig, defended them. Their arrest records were expunged from
court documents; thus, their prospects for future employment would not be
affected.

Demonstrations in the city continued through 1963. Meanwhile, in
1962, the city built Erlanger Hospital with a Carver Negro wing to replace the
old Jim Crow facility.

[*]

During the 1960–62 period, what had been happening in Nashville, Knoxville,
and Chattanooga spread to smaller towns in Tennessee—even those in the
eastern part of the state, where the black communities were relatively small.
At Morristown College, a junior college for Negroes, both the student government association and the college president endorsed Dr. King's nonviolent
philosophy and made an early decision to work with local white leaders rather
than launch public demonstrations. In nearby Johnson City, a railroad town
incorporated in 1869 and named for President Andrew Johnson, the Christian Community Relations Committee and the Johnson City–Washington
County Ministerial Association made similar pledges at weekly meetings. One
speaker was inspired to remark on the "splendid racial tone seen in Johnson
City." Yet, as other speakers noted, not all public places in town were open to
Negroes. It was reported, for example, that the two drive-in movie theaters,
which had traditionally allowed the community's few black citizens to enter
without controversy, had begun enforcing segregation practices. On the other

hand, twelve Negro youngsters had recently entered restaurants to see if they would be served, and at least one store did so. Johnson City's lone Negro doctor, Eugene Kilgore, reported that he had no problem treating patients of both races but declared that local Negroes still needed a voter-registration drive. Another resident, Bruce Anderson, said that Negroes were denied equal jobs and working privileges in the city.

In the West Tennessee town of Jackson (whose population was more than 35 percent Negro), demonstrations were initiated by students from Lane College, a historically black school affiliated with the CME Church, whose headquarters and publishing house were also based in Jackson. The protests began on October 13, 1960, when students who refused to observe the Jim Crow arrangements on city buses were arrested. The arrests led to a boycott that, within days, forced the private bus company to desegregate its seating. Then, on October 27, five students took seats at the Woolworth's lunch counter at around 11:00 A.M., and when white employees immediately closed the counter, they remained seated for three hours, reading books and the Bible. Eventually a white mob gathered and dragged the students from the store. At the McLellan's store nearby, five other students took seats at the lunch counter that afternoon; the manager called the police, who arrested the students. The demonstrations continued in the days ahead, and there were more arrests and abuse from white segregationists, who kicked the students, cursed them, burned them with cigarettes and coffee, spat on them, and pelted them with eggs and tulip bulbs. Among the demonstrators was Wesley McClure, a freshman who later became a president of Lane College. Albert Porter, a bookkeeper at Lane, and his wife, Fanye, served as leaders and advisors for the students and persuaded some faculty members to become involved. Porter, along with Lane professors such as Allan Ward (who was white) and Essie Percy, met with a local group of white Methodist women, and a biracial human relations council was eventually formed. Lane professor Preston E. Stewart was fined fifteen dollars for taking a picture of a "Whites Only" sign on a soft drink machine. In spite of the arrests and reports that police sometimes did nothing when segregationists abused the demonstrators, the local police department, under Mayor Quinton Edwards, generally avoided the sort of police brutality that occurred in other cities such as Birmingham, Alabama.

The worst wave of arrests came on November 8, 1960, the day of the presidential election, when 144 people (including 66 women and 10 teenagers) were charged with "parading without a license" as they marched in downtown Jackson to protest the mistreatment of black voters in nearby Fayette and Haywood counties (see chapter 8). A month later, a thirty-year-old white man was arrested for firing a shotgun at the Lane College dormitory. Although sit-in demonstrations continued at Woolworth's in December, the student movement was shifting its focus to the registration of black voters. President Kennedy addressed the nation about civil rights on January 25, 1961, and mentioned the crisis in Haywood and Fayette counties. On March 11, 1961, the Jackson Greyhound Bus Terminal desegregated its lunch counters, but Woolworth's and other downtown eateries in Jackson held on to Jim Crow until after passage of the Civil Rights Bill of 1964.

The segregationist Tennessee Federation for Constitutional Government placed large advertisements in the *Jackson Sun*, which was owned by Sally Pigford and her family. Like the conservative *Nashville Banner*, the *Sun* adhered to the southern-elite notion that "outside agitators" were provoking discord among local Negroes, and it tried to suppress news of the Negro movement by burying stories in the back pages. The three Jackson radio stations—including WJAK, the "black station" owned by two white men, Alex and W. E. Leech—stuck to their normal news format and also ignored the civil rights stories. But the *Nashville Tennessean, Memphis Commercial Appeal*, and *Memphis Press-Scimitar* carried the stories more prominently. Only the threat of a black boycott and the convincing arguments by moderate white *Sun* reporters, such as John Parrish, would force the paper to become more inclusive and fair toward blacks, and offer more news coverage of the civil rights struggle by the mid-1960s.

[∗]

From 1954 to 1961, that phase of the civil rights movement which focused on desegregation of public facilities slowly developed effective methods in Tennessee to dismantle the most visible side of Jim Crow. In many ways, Memphis started the ball rolling in 1955, followed by Nashville, and then Knoxville and Chattanooga by 1960. But of all the local movements, the Nashville sit-ins were the most organized and set the standards for nonviolent protest. Chronicled in nationwide telecasts by the CBS and NBC networks in early 1961, the Nashville sit-ins became the model for all other sit-in demonstrations. The Southern Christian Leadership Conference, the Student Nonviolent Coordinating Committee, and other civil rights organizations would use tapes of the broadcasts to train citizens for public protest. The Nashville Student Movement received letters of commendation from Ralph Bunche, Harry Belafonte, Roy Wilkins, and many others from across the nation. Eleanor Roosevelt sent a telegram that read, "I hope you can continue without violence and with ever increasing success and you achieve your ends. Good wishes." Martin Luther King Jr., in a phone call to the Reverend Kelly Miller Smith, said, "Your victory in Nashville has been more meaningful than our Montgomery victory. You won on the basis of moral force alone, without your [NAACP] court cases being a decisive factor. The students conducted themselves in the best tradition of passive resistance."

Recent historical accounts have hailed the Nashville protests as one of the most important episodes in the entire civil rights movement. In his 1998 book, *Pillar of Fire: America in the King Years, 1963–65*, Taylor Branch called the Nashville students the advance troops of the sit-ins and the earliest legends within SNCC. In *Sweet Land of Liberty: The African-American Struggle for Civil Rights in the Twentieth Century*, also published in 1998, Robert Cook described the freedom struggle as one rooted in Nashville, Birmingham, and the Negro church. And in *An Easy Burden: The Civil Rights Movement and the Transformation of America* (1996), Andrew Young wrote, "Nashville: The students there were so disciplined that they regularly engaged in serious Bible study and discussed theories of social transformation before breakfast and the school day began. Their actions were rooted in deep personal faith and conviction." Still further insight into Nashville is offered by Robert Weisbrot, whose 1990 book, *Freedom Bound: A History of America's Civil Rights Movement*, contains this passage:

> As young blacks began to seek guiding principles as well as precedents for action, they paid particular notice to the distinctive sit-in campaign unfolding in Nashville. Unlike the freshmen [in North Carolina] whose act of naïve courage first sparked the sit-ins, the Nashville activists were somewhat older students or graduates who had held their first workshop in nonviolent resistance nearly a year before the protest in Greensboro. As inclined to grapple with Gandhian texts as with white authority, they emerged as models for a movement that, at barely two weeks of age, was fast growing in numbers and vigor yet remained very much in search of its moral bearings.

In 1960, L. F. Palmer, the managing editor of the *Memphis Tri-State Defender*, said, "In Nashville, like none of the other cities, students will look you in the eye and say 'I am ready to go to jail if it is necessary to receive our rights, or I am ready to die for my rights if necessary. We are not afraid anymore.'" Palmer took note of the strong religious overtones of the sit-in movements, in which the demonstrators loved to sing "We Shall Overcome."

And from one of the actual participants, James Lawson Jr., came this summation:

> The Nashville movement did, of course, affect the entire move-
> ment in the country and in the South. Martin King called our
> movement the model movement up to that time. Eventually,
> any number of us served the SCLC staff, including C. T. Vivian,
> Diane Nash, Jim Bevel, and Bernard Lafayette. I became director
> of nonviolent education for the SCLC. . . . Jim Bevel, Bernard
> Lafayette, and Diane Nash in particular became identified with
> the larger struggle for social justice and for peace here in the
> United States. . . . So the Nashville scene perhaps more than
> any single scene, with the possible exception of Montgomery in
> 1955–56, became . . . the most significant movement in terms
> of its ongoing effect across the country.

CHAPTER 5

LET NOBODY TURN ME AROUND

SIT-INS AND PUBLIC DEMONSTRATIONS
CONTINUE TO SPREAD

In order to promote some uniformity and Christian resistance to Jim Crow, the Reverend Kelly Miller Smith, other preachers, and laypersons completed the organization of the Tennessee chapter of the Southern Christian Leadership Conference in December 1960. Smith and W. A. Dennis of Chattanooga were elected vice presidents for Middle Tennessee. R. E. Jones of Knoxville became president. Benjamin Hooks and H. C. Bunton were elected vice presidents for West Tennessee. Catherine Burks, a student at Tennessee A&I State University, became secretary of the organization.

The SCLC would become one of several groups lending support to civil rights activists in the town of Lebanon in Wilson County, just twenty-five west of Nashville. The movement there had its beginnings with a local pastor, Cordell Hull Sloan (1931–1987), who was born in Nashville, attended public schools, and graduated from the Tennessee School for the Blind (Colored Division) after a brain tumor destroyed his eyesight. Sloan completed bachelor's and master's degrees at Tennessee A&I and attended Vanderbilt's Divinity School with James M. Lawson and others. In 1960, the Presbyterian Church assigned Sloan to organize a congregation in Lebanon. In the spring of 1961, when the Reverend Sloan and his son were passing by the white school in Lebanon, Cordell Jr. asked his father why he could not attend "that school."

Sloan gave the boy's question some thought in light of recent school desegregation cases in Tennessee and the stance of the federal government on the issue. He and a neighbor, Cathy White, took their children to the all-white McClain Elementary School but were turned away. On August 23, 1961, several other Negro students were turned away from the all-white high school. The Negro community supported a lawsuit. Roy Bailey, Jessie L. Bender, Ephraim Sweatt, Acie McFarland, and others mortgaged homes and land to raise the funds. Williams and Looby were attorneys for the plaintiffs in *Sloan et al. v. The Tenth School District of Wilson County, Tennessee.* In September, the federal court ordered the desegregation of the schools. The Negro high school finally ceased to exist in 1969–70.

Some 150 Negro and white students from American Baptist, Fisk University, Tennessee A&I, Meharry Medical College, Vanderbilt University, and George Peabody College became involved in marching on segregated movie theaters in Lebanon in 1962. Hate mail and telephoned death threats almost forced Sloan, who was involved in all aspects of the Lebanon movement, to send his family to live with his mother in Nashville. Some whites in and out of Lebanon gave support, and money and letters of support arrived from Martin Luther King Jr., the Southern Christian Leadership Conference, the Congress of Racial Equality, the Nashville Christian Leadership Council, the Student Nonviolent Coordinating Committee, and others.

By the summer of 1962, Negroes were conducting regular public demonstrations to desegregate the entire town of Lebanon. Cathy and F. Paul White allowed meetings in their home. Pickett Chapel Church became the main gathering place until race radicals threatened to blow it up. Meetings shifted to an office building owned by John Glover, a Negro doctor. Police arrested many demonstrators, including Fred Brooks of Tennessee A&I State University. Even a reporter for the *Nashville City Examiner* was arrested for carrying a rifle in his car to protect himself. Aided by the Wilson County Committee for Christian Action and college students from Nashville (who conducted nonviolent workshops for the demonstrators), the Lebanon protests spread to the segregated water fountains of Rogers Brothers Grocery Store. Tennessee National Guardsmen entered the town after shots were fired from inside the Glover building, where blacks were holding a meeting and which had been targeted by some whites.

Lebanon lost the Reverend Sloan's leadership when he was moved to a Presbyterian church in Chattanooga in June 1962; four years later he would leave Tennessee altogether to assume a pastorate in Pennsylvania. Others, however, carried on what he had helped start. There were more arrests (with the names of arrestees published in the *Tennessean* on September 13, 1963), and some teachers were fired for their participation in the protests. Mayor Charles D. Lloyd finally appointed a biracial committee to ease the desegregation of Lebanon by 1965.

[*]

When he became president of CORE on February 1, 1961, James Farmer wanted the organization to dramatize the recent Supreme Court decision that extended the 1946 *Morgan v. Virginia* ruling against segregation in interstate bus travel. On March 6, 1961, President John F. Kennedy issued an executive order that "forbade discrimination because of race, creed, color, or national origin." Kennedy had promised this to the Negro leaders who supported his election campaign the year before. But CORE and Farmer wanted more. They sought to pressure Kennedy to do something about enforcing the laws against segregated interstate travel and thus decided to proceed with a Freedom Ride through the heart of the Deep South. Perhaps this exercise—in which black and white riders would join together and demand equal service on buses, in terminals, and at lunch counters—would provoke the racists in the South and, in turn, force the federal government to intervene more forcefully in the civil rights movement. In announcing the project, the *Nashville Commentator* (Apr. 15, 1961) quoted Farmer: "Whites will sit and eat in 'Colored Sections' and Negroes will sit and eat in 'White Sections.' They will refuse to accept segregation in any form." The NAACP opposed the tactic for fear of "wholesale slaughter with no good achieved." Nonetheless, the first Freedom Rides left as scheduled from Washington, D.C., on May 4, 1961.

The Freedom Riders comprised sixteen interracial demonstrators paying fares on a couple of buses, one owned by Greyhound and the other by Trailways. The buses traveled down the East Coast and through the Upper South without major incident. One rider was John Lewis, who left the bus in Nashville to handle some personal matters. A group of mostly fresh riders continued the trip after its stop in Atlanta, where King and other SCLC officials had given them names of some SCLC contacts in towns along the way. The trip proceeded uneventfully until May 14, when the riders came under attack at Anniston, Alabama. After the first bus reached the town, terrorists chased it down, surrounded it, broke its windows, and set the vehicle on fire. The second bus, arriving in Anniston an hour later, was forced on to Birmingham after some Klansmen boarded it and brutally beat several riders; when the bus arrived in Birmingham, a mob attacked them again. One Freedom Rider required dozens of stitches to close the wounds in his head. The city police commissioner, Eugene "Bull" Connor, explained sarcastically that no policemen were at the bus station to control the mob because it was Mother's Day. The Reverend Fred Shuttlesworth, a fiery young civil rights leader and head of the local SCLC chapter, led an armed caravan from Birmingham to rescue the stranded riders in Anniston. He hid them in Birmingham homes until CORE could have them flown to New Orleans. The flight was delayed several hours because of bomb threats, and racists in Louisiana threatened violence if the Freedom Riders came there. Farmer decided to end the project because he felt that it had accomplished its purpose: to show the federal government that it had to deal with the southern states and make them respect the Constitution and the spirit of *Brown*.

Diane Nash, however, contacted Farmer and then the Reverend Kelly Miller Smith to inform them that the Student Nonviolent Coordinating Committee was taking over the Freedom Rides. Both Farmer and Smith feared that such a move would be suicidal, but Nash believed that the movement would suffer a devastating blow if segregationists could use mob violence to disrupt the project. The new Kennedy administration also felt that SNCC's decision would get many people killed. Smith quickly called an NCLC executive board meeting that included Nash, Bevel, J. Metz Rollins, Will Campbell, and Andrew White in the discussions. Rollins had supervised the students during their first nonviolence workshops and practice sit-ins with Lawson in November-December 1959. He had come from Florida to Nashville in 1956 as a field worker with the United Presbyterian Churches and later would become director of the National Committee of Black Churchmen. He remembered staying up until 3:00 A.M., "arguing where the will of the students prevailed." The students were going it alone if the adults did not support them. The NCLC executive committee voted to give nine hundred dollars to support the students and their Freedom Rides project. Nash, Lewis, and others rushed off to prepare to send volunteers to Birmingham. The NCLC executive board, meeting in Smith's office in First Colored Baptist Church, also agreed to have "a heart-to-heart talk with Diane Nash, James Bevel, and Leo Lillard" about the activities at the local SNCC offices. Rollins recalled that "Nashville . . . became like a part of the Underground Railroad in reverse"—sending and financing students on the Freedom Rides into the Deep South.

Nash selected an integrated group of Nashville sit-in veterans to continue the rides: William Barbee, Paul Brooks, Catherine Burks, Charles Butt, Allen Cason, Lucretia R. Collins, William Harbour, John Lewis, Mary McCollum, Henry Thomas, and Jim Zwerg. A white exchange student attending Fisk from Beloit College in Wisconsin, Zwerg telephoned his parents to announce his decision. "I have got to do this," he told his mother, "though I may be dead tomorrow." He recalled that his mother hung up the telephone, exclaiming that this news would kill his sick father.

On May 17, at 6:30 A.M., the handpicked volunteers boarded the bus in Nashville and made their way to Birmingham. Bull Connor stopped the bus before it entered Birmingham, arrested the riders, and placed them in jail. Connor accused Shuttlesworth of helping the young protesters. During the early hours of May 19, several of them were awakened in their cells, loaded into three cars, and taken to the Alabama-Tennessee border. "This is the Tennessee state line; now cross it, and save this state and yourself a lot of trouble," said Connor. Catherine Burks, a student from Tennessee A&I, shouted, "We will be back." Connor and his men laughed and drove off in the darkness back to Birmingham.

Acting on instinct, the stranded riders carefully chose what appeared to be a safe house—and, as it turned out, it belonged to a Negro couple, who allowed them to use their telephone to contact Nash. She told them to stay put and that someone would pick them up. Leo (Kwame) Lillard, a graduating senior at Tennessee A&I, drove a large car from Nashville, traveling by himself in the darkness so that there would be enough room to squeeze all the riders into the vehicle. It was a dangerous task: A Negro traveling through rural Alabama at night could be stopped by ordinary (but "deputized") farmers who would question him, perhaps take him to jail for some imaginary offense, beat him up a little, and divide a fine with the local justice of peace. Lillard recalled:

> I was scared, but I stopped at a little road coming off the highway
> near the Alabama-Tennessee state line where a small cluster of
> houses appeared on the horizon. I knew if I selected the wrong
> house, where whites lived—it would be over for me [because they
> would call the local sheriff]. But I chose the oldest house, and
> knocked on the door. That was the right house! I picked up five
> Freedom Riders and drove them to the home of Shuttlesworth
> in Birmingham. He [Shuttlesworth] is the unsung hero of the
> Freedom Rides.

Lillard also recalled that the white students had been sent home by Connor and that two others were still in jail. It seemed that Connor had purposely picked Tennessee A&I State University students to transport to the state line; perhaps he expected them to meet quick punishment as soon as they crossed into Tennessee. Had Connor and the governor of Alabama communicated with Governor Ellington? Whatever the case, the students had remained on the Alabama side of the border, while Diane Nash had telephoned Shuttlesworth, using code language: "The chickens are being shipped." He advised her to cancel further plans because someone might be killed. But Nash held firm, contending that the movement would die if the Freedom Riders allowed violence to stop them. Anyway, the students had decided to continue. She and Shuttlesworth spoke in code because they believed that Hoover's FBI and other agencies might be listening through wiretaps, whether legally authorized or not.

Truly, Fred Shuttlesworth was a brave man in the middle of racist Alabama. After welcoming the students and Lillard early that morning, Shuttlesworth took them to the bus terminal where about ten new Freedom Riders waited; some of them had come into town by train and were already there waiting for a bus. No driver would dare take any of them if they said they were connected to CORE or SNCC. The Freedom Riders sat on the benches, singing civil rights songs and quieting their fears. Shuttlesworth would quarter them in private homes. These young people vowed not to leave Birmingham except on an integrated bus.

U.S. Attorney General Robert Kennedy threatened city and state officials with arrest on federal charges if they interfered again with the Freedom Rides. The federal government used emissary John Seigenthaler to negotiate with Alabama governor John Patterson over the release of the bus. The students urged Martin Luther King Jr. to accompany them, but he declined the offer. This aroused some doubts among the students as to King's effectiveness and that of the SCLC; it seemed to them that the SCLC was rushing to the scenes of crisis and gathering publicity without assuming the same degree of risk. There was also some confusion because what was initially a CORE project had become one sponsored by the SNCC and NCLC, although the news media still believed it was a CORE project.

Finally, on May 20, after more volunteers arrived, a Freedom Ride bus left the Greyhound terminal and headed for Montgomery. A caravan of police, highway patrol cars, and even a police airplane escorted the bus until it reached the Montgomery outskirts. At the terminal in Montgomery, however, local law enforcement authorities had allowed a trap to be set. John Lewis recalled that the terminal looked quiet until a mob emerged from hiding and descended on the alighting passengers, shouting, "Git dem' niggers. Git dem' niggers." As Lewis recalled, "To this day I don't know where all those people came from." William Harbour suffered a gash in his head when the bus driver pushed him into the windshield. Lewis and Zwerg were badly bloodied. Siegenthaler, the federal official who had accompanied the riders, was knocked unconscious after he had tried to push one of the female students into a cab before the mob pounced on them. He and Zwerg lay bleeding with black eyes, while the police claimed that the ambulance companies' vehicles were all broken down. The injured went to a hospital in police cars. Zwerg's pastor from Wisconsin soon came south to accompany him from the Alabama hospital to Nashville so that he could complete his examinations at Fisk. And as Zwerg's mother had feared, the boy's father did suffer a heart attack after seeing his son on the national news.

Seigenthaler also recovered and eventually returned to Washington. A native of Nashville, Seigenthaler was educated in parochial schools and Peabody College, served in the military, and went to work as a reporter at the *Tennessean* in 1949. He met Robert F. Kennedy while working on a union corruption story in 1959 when Kennedy was engaged in a similar investigation for the United States Senate. Seigenthaler helped with John F. Kennedy's presidential campaign in 1960 and joined the administration as an assistant in the Department of Justice. With his pronounced southern accent, Seigenthaler became one of the administration's key liaisons with both civil rights groups and southern politicians, urging moderation and explaining the federal laws that pertained to their actions.

Ironically, while the mob beat the twenty-one demonstrators in Montgomery, FBI agents—who, like Seigenthaler, were employees of the Department of Justice—stood across the street, taking notes. FBI director J. Edgar Hoover believed that his agency was created to gather intelligence and not to maintain local law and order. John Lewis later said, "I got the feeling . . . that even people within the Department of Justice had somewhat of a mistrust, distrust for their own FBI agents." Meanwhile, the Freedom Ride students went on a hunger strike and defiantly announced that they would leave Alabama only on an "integrated bus." Shuttlesworth, who also had been arrested, said that more Freedom Riders would come—in "wave after wave" if necessary. It would be May 24 before the Freedom Riders left Montgomery.

Opinions varied about the events in Birmingham and Montgomery. Editorialists for the *Tennessean* believed the affair in Alabama had "damaged their state, the South, and the nation" and called it "the kind of thing which makes the United States an object of criticism throughout the world." It did look like a scene from a war zone, and much of the nation was shocked at seeing the kind of barbarism practiced in Alabama. "Violence usually serves to strengthen us," Diane Nash said. "I think the federal government should take action." An opposite point of view was expressed by Bull Connor: "I have said for the last twenty years [or since the Southern Conference for Human Welfare had first met in Birmingham in 1938] that these out-of-town meddlers were going to cause bloodshed if they kept meddling in the South's business." Governor Patterson seemed unwilling to stop the violence, and he quickly blamed the Kennedy brothers for protecting the Freedom Riders. Patterson variously labeled the students a "group of troublemakers," "agitators," "Communists," and a "conspiracy to violate customs, traditions, and laws of Alabama." On May 26, the Alabama secretary of state sent a copy of a legislative resolution to Tennessee governor Buford Ellington condemning the Freedom Rides: "Violence and civil disorder have been brought in recent days to our state as a result of outside conspiracies against our [segregation] laws." Alabama had already moved to get students at Alabama State University expelled for participating in civil rights demonstrations. And in Tennessee, where most of the Negro students involved in the sit-ins and the Freedom Rides attended Tennessee A&I State University, the state commissioner of education notified public college presidents of new rules approved in April to expel any student arrested and convicted of breaking laws, missing classes, or engaging in bad personal conduct. Such threats angered James Bevel, among others. "Disciplinary action about what and for what?" he asked before a mass meeting at St. John AME Church. "Taking a bus ride as a citizen to New Orleans?"

Other responses to the Freedom Rides ranged from supportive to neutral. At Fisk, President Stephen Wright said that no disciplinary action would be taken against any students, including the white exchange students Susan Herrman and Jim Zwerg. Similarly, President Maynard P. Turner of the American Baptist Theological Seminary said that he would not punish any student for participating in the rides. Officials at Peabody College issued a statement saying that the school "neither condoned nor disapproved" of the student movement. One Peabody student who participated in the Freedom Rides, Nashville native Susan Wilbur, explained her involvement by recalling that students from A&I had come to Peabody to enlist whites to help in the movement. "I have always felt that segregation is wrong," she said, "and this was something we could do."

The Kennedy administration sent six hundred federal marshals to Montgomery to protect the Freedom Riders and their leaders. On May 21, after the news media alerted them to a mass meeting at Ralph Abernathy's First Baptist Church in Montgomery, where King was scheduled to speak, thousands of angry whites surrounded the church. When King stood outside the door of the church to survey the crowd, he was met with hurled stones and bottles, shouts of "Nigger King," rebel yells, and displays of Confederate flags. A car was set on fire. With an audience of about twelve hundred people trapped inside the church, the marshals repeatedly used tear gas to keep the crowd at bay. The mob threw the tear gas canisters back at the marshals and surged toward the church. King told the civil rights leaders that they would have to give themselves up to the mob if the doors were breached; perhaps, he thought, that would insure the safe exit of the members of the audience. FBI agents watched and took notes but obeyed Hoover's policy not to interfere with local law enforcement. Hoover, for his part, did not approve of the civil rights movement, and he especially disapproved of King.

At about 3:00 A.M. on May 22, King called U.S. Attorney General Robert Kennedy, who in turn called Governor Patterson with a stern message. Patterson responded by ordering state troopers and the Alabama National Guard to impose martial law, disperse the crowd, and help the Negroes leave the church and go home. Many were transported in the backs of National Guard trucks at about 4:00 A.M. A stunned Robert Kennedy called for a cooling-off period. James Farmer, who followed the fiery Shuttlesworth through a back way into the church, bullying his way past a less militant part of the mob, said, "We [blacks] have been cooling off for 350 years." Diane Nash wanted to stage a massive march through Montgomery, but King and the other leaders vetoed the idea.

Back in Nashville, as some students were picketing the local Greyhound and Trailways bus stations, the Reverend Smith called the NCLC executive committee back into session to discuss "the Alabama situation," while assuring newspaper reporters, whom they considered meddlers, that the session was just a regular meeting at First Colored Baptist. Meanwhile, on the night of May 22, a large crowd at the First Community Church on Knowles Street heard an address by the Reverend J. Metz Rollins, who had just returned from Alabama. After the arrests on May 17, the NCLC executive committee had voted to send Smith to Birmingham to check on the jailed students, but because he was needed in Nashville to raise money, Rollins, a Presbyterian minister, went in his place. Rollins told the crowd that the SCLC had responded marvelously by hiring local legal counsel and that Shuttlesworth, with whom he had met during his trip, had protected the students.

Although Smith had feared that his friend Martin Luther King Jr. had not intended to get SCLC affiliates involved in a project such as the Freedom Rides, King himself had rushed to Montgomery to lend support during the crisis despite budgetary problems within his organization. In the meantime, the Congress of Racial Equality voted to allocate money for the project—

perhaps to maintain its legitimate claim on the historic Freedom Rides. On May 23, Nash, Lewis, King, Abernathy, and Farmer announced that the rides would continue, and at the last minute, Farmer decided to join the riders on the buses. By this point, Nash had become head of the "Coordinating Center" for the Freedom Rides. And the same NCLC files that list her in that position also list the coordinating committee heads and give telephone numbers for SCLC, CORE, NCLC, and SNCC, as well as for coordinators in Atlanta, Montgomery, New Orleans, and Jackson, Mississippi. Clearly, the network of organizations supporting and coordinating the Freedom Rides had become quite extensive and diverse.

Diane Nash and other leaders of the Student Nonviolent Coordinating Committee were wary of Abernathy and King. The students felt that many people had given money to the SCLC in the belief that some or all of it would go to help the student protests. SNCC leaders, who argued that they had done more for the civil rights movement than King's organization, believed that the SCLC was not passing on to SNCC its share of the money. Some forty-two years later, Diane Nash recalled, "Martin was *not* the leader of the movement. He was the *spokesman*. Young people were upset with Martin and the SCLC for not moving fast enough. It was not Martin Luther King Jr.'s movement; it was a *people's* movement." Nash recalled contacting singer Harry Belafonte about participating in the Freedom Rides, but he declined, preferring instead to help raise money for the movement. Months later, according to Nash, he did invite her and other students to meet with him, actor Sidney Poitier, and others in New York.

When some of the original Freedom Riders came back to Nashville by car on about May 22, they appeared bruised, battered, and quite shaken by the ordeal. Upon returning to the Tennessee A&I campus, Curtis Murphy told anxious reporters that the Freedom Rides would continue despite Robert Kennedy's pleas that they stop lest more violence occur. Bomb threats arrived at the local SNCC headquarters. Lawson led a nonviolence workshop and recruitment session at First Baptist. He prepared for the dangerous mission into Alabama and left with reinforcements: C. T. Vivian of the Community Church, Alex M. Anderson of Clark Memorial Methodist Church, J. L. Copeland of Mt. Zion Baptist Church, and Grady Donald of Kayne Avenue Baptist Church, as well as James Bevel and four other college students.

Around this time, the South's largest religious denomination, the Southern Baptist Convention (SBC), which was headquartered in Nashville, was holding its annual meeting in St. Louis. The SBC surprised civil rights leaders by issuing a critical statement about "unwarranted provocation" in reference to the Alabama riot. When an African missionary was invited to speak at the podium, he was indignant enough to remind the delegates that the SBC's missionaries claimed that they loved the Africans. Why, he asked, could they not also love African Americans, even those in Birmingham? The SBC president quickly responded that Southern Baptists loved all people.

The federal government finally negotiated a release of the buses, secured drivers, and provided protection through federal law enforcement agents. Governor Patterson obeyed President Kennedy's directive not to interfere with the riders. Lewis and other students wrote the names of their next of kin on pieces of paper and handed them to people in the crowd just before their bus left the Montgomery station on May 24 and headed toward the darkness and uncertainty of Mississippi.

Later that day, the Freedom Riders, including five of the original riders from Nashville, arrived safely in Jackson, Mississippi, on two buses. Frederick Leonard, a student at Tennessee A&I, said, "They never stopped us . . . and they passed us right through the white terminal [waiting room] into the paddy wagon and into jail." Their trial was held on May 25. The judge turned his back to the defense attorneys as they argued the Freedom Riders' case, and when they were finished, he turned around and coldly announced sixty days in prison and a two-hundred-dollar fine for each and every Freedom Rider. On June 5, the jail terms were suspended, but some of the students had to work off their fines at three dollars a day at the notorious state penitentiary, the Parchman Farm. Lawson made bail and returned to Nashville, reporting that five of the riders were beaten by the guards in "an effort to intimidate us" at the prison farm. Meanwhile, new busloads of Freedom Riders had begun flooding into Jackson, and the arrests and jailings continued. In all, more than three hundred riders were arrested.

A naïve Robert Kennedy, in negotiations with Mississippi senator James Eastland, promised that the federal government would not use force in the state, as it had in Alabama, if there was no violence against the Freedom Riders. The dishonest Mississippi officials had something else in mind, and Kennedy, a New Englander who was not used to dealing with southern whites, failed to realize that authorities in Mississippi were mostly hardcore racists who were still fighting the Civil War nearly a hundred years after it had ended. They truly believed that they were subject only to decadent nineteenth-century state laws and not to those of the United States or any other "Yankee land." (Yet, these same racist officials had no objections to partaking of any federal monetary blessings, especially since Mississippi was the nation's most poverty-stricken state.) Thus, the arrangement that Mississippi authorities had worked out with Kennedy was bogus, designed mainly to avoid the embarrassment that a show of federal force on their territory would bring. Naturally, SNCC leaders were angry at the Kennedy administration for brokering the deal that allowed for the arrest of the Freedom Riders. SNCC would never forgive the Kennedy brothers.

On May 29, President Kennedy announced that he would ask the Interstate Commerce Commission (ICC) to declare segregation on interstate facilities null and void. The ICC did so on September 22, effective November 1, 1961. Meanwhile, as the *Memphis Press-Scimitar* reported on June 3, the Greyhound Bus Company declared that there was no segregation policy in any of its buses and facilities.

NCLC officers met with SNCC leaders at the latter's Jefferson Street office to review the situation and plan a course for further action, but Diane Nash revealed that Robert Kennedy wanted to meet with the Freedom Ride leaders on Friday, June 16, in Washington, D.C. She also informed the NCLC officers that the students planned a "Freedom Fast" for June 17 in Washington to force President Kennedy "to make a firm statement regarding civil rights of Freedom Riders, and that there are no further arrests on interstate travel." Lawson also wanted Negroes from Mississippi to start Freedom Rides on intrastate facilities: "Unless there are some people who are willing to do something about their tragic segregated plight, there is little that can be done quickly. Indigenous leadership is a must, and without it no significant gains are possible." James Bevel agreed: "If we cannot get Jackson people involved, we should get the Freedom Riders out of jail [and end the movement]." The NCLC voted to send Lawson with Nash, Bevel, and Joseph Ross, another SNCC member, to Mississippi in order to train and mobilize nonviolent local leadership to help with the struggle. The NCLC adopted the report, though it had no control over what SNCC was planning.

After being fined and sentenced to sixty days in prison, almost all the Freedom Riders were ultimately released. Civil rights lawyers got some demonstrators released on probation and shorter sentences. CORE was nearly bankrupted by the legal costs. The NAACP helped with its special fund, and the SCLC contributed eight thousand dollars. When some of the released students had a layover in Memphis as they traveled back to college in Nashville, large daily newspapers around the country obtained photographs of them from the Memphis papers. And as their faces, names, and arrest records were flashed to the public, they were depicted not as heroes but as troublemakers. Among those pictured were A&I students Lester G. McKinney, William

Mitchell, Allen Cason, and Larry Hunger, as well as Albert Dunn and William Barbee of American Baptist Seminary.

Governor Ellington was under intense pressure from segregationists and the governor of Alabama to take action against the students who had "invaded" Alabama and Mississippi. A number of A&I students—including Lucretia R. Collins, Carl Bush, Rudolph Graham, and Charles Butler—feared that they would not be allowed to graduate, but President Davis argued that Tennessee could not legally refuse to grant a diploma to a student who had completed all requirements as specified in the university's catalog. To do so would violate a legal contract. For their part, A&I faculty members refused to count the Freedom Riders as absent and even gave the students opportunities to make up missed work and exams.

Lucretia Collins, for one, posted five hundred dollars bond in Mississippi, flew to Memphis, and then traveled by bus to Nashville in time for exams and graduation. Intrusive reporters included a photograph of her and a friend in graduation attire. The A&I commencement exercises on May 29 were delayed two hours when students stood outside Kean Hall, refusing to march into the graduation arena unless all graduating seniors, including Freedom Riders, were allowed to receive their degrees at the last minute. It seemed that the governor, not Walter Davis, held the future of these young people in his hands. Faculty members, observing tradition, would also not move the processional line unless the students marched first. But an agreement was finally worked out, and amidst a loud cheer, the students marched into the arena to complete the graduation ceremonies. Ted R. Poston, an A&I graduate and *New York Post* reporter who had exposed Jim Crow brutalities in rural West Tennessee, was the commencement speaker.

Tennessee officials received numerous letters and telegrams pressuring them to take action against students and administrators at Tennessee A&I. One Nashville letter writer spoke for many conservative whites by demanding that Ellington and the State Board of Education enforce rules and regulations about class attendance and conduct against students who participated in the "assault on Alabama." Another said that a "large number of the students at Tennessee A&I seem to be more interested in their radical activities than in a concentrated pursuit of the education for which they are enrolled" and suggested that students from out of state, such as those from Michigan and California, should be "sent home." This familiar refrain of "outside agitation" was echoed throughout many of the letters. As a Memphis letter writer put it, "I am protesting against these so called Freedom Riders going all over the South stirring up trouble." Another wrote, "Such indoctrinated young 'carpetbaggers' and racial agitators have no place in any of the student bodies in Tennessee and should be finally removed from there as enemies of our beloved state and [southern] heritage." Some called for an investigation of Tennessee A&I itself, with one writer declaring, "The authorities at A&I must have given the green light *sub silento* to the troublemakers who invaded a sister state." Another called it "an offense to white taxpayers to support these students who comfort Communism and the NAACP." And on June 5, one man wrote to the commissioner of education to say, "Being a taxpayer, I am very much against the Nigger Freedom 'Raiders' being allowed to attend the A&I State institution that is supported by the Tax Payer money. I am for expelling the Niggers taking part in the agitation." In a form letter on June 9, Education Commissioner Joe Morgan assured the angry man that policies had been passed to deal with the students. It appeared that much of the letter writing had been instigated and coordinated by some segregationist organizations that even supplied the language for the letters: "taxpayers" and "tax-supported institution" were among the common words and phrases used. One woman admitted, "I am a member of Citizens for Constitutional Government." At least one letter came from a prominent Nashville businessman: the president of the Southern Colonial Furniture Manufacturing Company in Nashville wrote in support of expelling the Freedom Riders.

Although many letters condemned the students' actions, not all were unsympathetic. As James B. Thornton of Nashville asked on May 22: "Is it a crime for anyone to demand their rights?" Another writer urged the governor not to expel the students and thus identify Tennessee with the "bad elements" in Alabama. And one member of the State Board of Education's committee on academic policies, D. T. Wolcott, wrote angry letters to Commissioner Morgan and Governor Ellington about the intent to expel the students. He said:

> These policies were used as excuses to punish some Negro students
> and frighten others from exercising their [constitutional] privi-
> leges as American citizens on an equal basis with white people.
> The present administrations of Alabama and Mississippi may be
> grateful for this gesture of accord . . . You should be aware that
> in a decade or so the majority of Tennesseans will not honor the
> present state administrations for any act of discrimination. I cer-
> tainly hope the governor's administration will do all it can to per-
> mit equal treatment for all its citizens rather than to favor the few
> who wish to preserve the [Confederate] pride and [racial] preju-
> dice of yesterday.

Relations between the older civil rights activists and the students were not without their own tensions. The NCLC executive board had considered suspending the Freedom Rides, but the students had defiantly voted to continue them. At one point, Diane Nash diverted the NCLC's focus by telling them to do something about the condition of the student's office on Jefferson Street. "Students are assuming the role of adults," she complained, and they needed secretarial help. Increasingly worried about the battle raging in Mississippi, she dashed off in June to Jackson, where Bevel and Marion Barry had established nonviolence workshops. Kelly Miller Smith was unable to contact her there. Other NCLC officers complained that the students were not communicating to them about the situation in Mississippi. Rank-and-file SNCC members responded by complaining that Negro adults were not involved enough. At James Lawson's urging, the NCLC agreed to reimburse the original Freedom Riders for monetary losses: the organization paid William Harbour, for example, $38.50 for loss of property and also covered Jim Zwerg's $250.00 hospital bill. The NCLC also gave funds to John Lewis and Harbour to conduct nonviolence workshops and recruit students at the University of Minnesota. At the July 15 meeting of the NCLC, the officers voted to return their efforts to the local fight against Jim Crow. Lawson suggested a "total strategy" that would target hotels, restaurants, and public and private employment. He eagerly began to develop a set of comprehensive plans.

Around June 1, the administration of A&I convened a disciplinary committee consisting of Alger Boswell, Joseph A. Payne, Mable B. Crooks, Lewis R. Holland, Robert M. Murrell, Fred Bright, and M. L. Claiborne. All but Bright and Claiborne were top administrators. The committee began the process of expelling the students for having been "arrested and convicted for violating a Mississippi law and are now in litigation to prove or disprove the validity of that arrest and conviction, and in light of the policy of the State Board of Education must be suspended." On June 10, according to the *Memphis World*, A&I had placed fourteen students on the punishment list for taking part in the Freedom Rides and being arrested in Mississippi on breach-of-peace charges. On June 26, 1961, President Davis sent a single-spaced, double-column, five-page list of students to Joe Morgan at the State Board of Education, including ones with "10 quarters with a minimum scholarship standard 2.00," who were barred from re-enrolling at the university. Davis noted the fourteen students "jailed in Mississippi." A letter from Boswell, the head of the disciplinary committee, was attached to the list, showing which students had *already* been expelled. Among thirteen students on the list of definite expulsions, seven were from out of state.

The university's action against the students drew criticism from far and wide. "There are times when the most responsible members of society are the rebels, the insurgents, the law-breakers," said speaker Truman Douglass at the June 1961 Fisk commencement, "because society has settled down to tolerate injustice and iniquity and strong measures are needed to disturb the complacency." A member of CORE in Ohio wrote a letter of protest to Morgan, saying that the suspension of Pauline Knight (whose name had been mentioned in news reports) and other Freedom Riders for their beliefs was morally wrong: "Some of us Northerners dislike the racial views of some mountain boys who come here to take jobs away from our people, but we prefer to educate them to have 'better racial attitudes' than punish them." The NCLC and SNCC appointed a committee, among them Leo (Kwame) Lillard and the Reverend Smith, to meet with Morgan and Ellington and to demand that the state board rescind its order to dismiss the A&I students. However, the two state officials refused to receive the committee. In one attempt to reach the governor, SNCC spokesman John Lewis was told by Ellington's secretary that the governor would be out of town for a week. Hundreds of people—citizens as well as students and a few faculty members from Fisk, Tennessee State, and local high schools—marched on the State Capitol, singing civil rights songs and protesting the dismissals. Carl T. Rowan, a former A&I student and then a deputy assistant U.S. secretary of state for public affairs in the Kennedy administration, rejected an invitation to speak at the August 13, 1961, summer commencement at A&I, saying, "There is no secret about it—we all know they expelled 14 Tennessee State students for participating in the Freedom Rides. I attended school there for one year, but I disagree with their policy. My views [on civil rights] are known—I felt no useful purpose could be served at such a time by a speech, which would have embarrassed the administration."

The Williams and Looby law firm filed a suit in federal district court against President Davis, Governor Ellington, Joe Morgan, and the SBOE. Morgan assured other members of the board that the state attorney general would defend them and not to worry. The suit of *Pauline E. Knight, et al. v. State Board of Education for the State of Tennessee, et al.* was argued in court in October 1961. (Knight, the student named in the title of the suit, was from Nashville and about to graduate.) The state attorney general angrily claimed that the dismissals had nothing to do with race as Avon Williams, the attorney for the plaintiffs, contended. Williams was an expert at drawing angry white responses by exposing how ugly and personal racial prejudice was; often such responses simply confirmed what Williams was saying. On October 15, Judge William Ernest Miller ordered the state to allow the students to re-enroll at Tennessee A&I, pointing out that the students had been convicted under the state policies of "personal misconduct" in Alabama and Mississippi. He concluded that no misconduct had occurred in Tennessee or on the A&I campus; he also found that the university's disciplinary committee had not observed the students' right to due process. Morgan advised the board to comply with the order and told Davis to inform the students that they still could be expelled if they committed any infractions in Tennessee or if the state successfully appealed the decision in the Sixth Circuit Court.

[*]

On August 5, a few days after a SNCC leadership conference in Nashville, new demonstrations were mounted at various H. G. Hill's stores. Diane Nash, John Lewis, Andy Burns, Ruby Smith, Willie J. Thomas, and several others were arrested. James McDonald and Larry Hunter were among five persons hospitalized after altercations with policemen and thugs. Following a mass meeting called by the NCLC at the First Colored Baptist Church, nearly two hundred persons, including NCLC members and college students, staged a sit-down at the Nashville police station to protest police brutality. The police chief said that officers "only arrested those who violated the law." Reverend Smith told the newspapers: "It is strange the mayor would always be out of town when there is trouble." Some white women from the Highlander center were at the sit-down demonstration, but they were careful to avoid trouble. Highlander was waiting for the U.S. Supreme Court to act on its appeal of the Tennessee court decision to close the center. On August 11, Highlander held a workshop for SNCC leaders. Guy Carawan, a Highlander activist and folk-singer, helped to provide musical cadence and spiritual unity to the movement by popularizing and expanding "We Shall Overcome" and other songs. Diane Nash stayed in jail, but Reverend Smith arranged for her to have "tooth paste, book, ball point and writing paper." After her release, she headed to Mississippi to help in the voter registration drives that had begun on August 7. John Lewis, who became the new head of the Nashville Student Movement in September, later recalled, "The movement in Nashville actually shrank that year."

Upon returning to the A&I campus in September, students showed their displeasure about the treatment of the Freedom Riders and the continued resistance to desegregation of all downtown businesses. One newspaper headline said, "A&I Students Resent Board's Ruling." Some two hundred students demonstrated outside President Davis's office, singing, "Take me to jail, I shall not be removed." On Monday night, September 11, they gathered in front of the iron gates on Centennial Boulevard, singing civil rights songs and holding signs bearing slogans such as "Faculty do you Support Segregation?" and "A&I, Which side you on?"

The freedom riders returning to A&I included Catherine Burks (later Brooks), Frederick Leonard, Ernest Patton, Clarence Wright, and Charles Butler. The A&I student newspaper pictured the students chatting during a break outside the court room. Two students remained on academic suspension. Lester McKinney, Mary Jean Smith, William Mitchell, Larry Hunter, Etta Simpson, Frances Wilson, William Harbour, and Allen Cason did not immediately return. When asked if they would participate in another Freedom Ride again, the students gave an enthusiastic "Yes!"

The Nashville Christian Leadership Conference was now faced with financial burdens of the Freedom Rides, as well as one sticky matter that alarmed NCLC preachers: four or five students, male and female, had taken to living in the SNCC space on Jefferson Street, which was rented with NCLC funds. This embarrassment led the executive board of NCLC to close the office. At the time, the main SNCC leaders were all down in Mississippi, organizing voters and recruiting white helpers. The financially strapped NCLC asked the SCLC to share the Freedom Ride expenses, but an SCLC official replied that they had no more money. NCLC members then proposed sending money to SCLC to help save the parent organization. Lawson, however, suggested that Smith call the SCLC himself to determine whether funds might in fact be forthcoming to the NCLC. This time the answer was yes, and three thousand dollars soon arrived. CORE, meanwhile, tried to cut expenses by recommending that the students, who were being recalled to Mississippi for trial, take the jail sentences and release some bail money.

The SCLC held its convention in Nashville on September 27, 1961, when the NCLC and SCLC took the opportunity to cosponsor a fund-raising concert by Harry Belafonte at the Ryman Auditorium and a "Freedom Mass Meeting" at the War Memorial Building. Lawson began pushing the two organizations to recruit a nonviolent army of ten thousand to carry the fight through the South. But King and other leaders thought that this tactic would only provoke race radicals to greater violence. In December 1961, SCLC, NCLC, and the American Baptist Convention announced five-hundred-dollar scholarships to help Cason and other Freedom Riders. They scheduled the scholarship ceremony for the Ryman Auditorium.

To redirect attention to Nashville, a number of local groups met on October 21 to form the "ad hoc Coordinating Council." President Wright of

Fisk agreed to serve as chairman. But the council was hopeless, concluded John Lewis, who believed that the NAACP, SCLC, NSM, SNCC, and other civil rights group would never obey a central authority. Still, the NCLC voted to remain in the council, make suggestions to it, and continue specific NCLC activities. The NCLC board added some white members, Will D. Campbell and Walter Harrelson, a Vanderbilt divinity professor, who served on a team to negotiate desegregation plans with Nashville power brokers. In the meantime, James Lawson worked on developing a "Blueprint for Action" in Nashville, and late in 1961, Kelly Miller Smith announced that he would step down as NCLC president to allow the "leadership to rotate" as the SNCC did with its officers.

National NAACP leaders remained suspicious of the student movement. Thurgood Marshall reportedly told local civil rights lawyers that the student demonstrations in Nashville would work against the NAACP's court initiatives. Some students remembered being chided by Marshall when he spoke in Nashville. "If someone offers to get you out [of jail], man, get out," he told them. And according to John Lewis, Roy Wilkins of the NAACP did not trust SNCC and SCLC people and was especially jealous of King for hogging the national spotlight. The NAACP also avoided contact with the Southern Students Organization Committee, formed in Nashville by two white Methodists, because the organization "seemed to have socialist leanings."

The Freedom Rides became one of the most memorable chapters in the civil rights movement, and it continues to be celebrated. For instance, on May 10–12, 2001, "The 40th Anniversary Ride to Freedom, 1961–2001" was held, beginning in Washington, D.C., with programs in Atlanta, Anniston, Birmingham, and Montgomery. Congressman John Lewis of Atlanta led the reunion that was designed to teach young people about the civil rights movement. Jim Zwerg, aged sixty-one, participated in the program, which was sponsored by several corporations, including the Greyhound Bus Company. In the printed program, Greyhound's president declared, "Retracing this historic journey on its 40th anniversary gives us the opportunity to recognize and honor those who started it. But we must also remember that they were stopped short of their destination. The last leg of their journey remains un-traveled. It is up to us to advance the journey, to continue to build a nation of communities and companies with fair and equal opportunity for everyone, to be the shoulders that will lift up the next generation. As we do this, we pay tribute to the Freedom Riders."

However, in the midst of such attention, Nashville has often been overlooked. No events were held there during the fortieth-anniversary celebrations in spring 2001. And in November 2001, a Freedom Riders Reunion was held at Tougaloo College, Mississippi, with little mention of Nashville's role. Also, most books on the civil rights movement give no credit to the NCLC for financing the Freedom Ride project and the pivotal role played by the NSM and the SNCC leaders from Tennessee.

[*]

In Nashville in February 1962, the NCLC and local college students held "sleep-ins" at Jim Crow hotels, launched more economic boycotts, and held "stand-ins" at segregated theaters. C. M. Hayes, the NAACP branch president and a member of the NCLC board, was pushing a selective boycott, while urging Negroes to "continue to support independent Negro businesses." Bernard Lafayette headed to Selma, Alabama, to help with the SNCC effort to galvanize the Negroes there. Reverend Smith and Will Campbell became members of the mayor's Human Relations Committee to handle biracial problems. Smith, Campbell, Lawson, Looby, Andrew White, Avon Williams, Lewis, Lafayette, and twenty-one others held a meeting to discuss ways the local NAACP and NCLC could cooperate. Looby convinced them it was best for each organization to operate in its own sphere.

Kelly Miller Smith remained effective in negotiating desegregation settlements with reluctant storeowners. Smith persuaded L. D. Langford to open his restaurant in the WLAC Towers to Negro diners. Reluctant at first, Langford told Smith that he had nothing against "colored people," including his Negro maid of sixteen years, but added, "Some southern whites could break a restaurant if they refused to eat with colored people." He explained, "If we all open up, then they can either eat with them or stay home, which some will do. If Langford's lets those [Negroes] in, the whites will go to Cross Keys Restaurant." He said that the Restaurant Association had voted against integration and that the head of the association would not budge, especially against the management of Cross Keys and the B&W Cafeteria. The latter two owners were radically opposed to admitting Negroes.

Smith asked Langford if it would help to send controlled groups of well-trained demonstrators to Langford's Restaurant. "Send no one until I talk to the others," the proprietor answered. "The integrated restaurants are losing money, and one of the owners only did it because he is running for public office." Smith then said, "I believe it would be better to keep all this out of the papers." Langford agreed that one had "to educate some people, first," adding, "It [desegregation] is definitely coming, and right-thinking people should accept it." Smith said, "We want to make it as painless as possible for the restaurant owners." He agreed to send his best-trained demonstrators, and Langford told him that his personnel would not attack anyone. But, he added, "We are a little afraid of what some of our customers might do." He asked Smith to avoid the profitable lunch hour and use the less profitable late-evening hours for the demonstrations. Smith said he would consult with the NCLC board, while Langford said he would talk to Restaurant Association members. Smith asked Langford's to let the other business owners know the NCLC would work with them through the desegregation process. And in 1963, Langford did desegregate his restaurant, an action for which Smith sent him a letter: "We appreciate the courageous stand you have made in the interest of all citizens of this community. It is still the goal of NCLC and shall remain our goal to make Nashville the beloved community, a city without a Color Line."

In 1962, the NCLC was developing other tactics. C. T. Vivian came up with the idea of "kneel-ins," which would take the movement to white Christians and compel them to make a moral decision. If members of white churches turned Negroes away, the demonstrators were instructed to go outside the building and kneel and pray. "Drop-ins" on segregated restaurants was another new tactic: women were to stop by a segregated restaurant and ask for service; if refused, they were to ask for the manager, leave a protest note, and then vacate the premises. Unfortunately, in August the NCLC lost its strategist. The Methodist Church assigned James M. Lawson Jr. to a Memphis church. The NCLC issued a statement that read in part: "In the position of Projects Committee Chairman, James Lawson has been the chief person responsible for the nonviolence training of participants in the Nashville desegregation movement. It was his suggestion that nonviolence become one of the tenets of the Nashville Christian Leadership Council."

By then, the NCLC was complaining that the *Banner* and the *Tennessean* were not reporting on the local civil rights movement and that the police did nothing about the recent attacks by thugs on young demonstrators. The mass meetings at local churches continued, while Looby lost the vote in the city council for an anti-discrimination bill—even though the recent turning away of ten young Negro women from the Central YWCA showed how badly such local laws were needed. Meanwhile, A&I students Lester McKinney and Frederick Leonard were arrested for trying to enter the Tic Toc restaurant. An employee met them at the door and reportedly said, "We don't serve Niggers here, and you isn't going to get inside." The students sat down on the sidewalk. John Lewis was arrested with them.

Diane Nash, Jessie Bevel, Marion Barry, and other SNCC leaders were pushing a movement in Mississippi to get the Negroes—52 percent of the state's population—to register and vote. Most Negroes in Mississippi were afraid to speak to the student organizers at all. The jails filled up with SNCC volunteers, often with twelve persons sleeping on a concrete floor in a cell, eating rice and gravy in a flat pan with dry bread and drinking water from a faucet. When jail sentences of sixty days or more did not seem to work, Mississippi's race radicals resorted to outright violence and even murder of civil rights workers, black and white.

In December 1962, noting the upcoming one hundredth anniversary of the Emancipation Proclamation, President Kennedy again asked all Americans to respect the rights of all citizens, regardless of creed, color, or religion. When the anniversary occurred on January 1, 1963, the NAACP's slogan— "Free by '63"—had not been fulfilled, and white supremacy still reigned. On February 28, Kennedy presented a special message to Congress on civil rights, borrowing from Justice John Marshall Harlan's dissenting opinion in the 1896 *Plessy* decision: "Our Constitution is colorblind and neither knows nor tolerates classes among citizens." JFK's remarks sounded much like the strong statement President James A. Garfield had made in 1881 after being petitioned by J. C. Napier and other black Tennesseans. "There is no middle ground for the Negro race between slavery and equal citizenship," Garfield said. "There can be no permanent disenfranchised peasantry in the United States." Kennedy reminded Congress that it had obligations to pass civil rights legislation. The *Report of the U.S. Commission on Civil Rights* (1963) recommended removal of "all vestiges of racial discrimination, adoption of affirmative programs . . . Although the nation's struggle to redeem the promise of its ideals is primarily a domestic problem, it is also of worldwide concern. The nation now appears to be moving toward the eradication of slavery's lingering after effects. At this time in our history, we must fulfill the promise of America to all this country's citizens, or give up our best hope for national greatness."

The NCLC found itself dealing mostly with a new generation of young people not trained so carefully in discipline and nonviolence. By early 1963, students from Pearl High School and local colleges were gathering at 8:30 A.M. at First Colored Baptist Church and marching on downtown stores still opposed to integration. At Tennessee A&I, the campus newspaper, the *Meter,* was publishing pictures of the demonstrations, and leaders on the campus were filling the void left by the most experienced of the SNCC leaders who had gone to Mississippi. Some marches resulted in violence between Negro and white youths. Black youngsters grabbed police billy clubs and pushed the whites who were spitting on them and yelling racist epithets. One student, fearing another sermon, refused to return to the staging area, saying, "I am not going back to that church." And indeed, before a gathering at his church, Smith said, "Violence is a negative and destructive force which seriously hampers the positive and creative forces working toward the resolution of our problems." He assured the press: "We deplore violence." The audience sang "We Shall Overcome" and prayed.

A rock-throwing battle in the spring of 1963 between carloads of verbally abusive white youths circling FCBC and young demonstrators caused the NCLC to move some of its meetings, because, according to an NCLC memorandum, FCBC "was rapidly becoming a hated symbol of the movement. We are afraid someone might want to destroy it." One newspaper claimed that seven hundred students skipped classes at Negro high schools and Tennessee State to participate in illegal demonstrations. Williams and Looby tried unsuccessfully to get Criminal Court Judge John L. Draper to allow a retrial of nine demonstrators. John Lewis and other student leaders met with the mayor, who asked for a moratorium on the demonstrations until the Human Relations Committee could meet. The Nashville NAACP, NCLC, and the Human Relations Committee all supported the moratorium. Lewis said, "There are definite signs we are moving into the beloved community and we will get there. . . . It is this reality of purpose I believe our young people need in order to rededicate their lives and their sacred honor. Our aim is to desegregate all public places in Nashville. That will enable us to move from desegregation to integration. Through disciplined action, we can transform this community."

The NCLC and other local civil rights groups tried to keep the NSM participants in the fold of a nonviolent movement. In 1963, John Lewis was inaugurated as an officer in the NCLC, along with Kelly Miller Smith, Mrs. Matthew Walker, Mrs. J. B. Singleton, Vivian Horsely, Mrs. William Wheeler, Reverend A. M. Anderson, Elder H. E. Braden, Reverend J. Metz Rollins, Reverend Grady Donald, and Frankie M. Blakely, who was named executive secretary. The organization demanded more Negro policemen and promotions for existing ones and also voted to hire John Lewis at forty dollars a week to officially coordinate the student activities. Lewis, however, shortly resigned his positions to become national head of SNCC in Atlanta. "It is not that I am leaving you," he said, "but rather joining you in a fuller sense." Lester McKinney, a student at Tennessee State, replaced Lewis at the NCLC, and another student, Paul Brooks, was placed on the NCLC board. Both promised the older members that they would be invited to student meetings and that demonstrators would be better coordinated. "Our ultimate concern," Smith said, "is to move 'Toward the Beloved Community' . . . in Nashville."

The NCLC allowed public demonstrations to continue, but they coupled them with an economic boycott. In April 1963, the NCLC urged all Negroes to keep their money in their pockets until they gained total and complete freedom. "Indications are strong," said Smith, "that the economic boycott launched several weeks ago by the Council is beginning to have its effect." And Vivian Henderson called employment "still the number one problem here." Students from Vanderbilt and Peabody, among white colleges, participated in the downtown marches. The NCLC supported the student demonstrations at the B&W Cafeteria in May.

The economic aspect of the Nashville protests was certainly in keeping with the aims of the larger civil rights movement. "The damage to Negroes is psychological," said James Farmer of CORE, "and it is also economic." Or, as Will Campbell put it, "The heart of the racial problem is economic. Many Negroes are in revolt, not because they are discriminated against but because they are poor." Even so, to many engaged in the struggle, problems of perception remained essential. Malcolm X said, "You will never get the American white man to accept the so-called Negro as an integrated part of his society until the image of the Negro the white man has is changed, and until the image that the Negro has of himself also is changed."

As the demonstrations continued, there was some help from the U.S. Supreme Court, which declared that arrest and conviction of peaceful sit-in demonstrators was unconstitutional. In May 1963, the court ruled in *Peterson v. Greenville* that when police become involved in removing demonstrators from private establishments, discrimination is then supported by local laws, customs, and public officials.

Apart from the societal injustices the Nashville demonstrations were confronting, activists also had to deal with the persistence of generational tensions within the movement itself. Often, once a targeted demonstration ended, the youngsters, instead of returning to First Baptist, went on their own to stores not on the list, which caused some businessmen to bemoan "blanket boycotts after some of us had made desegregation agreements." The church trustees also began to complain about cigarette butts left in the sanctuary, profanity, rock throwing, soft drink bottles on the church grounds, unauthorized use of the church kitchen, interruption of the church secretary's daily duties, and the inclusion of some individuals who provoked violence from white thugs and radicals. On May 14, 1963, Smith wrote the NCLC board: "The facilities of First Baptist Church shall not—from the present—be available as a launching place for demonstrations. (This should not be construed to mean that First Baptist is 'out of the movement' or that this is a permanent arrangement.)" He was concerned that the "image of the church is getting somewhat out of balance."

Possible infiltration of the movement became yet another concern. Certain people were suspected of being employed by government intelligence agencies or racist organizations. It was feared that such entities had placed "volunteers" within the movement whose mission was to carry out sabotage and espionage. Responding to this ominous possibility, Reverend Smith suggested some intensive nonviolence workshops, reform of the movement's objectives and relationships, and filming of demonstrations to pick out individuals "who identify with the movement but whose motives are different." The NCLC board recommended that more college students supervise the secondary school students and bring them back to the church after the demonstrations. On June 1963, Smith announced that the boycott had been lifted but that Negroes should avoid doing business where they had made no gains in employment, including the YMCA, YWCA, Baptist Hospital, St. Thomas Hospital, and most of the city's hotels.

It appeared in September 1963 that the Nashville movement was losing another one of its top leaders when the Reverend Kelly Miller Smith went to Cleveland to assume a new pastorate. "The progress of civil rights in Nashville has been encouraging, but not always as rapid as it could have been," said Smith in his farewell speech at First Colored Baptist Church. Smith left Nashville just as Vivian was departing for Chattanooga and the Reverend Claude Walker and the Reverend J. Metz Rollins, two other strong leaders, were also leaving the city. When students were pictured at First Colored Baptist Church with upraised fists in a militant, black power stance, vowing to continue the marches, the mayor said that no such displays would have happened if the Reverend Smith had still been in town. Some claimed that Smith had only left Nashville to allow some militancy to creep into the local movement without compromising his peaceful reputation. However, Smith would not be gone for long. When FCBC members voted to bring him back to their pulpit, he accepted their offer and returned to Nashville in January 1964. And later that year, Vivian, Metz, and John Lewis would return briefly to help out after they heard news reports of police brutality against high-school-age demonstrators in Nashville.

[∗]

During this time, of course, Nashville was hardly alone among Tennessee cities in the ongoing civil rights struggle. About 130 miles southeast of the capital, the Chattanooga NAACP and other local activists tested the limits of segregation in May 1963 with demonstrations at downtown stores, theaters, and cafeterias. Whites typically responded by turning them away or otherwise refusing them service, and a few demonstrators, including the Reverend A. Eberhardt, were arrested at Krystal Restaurant. At the S&W Cafeteria, workers blocked the doors, allowing only white customers to enter. At other businesses, Negroes were refused service as they sat at tables by themselves.

To quiet racial tensions in Chattanooga, C. B. Robinson and others met with the police chief, while James Mapp, the Reverend Cordell H. Sloan (chair of the local CORE chapter), and other leaders answered the Mayor Ralph Kelly's call to discuss recent sit-in demonstrations. Mapp and the local NAACP declared a truce with the city and noted, "Negroes reportedly have made some gains though negotiations started as the result of the truce agreement." Mapp called for a freedom rally at Orchard Knob Baptist Church to raise funds and help families in the Birmingham movement. In June, Mapp, Sloan, Robinson, and others met with the mayor, representatives of the Chamber of Commerce, and others to work out more desegregation. To resist these efforts, the White Citizens Council also met with the mayor, demanding that the police "do their duty." The mayor, who had sponsored segregation legislation when he was a state representative, now pledged to do "what is best for the city," pointing out the need for law, order, racial peace, new industry, and new jobs for Chattanooga. In July 1963, some seventy restaurants and establishments agreed to desegregate. The mayor and the city commission declared all facilities open regardless of race and color. The mayor told a local Lions Club luncheon that Chattanooga had been called "an oasis in a desert of trouble."

That same summer, C. B. Robinson became one of a number of Negro leaders to meet with President Kennedy as he was pressing Congress to pass a new civil rights bill. A June 15 telegram from the president invited Robinson and other education leaders to the White House later that month. Chattanooga teachers and union organizations helped raise travel money for Robinson, and they publicized the invitation widely to show that a local Negro leader had national clout. Upon arriving in Washington on a Greyhound bus, he first walked to the offices of union labor chiefs he knew. Shortly afterward, at the meeting with Kennedy, the president laid out his legislative program, which included proposals for improving education and race relations in the country. Tennessee civil rights lawyers R. E. Lillard, R. B. Sugarmon, and

A. W. Willis Jr. were also among the invitees. That same month, Kennedy made a major televised speech on the race issue, saying in part, "We preach freedom here at home, but are we to say to the world and, much more importantly, to each other that this is a land of the free except for the Negroes; that we have no class or caste system, no ghettos, no master race except with respect to Negroes?" Back in Chattanooga, Robinson sent a "Thank You" letter to the president.

[*]

It was also during the spring and summer of 1963 that A. Philip Randolph and other civil rights leaders began organizing a "March on Washington" to exert greater pressure on Congress for passage of Kennedy's civil rights legislation. Randolph's Brotherhood of Sleeping Car Porters had become part of the AFL-CIO body of labor unions, which had supported the *Brown* decision and even declared in the *AFL-CIO News* (Dec. 17, 1955): "The AFL-CIO always believes in the principle and practice of equal rights for all, regardless of race, color, creed or national origin." Randolph had begun working on the idea of the Washington march in March but felt it was best for the NAACP to take the lead, since that organization, above all others, had truly begun the civil rights movement in the 1930s. In planning the march, Roy Wilkins agreed to call the initial meeting at the NAACP's New York office, inviting CORE, SCLC, and SNCC as principal co-organizers. The SCLC, only five years old at that time, was included because other civil rights leaders did not dare exclude Dr. King, whom they needed for broad media attention and the support of southern black churches. And, of course, the students would raise a public outcry if SNCC was left out. White liberal leaders and their organizations, such as the American Jewish Congress and the National Council of Churches, were also included to dispel white liberal opposition to the idea of the march. These whites, Kennedy among them, feared that black radicals might be featured too prominently as speakers and that this would further galvanize white resistance to the civil rights movement.

The Reverend C. T. Vivian served as Tennessee chairman of the March on Washington. One Washington-bound bus left from Tennessee Voters Council headquarters on Ninth Street in Chattanooga, while delegates from Fayette County, Memphis, and other parts of Tennessee went to Nashville, where buses picked up hundreds of march participants on August 27. Delores Wilkinson, a member of FCBC, remembered leaving a week earlier from Nashville to help "make signs once we arrived in D.C." Arriving on buses and trains and in private cars, hundreds of thousands of people converged at the Lincoln Memorial on August 28. It was the largest gathering of people for a civil rights demonstration in the history of the nation, and it came just one day after the death, in Africa, of the famed black leader, author, and NAACP cofounder W. E. B. DuBois. Many congressmen who opposed civil rights legislation had left town rather than witness the spectacle of unwanted Negroes marching on the U.S. capital. A long line of noted civil rights leaders addressed the huge crowd. John Lewis agreed to tone down the militant speech he had originally intended to give so as not to offend any white supporters. James Farmer was absent, having been jailed in Louisiana for civil rights protests. Martin Luther King Jr. was the last in a long list of speakers, capturing the spotlight with his famous "I Have a Dream" speech. President Kennedy met with the leaders of the march that day and renewed his promises to push the civil rights bill.

There were various reactions to the march. One negative assessment came from Malcolm X, an opponent of social integration and a spokesman for the Nation of Islam, a separatist organization. He had not been invited to participate in the march and called it a farce:

> The white liberals took over the March on Washington, weakened its impact, and changed its course; by changing the participants and the contents, they were able to change the very nature of the march itself. The whites didn't integrate it; they infiltrated it. It ceased to be a black march; it ceased to be militant; it ceased to be angry; it ceased to be impatient. In fact it ceased to be a march. It became a picnic, an outing with a festive, circus like atmosphere. White liberals who joined the march led the marchers *away* from the White House, the Senate, the Congress, Capitol Hill, and *away* from victory. They told those Negroes what signs to carry, what songs to sing, what speeches to make, and then told the marchers to be sure to get out of town by sundown, and all of them were out of town by sundown.

The day after the march, the *Union City Daily Messenger* in Obion County reported, "Demonstrators, tired and quiet, headed home in their special buses and trains. By 9 A.M., D.C. police reported the city normal." John Lewis said the March on Washington "was a truly stunning spectacle in terms of showing America and the world the size and the strength and the spirit of our movement." A. Philip Randolph declared, "The march has already achieved its objectives. It has awakened and aroused the conscience of the nation." The *Nashville Banner* expressed fears about more Negro militancy, and one FBI memorandum said, "In light of King's powerful and demagogic speech yesterday . . . he stands head and shoulders over all other Negro leaders put together when it comes to influencing great masses of Negroes. We must mark him now, if we have not done so before, as the most dangerous Negro of the future in this nation from the standpoint of communism, the Negro, and national security."

In April 1963, the SCLC already had begun demonstrations in Birmingham, demanding fair employment, desegregation of public facilities, and dropping charges against the demonstrators. Then, barely two weeks after the March on Washington, radical segregationists took control of Birmingham and used bombs to murder four Negro children in a Sunday school classroom on September 15. It was the city's twenty-ninth bombing since 1951. Lawson went to Birmingham to lend support. SNCC personnel arrived with renewed plans to march on that town, but Fred Shuttlesworth, King, and other leaders would not allow a march to overshadow the funeral for the four little girls. The Reverend Shuttlesworth was concerned that "we not lose the initiative in our struggle." The Nashville Christian Leadership Council voted to send money to the girls' families. Even the *Banner's* James G. Stahlman was listed as contributing $250 of the $402.50 raised among Nashville's downtown businessmen. The *Tennessean* gave $20. King, Shuttlesworth, and others met with Kennedy at the White House and received his assurances that the government "would not stand idly by and allow the lives and property and rights of Negro citizens to be trampled." The president sent hundreds of federal officers to Birmingham.

But on the fateful day of November 22, just two months later, President Kennedy was murdered while riding in a motorcade in Dallas. Unfortunately, he died before a civil rights bill could be passed into law; the legislation had not escaped the delaying tactics of southern obstructionists and other racial conservatives in Congress. As the president's death was dramatized on television, many in the Negro community in Tennessee and elsewhere mourned the loss, feeling that the Kennedy administration had reached out to black citizens and their causes. Others, however, felt that he had not done enough, and SNCC, for one, did not send an official delegation to the funeral.

[*]

In Nashville, NCLC leaders were trying to find a new direction for the movement. They continued to deal with some token desegregated establishments, including Hill's Stores. The NCLC put together a biracial negotiating team, consisting of Walter Harrelson, Delois Wilkinson, Elizabeth Harbour, and seven others, which divided into groups of three and approached downtown businessmen. Kelly Miller Smith was voted back on to the NCLC board. Marion Barry, meanwhile, asked NCLC to sponsor another student retreat in Nashville; such a meeting, he thought, could reaffirm SNCC's commitment to the nonviolent movement. In February 1964, Inman Otey of NCLC, Lester McKinney of the local SNCC, and A. M. Anderson of Clark Memorial Church invited John Lewis, the head of SNCC, to speak at the Freedom Rally at Mount Zion Baptist Church. Lewis told the audience to "work for more civil rights. The federal government must step in and oversee voter registration the same way it got James Meredith into the University of Mississippi if need be." NCLC leaders held other mass meetings, including one at Fisk University in early May at which Dr. King warned of "another sweltering summer of discontent." At one rally, a Vanderbilt faculty member spoke for freedom and justice. Two former Nashvillians, C. T. Vivian and J. Metz Rollins, visited the city and urged local Negroes to end "Stand Stillism." A Nashville rabbi, Randall Falk, banded with church leaders to call for biracial church services and other measures.

The downtown marches in Nashville were becoming disorganized and less disciplined, forcing FCBC to issue new regulations for use of its facilities: no grade school students were allowed; smoking in the sanctuary and damage to the building would not be tolerated; and there was to be no unauthorized use of the telephone, kitchen, or organ. "First Baptist Church," the trustees said, "has been and still is deeply involved in the purposeful activities of NCLC and the Student Nonviolent Movement. It has provided a physical base for your operations. In order to continue using these facilities, great care must be exercised on the part of the users in protecting the physical properties of the church. We feel that you're interested in preserving these facilities rather than destroying them."

At the state capitol, Frank Clement, previously a two-term governor (1953–59), returned to the office in 1963, succeeding Buford Ellington. By executive order on July 1 of that year, Clement created the Tennessee Commission on Human Relations (TCHR) to work for improved race relations. However, the TCHR had little power, except to try to persuade state agencies to comply with desegregation directives.

By the spring of 1964, the tenth anniversary of *Brown*, Negro leaders were upset with Clement's stalling on approval of recent recommendations by the TCHR, which urged total desegregation of all schools and public accommodations. Since 1954, only 44 of Tennessee's 144 school districts had been desegregated. Negro leaders also wanted Clement to sign a bill establishing a code of fair employment, but the governor refused to do so on grounds that the bill was vaguely in conflict with Tennessee law. A. W. Willis, vice chairman of the commission, joined others in criticizing Clement for "foot dragging on civil rights," saying, "It is time for the state to step out and take the lead." Clement, however, was nervously waiting for federal civil rights legislation to pass and take him off the hook. At the municipal level in 1964, Councilman R. E. Lillard took up the anti-discrimination bill Z. A. Looby had previously pushed, because the new mayor, Beverly Briley, continued to stall the legislation despite protest demonstrations in front of his office.

Andrew White, an AME Church minister, headed the NCLC in what would prove to be its final year. "We are in a fierce struggle here in Nashville," the Reverend White said, as he complained of "token Integration in Nashville, which is the new term that might well characterize Nashville unless we Negroes wake up and do more than we are now doing. It allows for *some* breakdown of racial segregation but seeks to *preserve*, in practice, the established patterns of segregation. It is intended to prevent sizable social change, which favors the Negro. Progress in desegregation is achieved in direct ratio to the pressure exerted by Negroes." In the four years since the original sit-in demonstrations, some restaurants in the downtown Arcade, a shopping mall, still refused to serve or hire the poor and working-class blacks who rode the city buses and frequented the Arcade. "NCLC must continue its efforts toward a greater understanding and tolerance of all mankind," White said. He sent a protest letter to the city, charging that the arrests of young civil rights demonstrators on April 20 was "definitely characterized by police brutality." White asked for an investigation, which the police chief reluctantly agreed to do, while telling White that such accusations had better be based on good evidence and not on mere emotions. NCLC officers began cooperating with other church associations, including the National Council of Churches' Commission on Religion and Race, to further change things in Nashville, and they met with the local Interdenominational Ministers Alliance to determine how involved they should be in the 1964 presidential elections and how to interface with recently formed Negro organizations.

The NCLC had entered 1964 with a deficit of $3,218. White asked local Negro sororities and fraternities to send funds, saying, "The future of the NCLC is at stake. There are many court cases still pending in our city. We would not want to fold and leave the students to serve time, who fought so hard for the rights of us all." The organizations responded, and so did some white churches, including the First Unitarian Church. White even sent some of the money to the SCLC to help ease the parent organization's own financial difficulties. "In triumph and defeat, in hope and despair," King responded, "your [NCLC] partnership in our common struggle has helped to keep us going." Much of White's time was taken up in meetings with Looby and Williams, arranging bail and court dates for demonstrators on bond. Many of the protesters went home for the summer break, but White wrote letters and sent checks to pay for their bus fares back to Nashville.

[*]

While Lawson, Smith, the NCLC, and the college students were finally getting black Nashville to move against segregated establishments in late 1959, the movement against Jim Crow by adult leaders in Memphis was well on its way to maturity. On January 6, 1960, in an elaborate downtown ceremony that drew more than a thousand spectators, Henry Loeb took the oath as Memphis mayor; a set of independent commissioners and new school board members were also sworn in. All of these officials were hardcore segregationists who meant to hold the line against any Negro uprising in Memphis—the "capital" of the Mississippi Delta. Federal District Judge Marion S. Boyd was still sitting on the city bus desegregation suit that O. Z. Evers had initiated in 1956, as well as on Jessie Turner's 1959 suit to desegregate the public libraries. Boyd also ignored repeated inquiries by H. T. Lockard about Tarlease Matthews's suit against the Jim Crow city zoo and parks. With the local federal judge seemingly behind them and the Negro's 1959 attempt to share political power having met disappointment, city government officials felt confident that Jim Crow would prevail and live long and heartily in Memphis, Tennessee.

However, the Negro leaders of Memphis were determined to continue their push for equality and justice. On January 16, 1960, the *World* reported that O. Z. Evers, leader of the Binghamton Civic League, had begun unionizing the twelve hundred Negro city garbage workers. "I think it's a shame and a disgrace," he said, "for a man in this day and age not to be able to take home at least a $60 per week check." Evers worked with the International Brotherhood Teamsters of America, Local No. 94, to sign up about 150 garbage workers, and held a rally at which Teamsters addressed drew a crowd of two hundred, according the *Tri-State Defender* (Mar. 19, 1960). Evers tried to meet with Public Commissioner William Farris, who refused to recognize Evers as a union representative. Farris claimed that the garbage men wanted nothing to do with a union, bragging that they made $1.40 to $1.44 per hour and received $92.00 per year in fringe benefits.

On January 10, 1960, NAACP officers and other Negro leaders were turned away when they tried to attend an auto show sponsored by the Memphis Automobile Dealers' Association at the city's downtown Ellis Auditorium. Neither elite-class Negroes nor any other blacks were welcome to mingle with whites of whatever class in Memphis. At a mass meeting at the Pentecostal Temple Church of God in Christ that followed, Ben Hooks, A. W. Willis, and Jessie H. Turner, chairman of the local NAACP, were selected to head the yet-to-be named "protest group," according to the *Memphis World* (Jan. 20, 1960). W. O. Speight and Vasco Smith manned a table that collected $157 for legal fees. The group's leaders then called a meeting on January 22 at the offices of the North Carolina Mutual Insurance Company branch at 571 Vance Avenue. At a later mass meeting at the nearby Mt. Nebo Baptist Church on Vance, the group took the informal name "Memphis and Shelby County Improvement League," with R. B. Sugarmon and Hooks as head officers. Hooks and Sugarmon issued a statement: "The City of Memphis consistently and repeatedly denies the Negro citizens their constitutional rights and equal protection under the laws." The *World* (Feb. 2, 1960) called for total desegregation of the city.

The civil rights movement was becoming infectious across Tennessee, reaching even deeper into Memphis. On February 27—the day on which dozens of Nashville sit-in demonstrators were arrested and jailed—the *World* reported that the Memphis Board of Censors had banned the movie *Island in the Sun* from showing in Beale Street theaters or anywhere in Memphis because it depicted interracial love between characters played by Harry Belafonte and Joan Fontaine. By March 2, the *Memphis World* was carrying pictures and stories of the student sit-ins in Nashville; one large photograph showed the Nashville demonstrators sitting at the McLellan's lunch counter reading books. The newspaper was also devoting ample space to the Negro voter-registration movement in adjacent Fayette and Haywood counties and related mass meetings at Clayborn Temple AME Church near Beale Street.

Demonstrators from LeMoyne College began their own sit-in movement in Memphis on March 18, when about twelve students took seats at McLellan's lunch counter on Main Street; they left without being arrested after the manager closed the counter. The next day, LeMoyne students entered the white library branches on Front Street and Peabody Street because they "needed some more books for their term papers and study." Some students from the other historically black college in Memphis, Owen Junior College, would join the demonstrations. The Brooks Memorial Art Galley on Poplar Avenue was also targeted for a sit-in by the young protestors. Some thirty-six students were arrested and jailed for loitering, disorderly conduct, and breach of peace, among them Ernestine Lee, "Miss LeMoyne." These so-called foot soldiers who started the Memphis movement also included Ronald S. Anderson, Claree Avant, Rosetta J. Bonds, Jean F. Brown, James Cleaves, Frank Cole, Mattie M. Daniels, Charles Gregory, Bernice Hightower, Carol A. Hooks, Rose Lee Ingram, Jo Iris, Willie Jamerson, Bernie May Johnson, Johnnie Naylor, Virginia Owens, Harold O. Ransom, Kathy J. Robinson, Darnell L. Thomas, Dorothy Truitt, and Curtis Williams. Several newspeople were arrested just for covering the protests and "talking too loud," including editors and photographers for the *Memphis World* and *Tri-State Defender*, which duly reported the arrests (see *World*, Mar. 23, 1960, and *Defender*, Mar. 26, 1960). This event galvanized the black community, and D. S. Cunningham, other NAACP officers, and nearly two hundred others showed up outside the Shelby County jail, where the forty-one persons were released the next morning.

A trial was held for some of the arrested student demonstrators on Monday, March 21. Nearly two thousand Negro spectators, who could not get in the courtroom, marched to Mt. Olive CME Church, prayed, and waited for the outcome. (The church's congregation was the largest of its denomination in Memphis; its pastor since 1953 was Henry Clay Bunton, an Alabama native, product of Miles College and Florida A&M State College, and World War II veteran.) With many people stopping by the church and contributing money, the impromptu meeting on the day of the trial raised three thousand dollars toward legal fees. "The day has finally arrived," Vasco Smith declared. "People are shedding tears of joy!" In an apparent reference to the hard-nosed William Farris, the Reverend R. W. Norsworthy, pastor of Mt. Moriah Baptist Church, said, "We are not annoyed by this backward-looking white man." At the trial, Attorney R. B. Sugarmon asked, "Where are the persons they disturbed?" The judge fined the defendants fifty-one dollars each. The *World* published the students' photographs to hail them as heroes, but some employers reportedly used the information to fire students from part-time jobs. The persons arrested at the March 22 Brooks Memorial Art Gallery sit-in demonstrations would be tried on April 6. Praising the demonstrators in its March 30 issue, the *World* said, "It was inevitable that the student sit-downs throughout the South would come to Memphis. Young people everywhere are stirred with a mission and a sense of freedom, and unlike those of a generation ago, have the courage to attempt to do something about racial oppression in the face of great personal danger. The students are to be commended for the orderly and intelligent way in which they conducted themselves."

Attorneys J. F. Estes, R. B. Sugarmon, Ben Hooks, A. W. Willis, Ben Jones, and S. A. Wilbun represented the students in a meeting with Mayor Henry Loeb and the city commissioners. They relayed the students' demands for full desegregation of the city's public facilities. Commissioner Farris declared flatly that he had been elected to "uphold segregation," deeply offending the Negro lawyers. The Memphis Committee on Human Relations (MCHR), which included former mayor Edmund Orgill, Lucius Burch, and other white progressives, had attempted to persuade Loeb to compromise with the Negroes. But he remained stubborn, and Farris absolutely would not give in. Things were "happening so fast" on the civil rights front that the *Tri-State Defender* announced that it would publish a weekly series on the sit-in movement across the South.

The *World* (Apr. 2, 1960) also reported on a March 29 mass rally at Mt. Olive CME Church, where the Interdenominational Ministers' Alliance pledged support for the $100,000 "Freedom Fund" to desegregate Memphis. The Negro churches pledged thousands of dollars each. This time, more than four thousand people showed up. By April 16, $4,279 had been raised. The *World* reported on April 23 that thousands had marched in protest of the bombing of Z. A. Looby's home in Nashville and that the Race Relations Institute was slated to meet at Fisk on June 20 through July 7. Meanwhile, by May, members of the NAACP youth chapter in Memphis were picketing downtown Jim Crow establishments with signs saying, "This store integrates your money and segregates you."

Also in May, eleven citizens filed *I. T. Watson et al. v. City of Memphis et al.* in federal district court. The plaintiffs asked for declaratory and injunctive relief that would result in immediate desegregation of public parks and other publicly owned or operated recreational facilities. True to form, Judge Boyd gave no immediate relief, but he did order the city to submit a gradual desegregation plan by the end of 1960. Willis, Hooks, and other attorneys appealed to the Sixth Circuit Court in 1961. The appeals court, however, would uphold Boyd's approach, forcing the Negroes in 1962 to carry the appeals to the final tribunal, the U.S. Supreme Court, which would agree to hear the case. Memphis desegregated the libraries in May 1961 but required segregated restrooms on the assumption that Negroes were heavy disease carriers. Turner, who had filed the original case in 1958, appealed to Federal District Judge William E. Miller, who ultimately ruled against the city.

For the sixth anniversary of *Brown*, the NAACP announced that Roy Wilkins, director of the national office, would be the speaker at a freedom rally at the Mason Temple in Memphis. As the *World* reported (May 21, 1960), more than four thousand persons attended the May 17 event, where Wilkins declared, "The students have shown they are through with segregation." With the Memphis NAACP out front and in support of the local sit-ins, Wilkins would have to refute Marshall's rebuke of the Nashville sit-in students and eventually allow the NAACP to embrace civil disobedience tactics against unjust Jim Crow laws. When students picketed Woolworth's at 59 Main Street and other downtown lunch counters in Memphis, NAACP lawyer Sugarmon expressed pride in their actions: "Instead of advising them, I feel they have taught me [something]." The freedom banquet included a report on the recent membership drive, which also sought to register black voters. The drive, led by the Reverend David S. Cunningham, pastor of Collins Chapel CME Church, had increased local NAACP membership from 5,246 to 6,750, including 655 youth members.

Maxine Smith was in charge of daily NAACP operations and protest activities. In August 1960, the local NAACP threatened to boycott WDIA, a "black-formatted radio station" owned by whites, because it continued to offer programs and events that "encouraged segregation"; this pressure caused the station managers to cancel one such event they were planning. Around August 20, three Negroes were jailed and fined twenty-five dollars by a city judge, Beverly Boushe, for "disorderly conduct"—visiting the city zoo on a day reserved for whites. Lockard, C. O. Horton, and B. J. Jones, defended the men, and on appeal, Judge William B. Ingram dismissed some of the charges. Indeed, city attorneys could find no law requiring the zoo to be segregated. Ingram, however, would be chastised by Mayor Loeb and Police Commissioner Claude Armour for "harassing the policemen in court" in front of Negroes. (Ingram, incidentally, would succeed Loeb as mayor, with huge black voter support.) Federal Judge Boyd continued to sit on the public parks case and the bus case. Around August 27, as the *Memphis Tri-State Defender* reported, Turner, O. D. Dodson, Vasco Smith, the quiet-spoken J. L. Netters (pastor of Mt. Vernon Baptist Church), and S. B. Kyles were arrested for refusing to move to the back of a bus; they were trying to "arouse other Negroes and keep the movement going in Memphis," they explained.

Another mass meeting was held in September at Mt. Olive Church, where it was decided to continue the protests until there were positive results. After enduring lengthy picketing, court litigation, and loss of revenues, on September 15, 1960, the Memphis Transit Authority gave in and desegregated the city bus system. Although a Negro man was arrested just a few days later for sitting in the front section of a bus, the transit chief apologized and said that the driver for that shift did not know about the new policy. On October 19, 1960, the *World* reported the announcement that the public libraries would be integrated. An embittered city official said, "We have opened the libraries [to all citizens]. I am a segregationist and I am going to do everything I can to hold on to what we [whites] have got. But I am going to do it legally. We will not go beyond the law." The Memphis Citizens' Council published a resolution in newspapers, opposing integration of the fairgrounds because "intermixing of black and white people would cause violence and loss of trade." City officials, ever fearful of miscegenation, stuck to the segregation rules for the fairgrounds.

In December 1960, Vasco Smith became president of the local NAACP by defeating O. Z. Evers for the position. Smith then joined with A. Maceo Walker, Jessie H. Turner, Roy Love, D. S. Cunningham, H. C. Nabrit, Smith, and C. C. Sawyer to test the fancy restaurant at Goldsmith's Department Store. The employees denied service to these well-dressed, elite Negroes. However, the management met with them, commended the men for handling the situation with "such calm and graciousness," and assured them that the owner would call a meeting to discuss the problem. "Prominent Negroes threatened to encourage a boycott of department stores," exclaimed the *Shelbyville Times-Gazette* on December 2. "The plan revealed after eight Negroes refused service on Thursday at Goldsmith's Department Store." A Jewish family that had migrated from Germany to Memphis in 1867 operated Goldsmith's, and Negroes heavily patronized this business, partly because of its liberal charge card system.

From Beale Street to Main Street, Negroes comprised many of the customers for Jewish merchants, but the large and prosperous Jewish community in Memphis offered no organized support for the Negro's civil rights battles. However, a few individuals among Memphis's Jewish leaders did help in the movement, according to Selma S. Lewis in *A Biblical People in the Bible Belt* (1998). Rabbi James Wax of Temple Israel and Lester Rosen, an insurance executive and supporter of the National Urban League, served on the Memphis Race Relations Committee in 1959. However, as Lewis wrote, the presence of a large black population "created a buffer for the Jews, and prejudice against the Jewish minority was, to a great extent, displaced by this more visible and more threatening minority [blacks]." She further noted: "Jews traditionally had been in the forefront of national movements for the advancement of civil rights, and Jewish Memphians were no exception. But in the South, those whose souls had been deepest in southern land often, paradoxically, felt the least secure, the least willing to risk the aftermath of the demands of

Judaism and of conscience. Most Jews 'ran for cover first,' when the civil rights movement began."

J. H. Turner appealed to local ministers to help raise more "freedom funds" for legal assistance. Bishop J. O. Patterson personally recruited fifty ministers for the effort, and Billy Kyle headed the Freedom Committee. Other ministers made their churches available for Thursday night rallies. "I am a citizen and I am in it up to my elbows, walk-in, sit-in, or stand-in, I am ready!" said the Reverend Roy Love. On December 22, the world-famous gospel singer Mahalia Jackson arrived to donate her services at a Freedom Fund rally. Maxine Smith organized the ladies clubs to continue downtown picketing and persuade Negroes to turn in their charge cards at segregated department stores. The motto was "If you're Black, take it back." The club women planned to mobilize five thousand volunteer picketers and cause a 25 percent decrease in business.

Throughout the spring of 1961, a variety of activities kept participants in the movement busy. According to the *World* (Feb. 25, 1961), one local group, the Volunteer Citizens' Association, called for Negro representation on the City Commission and the Memphis Transit Authority. In the branch NAACP report of April 10–May 2, 1961, Smith reported an intensifying membership campaign to bolster the Freedom Movement. Volunteer workers were recruited through various meetings across the city, including one at Mt. Olive CME Church on May 10 and a special program on May 21 at which the Pentecostal Temple provided the music. The choir from that church was guaranteed to draw a crowd, especially with younger people who enjoyed the music and the lively gatherings. LeMoyne College NAACP members recruited more pickets. Handbills were being printed. "Stay Away from Downtown [stores]" was the slogan. The NAACP youth adviser, Mrs. Russell B. Sugarmon, held the youth work committee meetings at her home. The local NAACP's political action committee continued to send complaints of police brutality to the U.S. Justice Department, the FBI, and Police Commissioner Claude Armour. The local NAACP convinced Sam Cooke and other rhythm-and-blues performers to cancel an appearance scheduled by a local white club that used segregated seating. Clarence Mitchell of the national NAACP office in Washington, D.C., spoke to thousands at the local branch's *Brown* anniversary dinner on May 21, 1961, at the Mason Temple. Four employers of North Carolina Mutual Insurance Company's branch office were arrested for "loitering and disorderly conduct" after attempting to use the Fairgrounds facilities. Local NAACP lawyers posted the $308 in bonds and argued the cases. The NAACP offices moved to larger quarters at 234 Hernando in the Universal Life Insurance

Company Building. Maxine Smith met with the Inter-Ministerial Alliance to remind preachers to push the "Stay Away from Downtown" theme in the Sunday sermons, and she became busy investigating job discrimination in the telephone company and the local U.S. Post Office.

By the summer of 1961, the NAACP and community leaders in Memphis engaged youngsters, preachers, all social classes, and numerous women in the movement. There was also a concerted effort to maintain discipline, nonviolence, and order in the various activities. To this end, H. C. Nabrit, Vasco Smith, J. H. Turner, Melvin Robinson, and Eddie Meacham (editor of the *Memphis Press-Scimitar*) served as speakers in a local "School for Sit-ins and Pickets." In demonstrations from June 22 through 29, more sit-ins occurred at several downtown department stores, including Goldsmith's, Bry's, Lowenstein's, Gerber's, and Walgreen's, where lunch counters were closed to the protesters. One hundred fifty pickets led by J. H. Turner carried signs reading, "Don't buy here," while Police Commissioner Armour said he was willing to arrest protestors if store owners were willing to prosecute. Younger demonstrators were sent to juvenile court. In mid-June, Memphis's first Negro bus driver was hired—John L. Smith, a graduate of Booker T. Washington High School. On June 29, a Torchlight March for Freedom was staged from Clayborn Temple to downtown stores. The Ministers' March for Freedom took place on July 7, while on July 17, sit-ins occurred at Union and Grand Central railroad stations. However, the stations began issuing tickets on a nonsegregated basis—the result of mounting federal pressure against Jim Crow restrictions on interstate travel. Over the course of several evenings, the Ladies March for Freedom took place. Local leaders held weekly Neighborhood Freedom Rallies and bombarded city officials with protest letters. Stories about atrocious police brutality in Memphis were sent to local and national newspapers. By August 20, nearly twenty-five people a day were being arrested in the Memphis demonstrations while the churches contributed bail money. Among those arrested was Laurie Sugarmon, the wife of R. B. Sugarmon. Also in August, A. Maceo Walker was named to the three-person policy-making board of the Metropolitan Transit Authority after Loeb's forces rejected A. W. Willis Jr. as the nominee.

The Memphis NAACP was united in purpose and goals. The NAACP had changed its mind—at least in Tennessee—about the methods that Thurgood Marshall had described as disruptive to the NAACP's legal assault on Jim Crow. The Tennessee State Convention of NAACP branches was scheduled to convene at Nashville's Pleasant Green Baptist Church on Jefferson Street on September 29 through October 2; the meeting included workshops on "The Role of the Branch in Desegregation of Lunch Counters and other Public Facilities," "Getting out the Vote," and other topics.

To avoid conflict with the September 1961 opening of the first integrated schools in Memphis, the local NAACP suspended its downtown demonstrations. Mayor Loeb was upset by the NAACP's persistent public marches, but he seemed to moderate his view of desegregation. The *Tri-State Defender* (Aug. 12, 1961) reported that Loeb, when speaking to the local Rotary Club, said, "Some intemperate people of both races are trying to hang the tag of racial prejudice around my neck. . . . I choose to be with the moderate, decent, level-headed people who desire to elevate all races. I promise the course of moderation with diligence and determination for Memphis and all of us." A week later, one of the last of the area's former slaves, Mittie Johnson (b. 1849), passed away in Memphis's John Gaston Hospital—her death signaled to the new generation to keep fighting for a new day and a new deal in Memphis and the Mississippi Delta.

Students at Owen Junior College and LeMoyne College, as well as members of the Masons, Eastern Star, and local civic clubs, were recruited to resume the weekly downtown protests by October. After servicemen from the nearby Millington Naval Base attacked some of the demonstrators, the post commander sent military police to the city and assured the NAACP that the U.S. Navy would not tolerate racist behavior among its personnel. The navy was notorious for racism against Negroes, having a large proportion of southern whites in its ranks; the Navy cap was often proudly referred to as "the Dixie cup." On October 8, a segregated baseball game was postponed after Smith sent a protest letter to event sponsors, the East Memphis Sertoma Club. On November 5, Percy Sutton, president of the New York City NAACP branch, was the speaker for a freedom program at Metropolitan Baptist Church. The branch NAACP called off all downtown demonstrations in late November to allow for the Christmas shopping season and to negotiate with merchants, according to the *World* (Nov. 25, 1961). Around this time, Bishop Charles Mason, founder of the Church of God in Christ denomination, died at age ninety-nine, and some twenty-five thousand faithful Christians would flood the city to view his body at Mason Temple, which continued to be a meeting place for civil rights movement activists.

In 1962, public library branches, the Brooks Museum, and the city zoo were opened to people regardless of color. Nine Negro bus drivers were hired. The Federal Reserve Bank hired two Negroes, the county hired a Negro tax appraiser, and Negro clerks were hired at downtown stores. Turner, Northcross, Sugarmon, and Maxine Smith met with Southern Bell Telephone and Telegraph Company executives from the Memphis and Nashville offices to discuss hiring Negro linesmen and operators, but company executives said they were not yet ready to do that. On February 6, Vasco Smith, Mrs. Jessie H. Turner, and other leaders tested the desegregation of twenty-nine department store restaurants. Many of them still refused service to Negro customers.

On February 27, 1962, the federal court heard the case of *Turner v. City of Memphis, et al.*, which challenged segregation at the airport restaurant. On March 26, the court ruled that the Dobbs House Restaurant under question, while operated by a private company, was leased by the city to the airport. Constance Baker Motley and other Legal Defense Fund lawyers successfully countered the defense's argument that Tennessee law allowed restaurants and hotels to exclude persons "for any reason whatsoever." A native of Connecticut, Motley had attended Fisk before completing New York University and then law school at Columbia University; in 1966 she became the first African American woman appointed to the federal district court.

Problems with Jim Crow remained: police brutality was rampant; Negroes still were excluded from grand juries; job opportunities for Negro high school and college graduates was quite restricted; new housing was closed to middle- and upper-class Negroes; and some individual stores remained holdouts against desegregation. Maxine Smith and the Memphis NAACP even protested a segregated religious crusade held at the city auditorium by the Reverend Oral Roberts. They sent letters to the president, the federal Committee on Equal Employment, and the U.S. secretary of labor protesting continuing racial discrimination in Memphis, and asked that the State of Tennessee's Employment Office be forced to stop discrimination and segregation in its facilities.

Much of the work of the Memphis NAACP was done through letters of protest to specific owners and to the newspapers. Negroes could expect little help from the governor. The local NAACP also dealt with the Tennessee courts on a cautious basis. It was best to appeal to federal courts and send protests to federal agencies. There were three local NAACP suits in the Tennessee Supreme Court, the Circuit Court, and the U.S. Supreme Court. On March 7, 1962, the Tennessee Supreme Court upheld convictions of Negro demonstrators who had protested segregated music concerts at the Overton Park Shell. Out of 318 sit-in cases held in Memphis courts between 1960 and 1962, 163 received convictions, and 155 were dismissed. Some 191 city fines were appealed, and 119 were dismissed. Of 123 arrests on State of Tennessee charges, 93 were dismissed, and 30 were indicted. On March 23, the Sixth Circuit Court overruled Judge Boyd on one Memphis case. In her 1963 reports, Maxine Smith noted that two NAACP-affiliated attorneys were named assistant legal counsel to the Charter Commission and the U.S. attorney's staff in Shelby County, that several movie houses had desegregated their facilities, and that city officials had made token desegregation arrangements at the local fairgrounds.

The most significant legal case involving Memphis was finally decided at the highest level in 1963. On May 17–18, 1963, the case of *Watson et al. v. City of Memphis et al.* was heard before the United States Supreme Court, with Constance Baker Motley arguing the plaintiff's case, assisted by Derrick A. Bell Jr. and H. T. Lockard. The City of Memphis argued that gradual desegregation on a facility-by-facility basis was necessary to prevent interracial disturbances, violence, riots, and community turmoil. In its ruling in the *Watson* case, the high court handed down a landmark decision that affected municipal desegregation across the nation:

> Memphis owns 131 parks, all of which are operated by the Memphis Park Commission. Of these, only 25 were at the time of trial open to use without regard to race, 58 were restricted to use by whites and 25 to use by Negroes; the remaining 23 parks were undeveloped raw land. Subject to exceptions, neighborhood parks were generally segregated according to the racial character of the area in which located. The City Park Commission also operates a number of additional recreational facilities, by far the largest share of which was found to be racially segregated. Though a zoo, an art gallery and certain boating and other facilities are now desegregated, about two-thirds (40) of the 61 city-owned playgrounds were at the time of trial reserved for whites only, and the remainder were set aside for Negro use. Thirty of the 56 playgrounds and other facilities operated by the municipal Park Commission on property owned by churches, private groups, or the School Board were set aside for the exclusive use of whites, while 26 were reserved for Negroes. All 12 of the municipal community centers were segregated. . . . While several of these properties have been desegregated since the filing of suit the general pattern of racial segregation in such public recreational facilities persists. There is an unmistakable and pervasive pattern of local segregation, which, in fact the city makes no attempt to deny, but merely attempts to justify as necessary for the time being. Goodwill between the races in Memphis would best be preserved and extended by the observance and protection, not the denial, of the basic constitutional rights [of all citizens].

The court argued that *Brown II* (1955) had set a precedent for proceeding with "all deliberate speed" in desegregation of public facilities but that it was "never contemplated that the concept of 'deliberate speed' would countenance indefinite delay in elimination of racial barriers in schools, let alone other public facilities not involving the same physical problems or comparable conditions." The court declared that citizens whose rights were being violated must have immediate relief; they could not wait for gradual relief.

The court countered each argument by the Memphis defendants to deter other southern governments from attempting the same delays in desegregation. In response to the Memphis argument about using a gradual plan to avoid violence, the court said: "Constitutional rights may not be denied simply because of hostility to their assertion or exercise." The city also argued that some parks and playgrounds would have to be closed until added supervision and an increased budget could be provided if immediate desegregation was ordered, thus depriving some children of their right to use of nearby parks and playgrounds. But the Supreme Court rejected this flimsy argument: "Vindication of conceded constitutional rights cannot be made dependent upon any theory that it is less expensive to deny than to afford them." The court also rejected the Memphis government's theory of proportional allocation of facilities by race: "The sufficiency of Negro facilities is beside the point; it is the segregation by race that is unconstitutional." The court made a point to say with finality that the *Plessy* principle of "separate but equal" was dead. To the city's argument that it was waiting on the Tennessee Supreme Court to rule on racially restrictive covenants contained in the private deeds to some park properties given to the city, the Court replied, "The outcome of the state suit is irrelevant to whether the city may constitutionally enforce the segregation [deal], regardless of the effect which desegregation may have on its title." This part of the *Watson* opinion asserted that state statutes, state supreme court decisions, and private covenants supporting segregation by race were null and void.

The high court also said, "Under the facts of this case, the District Court's undoubted discretion in the fashioning and timing of equitable relief was not called into play; rather, affirmative judicial action was required to vindicate plain and present constitutional rights. Today, no less than 50 years ago, the solution to the problems growing out of race relations 'cannot be promoted by depriving citizens of their constitutional rights and privileges,' *Buchanan v. Warley, supra, 245 U.S.*, at 80–81." The *Watson* case, in the words of Alfred H. Kelly and Winfred A. Harbison, was where "the Court demonstrated a consistent determination not to allow subterfuge or delay to frustrate integration of public facilities."

Meanwhile, the Memphis Race Relations Committee was busy trying to prove that better race relations would be good for everyone and would promote a thriving local economy. Edward J. Meeman, editor of the *Press-Scimitar*, wrote, "When we upgrade a large part of our population, the South will raise its standard of living, improve the labor supply, become an area with greater attractions to industry and distributive commerce, and provide a greater prosperity for all of us who live here and the peace of mind that comes from friendship and cooperation between the races." The *Press-Scimitar* proclaimed Memphis "a model in peaceful desegregation." The newspapers reported sixteen Negro bus drivers employed by the Memphis Transit Authority; also, twenty-eight policemen and three county sheriff deputies had been hired. The *Press-Scimitar* declared, "Memphis Provides More and Better Jobs for Negroes [in downtown businesses]." On June 4, 1963, the paper reported, "Gerber's department store finally desegregated its dining facility."

By 1964, that aspect of the civil rights movement involving public demonstrations still had a long way to go in Tennessee. And by the late 1960s, white resistance would turn violent while paradoxically provoking black violence.

CHAPTER 6
THE KING GOD DIDN'T SAVE

THE MOVEMENT TURNS VIOLENT
IN TENNESSEE

At last, amid cheers on July 2, 1964, less than eight months after Kennedy's death, Congress approved the Civil Rights Act of 1964. President Lyndon B. Johnson signed the bill the same day. Roy Wilkins called it "the Magna Carta of human rights." Governor Frank Clement of Tennessee must have breathed a sigh of relief, as he and Mayor Beverley Briley of Nashville urged compliance with the law. The death of Kennedy, the violent events that transpired in Alabama and Mississippi, the retaliation against Negroes in Fayette and Haywood counties, and recent murders of civil rights workers—all of these events undoubtedly had much to do with Johnson's persuading Congress to pass the bill. A headline in the *Clarksville Chronicle* of July 3, 1964 read, "Civil Rights Bill Becomes New Law of the Land." CORE and SNCC began tests of segregated businesses the next day. The law conferred jurisdiction upon the federal district courts to provide injunctive relief against discrimination in public accommodations (Title II), extended the Commission on Civil Rights, established a Commission on Equal Employment Opportunity, and provided specific guarantees of nondiscrimination in education (Title IV), federally assisted activities (Title VI), and employment opportunity (Title VII). Nonetheless, in Tennessee the civil rights movement was far from being over.

By the 1960s, as blacks stopped the Great Migration to the North and as many of those who had reached retirement age returned to their extended families in the South, the region's black population percentage began to increase again. Because of this shift, coupled with white flight to the suburbs, Memphis would become a majority-black city. In late 1964, the Memphis NAACP found segregation existing in a city-owned hospital, where a white nurse was making a distinction between "white" and "black" patients by erasing the titles of "Mr." and "Mrs." before the Negro registrants' names so that they could then be placed in different wards of the hospital. The Memphis Retail Association continued to resist the integration of restaurants with this claim: "A sight of a party of a dozen Negroes was sure to alienate white customers." The retailers were also afraid that the Memphis White Citizens Council and other segregationist groups would circulate a list of "Segregated Restaurants for White Customers." In the annual NAACP report for 1965, Maxine Smith noted, "We have targeted 'token' desegregation in local schools, employment discrimination in the justice system, hospitals, housing, and employment, and police brutality." Despite the passage of the 1964 Civil Rights Act, the NAACP branch "found it extremely necessary to remain alert and active in its role of assuring the implementation of acts and bills passed in the areas of civil rights, voting rights, poverty, etc. . . . The influence of the branch has extended far beyond the boundaries of this community [and into rural areas]."

The Ku Klux Klan was growing in membership. In October and November 1965, Congress held hearings before the Committee on Un-American Activities in the House of Representatives. Ironically, suspected Klansmen invoked the Fifth Amendment to avoid testifying about their clandestine, terrorist activities against isolated citizens, church buildings, and civil rights workers. Congress was compelled to complete a report entitled "Activities of the Ku Klux Klan Organization in the United States" (1965). The report's maps showed many racist organizations in Tennessee, including the Dixie Klan, Inc., the Knights of the KKK ("Old Hickory Club") in Chattanooga, and KKK chapters in Maryville, Knoxville, Etowah, Harriman, and Sevierville, among other places.

Many civil rights leaders, including Martin Luther King Jr., were starting to fret, too, about the escalation of the war in Vietnam during the middle to late 1960s. They believed that rising protests against the war by political leftists, radicals, and anarchists were diverting the news media's attention away from the ongoing civil rights movement. The war was also driving a wedge between the federal government and black young people, who were angry about being drafted more frequently by all-white draft boards than were whites. Whites were reportedly more able to join the National Guard or receive more deferments, more stateside military assignments, and a bigger share of the work behind combat lines. Blacks made up 11 percent of the armed forces but 25 percent of those troops sent to Vietnam. Military commanders reportedly sent black servicemen into the most dangerous combat assignments in Vietnam, which caused them to suffer a disproportionate number of casualties. Blacks were also disproportionately represented among the dishonorable and "less than honorable" discharges from the service. Thus, when they returned home, these veterans were often denied various military benefits, including medical care, housing loans, and education assistance.

SNCC became involved in the antiwar movement, and Diane Nash caught the attention of national intelligence agencies when she visited North Vietnam in 1966. Recalling that turbulent time in a Nashville speech on October 4, 2003, she said that government agents had tapped her telephones and opened her mail, while she made no secret of her antiwar views. SNCC began asking, "Where is the draft for the freedom fight in the United States?" On January 6, 1966, a SNCC pamphlet denounced the Vietnam War: "The Student Non-Violent Coordinating Committee assumes its right to dissent with United States foreign policy on any issue, and states its opposition to U.S. involvement in . . . Vietnam. We the SNCC have been involved in the black people's struggle for liberation and self-determination in this country for the past five years. Our work, particularly in the South, taught us that the U.S. government has never guaranteed the freedom of oppressed citizens, and is not yet truly determined to end the rule of terror and oppression within its own borders."

SNCC leaders became increasingly militant in the push for civil rights, and one of its flyers read: "White people who desire change in this country should go where that problem [of racism] is most manifest. The problem is not in the Black Community. Thus an all-Black project is needed in order for the people to free themselves." SNCC then began using a new slogan—Black Power—to emphasize color consciousness among African Americans and to bring the civil rights movement's decision-making process to the local level. Younger African Americans began to insist on the use of the militant word *black* instead of *Negro* and *colored*. The word *black* encouraged African Americans to be defiant and to resist the notion that *white* was better. SNCC taught young blacks to rebel against the idea that the history and cultural heritage of people of color had no value in America. The increasingly popular Afro-style haircut symbolized racial pride, but it struck fear in whites, who saw Negroes with large Afros as militants who had rejected white culture.

At Tennessee State, about four hundred impatient students launched protests in 1966 over facilities and the quality of teaching, forcing President

W. S. Davis to form a student-faculty committee to address the problems. Davis called a campus-wide meeting and responded with promises and solutions to fix the problems. A mile up the street, approximately five hundred students demonstrated at Fisk, causing the newly appointed acting president, James R. Lawson (no relation to James M. Lawson Jr.), to hear their demands. "What I expect and implore from the students both individually and collectively is basic loyalty to the university, self-respect and restraint and general belief in the democratic process," Lawson said.

In 1967 Governor Clement left office, making way for the return of Buford Ellington (who would serve from 1967 to 1971) to the governorship. In his farewell address to the General Assembly on January 11, Clement said:

> And as I bow out on January 16 and turn the helm of the Ship
> of State over to my successor, Governor Ellington, I can say with
> a clear conscience that when the 'storm clouds' came during the
> ten years I have served as your governor—whether it was at Clin-
> ton to protect the child to whom nature had given a dark skin—
> or whether it was to protect lives and property at Lawrenceburg
> where law and order had broken down, and local officers could
> no longer hold the line [against labor union disturbances]—I did
> what I thought was right and in the best interest of Tennessee
> and Tennesseans.

An organizer for SNCC arrived in Nashville to rekindle the local chapter, which had become inactive after the passage of recent civil rights legislation. Tennessee State's Frederick Brooks became its head. The national group, meanwhile, would organize National Black Power Conferences throughout the country. George W. Ware, the campus coordinator for SNCC at Tennessee State, gave the *Meter* an interview on December 13, 1966, to explain "Black Power":

> To SNCC, Black Power means that Negroes must begin to
> develop methods of exerting influence over their own lives.
> The first thing which must be done is that black people begin to
> become unified, because we are oppressed as a group and we must
> oppose our oppressors as a group. There is power in numbers and
> we must use this power to develop political influence through
> which we may develop the economic power which we don't have
> now. . . . Black Power is given an erroneous definition by the
> American white press. Whites have power, and since we are
> in fact black, then that power would be Black Power.

Ware denied that SNCC had put whites out of the organization. "They left," he said, adding, "We say to white people that instead of trying to orga-nize the black communities, they should go into the white communities and work to remove the deeply-rooted racism which is where the problem is. We are just pro-black . . . Black Power is a call, perhaps, the last call, to the black middle class to come home . . . and make common cause with the black have-nots."

Stokely Carmichael, the new national head of SNCC, was scheduled to speak at the Vanderbilt University Impact Symposium on Saturday, April 8, 1967. U.S. Senator Strom Thurmond of South Carolina, a notorious spokes-man for segregation, and Martin Luther King Jr. were also scheduled speakers. George Ware planned to have Carmichael, a graduate of Howard University and a native of Trinidad, speak at Fisk University and Tennessee A&I as well. Ware hoped that Carmichael's appearance would help revive the Nashville chapter of SNCC and once more involve local students in the civil rights movement.

By April 4, James G. Stahlman's *Nashville Banner* had started a cam-paign to discredit Carmichael and prevent his appearance at Vanderbilt. On its front page, the *Banner* said that Carmichael had recently called for the overthrow of the U.S. government in a speech at Miles College, a historically black institution in Alabama. Thomas Anderson, a Vanderbilt graduate and a member of the national council of the ultra-conservative, anti-Communist John Birch Society called Carmichael a threat to the ideals of western civiliza-tion: "The search for truth does not include any right to deliberately destroy the external verities upon which our civilization was founded, and by which it has prospered beyond any civilization in history." Dan Bayes, Tennessee coor-dinator for the John Birch Society, addressed Nashville's Downtown Optimist Club on April 6, calling Carmichael "more Red [Communist] than black," according to the *Tennessean* (Apr. 7, 1967).

Governor Ellington was not saying anything publicly about Carmichael, but Stahlman and the *Banner* were among Ellington's political supporters. Perpetuating negative images of African Americans and Carmichael, both the *Banner* and the *Tennessean* were lily-white in journalistic philosophy— much like many other white-owned southern newspapers that had refused to hire blacks in meaningful jobs as late as 1967 and whose news columns, apart from sports coverage, usually depicted black citizens as troublemakers, contro-versial figures, or criminals (often photographed in handcuffs). The occasional positive story was typically relegated to the inside pages. Local blacks viewed the *Tennessean* in a more favorable light than the *Banner*, but this newspaper, too, could be anti-black and racially biased. At best, its editors were paternalistic toward black people.

The Tennessee General Assembly began debate on a resolution opposing Carmichael's speech at Vanderbilt. Black legislators A. W. Willis, R. B. Sugarmon, J. O. Patterson Jr., and Dorothy Brown spoke against the proposal. In a lengthy speech on the floor of the House, Brown said, "The American Negro has been the most patient minority group within our borders." As the *Banner* reported on April 6, Thomas Wiseman of Tullahoma was one of the few white state legislators who argued for freedom of speech and Carmichael's right to speak. Some four hundred faculty members and students petitioned against the General Assembly resolution, declaring, "We therefore reaffirm the invitation to Stokely Carmichael." The *Banner* published the names of the petitioners and appeared to be angry at Bob Eager, chairman of the symposium, for not calling the whole thing off.

Officials at Fisk University and Tennessee A&I State University wanted to prohibit Carmichael from coming to their campuses. Fisk students, however, threatened to move the event to a nearby church, while the A&I Student Government Association said it would hold its rally outside if Carmichael was denied entrance to a campus building, as Joseph Payne, vice president for student affairs, had threatened to do. Nevertheless, on Thursday night, April 6, Carmichael addressed a huge audience in the Fisk University gymnasium. "They cheered everything he said," the *Banner* reported the next day. On that morning, April 7, Carmichael spoke to board members of the Southern Conference Education Fund (a remnant of the long-defunct Southern Conference for Human Welfare), outlining to them and director Carl Braden the goals and philosophy of SNCC. The *Banner* (Apr. 7) claimed that Braden and his organization were allied with communists. That night, Carmichael spoke in Kean Hall at Tennessee State, where student organizers forced a white newspaper reporter to leave the center of the floor and take a seat; they believed that white reporters were documenting the audience for state and federal intelligence agencies and had sometimes tried to intimidate the most timid blacks into not attending civil rights meetings. But the young blacks had no fear of these white editors, publishers, and reporters, and indeed they wanted to use them to gain valuable publicity for the movement.

The *Banner* (Apr. 8) claimed that Carmichael had referred to "the Honkies of the *Banner*" and had called Stahlman's hero, Republican presidential hopeful Richard M. Nixon, "Honky Nixon." According to the *Banner*, Carmichael had admonished the students to stop acting white: "You got to be one or the other: 'black' or 'white' [in racially divided America]." Carmichael told the Fisk audience that black people had to stop allowing white people to decide who could speak on black college campuses.

At the Vanderbilt Symposium on Friday night, King declared, "There is nothing more dangerous than the man who feels he has no status. This breeds a deep desperation. The Negro cannot lift himself by his bootstraps, because he has been left bootless." Carmichael attended King's speech, and afterwards he and King briefly discussed King's insistence on using nonviolence to advance integration. The *Tennessean's* coverage (Apr. 8) emphasized King's preference for nonviolence. On Saturday morning, Strom Thurmond focused on the controversy over the Vietnam War, blaming King and others for criticizing American involvement. He also blamed the nation's riots on the civil rights leaders.

Carmichael, who later would label the military draft "Black urban removal," finally addressed the symposium at 3:00 P.M. He had led a student workshop at Fisk that morning. The *Banner*, by then, had sufficiently painted him as anti-white and "a Trinidad-born character." During his speech, a white male stood up and unfurled a Confederate flag—a sure symbol of rebellion against the American nation and its human values, as well as a display of white southern hatred for the Negro. There were rumors of bomb threats at Vanderbilt. "I am nonviolent right now," Carmichael said, "but if a white man tries to put his arm on me, I am going to break his arm. I am not now and never have been a pacifist. I will not bow down my head and let them beat me until they become civilized. Segregated schools and the ghetto are products not of Black Power but of the absence of a group without power to organize their community." Carmichael had only coined the phrase "Black Power" the previous year and had even persuaded Martin Luther King Jr. to start using the word "black," although King still opposed the use of the phrase Black Power.

Later that Saturday night, trouble began on street corners in the north Nashville community near Fisk, Meharry, and Tennessee State. The weekend temperature had reached nearly 87 degrees. Carmichael reportedly accused students at Fisk of trying to look "light, bright, and damned near white" instead of embracing black culture. He said that white donors controlled Fisk, an accusation that President Lawson angrily denied. Policemen apparently were stationed throughout the Fisk–Meharry–Tennessee State area. Inman Otey and other former Tennessee State students recalled that the police and reporters showed up at the same time. The police raided places "looking for marijuana."

The *Meter* reported that bricks and bottles started to fly toward passing cars. Students on the corners of 17th and 18th and Jefferson made the scene look like a summer street party. Policemen were hit by hurled objects, and in reaction to some firecrackers thrown from a window, they fired into the dormitories at Tennessee State. They raided the dormitories, "looking for weapons" and destroying the students' rooms. James Montgomery, the Student Government Association president, got between the policemen and students to prevent the cops from using rifle butts on the students' heads. No major weapons were found by the police. The disturbance quieted down, but it began again the next night. The *Tennessean* published pictures of piles of lumber burning in front of the student union building. The Air Force ROTC building on campus nearly burned to the ground. But cadets, football players, and staff members helped save the facility, and the head football coach organized some of his players to patrol the campus to prevent any other disturbances. One particular police captain spread the notion of "a Communist conspiracy in Nashville." Some white race radicals entered the black neighborhoods but were arrested after they fired shots from a speeding car. The presidents of the local Negro colleges barred outsiders from the campuses. Thirty-six persons were arrested in two nights of rioting. Looby, Williams, and other NAACP lawyers had to defend the students despite the fact that they had resorted to violence. This, they believed, would alienate many white supporters from the civil rights movement.

On April 10, the *Banner* devoted its entire front page to the riots, with photographs and an editorial denouncing Carmichael. "The police knew Carmichael came to bring trouble," the *Banner* said. The *Tennessean*, in earlier coverage of the riots (Apr. 9), included a photograph of Carmichael that made him appear almost Hitler-like. Carmichael was not in Nashville when the worst disturbances occurred, having traveled on to Knoxville for another speaking appearance.

Governor Ellington was prepared to deal quickly and firmly with the students this time. Faculty member Jamye C. Williams and her husband, McDonald, recalled that after returning to the A&I campus from lunch one day shortly after the riots, they found the place blocked by tanks and troops sent by Ellington. Only Tennessee A&I students, faculty, and employees were admitted onto the campus. The students were playing music in front of the ROTC building and dancing, with some running into the middle of Centennial Boulevard toward the troops and taunting them. The *Meter* published pictures of soldiers and their automatic weapons on campus. Jamye Williams, along with James Montgomery and others, including the vice president for student affairs, visited the governor's office, where Ellington promised to recall the troops if the students would stop the demonstrations. Returning to campus, Montgomery persuaded the students to go into the gymnasium, and the troops, transports, and tanks left. Minor incidents continued through April 11. In all, about ninety people were detained by police since the disturbances began on April 8.

To discuss the events and further ease tensions, local civil rights organizations held a meeting at St. John AME Church on April 19, with Andrew White of the NCLC and Mansfield Douglass of the NAACP presiding. White blamed social problems and employment discrimination against young Negroes for the conditions that produced the riot. Some NAACP leaders believed that "the term Black Power arranges race against race on the basis of skin color" and that this militancy had thrown the movement "off course just when Negroes in Alabama and Mississippi were getting their hands on the ballot." Edwin H. Mitchell, who led the city's Human Relations Commission and who had been hit by a rock when he tried to calm some students near Fisk, told the *Tennessean* that Carmichael deserved to be criticized but that the riot in fact resulted from poor economic conditions, lack of quality police and municipal services, and unfair treatment of blacks in Nashville. The *Banner* reprinted the *Tennessean* story but cut the part of Mitchell's remarks that criticized the white community. Howard Congregational Church held a forum to allow the students to air their grievances. Black Power advocates criticized Mitchell, Mansfield Douglass, and Inman Otey for failing to push the black agenda among city officials. Ironically, on the night of the riot, Otey was arrested for "speeding" and roughed up by policemen, and the Otey family store was looted by rioters. Some student leaders concluded that adult black leaders were mere "vote deliverers who answer to the white press." The Nashville Interdenominational Ministerial Alliance issued a statement supporting the students' accounts of events and said that the real causes of the riots "were in existence long before Carmichael was born." In the end, said a Tennessee A&I dean, "We just don't know what happened." He believed that the presence of riot police had triggered the disturbances.

Mayor Briley accused Carmichael of starting the disturbances. The police arrested SNCC leader George Ware for inciting a riot. On April 20, the *Tennessean* published a letter from one Nashvillian who said, "I am sick of the whole catalogue of weirdoes running around badmouthing the United States, from the whining draft-dodgers to the finks of Berkeley, but most of all I am sick of Stokely Carmichael and those ministers of the gospel, Adam Clayton Powell and Martin Luther King Jr."

In the wake of the disturbances and Carmichael's visit to Nashville, the *Banner* stoked a controversy over an honorarium payment to Carmichael out of the A&I student activity fund and whether the SNCC leader had been compensated with state money. *Banner* publisher James Stahlman obtained a copy of the check that allegedly was found in the SNCC station wagon in which Ware and A&I student Eugene Anderson had been arrested. (The two had acted as Carmichael's bodyguards during his visit to Nashville.) Stahlman investigated Davis's side of the matter and wrote to an official: "Dr. Walter S. Davis, president of A&I University, told Charlie Moss [executive editor of the *Banner*] that he was forced by a petition of 3,000 of his 5,000 students to give Stokely Carmichael the $300 honorarium check." Stahlman said that Davis had recalled that Carmichael could not understand why a black man could speak at Vanderbilt but not at Fisk or Tennessee State. According to Stahlman, Davis claimed to have prevented some Tennessee State students from going over to Vanderbilt "to assault the student body there." Meanwhile, state officials investigating the check controversy were told that two A&I alumni had come forth with money to cover Carmichael's honorarium and that no state funds were involved. President Davis had accepted their check and directed the A&I business manager to deposit it to the student activity fund.

In addition to a copy of the check to Carmichael, Stahlman had a list of seven Tennessee residents and twelve out-of-state students who had been arrested during the riots, as well as a list of people who worked with SNCC. To conservative whites like Stahlman, such lists seemed to be further evidence that outside troublemakers were behind civil disturbances in Tennessee. Indeed, the Ellington administration would respond with reactionary legislation to limit out-of-state enrollment at state colleges to 15 percent. This move especially targeted A&I, whose reputation had attracted large numbers of students from outside Tennessee—considerably more, in fact, than the white public colleges and universities in the state had drawn.

The governor's position became clear at a press conference on April 20. During his new term, which had begun in January, Ellington seemed intent on doing a more effective job to contain civil rights agitation in Tennessee than when he had previously served as governor from 1959 to 1963. "Major Changes Slated at A&I by Ellington," said the *Tennessean* headline (Apr. 21, 1967) above its story on the press conference. At that session, Ellington complained that the proportion of out-of-state students at A&I—36 percent of the student body—was "too big a percentage" and that it might even be higher because of some students illegally declaring in-state residency. Ellington also said that the proposed state commission on higher education might look into the possibility of combining Tennessee A&I and the University of Tennessee at Nashville.

James Montgomery, SGA president, responded that Black Power was not the cause of the unrest, as President Davis had reported to Ellington, but that the disturbances had resulted from a lack of support from state officials for the university and its programs. The *Vox Populi*, a new student newspaper emerged on the A&I campus as an alternative to the *Meter*, which was controlled by the university. Ellington's remarks started a thirty-eight-year debate about whether whites would try to take over Tennessee State and end its days as historically black university. Later in April 1967, one student said, "I think the administration [of Davis] is under pressure from the people downtown." On the afternoon of April 14, hundreds of students from Fisk and Tennessee State had marched on the mayor's office, protesting the placement of blame for the riots on the blacks.

On April 21, 1967, attorneys for SNCC filed *Frederick Brooks, et al. v. Beverly Briley, etc., et al.*, charging the city with conspiracy to violate the 1964 civil rights law, to violate federal rights of Nashville's eighty-three thousand black citizens. The suit asked Federal District Judge William E. Miller to appoint a three-judge panel to ascertain if specific statutes of Tennessee, including vagrancy acts and a local ordinance prohibiting assembly of two or more persons to annoy or disturb travelers, were constitutional. The Middle Tennessee chapter of the American Civil Liberties Union asked to join the suit in support of the students, according to the *Tennessean* (Apr. 26, 1967). SNCC, however, would not win the suit.

The city and the state did institute some positive changes as a result of the riots. On May 17, the mayor announced a permanent Metro Human Relations Commission, which included Will E. Campbell, Herman Long, J. E. Lowery, Inman Otey, Kelly M. Smith, and Mrs. Matthew Walker, among others. In May, the General Assembly approved a bill to create the Tennessee Commission on Human Development (TCHD); this panel would replace former governor Clement's Human Relations Committee, which Ellington had allowed to lapse. The new TCHD was to go into effect on July 1, 1967, with five members from each of the state's grand divisions (West, Middle, and East Tennessee) and a full-time executive secretary. For now, racial tensions had cooled off in Nashville and elsewhere in Tennessee.

In June 1967, the state commissioner of education fired the business manager at Tennessee State. The governor had apparently meant to make changes at A&I soon after he took office in January, ordering an audit at the university weeks before the riots. Ellington seemed to be moving to gain more control of the institution—that rebellious Tennessee A&I State University with all those black out-of-state troublemakers. In truth, the business manager was in trouble because he had signed the Carmichael honorarium check. Soon Ellington, without consulting university administrators, secretly hired a black man, Arthur Danner from Alabama, to take over A&I finances after a white state employee temporarily did the job. While the governor might have preferred to place a white in the position permanently, it was too risky for now, because the students would surely protest. But blacks found out about Ellington's secret maneuvers. On July 6, Danner received an anonymous letter that warned him not to cooperate with the white state officials: "Son . . . the white people may offer you protection and 'Super Tom' President Davis will help you get adjusted, but you should know his days are numbered here. Don't be a Young Uncle Tom; stay where you are if you know what is good for you and your family." Danner sent a copy of the letter to the Tennessee education commissioner and said on July 8 that he had "stayed clear of making any comments" to A&I alumni in Alabama who had asked him about taking the job at Tennessee State. The daily newspapers cooperated with Ellington's administration, announcing the appointment without mentioning that the university had not participated in the selection. Danner would receive a high salary and a house at cheap rent on campus, and he would report directly to the state commissioner of education.

The same month the business manager was fired, Tennessee A&I State officials again began expelling student demonstrators, including James M. Booth, Fred Brooks, and Kenneth R. Jones, for taking part in the riots. Brooks was suspended for "abusive language to the faculty and administration, public drunkenness, and participating in a riot." President Davis reported to the disciplinary committee that Brooks had said, "We came here to eliminate you and tear this joint down," as the activists demonstrated in front of the president's house and the cafeteria at the Women's Building. On August 9, the dean of students sent a list of seventy-nine students who allegedly participated in the April disturbances with Brooks to the registrar with a note: "Tuition and fees should *not* be *accepted*." The chairman of the disciplinary committee said, "We believe in free speech, but we cannot allow students to interfere with other students." He claimed that these "other students" had been harassed for not joining the demonstrations.

Militant leaders accused some students of being Uncle Toms and told them that they had to choose sides in the war against racism. A campus flyer dated August 17, 1967, proclaimed, "The great white fathers downtown have given the ultimatum to the administrators of this school. They have begun the conspiracy to seize total control of the puppet administration and the student body. Student names in the *Tennessean* and *Banner* in connection with the April disturbances [are] being used to dismiss students from A&I;

legislation passed to decrease A&I out-of-state enrollment; increased dormitory fees. Cast your vote for student power!!!" In October, the first permanent head of campus security forces was hired at Tennessee State. Feeling the pressure, Davis left in December for the family farm in Canton, Mississippi, and took sick leave in January 1968. In May, he submitted his resignation, effective that September.

At Vanderbilt University, Chancellor Alexander Heard defended freedom of speech on the campus. Vanderbilt trustee and *Banner* publisher James Stahlman, however, was not only upset about the Carmichael affair, but he and some fellow trustees also worried about the radical Students for a Democratic Society (SDS) chapter on campus. The SDS objected to Dow Chemical Company recruiting at Vanderbilt, because the company manufactured napalm, which was being used "to burn people to death" in Vietnam. SDS members threatened to burn a cat with gasoline on campus to demonstrate their point. A member of the Stahlman faction on the Board of Trustees said that the radicals "damn well will suffer the consequences of their actions" if such a thing happened. Stahlman declared his belief that the Republican candidate, Richard M. Nixon, was the country's best hope in the 1968 November election. Many other whites who supported Nixon believed that he would end the civil rights movement.

Fred Brooks established a summer "Liberation School" in Nashville, and refused to take the oath to be drafted into the U.S. army, but city officials denied him any Model Cities federal funds to support the project. Like the NCLC, by 1969 SNCC had outgrown its effectiveness and quietly faded away. Historian Clayborne Carson, who acknowledged the death of SNCC at about this time, wrote:

> SNCC workers failed to resolve the enduring dilemmas that perplexed earlier radicals and revolutionaries, but they provided a surviving legacy. This legacy is most evident among black people in the Deep South communities where SNCC became enmeshed in strong local struggles. . . . Local black leaders, who gained new conceptions of themselves as a result of SNCC's work, carried on political movements after SNCC workers departed and the excitement of protest subsided. In other areas of the South where SNCC was active, the evidence of success is less dramatic, but there is no doubt that an important and irreversible change occurred among black people during the 1960s.

Despite the loss of SNCC, the civil rights movement was not over. The movement focused on concerns that had not been addressed by sit-ins, voter drives, and legislation. For instance, in the late 1960s, Avon N. Williams Jr. and the NAACP responded to requests by community leaders to file a lawsuit, *Nashville I-40 Steering Committee v. Ellington*, seeking injunctive relief against the form that interstate highway construction through Nashville was taking. A number of stalwarts from the community near Fisk and Tennessee State— including Jamye and McDonald Williams, other professors, and activists Edwin Mitchell, Mrs. C. M. McGruder, Mrs. C. J. Walker, and Evelyn Sugg— organized the group opposing Interstate 40 and elected Flournoy Coles president. They believed that state transportation officials had unfairly restricted the on and off ramps and that the interstate was being used to isolate black residents. The officials countered that they had published notices of the route of the highway. Inman E. Otey, president of the Middle Tennessee Business Association, developed much of the proof in the plaintiffs' case. But the millions of dollars already spent buying the right of way helped the defendants to prevail despite substantial evidence of racial discrimination. More than thirty years later, a local white leader, Nelson Andrews, said of the controversy: "I felt for some time . . . we were doing some dumb things in this community because we were all looking at things from our own point of view, and there wasn't any sense of the total community in looking at things. If there was one thing that triggered it for me was putting I-40 through North Nashville; [we] cut it in two and . . . [and] took a growth pattern and stopped it dead in its tracks." He was explaining why he and others had formed Leadership Nashville to train the city's new leaders and teach them to "do it better."

[∗]

Over in Memphis, Maxine Smith of the NAACP provided leadership on several fronts in March 1967. She charged the federal marshal's office and the county sheriff with discriminatory hiring and assignment of black deputies. Then she opposed certain appointments to the Shelby County Board of Education because of the appointees' dismal records on race relations. She also began an investigation into the employment practices at the local RCA manufacturing plant. In April, three hundred people marched on city hall, protesting the recent deaths of Negroes at the hands of the police, which forced an internal investigation into police brutality. The NAACP called for a police review board. In July, the NAACP called for the mayor to fire all the park commissioners for keeping the swimming pools closed four years after the *Watson* decision. In August 1967, blacks reported to the local NAACP that seating segregation remained in the city auditorium. The Tennessee Advisory

Committee to the U.S. Commission on Civil Rights published a report, *Employment, and Administration of Justice and Health Services in Memphis–Shelby County, Tennessee* (1967), which gave credibility to the local NAACP's claims of widespread employment discrimination.

Discrimination was most certainly rampant in the city's sanitation department. For example, on rainy days, Negro garbagemen, who made up 98 percent of the public sanitation workers in Memphis, were routinely paid for two hours of work and sent home, whereas the white workers were encouraged to stay around a little longer and receive a day's pay. White men (often less educated than some of the Negro workers) drove the trucks and earned higher wages, while the Negroes walked behind, lifting and emptying the heavy garbage cans.

Ernest Parker of South Memphis was one such garbageman. He earned less than $1.50 an hour at age fifty. He would arrive at home, pull off his tall rubber boots to rest his tired feet, sit on the front porch on his side of a rented shotgun frame duplex, and wave and chat with the neighbors on Ford Place. Sometimes, a passing youngster would run to the little store a block away on the southwest corner of Porter and Williams streets to get "some real cold Royal Crown Colas" for Parker in return for a nickel tip. Both youngsters and the grownups respected "Mr. Parker" because he had a steady job—a nasty, hard one to be sure, but nevertheless a city job. His wife, a domestic worker, was a "good-looking brown-skin woman," elegant and strong. The couple dreamed the same dreams as other Americans and aspired for success. Parker had managed to buy a used Cadillac, which he and his wife had proudly driven around for a month or so. But it had broken down and sat rusting in the backyard, refusing to run another mile. The Parkers and a third of the Negro families in Memphis were living below the poverty level, and yet they, "the working poor," worked every day—and as hard as the white families. At the pool hall, the movie theater, Harlem House Restaurant, the busy shoe repair shop, the noisy barbershop, the Jewish-owned variety store, the neighborhood bar, and an infamous and lively shoeshine shop on the nearby corner of Mississippi Boulevard and Walker Avenue, these Memphis residents talked about the plight of sanitation workers and supported their cause.

On February 12, some 1,375 garbage workers and the all-Negro Memphis Local 1733 of the American Federation of State, Local, and Municipal Employees (AFSCME), a union affiliated with the AFL-CIO, declared a strike, demanding better wages and improved working conditions. T. O. Jones, a garbageman since 1959, effectively organized the strikers. On February 19, political clubs and the NAACP endorsed the strike and participated in nightly meetings at area churches. City councilman Fred Davis, who chaired the committee on public works, attempted to conduct a hearing on the matter on the morning of February 22, but 700 fiery activists overcrowded the meeting room and shouted Davis down; he ordered the meeting closed. O. Z. Evers shouted, "We are going to stay right here." The crowd began singing, "We Shall Not Be Moved," and ordered cold cuts, bread, mustard, mayonnaise, and began their lunch on the large conference table. The *Memphis Commercial Appeal* (Feb. 23, 1968) cried, "Threat of Anarchy."

Meanwhile, on March 1, 1968, the National Advisory Commission on Civil Disorders turned in its final report, which stated, "Our nation is moving toward two societies, one black, one white—separate and unequal."

The A. Philip Randolph Institute and the labor unions came to the aid of the Memphis sanitation workers. The Negro union members at the Memphis Furniture Factory would give aid to the strikers. Jessie H. Turner and the local NAACP arranged for Roy Wilkins to speak to thousands at Mason Temple on March 14, 1968. Yet, Mayor Henry Loeb refused the good offices of the Memphis Committee on Community Relations, and he paid no attention to a request by the Catholic Council on Human Relations to settle the dispute. After an attempted march by strikers and their supporters turned into a police free-for-all, Maxine Smith said, "The police went crazy like savages. One girl, a billy club just gouged her head out." Jailed Negro women were humiliated when the police forced them to use the men's restrooms.

James M. Lawson Jr. was now in Memphis. Ever since the Methodist Church had transferred him there in 1962 from the Nashville area, he was stunned to see the continuing effects of Jim Crow in this larger city. Afro-Memphis was a far more complex community, with many political factions, than the smaller black community in Nashville. Lawson became a new force in the Memphis movement after becoming pastor of the Centenary Methodist Church at 584 McLemore. He began pushing for more NAACP confrontation with the city governmental agencies. He formed Community on the Move for Equality (COME) and started action groups to help address the high poverty, inadequate health facilities, indecent housing, and unequal education. Lawson approached the school board with an NAACP delegation and organized hundreds of people to picket the business of the school board president. Many people called him a troublemaker, but for Lawson the demonstrations were "a stride towards freedom." He explained that Moses, Jeremiah, Jesus Christ, and Thomas Paine had used public demonstrations to fight the wicked.

Lawson convinced local ministers to endorse the garbage strike, and COME spearheaded an economic boycott, which included the Loeb's Bar-B-

Cue chain, owned by members of the mayor's family, to force the mayor to negotiate with the garbagemen. Lawson asked Martin Luther King Jr. to come to Memphis immediately and speak for the garbage strikers. However, King and SCLC officers were touring the country to gain support for their proposed Poor People's March on Washington, D.C.; this effort was mounted in the realization that, in the aftermath of the Civil Rights Bill of 1964, the civil rights movement had to focus on lifting blacks to economic parity with whites. The SCLC leadership saw this as the real prerequisite to ridding the nation of racial discrimination, and in this regard, King would see eye to eye with Richard M. Nixon, who was running for president at the time. The SCLC leaders were reluctant to divert attention from these objectives to come to Memphis, but Lawson had rendered many valuable services to the SCLC and King. Now, the SCLC's help—more specifically, the national recognition and charisma of King—was desperately needed to keep the Memphis garbage strike alive.

King did come to Memphis, speaking at Mason Temple on March 18. He was so moved by the crowd of thousands that he pledged to return on Friday, March 22, and lead a march. On that particular day, however, it snowed nearly sixteen inches. Cars and buses were backed up for miles into Arkansas as they tried to reach the Mississippi River bridge entrance into Memphis. The march was postponed and rescheduled for the following week. On March 28, the snow was gone, and the weather was hot. The marchers were delayed by several hours as they waited for King to arrive from the airport. Young leaders inside Clayborn Temple fired up some high school students. Reportedly, students had broken past their principals and teachers and went to other high schools, urging the students to go downtown and join the march. The young people did not appreciate the slow pace of events.

When the march began that day and turned from Hernando Street west onto Beale Street toward Main Street and the Mississippi River, there was disorganization, crowding, and pushing. Many street people and neighborhood drunks also joined the march since it was such a sunny day. No one would later admit where the leaders of the unruly faction came from, but at the rear of the crowd, some young people began snatching the large sticks from the protest signs and systematically breaking display windows. Lawson left King and ran to the back of the crowd to find out what was happening. He was mortified to see the broken windows and the police doing nothing about it. Fearing a setup, Lawson quickly returned to the front of the crowd and shouted for King to leave the scene. In his book *Orders to Kill: The Truth behind the Murder of Martin Luther King, Jr.* (1995), William F. Pepper wrote that the policemen were given an order not to break ranks and not to go after the *first* group of people breaking windows. And thus the march turned into a riot: tear gas hit the marchers taking refuge in Clayborn Temple; sixteen-year-old Larry Payne lost his life; at least sixty-two people suffered injuries; and one hundred people went to jail. When the way to the nearby Lorraine Motel was blocked, King was rushed by car to the electronically bugged River Bluff Holiday Inn.

King's people believed that local young militants started the riot. Charles L. Cabbage, a leader of the student organization, the Invaders, was called to the Holiday Inn to meet King and his assistant, Ralph Abernathy. J. Edgar Hoover's FBI agents, assigned to follow King, listened to the meeting via bugging devices, and some of the Invaders were FBI informants. Abernathy accused the Invaders of starting the trouble, but they denied the charge, even though Cabbage admitted that Lawson had refused to talk to the Invaders as partners in the movement. The Invaders consisted of some students at LeMoyne College, Memphis State University, and local high schools. The group focused on community work, the youth, and "black consciousness." SCLC leaders made peace with the Invaders and pledged to give them support if they agreed to insure nonviolence at the next march. King was secreted out of the city, vowing to return and prove that a peaceful march could take place. Lawson was embarrassed by the episode.

The riots tarnished King's image, particularly his credibility with regard to nonviolence. The *Whitehaven-Southaven Star* (Apr. 4, 1968), a neighborhood suburban newspaper in Memphis, published an article entitled "Africa's Bush Country Seemed Not Far Away Last Thursday." The article, which was reprinted in several local suburban papers, said, "We walked in the wake of unlashed animalistic destruction last Thursday . . . down Main Street and into Beale, in Memphis. Martin Luther King had conducted one more of his 'non-violent' marches; rather he had incited another of his marches." The writers also blamed union leaders for supporting the strike that led to the riot, and they mentioned that William Loeb, brother of Mayor Loeb, needlessly suffered destruction of his barbecue sandwich shop. U.S. Senator Robert Byrd of West Virginia said on the day following the riot: "Yesterday, the Nation was given a preview of what may be in store for this city by the outrageous and despicable riot that Martin Luther King helped to bring about in Memphis, Tennessee." West Tennessee congressmen Dan Kuykendall, Robert Everett, and Ray Blanton verbally attacked King on the floor of the House of Representatives, and they joined other congressmen in a failed attempt to outlaw the proposed Poor Peoples' March on the capital.

Memphis was placed on alert for the funeral of Larry Payne, which was held at Clayborn Temple with thousands in attendance. The policeman who shot the young man said that Payne had come at him "with the biggest knife I ever saw." Negroes were angered by this claim, believing, with justification, that Memphis policemen carried weapons to plant on any Negro they shot. Hardly anyone expected anything to be done about a white policeman murdering a black boy in Memphis. But no significant violent incidents followed the funeral.

SCLC leaders concluded that success in Memphis could perhaps quiet congressional opposition to the Poor People's March. They postponed that demonstration and scheduled a peaceful march for Memphis for Monday, April 8. But there were some bad omens. In Knoxville, some youngsters began a minor riot by throwing rocks at cars and businesses after an NAACP block party. No one knew the rock throwers as members of the community—which was highly unusual in a black community. On Sunday evening, March 31, President Johnson announced to a shocked nation that he would not run for reelection and that the bombing in Vietnam would be halted. Before King returned, a National Guard unit from nearby Milan had been sent into Memphis.

On April 2, 1968, King and his people returned to Memphis. They conferred with Lawson, NAACP leaders, and local ministers, and spoke to small groups at the churches. King was influenced to stay at the low-budget Lorraine Motel at 406 Mulberry Street, which was owned and operated by Walter and Lorraine Bailey. A three-story brick apartment building faced the motel. Mulberry Street was off a less-traveled part of Main Street and near train stations, warehouses, small businesses, and cheap rooming houses. Some local NAACP officials knew that the FBI had been spying on civil rights activities, and local police and federal spies were watching King and his people at the Lorraine Motel. Someone wanted the *Commercial Appeal* to run a paid advertisement with that notable 1957 picture of King at a Highlander Folk School Labor Day workshop, but the editor refused.

On the night of April 3, King gave his famous "I've been to the Mountaintop" speech at Mason Temple. He had not intended to speak, but he honored persistent requests to "say a few words." His eyes swelled with tears and fatigue, and confusion showed on his face. Two FBI agents were in the audience when King said:

> I am delighted to see each of you here tonight in spite of a storm warning. You reveal that you are determined to go on anyhow.

THE MOVEMENT TURNS VIOLENT

Something is happening in Memphis, something is happening in
the World . . . We aren't engaged in any negative protest and in
any negative arguments with anybody. We are saying that we are
determined to be men. We are determined to be people. We are
saying that we are God's children. And that we don't have to live
like we are forced to live . . . Now we're going to march again,
and we've got to march again, in order to put the issue where it
is supposed to be. . . . We aren't going to let any mace stop us.
We are masters in our nonviolent movement in disarming police
forces; they don't know what to do. That couldn't stop us [in
Birmingham]. And we just went on before the dogs and we would
look at them; and we'd go on before the water hoses and we
would look at it, and we'd just go on singing "Over my head I
see freedom in the air." We don't have to argue with anybody.
We don't have to curse and go around acting bad with our words.
We don't need any bricks and bottles . . . And our agenda calls
for withdrawing economic support from you . . . And then I got
into Memphis. And some began to say the threats, or talk about
the threats that were out. What would happen to me from some
of our sick white brothers? Well, I don't know what will happen
now. We've got some difficult days ahead. But it doesn't matter
with me now, because I've been to the mountaintop. And I don't
mind. Like anybody, I would like to live a long life. Longevity has
its place. But I'm not concerned about that now. I just want to do
God's will. And he's allowed me to go up to the mountain. And
I've looked over. And I've seen the Promised Land. I may not
get there with you. But I want you to know tonight that we, as
a people will get to the Promised Land. And I'm happy, tonight.
I'm not worried about anything. I'm not fearing any man: Mine
eyes have seen the glory of the coming of the Lord.

Benjamin L. Hooks had left a funeral and gone to Mason Temple to hear
King. Hooks recalled "the raining and lightening, gloomy, thunder, wind
howling, and could hear the rain on the auditorium's tin roof. I shall never
forget it as long as I live. I never heard him speak with such fervor and emotion
as that night. Little did I know this would be the last speech Dr. King would
make on this earth?" Hooks continued: "I now realize in the last 30 years that
Dr. King was right when he said on the night of April 3: 'We have some dark
and difficult days ahead.'"

On the morning of April 4, a biracial group of ministers met at Blair T.
Hunt's church to discuss the situation. The SCLC leaders met again with

Charles Cabbage and colleagues, who agreed not to take a prominent place in the march but would serve as monitors to help control the crowd. The FBI was asking President Johnson for more wiretaps to get information to discredit King. City officials were busy moving black firemen and policemen to new but distant posts. The black detective squad assigned to King during recent visits to Memphis was not assigned to him this time. Mayor Loeb was leaving town, "headed to Ole Miss University to make a speech."

After spending all day in court trying to nullify a ban against the march, the SCLC leaders decided to go to Reverend Billy Kyle's house for a big soul food feast. This would help Dr. King relax and put him in a jovial mood. They were to join Maxine and Vasco Smith and fifteen others at Kyle's place before the next mass meeting. The group relaxed and let their guard down, perhaps too much. King went to the balcony of the motel, while the group waited for Abernathy to put on his tie and come out of the room. As King leaned over the balcony to joke with Jessie Jackson and a car of SCLC people, he was hit by a single rifle shot. A few staff members numbly tried to scoop up some of the blood and place it in a jar; others hysterically screamed for the police, pointing animatedly west, toward the direction of the gunshot—that cheap rental apartment building, where a bathroom window had a direct view of King on the balcony. King lay there with a crushed cigarette in his frozen hand. Law enforcement officials appeared from out of the shadows.

Maxine Smith arrived at the motel to join the trip to Kyle's house only to find that King had been taken to the hospital. Mayor Loeb, who was furtively traveling in Mississippi, turned around at the news of the shooting. Lawson had been speaking at a local college, and only after returning home did he hear the news on the television. He headed to WDIA Radio Station to urge calm in the black community. An hour later, Dr. Martin Luther King Jr. died in the hospital. Reports crackled on police radios that a white Mustang was being pursued north of the scene. But natives of the city knew that it would be foolish to head in that direction to exit Memphis and get out of Tennessee. And indeed, the report proved false, perhaps a decoy. The origin of the radio transmissions remained a mystery, according to Frank Holloman, the commissioner of fire and police. Robert F. Kennedy, the former attorney general and now a U.S. senator from New York (as well as a candidate for the Democratic presidential nomination), promised Coretta King to help move the body to Atlanta. Kennedy, his wife, and Jacqueline Kennedy would attend the funeral. Ellington sent a telegram to Coretta King: "Every action possible is being taken to apprehend the person or persons responsible for this horrible crime. My office is at your disposal for any service we may render."

Rioting broke out in Memphis and across the nation—an expression of frustration among politically impotent black citizens. King's death came on the heels of a near riot in Nashville after police invaded a student apartment on Hermosa Street, where shooting erupted, two persons died, and the police began beating and brutalizing young black men. In front of the Air Force ROTC Building, the Student Government Association president at Tennessee A&I calmed an angry crowd and persuaded the students to return to their dormitories. A small riot occurred at Osage and 23rd Avenue North, after police shot a drunken man. Forty persons were arrested for curfew violations. Five whites, including an A&I professor, reportedly were arrested for attempting to march on Governor Ellington's mansion.

Memphis sent official representatives to the funeral in Atlanta. A prominent local businessman loaned his jet and furnished a rental car in Atlanta for the delegation. The AFSCME sent its own delegation. The Memphis NAACP sponsored four buses to go to Atlanta. Richard Nixon attended the funeral.

On Sunday, April 7, the national day of mourning for King was observed in Memphis. James Lawson, speaking at one of the programs, said, "And no matter how much we try, from now on until there is no longer any written history, Memphis will be known as the place where Martin Luther King was crucified." The city was filled with national civil rights and union leaders. Five hundred angry students marched on downtown Chattanooga after a memorial service for King. Some looting occurred in the area, and twenty-seven persons were arrested. In East Tennessee, the students at Morristown College honored King by issuing a resolution to respect his nonviolent principles, and they and the college president appeared in a joint photograph in the Morristown newspaper to calm the local people.

Blacks were angry not only about King's death but also about so many whites' rejoicing in the murder. These whites openly epitomized arrogant ethnic power and racial hatred; they hoped that the murder would end the Negro's civil rights movement. "I do not share a high regard for Dr. King," said Senator Strom Thurmond. "He pretended to be nonviolent." And an article in the *Whitehaven-Southaven Star* (Apr. 11, 1968) said, "He [King] exploited his people as truly as did the union leaders, and as have the Lawsons, the Abernathys, the Carmichaels, and the Rap Browns."

President Johnson sent federal labor officials to Memphis to help negotiate an end to the strike. Mayor Loeb said that the city could only give an eight-cent-per-hour raise and not the forty-five-cent raise the strikers were requesting. He also that it would not deduct union dues from the city paychecks for the men; this provision would make it easier for the union to collect dues by receiving one check from the city rather than separate checks from individual members. The pastors from four of Memphis's largest Southern Baptist churches expressed sorrow over King's death and supported a ministers' march on the mayor's office demanding a negotiated end to the strike. On April 16, the Memphis garbage workers received recognition of their union, deduction of union dues through their credit union, a raise of fifteen cents, and eligibility for promotions. Councilman J. O. Patterson said, "We [city officials] could have avoided all this, including the death of Dr. King."

To commemorate King's death, Ralph Abernathy returned to Memphis to lead a mass rally on Good Friday, April 4, 1969. He contended that evidence had been found that some of the troublemakers who had started the first riot in Memphis were inspired by the FBI. According to Abernathy, King had said, "Ralph, I want to get out of Memphis. You've got to get me out of Memphis." Of King's murder, Abernathy commented, "There has been a crucifixion in our nation, but here in this spring season as we see the blossoms and smell the fresh air we know that the Resurrection will shortly appear." Andrew Young seemed to imply that Lawson was partly to blame for the disorder by not properly preparing for the march and not staffing it with marshals to keep the crowd peaceful. Young believed that the whole movement was the assassin's target, but he did not admit that the FBI was involved in the harassment. Meanwhile, Lawson said, "The plantation theory of government for the most part still dominates. We have made small beginnings in terms of black and white people waking up and trying to remake the city [of Memphis] into a humane place." At a SNCC press conference, Stokely Carmichael said, "When white America killed Dr. King, she declared war on us [black people]."

In 1969, there was speculation that King's murder was the result of a conspiracy among government officials and that it perhaps involved some downtown businessmen. It is estimated that the FBI and other federal intelligence agencies enrolled thousands of informants for spying on civil rights activities. Clarence R. Kelly, Hoover's successor as FBI director, publicly said that a group of FBI agents were responsible for harassing King and that they "should be brought to account." Newspapers in Memphis criticized King for staying in "a luxury hotel"; these criticisms were reportedly inspired by calls to the papers from undisclosed persons. Of Robert Kennedy and King, author John A. Williams said, "Hoover hated both men. . . . The press turns out to have been a co-conspirator."

J. Edgar Hoover believed that the civil rights movement was the work of Communists, and he especially targeted King, whose file would include sixteen FBI tapes of wiretaps approved by presidents and attorney generals of the United States. King had been critical of the FBI for not doing enough to find and arrest people suspected of bombing and murdering civil rights leaders, and in a letter to Hoover he wrote, "I have sincerely questioned the effectiveness of the FBI in racial incidents, particularly where bombings and brutalities against Negroes are at issue. . . . I will be happy to discuss this question with you at length in the near future." Hoover, King, and Abernathy reportedly met for a discussion in a meeting at the FBI offices on December 1, 1964, just days before King would leave for Sweden to receive the Nobel Peace Prize. But southern district FBI agents continued wiretaps on his hotel rooms, home, and private life. They prepared a file on "Martin Luther King Jr.: His Personal Conduct" and leaked it to his wife, the press, and to Negro Baptist church leaders.

[*]

Hoover reportedly gained the friendship of fellow moralist Joseph H. Jackson, the president of the National Baptist Convention, U.S.A., Inc. (NBCI), which was centered in Nashville. However, civil rights leaders held the Reverend Jackson at a distance. In 1956, when Jackson sent a barrage of letters to black leaders urging them to celebrate the second anniversary of the *Brown* court decision, Charles S. Johnson at Fisk answered apprehensively: "To me, this [*Brown*] decision is a national moral victory. My only concern—which has no elegance for a responsible and powerful organization of Christians such as your organization of Baptists represents—is that this historical development in the process of maturing American democracy, should not be exploited for fortuitous reasons merely of gaining public attention." In 1960, Jackson engineered a move that ousted Martin Luther King Jr. as an officer in this black Baptist convention "because of the type of militant campaign carried on against his [King's] own denomination and his own race." Jackson said, "All protest being directed according to the Constitution of the United States will be of such caliber that hostile forces of the nation and enemies of a democratic society will not join with us and use our methods and techniques for the purpose of weakening and destroying the nation. The [USA] convention by its actions rejected nonviolent civil disobedience as the best tool to use in the struggle for first-class citizenship. In a democratic social order, one cannot harmonize disobedience with nonviolence."

Two black ministers from Memphis, S. A. Owens and R. W. Norsworthy, held offices in the NBCI; yet, at the same time they were supporters of the

NAACP and the SCLC. Owens resigned his office in the Baptist convention while Norsworthy remained. King supporters tried to elect a new NBCI president, but Jackson was reelected at the September convention where his supporters often stood on the seats and began shouting "by acclamation, by acclamation," thus aborting the democratic electoral process. When pro-King delegates persisted in demanding fair and open elections in 1961, a fight broke out at the podium. The Jackson forces closed the convention without electing a president by ballot. In October they met in "executive session" and declared another term for Jackson. This outraged democratic reformers, who exited the NBCI and formed the National Progressive Baptist Convention, Inc. (NPBCI), on November 15, 1961.

Kelly Miller Smith and his First Baptist Church in Nashville were supporters of the NPBCI, favoring church involvement in civil rights activities. In his book *Social Crisis Preaching* (1984), Smith said:

> During the Civil Rights Era of the sixties, many communities held mass meetings for the purpose of providing information on the progress of the 'movement,' for the recruitment of participants, for raising funds, and for providing inspiration and encouragement. Speakers on those occasions were usually ministers who rose to uncommon heights in the presentation of their mass meeting sermons. . . . Preaching, in spite of its fragility and other problems, is a viable means for addressing critical social issues. . . . The social crisis sermon . . . is a call to action.

The National Baptist Convention of America (NBCA), which had split with the NBCI in 1915, was affiliated closely with the National Baptist Publishing Board in Nashville. Both black Baptist agencies supported civil disobedience tactics. "The present condition through which we as a race are passing should encourage us as a group to take every advantage to assert our claim and right to full status of first-class citizens in this country for which our sons have bled and died," the president of the NBCA, C. D. Pettaway, said, "The day of the 'Uncle Tom' is gone forever."

Despite support from black churches, the modern civil rights movement in Tennessee did not have the public and moral support of most of the white church organizations; for many years white Christians generally did not connect race, morality, civil rights, and Christian principles within their religious philosophy. The Southern Baptist Convention had originated out of opposition to the Northern Baptists' antislavery positions in 1845, and for decades afterward, it saw no contradiction in being Christian, owning slaves, and being opposed to racial integration after slavery. In 1955, the SBC did offer a mild endorsement of *Brown* as being "in harmony with the constitutional guarantee of equality," and later it gave no official support to the Christian academy movement that arose in massive resistance to school desegregation. And in 1958, the president of the SBC said, "I realize that we [white Southern Baptists] cannot have complete unanimity in these matters, but it would be tragic for us to assume that we can function as a Christian body without assigning to trusted representatives of the convention the task of pointing out our Christian duty with respect to social evils and current evils. Discontent of the minority [Negroes] is the symptom of an illness which affects the nation and the world." In February 1959, the SBC hosted Negro Baptist convention representatives in a meeting in Nashville to discuss some common understanding of the civil rights movement. In 1961, however, the SBC spoke against the Freedom Rides. Finally, at its June 20–22, 1995, session in Atlanta, the SBC approved *Resolution No. 1—On Racial Reconciliation*: "Whereas, Our relationship to African Americans has been hindered from the beginning by the role that slavery played in the formation of the Southern Baptist Convention . . . therefore, be it resolved, that we . . . unwaveringly denounce racism, in all its forms, as deplorable sin."

It was only after the civil rights movement transformed itself into public protest that the churches begin to feel any pressure to support the Negro's fight for justice. The National Council of Churches launched some of their civil rights strategies from Tennessee. On June 7, 1963, the general board of the NCC established a commission on religion and race. The National Jewish Congress, United Methodist Church, United Presbyterian Church, U.S.A., and United Church of Christ also established civil rights commissions. In April 1969, SNCC leader James Forman held the National Black Power Conference and demanded that white churches either give funds or pay reparations for rehabilitation of the black community. The Black Power movement led to the creation of black caucuses within the white church organizations, including the Black Methodists for Church Renewal, which was led by James Lawson within the United Methodist Church.

[∗]

In Memphis, the protests continued after King's death. The Memphis NACCP filed sixty-six complaints of brutality against local police, county sheriff deputies, state troopers, and National Guardsmen, and it campaigned against racially biased books in the school system, sent letters of protest to the mayor, recruited picketers to block garbage trucks, tied up city hall telephones, and boycotted downtown businesses. All these activities "have sharply increased the work and involvement of the Memphis Branch NAACP," said Maxine Smith. John Lewis was glad to see the end of 1968, "that horrific year."

Reflecting on the movement after the King assassination, John A. Williams said, "[T]he thing for conspirators and conspirators-to-be to remember is that there will always come along another Cinqué, another Gabriel, another John Brown, another Nat Turner, another Martin King. The Chain must have many links, and Martin King was but one of them."

From left, Norman Hill Sr., William Radcliffe, and Norman Hill Jr., wearing the uniforms of the U.S. Colored Troops, participate in the 1998 dedication of the monument commemorating the Battle of Nashville (1864). Courtesy of Norman Hill Sr.

Beale Street Baptist Church, where union leader A. Philip Randolph spoke in 1944 during a visit to Memphis. Photo by the author.

Kennerly Public School for Negroes, built in 1949, as it appears today, in Sewanee, Tennessee. Photo by the author.

Nashville Colored YMCA, 1950. From the *Nashville Globe*.

Reporters outside First Colored Baptist Church, Nashville, 1960. Courtesy of the Metro Nashville–Davidson County Archives.

Maxine Smith (second from left) and Vasco Smith (third from left) test a newly desegregated restaurant with friends in Memphis, 1961. Courtesy of Memphis–Shelby County Library and Information Center, Memphis and Shelby County Room.

James M. Lawson (far left), Maxine Smith (center), Harold Middlebrook (far right), and others participate in Ministers' March for Civil Rights in downtown Memphis, 1962. Courtesy of Memphis–Shelby County Library and Information Center, Memphis and Shelby County Room.

John Lewis, head of Nashville Student Movement, during downtown demonstrations, 1963. Courtesy of the Metro Nashville–Davidson County Archives.

Nashville police subdue civil rights demonstrator, 1963. Courtesy of the Metro Nashville–Davidson County Archive.

Nashville police drag a sit-in demonstrator, 1963. Courtesy of the Metro Nashville–Davidson County Archives.

Student civil rights demonstrators in downtown Nashville, 1963. Courtesy of the Metro Nashville–Davidson County Archives.

Observers watch civil rights demonstrators at Davidson County Court House, 1963. Courtesy of the Metro Nashville–Davidson County Archives.

White college students support civil rights movement in Nashville, 1963. Courtesy of the Metro Nashville–Davidson County Archives.

Sanitation workers march in Memphis, 1968. Courtesy of the University of Memphis Library.

Martin Luther King Jr. speaks at Mason Temple, Memphis, during the sanitation workers' strike, 1968. Courtesy of the University of Memphis Library.

During the controversy over the merger of Tennessee State University with UT Nashville, students march to the Federal Courthouse in Nashville, 1974. Courtesy of the Tennessee State University Library.

THE BLACK REPUBLICANS

CIVIL RIGHTS AND POLITICS
IN TENNESSEE

Each generation of African Americans sought salvation in politics and the economic rewards such power could bestow and protect. Even in antebellum times free Negroes voted in elections, paid taxes, and served their required time in local militias. But the few (5 percent) free Negroes, most of them women and children, had no real impact on the early political system. After the 1831 Nat Turner slave rebellion, free Negroes, slaves, and Indians were viewed as even greater threats to the economic ambitions of the white man. During the 1834 constitutional convention, some delegates included a constitutional provision that the legislature could pass no laws to free slaves without the permission of their owners; also, a delegate inserted the word "white" into the clause "males 21 years of age" for voting requirements. In March 1835, the people voted to accept these changes. Until then, free Negroes had voted for the Whig Party and against the Democratic Party of President Andrew Jackson. Whigs included more wealthy slave owners than did the Democrats, and yet the Whigs were more willing to compromise over the expansion of slavery than to destroy the American Union over the issue. The Democrats were more obsessive about slavery and race matters, and they talked openly about secession and war to preserve "state's rights."

In this age of Jacksonian Democracy, American politics simply was an orderly process to distribute and transfer power and peacefully divide the spoils of a rich land among the "People of Plenty." The predominant number of new inhabitants—people from Europe—felt, of course, that the New World's land and its riches belonged to those who had the sheer and naked power to maintain control. By the 1830s, European settlers were throwing off the tattered rags of white bondage—indentured servitude, redemption contracts, and convict contracts—that allowed most of them to come to America. But the settlers of African origins were bogged down with the issues of slavery and freedom, and until the former was dead, the latter was obtained, and racism against free Negroes was outlawed, persons of African descent could not enjoy any of America's political spoils, and none of them could be respected as economic equals in American society.

Informed Negroes closely watched the presidential election of 1856, when the issue of slavery was openly debated. Indeed, the parties and sections of the country had been trying to settle the slavery issues through a series of compromises: the Northwest Ordinance (1785), Constitution compromises (1787), the Missouri Compromise (1820), the Compromise of 1850, and the Kansas-Nebraska Act (1854). Political debates in 1856 indicated that an alternative existed to the Democratic and Whig parties, that freedom for persons of African descent was possible in the not-too-distant future, and that not all white men believed it was necessary to shut out all other Americans from accessing the spoils of a rich land. The Republican Party, founded in 1854, sponsored a candidate. However, realizing that politics was dangerous for the Negro but necessary for white men, vigilantes ran Negroes away from the 1856 street-corner political debates. The Democratic candidate, James Buchanan of Pennsylvania, who was sympathetic to the slave states, won the 1856 election. When rumors of slave rebellion swept Tennessee, many slaves were accused and jailed, and some were hanged. Prosperous Negroes were victimized during the 1856 race riot in Nashville.

In October 1859, the abolitionist John Brown, educated in the antislavery seminaries of Cincinnati, led a raid on the U.S. arsenal at Harpers Ferry, Virginia, with the aim of liberating slaves through armed insurrection. After being captured along with some free Negro compatriots from Ohio, Brown was tried and hanged and thus became a martyr to the antislavery cause. The following year, the Republican candidate, Abraham Lincoln of Illinois, won the November presidential election. In December, South Carolina became the first state to break with the Union. Eventually, eleven of the fifteen slave states seceded. Once the Civil War started, slavery began to crumble, and Congress passed the Confiscation Acts of 1861 and 1862, which allowed Union armies to retain fugitive slaves. President Lincoln issued the Emancipation

Proclamation on January 1, 1863. In response, Jefferson Davis, the president of the Confederacy, declared that all free Negroes must submit to slavery.

The Union army, however, had easily occupied Tennessee in February 1862, producing a favorable environment for the Negro's renewed political participation. Federal forces in Tennessee included 20,133 Negro soldiers, whose honorable service gave credence to the Negro's demands for freedom and citizenship. In August 1864, the state's Negro leaders held their first political rally under the shadow of Fort Gillem, now the site of Fisk University. That fall, they sent delegates to the National Colored Men's Convention at Syracuse, New York, where they met with such prominent figures as Frederick Douglass and John Mercer Langston. The National Equal Rights League was formed at this meeting. Upon returning to Tennessee, the leaders petitioned Military Governor Andrew Johnson to declare a "Tennessee Emancipation Proclamation." On Thanksgiving Day 1864, the Tennessee chapter of the National Equal Rights League was formed to push for full freedom and equal citizenship through constitutional amendment. During the November 1864 presidential elections, the Tennessee Negro leaders held a mock election, giving all but four of their votes to Lincoln. For the January 1865 Emancipation Proclamation celebration in Nashville, they hosted a visit by Langston, who met with Governor Johnson about Negro issues. Tennessee voters abolished slavery in March 1865. By December 13, 1865, the required number of states had approved the Thirteenth Amendment to the U.S. Constitution, thus outlawing slavery throughout the nation. Next, Congress passed the 1866 Civil Rights Bill, giving freedmen citizenship, equal protection of the laws, and due process of the laws. The *Paris (Tennessee) Intelligencer* of February 16, 1867 said that was "like the gathering of dusk" when Negroes packed the state House of Representatives gallery during the debate on the suffrage bill that would extend voting rights to Negroes. The bill passed the Tennessee General Assembly on February 25, 1867. Negro leaders held a political mass meeting in March 1867 in the state capital. They and the Radical Republicans—those members of the party who had been most strongly in favor of abolition and of extending full citizenship rights to Negroes—took control of the local government in September, and two Negroes were elected to the Nashville City Council. The state militia had to be employed to escort the new government into City Hall. A few Negroes, such as Elias Polk (a former slave servant to President James K. Polk), formed Colored Democratic Clubs and cooperated with their white friends to oppose the "carpetbaggers."

In Tennessee and elsewhere, however, almost all Negro voters would remain loyal Republicans for decades to come. In November 1868, they voted in their first presidential election since 1832, casting nearly all their votes for Ulysses S. Grant, the former general and Republican candidate. Negroes won various offices in Tennessee throughout Reconstruction. In 1868, W. S. McTier was elected to the Maryville Board of Aldermen, while Edward Shaw was elected to the Shelby County Commission in 1869. "Teach them [the Republicans] that you [blacks] have rights to be respected," Shaw told his supporters. In the presidential election year of 1876, Francis Yardley of Knoxville ran for governor. Five Negroes were elected to the Nashville City Council in 1868, and between 1878 and 1885, the council consistently included two or three Negroes. Blacks sat in the Knoxville City Council until 1890. Josiah T. Settles, a graduate of Howard University Law School, joined the criminal court of Shelby County in 1887. G. H. Clowens became a magistrate in the Thirteenth Judicial District of Memphis.

In 1872, Davidson County elected the first Negro, Sampson W. Keeble (a Republican), to the General Assembly; he served from 1873 to 1875. Between 1880 and 1893, Negroes won fourteen elections to the General Assembly. Nashville's Thomas Sykes became a state representative from 1881 to 1883, while Thomas F. Cassels (1881–83), Greene E. Evans (1885–87), William A. Fields (1885–87), Leonard Howard (1883–85), and Isham F. Norris (1891–93) represented Memphis–Shelby County. Evans was born in Fayette County, graduated from Fisk University, became a teacher, and then a mail carrier. John W. Boyd represented Tipton County from 1881 to 1883. Born into slavery of parents from Virginia, Boyd first became a magistrate in Civil District 10 in Tipton County, then won his seat in the General Assembly because of a split in the local Democratic Party. He used his term to try to get Jim Crow laws repealed and thereafter became a farmer and an informal lawyer. He was buried in the Negro cemetery near Mason. Samuel E. McElwee represented Haywood County (1883–89); Monroe Gooden (1887–89) and David F. Rivers (1883–87) represented Fayette County; and William C. Hodge (1885–87) and Styles Linton Hutchins (1887–89) represented Chattanooga–Hamilton County. Hodge was born in North Carolina in 1846 and came to Tennessee as a stonemason, served as a transfer agent at the railroad depot in Chattanooga, and became alderman for the Fourth Ward, serving from 1878 to 1887. Stiles Hutchins practiced law in Chattanooga until 1905. Jessie M. H. Graham was elected to the legislature from Montgomery County and seated on January 4, 1897, but the other legislators voted to unseat him because he "lacked sufficient residency in Tennessee," having lived for a while on the Kentucky side. He had attended Fisk University, taught school, and edited the *Clarksville*

Enterprise. Graham served as a lieutenant during World War I and thereafter helped form the American Legion Post No. 3 in Clarksville.

The Republican Negro legislators pushed to outlaw Jim Crow laws, repeal contract labor laws, and secure state funds to support Negro schools and colleges; they also worked to have Negro students included in Tennessee's expenditures of federal land grant funds. Cassels served on the House Education and Common Schools Committee; submitted a bill in June 1870 to repeal the law that prohibited sexual intercourse between whites, Negroes, mulattos, and "persons of mixed blood descended from the Negro race"; and introduced a bill to create the office of county superintendent of public roads and bridges. Sykes served on the Penitentiary Committee when Negro imprisonment increased significantly. He submitted bills to build a better prison, to dispense fairly the federal land grant funds to the University of Tennessee, and to force the Tennessee School for the Blind and Deaf to admit Negroes. Samuel McElwee served on the Military Affairs Committee, while Rivers was a member of the Federal Relations Committee. While serving on the Public Grounds and Buildings Committee, Norris presented a bill to prevent racial discrimination on the railroads. Negro legislators also supported bills in 1887 "to promote the freedom of elections and the parity of the ballot box."

During Reconstruction, a milieu of terror and political corruption prevailed under the neo-Confederate and Democratic Party administrations. James C. Napier of Nashville headed a delegation of Negroes to Washington in March 1870 to request federal help against white terrorism in Tennessee. In 1876, when President Rutherford B. Hayes visited Nashville, Napier again was the spokesman asking for "an equal chance" for the Negro. In 1881, a delegation of Tennessee Negroes met with newly elected President James A. Garfield, who told them that there would be no second-class citizens in America. Election fraud and efforts to restrict the Negro vote became a particular concern. In 1885, the Tennessee governor told the General Assembly that there were "great delays in forwarding election returns, [which served as] open channels to fraud, and should be strictly forbidden." Some election officers took up to three weeks before forwarding returns to the state office. In 1887, bills to "promote the freedom of elections and the parity of the ballot-box" were submitted in the General Assembly. In January 1889, the governor again asked the legislature to address the issues of fraud and cheating, noting, "Many men vote more than once and it is impossible to prevent it, hard to detect them, and more difficult to punish them." Voters could pick up their ballots from the headquarters of any party; Republicans thus warned Negro voters to "get your

ballot only from men you know." The governor suggested an election canvass-
ing board to better administer elections, but none was created at this time. A
state legislator from Fayette County sponsored a secret ballot bill in 1890 and
targeted urban counties with large numbers of Negro voters. The secret ballot
would hinder Negro voting in that illiterate persons could not read the printed
ballot or determine which box to place it in.

Of the various measures that white politicians—in Tennessee and
throughout the South—undertook to restrict Negro voting during the later
years of the nineteenth century, it was the poll tax that truly posed a major
problem for American democracy, more so even than literacy requirements.
Largely because of the poll tax, which made citizens literally pay for the right
to vote, a small minority of eligible voters, estimated at 17 to 30 percent, ultimately controlled the elections for all political offices in the impoverished
South. Poor and ordinary whites often stopped voting unless they lived in
areas where an enlarged Negro electorate might threaten white domination.
In these cases, white solidarity typically prevailed; however poor and ignorant
they might be, such voters were still "white," and that was what counted in the
South.

The *Plessy v. Ferguson* decision of 1896 left southern whites in charge to
determine *what* was equal and *who* was "white," "black," and "other"; however,
Plessy did not give southern governments the constitutional power to exclude
citizens from voting on the basis of race, class, and color. As it evolved, the
new constitutional concept of federal citizenship required the federal courts to
interpret whether voting was a part of the new post–Civil War national citizenship. In creating a federal citizenship category for freedmen, the Fourteenth
Amendment applied to all Americans, white or black. In *Ex parte Yarborough,
110 U.S. 651* (1884), the Supreme Court upheld federal legislation to protect
voting rights and to punish terrorists under the 1870–71 force acts. In *Williams
v. Mississippi* (1898), the court upheld literacy test requirements for voting,
mostly in response to Republican Party attempts to slow the swelling of northern Democratic Party ranks by dark-skinned immigrants (Jews, Italians, Poles,
and others) from southern and eastern Europe. Though of European descent,
these persons had not yet been admitted fully to the club designated as
"whites." In *Guinn v. United States* (1915), the Court struck down "grandfather
clauses" for voting, which protected the voting rights of illiterate whites, especially in the South where the inability to read and write was widespread.

Despite the poll tax, secret ballot laws, lynching, election fraud, literacy
tests, general terrorism by race radicals, and the benign neglect on racial issues
by Republican presidents, Negroes generally stuck with the Republican Party.

During his two terms as president (1901–9) Theodore Roosevelt disappointed Negroes with the subtle racism displayed by his administration, although he did try to break the ice by inviting Booker T. Washington to dinner at the White House. William Howard Taft (1909–13) wooed Negro voters by appointing many Negroes to positions in his administration. Herbert Hoover (1928–32), on the other hand, adopted a "lily-white" southern strategy designed to bring more whites into the state parties in the South. Nevertheless, loyal Negro Republicans did not even dream of abandoning the Republican Party until it abandoned them.

Colored Republican clubs continued to reign in Tennessee through the 1950s. In Chattanooga, under Walter C. Robinson, the Republican Colored Voters League of Greater Chattanooga remained the principal Negro political organization. Born in Alabama in 1893, Robinson was educated in the public schools of Chattanooga, wore fine suits, smoked expensive cigars, and published the *Chattanooga Observer*. He cooperated with the East Tennessee Colored Voters League meetings under Dr. W. S. E. Hardy and Webster L. Porter, editor of the *East Tennessee News* based in Knoxville. Porter started the newspaper in 1907 and continued it through the 1940s to galvanize Negroes throughout East Tennessee "who are interested in the progress of the Negro racial group." Robinson tried to gain a seat on the executive committee of the Tennessee Republican Party, but first J. C. Napier and then Robert R. Church Jr. held the designated Negro seat. In 1932, in the West Tennessee district Republican meeting, the "lily-white element" opposed Church for the seat, but he held on for ten more years. In Nashville, Henry Allen Boyd succeeded J. C. Napier as head of the Negro Republican club, and Z. A. Looby joined him as a leader. And in Knoxville, Negroes had known no other party but the Republicans since the days of Francis Yardley, the city's most prominent Negro official during Reconstruction.

Meanwhile, however, the Democratic Party was ideologically shifting its base to the North, and by 1932 this realigned party came to power and became a factor in changing the South's political economy. Northern Democrats pushed to eliminate the poll tax, while labor unions and liberal New Dealers made efforts to dismantle the worst aspects of Jim Crow. New Deal union leaders believed that as long as Jim Crow was in place, southern employers could maintain poor conditions and depressed wages for all workers. As the *Memphis World* noted, "Jim Crow wages hurt the entire region, embarrassed the South, and kept the white worker down, too."

Prior to the election of Franklin D. Roosevelt and the initiation of the New Deal, FDR's predecessor, Herbert Hoover, had attempted to curry favor among the nation's Negro voters. According to the *World* (Oct. 19, 1932), he responded to criticism about his racial policies by inviting 150 Negro Republicans to meet with the Republican National Committee, visit the White House, and pose for a group picture with the president (which the *World* printed). He meant to assure blacks that the party platform and the president still insisted on the protection of Negro rights. This protection, Hoover said, was the tradition of the Republican Party "for 70 years." Hoover's last-minute gesture was not enough to hold the Negro vote for the Republicans, however. Negroes would increasingly vote for Democrats. In the November 8 election, in fact, Negro candidates won Democratic legislative seats in Indiana and New York, while in Michigan, Negro Republican candidates lost state elections, in part because of the shift of the Negro vote to the Democrats.

Roosevelt himself came to Nashville in November 1934, and prominent Negro Republicans were there to greet him. William J. Hale, then president of Tennessee A&I and a native of the heavily Republican Alcoa-Maryville area of East Tennessee, invited his confidante Walter C. Robinson to Nashville for the presidential visit. Hale, who had been a school principal in Chattanooga when he was chosen to head the Negro college in 1911, also headed the Negro division of the Tennessee Commission on Interracial Cooperation from 1919 to 1943. J. C. Napier saluted FDR with a speech as the president and his entourage sat in their cars in front of Fisk University's Jubilee Hall. Later, the city's Democratic mayor recommended Napier to a seat on a city commission, but Kenneth McKellar, a Democratic U.S. senator from Tennessee, preferred a Negro Democrat, Coyness L. Ennix.

New Dealers promoted the inclusion of Negroes in federally financed projects during the Great Depression, but the actual record was mixed at best. Under the auspices of the NAACP, Charles Hamilton Houston and John P. Davis undertook a critique of the "lily-white Tennessee Valley Authority." Their report, published in the NAACP's *Crisis* magazine in October 1934, observed, "In almost every activity the Negro is either systematically excluded or else discreetly overlooked. Negroes must relentlessly attack and continue to attack discrimination in the TVA with relentless publicity, politically at law, and with whatever other means are at their disposal."

It was hard for New Dealers to change the racial practices of Jim Crow leaders without some convincing data. Thus, in June 1938, the National Emergency Council presented a sixty-four-page "Report on Economic Conditions in the South." The report noted that in thirteen southern states—comprising 36 million people, 29 percent of whom were Negroes—there was a 9 percent illiteracy rate, compared to 2 percent for the nation as a whole. It also observed that 66 percent of the South's tenant families were whites and went on to point out a number of dire conditions in the region: the South's waste of its splendid natural and human resources; the erosion of its soil; the crowding of its rural slums; the draining of its youngest blood and best talent; its ramshackle housing; its high incidence of pellagra (on which it had a virtual monopoly), as well as syphilis and malaria; its sparse schooling (and, in some cases, no schooling at all); its starvation wages and exploitation of the labor of women and children; its dependent farm tenants and brutalized, impoverished landowners; and its untaxed industries and tax-burdened people. In short, the report identified the grotesque paradox of a land "blessed by nature with immense wealth," yet one whose "people as a whole are the poorest in the country." Some critics of the report argued that it mixed Negroes into the averages and that such data dragged the white South down. But others pointed out that the Negro had no monopoly on southern poverty. Even FDR said that "three-quarters of the whites in the South" could not vote as a result of poll taxes and other practices. However, after New Deal Democrats suffered election losses in the South in 1938, FDR backed away from public criticism and began to soft-pedal civil rights issues.

On the other hand, the president's wife, Eleanor, was a strong advocate for humanitarian issues and did not back down. In November 1938, she met in Birmingham with southern liberals who supported New Deal reforms; out of this meeting the Southern Conference on Human Welfare (SCHW) was formed. In 1939, the SCHW supported a poor white man to challenge the Tennessee poll tax in an unsuccessful legal action. Various southern progressives—U.S. Representatives Estes Kefauver of Tennessee and Lyndon B. Johnson of Texas, the *Nashville Globe* (Apr. 27, 1941), and the Tennessee Press Association—supported this move against the poll tax. Yet, Tennessee's one-dollar requirement remained until a Tennessee constitutional convention repealed it in 1953. Local jurisdictions could charge another dollar.

[*]

The poll tax was advantageous to political machines like the one in Memphis, headed by Edward Hull Crump (1874–1954). Born in Holly Springs, Mississippi, the son of a planter and former Confederate Army officer, Crump arrived in Memphis as a poor teenage worker, but by 1905 he had gained a seat on the City Council. He would become mayor in 1909–15. For the 1909 election, a Negro musician, William C. Handy (1873–1958), composed a popular campaign song, "Mr. Crump," which was renamed "The Memphis Blues" and published in 1912, propelling Handy to national fame as "the father of the Blues." Crump was forced out of office through a recall election in 1915, but he became a millionaire businessman. In 1927, he reentered local politics and served as a congressman from 1930 to 1934. After his brief career in Washington, Crump put together a political machine and became "boss for life." He was so powerful that in 1940 he "stood in" for his favorite candidate for mayor, won the election, and then resigned so that his man, Walter Chandler, could be appointed to the office. The machine was notorious for bringing truckloads of Negroes (38 percent of Shelby County's registered voters by 1932) to the polls to help keep Crump's candidates in office. The Crump machine rewarded Negro supporters with firewood, coal for fuel, food baskets, and whiskey, but no political jobs. Memphis had neither black policemen nor black fire fighters on the city payroll.

Robert R. Church Jr. and George W. "Lieutenant" Lee headed the Negro Republican Club in Memphis, but despite their party affiliation, they joined with Crump's Democratic machine to gain some local political spoils, especially after Roosevelt won the presidency in 1932. As early as 1911, Church and others had formed the Colored Citizens Association, conducted a voter registration drive, and consulted with Mayor Crump about parks and paved streets in the Negro community. Church owned the Solvent Savings Bank, the Beale Street Park and Auditorium, several other businesses, and vast real estate holdings consisting of rental houses he had inherited from his father. He was one of the organizers of the Lincoln Republican League in 1916 and the Memphis Branch NAACP in 1917. Lee, upon arriving in Memphis in 1919 from his native Mississippi, teamed up with the Republican League and became a salesman for two regional Negro life insurance companies. His real local fame came through his military commission in World War I and through publishing the book *Beale Street: Where the Blues Began* (1934). Church and Lee allowed the NAACP branch to languish until it was "dead as a pharaoh." Indeed, Crump and his machine did not like the NAACP, the Urban League, or any biracial groups operating in Memphis. Joseph E. Walker revived the chapter in 1933, and the "shabby NAACP local organization took cognizance of its unimpressive record" (in the words of the *Memphis World*) and called a meeting at the Metropolitan Baptist Church to raise memberships. Ira Latimer, S. A. Owens, and others invited James Weldon Johnson, "father of the Harlem Renaissance," to travel from Fisk University, his new home, to address a Memphis NAACP rally. Before joining the Fisk faculty as professor of creative literature, Johnson had served as NAACP secretary at its national headquarters in New York.

The Crump machine used its control of the police force both to reward friends and punish enemies. When intimidation, tough talk, threats, and warnings did not work against its foes, the Crump machine allowed police brutality to prevail. Memphis policemen were known to handcuff Negroes to cars and beat them mercilessly, pin their heads in rolled-up police car windows while driving down a railroad track, and force them to confess to crimes they did not commit. In January 1938, at least three Negro men, including mail-man George W. Brooks, died at the hands of police. The Youth Council chapter of the NAACP at LeMoyne College sent Boss Crump a letter in protest, but he ignored the message. Whenever Negroes tried to get "sassy," the city allowed Beale Street to deteriorate, threatened renegade Negro preachers about their "civil rights sermons," and arrested and jailed Negro men by the truckloads at cafés and "juke joints." Reminiscent of slave patrols (the "patty rollers"), the "paddy wagons"—as Negroes called these padded, black-painted trucks—often waited for reinforcements outside Negro establishments before hauling all the patrons to jail. However, businessmen and employers, if they were not enemies of Boss Crump, were allowed to get Negroes out of jail so that they would not miss a day of work and thus hurt profits. And in 1933, when Robert Church Jr. was harassed by policemen and arrested for reckless driving, his allegiance to Crump got the charges dismissed.

[*]

Following the 1936 presidential election, the Crump machine would use New Deal funds to win favor with Negro voters. Over the next seven years, the machine used federal money to construct low-income housing for Negroes, including Dixie Homes, Foote Homes, and Lemoyne Gardens. Federal funds helped to build new schools and expand others, as well as construct playgrounds, parks, clinics, and recreational areas for local Negroes. But the machine withheld some New Deal money that would require racial mixing and kept Negroes from being hired in meaningful, skilled jobs created by New Deal training programs. And while white subdivisions spurted in Memphis, black private housing remained financially restricted and limited by Jim Crow laws and customs.

The power of the Crump machine extended to state elections. Although Crump had supported Gordon L. Browning as governor in 1936, the relationship soon soured, and Browning, as much a political boss as Crump was, launched an anti-Crump campaign in 1937. Browning even dared to send a crime commission to hold hearings in Shelby County, as well as National

Guard troops to supervise elections in Memphis. So, with Crump flexing his political muscle, Browning's bid for reelection in 1938 failed. He lost in the August Democratic primaries to William Prentice Cooper, a Crump man, who went on to become governor from 1939 to 1945. Though educated in northern colleges, Cooper also held deep racial prejudices, and like the Crump machine, he was no friend to the Negro and the civil rights movement.

After the elections of 1936, Crump no longer needed the Negro Republican leaders Church and Lee; his machine had control of the Negro vote by now. Besides, Church had become close to some of the civil rights leaders who encouraged criticism of the Negro's pitiful conditions.

In February 1940, the NAACP sent William H. Hastie, the federal judge of the Virgin Islands, into Tennessee to speak at NAACP membership drives, including one hosted in Nashville by J. Frankie Pierce, the head of the Federation of Colored Women's Clubs. Hastie criticized the treatment of Negroes in the South. Mrs. A. D. Byas headed the federation in Memphis, but Hastie did not speak in that city, where Crump was outraged when Church supported the Republican candidate, Wendell L. Willkie, for president in 1940. There was fear that Willkie would stop FDR from gaining an unprecedented third presidential term; moreover, Willkie dared to criticize the big city bosses and the political corruption they brewed. For the most part, Church stayed out of town during the campaign; since 1938, he had been mainly in Pennsylvania, helping the Republicans there. Lee also kept a low profile. However, J. B. Martin, a pharmacist and head of the National Negro Baseball League, helped Republicans with the local campaign. Roosevelt won a third term as president.

As long as he had enjoyed the Crump machine's favor, Church had not had to pay property taxes, but now the city sent him a bill for more than eighty thousand dollars in overdue taxes. When he could not liquidate his assets fast enough to pay the bill, the city quickly confiscated his properties. Church moved to Chicago in November 1940, taking his sister, Annette, with him, and joining his daughter, Roberta, who was employed there as a city social worker. While living on Champlain Avenue with his family, Church used his local contacts, such as J. B. Martin, to relay anti-machine messages into Memphis. Discovering this, the police began searching all customers who entered Martin's South Memphis Drug Store, claiming that they were looking for illegal drugs and weapons. This tactic, which local newspapers protested, did little to frighten off Martin. But the druggist had forgotten that the machine had allowed him to post bail money for prisoners without a license. Martin learned from a friendly source that the city was going to bring charges against him for operating as a bail bondsman without a permit. Martin fled Memphis by airplane on December 20, 1940. Similar police tactics caused Elmer Atkinson to close his café on Beale Street and flee to Chicago. Martin and Church protested to the U.S. Department of Justice. But Crump said, "We are not going to let the *Press-Scimitar* or any New York [NAACP] or any other foreign influence interfere with us [in Memphis]." The city changed the name of the Church Park Auditorium to the "Beale Street Park." The elder Church had built the park at the turn of the century, when the city did not allow Negroes in public parks; his son had, in turn, sold it to the city. And, in January 1941, as the local newspapers took pictures, the Fire Department burned the vacated Church family mansion at 384 South Lauderdale Street as a public "practice session" for some fifteen hundred delegates attending a national fire inspection convention.

As the local fortunes of Church declined, those of another black Memphian were on the rise. With the help of two whites (lawyer William H. Foote and Democratic leader Frank Rice), the insurance executive Joseph E. Walker, who started out as a Republican, formed the Shelby County Democratic Club in 1936. Walker won favor with the Democrats by heading the Negroes-for-FDR campaign in the county. Walker had helped to found the Universal Life Insurance Company in 1923 at 234 Hernando Street, claiming $843,552 in company assets and $572,966 in premiums by 1931. Born in Mississippi and educated at Alcorn A&M College, Walker taught school, completed Meharry Medical College, practiced medicine, became president of Delta Penny Savings Bank in Indianola from 1912 to 1922, a delegate to the National Republican Convention in 1916, and president of the Mississippi Life Insurance Company from 1917 to 1923. In Memphis, he became president of the National Negro Insurance Association in 1926, co-organized the Memphis Welfare League chapter, and was president of the National Negro Business League from 1939 until 1944. A quiet agitator for Negro equality, he used the offices of his insurance company to hold meetings for the Business League, Colored Chamber of Commerce, and the Independent Business and Civic Association (IBCA), which sought to promote the business interests and the "civic [civil] rights of colored people in Memphis." The *World* (Apr. 1, 1932) reported that Walker's IBCA engaged students at LeMoyne College to help canvass Negro homes and produce a record of Negro economic conditions in Memphis, where rural Negroes had settled after fleeing the effects of the agricultural depression. Walker would resign his chairmanship of the Colored Democratic Club in May 1944, claiming that he wanted to devote time to promoting the War Bonds drive within the Negro community. He sent copies of the letter of resignation to his local white Democratic benefactors, including Crump.

242

On the national level, A. Philip Randolph, Walter White of the NAACP, and other Negro leaders were trying to pull together the Negro vote into an effective bloc that would increase pressure on Roosevelt to take stronger civil rights initiatives. In January 1943, after race riots between Negro and white soldiers broke out in several camps, the Fraternal Council of Negro Churches met in Chicago and called for an end to employment discrimination and for the president to appoint a committee to study the pathetic conditions of Negro communities. In February, William H. Hastie resigned his position of Negro civilian aide to the secretary of war to protest open discrimination against Negroes in military camps and defense industries. "His courage and fortitude smack of a new type of [Negro] leadership," said the *Memphis World*. Randolph appeared in Nashville on April 25, 1943, speaking at the St. John AME Church on "The Negro and the War." The local chapter of the Brotherhood of Sleeping Car Porters sponsored his visit. The union members were encouraged by Robert K. Carr's *Federal Protection of Civil Rights: Quest for a Sword* (1940), which called for the courts to invoke "both a shield and a sword" to insure Negro rights throughout America. The *Memphis World* called for Roosevelt to protect Negro citizens against all discrimination.

Several months after his appearance in Nashville, Randolph would come to Memphis. He was scheduled to speak at Mt. Nebo Baptist Church on Sunday afternoon, November 7, 1943—his first visit to the city. In a November 3 article detailing his schedule, the *World* observed, "Mr. Randolph has taken the lead in racial matters, and his visit should be regarded as a milestone in the progress of the Memphis Negro. Mr. Randolph's appearance here should be [important] in the progress of the Negro race. He helped get [FDR's] Executive Order 8802, 'a second Emancipation Proclamation.'" But then, as the *World* subsequently announced, the mass meeting at Mt. Nebo was cancelled. The reason was harassment from Crump's organization, which considered Randolph a dangerous radical. To stop the labor leader from speaking in Memphis, the machine had bundled nearly twenty Negro leaders in a jail cell where the sheriff, the police commissioner, and the local attorney general lectured them, calling Randolph a troublemaker whose visit to Memphis would result in a race riot. Blair T. Hunt, George W. Lee, Alonzo Locke, and others reportedly agreed to cooperate. Locke was headwaiter at the Peabody Hotel and supervisor of three hundred Negro workers there; he was known as the "Race Ambassador of Goodwill at the South's Largest and Finest Hotel." The machine would name a local elementary school for him. Hunt, who was born in Memphis in 1887, attended LeMoyne Institute, received degrees from Morehouse College and Howard University, and became a schoolteacher in 1913, a lieutenant in World War I, pastor of the Mississippi Boulevard Christian Church, principal of LaRose Elementary School, and in 1932 principal of the Booker T. Washington High School, the city's largest such school for Negroes. Black citizens with something "to say something to Mr. Crump" reportedly had to speak first to "Professor Hunt." Hunt downplayed the Crump machine's strong-arm tactics, explaining that what happened at the meeting, as reported by the *Press-Scimitar,* was simply not true, even as he admitted that he and others did meet with "some city and county officials" at the Shelby County Criminal Court Building. A city official also confirmed that "We met with representative Negro citizens, hoping never to have any race trouble here."

Nevertheless, Randolph tarried in Memphis from November 7 through 9, 1943, speaking to Negro activists. He spoke on November 7 to a local Brotherhood of Sleeping Car Porters rally at Mason Temple, owned by the Church of God in Christ and headed by its founder, Bishop Charles Mason. The local Brotherhood was headed by H. F. Patton. After being escorted to the podium by Cornelius Maiden of the Memphis American Federation of Labor and Benjamin F. Bell of the Memphis Urban League, Randolph told the audience, "If the American soldiers for both races fight for the right of free expression, free assembly, and free thought, it is our duty on the home front to keep, with the sacrifice of our lives, those democratic principles and actions which made America great." Randolph spoke two days later to a Southern Tenant Farmers Union meeting at Greater White Stone Baptist Church on Wellington Street. There he declared, "In this world the enemies of the freedom loving peoples are the fascists who are avowed to drive freedom of speech and freedom of assembly underground." Bell also addressed that audience, proclaiming that the Urban League would help find jobs for the fifty thousand displaced tenant farmers in the Delta. The local Urban League did request an investigation from the War Manpower Management Office of the Memphis U.S. Office of Employment Services for denying skilled and semi-skilled jobs to Negroes. Bell's militancy irritated Urban League officers at the national office, however, and he certainly attracted an unfavorable eye from the Crump machine.

The anti–civil rights efforts of Crump and others like him failed to stop the movement. Speaking in Denver in late 1943, Randolph again threatened a March on Washington in a "direct nonviolent protest" against America's treatment of the Negro. American newsreels were suppressing this news and the president's recent visits to the Negro troops' camps. The Negro lawyers' association decided on January 14, 1944, to push for "legislation to secure and safeguard our civil rights and repeal legislation hostile to the welfare of the race." As part of its "twelve-point program," the association set objectives of publishing a guide listing Negro lawyers and launching "a vigorous fight against the poll tax in the South." In March 1944, the editor of the *Broadcaster*, the journal for the Tennessee Negro Teachers' Association, said, "Throughout the state there is ample evidence that Negroes are growing increasingly restive under the conditions that deprive them of direct representation in the government." In Washington, D.C., Robert Church was busy pushing a civil rights plank in the Republican Party's platform. Randolph invited Church to join the national council for a lobbying group, the Permanent Fair Employment Practices Committee, which was pushing for federal legislation against job discrimination. Church became founding chairman in 1944 of the Republican American Committee, a group of two hundred Negro Republican leaders from thirty-two states who united to pressure Republican congressmen to help enact civil rights legislation. Randolph opened an office in Washington around that time, and Church, who maintained his residence in Chicago, stayed in hotels while working for the group in the national capital.

After the embarrassing events of November 1943, some civil rights advocates, especially B. F. Bell, were working quietly but determinedly to oppose Crump and find a sponsor for a return trip to Memphis by Randolph. Local supporters of a Randolph visit were the *Memphis World*, which had connections to its publishing base in Atlanta; Robert Church, a personal friend of Randolph's; and George Albert Long, the pastor of Beale Street Baptist Church, who was openly critical of race relations in Boss Crump's town. On March 6, 1944, the American Federation of Labor (AFL), under William Green, announced that Randolph would appear in Memphis in April, and speak on behalf of the sacrifices of millions of southern workers.

Lev Loring, the president of the Memphis Trades and Labor Council, was apparently enlisted to voice opposition to Randolph's visit. According to the *Memphis Labor Review* (Mar. 17, 1944), Loring, who also headed the Memphis Plumbers' Union, brokered "a unanimous resolution" opposing Randolph's visit to Memphis, because "Randolph is regarded as an agitator and demagogue." Loring enlisted the support of J. L. Essary, president of the Tennessee State Federation of Labor, who said that Green had no authority to call a mass meeting in Tennessee and require members of the state unions to attend. "We are our own boss," he said. On March 10, the *Memphis Labor Review* called Randolph "a graduate of Harvard and an opportunist" who was "advocating social equality for the people of his race." The publication then carried no further news about Randolph. Mayor Walter Chandler, a Crump man, and the State Labor Department seemed to get along with these kinds of conservative unions.

Green was determined that the AFL and its civil rights advocacy would not be defeated by a local southern union chief and Crump. He said that the AFL "believes in freedom of speech" and that Loring did not reflect the organization's racial attitudes. According to the AFL, "Mr. Loring has not gained any appreciable benefits for workers white or colored in Memphis," compared to the progressive advances made on behalf of labor everywhere by Randolph. The *Memphis World* reported the AFL's announcement that "Randolph will speak in Memphis" on April 3 (although, as it turned out, he would actually speak several days earlier). George Googet, organizer for the AFL Southern Regional District, was sent to Memphis to help Cornelius Maiden, local AFL organizer, get the union members to the rally. Although he had been fired as head of the local National Urban League, Bell helped contact local unions and especially black union members. Reportedly, two Negroes, either sponsored by a local union or the Crump machine, were sent to AFL headquarters in Washington, D.C., to argue the case for not sending Randolph to Memphis. Randolph later would accuse the Crump forces of using "Negro stooges to pull its chestnuts out of the fire." Lieutenant Lee hurriedly informed Robert Church by letter about the tense developments, saying that anything was "liable to happen" if Randolph indeed decided to return to Memphis. Church probably marveled at Lee's sitting on the sidelines.

The AFL rally was held on the evening of March 31, 1944, at the Beale Street Baptist Church, adjacent to Church Park. George Albert Long was the pastor of this church, which had been founded in 1866. The Reverend Long was a member of neither the local NAACP nor the National Urban League chapter, but he was a loyal Republican. A native of Phillips County, Arkansas, and a graduate of Arkansas Baptist College in Little Rock, he had headed churches in Illinois and Indiana before coming to Memphis in March 1937. The house was packed with a friendly and racially mixed audience, and Bell was one of the men who escorted Randolph to the podium. More than "one thousand" cheered Randolph, who proclaimed: "I have returned to Memphis because I consider it my constitutional right, my democratic privilege, and my moral duty. A government of law and free men could not come into existence or long endure were men not free to freely express their convictions concerning men and measures. Memphis is under the absolute control of E. H. Crump, the political boss of the city and Shelby County and perhaps the State. Mr. Crump out-Hitlers [sic] Hitler." Randolph criticized timid Negro leaders in Memphis, and he declared that Crump had lied about responses to his speeches. No riots, he pointed out, had followed any speech he had ever made.

"This is white man's country, and always will be," said the outraged sheriff, Oliver Perry, "and any Negro who doesn't agree to this better move on." He added that he wished he had been at the rally so that he could "pull that Negro out the pulpit." When asked why the Crump machine opposed freedom of speech, Perry said, "Freedom of speech doesn't give anyone the license to lie, and incite riots, and that's what they were doing." Crump said that reports of Negro leaders being corralled into a jail cell were "a willful lie" and that Randolph did not mention good things he had done for Negroes, such as police cleanup of Beale Street crime and stopping senseless fights and shootings at Negro football games. He assailed the Reverend Long for desecrating the church by allowing it to be used "for spreading racial hatred," adding, "The town will be better off without that type of citizen, including the preacher who gave permission to hold that meeting in his church." According to the *World*, Crump's Negro henchmen refused to be interviewed.

Responding to Crump's attacks, Long said, "I have heard rumors that I am to be hounded by the police and the First Baptist Church on Beale would be condemned because I allowed A. Philip Randolph to speak at the church as one of the mediums of breaking me down and running me out of town. I am trying to buy a home at 322 Vance Avenue and with God's help I am planning to stay here." The minister said that there had been no riots and that the audience left the church in a spirit of love instead of hate: "I am not an imported rabble-rouser. When Mr. Crump speaks of my abiding the consequences, I am fully cognizant of what he means. I have made up my mind. Now, as for the town being better off without me, I did not ask Mr. Crump could I come to this town, and I am not going to ask him may I stay. The issue raised by Mr. E. H. Crump in Memphis is the issue around the world—Freedom! Thousands of my group are dying around the world for that freedom. If they can take it there, I can take it here!"

Long charged Crump with violating the Bill of Rights, having the police beat up citizens, arresting Negroes on baseless charges, denying them jobs in the city government, and sending the police to invade private homes. He declared, "Christ, not Crump, is my Boss." An editorial in the *Nashville Globe* opined: "Crump is a veritable cry baby, and a regular punch drunk. The colored leaders of Memphis are more afraid of Mr. Crump than they are of the devil, and that's why Randolph was forced to move his speech to Beale Street Baptist Church. Mr. Crump, who Mississippi produced, should stop crying and get ready, because the civil rights movement [i.e. equalization of teachers' salaries and other reforms] is continuing to progress." Unidentified black assailants attacked and beat the Reverend Long. In the late spring of 1944, the city cited his church for thousands of dollars of city code violations. Henry Allen Boyd, editor of the *Nashville Globe*, head of the National Baptist Publishing Board, and president of Citizens Bank in Nashville, announced that black Baptists would help Beale Street Baptist Church cope with the financial crisis brought on by this harassment.

The Crump machine increased police pressure on all the city's Negroes. The *Memphis Press-Scimitar* reported some typical episodes on April 3, 1944. In one case, a Negro man driving a new car was stopped by two policemen, who charged him with "defective brakes" and told him to make a periodic payment of ten dollars to the policemen or go to jail. When the policemen came to the man's place of employment to collect the money, the proprietor swore out a complaint, but a departmental investigation declared the officers' innocence. In another case, J. B. Martin was intimidated when he returned to Memphis to watch a Negro League baseball game. Although he co-owned the facility and the local team with his brothers, the police entered the stadium, escorted him outside, and told him harshly that he was to leave town or go to jail. He left town. That same year, the city published, with unintentional irony, a report entitled *Benefits and Opportunities for Colored People in the City of Memphis*.

In September, the National Baptist Convention of America held its annual session at Beale Street Baptist Church, where the Reverend Long "gave a stirring speech." The Negro Baptists intended to signal to the Crump machine that George A. Long was within their protection. The convention invited Reverend Long to speak at churches throughout the region.

In the November 1944 election, Roosevelt was reelected for his fourth term and gained the majority of the urban Negro vote. But this was not a sign that Negroes were abandoning the Republicans or the civil rights movement. Robert Church attended the Republican conventions on his own. He blamed the GOP for losing the 1944 election because they had left the Negro out of the party: "You can't use the same bait to catch colored voters in 1946 that you used in 1920." He asked the party for a one-hundred-thousand-dollar fund to educate Negro Republicans on the real political issues. The Republican platform promised to permanently establish the federal Fair Employment Practices Board and address the problems of Negro poverty—the "real cause of his low position in American society."

William Hastie and the Washington, D.C., chapter of the NAACP wrote to FDR to say that the segregated inaugural activities of 1941 should not be repeated: "We believe it desperately important for our domestic progress and for our international prestige in these most difficult times that our national government repeatedly and consistently demonstrate its adherence in action as well as in words to the principles of genuine democracy." The CIO asked for non-bias clauses in all union contracts. Meanwhile, the ever-active A. Philip Randolph was invited to give speeches in Nashville.

While the *World's* editor, Lewis O. Swinger, was serving in the U.S. Army's public affairs unit, acting editor Nat D. Williams attracted national attention with his column "On Beale Street." Williams had served for a month during the war in Washington, D.C., on the Negro newspaper unit to advertise the bond drive, and for a time he had worked on a newspaper in New York City with his former Tennessee A&I classmate Ted Poston. Williams used his columns in the *World* both to promote the cause of civil rights and, on occasion, to take his fellow Negroes to task. On the one hand (and partly as a way to divert the Crump machine's attention), he could be critical of blacks, as when he criticized working-class Negro misbehavior downtown. In "Crime Report Shows That Life Here Is Cheap," Williams noted that Negroes represented 85 percent of the violent deaths in the city. But he also used the occasion to point out that Democrats were being forced toward moderation and even conservatism by powerful southern congressmen in the party. He thus focused the attention of local Negroes on important developments that were affecting their struggle for equality and justice, while managing to avoid direct criticisms of the Crump machine. A strong presence in the community, Williams also headed the weekly "Amateur Hour" at a Beale Street movie theater and hosted many of the radio shows that originated from Beale Street.

The end of the war and the return of the troops had some leaders, including Randolph and Roy Wilkins of the NAACP, warning of new racial clashes in America. As the *World,* which continued to encourage changes in race relations, reported in September 1945, the National Conference of Christians and Jews had begun raising money to "avert a calamity of post-war hate movements." Harry S. Truman, who had assumed the presidency in April upon the death of FDR, asked Congress to approve a permanent Fair Employment Practices Commission. In 1946, control of both houses of Congress would fall into Republican hands, hampering Truman's efforts to push for certain types of legislation.

From his base in Memphis, Boss Crump was busy pulling some tricks to win support for his county and state tickets, and as always, that included efforts to manipulate black voters. Police attacks on Negroes decreased. The Reverend J. L. Campbell and Blair T. Hunt held a Negro parade for Crump in 1946, and repeated the machine's message about good schools, clean streets, swimming pools, and public housing projects for Negroes. Memphis, they said, was "one of the few areas in the South where the Negro voter is invited and expected to participate in a Democratic campaign. These things do not just happen, but they came as a result of a beneficent political organization by Honorable E. H. Crump, Sr." But some white citizens were growing tired of Crump and machine politics in general. The *Nashville Banner* wrote sarcastically of "Mr. Crump—that's what every Memphian calls him—bragging about the hospitals, nice streets, parks, swimming pools, and cleanliness of Memphis," while the *Maryville Times* observed, "Tennessee is in a bad way with political machines controlling the affairs of the State. Election thefts have gone on undisturbed for years. In some counties men and women have been afraid to go to the polls and vote." In McMinn County, a huge crowd of World War II veterans actually rebelled and overthrew the local political machine, firing on their homes, locking some deputies in the jail, and causing Governor James Nance McCord to send troops into the county to quell the uprising. McCord beefed up the Young Democrats Club, placing Frank G. Clement as president of the unit, perhaps to counter the growing political threat from World War II veterans. McCord then favored election reform.

Civil rights leaders believed things would not change until the Negro used his voting power to affect that change. The Memphis NAACP membership drive, which was launched in February 1947 to commemorate Negro History Week and the birthdays of Abraham Lincoln and Frederick Douglass, brought the list to six thousand. Helen Hayes, a local schoolteacher, won first prize for signing up the most memberships. The NAACP was keeping an especially close eye at the time on the all-Negro town of Mound Bayou, Mississippi, where whites disqualified all 65 voters, leaving only 335 Negro votes counted in the whole state. Neo-Confederate Mississippi believed it was untouchable.

The Memphis chapter of the Brotherhood of Sleeping Car Porters continued to meet in Mason Temple every third Monday. With their jobs on the trains, the union's members could easily see the differences between life in the North and the South. On September 14, 1947, they brought Randolph back to Memphis to speak at Beale Street Baptist Church—a move that, of course, further annoyed Boss Crump. As before, the rally was billed as "a labor clinic." The local NAACP was raising funds for Adelaide Hudson, a Negro housewife, who was beaten badly in her home by the Memphis police for "talking back." Randolph pledged help from the Memphis Brotherhood and urged people to write Congress for passage of a permanent fair employment practices act. Governor McCord had branded the bill as Communist-influenced. Crump compared "good Negroes" to those he called troublemakers. When a speaker for

"Race Relations Sunday" at a local church lauded "local Negro progress" and cited the "better schools, parks, low cost housing, and playgrounds," Crump made sure the man received favorable press coverage for his "good views on race relations."

In October 1947, St. Andrew AME Church brought the civil rights lawyer Harold Flowers of Pine Bluff, Arkansas, to Memphis as its Youth Day speaker. Flowers was state NAACP president in Arkansas and chairman of the Arkansas branch of the Southern Conference on Human Welfare, and his visit helped to boost the participation of local young people in the movement. The Youth Council of the local NAACP was reactivated on November 9, 1947, under student Edgar Hawkins and the local NAACP president, Utillis Phillips. Jessie Owens, the track-and-field star, spoke at the occasion.

Late that same year, the Reverend George Albert Long announced that he was leaving Beale Street Baptist Church. Just a few months earlier, on March 26–30, he had celebrated his tenth anniversary at the church. The *National Baptist Union-Review* published a photograph of Long and praised him for accomplishing "great good [in religion and civil rights] in Memphis." Reverend Long said he was headed to Detroit to pastor Mt. Tabor Missionary Baptist Church but made it clear that he was no political exile: "I dared to speak what was right for my people. I am not leaving here under pressure or threats [from Boss Crump]." Long's church in Detroit would host the Negro Baptists as they moved their annual meetings to northern cities and the more racially accommodating hotels there. Long became an officer in the convention.

In one sense, the Reverend Long's move to Detroit was part of a ongoing trend. Jim Crow, corrupt politics, criminal injustice, poverty, white terrorism in the form of lynching, and lack of cultural and educational opportunities continued to cause southern Negroes to engage in the Great Migration by the millions. The *Chicago Defender* urged Negroes to leave the oppressive South and come to Chicago, where the Negro population grew from 277,731 in 1940 to 812,637 by 1960. The Negro's share of the southern population, which amounted to one-third in 1860, had shrunk to 22 percent by 1950. Elma Stuckey, author of *The Big Gate* (1976), recalled that she and her family left Memphis in 1945 and moved to Chicago "for greater opportunities especially for our children." The *Defender* associated past racial trouble in the South with the number of new Negro arrivals in Chicago.

In December 1947, Boss Crump tossed a new bone to his supporters in the black community by announcing that sixty thousand dollars would be given to the fund for Negro blind people. Hunt and other Negro friends of

Crump held a huge meeting in the auditorium of Booker T. Washington High School. They sent a resolution of "appreciation for the interest of Mr. Crump" in the welfare of the Negro community. There was another reason for celebration among Crump's Negro friends. Benjamin F. Bell, head of the local National Urban League office, was succeeded by the Reverend James A. McDaniel. A native of Chicago with a graduate degree in social work, Bell was a former researcher with the Gunnar Myrdal project and in 1943 became the successor to the late Lucien J. Searcy as head of the Memphis Urban League. Bell had set out to make the organization more active in promoting civil rights, but he was ahead of his time in Memphis. McDaniel, perhaps, was more to Crump's liking.

Politics and race relations seemed to be improving in the country and in Tennessee by the late 1940s. The *Chattanooga Labor World* announced the formation of a local poll tax committee to help pay the tax and register more voters. NAACP officials appeared in Washington to speak against the poll tax. They informed both Truman and a congressional committee of the political corruption that this taxing device caused in the South. They pointed out that southern politicians, whose considerable power in Congress gave them disproportionate control over legislation that affected the entire country, were in fact elected by only a small percentage of the South's eligible voters. A presidential committee's report, *To Secure These Rights* (1947), indicted many such un-American practices: "An American diplomat cannot argue for free elections in foreign lands without meeting the challenge that in sections of America, qualified voters [i.e., Negroes] do not have access to the polls." The report included sweeping recommendations. To counter the argument that the Negro's civil rights movement was Communist-inspired, Randolph told Truman that segregation and racial discrimination represented the most powerful weapon for Communist Russia. However, a March 1948 Gallup Poll said that 56 percent of those polled did not favor a civil rights program.

During the election year of 1948, Crump's dominance of Memphis and his sway over Tennessee politics drew new fire in other parts of the state. An editorial in the *Chattanooga Times* charged that "Crump, calmly assuming the acceptance of his political dictatorship, has built Memphis and developed wealth there at the expense of the rest of the state." And while Crump used Negroes for his own political purposes, his machine showed no tolerance when a few of them stood on a sidewalk in August 1948 to listen to a Democratic Party rally in Court Square on Second and Main streets. Policemen ran them off. They were not allowed to enter the beautifully landscaped Court Square public park.

The spirits of the city's black citizens rose when Negro heroes came to town. Joe Louis visited Memphis during his southern exhibition tour in 1948 and attended the Booker T. Washington–Manassas High School football game. Louis's achievements—defeating white men in the boxing ring—imparted hope to the Negro community. He was not, however, an articulate speaker, and he did not make civil rights speeches as Jessie Owens, Jackie Robinson, and Paul Robeson did. But as the *Globe* often noted, a few Jim Crow barriers seemed to melt away whenever Louis visited a southern town and whites and blacks gathered to see him. Paul Robeson, on the other hand, was called a Communist by the white newspapers when he came to Memphis to speak. Responding to such criticisms in his "Down on Beale Street" column, Nat Williams praised Robeson as a courageous man who stood up for the rights of his people, adding that black Americans "want to see a Negro who is willing to be a martyr for the race."

That August the death of a local Negro at the hands of the Memphis police drew this response from the *World*: "The killing of James Murphy is not a single isolated incident which has involved mistreatment of citizens and violation of their civil rights by policemen on the Memphis Police Force." Surprisingly, this particular protest against police murders and brutal Jim Crow incidents was enough to influence Crump and the city to appoint thirteen Negro men to the police academy. Later that year, nine of them made their debut as a walking patrol on Beale Street, and two more were assigned a police car and sent to a black neighborhood.

During the summer of 1948, outside the halls of the Democratic and Republican national conventions, A. Philip Randolph led picket lines protesting segregation in the armed forces. The signs read, "Prison Is Better than Army Jim Crow Service," "We Demand an Executive Order Outlawing Military Segregation," and "Don't Join Jim Crow Army." Truman vowed to continue the New Deal liberalism that FDR had started, and he even proposed a civil rights bill. Both parties included a civil rights plank in their platforms during the summer of 1948, but the race issue split the Democratic Party, which had been the home of southerners since Andrew Jackson's time. Conservative Democrats refuted the party's civil rights plank and left the convention. They later met at Birmingham and formed the States' Rights (or "Dixiecrat") Party with Governor Strom Thurmond of South Carolina as their presidential nominee. Thurmond ran on a strict segregationist platform. Representing a much more liberal side of the political spectrum and a different sort of split from the Democratic Party, former vice president Henry A. Wallace was also in the race, running as the Progressive Party candidate.

In Memphis, the Reverend Dwight V. Kyle of Avery Chapel AME Church ran for Congress on the Progressive Party ticket. Kyle had been assigned to Memphis in 1945. He and J. Benjamin Dove were among the young Negro preachers who frequented the home of F. Douglass Coleman Sr., the pastor of St. Andrew AME Church. About thirteen years later, Coleman's daughter, Jamye, would become secretary for the Tennessee Voters Council. Kyle said, "I favor complete integration of the Negro into American life as a citizen and as an individual. I am for total equality for the Negro." But the Negro voters were harassed in 1948 by Republican poll watchers, who challenged them to see whether they had a poll tax receipt and whether each black voter lived in the proper district. Lieutenant Lee stayed on the sidelines as he went through a bitter divorce. The Crump machine employed its usual electoral tactics, including rewards for cooperative Negro preachers. Kyle and another man were the only "two local Negro preachers to refuse Crump's $50" during the 1948 election.

The 1948 election was considered a defeat for Crump. After beating Crump's man, incumbent James Nance McCord, in the Democratic primary, Gordon Browning won the governor's office, defeating the Republican candidate, country singer Roy Acuff, in the general election. Browning's victory avenged his previous losses to the Crump machine. (Browning easily won reelection two years later when the Republicans had no candidate for governor.) Browning instituted some minor election reform but lost the battle to repeal the poll tax. The senatorial race that year was won by Estes Kefauver, a U.S. representative from Chattanooga. Crump claimed that Kefauver backed the Communist labor unions, had radical affiliations with the SCHW, and supported Negro rights. Kefauver denied the charges. J. E. Walker went against the Crump machine and endorsed Kefauver, who received 42 percent of the vote (a plurality), beating the Crump candidate and the Dixiecrat candidate. The forty-five-year old Kefauver was a Yale University Law School graduate and a practicing attorney in Chattanooga; he had been state commissioner of finance in 1939 prior to serving in the U.S. House of Representatives from 1939 to 1948. He walked a careful line to keep his national political dreams alive, voting against both anti-lynching and fair employment practices commission bills. National headlines said of his victory, "Kefauver Beats Crump."

In the presidential race, Truman took his campaign directly to the people, and although his margin of victory was the smallest since 1916, he won the November 1948 election when almost everyone else, including newspapers and the Gallup Poll, predicted he would lose. With the Democratic Party split by Thurmond, Wallace, and the race issue, Truman was expected to lose. But Truman's campaign emphasized his experience in foreign policy, dealing with the international Communist threat, and his attacks on the alliance between Republicans and Wall Street. The West and the Midwest voted Democratic, and Truman defeated Republican Thomas C. Dewey with 49.5 percent of the popular vote, as opposed to Dewey's 45.1 percent. Truman garnered 303 electoral votes to Dewey's 189. Wallace carried no states and thus received no electoral votes. Truman beat Dewey in Tennessee by 49 to 37 percent. Thurmond and his Confederate-flag-waving party gained 1,169,063 votes (2 percent of the total) and 39 electoral votes, beating Truman and Dewey in some southern states. Fifty-three percent of the eligible electorate voted that year.

[*]

The record of service and loyalty to America by some one million Negro military personnel during the recent war encouraged many in the civil rights movement to look toward the federal government for relief, notwithstanding the political threat from Strom Thurmond's backward-looking Dixiecrats. The Supreme Court case of *Shelley v. Kraemer* (1948) concluded that even private covenants could not be used to keep Negroes out of residential neighborhoods. Real estate agents and landlords still maintained a code not to sell or rent to minorities who might prove to be "inharmonious elements" in a community development. Similarly, the banks generally refused to give Negroes any housing loans. Less than 5 percent of the nation's suburban neighborhoods included Negro home owners. Truman directed the Federal Housing Administration to stop financing mortgages on property with racially restrictive covenants. The U.S. Census of 1950 listed the 1949 median income for Memphis Negroes at 43.6 percent of the median income for whites. In January 1949, the federal government appointed two Negroes as postal clerks in the downtown post office. The Negroes, both veterans of World War II and former students at LeMoyne College, were placed on the night shift to ease integration of the facility, but at least they made more money on that shift.

Civil rights leaders pushed harder for repeal of the poll tax. In Chattanooga, C. B. Robinson used his Negro Teachers' Association office to send letters to local political candidates, asking if they supported the repeal of the poll tax. Coyness L. Ennix headed the Solid Block Party movement to organize fellow Negroes in Nashville for weekly visits and petitions to the General Assembly, where they crowded the visitors' galleries in support of the poll tax repeal bill. Ennix edited the *Block Bulletin*, which urged its readers: "Join Solid

Block and NAACP. To move ahead in the years to come, we must protect rights for everyone." Among the civil rights initiatives Solid Block promoted were "Negro policemen and sheriff deputies, a high school for South Nashville, the employment of Negroes in state and local government, Negro bus drivers, and improved city services to the Negro community."

Under Governor Browning's election reforms, including voter registration at any time and new kinds of voting boxes to deter cheating, Negro voter participation did begin to show increases. But the segregationist Browning was trying to use Negro votes as Boss Crump had so effectively used them. The Nashville City-County Democratic Civic League began to register Negro voters to support Browning in the 1950 governor's race, causing their numbers in Davidson County to double. Negroes were using Browning as much as he intended to use them. The *Block Bulletin* criticized Browning for not speaking out about employment discrimination against Negroes, who were "confined to 'white-coat' class" as butlers, waiters, and menial laborers.

The General Assembly did amend the Nashville charter to allow single-district council seats. Negroes ran for the Nashville City Council in 1951. "Council Candidates in Hot Fight," proclaimed the *Globe* on April 20. Ennix opposed Z. A. Looby in his district, and reminded the voters that he had led the Negro's movement to repeal the poll tax. On a radio show, Looby responded, "This is not a time for division. This is a time for us to get together. I shall continue to fight for equality no matter what the outcome of this election." Looby was more concerned that Negroes "have not had representation in the city council in nearly fifty years." Robert E. Lillard simply advocated "continued good race relations for the community and the city at large." Looby, a Republican, and Lillard, a Democrat, both won seats on the city council. The *Globe* reported that Negro voters also helped elect mayoral candidate Ben West, who appointed Ennix to the school board and hired Negroes in the police department.

In Memphis, J. E. Walker ran for election to the school board in 1951, challenging a slate of Crump–approved candidates, but he attracted only a third of registered Negro voters and almost no white votes. Walker tried to convince Negro leaders that they had to unite their vote, but he lost even the Negro precincts. About 22,000 of the 106,000 registered voters were Negroes. The preface to the Memphis Negro Chamber of Commerce's publication *Negro Classified Business Directory of Memphis* (1952) said, "The problem of the Negro is not Mass problem, it is a leadership problem. The Mass is ready for a forward march far beyond the ability of the leadership to direct without a focused vision."

George W. Lee had focused his attention to starting the Annual Blues Bowl competition for high school football, with W. C. Handy, the "father of the blues," making an annual trip from his home in New York City to attend the games and present the honors to the winner. Crump was still fond of Handy, who had once written a campaign theme song for him. Lee and his associates used the game's proceeds to distribute truckloads of food to needy families, to maintain political visibility among Negro voters, and to allow Lee to keep a political war chest to use when the time came to act in Memphis. (That time would come just a few years later, when, as the *Nashville Globe* would report [June 22, 1956], Lee, Walker, and other black leaders in Memphis would launch a campaign "seeking 70,000" Negro voters.)

Lieutenant Lee, R. Q. Venson (a Negro dentist), and others were still fighting for Negroes to remain a vital part of the Tennessee Republican Party. Lee received word that Shelby County Republicans intended to elect all white delegates to the 1952 National Republican Convention so that the annoying civil rights message would not embarrass the South. Some Republicans were trying to woo the Thurmond Democrats and other racial conservatives into the party. Word leaked out to Lee that this faction had met at the Hotel King Cotton. (Since Negroes were the porters, waiters, and majority workers in the Memphis hotels, they, like railroad porters and black insurance agents, relayed important information about whites' meetings to black community leaders.) One rainy day, Lee countered the local "lily-white" Republican movement by recruiting six hundred Negroes to gather at his Beale Street office. They boarded chartered streetcars to the Criminal Court Office Building and packed the Shelby County Republican Convention three hours before the meeting opened. "I was able to get a crowd to the meeting," Lee told the *Press-Scimitar*. "The only way a minority group can protest its rights is to turn out in large numbers." Lee used thirty-five hundred dollars from Blues Bowl proceeds to register Negro voters, sending them to the courthouse, with hundreds standing in line from Washington to Adams Street. "I will take my chances on getting my share of them to vote Republican," he said, asserting that Negroes had kept the Republican Party alive during the New Deal's domination of politics.

Robert Church criticized Lee for taking part in the Non-Partisan Voters League, saying, "There is no such group. Every member . . . votes either Republican or Democrat. Let me again urge you to have a Colored Republican . . . designated as your candidate, that is if you are still a Republican." Lee had developed this new political alliance with J. E. Walker, a Democrat, to produce a formidable black voting bloc in Memphis. Church thus felt he no longer could depend on Lee to marshal black Republican voters in the city. He returned to Boss Crump's town in October 1951 and registered as a voter, citing his property on St. Paul Avenue as his residence. Church's intent was to take one of the four Shelby County delegation seats on the State Republican Executive Committee and become an official delegate to the Republican National Convention in support of General Dwight D. Eisenhower's bid for the presidency. To Church, Ike represented the best hope since Hoover of bringing black voters back to the Republican Party, their ancestral political home.

Months later, in April 1952, Church was staying at a Memphis hotel and holding court with local black Republicans and Matthew Thornton Sr., "the Mayor of Beale Street." Thornton had helped Church to establish the Lincoln League Republican Club and the local NAACP. He maintained his "mayor's office" in the Beale Street Auditorium, and he later led the successful effort to restore the Church family name to the Beale Street Park. Church promised Thornton that he would be placed in charge of the local black Republican campaign for Eisenhower. Crump was old and sick now, and while his machine was still intact, it lacked the strong personalities who might otherwise have run Church out of town. Besides, Church was smart enough to move back and forth from Washington and Chicago and spend as little time in Memphis as possible. However, on April 17, while talking strategy with Thornton from his Memphis hotel room, Church suffered a heart attack and died. The next day, the *Commercial Appeal* and the *Press-Scimitar* carried large stories on his life and death. He was buried in Memphis.

With Church's death, Lee expected to take the seat on the Republican State Executive Committee. However, Church's daughter Roberta traveled from Illinois, reestablished her claim to Tennessee residency, and won the seat in June 1952. But the Republicans never used her services in Tennessee, although she did campaign for the party's nominee, Eisenhower, around Chicago. Lee managed to get two black Republicans, T. H. Hayes and Ben Hooks, on the committee to welcome Eisenhower to Memphis during the campaign. In November 1952, the Republicans did not carry any Memphis Negro precincts even though Tennessee as a state "went Republican" in the presidential election for the first time since 1928. The Democrats beat the Republicans 19,592 votes to 9,309 votes in Memphis's Negro precincts, and won other contests in Shelby County. That same year, Representative Albert Gore Sr. beat the Crump candidate for the U.S. Senate in the Democratic primary and went on to win the general election. Lee attended Ike's inaugural, but he got none of the Republican spoils.

Roberta Church mounted a letter-writing campaign to Eisenhower's party leaders to remind the recipients of her late father's loyalty to the party. She received support from U.S. Representative Howard Baker Sr., a Republican from East Tennessee, to gain a minor job under Eisenhower in July 1953. She remained in that position until the Democrats came to power in 1961; after that she gained civil service status and returned to a political appointment under Richard M. Nixon, serving in federal positions until retiring and moving back to Memphis in 1982.

In 1954, several Negro candidates from Memphis ran for seats in the state legislature, including C. D. Hayes, a graduate of Wilberforce University and part owner of Hayes Funeral Home, and Roy Love, minister at Mount Nebo Baptist Church since 1926. Lieutenant Lee's organization also decided to run candidates for the legislature. Rather than split the Negro vote, Hayes withdrew his candidacy, and on October 30, he said, "I feel I have accomplished my objective in getting attention called to the desirability of Negro candidates for office." Love was deemed ineligible by a state rule of the time barring ministers from holding public office. The remaining state legislative candidates—Benjamin L. Hooks, Theodore Spencer, and W. C. Weathers—were Lee's men. None won public office, but the registration drives raised local Negro votes to fifty thousand.

To further Negro voter power across Tennessee in the 1956 presidential election, the black leaders in Memphis took the lead. On April 17, Joseph E. Walker wrote to W. C. Robinson, urging him to cooperate with Looby and Meredith Day, a Nashville businessman and a leader in that city's NAACP chapter since 1937, to get people to vote in the Republican primary. Although Walker was a Democrat, he sought to unite Negro voters and thus put pressure on white politicians and win some elective and appointive public offices for Negroes. "I am sure men of the pro-segregationist group will do what they can to block the small progress we are making," Walker said. Robinson replied to Walker's letter on April 20, saying, "It is a terrific struggle to influence many Negroes who recently came into our community from states farther south [Alabama, Georgia, and Mississippi] where the right for the Negro to vote undisturbed is very limited. But it is worth all that we can put into it to help make democracy work in Tennessee and the nation." Robinson then wrote to Lieutenant Lee on October 16, telling him, "I believe we can and will carry the state, again for Eisenhower and Nixon." He warned Lee, "Your district manager, Walter D. Parks, for the Atlanta Life Insurance Company here, is for the Democrats [unless] maybe you could cool him off a little by dropping him a note." Before an audience in Indiana, Robinson declared, "The hope of the

Negro people in America is the reelection of Eisenhower and Nixon and election of a Republican Congress."

The Republicans gave Lee thousands of dollars to head up the Negro division of the Eisenhower campaign throughout Tennessee. In November, local newspapers reported that Eisenhower had won Shelby County, including a majority of votes from twenty-three predominantly Negro precincts. In those precincts, Eisenhower beat the Democratic candidate, Adlai Stevenson, with 16,802 votes to Stevenson's 14,131. Stevenson had picked Kefauver as the vice presidential candidate, but the Tennessee senator did nothing to help Stevenson attract black votes. Lee had 225 doorbell ringers, 101 "ministers for Ike," 89 telegrams to church ministers to read a get-out-the-vote message to the congregations on Sundays, 89,000 pieces of literature, and 39 rallies in the 38 Negro precincts. Ward 61 gave Ike 607 votes compared to 381 votes for Stevenson. Lee's organization again ran some Negroes for the legislature to keep up Negro voter enthusiasm. Lee was enjoying the political spotlight, overshadowing Roberta Church, who had ventured back into Memphis to say good things about Eisenhower. In 1956, Lee was credited with Ike's margin of victory in Shelby County because he had managed to get 54 percent of the local Negro vote for the incumbent president. This was the last time a Republican presidential candidate carried a majority of the African American vote in Tennessee. Eisenhower was reelected with 57.6 percent of the national vote, winning 457 electoral votes to Adlai Stevenson's 73. Voter participation that year was 60.6 percent of the eligible electorate.

Lee believed that Eisenhower was the remedy to Hoover's failed policies toward the Negro and that, under Ike, Negroes would come home to the Republican Party. And in 1956, as Lee was working for Ike's reelection, the Republicans got a small post office at 856 Mississippi Street named for him; it opened on July 29 with a parade and a program at Mason Temple. Just two years later, however, Lee was nearly finished as a political force in Tennessee. His organization ran W. R. Bradford, Sam Qualls Jr., B. F. McCleave, and R. Q. Venson for state house seats, but less than a fourth of registered Negroes turned out to vote.

[*]

Jim Crow's legacy still had its grip on blacks: (1) Most Negroes remained complacent and skeptical about registering to vote; and (2) many Negro registrants, in Tennessee and elsewhere, often did not show up at the voting booths to cast their votes. It took considerable resources to register them and then get them to the polls. As H. A. Boyd had noted in 1940, "The people who do not vote will always be controlled by those who do vote."

While the NAACP in Tennessee did not at first endorse civil disobedience as a way of augmenting its legal tactics against Jim Crow, it did combine legal tactics and politics to help Negroes achieve equal rights. In January 1959, the revived Memphis NAACP launched a combined membership and voter-registration drive. Several years earlier, the Memphis NAACP had elected a preacher, Van J. Malone, as its head for the first time in its history. Ministers would prove to be very effective in galvanizing the masses from the pulpit. The Citizens Non-Partisan Registration Committee also urged Negroes to "Register Now." At a meeting at LeMoyne College, the Memphis Urban League called for better jobs, better housing, and better health care for Negro citizens. Meanwhile, two hundred people attending a Citizens Non-Partisan meeting were told by a Universal Life Insurance Company executive: "I feel that proper exercising of the ballot is the surest road to freedom." The local NAACP urged the Negro churches to declare a "Citizens Sunday." The Reverend Malone said, "[Voting] is a duty." Cash prizes would be awarded to the groups registering the most voters. W. C. Patton and I. A. Watson directed the drive for thirty thousand new voters by September. In New York, the NAACP was planning a national campaign to gain three million new voters. On March 4, 1959, Perry A. Stephens, head of the Chattanooga chapter of the NAACP, died after an extended illness. But James Mapp, C.B. Robinson, and others picked up the movement.

[*]

In 1959, five Negro leaders announced their candidacy for public offices in Memphis. The Reverend L. A. Hamblen, head of a large Baptist Church near the Dixie Homes Housing Project in North Memphis, gave his support. Ben Hooks announced his candidacy for juvenile court judge. A graduate of Booker T. Washington High School and LeMoyne College, Hooks attended Howard University before entering the military in 1943; three years after the war, he completed law school at DePaul University and in 1955 became co-founder of Memphis's Mutual Federal Savings and Loan Association. Henry C. Bunton, pastor of Mt. Olive CME Church and a graduate of Florida A&M State College, ran for a school board seat. Elihue Standback, a print shop owner, public accountant, and member of the Binghamton Civic Club, ran for tax assessor. Roy Love, a trustee of both S. A. Owen Junior College and Griggs Business College, announced for the school board. R. B. Sugarmon announced his candidacy for commissioner of public works.

The most controversial of the Negro candidates was O. Z. Evers, a postal worker and president of the Binghamton Civic Club, who announced his candidacy for city commissioner. He had lived in Chicago before coming to Memphis and had a bus desegregation suit pending against the city. "Seemingly," Evers said, "our federal judges here in Memphis are timing the hearings [of civil rights cases] to the advantage of segregationists. Integration [as decreed by the *Brown* decision] is the law of the land, and when I take my oath of office, I will be taking the oath to uphold the law of the land." The city disqualified Evers's candidacy by changing the election date from November to August 20, which left him two months shy of meeting the city's five-year residency requirement. "I believe it was the first time I ever cried since calling myself a man," Evers said. "I was not crying for myself alone, I was thinking about all the good people working in my behalf and the Negro as a whole." He cried for his wife and five children. Their savings were gone, and one hundred thousand pieces of campaign literature were no good. "They can stop me," he observed defiantly, "but they cannot stop integration. As long as I have breath in my body I will be fighting for the civil rights of my people. We must not let defeat discourage us." Evers asked the people to support the "Volunteer Ticket," as the slate of Negro candidates was collectively known, by going to the polls and voting. When the local White Citizens Council applied pressure to have Evers fired from his federal job, the Binghamton Civic Club started a legal defense fund to help him hire an attorney, but on November 20, 1959, he would be fired.

At a meeting of the Citizens Leadership Council in the Universal Life Insurance Company building during the early summer of 1959, the two insurance executives, Joseph E. Walker and Lieutenant Lee, headed a bipartisan effort to support the announced candidates. The council endorsed the slate of Negro office-seekers, and Walker agreed to take a leading role in financing the campaign. On July 18, the council announced the kickoff celebration at the headquarters at 390 Beale Street. On July 22, Lee addressed a political rally for the Volunteer Ticket at Mt. Olive CME Church, where he said that "Negroes want full political participation and will not accept paternalism with a handout." But Lee, perhaps remembering those tough days during Boss Crump's time, was careful to say that Negroes were willing to work with white people in brotherhood and love and to compete with them as individuals but "not as a racial group." E. Frederick Morrow, an assistant to Eisenhower and the highest-ranking Negro in the administration, arrived in Memphis to speak.

The Volunteer Ticket called for good jobs, decent housing "in all sections of town," an end to police brutality, admission of Negroes to licensed trades, improved services at the city's hospitals, public schools for problem children, objective criteria for hiring public school teachers, full compliance with the *Brown* decision, and a focus on the issues of justice and injustice. Some citizens seemed alarmed at the Negro's attempt to vote en bloc, but Lee responded by telling "inquiring white friends" that the reason behind the Negro candidacies was to select individuals who knew the Negro community and its interests. On July 31, Martin Luther King Jr. and gospel singer Mahalia Jackson headed the guest list at the Freedom Rally at Mason Temple, where thousands showed up to support the political movement. "Their election will give impetus to our civil rights struggle," King said of the candidates. "We have a date with destiny." Lee followed King's speech by saying, "I want the same kind of freedom that flows in Chickasaw Gardens [the elite, wealthy white neighborhood in east Memphis]. I want that freedom that makes a Negro man a man, and a Negro woman a lady, who can walk the streets with dignity." And candidate Sugarmon said, "We are bringing a brand new day to Memphis. You have heard that democracy cannot work in this Dixie town, but we are here to put an end to that lie. Mr. Crump is dead, machine rule is dead, and we are going to bury segregation on August 20. Ben L. Hooks is going to preach the funeral but there will not be much mourning." Hooks again spoke with caution and a fear of an impending loss, because "there are still a lot of Uncle Toms around." Vasco Smith and S. A. Owens were also among the long line of NAACP speakers. Prayer services were held at the churches, including the Mt. Moriah Baptist Church. Daisy Bates was the speaker at the Freedom Banquet at Club Ebony.

The entire Volunteer Ticket went down in defeat, in part because the Negroes did not turn out to vote "55,000 strong" as asked. Five days before the election, the *Tri-State Defender* had warned, "Henry Loeb is going to do nothing for the Negro if he is chosen mayor." Just as Hooks feared, some Negro preachers did nothing against the movement, but they also did nothing to help. White politicians had launched a successful whisper campaign that the Volunteer Ticket was the "NAACP Ticket" and that the NAACP was "Communist inspired." Employers, especially white women who hired maids and laborers, had strong influence over docile Negro workers. The Volunteer Ticket printed thirty thousand pieces of literature, but white leaders printed wallet-size lists of Negro candidates for voters to take to the polls. Loeb, a current commissioner, won a landslide victory after mayoral candidate Edmund Orgill withdrew "for health reasons." (In 1950, the *Nashville Globe* had predicted that Memphis Negroes might "come into their own" under Orgill.) More than 70 percent of registered white voters cast ballots in the election, compared to 62 percent of registered Negroes. In the race for public works commissioner, Sugarmon got 35,268 votes, as compared to 58,943 for avowed segregationist William "Bill" Farris. Of all the Negro candidates, Sugarmon came closest to winning his contest.

Sugarmon's wife, Laurie, was especially hurt by the outcome of the election because she had "worked twelve hours a day" hosting Coke parties, poring over voting lists, and organizing women and young helpers. The youth chapter of the NACCP held their meetings in her home. A graduate of a prestigious women's college in Massachusetts, Mrs. Sugarmon said, "The challenge today is not to die [in Memphis], but to live." Notwithstanding the bitter defeat, she believed that her husband was a winner in other ways. And Sugarmon himself reflected, "We won everything but the election. The tremendous unity shown by the Negroes in the campaign can only show the city that the colored citizens—almost 40 percent of the population—are a group to be reckoned with." He said the whites indeed "had kept [their 1956 promise] to ['Keep] Memphis down in Dixie.'" For his part, Lee said, "Memphis government is now compelled to give the Negro true representation in governmental affairs. We have created an atmosphere in which we will get more respect from the whites."

If the whites had not been mobilized racially and black turnout had been as projected, the total vote for Sugarmon would have won the election, but whites saw a black bloc vote as a threat to their power. When local dailies accused Lee of promoting racial bloc voting, he said, "I deplore a racial vote on a bloc basis, but Negroes desire to participate in our public life. Until the present, as we all know, such has been impossible [in Memphis]." Perhaps what the *Globe* had said on April 20, 1956, was still true: "Nashville Negroes appeared to cast more votes than the [black] Memphians who had little or nothing tangible to show for their prowess."

Nat D. Williams reflected that the election had brought the white community together like never before to strike a blow against the attempts of Negroes to rise in Memphis. The *Tri-State Defender*'s editor, L. F. Palmer, who called himself "a newcomer to the city," took middle- and upper-class Negroes to task for not doing more to get out the vote. But, in his view, it was still a "Crusade for Freedom." The Memphis elections even caught the attention of the *Washington Post,* which noted, "Negro leaders aren't singing the blues on Beale Street these days. At long last, they figure the Negro vote had come of age in Memphis." Writing in the *Defender* (Mar. 12, 1960), Williams said, "Things are happening so fast on the racial front until it's easy to get the impression that one is not in the mainstream of things. The time has come for every individual Negro to come out in his true colors."

CHAPTER 8

THE BLACK DEMOCRATS

CIVIL RIGHTS AND POLITICS
IN TENNESSEE

Negro leaders in Memphis definitely had the political fever by 1960. O. Z. Evers applied as a candidate for the minor office of constable in the first district, but the authorities disqualified him for actually "living in district two." J. H. Turner and Alexander Gladney became candidates for the local Democratic executive committee after A. Maceo Walker (Joseph E. Walker's son) withdrew his name. By July 1960, some 66,736 Negroes and 216,075 whites were registered to vote in the city. By August 1960, Negroes constituted about 31 percent of eligible voters in Memphis. Some 26 of 172 precincts had fewer than 10 percent white registered voters. Only 41 percent of the registered Negro voters in those 26 precincts actually voted, compared to 56.2 percent of the white registered voters. Only 41.7 percent of the 72,372 registered Negroes voted in the Democratic primary that Senator Kefauver won by 64,253 to 53,421 votes. "If the Negro voters had turned out at the rate of the white voters, there would have been 10,490 more Negro votes," said the *World*. A. W. Willis lost his bid for a city-at-large Shelby County Court seat, but he drew a good many white votes in his 26,369-vote total. In 1960, the Shelby County sheriff announced the training of the first Negro deputies.

Thirty miles east of Memphis, in rural West Tennessee, Jim Crow remained an arrogant and brutal presence, especially in Haywood County, where Negroes had been accorded no civil rights since the 1880s. Negroes saw

"Mr. Crump" in every white man in Haywood County. In May 1940, they organized an NAACP chapter in Brownsville and began a voter registration drive in the county. When race radicals heard about the attempts to register Negroes at the courthouse, they cut off credit to Negro leaders, fired some workers, and even opened mail related to the NAACP. After they got word that Negroes had traveled in a caravan of cars into Memphis to hold their meeting, some whites burst into a Negro café, held the patrons at gunpoint, and forced some of them to name the leaders of the movement. Negro leaders spoke with the president of the Brownsville Bank, whom they considered to be a moderate white man; he told them, "You have a right to vote. . . . [But] These rednecks, there is no telling what they will do."

A few days later, on a Saturday, a white mob gathered at the courthouse, formed a caravan, and then drove menacingly in front of Negro businesses, looking for the Reverend Buster Walker, an activist in the Brownsville NAACP. Civil rights attorney J. Emmett Ballard of Jackson took Walker to Jackson for safety. Negroes warned Elisha Davis, another activist, who closed his filling station and was secretly driven to Jackson. Later, a mob found Davis, took him from his home early in the morning of June 15, threatened his life, and ordered him to leave the county after he gave the names of other NAACP members. Truck drivers, procurers, federally funded WPA workers, farmers, and county officials were among those in the mob.

On June 23, 1940, the body of thirty-three-year-old Elbert Williams, a laundry worker and an NAACP leader, was found by a fisherman in the Hatchee River with a rope around his neck attached to a heavy limb. A mob had beaten and shot Williams, stripped the body to the underwear, and thrown it in the river. Walker and a half-dozen other Negroes fled to Chicago and reported the lynching to the *Chicago Defender.* Walter White of the NAACP arrived in Memphis to confer with the U.S. attorney. White sent information about the lynching to President Roosevelt, and the NAACP-LDF assigned two lawyers to assist Buster Walker in approaching the U.S. Department of Justice about an investigation. Thurgood Marshall traveled to Haywood County in December 1941, but despite his pleas for a thorough investigation, the FBI stalled and then closed the case in 1942. The NAACP Convention delegates, meeting in Philadelphia, contributed money to help Buster Walker.

Roosevelt narrowly carried Haywood County in 1940. Thereafter, the rapidly changing faces of American politics strongly affected the attitude of the federal government toward the issue of civil rights. By 1943, two Negroes, William Dawson of Chicago and Adam Clayton Powell Jr. of New York City, both Democrats, held seats in the U.S. Congress. And by 1946, Negroes held seats in ten state legislatures. In 1954, Charles C. Diggs Jr. of Detroit, another

Democrat, won election to the Congress. Charles H. Mahoney was the first Negro to serve as permanent delegate to the United Nations. Ralph Bunche was named United Nations undersecretary general and received the Nobel Peace Prize in 1950. In 1958, Clifton R. Wharton Sr. became the first Negro to head a U.S. embassy when he became minister to Romania. Robert N. Nix, Democrat of Pennsylvania, became the fourth Negro elected to Congress.

In July 1959, attorney James Franklin Estes of Memphis escorted a six-person delegation from Haywood County to Nashville to testify before the State Election Commission. The *Brownsville States-Graphic* newspaper in Haywood County said that its reporter could "get their names," perhaps to target them for retaliation, and believed them to be the same people—Currie P. Boyd, T. O. Crews, Odell Sanders, Billy Martin Peterson, the Reverend Newborn, and Becky [Bettye] Douglass—who were turned away from registering to vote a few weeks before. Those Negroes were not the ones who made up the delegation, however. That group actually consisted of members of the newly formed Haywood County Civic and Welfare League (HCCWL): Sherman H. Coleman, the Reverend George W. Douglass, James Bond, George Gray, Thad Turner, and Joe L. Sanderson. The delegation asked for a change in the county's voting practices and for appointment of a new election commission. County officials argued that the commission was inactive at this time, because the two political parties had failed to replace members who resigned. Officials threatened Estes with arrest if he appeared anywhere in Haywood County. Racial conflict increased in the county when a Negro farmer, forty-nine-year-old Willie M. Jones, shot and killed the sheriff in July 1959. The *States-Graphic* (Oct. 23, 1959) ran pictures, one of Jones sitting on his porch and another showing a deputy pointing at the front-door screen from which the shot allegedly originated. Jones claimed that the shot was fired from the *back* door after the sheriff tore off the screen and pointed a pistol into the room. Jones was convicted of murder but appealed his case, contending that the sheriff's body had been moved to the front porch to make it appear that he could have identified the sheriff before the shooting. Jones eventually had his sentence reduced to manslaughter and received a two-year jail term, which included time already served.

Haywood County's population declined by twelve hundred between 1950 and 1960, dropping to only nineteen thousand citizens, while Memphis gained citizens and the Tennessee population increased by nearly nine hundred thousand. The local newspaper carried photographs of the work on nearby Interstate 40 Highway and new automobiles with fins and wings to speed passengers to distant places. Such developments added rural Negroes to the Great Migration to the North, and they opened Haywood County to the outside world. Negroes, although they were in the majority in Haywood County, had no local newspaper of their own. They had to rely on such publications as the *Chicago Defender* and *Tri-State Defender* in Memphis.

[*]

In nearby Memphis in January 1960, the national offices of the NAACP and the SCLC announced that they were teaming up to launch another nationwide voter registration campaign to add two million new voters to the rolls. This was part of the NAACP's campaign called "free by '63" in honor of the approaching one hundredth anniversary of the Emancipation Proclamation. Lieutenant Lee, Maceo Walker, and others spoke at the Ninety-seventh Emancipation Day Proclamation program at the Ellis Auditorium and urged the audience to register to vote. On the other side of Ellis Auditorium, ironically, the mayor-elect, Henry Loeb, and the new school board members were being sworn into office—it was an all-white Memphis government.

Some Colored Methodist Episcopal (CME) Church leaders began to promote the NAACP's work, although the CME, which grew out of the conservative white Methodist Episcopal Church South in 1866, had been criticized for not engaging in earlier phases of the civil rights movement. Henry C. Bunton had come to Memphis in 1953 to be assigned pastor of Mt. Olive CME Church, and by 1959 he was a leader and officer in King's Southern Christian Leadership Conference. The Reverend Bunton attended SCLC regional meetings and was also a frequent speaker in churches throughout Tennessee. As associate editor of the *Christian Index,* he was able as well to influence the CME Church to become involved in Christian social activism and nonviolent protest against Jim Crow. "The ballot is the legal weapon with which we are armed to fight our battle to be free, to be recognized as Americans with full citizenship status," declared the *Christian Index* on January 21, 1960. "This is the place where many of us show our disrespect for all that we mean by civil rights. Some organization should be created in our churches for the purpose of urging our members and all who worship with us to register, consider the issues, and vote in all elections where our interest is involved." During its General Conference on May 12, 1960, the CME substituted the word "Christian" for the word "Colored" in its name. Church leaders urged the congregations to adopt the spirit of *Brown* and become "The 'stalking Negro,' who must march until the last vestige of segregation has been crushed."

Although other local papers in Memphis were filled with news about the Negro's struggle for civil rights during the late 1950s and early 1960s, the Jewish paper, the *Hebrew Watchman*, carried no mention of it. White radicalism in Memphis could be a formidable force against friends of the Negro. Thus, members of synagogues in Memphis concentrated on national and international issues, such as the crisis in Israel, the recent anti-discrimination resolution by the United Nations, and the question "Can a Jew be elected president?"

[*]

But if Jewish Memphians looked carefully, they would see a fierce struggle against injustice brewing in their own backyard in Haywood County. On February 26, 1960, the State Election Commission approved a three-member county election commission. But some landowners sent eviction notices to certain tenant farmers as part of a concerted effort to harass and intimidate Negro voters. Approximately 437 farmers in Haywood County were over sixty-five years old, and most of them had nowhere to go if the landowner evicted them. Negro tenants had no retirement benefits, and the New Deal's Social Security regulations did not cover such workers. They usually received their pay in cash without checks, stubs, and receipts. Local druggists refused to sell medicine—even for sick babies—to the Negroes who had been marked for eviction, forcing them to go to Memphis or Jackson. Negroes on this blacklist were denied the right to buy groceries, purchase clothes, and secure bank loans to put in new crops. Negro school cafeteria workers were dismissed after registering to vote. Law officials patrolled the roads, turning back delivery trucks. "They want to run us out of the county, but we chose to remain," Currie Boyd said. "This is our home, and we believe in democracy. We know that God is on our side. We know that if we persist, justice will win over injustice." Boyd, who had earned a Ph.D. degree, had returned home in 1957, determined to change things. "In Fayette County," he said, "Negro teachers are at the mercy of the superintendent, because the county gave them no contracts—a violation of state law. The economic squeeze is hurting all Negroes and is hurting the county." Boyd also wanted to have the Confederate statue removed from the courthouse grounds.

The U.S. Commission on Civil Rights already had found that there were at least one hundred hardcore counties in the South, including Fayette and Haywood in Tennessee, which resisted the registration of Negro voters. Southern officials had ignored the 1957 Civil Rights Act, which was supposed to protect black voters. But no one ever registered under that act. The Commission on Civil Rights recommended a stronger act, only to have southern members of Congress resist the change. Senator Estes Kefauver voted with the southern congressional bloc about 83 percent of the time during debates on the 1960 civil rights bill. A. Philip Randolph, Martin Luther King Jr., and Bayard Rustin organized the "March on the Conventions Movement for Freedom Now" and held twenty-four-hour vigils outside the convention halls of the two major parties during the summer of 1960. Congress passed the 1960 Civil Rights Act, and it was signed by Eisenhower. It provided a system of voter referees appointed by federal courts and a provision that if a registrar resigned after a voter had filed a complaint, the county could be sued. The voting records had to be preserved for twenty-two months after the election, and anyone who defaced churches, synagogues, and other buildings in acts of terrorism could be punished under federal law.

Roy Wilkins announced that truckloads of supplies were being sent to besieged tenant families in Haywood County. The Memphis branch NAACP and the black churches and communities in Nashville and Memphis gathered food and clothing, while the Looby-Williams law office helped prepare a lawsuit. Members of SNCC ran trucks back and forth from Nashville to West Tennessee, delivering clothing, food, and supplies. The Memphis NAACP filed race discrimination charges with the Tennessee government, the State Election Commission, and the U.S. Department of Justice on behalf of Negroes in Haywood County who had been forced to stand in line for hours on May 19 just to register to vote. The Congress of Racial Equality sent a field secretary to confirm reports that major oil companies were refusing to supply gas to Negro customers. CORE chapters in Los Angeles, St. Louis, New York, and the Chicago Emergency Relief Committee sent sixty tons of food, medicine, and clothing. By July 1960, 235 of 620 people registered to vote in Haywood County were Negroes. The *World* criticized the low voter turnout among Memphis's Negroes, while noting, "Elsewhere in the nation citizens are being begged to register and vote. In Fayette County, and in many sections of the South, colored citizens are being dared to attempt it and punished if they succeed."

In Haywood County, the number of Negro farmers had declined from 2,709 in 1954 to 2,037 by 1959, and Negroes owned much less land than the minority whites. In *The Black Rural Landowner—Endangered Species* (1979), Tennessee State University professors Leo McGee and Robert Boone wrote, "Part of the reason [for the lower levels of land ownership] was chicanery perpetuated under unscrupulous lawyers, land spectators, and county officials." Most Negro landowners had purchased their land from other Negroes, and most Negro farmers were tenants. Whereas many of the Negro tenants who remained on the land were older persons, the average white farmer was about forty-five years old and had been taught to uphold the tradition of white supremacy. The 1960 agriculture season had been a good one, after years of revival by New Deal programs, and the white farmers in Haywood County reaped millions of dollars in sales. They could easily refuse to renew the share-crop contracts of targeted Negro tenants.

Currie P. Boyd appealed in the *Nashville News-Star* (June 26, 1960) for donations to be sent to Tri-State Bank and Trust Company (formed by Maceo Walker, Joseph E. Walker, and others in 1946) in Memphis or to the HCCWL in Stanton. Boyd asked that letters be sent to U.S. Attorney General William P. Rogers because "He is the one to put teeth into it." NAACP lawyers asked that two Memphis FBI agents be removed from the investigation because of their racial prejudices. On September 13, 1960, the Civil Rights Division of the U.S. Department of Justice asked the local district court to issue injunctions against twenty-seven individuals and two banks. This was the first time that the Civil Rights Act of 1960 was invoked. The *States-Graphic* declared it a shame that white citizens were being forced to endure a waste of time and money in defending their rights; the paper accused the federal government of moving toward a "police state" by seeking injunctions to force "private citizens to whom they shall lend and sell, who they shall house and feed, and whom they shall employ." Democrats won the November election in the county. The *States-Graphic* reported, "Some 850 Negroes [among nearly 3,400 voters] of the county, the majority of whom voted in their first presidential election, apparently aided the Democratic victory as evidenced by District 9, which has a majority of Negro voters."

Negroes in Haywood County continued to endure harassment as legal action was taken against those who harassed them. Radicals tried to put Odell Sanders's grocery out of business, and shots were fired into the laundry business owned by Sanders and Boyd. On December 23, 1960, the *States-Graphic* reported that sixty-one defendants, including two local banks, the county's school superintendent, and the mayor of Brownsville, had been charged with federal civil rights violations. U.S. marshals served injunctions throughout the county, causing a stir among the citizens, but the case landed in the district court of Judge Marion S. Boyd, who said that serving an immediate injunction was like "cutting a man's water and lights off without warning." Judge Boyd declared that the Civil Rights Act had no power to force a man to renew a private contract with his tenants, thus ignoring the Justice Department's request that the defendants be prohibited from punishing the Negro tenants for registering to vote. Boyd required the federal government to "be more specific in the allegations and complaints." When asked on the stand about the "blacklist" of evicted tenants, defendants "took the Fifth" and refused to answer. On May 2, 1962, the appeal by plaintiffs to the Sixth Circuit Court resulted in a judgment against fifty individuals and four corporations.

[*]

Adjacent to Haywood County was Fayette County— also a rural area, with a society much like that of Mississippi, which lay just across its southern border. In 1860 Negroes had constituted 67 percent of the population in Fayette County. After emancipation, Negroes were quite organized and participated fully in the county's politics. Monroe Gooden was elected to represent Fayette County in the General Assembly from 1887 to 1889, as was David Foote Rivers, who served for two terms from 1883 to 1887. Gooden (1848–1915), a Negro farmer and cotton gin owner near Somerville, was thought to be a Democrat. Rivers (1859–1941) was an Alabama-born Republican who attended Roger Williams University and came to Fayette County by way of Mississippi. Whites tried unsuccessfully to contest his seat on the grounds that the time he spent in school in Nashville made him a nonresident of Fayette County. At any rate, Rivers fled the county before completing his second term, believing that white race radicals would kill him. He taught at Roger Williams before going to Kansas City, Missouri, in 1893 to pastor a church. He headed Baptist churches in Washington, D.C., and New York, where he died. His son Francis E. Rivers became a member of the New York General Assembly and an assistant district attorney. Once the whites took back political power in Fayette County in 1887, they moved definitively to exclude the Negro as a political participant and an economic competitor. By 1960, Negroes still made up 68.9 percent of the county's population, but whites held nearly 90 percent of the land there. The people of Fayette County were the poorest in all of Tennessee, and in 1958 the per capita income was only $547, compared to $1,439 for the state as a whole and $2,057 for the country. Since 1954, the number of farms in Fayette County had declined to 3,451, averaging 109 acres each; they raised soybeans, okra, peas, cattle, hogs, and plenty of cotton. The county lost nearly 12 percent of its population between 1950 and 1960, when its population was 24,577 people. In 1890 it had been 31,871. Many sharecroppers and tenants migrated to nearby Memphis, and after World War II, many Negroes from Fayette County joined the Great Migration to the North.

Around 1959, Fayette County authorities learned that Burton Dodson, a Negro wanted for murder since 1941, was living in East St. Louis, Illinois. Dodson had escaped in a hail of gunfire when a white lynch mob, including law enforcement officers, came to his house. County officials had Dodson brought back to Tennessee for trial. Perhaps emboldened by news of the civil rights movement elsewhere, Negroes came out of the fields and crowded the county courthouse in Somerville. Two young Negro farmers, John McFerrin and Harpman Jameson, were among those who attended the trial. They were so impressed by the black turnout and the interest in seeing justice done that they led an effort to raise funds for Dodson's defense. Attorney James Franklin Estes, who was defending Dodson, also helped them to form a permanent organization, the Fayette County Civic and Welfare League (FCCWL). Scott Franklin, Floyd Franklin, John Lewis, and others from small towns in Fayette County helped lead the FCCWL. Estes managed to limit Dodson's prison term to ten years.

John McFerrin became a key leader of the local civil rights movement. Born in 1925 in Fayette County, he was descended from slaves who had been brought on covered wagons from North Carolina as part of the domestic slave trade in the 1820s. McFerrin's wife, Viola, was a 1951 graduate of Fayette County Training School for Negroes and a registered nurse. The couple farmed a mere eight acres of corn and cotton, and John had to cut lumber in nearby Mississippi to make ends meet. One day, when cutting timber on a white man's land in Mississippi, McFerrin, a veteran of World War II in the European theater, discovered three Negro families living in mud huts in the woods and making a living by selling bootleg whiskey. The children had no idea that such a thing as school even existed. McFerrin was floored: "It was outright slavery in Mississippi just miles from my home in Tennessee." Disgusted, he refused to accept the logs he had cut and would have done so even if the white landowner had given them to him "for free."

In May and June 1959, operating out of the home and then the tiny grocery store of John and Viola McFerrin, the FCCWL began to persuade even more Negroes to register to vote. Just prior to the August 1, 1959, primary, the Fayette County Democratic executive committee resolved that only "known white Democrats" could participate in the election. The Negroes were given a printed notice to that effect and turned away from the voting boxes. In response, the federal government filed discrimination charges against nineteen whites on November 16, 1959, after twelve Negroes were willing to testify that they had been denied the right to vote in the primary.

In October and November, white farmers began displacing Negro sharecropper families, particularly those who had registered to vote. On February 13, 1960, R. H. Powell, Shepherd Towles, the Reverend J. Dowdy, and John McFerrin appeared with attorney Estes to deny newspaper accounts that no Negroes had shown up to register to vote; in fact, two hundred Negroes had crowded the courthouse but received the runaround from election officials. McFerrin, Jameson, C. P. Boyd, Sanders, and Estes drove nonstop to Washington, D.C., to demand federal action under the Civil Rights Act. After submitting their petition to officials, they did not linger in Washington but instead, to save money, drove directly back to West Tennessee.

Upon his return from the Washington trip, McFerrin told local Negroes to put their automobiles in good shape because of reports that county law enforcement officers planned to stop Negroes traveling through the county. Drivers might be stropped and harassed for the least reason, such as allegedly having a broken taillight. Some might even be arrested on trumped-up charges. On February 20, the *Memphis World* spread the warning. Relatives from Memphis would fill their cars to overflowing and carry extra cans of gasoline with them before venturing into Fayette County, where they were careful to obey the speed limits and watch for the patrol cars. As in the days of abolitionism and the Underground Railroad, any whites who supported Negroes also suffered economic sanctions, and fear gripped citizens in the countryside. "I hardly think you can get that feeling of oppression until you have been oppressed," C. P. Boyd said. McFerrin used his cinderblock grocery store to extend supplies, gasoline, and credit to Negro workers. Landowners placed McFerrin's picture in local buildings. Negroes who tried to register to vote were placed in the back of the line, as whites were allowed to register first. County officials would close their offices before all the Negroes could be registered, forcing them to return the next day and stand in line again.

Like the people he was trying to help, attorney James F. Estes also became a marked man in Fayette County. Born in nearby Jackson, Estes (1919–1967) completed public schools there, graduated from Lane College, and received his law degree from Marquette University. He served as an officer in the U.S. Army and practiced law in Wisconsin before returning home. In 1946, Estes headed the Tennessee Negro Veterans Association and with other Negro veterans petitioned Governor McCord for inclusion in the state National Guard units that were being formed after World War II. In 1948, Estes became an attorney and pastor of Vance Avenue Baptist Church. In March 1960, he arranged a large rally at Clayborn Temple in Memphis to gain wider support from that community for the besieged people in the neighboring rural counties. About two hundred Negro farmers from Fayette and Haywood counties participated in the rally. The Reverend W. Herbert Brewster of East Trigg Avenue Baptist Church and the Reverend Samuel Herring were among the speakers. "We are not afraid," the farmers said, vowing, "We will stand together." Estes said, "What affects Negroes in Fayette and Haywood counties will affect Negroes in Memphis."

Landowners so intimidated Negro storekeepers that Odell Sanders, for one, had nothing to sell and had to close his store in Brownsville. A national oil company removed Scott Franklin's gasoline pumps at his store. But a man from an oil company appeared at McFerrin's house and offered to sell gasoline for cash if local Negroes could furnish a driver or two to transport it. McFerrin recalled that Negroes came from everywhere to his store when the two trucks carrying gasoline arrived. Amid a festival-like atmosphere, they filled up their automobiles. Meanwhile, Viola McFerrin had to deliver her third child, Claudia, in Memphis, and no white merchant in Fayette County would sell her products or services for the infant. Estes asked President Eisenhower to declare the two counties federal disaster areas so that families could receive food, farm supplies, credit, and health care. The *Fayette County Falcon* predicted that federal interference might prevent the county primary election from being held.

Fayette County election officials and the U.S. Justice Department reached an agreement, however. The State Election Commission appointed a new Fayette County Election Commission on May 20, and registration of voters resumed in June. The Tennessee Advisory Committee to the U.S. Civil Rights Commission invoked the federal statute and sent a request to the chairman of the Fayette County commission to provide figures on the "number of white and Negro voters now registered in the county and the number of voters from each group who recently voted." Fayette County officials had been supplying lists of Negro voters to the sheriff, who would harass and arrest them and then send a list of arrests to employers. The Justice Department sent two attorneys to check records at the courthouse and review the amounts of fines assessed in recent arrests. On May 25–28, several FCCWL members attended a retreat at Highlander Folk School and subsequently established citizenship classes in Fayette County. "This is a struggle for democracy," a Highlander spokesman said. "The white person's commitment should be as total as the Negro's." According to the *World* (June 8, 1960), about seventy-five blacks and whites attended the Highlander workshops.

Ted R. Poston, who had covered the Little Rock school integration crisis, wrote a series of articles for the *New York Post* to bring national attention to the anti-democratic practices in rural West Tennessee. He, like Carl T. Rowan of the *Minneapolis Tribune*, was sent south to cover civil rights activities. These two former Tennessee A&I students were gifted at writing stories that would touch the hearts and minds of citizens. Theodore Roosevelt Augustus Poston

(1906–1974) was born in Hopkinsville, Kentucky, and after college he moved to New York to join his brother. Poston wrote for the *Pittsburgh Courier* and the weekly *Amsterdam News* in Harlem, became a nationally celebrated journalist at the *New York Post*, won journalism awards in 1949, and was nominated for the Pulitzer Prize.

In August 1960, news reporters and the NBC television network were present when the Fayette County election commission held voter registration. Hundreds of Negroes showed up. The *Falcon* reported, "The eyes of the Nation were on Fayette County Wednesday." Most whites avoided the news media, a decision that stemmed not from guilt about terrorist activities but from defiance of "outsiders." Courthouse workers locked the restrooms in the building, and from the roof they poured paint, red pepper, and coffee on the Negroes standing in line. Despite the summer heat that caused some elderly people and women to faint, 450 Negroes were added to the voter registration rolls, bringing their total to 1,650 voters. John McFerrin said, "The people of the Tennessee town [Somerville] on the border of Mississippi have become world famous for their stand [against the Negro's constitutional rights]." He said that Negroes still had to travel to Memphis or Jackson to get supplies and that the FCCWL needed donations of money and gasoline to travel to the fifteen districts and keep the communication lines open. The Memphis branch NAACP distributed food to about seventy-five families, while four hundred new voters were registered.

Fayette County citizens voted heavily in November 1960, when local officials counted the ballots and reported the results under watchful federal eyes. The heaviest Negro voting was in Langtown, where almost all of the 180 votes were cast for John F. Kennedy, and in the Seventh Civil District where 120 Negroes cast ballots. Kennedy beat Richard M. Nixon by 1,871 to 1,188 votes in the county, winning in the heavily Negro Nut Bush precinct (the former home of pop singer Tina Turner) by 44 to 41 votes and gaining the largest vote in other predominantly black districts. Throughout America, 68 percent of the Negro voters cast ballots for Kennedy, while 52 percent of white voters sided with Nixon. Kennedy won with 49.9 percent of the popular vote to Nixon's 49.6 percent, gaining 303 electoral votes to Nixon's 219. Voter participation was 62.8 percent.

In December, notices went out to over four hundred sharecroppers and tenants in Fayette County that they must move off the land by the first of the year. The landowners claimed that effective weed-killing chemicals and new cotton-picking machines had displaced the workers. Senator Kefauver, who claimed he did not believe such atrocities were happening in Tennessee, soon asked federal agencies and the American Red Cross to assist evicted families. John S. Wilder, a state senator who was born in Fayette County in 1921 and chaired the board of supervisors of the Fayette County Soil Conservation District, became one of the few whites willing to help blacks. The Wilder family owned a five-thousand-acre farm, a service station, and several other businesses in Mason. Wilder refused to participate in the eviction campaign or call in crop loans on more than three hundred Negro farmers, even though a local church placed pressure on him.

On December 14, 1960, the U.S. Department of Justice filed *U.S. of America v. Herbert Atkeison, et al.* against forty-five landowners, twenty-four merchants, and a bank in Fayette County, charging them with conspiring to deny Negro citizens the right to register and vote. John Doar argued for the plaintiffs, and Lucius E. Burch Jr. was attorney for the defendants. County election commission members and the registrar decided to resign because, as the *Falcon* reported, "These [federal] investigations have increased the demand on our time to a point where we can no longer serve." Burch argued that farmers should be allowed to evict any tenants to economize and save money. Judge Boyd refused to issue a federal court order to prevent the eviction of Negro tenants, but he did issue an order to prohibit the defendants "from preventing citizens of the United States, on account of their race or color, who are qualified to vote in Fayette County, from effectively participating in any election." Boyd knew what the real problem was, but he chose to ignore the evictions as tools to deny voting rights, and he continued to argue about violating the owners' property and contractual rights. Plaintiffs appealed to the Sixth Circuit Court, which partly reversed Boyd's decision by restraining the landowners from evicting tenants except for legitimate reasons. Boyd allowed landowners "who are hurting the most" to individually appeal the restraining order. A week later, the defendants' lawyer asked Boyd to allow six more landowners to evict their Negro tenants for "legitimate cause."

By late December 1960, an encampment of about twenty-five evicted families living in tents—which became known as "Tent City"—was established along the Somerville–Macon Road on Shepard Towles's property near Moscow. Towles was risking his life to help the evictees, but he could not bear to see fellow Negroes and their children freeze in the cold weather so near to Christmas. The origin of the fourteen tents was kept secret. Twenty adults and fifty-six children were living in Tent City by January 1961. The *Falcon* complained, "An amazing flood of publicity has spread over the United States within the past two weeks about 'Tent City.'" More news media came into the county after some shots were fired into the tents, reported the *World* (Jan. 4,

1961). One Negro was admitted to a Memphis hospital. Three youths set off explosions along the road, causing Tent City residents to fire on them. Another encampment was established along State Highway 57 on land just east of the Moscow town limits. The president of the Memphis NAACP attended meetings in New York and Washington, D.C., to obtain federal and corporate assistance. A New York radio station collected a host of goods. The Memphis NAACP branch and local churches acted as collection centers. A caravan of trucks soon arrived at Tent City with food and clothing. The *Falcon* claimed that these supplies had been withheld from Negroes not registered to vote, and FCCWL officials were in dispute about how to distribute the goods. The CORE field secretary tried to mediate the disagreement, but the fight split the FCCWL, causing McFerrin to form a new organization with a different name and to replace attorney Estes. The leaders soon established an equitable system of distributing supplies and used incoming funds for scholarships and adult education classes. The funds also helped to establish a permanent office for McFerrin's organization, the Fayette County Civic League. Judge Marion Boyd began hearings on January 16, 1961, to allow the white farmers, "one by one," give legal reasons for evicting Negro tenants.

McFerrin spoke at Nashville's St. John AME Church on February 2, 1961, bringing evicted tenant Georgia Mae Turner to tell the audience how she was forced to live in a tent. The AFL-CIO sent a representative from the United Packinghouse Workers Union to investigate the conditions in the tent city and order supplies for the residents. The Ann Arbor, Michigan, affiliate of CORE donated $377 to help volunteers install floors in the tents. SNCC continued to run a supply convoy from Nashville. "In the deepest sense," said Walter P. Reuther, president of the AFL-CIO, "the men and women of Tent City are fighting for the civil rights of all Americans and they are writing a bold chapter in the continuing narrative of American democracy." On January 19, the *Falcon* said it would no longer give Tent City publicity that would provoke outside news media to exploit a local matter.

Joseph H. Jackson, the president of the National Baptist Convention, Inc. (NBCI), entered the fray. Jackson, whose convention had been pushing voter registration as a "proper" civil rights tool, also intended to show that economic programs—and not "un-Christian" civil disobedience—were the best ways to push the civil rights movement. In March 1961, Jackson announced that NBCI was buying a "National Baptist Freedom Farm" in Fayette County. The place was dedicated on March 22, 1961, and additional acres were added several years later. The NBCI provided loans for the tenants to start their crops. Several families eventually bought their own land.

In June the Kennedy administration ordered the United States Department of Agriculture to send food to fourteen thousand Negroes in the two counties, and it allowed the Department of Justice to continue the lawsuits against the landowners. Cynthia Rawls, with help from Ollie S. Bond and others, reestablished the NAACP chapter in Brownsville on May 7, 1961, and by October, more than twenty-eight hundred Negroes were registered to vote. They were among the seven thousand people who voted in the primary elections that fall—the first primary election for Negroes in Fayette County. On July 27, 1962, the court cases against seventy-four individuals and one bank were ended by consent decree. The defendants agreed not to interfere with the rights of other citizens.

[*]

Again, Negro leaders in Memphis became central to the Democrats becoming the majority party among blacks. Yet, until 1959, as demonstrated by Robert R. Church Jr. and G. W. Lee, Memphis Negroes were loyal Republicans. Between 1881 and 1893, Thomas Frank Cassels, Greene E. Evans, William A. Fields, Leonard Howard, and Isham F. Norris, all members of the GOP, had represented Memphis–Shelby County in the General Assembly. Cassels, who had served as assistant attorney general in Memphis in 1878, served on the education and common school committee of the House. He submitted a bill to repeal the 1870 law that had prohibited sexual intercourse between whites and Negroes, mulattos, and other persons of mixed blood descended from Negroes. Born in Kentucky in 1843 and educated at Oberlin College, Cassels also submitted a bill to create the office of county superintendent of public roads and bridges, and he fought tax discrimination against Memphis. Evans was born in Fayette County in 1848 and graduated from Fisk University. He was a member of the Jubilee Singers (the famed choral group based at Fisk), a schoolteacher, a mail agent, and a deputy wharfmaster. Fields was born in Tennessee in 1852 and made his living as a farmer and schoolteacher in Shelby County. Howard was a porter at the Gayoso Hotel and a janitor at the Customs House. Little information is known about Norris, but he was a wealthy man who dealt in coal, wood, and groceries, and served on the House Committee on Grounds and Buildings.

During the 1960 presidential campaign, the Shelby County Democratic Club cosponsored Senator John F. Kennedy's visit to Memphis. The work by the late Joseph E. Walker and his Democratic Club since 1936 was about to bear fruit. J. H. Turner, A. Maceo Walker, R. B. Sugarmon, and other Negro leaders, as well as Governor Ellington and Senators Gore and Kefauver, among others, met Kennedy's plane at the Memphis Airport. Eleven students from LeMoyne College and Griggs Business College, including twenty-two-year-old Ollie Neal, were arrested at the Dobbs House Restaurant in the airport for conducting a sit-in demonstration. Turner informed Kennedy of what was going on, but he waved it off, and said, "I saw the incident." The students were holding placards: "Discrimination Still Exists in Memphis," "Negroes Want Freedom," and "Is America the Land of the Free?" Kennedy would be criticized for not stopping on Beale Street to pay respects to the W. C. Handy Memorial and Matthew Thornton Sr., the "Mayor of Beale Street." Nonetheless, the *Tri-State Defender* promoted Kennedy.

The Republican presidential candidate, Vice President Richard M. Nixon, visited Memphis five days after Kennedy was there. Lieutenant Lee had attended the Republican convention in Chicago in July 1960 and was convinced that Nixon would "do right by Negroes." As the *World* (Dec. 9, 1961) reported, he criticized another GOP contender, Senator Barry Goldwater, for ignoring Negro voters, saying, "When a Republican leader disregards our party's heritage and our party's regularity and you join the cry of the White Citizens' Council and other intolerant groups of 'Down with the Negro' we have a special spectacle that calls for tears." For the third consecutive presidential election, the Republicans appointed Lee to be chairman of minority groups for Tennessee. In September, local Republicans opened their campaign headquarters on Main Street with an integrated staff. Willie Dunn and Edgar Young headed the Young Colored Republican Club for Nixon. Lee and others influenced Nixon's motorcade to travel down Beale Street and stop at the Handy Park Memorial, where Nixon placed a wreath, listened to a hot band play the "St. Louis Blues" by W. C. Handy, and posed for pictures with Negro Republican leaders: "Let us make our country a shining example for the world to see." The *Memphis World* boasted that Nixon had attracted much larger crowds than Kennedy had drawn, and the paper also reported on October 21, 1960, that Benjamin Hooks had congratulated Nixon for his stand on civil rights issues.

On October 26, 1960, the Republicans also brought baseball star Jackie Robinson to Memphis, where he told a rally at Mason Temple that "Kennedy goes the way the wind blows." The *World* carried a full page of photographs of his Memphis visit. Robinson was notable for being able to attract ordinary Negroes and to connect politics, sports, and civil rights. Memphis was a baseball town, with a Negro League team and the Martin Baseball Stadium.

Explaining his view of civil rights, Robinson once declared:

> Negroes are not seeking anything, which is not good for the
> nation as well as us. For America to be 100 percent strong—
> economically, defensively, and morally—we cannot afford the
> waste of having second- and third-class citizens. Civil rights by
> any means are not the only issues that concern me—nor, I think
> any other Negro. As Americans, we have as much at stake in
> this country as anyone else. But since effective participation
> in a democracy is based upon enjoyment of basic freedoms that
> everyone else takes for granted, we need make no apologies for
> being especially interested in catching up on civil rights. We
> cannot wait until men's hearts are changed to enjoy our consti-
> tutional rights.

In the general election, Kennedy received 63 percent of Negro votes across the country, while Nixon received the majority of white votes. Most local whites voted for the Republicans, giving Nixon Shelby County by 87,181 votes to Kennedy's 86,265. But two-thirds of the local Negro votes were for Kennedy, and in some black precincts, JFK gained 95 percent of the vote. The Republicans won no Negro precincts, signaling the end for viable Negro Republican organizations. But 75 percent of eligible Negroes in the South were still not voting. In Mississippi, that statistic was 99 percent. "Negro citizens," said Roy Wilkins, "will expect the new administration . . . to address itself to civil rights and race matters as well as other matters." In 1961, representatives of the Kennedy administration met with leaders of the West Tennessee black movement and decided to support its voter registration efforts. Justice Department officials participated in southern meetings that led to the creation of the Voter Education Project (VEP), a legal agency. The Justice Department increased the staff of lawyers to handle voting-rights litigation. The impact of the VEP and the movement to organize Negro politics did what the Negro Republicans had not been able to do: unite Negro voters across the state.

In Nashville, the younger Negroes (who could not vote until reaching the age of twenty-one) were fired up by the ongoing intensity of the sit-in demonstrations, and they were no longer tolerant of old political leaders. When R. E. Lillard and C. L. Ennix endorsed a conservative white candidate in 1960, the Nashville Student Movement Advisory Council sent a harsh reprimand: "We the students of Nashville, who you defended so vigorously during our sit-in demonstrations, are astounded and dismayed at your public endorsement of a man who has voted for the evils we are trying to eliminate." Marion

Barry signed the letter. The *Nashville News-Star*, a Negro newspaper, said, "Our vote can teach local politicians how to respect the Negro's rights." Most black leaders in Nashville endorsed Richard Fulton, a young liberal Democrat, for Congress. They also supported the reelection of Kefauver. M. G. Blakemore, who later practiced law with Looby, announced for a seat in the General Assembly. When two liberals (including Kefauver) defeated racially conservative opponents in the August primary, the *News-Star* (Aug. 14, 1960) wrote, "Segregation is dead as a major political issue in this state. No longer can a little political figure ride into office on the basis of hate and racial disunity. . . . What Memphis did [in 1959] by rallying around Sugarmon should not go unnoticed in Nashville. He became a symbol of the Negro's political hopes."

Sugarmon and Willis soon persuaded Nashville's Negro politicians to join with them in the formation of a statewide political organization, which would be officially named the Tennessee Voters' Council (TVC) in 1962. Avon Williams, Vivian Henderson (director of the Race Relations Institute at Fisk), and local NAACP leaders were all involved in the planning, with Henderson, according to Williams, acting as the chief political strategist. The groundwork for a statewide organization had actually been laid several years earlier, in March 1959, when Memphians W. C. Patton, Willa McWilliams, James T. Walker, and Charles F. Williams led the Tennessee Leadership Conference for Political Action on the Fisk campus. A strange turnaround was in progress: Since 1867 Negro leaders in Nashville had dominated political leadership in Afro-Tennessee, but Memphis was trying to take the lead, although winning political offices in the Delta city would still be difficult. Robert E. Lillard, Harold Love, Z. Alexander Looby, John Driver, and Mansfield Douglass held Nashville city council seats in 1962 because Nashville used wards and five at-large districts to elect council members, while Memphis effectively used at-large elections, the city commission government system, and a white voter bloc to keep Negroes from sharing local political power.

The nonpartisan Davidson County Independent Political Council (DCIPC) was launched in April 1962 with a mass meeting at Nashville's Ryman Auditorium, where Jackie Robinson delivered the principal address without charge. Wiley Branton, who had just moved from his civil rights law practice in Pine Bluff, Arkansas, to take over the new Voter Education Project headquarters in Atlanta, spoke at the rally. Nashville's Negro Republican Club died as Negro Democrats became dominant.

The Memphis group had actually designed the TVC to unite the black vote to help Democrat Frank Clement in his latest gubernatorial bid. Clement had won his first two-year term as governor in 1952, beating Gordon Browning. When the state constitution was changed in 1953, Clement won election in November 1954 as the first governor to be able to serve a four-year term. Buford Ellington, a conservative Democrat whose support came mostly from rural elements, won election as governor in 1958. Clement was returned to the governor's office in 1962 for his last four-year term. Clement, once elected, formed the State Human Relations Commission, appointed Benjamin Hooks as a criminal court judge, and placed Harold West, president of Meharry Medical College, on the State Board of Education. In 1962, when Kefauver died, Governor Clement decided to run for the vacated U.S. Senate seat, but Ross Bass, a Democratic congressman since 1954, also wanted the seat. Bass had attracted Negro support, and by winning Shelby County, gaining fifty thousand votes in Davidson County, and winning other urban areas, he defeated Clement for the remaining two years of the senatorial term. But Clement challenged Bass for the seat when the election for a full term approached. This time Clement won the Democratic nomination but lost the seat to a Republican, Howard Baker Jr. When Avon Williams and the Negro political leaders in Nashville came to realize the real meaning of all this, they felt they had been used by the black leaders in Memphis, especially because they had promised Looby a state Supreme Court seat but had failed to deliver the votes to help him win.

The Avon Williams group was concerned that Negroes had no representation in the General Assembly and held no appointive political positions in Tennessee. However, if the state districts had been apportioned properly, the fact that 70 percent of the state's Negroes were concentrated in West Tennessee and particularly in Memphis would probably have resulted in the election of a few black state legislators. Since 1900, the Tennessee population experienced tremendous growth and redistribution from the rural to the urban areas. In 1901, the population was 2,020,616, of whom 487,380 were eligible to vote. The 1960 federal census reported the state's population at 3,567,089, of whom 2,092,891 were eligible to vote. Rural Tennessee lost 25,000 Negroes and 112,000 whites between 1950 and 1960 alone as the agricultural areas suffered economic decline and the population migrated into cities and towns. Nashville, for instance, gained 56,000 Negroes and 200,000 whites between 1940 and 1950. But Tennessee had not been redistricted in decades, giving the rural areas more legislative power than they deserved and the Negroes none at all. Thirty-seven percent of the voters elected twenty of the thirty-three state senators while 40 percent of the voters elected sixty-three of the ninety-nine members of the state House of Representatives. Shelby County had three state representatives instead of the seven to which it would have been entitled had the legislative districting represented the population more fairly. In effect, a single vote in Moore County was worth nineteen votes in Hamilton County. One vote in Stewart or Chester County was worth nearly eight times a single vote in Shelby or Knox County. Rural, conservative legislators dominated the General Assembly and refused to allow a redistricting plan that would diminish their agrarian, ideological, and racial power.

The needed changes came about through the landmark Supreme Court decision of *Baker v. Carr.* The NAACP submitted an amicus brief for "one man, one vote," and the Leadership Conference on Civil Rights lobbied on behalf of ninety national organizations for the *Baker* case, as well as a new civil rights bill to replace the 1960 Civil Rights Act. The *Baker* plaintiffs claimed that because of the debasement of their votes, they were being denied equal protection of the laws accorded them by the Fourteenth Amendment. Negroes suffered because of no representation at all. Cities like Nashville joined the suit as plaintiffs. But the district court dismissed the suit "for lack of jurisdiction." After appeal to the U.S. Supreme Court, the ruling in *Baker v. Carr, 369 U.S. 186,* was handed down in March 1962. It established the "one-man, one-vote" concept, which required equal legislative districts to be drawn voluntarily by the states or done otherwise by district courts. The decision said in part:

> The relative standings of the counties in terms of qualified voters have changed significantly. It is primarily the continued application of the 1901 Apportionment Act to this shifted and enlarged voting population which gives rise to the present controversy. Indeed, the complaint alleges that the 1901 statute, even as of the time of its passage, made no apportionment of Representatives and Senators in accordance with the constitutional formula, but instead arbitrarily and capriciously apportioned representatives in the Senate and House without reference . . . to any logical or reasonable formula whatever. . . . The United States shall guarantee to every state in this union a Republican form of government and shall protect each of them against invasion, and on application of the legislature, or of the executive (when the legislature cannot be convened) against domestic violence.

The justices rejected the Tennessee reapportionment plan and ordered that districts be evenly divided by 1965 even if it meant crossing county lines. Governor Ellington called a special legislative session to meet on May 26, 1962. The legislature called for a constitutional convention, which the voters approved. *Baker* established that the equal protection clause of the Fourteenth Amendment to protect freedmen now went beyond the protection of "a particular race or nationality for oppressive treatment."

From 1961 to 1963, black and white college students, mostly under the auspices of CORE and SNCC, would spend their summers living with Negro families while registering more than four thousand new voters in West Tennessee. Sometimes they were arrested for trespassing when trying to reach sharecroppers and laborers on private farms. In July 1963, the Ku Klux Klan conducted public marches in Somerville, waving Confederate flags. One civil rights demonstrator was scalded with hot coffee in a Somerville restaurant. Odell Sanders's home was bombed, and many people believed that county officials were stuffing ballot boxes and remotely registering white voters in places other than the courthouse. Some 97.8 percent of whites and 33.5 percent of Negroes were registered in Haywood County, while Fayette County had 72.1 percent of whites and 40.8 percent of Negroes registered to vote. Black youngsters were still being harassed because of their public protests. Negroes won elections for 37 percent of the commissioners (about three seats) in Fayette County and a minority of seats on town councils.

In October 1965, when the federally funded Fayette County Economic Development Commission began efforts to help eliminate poverty, blacks were still mostly landless and poor. More than 95 percent of their income derived from agriculture. Economic rehabilitation programs reached only half of the Negro population mainly because they had no radio station and no newspaper. Many of them lived in tenants' shacks in hard-to-reach areas of private property. They usually had no water and sewer lines. Schools and Negro churches helped with communications, but white churches refused to participate.

Yet, despite such problems, the U.S. Commission on Civil Rights recommended dropping Tennessee from the list of eight states in which Negro access to the ballot was said to be impeded in the *1961 Voting Report*. At the same time, the Memphis NAACP chartered chapters at Dyersburg and Ripley and in Tipton County. R. B. Sugarmon and Maxine Smith, among other Memphis NAACP leaders, participated in expanded voter registration meetings with representatives from surrounding counties. Tipton County, where the movement had not yet impacted Negroes, sent twenty-one representatives to one meeting.

Memphis Negroes continued their political struggle at home. A. Maceo Walker was appointed to the Memphis Transit Authority in August 1961, forcing him to resign as chairman of the Shelby County Democratic Club. Frank

Kilpatrick relaced him as head of the partisan organization. Benjamin L. Hooks lost a tight race—receiving 41,948 votes to his opponent's 43,209—for a city court post. Hollis Price was defeated, 61,019 to 40,518, for a school board position. Price, who in 1943 became the first Negro to head LeMoyne College, said, "Many Negroes avoid saying that things have improved, because so much more needs to be done and we do not want to feel that we can stop where we are. But everybody knows we have come a long way in three years, and I don't mind telling you I think it is tremendous." The Memphis NAACP hired an office secretary and appointed a campaign coordinator and divisional chairmen to kick off a voter registration campaign at the climax of the 1962 membership drive. They began a door-to-door canvas, hired women to work at the courthouse during the purchase of automobile tags, invited the head of the Legal Defense Fund as speaker for the May 20, 1962, banquet to commemorate *Brown*, and got radio station WLOK to broadcast the Lincoln Day tapes. By 1963, Hooks had joined the public defender's office, and the new mayor, William B. Ingram, appointed ten Negroes to various commissions, committees, and city agencies. Lieutenant Lee had taken a back seat to local Negro Democrats, but he continued to participate in the Republican conventions and use his influence to advance the Negro's concerns. He appealed to the GOP to avoid a "lily-white label" and reject the racial rhetoric of Barry Goldwater.

But it was clear by then that blacks favored the Democrats. *The 780 Countdown* in Nashville noted that the Kennedy administration had sent Negro aide Andrew T. Hatcher to speak for the Davidson County Democratic League rally in June 1962. On November 11, 1963, C. B. Robinson, head of the Negro teachers' association in Tennessee, sent letters to all members reminding them to vote, a message he reiterated on December 16, 1963, when he urged school principals to make sure that their teachers were registered to vote. The director for political education of the AFL-CIO in Washington, D.C., sent money to Robinson to help with his "Get Out the Vote" efforts in Chattanooga–Hamilton County. Negro leaders were coming to expect the Democrats to do something to help improve their people's conditions. In Knoxville, half of the Negro homes were substandard, and in Memphis the Negro family of four earned only 44 percent of the income for white families. In Tennessee, the endless voter registration campaigns had managed to register about two-thirds of eligible Negroes by 1960 and nearly 70 percent of them by 1964. But getting black people to the polls to actually cast their votes remained a big problem. Blacks held only forty-three elective posts in Tennessee.

On June 27, 1964, when TVC held its convention at Fisk University, Avon Williams complained, "We made Frank Clement governor [in 1962], and he betrayed us. He lied and refused to sign the recommendations of his own human rights commission." Willis, Charles F. Williams, and other Memphis delegates defended Clement. Willis, Sugarmon, J. H. Turner, R. E. Lillard, and Harold Love were among seven Negroes in the sixty-four-person delegation to go to the 1964 National Democratic Convention. Governor Clement would chair the Tennessee delegation. Thomas E. Poag, a dean at Tennessee A&I State University, spoke up for Clement, prompting an angry Avon Williams to say, "You're a disgrace to this organization [TVC] and you ought to come off that stage and leave this meeting." The Reverend Charles F. Williams, who headed a Masonic lodge of which Poag was a member, and others walked out of the meeting and formed a rival state organization, the Independent Voters League.

TVC came to be dominated by Avon Williams and his circle in Middle Tennessee. Jamye Coleman Williams and her husband, McDonald Williams, recalled the importance of the Tennessee Voters Council. Jamye Williams, whose father had nurtured young activist preachers in Memphis during the 1948 elections, became secretary of the TVC after Avon Williams called her at the A&I campus one Saturday morning. She recalled that TVC mailings were initially sent to only twenty-five or thirty-five people, but soon the mailing list numbered in the hundreds. McDonald Williams said that some people viewed the TVC as a "paper tiger," but politicians, both Republicans and Democrats, sought the group's endorsement. Avon Williams would convene the TVC meeting in Park Johnson Auditorium at Fisk, divide the delegates according to the three grand divisions of the state (east, middle, and west), and have them interview candidates and take a vote. "The main questions were your views on race relations and who financed you," said Jamye Williams. Avon Williams's direct and bold manner of questioning whites angered some candidates.

Over in Memphis, George W. Lee believed that Barry Goldwater's supporters had prevented his election to the state Republican executive committee. Lee argued that members of the John Birch Society, the White Citizens Council, and other racial conservatives were seeking "to take control" of the Republican Party. Lee battled the "old guard Republicans" for a seat in the Republican National Convention, and after he failed, he cried foul, declaring that Tennessee would have no Negro representation at the 1964 convention. Local Republican leaders said that no Negroes were elected to the national convention because Lee and two hundred Negroes had walked out of the

Shelby County convention. Lee denied that it had happened that way. He attended the national convention in San Francisco anyway and protested unsuccessfully for a seat. "It will be a great tragedy for the Republican Party, the Negro and the nation if the Republicans become a white man's party," he said.

The Democrats mobilized effectively for the 1964 election. The Davidson County Independent Political Council supported Dick Fulton's successful reelection to Congress. The TVC supported the Democratic candidate for president. Looby and Lee finally put their party loyalty aside and refused to campaign for Goldwater. With heavy black voter turnout, the Republicans lost so badly in Shelby County that they threatened to challenge the results. "LBJ Scores Crushing Victory," said the *Jackson Sun*. Madison County went Republican, but four black precincts helped the Democrats to carry the city of Jackson. Lyndon B. Johnson carried Tennessee and won the nation with 486 electoral votes to Goldwater's 52. Johnson received 61.1 percent of the popular vote with 61.7 percent voter participation. The *Sun* (Nov. 4, 1964) observed, "Voting was particularly heavy in precincts where Negro registration is high."

In 1964, H. T. Lockard won election to the Shelby County government. A graduate of LeMoyne College and the Lincoln University Law School in Missouri, Lockard would also serve as an administrative assistant to Governor Buford Ellington, beginning in 1967. A. W. Willis Jr. was elected a state representative—the first Negro since 1893. Willis (1925–1988) served two terms in the General Assembly until 1969, representing the Fifth District. He was born in Birmingham, completed Talladega College and the University of Wisconsin School of Law, served in the U.S. Army, and joined the Pentecostal Church of God in Christ. His late father was vice president of Universal Life Insurance Company.

The Democrats helped in 1964 to secure ratification of the Twenty-fourth Amendment to the Constitution, which outlawed all poll taxes on both the state and federal levels. Virginia tried to place registration requirements on voters that would defeat the amendment, but in 1965 the U.S. Supreme Court declared such laws unconstitutional. In Tennessee, between 1960 and 1965, black registrants had increased by 21.6 percent. The Tennessee Constitutional Convention was scheduled for July 26, 1965, to review the legislative parts of the state constitution and comply with *Baker*. On November 8, 1966, the voters ratified nine proposals, including the use of geography, political subdivision, substantially equal population, and other criteria in drawing legislative districts.

In August 1965, Congress had passed President Johnson's proposed Voting Rights Act, which banned a variety of methods that states used to deny blacks the right to vote, including Mississippi's undemocratic literacy test. As a result of this legislation, the number of Negro voters in the South increased from 1.5 million to 3.1 million over the next four years. Tennessee's percentage of registered black voters climbed from 59 percent in 1960 to 73 percent by 1968, compared to 14 to 57 percent in Mississippi, 14 to 57 percent in Alabama, 29 to 56 percent in Georgia, and 16 to 51 percent in South Carolina during the same time period. But neither the 1964 Civil Rights Act nor the 1965 Voting Rights Act guaranteed justice, removed oppressive poverty, provided jobs, or ensured a higher standard of living.

At the March 1966 TVC meeting, Willis said that Negroes needed more candidates for the General Assembly, contending that the third congressional district seat was lost to Republican Bill Brock "because we were not united." TVC then developed a strategy that would focus on *where* to run Negro candidates.

As a result of reapportionment, the 1965 Voting Rights Act, and the sharpening of political organizations by Negro leaders, four blacks joined Willis in the General Assembly. Dorothy Lavinia Brown, a physician in Nashville, became the first Negro woman elected to the state house. Brown was born in 1919 in Troy, New York, and reared in an orphans' home. She graduated from Bennett College in North Carolina and received her medical degree from Meharry Medical College, becoming the first Negro woman to practice general surgery in the South. She came under great criticism for introducing a bill to legalize abortions in Tennessee, and Brown's enemies circulated rumors that she performed abortions in her medical office in north Nashville. M. G. Blakemore finally won election in 1966 to the General Assembly, having made several unsuccessful earlier bids. Blakemore (1912–1972) was born in Franklin, attended public schools in Nashville, and graduated from Tennessee A&I State College before receiving the dentistry degree from Meharry Medical College and a law degree from the recently desegregated Nashville Night Law School. He and Avon Williams were both members of St. Andrews Presbyterian Church. Blakemore served one term until 1969. Russell B. Sugarmon Jr. was elected to the state house, serving one term. He was born in 1929 in Memphis, attended Morehouse College for one year before completing Rutgers University, receiving a law degree from Harvard University, and doing graduate work at Boston University. Sugarmon established his law practice in Memphis in 1956, and eleven years later he was elected judge of Shelby County

General Sessions Court. In the period from 1966 to 1976, Maxine Smith pointed out that two of the Negro representatives elected from Memphis, Sugarmon and Willis, were local NAACP board members and that all three were local NAACP lawyers. Robert J. Booker of Knoxville won a General Assembly seat in 1966 and served until 1971. He was born in 1935 in Knoxville, attended public schools, and in 1962 graduated from Knoxville College, where he served as student government president and helped lead the local civil rights movement. Booker spent a summer in Africa and edited the *Knoxville Examiner*.

Blacks won election to more public offices in Memphis by 1967. The restructuring of the Memphis government, which replaced the commission form of government with at-large elections and required a mayor with executive powers and thirteen councilmen with four-year terms, finally made local public office possible for blacks. Fred Davis, J. O. Patterson, and James Netters became Memphis's first black city councilmen since Reconstruction. A. W. Willis Jr. ran for mayor, and in a *Look* magazine article entitled the "Black Movement" (Sept. 30, 1967), Willis was called "the black boss Crump." Paying no attention to the negative reference, Willis said, "We have done pretty well in politics, but if we do not get where the real power is, in business and finance, we will always be on somebody's plantation." He entered the August primary, hoping that the five white candidates would split the white bloc vote and allow him to win outright. But the Shelby County Democratic Club simply did not get out the seventy-nine thousand Negro voters in Memphis: nearly half of them, 47 percent, did not vote, whereas nearly 70 percent of the registered white voters cast ballots. Many Negroes voted for the incumbent mayor, William B. Ingram, because of a defeatist attitude: "Why vote for a Negro, when you know a Negro cannot be elected mayor in Memphis?" Willis received less than a fourth of the Negro votes, and came in fourth. O. Z. Evers opened a headquarters on McLemore Street and supported Ingram, and when Willis lost, Evers called during a radio talk show to persuade him to support Ingram in the runoff election. "No matter who is elected mayor," Willis said, "we are going to march on City Hall every week and give this city some democracy." The *Tri-State Defender* endorsed the incumbent: "Let us at this time make VOTES COUNT." Loeb, who came out of political retirement, faced the incumbent in the runoff election and won, 78,740 votes to 66,628.

Henry Loeb III was a fourth-generation member of a Jewish merchant family that started the Loeb Shirt Company. He returned to the family's business after serving as commissioner of public works from 1956 to 1959 and mayor

291

from 1960 to 1963. Loeb never professed to be a part of Memphis's Jewish minority but sought to be identified as an assimilated American. Perhaps he disapproved of the Negro's clinging to color and race instead of assimilating as he and other local Jews had done. But many blacks perceived Loeb's attitude as anti-Negro, and thus some of them detested him with a passion. The NAACP chapter and the Shelby County Democratic Club, which were angry at Loeb for not appointing any blacks to his administration, reacted especially badly to his reelection.

Meanwhile, in rural Giles County in Middle Tennessee, James Brown and the Reverends J. W. Starling and A. P. King were pushing Negroes to register and vote. Brown was chairman of the Giles and Lawrence County Voter Education and Registration Project, a leader in the TVC, and a close colleague of Avon Williams. Brown found that poverty among rural Negroes hindered efforts to organize them politically; thus he and others engaged in a three-year fight against local officials to get a federal economic opportunity office opened in Pulaski to help poor families.

[∗]

On April 11, 1968, President Johnson signed the Open Housing Act, a new civil rights law aimed at expanding housing opportunities for blacks. As a result, fair housing cases became a new and frequent concern for black civil rights lawyers. Blacks who were economically able began to seek better and bigger houses in the suburbs, and this out-migration may have had a negative effect by leaving many inner-city neighborhoods without the educated leadership needed to sustain organized activism. The poorest of black youngsters no longer had enough successful role models in their neighborhoods as the more successful and wealthier blacks opted for the suburbs. Yet, some black role models, and civil rights leaders in particular, such as Avon Williams, remained in central-city neighborhoods.

Later in 1968, Williams and J. O. Patterson Jr. of Memphis won two new seats in Tennessee Senate. The previous year, under pressure from a federal district court in Middle Tennessee, the General Assembly concluded a plan for legislative redistricting. The court ordered districts with a limit of no more than 5,000 above or below the average of 396,343 people per district. This resulted in two predominantly black senate districts. Even during Reconstruction, no Negroes had served in the Tennessee senate. Williams won the Middle Tennessee seat in the nineteenth district, after Mansfield Douglass persuaded him to run against Dorothy Brown. She gave up her house seat and organized a well-financed senate campaign with much white support; however, some whites likely remembered the passionate speech she had given in the General Assembly in April 1967 against a resolution to prevent Stokely Carmichael from speaking in Nashville. Williams, for his part, had blasted Carmichael and his local "bully boys" for contributing to the 1967 riot. Months later, Williams opposed the mayor's claim that Carmichael had caused the riot. For campaign coordinator, Williams chose Edwin H. Mitchell, who headed the Metro Human Relations Commission and was a physician at Meharry's Hubbard Hospital. Williams, because of his role as an NAACP civil rights lawyer who had won numerous cases since 1950, came off as the candidate who would better protect blacks' civil rights, and he seemed to have the support of the editor of the *Tennessean*. As soon as Williams took office in January 1969, he sponsored a senate resolution honoring the late Martin Luther King Jr. Indeed, with the arrival of more black legislators, some twenty-five civil rights bills would be proposed in the Tennessee General Assembly by 1969. Meanwhile, Patterson won in the new twenty-ninth district in West Tennessee. The son of a bishop in the Church of God in Christ, Patterson was a graduate of Fisk University and the DePaul University School of Law.

The Republicans won the presidential election of November 5, 1968, after Johnson declined to run for a second term. The Democratic candidate, Vice President Hubert H. Humphrey, came in third in Tennessee, behind Nixon and Alabama governor George Wallace, who was running as a third-party candidate. Wallace won in congressional Districts Five through Eight, including Shelby County, and Nixon took Districts One through Four. Voter participation dropped to 60.7 percent that year, when Wallace took 13.5 percent of the total votes cast; this allowed Nixon to take office with only 43.4 percent of the popular vote but with 301 electoral votes to 191 for Humphrey and 46 for Wallace.

Nixon tried to redirect the civil rights movement, believing that social separatism persisted in America because of personal and group choice. He preferred to help blacks become economic equals through government programs, quotas, set-asides, and initiatives to create a strong black middle class with small businesses of its own. Nixon believed that this would give blacks leverage in a multiracial society, and once all racial barriers were removed, blacks and whites could decide their own levels of social interaction. Nixon was a life member of the NAACP and no racist. He feared a society divided into racial factions. Many conservatives in the Republican Party would later blame him for extending the Negro's civil rights movement, even though many of his policies also drew criticism from black leaders while he was in office. But whatever else he was, Nixon was a skillful politician who dared to take up the cause of blacks, especially in the economic arena.

[*]

As a state senator, Avon Williams became a friend with legislative leaders John S. Wilder of Fayette County and Thomas Garland of East Tennessee. Ironically, the latter friendship began when Williams opposed Garland's efforts to pass a bill that would place a one-year statute of limitations on legal damages sought in civil rights actions against local sheriffs. Williams argued that the legislation could be used in equity cases such as school desegregation and other types of racial discrimination (i.e., housing). In *Jones v. Mayer Co.* (1969), however, the U.S. Supreme Court ruled that racial discrimination in the public and private sale and lease of housing was unconstitutional. As an attorney, Williams assumed many housing cases, and as a legislator, he sponsored bills that opposed discrimination in housing. But Williams found the state senate to be a cold place for him and Patterson. Feeling that the major newspapers ignored their accomplishments and played up their mistakes, Williams began his own newsletter to keep his constituents informed.

Several new African American faces had entered the Tennessee House of Representatives: Alvin M. King of Memphis (1969–93), Harold M. Love of Nashville (1969–95), Ira H. Murphy of Memphis (1969–83), and James I. Taylor of Memphis (1969–71). A graduate of LeMoyne College, Taylor was a real estate broker, former teacher, NAACP member, World War II veteran, and former candidate for the Memphis city council. Murphy was born in 1928 in Memphis, attended the public schools there and Oakwood College in Alabama, and graduated from Tennessee A&I State College before completing bachelor and master's degrees in law at New York University. After serving in the U.S. Army during the Korean War, he returned to his law practice in Memphis but lost his law license. King was born in 1935 in Saint Louis and attended Lemoyne-Owen College and the University of Tennessee, Memphis. Love was born in 1919 in Nashville and completed Pearl High School and Tennessee A&I before receiving the master's degree from Fisk University. He also served in the U.S. Army during World War II, receiving a Distinguished Service Award and two battle stars.

When the 1965 Voting Rights Act was scheduled to expire on August 5, 1970, Congress extended the law and President Nixon signed the bill on June 22. Coverage was extended to electoral districts in six non-southern states. Some 90,331 Negroes were registered in Memphis–Shelby County by then, and in Mississippi Negro voter registration increased from 14 percent to nearly 60 percent.

The political aspects of the civil rights movement remained as turbulent as ever in Memphis. O. Z. Evers defiantly backed the white candidate for Shelby County sheriff in August 1970. Evers knew he was a thorn in the side of leading Negro politicians, who had little time to be bothered with him, especially after he accused the Memphis branch NAACP of moving too slow against Jim Crow. Then he filed a $1 million suit against Charles Evers (no relation), the recently elected black mayor of Fayette, Mississippi. As a guest speaker for the black candidate for Shelby County sheriff, Mayor Evers reportedly said, "A black man who makes statements like O. Z. Evers is just as much a racist and is not fit to be in our community." O. Z. Evers, who operated the Unity League Democratic Council, was accused of "being on the take" to support white candidates and divide the black vote. Local leaders could still not get half the registered black voters to the polls, while the whites continued their heavy voting patterns. "It [failure to vote] is a bad commentary on a people who have so long and so loudly clamored for the right to suffrage, and to be classified as first-class citizens," observed Nat D. Williams.

Among recognized black Republicans, only George W. Lee was holding on like a bulldog. Despite the Goldwater disaster, Lee said that he would back the GOP candidates for Congress, Dan Kuykendall and Howard Baker Jr., but added, "They must make as an issue the freedom of all men." Lee's remarks drew an arrogant response from a local campaign manager for the Republicans: "That's his [Lee's] problem, not ours." Lee had attended the 1968 Republican National Convention "in an unofficial capacity" and let it be known that he opposed "Ronald Reagan and the Goldwater types." After sending a hundred dollars to the Nixon campaign, Lee received an invitation to the inaugural festivities. His Lincoln League continued to endorse candidates in Memphis as late as 1971. In the late summer of 1976, while suffering an apparent heart attack, Lee lost control of his car, crashed into another automobile, and was killed. His body was buried in the Elmwood Cemetery where his former colleague, Robert Church Jr., and their archenemy, Boss Crump, had been interred.

CHAPTER 9

THE FRUSTRATED FELLOWSHIP

CIVIL RIGHTS AND AFRICAN AMERICAN POLITICS
IN TENNESSEE

In 1970 Winfield C. Dunn, a dentist from Memphis, became the first Republican to win the Tennessee governorship in half a century. Born in Mississippi, Dunn had graduated from "Ole Miss" and the dentistry program at the University of Tennessee, Memphis. From a strong Republican Party base in east Memphis, Dunn took advantage of the Nixon ascendancy. Tennessee politics—like that in much of the South—had entered a new phase.

By this time, the Tennessee Voters Council had become recognized as a critical endorsement for white politicians who desired the black vote. The TVC was meeting quarterly, with nearly forty representatives present from seventeen or eighteen of Tennessee's ninety-five counties. The organization cooperated with the NAACP in petitioning the Federal Communications Commission to deny renewal of licenses to radio and television stations that failed to include minorities in their programming and staffing. TVC also supported minority applications for Model Cities money and the A. Philip Randolph Institute's voter registration drive. It helped the NAACP to protest against certain conservative judges whom Nixon had nominated for the Supreme Court and petitioned Tennessee governors to close the notorious Pikeville School for juvenile delinquents and consult the TVC on such matters. In June 1971, the TVC groups in Middle Tennessee met under James

Brown, Berry Duncan, and James Caldwell to focus the goals for Pulaski, Shelbyville, Columbia, Hickman County, Marshall County, and Maury County. They concluded that blacks had to target banks and contractors that continued racial discrimination practices despite the 1964 Civil Rights Act.

Blacks now held thirteen seats in Congress. These officeholders organized the Congressional Black Caucus, holding their first national meeting in Nashville. The TVC, the DCIPC, and the informal state black caucus hosted the meeting, which included a joint banquet on December 11, 1971. Fannie Lou Hamer, organizer of the Freedom Party in Mississippi, was the speaker. Meanwhile, the seventy-two-year-old Z. Alexander Looby announced retirement from the City Council after twenty years: "I think I have made my contributions to social welfare, and now I am tired."

Tennesseans prepared for their first presidential primary in May 1972, when the Democrats were intent on finding a strong candidate to defeat Richard M. Nixon. George McGovern won the Democratic Party nomination, and his faction required local election for delegates instead of the old-style handpicking process. As a result, the 1972 Democratic Convention would have a large number of black delegates, including, from Tennessee, R. B. Sugarmon, Jessie Carter, and Maxine Smith of Memphis; Lillian and C. B. Robinson of Chattanooga; James and Ann Brown of Pulaski; Avon Williams of Nashville; and Paula Rucker of Murfreesboro. At the Democratic Convention, George Wallace refused the request from Avon Williams and a small delegation to be released from the Tennessee primary vote that he had won.

The 1972 presidential election was another repudiation of liberalism and approval of Nixon's promise to restrain social and civil rights reform. Nixon's campaign strategy was not to court the Negro vote but to neutralize it and frighten white Democrats into the Republican Party while continuing the rhetoric about racial discrimination. Though he remained supportive of black economic progress, Nixon fired some zealous civil rights officials in the government and asked Congress to do something to stop busing. Kenneth O'Reilly wrote, "What he [Nixon] did with that power on the racial front, as on the Watergate front, was a disgrace—an entirely separate disgrace." Nixon won reelection in 1972 with 60.7 percent of the vote and 521 electoral votes to McGovern's 17. Only 55.2 percent of American voters participated in the election, compared to more than 60 percent in each of the previous five presidential elections. The percentage would continue to drop during the next seven presidential elections. Nixon only received 11 percent of the black votes, but he swept the white South.

When the TVC held its quarterly meeting on December 9, 1972, not many representatives showed up. John McFerrin of Fayette County said he had heard that the white power structure intended to break the TVC by not giving it any money. The TVC's public endorsements of particular candidates, McFerrin said, were causing whites to vote against those candidates. Avon Williams seemed to agree that the TVC needed to "devise techniques whereby we may be more effective." The much older Shelby County Democratic Club had endorsed candidates who were not endorsed by the TVC. Some felt that Williams dominated the TVC and that his style of dealing with the candidates he interviewed was too rough. Some of Williams's handwritten notes in the TVC papers revealed his opinion that one Tennessee Supreme Court candidate was "racist [and] mediocre" and that he had "attempted to mistreat judges in his circuit." Another penciled note read, "Nothing to suggest he has changed [his] treatment of civil rights lawyers, and doesn't have sensitivity toward minorities." McFerrin suggested that TVC meetings be held across the state to improve participation in the organization. The real problem was that TVC could not back up its claims of delivering 200,000 or more voters. In the 1970 elections, only 40 percent (115,000) of the black voters turned out. "We did not set a fire under the black voters," James Brown said. "Black voters need to be wooed by the candidates, although the white man thinks he can give us a budget at the last minute and we can still do a good job. Black TVC leaders are not magicians as some may think."

The Democratic-controlled General Assembly finally passed a reapportionment bill including more predominantly black districts, but legislators had to override the governor's veto. C. B. Robinson and others worked to gain reapportionment so that blacks in Chattanooga could have representation in the General Assembly. On March 16, 1973, Robinson wrote to Williams: "Your support and influence for the passage [of the bill for Chattanooga] will be appreciated." On April 9, 1974, Robinson wrote to TVC members: "As you know, the great progressive movement, which has brought the Negro to its present status, has just about been stopped by the present Republican administration. The president and the party leaders have a coalition with the southern extremists that are turning the clock of time backward. Unless we put forth maximum effort, it will continue." Robinson called for more Negroes to be placed on state commissions and hired as state highway patrolmen. He also wanted to change Chattanooga's status as the "only large city in Tennessee without a black representative in the state General Assembly," and to that end he announced that he would run for a legislative seat in August 1974. He established his campaign headquarters on Market Street and asked the wealthy, liberal John J. Hooker for financial help; Hooker did not respond. Teachers and unions supported Robinson, who won the election and took his seat in January 1975. His first bills targeted discrimination in housing and sought to stop racial discrimination in the granting of loans and insurance.

In his 1978 newsletter, *Legislative Report*, Avon Williams told his constituents: "One of my principal goals as your state senator has been to demonstrate and convince people that someone outside the system *can* substantially affect the system in ways that help black people and the average working citizen." His margins of victory in each election indicated that most constituents appreciated Williams's use of political office to continue to advance the civil rights movement. He reported several successful bills, including ones on slum housing, discrimination against poor and minority people by utility providers, and the repeal of racially discriminatory statutes from the Reconstruction era that included inheritance restrictions by race. He secured the requirement to teach African American history in the public schools and enactment of the Housing Rehabilitation Corporation to provide low-interest loans to help elderly and poor people repair and upgrade their homes. The latter was "one of my happiest achievements in the 1973 session," Williams said. He also sponsored a successful bill to increase the number of blacks on the Tennessee Highway Patrol, which had only 11 officers of color among 650 patrolmen. Other bills involved placing black students in the legislative internship program and eliminating racial designations on Tennessee driver's licenses. The black state legislators submitted bills for $1 million to build a new TSU business building and $170,000 to assume a TSU debt on an old dormitory converted to classroom space. In 1973, the Capitol Hill press voted Avon N. Williams Jr. one of the two most effective Tennessee legislators.

Williams and the Tennessee Voters Council interviewed candidates for the governor's primary in May 1974. When Ray Blanton, a former legislator and congressman with a segregationist record, appeared, Williams raked him across the fiery coals. However, Blanton claimed that only he could unite the Democratic Party and create more black participation. He would not guarantee TVC that the Tennessee Commission on Human Development would receive an increased budget or that TVC would be consulted on all black political appointments and other matters. Blanton promised to "end discrimination in all areas of state government" but also said he remained opposed to busing. Williams exploded, saying that Blanton had received TVC endorsements on three occasions "but treated TVC like a prostitute and emasculated the black vote by buying black persons to dilute the power of TVC." Blanton shot back with denials. Williams bluntly told Blanton not to "ignore TVC in the future." Among other candidates being interviewed, former state treasurer Thomas Wiseman, a Democrat, claimed endorsements by TVC affiliates in Franklin and Coffee counties. Wiseman said that he had opposed the General Assembly's efforts to stop Stokely Carmichael from speaking at Vanderbilt in April 1967. He also said that he had added ten blacks to his staff and that he opposed racial discrimination. Lamar Alexander, a Republican, promised that he would not use race as an issue and would be cooperative toward TVC. He said that he would be reluctant to eliminate Tennessee State University, which had been neglected over the years, and that he would not rule out TSU as the major state university in case of a court-ordered merger with UT Nashville.

During that same election year, 1974, several candidates challenged Williams's legislative seat, both in the primary and general elections, which led him to believe that some powerful whites had conspired to oust him from the General Assembly. Negative reports about him had begun to appear in the newspaper, he recalled, and he suspected that the editor of the *Tennessean*, for one, had withdrawn support for him because of the independent, militant stances he had been taking in the General Assembly on black and racial issues. Williams might well have forgotten just how racially minded Nashville's white establishment—including executives at the *Tennessean* and the *Banner*—could be. In the 1968 election, that establishment had apparently remembered Dorothy Brown's defense of Stokely Carmichael's right to speak in 1967 and thus gave her candidacy little, if any, support. And Williams won the senate seat instead. But once Williams showed his own independence in the senate chamber, the *Tennessean* editor and other white leaders were ready to turn on him, too. In fact, they had probably never wanted Williams, the outspoken civil rights lawyer, to become an elected official in the first place—unless he followed their paternalistic wishes.

Williams, however, had worked closely with the leaders in the legislature to ensure a favorable apportionment in his district, in which black voters represented 57 percent of the total. Williams even considered supporting for Tennessee the new punch-ballot computer system that Florida had adopted, and he gained assurance that prisoners convicted only of misdemeanors could vote. (North Nashville included the area's prisons for men and women, as well as its juvenile detention facilities, and almost half of the inmates were blacks.) Williams reminded citizens that he had secured a yearly appropriation of $80,000 through the Tennessee Arts Commission to help "endow the priceless art collection at Fisk University," that he had promoted a bill for the homeless, and that he had gained $3.72 million for Meharry Medical College. He had secured legislation to prohibit discrimination against handicapped

people and gained a 10 percent set-aside for minority contracts in state highway projects. The campaign literature for Williams included a photograph of
him, his daughter and son, a policeman, and neighbors staring at a burning cross left by unknown persons in front of the family's home. With 5,463
votes, Williams defeated his opponents Dorothy Brown (4,005 votes), Morris
Haddox (1,505 votes), and William Gregory Jr. (844 votes).

In July 1974, Tennessee's black legislators secured the creation of the
Office of Minority Affairs as a legislative auxiliary. The office was headed by
a director and provided a full-time staff to complete research related to minority citizens and to serve as a clearinghouse for information on state legislation
and give legislative response to minorities. In February 1975, the eleven members officially chartered the Tennessee Caucus of Black State Legislators.

[*]

In Memphis, black interest in the election was high. J. H. Turner became
the first black pro tempore of Shelby County government in 1974. In July,
Washington Butler, another Shelby County squire, announced his campaign
for governor. Butler, who had experience serving two terms on the Oak Ridge
City Council, was the first black gubernatorial candidate since William F.
Yardley in 1876. The West Tennessee Political Action Committee was formed
to mobilize blacks in thirty-three counties where 240,000 black voters resided.
Some 73 percent of all black voters lived in West Tennessee. Avon Williams
warned his fellow black Tennesseans that while things were better in 1974
than twenty years earlier, problems remained. He said that "in terms of real
change, the attitudes of white hate and attitudes of whites toward blacks
in general, the situation has not changed. Black people must look out for
themselves."

Also in 1974, Harold E. Ford of Memphis, who was serving his second
term in the legislature, became the Democratic nominee to oppose veteran
U.S. congressman Dan Kuykendall in the state's only predominantly black
congressional district. Ford had to run a tough campaign against a skilled and
well-financed Republican Party. He had little help from most Democratic
Party politicians. Leonard Small, S. A. Wilburn, and a few other black Republican leaders opened an office for the Kuykendall campaign in Southgate
Shopping Center. Ford developed a campaign plank on education, fair housing, higher minimum wages, Social Security reform, and fair crime bills. Ford
said that Kuykendall supported Nixon's racial policies, but he did not lean too
heavily on the race issue, refusing to attack the Democratic nominee for gov-

ernor, Ray Blanton. The popular singer Isaac Hayes and Tom Bradley, the black mayor of Los Angeles, publicly supported Ford's campaign, posing with him for a group picture in the *Tri-State Defender*. Local blacks were further galvanized in October, when two white Memphis policemen beat a young black man and then shot him ten times, killing him.

Newspaper pictures showed Kuykendall standing by a black female state worker, with Kuykendall claiming that he was responsible for more state appointments of blacks than any other politician. Lamar Alexander, who was running for governor against Blanton, also pursued the black vote with a full-page advertisement in the *Tri-State Defender* on October 5; it claimed, "Blanton endorsed by Governor George Wallace; Blacks Must Not Be Fooled." The Memphis chapter of People United to Save Humanity (PUSH) was charging racism and job discrimination against the *Press-Scimitar* and the *Commercial Appeal*. Ford, his son Harold Jr., his wife, and Isaac Hayes visited the polling places. Ford voted at the Riverview Community Center, where he received 1,013 votes to only 59 votes for Kuykendall.

On election night, Ford, his family, friends, supporters, Isaac Hayes, his brother John N. Ford (who won election to the state senate), and others waited at the campaign headquarters. Later the *Commercial Appeal* would cynically recall that the black elected officials "were legion in their absence" at the Ford headquarters on election night. Ford had put in eighteen to twenty hours a day during the campaign, and now his accountants were monitoring the vote tally. When the newspapers reported that Kuykendall was ahead by 5,000 votes, gloom settled over the Ford headquarters, because they had worked so hard to lose so badly. But Ford's vote counters were saying that the figures could not be true, that according to their calculations Ford should be ahead by 500 votes at least. Negroes voted late in the evening after coming home from work, they reasoned, and the late votes would mostly go to Ford. Some campaign workers believed that whites were up to the same sort of dirty tricks once employed by the Crump machine. As the frustration and suspicion grew, a disturbance nearly erupted; the situation quieted down when Ford said that he and some trusted assistants would call on the offices of the Shelby County Election Commission to confirm the returns.

"We came here to make sure it was a fair election," Ford said upon his arrival. A black worker at the Election Commission whispered to Ford that he should check the basement for uncounted boxes before he left the building. And sure enough, there they found six huge steel voting boxes with uncounted votes in them. The executive secretary of the Election Commission claimed that such mistakes had occurred during every election because of the inexperience of some election officials. The secretary claimed that these workers sometimes placed the manila envelopes containing the voting results in the steel boxes with the leftover supplies instead of handing them over to commission staff members. Ford's people watched and used their hand calculators as the election officials totaled the votes from the boxes and delivered the results to the upstairs computer room. Ford claimed that the voting results were found in a garbage can, but the election official said, "That's absurd." At campaign headquarters, John Ford held the telephone while Hayes and others leaned forward, trying to hear what Harold and the others had found at the Election Commission. When word came through the line that the missing votes had been found, there was jubilation and the smell of victory. The *Press-Scimitar* soon declared, "Harold Ford Stuns Kuykendall." Ford had won 67,715 votes, while 67,141 votes went to Kuykendall.

In the wake of the Watergate scandal, Republican candidates went down in flames all over the country. Alexander won Shelby County, but he lost the state. Democrats captured forty-four extra seats in the state house. Some 56 percent of the voters participated in the November election compared to 43 percent in the August primary. In 1972, during the Nixon sweep, Kuykendall had received 93,175 votes, compared to the 67,141 he drew in 1974. An independent white candidate attracted 987 votes in the '74 election, which Kuykendall's people believed would have provided the margin of victory. There was a light turnout in the white districts, where Kuykendall received 89 percent of the vote. Mixed districts gave Ford the edge, and he got 94 percent in the predominantly black districts. Ford won 47 percent of the working-class white vote, perhaps because of his slogans on the minimum wage and Social Security. "It's a pretty heavy price to pay for sneaking into [the Watergate] building," Kuykendall reportedly said of his defeat. Black Republicans were upset with the state party for "[w]illfully excluding blacks from the mainstream of party politics." Of Ford's brilliant congressional campaign, a local white politician said, "He taught us a few lessons." And regarding those black elected officials who were not at the Ford headquarters on election night, the *Commercial Appeal* said that they certainly would show up in the future.

Harold Eugene Ford was born in 1945 in Shelby County, graduated from Geter High School, received a bachelor's degree in business administration from Tennessee State, earned a mortuary science degree, an M.B.A. degree from Howard University, and worked in the family's N. J. Ford and Sons Funeral Parlors in Memphis. The year he was elected to Congress, all sixteen members of the Congressional Black Caucus had been reelected, and Ford went to Washington in December to meet with them. Ford took his seat in

January 1975 and was appointed to the Ways and Means Committee. He served in Congress for twelve years.

[*]

In January 1976, black politicians throughout the country formed the National Association of Black Elected Officials. "Today," said Maynard Jackson, the first black mayor of Atlanta, "civil rights organizations are substantially weakened due to a lack of funding and inadequate support by black people. This fact increases the urgency for a black political coalition on a national scale in order to sustain the political impetus [of the civil rights movement]."

The persistence of a racist and corrupt criminal justice system worried black politicians. Tennessee's black legislators proposed bills to make the police accountable for violating the civil rights of suspects, and when those failed, civil rights lawyers sought relief in the federal courts. The Supreme Court case of *Cleamtee Garner, et al. v. Memphis Police Department, et al.* (1976–85) finally brought an end to the ruthless behavior of Tennessee law enforcement authorities who used unnecessarily deadly force against black suspects. At about 10:45 on the night of October 3, 1974, a Memphis police officer shot Edward E. Garner—an eighth grader, age fifteen, five feet four inches tall, and weighing little more than a hundred pounds—in the back of the head. The youngster died at the hospital. The police claimed that while answering a burglary call, they encountered Garner trying to escape over a six-foot chain-link fence; ten dollars and a stolen purse were allegedly found on his person. With the help of NAACP lawyers, the youth's father, Cleamtee Garner, sued the police department, the mayor, officer Elton Hymon, and the City of Memphis on the grounds that they had used unnecessary force and violated the child's rights under the Fourth, Fifth, Sixth, Eighth, and Fourteenth Amendments. The city argued that the officer's actions were justified under state laws authorizing use of all necessary means to effect arrest. On September 29, 1976, the federal district court ruled no cause of action against the defendants. Attorneys Walter L. Bailey Jr. of Memphis, Avon N. Williams Jr. and Maurice E. Franklin of Nashville, and New York–based NAACP-LDF lawyers filed an immediate appeal. The Sixth Circuit Court agreed that the Tennessee statute gave the officer immunity and that the city could not be held liable; however, in light of the district court's refusal to reconsider the case based on a recent Supreme Court decision, *Monell v. New York City Dept. of Social Services* (1978), the Circuit Court reversed and remanded in 1983, on the grounds that the use of deadly force must meet the test of "probable cause

. . . to believe that the suspect [has committed a felony and] poses a threat to the safety of the officers or a danger to the community at large. . . . The Fourth Amendment [has] limitations on the use of deadly force against fleeing felons." In 1984, Tennessee entered the case to defend its statute: *Appellant v. Cleamtee Garner, etc., et al. Memphis Police Department, et al.* The arguments were heard in the U.S. Supreme Court on October 30, 1985. The high court said, "The use of deadly force to prevent the escape of all felony suspects, whatever the circumstances is constitutionally unreasonable. . . . A police officer may not seize an unarmed, non-dangerous suspect by shooting him dead. The Tennessee statute is unconstitutional insofar as it authorizes the use of deadly force against such fleeing suspects." The court dismissed liabilities against individuals but remanded the case to the lower court for possible liability against the police department and the city.

In his role as a state senator, Williams drafted a bill to make it unlawful to gather physical or statistical data on any person arrested prior to a conviction. He also proposed a freedom of information bill that would allow citizens to request and receive any public and/or court records on them. Other Negro state legislators requested hiring of black guards in the state prisons and legal services for prisoners. Fellow committee members failed to show up when Williams held a senate hearing on a bill to establish uniform standards in the police's use of deadly force. The NAACP southern regional director testified that 87 percent of the police's deadly force victims were blacks: "We must demand an end to the practice of 'trial by bullets.'" For a time Memphis policemen shot and killed three or four blacks per month, causing the city to be among the top ten in citizen complaints registered with the federal government. The Sixth Circuit Court overturned the Tennessee law that allowed policemen to shoot anyone suspected of fleeing any felony. "If there is a consensus on anything in the black community, it is on the indiscriminate use of deadly force by the police," said State Senator Edward Davis of Memphis.

During the 1976 election cycle, Williams directed TVC directors to help "elect in the May 25 primary as many black delegates to the [Democratic] National Convention as possible," and indeed, 16 percent of the delegates who attended the convention that nominated Jimmy Carter were black—an equitable representation. On June 22, 1976, the Tennessee Office of Minority Affairs sponsored a workshop on "Political, Economic, and Social Development," and continued this theme at the First Annual Black Caucus Retreat on November 19–20, 1976, at Paris Landing. Williams, John Ford and J. O. Patterson continued to spearhead civil rights legislation in the Tennessee Senate.

Elected in 1974, Democrat Leonard Ray Blanton was now governor of Tennessee. Blanton grew up poor in Hardin and McNairy counties, in West Tennessee's cotton fields. He completed the University of Tennessee and then operated a construction business in Adamsville. He was elected to Congress in 1966, serving three terms before being defeated in a run for the U.S. Senate by the incumbent, Howard Baker Jr., in 1972. Governor Blanton pushed some populist legislation, but the legislature's black caucus shunned him. In a letter to fellow caucus members on March 18, 1976, C. B. Robinson urged them to support the house speaker *and* the governor because of recent successes: estab-lishment of the Office of Minority Affairs, a salary for a director, and money for a Tennessee State University capital project. By August 27, however, Avon Williams was asking Blanton why funds for education of health personnel were being withdrawn and why no blacks had been appointed to certain state boards and commissions.

In 1978, Blanton appointed Robert E. Lillard as the first black judge in the First Circuit Court in the Tenth Judicial District from March through August 1978. Lillard had been the sole Negro member of the Nashville Bar Association, eventually its president, founder of the Tennessee Federation of Democratic Leagues, and a city councilman (1951–71) until he lost a bid to become vice mayor. But civil rights leaders considered Lillard too conserva-tive. Blanton also appointed Adolpho Augustus Birch Jr. to the Davidson County Criminal Court, where he served for nine years; he had previously served on the Davidson County General Sessions Court to which Ellington appointed him in 1969. A graduate of Howard University Law School, Birch was groomed by Lillard.

In September 1976 the TVC was parading candidates before its inter-view committees, which asked the question "How will you make yourself available to the black people?" In the presidential election that year, TVC and its affiliates across Tennessee endorsed the Democratic candidate, former gov-ernor Jimmy Carter of Georgia, who defeated President Gerald R. Ford by 297 to 240 electoral votes. Carter received 53 percent of Tennessee's votes. Black voters gave Carter a narrow edge in twelve states. Carter barely won with 50.1 percent of the votes nationwide in a 53.5 percent voter turnout. But Carter failed to nurture the sixteen-year-old relationship between Democrats and blacks. Rather than building on Nixon's economic approach of granting socioeconomic parity to blacks and creating among them a larger middle and entrepreneurial class, Carter's administration made a tactical error of trying to play down civil rights issues. As Kenneth O'Reilly wrote, "Whereas Adlai Stevenson once expected black gratitude (because he was not Eisenhower),

Carter expected the same because he was not Nixon. He never quite understood that civil rights leadership expected much more out of his administration in the first place." The TVC endorsed him for reelection in September 1980 because they feared the Republican candidate, Ronald Reagan, more than they liked Carter.

Democrats would lose the next governor's race in 1978. Senator Williams sensed that something was wrong after he received a letter from a citizen named Frances Broyles on April 28, 1977: "It is my desire as a taxpayer and resident of Williamson County, Tennessee to solicit your support in the immediate removal of Ray Blanton as Governor." The Blanton administration's apparent ingrained corruption, which triggered an FBI investigation into allegations that he had accepted bribes for pardons and paroles, even angered fellow Democrats. Legislative leaders decided that Lamar Alexander, the Republican who won the 1978 election, should be sworn in three days early because of Blanton's vows to pardon more prisoners. According to a February 21, 1979, analysis by Charles M. Traughber, chairman of the Board of Pardons and Parole, Blanton had more commutations and pardons than the previous three governors. Blanton had removed the authority of the board and allowed a corrupt system.

Alexander, the new governor, was a GOP moderate born in 1940 in Blount County in traditionally Republican East Tennessee. He would be the first governor to serve consecutive four-year terms in Tennessee under the new rules. He made education reform a priority, which gained him national attention. In a letter to Alexander, Avon Williams told him, "The TVC still wishes you to visit with us." Alexander already had met with the Agora Assembly— an elite black social club in Nashville, founded in 1922, of which Williams also was a member. After that meeting, on June 22, 1979, the governor had sent an amiable letter to Agora, saying, "The good exchange of ideas was both pleasant and useful." Meeting with the TVC as Williams requested, Alexander suggested that the organization become less partisan, affiliate with the NAACP, and influence blacks to vote for the best candidate. He agreed to strengthen Tennessee State University, with which the University of Tennessee at Nashville had recently merged, and to seek blacks to be hired at the state cabinet level.

Alexander appointed Francis S. Guess as the first black to head the Department of General Services and then the Department of Labor. Indeed, in appointing a black to a cabinet-level position, Alexander did what no Democratic administration had dared to do. Guess was a 1972 graduate of TSU, with a 1974 master's degree in business from Vanderbilt University, and a certificate from the senior executive program of Harvard University. He had also served in Vietnam. Through Alexander and Senator Howard Baker, he became a member of the U.S. Commission on Civil Rights and the Tennessee Commission on Human Development. Guess served as president of the Nashville chapter of the National Urban League, was a delegate to the National Republican Convention in 1984 and a member of the Republican Executive Committee of Tennessee in 1986, and received the award of merit from the Tennessee Caucus of Black State Legislators in 1985. In September 1981, Guess appeared before the TVC to outline what the administration was doing for black people. He said that Alexander had issued an executive order to prevent discrimination in hiring and that he appointed blacks to commissions and boards. Guess also said that the governor doubted the real interest of the Democratic Party in seeing blacks in meaningful positions. He pointed out that the Democratic speaker of the house, attorney general, lieutenant governor, state treasurer, and secretary of state—none of whom the governor had selected—had no blacks in important jobs. Avon Williams, who had a short temper, shot back that Guess was called to testify before TVC to say what *he*, as the commissioner of general services, was doing. Alexander had also appointed George A. Brown of Memphis as the first black to serve on the Tennessee Supreme Court for two months, but Brown lost in the next election. Guess mischievously pointed out to Williams and the TVC that Brown had lost the vote in Middle Tennessee. Williams did not like that remark either. Williams noted that Shelvie Rose, a black member of the county commissioners in Tipton County, had also become the county superintendent of roads. Williams meant to suggest to Guess that TVC was indeed helping blacks win public office.

According to Williams's newsletter, *Legislative Report*, acts in the Eighty-ninth General Assembly included a $9 million bond issue to build a physical education, recreation, and health building at TSU; a bill to increase the electoral chances of black legislative candidates in Chattanooga; and money for Meharry Medical College, among some twenty pieces of legislation sponsored and cosponsored by Williams and other black caucus members. And in the Ninetieth General Assembly, the black legislators had succeeded in securing passage of the State Civil Rights Act, which the governor signed on March 29, 1978. This legislation gave citizens the same protections on the state level that national civil rights bills had guaranteed on the federal level, and it increased the powers of the Tennessee Human Rights Commission (THRC). Williams and caucus members helped to pass legislation to include college faculty in the longevity pay plan for state employees. Williams, Representative Harold Love, and NAACP activist Curly M. McCruder stopped the placement of a prison work release center in North Nashville. Williams personally drove Lieutenant Governor John Wilder and Senator Douglas Henry, chairman of the Senate Finance Ways and Means Committee, through the neighborhood near the TSU, Fisk, and Meharry campuses. The chairman of the black caucus met twice with the governor, and after they agreed to support opposition to building the center in nearby Joelton, state officials stopped the project.

The TVC, the black caucus, and other black local political organizations were also concerned about black land ownership, loss of black farms in Tennessee, white domestic terrorism, black access to higher education, black political representation, and continuing black poverty. A two-man faculty team at Tennessee State University was put to work to study the problem and publish a study on it, and according to data distributed at the third annual retreat, nearly one-third of the black population remained among the working poor and people who sought public assistance. Some 62.7 percent of the 56,605 Tennessee families on welfare in 1973 were blacks, and another 2,500 black families joined the Tennessee welfare rolls in the 1974 economic recession. These figures had not improved four years later. At the 1978 black caucus retreat, the speaker, Joseph Lowery of the SCLC, said the continuing civil rights battle for equality included economics, education, morals, and ethics.

Blacks continued to win election to the legislature, thereby strengthening the political component of the civil rights movement. These men and women included Joseph E. Armstrong, Harper Brewer Jr., Lois DeBerry, Edward Davis, Roscoe Dixon, Charles Drew, Emmitt H. Ford, John N. Ford, Rufus E. Jones, Ulysses Jones Jr., Charles W. Pruitt, Mary Pruitt, C. B. Robinson, Larry Turner, Avon Williams, and Teddy Withers. Charles Pruitt, who died in 1985, was state representative for House District 58 in Nashville from 1971 to 1985. Pruitt was born in Huntsville, Alabama, moved to Nashville in 1949, worked for Western Electric Company, and became a community leader, holding meetings in his backyard. Lois M. DeBerry, representative for House District 91 in Memphis from 1973 through the present, was born in Memphis in 1945 and graduated from Lemoyne-Owen College. DeBerry would be cited nationally and locally for outstanding achievements and contributions to politics and women's leadership in America. She worked diligently on legislation to reform laws on parole eligibility, mandatory release times, and family visitation. The Women's Prison Support Committee under Victoria L. Webb and others worked closely with the caucus and DeBerry to relieve overcrowding in prisons and to give prisoners a chance to be rehabilitated and returned to society as productive persons. The DeBerry Correctional Institution was named in her honor. She led a protest against the governor in November 1979 when a top black administrator appeared to be demoted. "It is becoming a continuous pattern to take qualified blacks who have worked their way up and fire them or put them in new positions," she said. DeBerry was responsible for directing the annual caucus retreats, and she became speaker pro tempore of the House. Harper Brewer Jr., who represented House District 98 in Memphis from 1973 through 1987, was born in 1937 in Memphis and received bachelor's and master's degrees from Fisk University and a law degree from the YMCA Night Law School in Nashville. Brewer served as assistant majority leader and speaker *pro tempore* of the House. Senator John N. Ford, brother of Harold Ford, has represented District 29 in Memphis from 1975 through the present. He was born in 1942 in Memphis, graduated from Tennessee State University, received a master's degree from Memphis State University, and worked for several corporations as a financial analyst in Chicago before returning to Memphis in 1969. Senator Ford became a powerful political leader despite efforts by the white media to discredit him because of his masculine, aggressive, and arrogant behavior, which white racists detested in a black man. C. B. Robinson represented House District 28 from 1975 through 1993. Teddy Withers of Memphis, who represented House District 85 from 1975 through 1985, was born in Memphis in 1952 and graduated from Tennessee State University. Senator Edward Davis of Memphis represented Senate District 33 from 1979 through 1991; he was born in Germantown in 1935 and received his bachelor's degree in political science from Tennessee State in 1967. Rufus Jones represented House District 86 in Memphis from 1981 through 1996). Born in 1940 in Memphis, Jones graduated from Michigan State University in 1961, became a businessman, and served as chairman of the Tennessee black caucus. Roscoe Dixon represented House District 87 in Memphis from 1983 through 1994. Dixon was born in 1949 in Arkansas, received the bachelor's degree in political science from Memphis State University in 1975, and served as chairman of the black caucus. Charles Drew of Knoxville served House District 15 from 1983 through 1989 as the first Negro Republican elected to the General Assembly since Reconstruction. He completed Austin High School, the Knoxville Business College, and became a real estate broker. Mary J. Pruitt succeeded her husband, Charles, in Nashville's House District 58, serving from 1985 through the present. She was born in Williamson County in 1934, received two degrees in education from Tennessee State, became a teacher in the Metro Public Schools of Nashville–Davidson County, and became known as a powerful advocate for education and women's rights legislation. Larry Turner has represented House District 85 in Memphis from 1985 through the present. Turner was born in 1935 in West Memphis, Arkansas, but attended schools in Memphis, graduated from Memphis State University in 1976, and became secretary of the Ninety-sixth General Assembly. Ulysses Jones, who has represented House District 86 in Memphis from 1987 through the present, was born in 1951 in Memphis, attended Memphis State University, and became an officer in the Memphis Fire Department. Joseph E. Armstrong of Knoxville, who has represented House District 15 from 1989 through the present, was born in Knoxville in 1956, and graduated from the University of Tennessee.

[*]

In late 1979, Congressman Harold Ford notified Avon Williams and other black leaders in Tennessee that hundreds of jobs were available with the U.S. Census Bureau and that minorities needed to participate in the census because of the political consequences of drawing legislative districts to last for the next ten years. On March 29, 1979, Williams had already requested the data from the Davidson County Election Commission to make sure he was in a good position to maintain his seat, but one of the more conservative members on the election commission was angry that the data had been sent to Williams. The data showed that by 1979 the county had 174,595 white voters and 37,126 registered Negro voters and that most of the latter voters were in Williams's district. He later supported the bill by Senator John Ford to ensure a "fair drawing" of Harold Ford's congressional district, which had to add 80,000 people after the 1980 census. According to the agreement with U.S. Representative Ed Jones, Ford's district would be drawn to include more citizens in Whitehaven and the area around the penal farms in east Memphis. For Jones, a white Democrat, white voters in east Shelby County were combined with white voters in surrounding counties, but with enough friendly black voters drawn into Jones's district to offset any conservative white backlash.

In 1980, Tennessee's black politicians were asked to participate in the election of delegates for the Jimmy Carter–Walter Mondale ticket for the Democratic National Convention. The percentage of registered black voters had peaked in 1971 and declined by 1980. In Tennessee, they fell from 71 percent to percentages in the middle 60s. The Republican candidate, Ronald Reagan, defeated Carter, winning Tennessee with 49 percent of the vote. Nationally, Reagan received 50.7 percent of the popular vote and 489 of the total 538 electoral votes. Voter participation had dropped to a mere 52.6 percent. The Democrats lost the white male vote to the Republicans and were not able to offset this by increasing black voter turnout. White southerners saw the Republicans as the best party to protect their racial interests. Avon Williams and the TVC sent a letter to President Reagan, requesting that he appoint black personnel, support extension of the 1965 Voting Rights Bill, and "exert effective action to oppose and eliminate the Ku Klux Klan in its efforts to promote racial hatred, terrorism, and violence directed against black American citizens and other minorities in the United States." The letter seemed to presume that the seventy-year-old Reagan would be sympathetic to black concerns. But Republicans indeed were using coded language, like "American conservatism," to call for white male solidarity and a precisely calculated counterrevolution to the civil rights revolution. As Kenneth O'Reilly noted, "If Reagan's spoken promise was to get the government off the backs of the American people, his unspoken promise was to get the 'niggers' off the backs of the white middle and working classes. They had lost control over their schools and neighborhoods while paying taxes to support busing, Medicaid, public housing, assorted welfare programs, and civil rights enforcement lawyers at every level of government."

Tennessee's legislative black caucus asked the state's congressional delegation to support the National Black Caucus's petition to President Reagan regarding his intention in 1981 to weaken the renewal of the Voting Rights Act. "The Voting Rights Act of 1965 as amended in 1970 and 1975 has worked well for the past seventeen years," Harold Ford told his fellow congressmen. "I do not think that we are totally ready to say that it is no longer necessary, or the burden of proof of discrimination should be on the complaining party. This is not the time to retreat. The Act should be extended for ten additional years." Ed Jones and Ford sent letters to assure Avon Williams and the caucus that the bill would likely pass "without any watering down." Governor Alexander also sent a letter on October 19, 1981, to Lois DeBerry in which he stated, "Although I cannot attend this week's [black caucus] Retreat, I have urged President Reagan and our congressional delegation members to extend the 1965 Voting Rights Act." Reagan reluctantly complied and signed the bill.

That same year, former governor Ray Blanton was convicted of serious crimes connected with the pardons scandal and sent to a federal prison. He left prison impoverished, suffered a divorce, then remarried, and in 1986 was forced to work at odd jobs while trying to clear his name. He would pass away just ten years later.

[*]

In 1983, black leaders in Memphis had Jessie H. Turner and J. H. Turner Jr. complete an analysis of the November 2, 1982, election in Shelby County. This report yielded some important electoral data that could be used for future political strategies and election campaigns. In his 1982 reelection bid, Governor Alexander easily carried Memphis and Shelby County against his Democratic opponent, Randy Tyree of Knoxville. In Shelby County and Memphis, respectively, blacks gave the Democratic candidate 89 and 84 percent of their votes. Blacks gave Democrat Jim Sasser 98 percent of their votes for his win in the U.S. Senate race. Harold Ford gained 98.6 percent of the black votes and 38 percent of the white votes to win reelection to Congress against two opponents. The county had 357,000 registered voters, with 44 percent of them blacks who lived in Memphis. The turnout on that cool, rainy day was 63 percent white and 61 percent black. The black candidate for mayor, J. O. Patterson Jr., received 88,000 votes, 40 percent of the total, and won 94 percent of the black vote. Two white candidates, Dick Hackett and Mike Cody, respectively received 64,000 votes (29 percent of the total) and 56,200 (26 percent), and another candidate got the remainder, with the three of them splitting most of the white votes. Patterson had become chairman of the City Council and was acting mayor after Mayor Wyeth Chandler resigned on October 1, 1982. But Patterson had to struggle against the white bloc vote and three black candidates. He lost the runoff election to Hackett, who received 20 percent of the black vote and almost all white votes.

The *Chattanooga North Star* reported on July 10, 1982, that only 48.2 percent of eligible black voters in the South, compared to 52.8 percent for northern blacks, voted in the November 1980 elections. The increase in southern Negro poverty rates since 1968 was blamed for the problem. White voter turnout would drop to 47 percent, and only 50 percent of eligible voters overall bothered to vote in presidential elections. Yet, ironically, voter registration for blacks increased from 59 percent to 61 percent by the 1990s.

[*]

In the legislature by 1983, meanwhile, forty-two-year-old Rufus Jones of Memphis was trying to take the chairmanship of the black caucus away from the elderly C. B. Robinson of Chattanooga. The Memphis delegation made up most of the caucus, but they did not control the chairmanship. Avon Williams of Middle Tennessee, Alvin King of West Tennessee, and Charles Drew of East Tennessee formed the nominating committee. They agreed to another term for Robinson, with rotating chairmanships thereafter; the compromise quieted the sectional dispute down for the time being.

Governor Alexander and black legislators also came to odds. Alexander cut $150,000 from the budget of the Institute of African Affairs at Tennessee State University with this explanation: "Such isolated, piecemeal appropriations frustrate the aims of coordinated planning. Section 5 of this bill is such an appropriation." Black legislators knew that the predominantly white University of Tennessee received many such "piecemeal" appropriations for its programs but that it seldom suffered cuts by any governor. Also, in letters to Avon Williams and House Speaker Ned R. McWherter, Alexander explained that he had rejected bills to give state funding to Meharry Medical College's dentistry program because there was no money to make Meharry "a third public medical school in Tennessee." Yet, the white public medical schools were not breaking down doors to get to black candidates and ease the dearth of black health care workers in Tennessee. In a March 29, 1982, letter to Williams, Alexander explained that items for TSU and Meharry should "follow the allocation formula of the Tennessee Higher Education Commission" rather than "invite similar appeals [for funds] from every other institution of higher education in the state." But THEC leaders were not friendly to black requests or to Senator Williams. Alexander slashed other special interest appropriations in the name of fiscal conservatism. Avon Williams contended that Alexander was racially motivated and hypocritical for vetoing line items in the budget and other bills specifically sponsored by Williams. Alexander wrote to Williams again on June 12, 1984, saying that the veto power was to force the legislature to study the bills better. Caucus members also were angry because the state senate had rejected a bill establishing a holiday in honor of Martin Luther King Jr. Francis Guess and the Tennessee Human Rights Commission asked the senate to reconsider because "Dr. King was killed in Tennessee and Tennessee should not lag behind the rest of the country in declaring his birthday a holiday."

In November 1984, President Reagan defeated Democrat Walter Mondale, winning 58.8 percent of the vote. Some 53.1 percent of the voters participated. Reagan won 525 electoral votes to Mondale's mere 13 electoral votes. The TVC and other black organizations had endorsed Mondale, who won the black vote in Tennessee. TVC even had published a newsletter blasting the "ill effects of the Reagan administration" and urging blacks to "elect as many more [Democrats] as we can." But the TVC's influence was waning. The Caucus of Black State Legislators had the attention of the community.

Nevertheless, Williams presided over the TVC meeting at the Legislative Plaza on December 8, 1984, and proclaimed that TVC "intends to meet the challenge that will face black people in the years to come."

Williams hammered away at Alexander. On April 4, 1985, Williams wrote the governor to protest his support for "freedom of choice" in public school desegregation, because the concept would encourage resegregation of the schools. "On May 17, 1954," Williams said, "when you were 13 years of age, the U.S. Supreme Court struck down *de jure* racial segregation in the public schools of our nation, including Tennessee." Williams cited the Civil Rights Act of 1964, *Monroe v. City of Jackson, Tennessee,* and the ongoing case of school desegregation in Davidson County. "Probably due to your youth and racially segregated environment at the time, you may not have been aware of much of the foregoing. I am asking you to consequently withdraw and disavow said freedom-of-choice objective which you are seeking to impose as a principle and practice of public education," wrote Williams, who also issued a press release to embarrass the governor. On April 17, Alexander sent a reply: "I had expected to be opposed by suburban whites who did not want their school districts disturbed, but I had not expected to be opposed by you."

Republicans in Tennessee needed votes from moderate white independents and moderate Democrats and to keep down black voter turnout. Nevertheless, on February 12, 1986, Alexander sent greetings to the Fifteenth Annual Freedom Fund Banquet of the Nashville NAACP: "I am proud to lend my support to the Nashville Branch of the National Association for the Advancement of Colored People with whom I share a long-standing commitment to the advancement of those individuals who have historically been denied equal access of opportunity." After leaving the governor's office in 1987, Alexander would serve as president of the University of Tennessee and later as U.S. secretary of education before returning to legal practice and trying unsuccessfully to win the Republican presidential nomination. In November 2002, he won a seat in the United States Senate. Frances Guess went on to become a wealthy corporate executive in Nashville.

In the 1980s, the black caucus expanded its annual retreat, which allowed citizens and public officials to meet from Wednesday evening through noon Sunday in a relaxed setting, often at a state park facility or in Gatlinburg in the Smoky Mountains during the month of November. Lois DeBerry stated its striving purpose: "To bring together various segments of the community in an effort to inform the public of the need for governmental action to help solve the whole range of the state legal, social and economic problems." The retreats featured nationally known speakers, luncheons, banquets, panels, workshops, presentations and follow-up discussions, and suggestions for the caucus's legislative agenda on housing, community and economic develop‑ ment, health and social services, crime and corrections, higher education, youth activities, and K–12 education. Some three hundred citizens and public officials attended the retreat on October 22–24, 1982, when they gave the Award of Excellence to Tennesseans for Justice in Higher Education and its officers: David Acey and Carl Johnson of Memphis; Sterlin N. Adams and Raymond Richardson of Nashville; and Marvin Peek and James Robinson of Knoxville.

After each annual retreat, the black caucus and the Office of Minority Affairs, assisted by social scientists at Tennessee State University, published *The Report of Findings of the Legislative Retreat.* TSU's presidents, who attended the annual retreat without fail, supplied the meeting with faculty volunteers to record the sessions, compile data, operate recording and video equipment, host a banquet, and provide other resources. *The Report of Findings* gave the black legislators solid facts, accurate figures, and citizen input to push desired legislation at the next session of the Tennessee General Assembly.

The *1980 Report of Findings* included valuable data prepared by Avon Rollins, who oversaw the Tennessee Valley Authority's Minority Investment Forum and co-chaired the retreat's Task Force on Economic and Community Development. These statistics showed, for example, that in Knoxville in 1980, blacks accounted for 14.5 percent of the city's population but made up 31.5 percent of families earning less than $5,000 a year. For other Tennessee cities, the percentages in these same two categories, respectively, were as follows: for Nashville, 23.2 and 58.2; for Memphis, 47.6 and 81; for Jackson, 34.2 and 49.1; and for the Tri-Cities area (Johnson City, Kingsport, and Bristol), 2.1 and 3.2. In the nation as a whole (and not much better in Tennessee), blacks earned only 55 percent of the median income that a white family of four earned— first, because the structure of black families declined from 48 percent married couples in 1970 to 31 percent married couples in 1980 and, second, because of the high numbers of black males who were held in American jails and prisons, had criminal convictions, or were on parole. In general, then, African Amer‑ icans were economically unequal in the country of their birth; thus, the goal of "free by '83"—the 120th anniversary of the Emancipation Proclamation (1863)—was far from becoming a reality.

[∗]

Civil rights leaders were busy trying to get Martin Luther King Jr.'s birthday declared a national holiday. Reagan opposed the bill but reversed his stand after learning that Congress would approve it over his veto. But even as he agreed to sign the bill, he insinuated that in a generation FBI papers might reveal that King was a Communist. On November 2, 1983, in a well-publicized and much-photographed setting, the president signed the Martin Luther King Holiday Act as the wife and children of King and civil rights leaders looked on.

By 1983 the Tennessee black caucus had thirteen members, including Charles "Pete" Drew, born in 1938 in Knoxville. Drew chaired the Knoxville black caucus of elected officials, but in 1984 he became a vagabond among black political leaders when he switched to the Republican Party. Ironically, the predicament of this modern-day black Republican in a Democratic black caucus was historically comparable to that of any Negro proclaiming to be a "Democrat" in the 1880s—except that, in those days, such a maverick would have been pelted with tomatoes and rotten eggs. In the 1980s, however, Democratic detractors resigned themselves to whispering that Drew was just an opportunist. However, when Alexander and the Republicans made threats to cut a $1.1 million supplemental appropriation for TSU, Drew was able to save the item because he had voted with the Republicans to pass the governor's sales tax increase. The other members of the black caucus had opposed the tax increase because it placed a burden on poor people, many of them black. Drew also helped obtain final approval for the Tennessee Martin Luther King Jr. holiday legislation in 1985.

If George W. Lee of Memphis had still been alive, he certainly would have said that Goldwater and Reagan were mainly to blame for how black Americans came to view the Republican Party in such a negative light. Lieutenant Lee had denounced both men just before he died. Reagan was not a racist, but as his health slowly declined in his seventies, he became more and more detached from the daily operations of government, and this allowed mean-spirited conservatives in his administration to embark on law-breaking missions and clandestine attacks on the civil rights movement, seemingly with a vengeance. Gunnar Myrdal, who had published optimistic comments in the conclusion of An American Dilemma (1944), condemned Reagan for allowing America's racial situation to worsen. Myrdal said that white racism still thrived, that many blacks still remained trapped in dire economic straits, and that since his 1944 study the vicious circle still worked its evil in the America of the 1980s. Conservative Reaganites, however, used Myrdal's treatise of optimism to publish articles in newspapers and magazines claiming that the black middle-class really had grown and that this was proof that America was moving in a positive direction on race relations. In reality, black family income had declined by 5.2 percent. In May 1984, the NAACP and the National Urban League held a Black Family Summit Conference on the Fisk campus to address unemployment, acidic poverty, heavy reliance on state and federal welfare programs, and the deterioration of the black family structure that threatened recent civil rights gains. In their 1984 annual report, the NAACP's National Board of Directors made an unusual announcement that "the number one priority is the defeat of the . . . Reagan system . . . by casting every vote for the candidate most likely to achieve the goal."

[*]

On January 8, 1985, Rufus E. Jones of Memphis succeeded C. B. Robinson as chairman of the black caucus. There had been some discussion about how aggressive the caucus should be in protesting the failure of House Speaker Ned R. McWherter to appoint a black as chairman of a major committee. Jones wanted the caucus to have weekly meetings with the leadership of the General Assembly, hold periodic meetings with Alexander, and increase the caucus's staff to better interact with other legislative caucuses and monitor legislation in all committees.

In rural Haywood County, whites still controlled politics and the economy with an iron fist, even though blacks outnumbered them. However, whites gradually had to compromise with black leaders and give up some elected seats to prevent violations of federal civil rights laws. Odell Sanders ran unsuccessfully for an alderman seat in Brownsville in 1964; in 1968, he filed a federal lawsuit to place more blacks on the jury lists. In 1970, when four vacancies occurred on the Fayette County Commission government, whites gave in and placed two blacks, Sanders and W. D. Rawls, on the commission. Seeking more change, William King, who moved back to the county in 1972, became a staff member for Just Organized Neighborhood Area Headquarters (JONAH), a community organization founded by two Catholic nuns and assisted by Truly Mae Taylor. JONAH forced the county to court to place Willie Ross as road commissioner. Local whites had blackballed Ross, as they typically did to any black deemed too militant and outspoken to hold public office in the county. King would join the County Commission in 1983, bringing the number to three blacks, or one third of the commissioners. In 1986, Fred Sanders narrowly lost election for sheriff in a disputed vote. C. P. Bond ran for the state legislature in 1988 but came in third behind white candidate John S. Wilder and another candidate. Jean Carney ran for the state house in 1988 with the backing of the black caucus but lost to her opponent, 2,327 to 6,500, in this predominantly black county where, by 1990, registering blacks to vote and then actually getting them to the polls remained a Herculean task.

But in Haywood County—and more generally in West Tennessee, where 70 percent of the state's blacks still lived, with half of that number in Memphis—there remained another obstacle to their realizing parity in political power. Despite *Baker v. Carr* (1960), the political parties continued to gerrymander the state districts based on race. Sometimes these maneuvers favored African Americans, and sometimes they did not.

The racial gerrymandering of state house and senate districts, which generally protected incumbents, prompted a lawsuit—*ex rel. W. B. Lockert et al. v. Gentry Crowell, Secretary of State, et al.*—in which the NAACP-LDF joined the plaintiffs. The suit challenged the redistricting that had followed the 1980 census. Three senate seats representing predominantly black districts, two in Memphis and the seat held by Avon Williams in Nashville, remained intact from the redistricting. The white areas of east Shelby County, meanwhile, had been slashed off and added to Tipton and Lauderdale counties to form a predominantly white senate district. However, the predominantly black Haywood and Fayette counties (adjacent to Memphis–Shelby County) were combined with Chester, Hardeman, Henderson, Hardin, and McNairy counties, which would deny a senate seat to rural West Tennessee blacks. These blacks also suffered because the new map for house seats placed west Fayette County with predominantly white east Shelby County. Additionally, the reapportionment for the house placed north-central Fayette County (25,305 citizens) with Tipton County (32,747) to create District 81 and combined Haywood County (20,318) and Lauderdale County (24,555) to create District 82. The TVC joined *Amicus Curiae* in the court case, but when it was finally decided by the Tennessee Supreme Court in 1986, the legislative redrawings were upheld on the "one-man-one-vote" principle. One justice said, "It is not constitutionally permissible to discriminate *in favor* of black people any more than it is to discriminate *against* black people." At the least, however, blacks did not lose seats.

In the 1986 gubernatorial election, the Democratic candidate, Ned Ray McWherter, succeeded Lamar Alexander by defeating Winfield Dunn, who was attempting a political comeback. Although his rival in the Democratic primary had accused him of calling for rural whites to counter any heavy urban black voting, blacks voted heavily for McWherter in the general election. He had served seven unprecedented terms as Speaker of the Tennessee House of Representatives, and unlike Blanton, McWherter was able to come to an understanding with black legislators. He formed a formidable alliance with them, appointing blacks to chair committees and selecting Lois M. DeBerry as *pro tem* of the House. In 1987 he appointed Adolpho A. Birch Jr.

to the Tennessee Court of Criminal Appeals (making him the first black judge of that court) and six years later appointed him to the Tennessee Supreme Court to fill a vacancy left by Martha Craig Daughtry, who had received a federal judgeship. The first African American to serve on the state's highest court, he was later elected to a full term despite opposition from police associations and jealous lawyers. In 1996, Birch became the first black chief justice of the court.

From 1951 until his death in 1958, Joseph E. Walker had tried to involve Negro Republicans and Negro Democrats in a nonpartisan effort to face the formidable white voting bloc in Memphis. But, as previously noted, Robert R. Church Jr. opposed Walker's scheme, chastised G. W. Lee for participating in it, and even returned to Memphis to lead a black Republican resurgence before suffering that fatal heart attack. Ultimately, the city's black political leaders became loyal Democrats and, drawing on the organizational skills learned in 1959–60, united the black vote sufficiently to win more public offices. However, internal strife among various factions (as in the 1880s conflicts among black Republicans) would prevent Memphis blacks from realizing their full political power.

Nonetheless, beginning in 1967, local blacks won significant political victories. The John E. Ford family passed out sample ballots (as black Republicans had done in the 1880s) and developed other techniques to get mass numbers of black voters to the polls on election day; consequently, as the result of a well-oiled political machine, members of the Ford family would hold offices in the City Council, the county government, the General Assembly, and the U.S. Congress. Minerva J. Johnican, a former school librarian, held a seat on the Shelby County Commission (1975–82), served at large on the Memphis City Council (1983–87), and was a mayoral candidate in 1988. She ran against Congressman Harold Ford in 1982 and lost her County Commission seat in 1982 to a Ford-sponsored candidate, Julian Bolton. After making a comeback by winning a City Council seat, Johnican resigned to run for mayor and later won election as Shelby County criminal clerk in 1990. Odell Horton, R. B. Sugarmon, Fred Davis, J. O. Patterson Jr., James L. Netters, H. T. Lockard, and Vasco Smith, among others, were elected to various offices, including judgeships and seats on the City Council and County Commission in Memphis–Shelby County from 1967 through the 1990s. Michael Hooks won election as Shelby County assessor of taxes in 1988, and Janet Perry Hooks joined the City Council. In 1996, at age twenty-six, Harold Ford Jr., fresh out of the University of Michigan Law School, succeeded his father in Congress. Before getting his law degree, Harold Jr. had received a bachelor's degree in history at the University of Pennsylvania. Running for reelection to the Ninth Congressional District in 1998, he received 79 percent of the vote; in 2000 he ran unopposed. Harold Ford Jr. continued to serve in Congress through 2004 while planning to run for the U.S. Senate.

Despite such electoral victories, however, the economic position of black Memphians, except for the elite and middle classes, improved little, which led working-class blacks to push for better jobs and promotions in Memphis industries. Edward Lindsey, a worker at the Firestone plant in Memphis, recalled in 1989 how Negro workers had broken Jim Crow in the factory. Lindsey had been involved in the student sit-in demonstrations in Nashville in 1960 when he was a student at Tennessee A&I State University, but he subsequently dropped out, got married, and secured a job at Firestone in April 1963. At the time, the Firestone plant had segregated restrooms, showers, and even a partition in the cafeteria to keep Negro and white workers separated. Negroes were shut out of skilled and higher paying jobs, even if they had more education than the poor whites. "From the Crump machine on back, Memphis is a city that has been 'divide and conquer' [the Negro]," said Lindsey. Matthew Davis, another Firestone worker in Memphis, recalled, "They had some white guys out there being supervisors that could not write [their names]." Remembering Memphis as a segregated town, Clarence Coe, also a Firestone worker, said, "There is something about Memphis, I just cannot handle. I never went to Crump Stadium or to Memphis State University [because of the way they treated black people]." Negro workers at the Firestone plant protested the segregation and discriminatory practices, which soon ended, even though whites threatened to walk out. However, the union head simply told them, "Anyone who does not want to come back tomorrow can turn in their badge, now."

[*]

Housing and employment discrimination became the focus of the Tennessee Commission on Human Development (TCHD), which had been set up by the General Assembly in May 1967. On August 21, Ellington appointed fifteen people, five from each grand division of the state, to serve on the new commission, which replaced Clement's 1963 Tennessee Commission on Human Relations. The commission included at least seven blacks, including J. Emmett Ballard, Cornelius Jones, and T. W. Northcross. Jones, a graduate and former faculty member of Tennessee A&I State College, became the executive secretary of TCHD. In October 1967, the TCHD reported that the Oak Ridge City Council had passed a public accommodations ordinance prohibiting owners and proprietors of businesses from allowing "discrimination on the basis of individuals' race, color, ancestry, religion, or national origin, or to permit such a denial by any of his employees." The TCHD also promoted the establishment of human relations commissions for all Tennessee cities.

Only gradually did the TCHD, which was designed to satisfy provisions of the Civil Rights Act of 1964, become involved more directly in discrimination complaints. In 1968, the agency claimed that it had received only nine complaints on employment discrimination and that it had sent one of those cases to the federal Equal Employment Opportunity Commission. The other cases were either dropped by complainants or "conciliated by TCHD." Negroes especially were shut out of meaningful jobs with local, county, state, and federal agencies in Tennessee, and the TCHD worked on the problem. Negro employment in state government rose from 7.1 percent in 1962 to 10.5 percent by 1968, and white collar state jobs for Negroes rose from 13.08 percent to 20.2 percent. The TCHD also worked with the Tennessee Manufacturing Association, Tennessee Business Men's Association, and private industry to increase hiring and promotion opportunities for blacks. A "Governor's Conference on Human Development" was held to persuade the Tennessee Association of Realtors and others to respect and promote the federal Fair Housing Act of 1968. The TCHD informed the real estate industry of recent U.S. Supreme Court decisions that provided relief against discrimination in the sale, lease, and rental of housing.

The second governor's conference, held on May 15, 1970, addressed equal employment opportunities and affirmative-action measures. The TCHD newsletter announced that the Knoxville Roundtable of the National Conference of Christians and Jews had given James M. Lawson Jr. their "Brotherhood Award" for 1970. Attorney J. Emmett Ballard, the noted civil rights lawyer from Jackson, was elected as the first black chairman of the TCHD on September 28, 1970. A native of Jackson, he received degrees from Lane College and LaSalle University Law School and chaired the city's Community Relations Board. In January of the following year, Winfield Dunn, the newly elected governor, issued a mild statement on civil rights without mentioning race: "As Governor, I shall strive to insure the right of every citizen to achieve whatever station in life he seeks. I firmly believe that all citizens of our state should have the same . . . opportunities." But Dunn appointed no blacks to cabinet-level positions, except as a "Special Assistant to the Governor." On February 16, 1971, Dunn issued a fair employment directive "that no factors of race, religion, or sex are to be considered" and that hiring was to be "fair and impartial," but he did not consider affirmative-action measures. Dunn met with the TCHD, saying that he wanted the agency to become more than a mere trouble-shooting office. He asked for recommendations for nominees to fill nine TCHD vacancies and said, "The best example the State of Tennessee could set would be the example of making the employment practices measure up to certain standards as set by the TCHD as they relate to the racial scene in our state." TCHD received a grant from the U.S. Equal Employment Opportunity Commission (EEOC) to study hiring and recruitment procedures of employers.

In 1972, a high-ranking EEOC official met with the TCHD and declared that state government had the responsibility to assume leadership in eliminating employment discrimination. The TCHD had opened a regional office in Memphis in 1968 and another in Chattanooga in 1972. Black employment in state government rose to 12 percent by 1973, when 631,696 blacks constituted 16.1 percent of Tennessee's population. Still, in 1974, under Dunn, charges of job discrimination in Tennessee were up by 800 percent. TCHD began regional hearings to set priorities and define issues for the agency. In Chattanooga, James Mapp told the commissioners that blacks suffered housing discrimination and problems in education, government, and private business employment and pointed out that the Chattanooga state office for unemployment had no blacks in white-collar jobs. He said that real estate agents and property owners were enforcing segregation in local housing and were even harassing whites who allowed black visitors on their property. Housing segregation patterns made it difficult to maintain school desegregation without busing. Despite the efforts by the legislative black caucus and the TCHD, there was no let-up in white opposition to the civil rights movement in Tennessee, and the election of conservative governors did nothing to improve the situation.

The Tennessee Advisory Committee to the U.S. Commission on Civil Rights held an open meeting in the Fayette County town of Somerville on March 17–18, 1971, with the Reverend Samuel B. Kyles of Memphis chairing the group. The sheriff, chief of police, school board chair, and election commission chair refused to testify about the problems in Fayette County. Only one white person, Alice Coghill of the Community Action Program, testified before the committee. The investigation triggered a host of complaints about discrimination in law enforcement, continued mistreatment in the integrated schools, and voting rights violations. The vice president of the local NAACP said that too many Negroes were afraid to register complaints with the police and government officials. The committee recommended investigations by the U.S. Justice Department and the U.S. Civil Rights Commission.

Housing discrimination cases and the persistence of segregation continued to engage civil rights activists during the early and middle 1970s. The
American Civil Liberties Union (ACLU) chapter in Tennessee became
involved in housing cases, including one in which it handled a complaint that
a landlord in Chattanooga had evicted a tenant who had received black visitors in 1972. A black family in that city was also harassed by white tenants
after moving into a cheap duplex that same year. In *Franklin v. Collins* (1972),
a black law student at Vanderbilt brought a charge of housing discrimination.
Loan officers, bankers, real estate agents, and others steered blacks away from
buying houses and leasing apartments in white areas. Some hotel clerks sought
ways to segregate black customers to certain rooms and floors. Waiters in
chain restaurants would sometimes reserve a section for black customers or
refuse to wait on black customers until the white ones were served first. In
1974, an act to amend Tennessee Code Annotated Title 4, Chapter 21, embodied recent federal civil rights legislation, which further prohibited racial discrimination. Yet, in 1975, the TCHD concluded, "Racial division, unequal
and unfair practices exist in Tennessee today." It recommended that the "legislature should enact appropriate legislation in the areas of employment, housing, and public accommodations."

In March 1979, the General Assembly gave the Tennessee Human Rights
Commission (the successor to TCHD) enforcement powers to ensure fair and
equal treatment in employment, housing, and public accommodations for all
Tennesseans without regard to age, race, handicap, creed, color, religion, sex,
or national origin. 1995 legislation gave the commission monitoring compliance of Tennessee's equivalent of the Title VI of the Civil Rights Act of 1964.
THRC gained permanent legal counsel to represent complainants in administrative hearings and coordinate court actions with the state Attorney General's Office.

More and more black citizens did sue. Avon N. Williams's office of young
lawyers, including Julian Blackshear, handled several important employment
discrimination cases: *Mary Johnson v. Lillie Rubin Affiliates* (1972), *Newman et
al. v. Avoco Industries* (1975), and *Napoleon Batts et al. v. NLT Corporation*
(1984). But the federal courts were singing a conservative tune in the twenty-
plus years after *Brown*. In the case of *City of Memphis et al. v. Greene et al.*, the
city appealed a lower appeals court decision regarding complaints by black
residents that the city, since 1971, had closed certain streets in a white neighborhood to keep blacks from driving through the area. On April 20, 1981, the
U.S. Supreme Court reversed the earlier decision that had found the city's
practices discriminatory. Justice Thurgood Marshall dissented, offering the

opinion that the city's practices were in fact a "badge of slavery" in violation of the Thirteenth Amendment. In *Firefighters Local Union No 1784 v. Stotts et al.* (June 12, 1984), the high court sided with Memphis firefighters, contending that they should not be laid off to accommodate the affirmative-action hiring of blacks to make up for past discrimination. Again Marshall dissented.

[*]

In 1988, George H. W. Bush won the presidential election with 53.4 percent of the total vote and 489 electoral votes. Only 50.2 percent of American voters participated. Low voter turnouts turned elections in favor of the Republicans. Bush was criticized for allowing his campaign managers to use mean-spirited racial symbolism, which depicted blacks as criminals, to further galvanize the white solidarity movement. "Bush's quota wars [against affirmative action] involved a complicated backdrop and skirmishes that did not always involve the White House directly," noted Kenneth O'Reilly. "The president himself ignored straightforward civil rights issues and saw only a way to win elections by exploiting what everyone now agreed were divisive and explosive racial tensions." Dunn chaired Bush's successful election campaign in Tennessee.

Despite such conservative trends, the Tennessee Caucus of Black State Legislators had matured into an effective organization for pushing the minority agenda. The caucus's *1989 Legislative Report: Assessing the Impact of the 1988 Legislative Retreat* concluded that the participants accepted fifty-nine proposals. The caucus members later reviewed, consolidated, and refined the insights and suggestions from these proposals to introduce twenty-five bills, sixteen house resolutions, and twenty-three separate supplemental amendments to the general appropriations act. The resolutions and bills affected the Blues City Cultural Center, African American tourism in Tennessee, blacks in higher education, money for Meharry Medical College and Tennessee State University programs, fellowships for minority teachers, the Institute of African and Caribbean Affairs, the Memphis Blues Foundation, the TSU Center on Aging, Beck Cultural Exchange Center, the Free the Children Program, and the Minority Business Development Center, among other programs. The General Assembly enacted twelve of the twenty-five bills and adopted twelve of the sixteen resolutions; twenty-three of the supplemental appropriations were added to the 1989–90 general appropriations act. After accepting an award from the state senate on February 22, 1990, Avon Williams had a statement read that said in part: "Recent events at Tennessee State University and in Bordeaux show that the freedom [civil rights movement] spirit . . . lives on and is not dead." Williams was referring to some student protests that were underway at TSU and to the fight by Nashville's Bordeaux community against proposed zoning changes that would allow more garbage dumps and prisons in their neighborhood.

The Tennessee black caucus was invited to participate in the May 4, 1990, National Conference on Harassment of Black Elected and Appointed Officials, sponsored by the Congressional Black Caucus, which came after a series of indictments and arrests involving black politicians across the country. However, harassment did not deter the civil rights movement and its legislative advocates in Tennessee. In March 1990, black state senators cosponsored bills to (1) make affirmative action remedies for discrimination available in Chancery Court, (2) allow the Tennessee Human Rights Commission to hold hearings on alleged violations of civil rights by policemen, (3) revise the Tennessee housing discrimination law to conform with the federal Fair Housing Act amendments, (4) establish a Martin Luther King Jr. Day task force, and (5) authorize bond issues for facilities to be built at Tennessee State. These state senators were submitting so many bills that there was a failed attempt by other legislators to impose a rule of no more than nine bills per member.

The black caucus's Sixteenth Annual Legislative Retreat, held November 15–18, 1990, featured the theme "Retooling for the African American Family: Agenda for the 1990s." Activities included an award for the year's best example of a strong African American family in Tennessee. Governor McWherter offered "Special thanks to the Black Caucus and retreat participants for the roles they have played in the resolution of many state and local problems." More than seven thousand persons had participated in the retreats over the previous fifteen years, and the workshops had become large enough to move the meetings to the cities. Lois DeBerry, chairperson of the 1990 retreat, which was held in Chattanooga, told participants, "Although the retreat setting has changed, it is still our purpose to work, as hard as ever, to develop from you, input for a definitive legislative agenda for members of the Black Caucus to take to the General Assembly in January." The retreat honored Harry J. Reynolds, Chattanooga's first black school superintendent, who had begun serving in June 1988. Willie L. Brown Sr., the first black leader in the California State Assembly, was a guest speaker at one of the retreat luncheons. The retreat also honored twelve men and women who had forced the Chattanooga government to restructure so that blacks could have fair representation on the City Council. This development had resulted from the lawsuit *Brown, et al. v. City of Chattanooga*, which was filed in November 1987; in that case a federal judge struck down Chattanooga's seventy-nine-year-old at-large system of election. The judge ordered a new plan based on the Voting Rights Act of 1965 and the Fourteenth and Fifteenth Amendments. By June 11, 1990, there were four black city councilmen. One of the plaintiffs, Tommie Brown, a black professor of sociology at the University of Tennessee at Chattanooga, succeeded C. B. Robinson in the General Assembly.

In 1992, President George H. W. Bush drove another nail in the Republicans' coffin—as far as the black community was concerned—when he nominated a conservative African American, Clarence Thomas, to replace Thurgood Marshall on the U.S. Supreme Court. Justice Marshall had caused a stir in 1990 by publicly criticizing Bush for the appointment of conservative David Souter to the Supreme Court. With his health failing fast late in 1991, Marshall announced his retirement after twenty-four years on the bench. Opinion polls, which predicted an easy reelection for Bush after the recent success of Operation Desert Storm in the Middle East, influenced the eighty-three-year-old Marshall to make his retirement decision. Civil rights leaders bitterly opposed Thomas as Marshall's replacement because he had sided with conservatives on civil rights issues and because he was considered an abuser of women's rights, as well as an intellectual lightweight. Many saw him as one African American who had done nothing for the civil rights movement. Yet, Thomas was quick to brag about his background as a southern Negro born and raised in poverty. Earlier, the Reagan administration had placed Thomas in charge of the EEOC to move the agency away from class-action discrimination suits against big corporations, and Thomas had faithfully served there for eight years. President Bush promoted Thomas to the District of Columbia federal bench, usually a stepping stone to the Supreme Court. Like Clarence M. Pendleton Jr., the African American whom Reagan had appointed to head the U.S. Civil Rights Commission, Thomas contended that blacks should shun welfare, government assistance, and affirmative-action programs and that they should hoist themselves up the ladder of success by their mere bootstraps. Thomas really believed that he had advanced with no help, and his boss, President Reagan, had bragged that he was not against the New Deal but was intent on dismantling the Great Society program left by Lyndon Johnson and the Democrats. In this mean-spirited political milieu, the NAACP suspiciously backed away from strong opposition to the Thomas nomination— perhaps fearing that the Republicans would appoint no African American at all to the Supreme Court if Thomas were defeated. Thomas was confirmed by a 52–48 vote by the Republican-controlled U.S. Senate. Mary Frances Berry, a

Nashville native who served on the U.S. Civil Rights Commission (becoming its chair under President Bill Clinton), said of Thomas's rise to the high court: "The hallmark of black conservatives throughout our history—and the neoconservatives who became very visible in the 1980s—is to denounce African Americans who talk about race. . . . Thomas is there as an apologist for America's racism, [he is] not [there] to stand up for his own people."

It seemed that conservatives had taken revenge on civil rights leaders by using Clarence Thomas as an emblem to slap them in the face. However, in the 1992 election, in the midst of a bad economic recession, Bush lost his bid for reelection. His younger Democratic opponent, Arkansas governor Bill Clinton, presented himself as a centrist and as a man capable of fixing the economic and social mess left by Reagan and Bush. In a race that included independent candidate Ross Perot, Clinton appealed to minority voters and enough white voters to win with 43 percent of the popular vote and 370 electoral votes. Voter participation reached 55 percent that year. Clinton received nearly 95 percent of the black vote, as well as most of the minority and women's vote. As a student at Georgetown University, Clinton had seen buildings in Washington, D.C., burn during the riots that followed Martin Luther King Jr.'s murder in 1968. He left his dormitory room to help the Red Cross distribute needed food supplies to black victims. At Yale Law School, he chose a minority roommate and ate with black students in the cafeteria.

Just before leaving office, President Bush signed a letter written by a staff member that proclaimed Monday, January 18, 1993, as the Martin Luther King Jr. Federal Holiday. Speaking at King Day observances at Howard University (just three days before his inauguration on January 21), President-elect Clinton said, "I will try to follow the powerful example of Dr. King's conviction into these new responsibilities. Let us begin with energy and hope, with faith and discipline, and let us not quit until our work is done." Late that month, after Clinton was sworn in, Thurgood Marshall died. Clinton and his vice president, Al Gore Jr. of Tennessee, joined four thousand others for the funeral at the National Cathedral.

Tennessee, meanwhile, was becoming increasingly conservative in its politics. After Ned McWherter ended his second term as governor in 1995, state Democrats had no political stars left, and the Republicans controlled statewide elections. The only thing that kept Tennessee from going too far to the right was a Democratic-controlled General Assembly, with a highly active black caucus. Republican Donald Kenneth Sundquist was elected the new Tennessee governor in 1994 and would easily win a second term, serving through January 2003. Sundquist was born in Moline, Illinois, in 1936 and received a bachelor's degree from a Augustana College in Rock Island, Illinois, in 1957. After moving to Tennessee, he became the Bedford County chairman for the Goldwater campaign in 1964 and then chairman of the Tennessee Young Republican Federation. Sundquist served several terms in Congress. His two terms as governor would be plagued by state financial problems but no civil rights controversies. As no Democratic governor had done, Sundquist appointed two African Americans to cabinet-level positions: Donal Campbell was named commissioner of corrections, while Ruth Johnson was named commissioner of revenue. In November 2002, another northern native, former Nashville mayor Phillip Bredesen, won back the governor's seat for the Democrats with a combination of black, Democratic, and East Tennessee Republican voters.

Across America, nearly sixty thousand blacks—including a congressman from Mississippi—held elective public offices. Half of them were women. About twice as many African Americans held seats in Congress as did during the post-Reconstruction period of 1881–1901. Some 9.8 percent of Tennessee's legislators were African Americans and mostly men.

In addition to Thelma Harper, who replaced Avon Williams in the Nineteenth Senate District in 1992, other African Americans elected to the General Assembly in the 1990s included Representatives Tommie F. Brown of Chattanooga (1993–); Henri E. Brooks of Memphis (1993–); Bretran Thompson of Memphis (1993–95); Larry Miller of Memphis (1993–); Kathryn I. Bowers of Memphis (1995–); Edith T. Langster of Nashville (1995–); Joe Towns Jr. of Memphis (1995–); and John F. DeBerry Jr. of Memphis (1995–). Langster was born in Ohio in 1950, graduated from Tennessee State University, and served in the Nashville City Council before being elected to the General Assembly; she and Carolyn Baldwin Tucker, a member-at-large of the Nashville City Council, were the only black politicians to defend their alma mater, TSU, during a severe crisis in 2004 when it appeared that state officials might fire the university president and take control of the institution amid allegations of financial mismanagement and other complaints. Larry Miller was born in 1954 and was a former firefighter in Memphis. Henri Brooks often single-handedly kept the issues of black culture and history before the General Assembly in the form of bills, resolutions, monuments, and defiant personal actions—which, of course, drew resentment and even threats from racists, neo-Confederates, and black and white conservatives. The black caucus and its Task Force on Criminal Justice continued to wrestle with the racially oppressive court and prison system.

The Tennessee Supreme Court would establish the Commission on Racial and Ethnic Fairness on September 27, 1994, to "examine the Tennessee judicial system and identify issues relating to racial or ethnic fairness in that system." Tennessee participated in the National Conference on Eliminating Racial and Ethnic Bias in the Courts in 1995 and as a member of the National Consortium of Task Forces and Commissions on Racial and Ethnic Bias in the Courts. The Tennessee commission did not find "systemic bias" but did find evidence that "significant perceptions of bias and discrimination do exist in some aspects of our judicial system."

However, reporting on national trends in 2003, the NAACP-LDF concluded: "There is growing recognition in this country that our system of capital punishment is broken. Study after study finds that racial discrimination, inadequate defense services, prosecutorial misconduct and other arbitrary factors often play a large role in determining who is sent to death row. These factors, which influence who is charged and sentenced capitally, should not taint our system of justice. And yet, they do time and again, particularly where the ultimate sanction is concerned. Often the review process fails to remedy these errors." According to the report, white conservatives pushed a "War on Drugs" that seemed to be "a war on America's minorities," although whites comprised most of the drug users: while blacks made up 90 percent of all drug arrests, only 12.4 percent of drug users and dealers could be classified as blacks. Yet, more than 1 million blacks would be in prisons and jails by 2003.

[*]

Meeting in Gatlinburg on November 16–19, 1995, the Twenty-first Annual Legislative Retreat and Training Conference took up the theme "Reclaiming the Past, Inspiring the Present, and Shaping the Future." The *Report of Findings* for that year showed that 40 percent of the state's African American population still lived in Shelby County–Memphis. It also noted that more than 65 percent of Tennessee's black families had no married head of household; however, the black unemployment rate was down to 9.2 percent. The caucus held some mini-retreats and put its citizen task forces to work developing long-range strategic plans. At periodic meetings and during the annual retreat, the task forces would assess the progress of the long-range strategic plans and make adjustments to meet the benchmarks.

In the presidential election the following year, Bill Clinton won a second term, aided in no small part by 96 percent of the black voters. President Clinton claimed 50 percent of the total vote and 379 electoral votes. The

Republicans were as stunned by his reelection as they had been by his 1992 victory. Retiring governor Ned McWherter returned to his businesses and became a part-time Clinton adviser.

On November 19–22, 1998, the Twenty-fourth Annual Legislative Retreat met at Pigeon Forge. The participants honored the late A. W. Willis Jr. (1925–1988) with an awards banquet named for him. They hailed Willis as a master negotiator working quietly in private, as a near-genius who helped organize voter groups across Tennessee, as the attorney for the *Memphis City Schools* case, and as a brilliant businessman. The 1998 retreat also established the "Avon N. Williams Jr. Living Legend Award" for individuals who exhibited leadership and fought for human causes of dignity and equality.

Health care issues became important to black leaders after studies began to show that color or sex determined the level and frequency of medical care that individual Americans received. The Reverend Al Sharpton, a prominent civil rights activist in New York, identified health as the "new civil rights battlefront." President Clinton, in a 1998 radio address, declared, "Nowhere are the divisions of race and ethnicity more sharply drawn than in the health of our people." Conservatives countered with well-funded studies to dispute these findings and argue that the pathological lifestyles of blacks, not racism and racial discrimination, were the causes of the disparities in health care.

The Twenty-sixth Annual Retreat met in Nashville on November 16–19, 2000, with the theme "New Beginnings in the New Millennium: Assessment, Accountability." At this time, census data and government reports were showing per capita income for blacks as $15,197, compared to $25,278 for those designated as "whites," $12,306 for Hispanics, and $22,352 for Asian-Americans. The poverty rate for blacks was 22.1 percent, compared to 21.2 percent for Hispanics and 9.4 percent for whites, but the 2000 black poverty rate was 10 points lower than in the Reagan years. Some 18.5 percent of black Americans had no health insurance.

Tennessee's number of minority state legislators increased to eighteen. Johnny W. Shaw of Bolivar became the first black elected from rural West Tennessee since the late 1880s. Shaw received his early education in Fayette County before finishing high school in Hardeman County and was elected a county commissioner in 1994. Nathan Vaughn was elected from the Kingsport area as the eighteenth member of the caucus. African American legislators still included three in the senate: Roscoe Dixon and John Ford of Memphis and Thelma M. Harper of Nashville. The black members in the house (in addition to Shaw and Vaughn) were Joe Armstrong, Kathryn Inez Bowers, Henri E. Brooks, Tommie F. Brown, Barbara W. Cooper, Lois M. DeBerry,

John J. DeBerry, Ulysses S. Jones Jr., Edith Taylor Langster, Larry D. Miller, Mary Pruitt, Joe M. Towns, and Larry Turner.

[*]

At the turn of the millennium, much of the original, feisty leadership in Memphis was no longer around. O. Z Evers died at age seventy-six in 2001. Vasco Smith retired from his Shelby County commissioner position in 1994. H. T. Lockard and R. B. Sugarmon still were judges in the county, and Otis Higgs was a criminal court judge. Maxine Smith was preparing to leave the Memphis Board of Education in 1995 but would retain her 1994 appointment to the Tennessee Board of Regents. "The original problems we started out to solve have not been solved and now there are additional problems to put on top of them, to add to them," said Vasco Smith. "Where the solutions are to come from, I just do not know. I think a sense of despair [among blacks] is creating something we were not dealing with back then." On a good note, A. C. Wharton was elected mayor of Shelby County in 2003. Black politicians remained divided, however.

Willie Herenton had become the first African American mayor of Memphis in 1992. Twelve years later, on January 25, 2004, the *Nashville Tennessean* would note that Mayor Herenton was beginning his fourth term "undeterred by criticism." Herenton had held on to the mayor's seat for twelve years in the predominantly black city by building coalitions with the business community, gathering white voter support, trying to bridge the racial divide in Memphis, and fighting a running battle with his black opposition. He completed Lemoyne-Owen College, earned his doctorate at Southern Illinois University, and became a teacher and then the city's first black school superintendent. But his sudden rise to political prominence and the arrogant way he ignored his black critics caused clashes with the established black politicians. Yet, Herenton beat the establishment's black candidate for mayor in 1999. He continued to revitalize downtown Memphis and bring billions of dollars of investments into the city. By 2004, black politicians were at bitter odds with Mayor Herenton for reasons that were never publicly disclosed.

Black and white suburbanites in outer Shelby County were resisting any mergers with cantankerous Memphis, which had become more than 60 percent black. The inner black neighborhoods were characterized by slums, poverty, and crime. The outer rims of Memphis were growing and prospering. This process was producing two cities in Shelby County, two ethnic communities (one black; one white) that were as socio-economically separate and unequal as before the 1954 *Brown* decision. African Americans would soon outnumber whites by 1.3 percent in Memphis–Shelby County. By 2004, white flight was spilling over the state line into Mississippi.

In Tennessee's second-largest city, Nashville, the representation of African Americans on the City Council increased by the late 1990s. The Negro councilmen of Nashville who served from 1868 to 1885, included Randal Brown, Wiley Duke, Squire Fain, Charles C. Gowdy, William Long, John McGavock, James C. Napier, and James H. Sumner. But there was a long drought due to the imposition of Jim Crow until 1911–13 when Solomon P. Harris was elected to the council. Harris was the only elected Negro official in Tennessee at the time. Following the rebirth of local black politics in 1951, dozens of blacks had served in the Nashville City Council: Melvin Black, George Darden, Mansfield Douglas III, John L. Drivers, Howard Gentry Jr., Brenda Gilmore, Ronnie Greer, Troy Jones, Lawrence E. Hall, Thelma M. Harper, Frank Harrison Jr., James Hawkins, Saletta A. Holloway, Leon Q. Jackson, Lois Jordan, Edith T. Langster, Kwame Leo Lillard, Robert E. Lillard, Z. Alexander Looby, Jack London, Harold M. Love, Don Majors, Willis McCallister, Carlton Petway, Harvey Sims, Julius Sloss, Carolyn Tucker, Ludye Wallace, Edward L. Whitmore, and Vernon Winfrey. During the late 1990s, the Nashville administration of Mayor Bill Purcell included subtle themes of racial cooperation, modern populism, and neighborhood progressivism. Howard C. Gentry Jr., a TSU employee, and Carolyn B. Tucker, another TSU graduate and a retired Metro teacher, became the first two African Americans elected to one of the five at-large seats in the Metro Nashville–Davidson County City Council. Other minority councilmen in Nashville included Brenda Gilmore, Melvin Black, Don Majors, Lawrence E. Hall Jr., Ronnie Greer, Morris B. Haddox, and Saletta Holloway. African Americans made up 24 percent of Nashville–Davidson County's population in 2001. They held eleven (or 28 percent) of council seats and 22 percent of school board seats. When the 2000 census figures became available for redrawing of council districts, however, a fierce dispute broke out over an attempt by some officials to limit blacks to only seven districts instead of the eight districts African Americans claimed as equitable. The district plan was sent back to the drawing board. By 2003, Howard Gentry had won election as vice mayor.

[*]

In the national election of November 2000, there were reports and rumors about cheating, irregularities, and intimidation of minority voters, just as there had been in Reconstruction times. In November 2002, many of the disputed votes and some thrown-out votes originated in heavily black precincts across the country. America's conservative commentators argued that voters too ignorant to properly mark and cast a ballot deserved to have their votes discounted—an argument borrowed from the Reconstruction era, when literacy tests and multi-ballot box systems were designed to confuse and disqualify the freedmen. When a controversy over the election results in Florida extended into the early part of December, the Supreme Court decided to halt recounts in that state. Clarence Thomas cast the deciding vote in the 5–4 decision. Vice President Al Gore gained the majority of the popular vote—48.39 percent to 47.88 percent for George W. Bush, son of the forty-first president. Yet, as a result of the Supreme Court's unprecedented action regarding the Florida recount, Bush won the electoral college, 271–266. One Gore elector from Washington, D.C., abstained. Gore lost his home state, Tennessee, with its 11 electoral votes, although he did pick up 91 percent of the state's black vote. A Gore win in Tennessee or in one more state in the Northeast would have saved American democracy from worldwide embarrassment. It was clear by this time that Tennessee could no longer be taken for granted by the Democratic Party. Since Dwight Eisenhower's win in 1952, Republican presidential candidates had carried the state in several elections, and even George Wallace had won the state in 1968. Racial attitudes, meanwhile, were becoming increasingly similar to those in the Deep South as more job-seeking poor, working-class, and middle-class persons arrived from surrounding states and from blue-collar communities in the northern "rust belt."

The civil rights movement helped to transform the American political system since antebellum times. The Negro alliance with Republicans from 1867 to 1959—albeit a reluctant marriage on the part of white Republicans—helped to transform the American Constitution itself through the Thirteenth, Fourteenth, and Fifteenth Amendments. Despite the Compromise of 1877 with rebellious southerners, the North pushed toward nationalism, and the U.S. Supreme Court—notwithstanding *Plessy* (1896) and a few other retrograde decisions—continued to strengthen constitutional nationalism and federal citizenship. The northerners' drive for post–Civil War nationalism and the constitutional supremacy of federal citizenship would prove beneficial to the Negro's quest for equal citizenship. Indubitably, the New Deal, as well as President Truman's race commissions and executive orders against racial discrimination, contributed to the laying of a foundation for transforming American society and its economy into something it had never been before. These historical developments would serve as the real justification for nine justices to unanimously approve *Brown* in 1954. Even President Eisenhower's inter-state highway program and Congress's Civil Rights Acts of 1957 and 1960 positively changed a retrogressive South that truly was a social, cultural, and economic drag on twentieth-century America. Policies under Presidents Kennedy, Johnson, and even Nixon further developed this new, post–Civil War American socioeconomic system and made capitalism and democracy more inclusive.

The American civil rights movement proved that human inclusiveness—not exclusiveness, as proclaimed by conservatives and a plutocracy of greed—*strengthened* American democracy at home and extended it abroad (relative to the fight against Communism). Just as important, Tennessee's civil rights movement contributed a dynamic chapter to that American saga of human struggle and the ingenious human triumph over men's tendency to oppress fellow men. And so this Tennessee story belongs within the broader American and world history narrative about civil rights struggles and ultimate peace among humankind.

CHAPTER 10

MAHE TENNESSEE STATE EQUIVALENT TO UT FOR WHITE STUDENTS

DESEGREGATION OF HIGHER EDUCATION

The history of Negro access to higher education goes back to antebellum times. Free Negro citizens were barred from Nashville's public schools in 1853, and in early 1857, when common whites found that free Negro citizens were clandestinely operating their own schools and had done so intermittently since 1833, vigilantes persuaded the City Council to close them down. Some Negro families relocated to Ohio to educate their children. Franklin College, which was operated by Tolbert Fanning and his wife on the eastern outskirts of Nashville, included a curriculum of Christian ethics, manual labor, and basic courses for working-class whites, and they allowed a few free Negroes to work there and take some instruction.

Beginning in late 1863, northern missionaries established freedmen's schools in Tennessee—in Knoxville, Memphis, Nashville, and other places where large numbers of fugitive slaves resided in contraband camps protected by the Union army. In 1867, the General Assembly passed a common school law that led to the closing of many of the private freedmen schools. Missionary societies converted some freedmen's schools to pre-collegiate and then college-level programs: Nashville Normal and Theological Institute, or Roger Williams University (1866–1929); Fisk Free School, or Fisk University (1866–present); Central Tennessee College, or Walden University (1868–1922); and

Tennessee Manual Labor University (1868–74)—all located in Nashville. Other Tennessee freedmen schools included LeMoyne Institute or Lemoyne-Owen College (1872–present) in Memphis, Knoxville College (1875– present), Meharry Medical College (1876–present), and Lane College (1882– present) in Jackson. Fisk and Roger Williams produced college degrees by 1874; Knoxville and LeMoyne did so much later. None of the freedmen's colleges had Negro presidents, and there were very few Negro faculty members at these institutions.

Northern states had public colleges partly because of the Morrill Land Grant Act, which was passed on July 2, 1862, and which used money from sales of vast public lands to finance public colleges in each state. After the Civil War, Mississippi, South Carolina, and Virginia—controlled by Radical Republicans—were among the first of the former Confederate states to take advantage of the Morrill act. They shared funds with three Negro land-grant colleges.

Tennessee accepted federal land-grant funds in 1869 and designated the private East Tennessee University (ETU) in Knoxville to use the funds. After being elected to the General Assembly in the 1870s and 1880s, Negro state legislators secured resolutions that directed ETU trustees to provide "separate accommodations or instruction of any persons of color, who may be entitled to admission." In 1879, East Tennessee University became the University of Tennessee (UT). In 1881, three Negro legislators nominated students to attend UT under the 1869 act, but the trustees feared that admitting Negroes would deter whites from enrolling in this private school. They would have to "provide two sets of buildings, apparatus, libraries, and equipment and a double corps of instructors" to comply with state segregation laws. UT made arrangements with Fisk to educate Negro applicants. In 1884, Negro legislators asked that Morrill scholarship students be allowed to attend *any* Tennessee Negro college of their choice.

On August 30, 1890, when Congress amended the 1862 Morrill Land Grant Act, some language was inserted into the legislation to advocate equal access to public higher education for Negro citizens. This language sanctioned de jure racial segregation and helped to set the stage for *Plessy v. Ferguson* (1896)—the principle of "separate but equal." By 1899, Delaware, Florida, Georgia, Kentucky, Oklahoma, Louisiana, Maryland, and West Virginia accepted the terms, and fourteen more Negro colleges gained land-grant status but not equal collegiate programs.

To comply with the 1890 Morrill Act, for instance, the University of Tennessee established an "Industrial Department" at nearby Knoxville

College—a Presbyterian freedmen's school. The president of UT ordered admission standards "lenient to the colored man" and modified courses "to suit the requirements of the students of this race." The courses consisted of shop work, manual labor, and farm work, using Morrill funds to finance sixteen students in 1891–92. "We believe that this college [UT] now provides the 'brother in black' the kind of education which he needs most," said the UT president in 1893. UT became Tennessee's only pubic college in 1906. On March 6, 1908, the *Nashville Globe* protested "the inequitable distribution" of the Morrill Land Grant funds because "the UT does not admit Colored people of the state, and the Colored people of . . . have benefited very little by an appropriation that was made primarily in their interest." In the 1910 census, Negroes constituted 22 percent of the population; however, in 1911, UT received $68,960 in federal Morrill funds, while Knoxville College received only $10,350, or 15 percent of the total allocation.

A wealthy northern philanthropist, George Peabody (1795–1869), established the Peabody Education Fund to help train southern teachers and spread the improvement of education among Negroes and whites throughout the impoverished South. George Peabody Normal College, founded in 1875 in Nashville, received nearly $2.5 million from the Peabody Fund and $500,000 in state funds. Yet, except for a brief auxiliary program, Negro citizens were excluded from equal benefit of state tax and Peabody funds. The *Globe* (Jan. 18, 1907) protested that Tennessee excluded private Negro colleges from the Peabody Fund: "There was a time when the state paid for four or five students in Fisk University or Roger Williams University—this is not so now." Only one white college, Maryville College (1819–present), a Presbyterian school in the antislavery section of East Tennessee, had admitted Negroes until a state act in 1901 forbade such "race mixing." This sort of restriction was approved by the U.S. Supreme Court a few years later when it ruled, in *Berea College v. Kentucky* (1908), that even private schools could be compelled by state law to observe *Plessy v. Ferguson* (1896).

Southerners indeed knew that they needed to give attention to catching up to the progressive education movement in the North. Only 39 percent of Tennessee's counties offered four years of public high school; most counties provided no high school at all for Negroes and did not fund an equal number of months of school compared to that provided to white children. Some Tennessee progressives began an education reform movement in 1905 with the intent of establishing public normal schools that would compensate for the lack of higher grades in most counties. These normal schools would admit students in grammar school grades through high school, provide two years of college education in order to increase Tennessee's supply of teachers, and promote the opening of more public and private secondary schools throughout the state. These reform plans excluded Negro citizens.

In 1909, to counteract such exclusion, Henry Allen Boyd, James C. Napier, Richard H. Boyd, Benjamin Carr, Preston Taylor, and other Negro leaders formed a lobbying group called the Tennessee Agricultural and Industrial Normal School Association. They avoided mention of liberal arts education, and assured white leaders that a Negro normal school would be "like Tuskegee [Institute]," which emphasized manual labor, industrial arts, domestic science (home economics), and other non-threatening subjects. Napier argued that the school would help reduce the Negro criminal element and produce better citizens. Boyd said that Negro businesses needed mechanics, printers, and people trained in manual work. The reformers included a Negro school in the proposed legislation, but they assured other citizens that the institution would not be like existing private Negro colleges, which had prepared no more than "discontented propagators." To make sure that the state Negro school would have a narrowly focused program, the sponsors of the bill inserted into the institutional title a confining phrase, "Agricultural and Industrial," which was a step below the word "Mechanical" (engineering). The General Assembly passed the legislation on April 27, 1909.

Various towns competed to raise matching funds in order to have such a school established in their locale. In particular, Negro leaders in Chattanooga and Nashville battled to gain control of the Negro normal school. The Nashville group raised twenty thousand dollars in a door-to-door canvass, and persuaded the Davidson County government to appropriate some bonds. One county magistrate voted for the bonds because "[t]he old slaves had cared for the [white] folks at home when the old masters were out to [Civil] War." In January 1911 the state awarded the school to Nashville–Davidson County.

Tennessee A&I State Normal School for Negroes opened its doors on June 12, 1912, under President William Jasper Hale, who had led the state normal campaign in Chattanooga. The state superintendent visited the new school and reminded the faculty that Hampton and Tuskegee institutes were the best models to emulate. Such institutes were little more than glorified high schools, and only by 1915 would they be recognized as such by the Southern Association of Colleges and Schools (1895–present). Jim Crow practices mostly determined A&I's development. The respective state/county appropriations and donations for the four normal schools were as follows: Tennessee State A&I for Negroes, $46,279/$80,639; Middle Tennessee State Normal School,

$92,558/$180,000; East Tennessee State Normal School, $92,558/$151,875; and West Tennessee State Normal School, $92,558/money still being raised.

After J. C. Napier became U.S. Register of the Treasury in 1911, only then did he begin to attack this unfair treatment. He sent a letter in December of that year to President William H. Taft to point out the ways in which Negro citizens were not receiving equal benefits from federal land-grant and agricultural funds. He testified before the Agriculture and Forest Committee of the U.S. House of Representatives that Negro youth had no access to agricultural experiment stations. He said that he "personally found no Negro at Knoxville College that considered themselves a part of UT" and added, "We [Negroes] never have gotten a full portion of it [the Morrill funds]." Indeed, when Congress passed the Smith-Hughes Vocational Education Act in 1917, UT shared none of the money with Negro citizens. The General Education Board, Anna T. Jeanes Fund, John F. Slater Fund, and Julius Rosenwald Fund—northern philanthropic groups—supplemented the meager state funds at Tennessee State. Once the Negro school had granted its first bachelor's degrees in June 1924 and was renamed Tennessee A&I State Normal Teachers College in 1925, these philanthropic groups helped to build facilities fit for collegiate status.

A few private historically black colleges and a few white colleges in the North had to produce what few Negro college graduates completed master's and doctorate degrees. UT offered graduate programs, but Negro citizens had no access to them. At the demand of Negro teachers, who represented 17 percent of the state's public school teachers, Tennessee A&I State Teachers College started some graduate courses in 1935, but the State Board of Education stopped the process and ordered an outside study of the institution. The study was concluded in 1936, with the recommendation that Tennessee A&I upgrade the undergraduate program before offering graduate work. However, in 1937, William B. Redmond, a recent graduate of Tennessee A&I, became the NAACP plaintiff in *State of Tennessee Ex. Rel. William B. Redmond, II v. O. W. Hyman, et al.* A state judge, however, upheld the continued exclusion of Negroes by ruling that NAACP lawyers had made mistakes in filing the case. The General Assembly, in fear that the NAACP would refile *Redmond,* quickly passed legislation to grant scholarships for Negroes to attend out-of-state graduate schools. In 1939, the NAACP lawyers refiled the UT case but lost again. In light of the NAACP's recent victories in similar cases in several southern states, a 1941 act of the General Assembly authorized a graduate school at Tennessee A&I State College. In *State ex Rel, Joseph M. Michael,*

Complainant and Appellant, Knox County (1942), six Negro citizens filed cases in the state Supreme Court to force UT to admit them to graduate school. The Tennessee court ruled against them with these words: "The legislation of 1941 took no rights away from appellants; on the contrary the right to equality in education with white students was specifically recognized and the method by which those rights would be satisfied was set forth in the legislation." State officials formed a team of UT faculty members to help Tennessee A&I design graduate degrees. Tennessee spent $6,966.60 for out-of-state Negro scholarships in 1941–43. The financially strapped NAACP backed down.

President W. J. Hale refused to submit a budget for the proposed graduate school as recommended by the UT study team because state authorities intended to force him to use A&I reserve funds. Hale argued that there was not enough money to implement the recommendations. The authorities responded by auditing the college, finding $337,000 in surplus funds, and accusing Hale of financial mismanagement. On May 16, 1941, the state attorney general warned fellow officials: "Be reminded we are making an effort to give the Negro equal access to graduate work to relieve the University of Tennessee of the embarrassing question made by an application of Negroes for admission to UT. If there isn't anything wrong with the management of this [Negro] institution, and I am constrained to believe there is not anything radically wrong from the records before me, it would be a shame to besmirch the institution and do it irreparable damage by an ill advised, ill-considered, and inaccurate audit." The Negro graduate school was opened in June 1942. On August 27, 1943, however, state authorities did force Hale to resign on the grounds that he had misused funds.

Effective September 1, 1943, the commissioner of education appointed Walter S. Davis as acting president of Tennessee A&I. Davis was a 1931 A&I graduate and had recently received his Ph.D. degree from Cornell University. On September 15, 1943, the commissioner wrote to Davis, telling him to select competent faculty members as administrators to assist him and to proceed to build Tennessee A&I State College into a university for Negroes "equivalent to the University of Tennessee for white students." A dean at UT remained so frustrated by the slow progress in achieving this parity that he suggested in a letter on November 3, 1943, that the State of Tennessee cooperate with other southern states to "create a regional school to separately accommodate Negro graduate students." Tennessee authorities toyed with the idea of quickly setting up a law school at either Fisk University or A&I to accommodate three of the Negro plaintiffs in the lawsuit against UT. The dean of a hurriedly established public Negro law school in St. Louis was hired as a consultant. At the time, however, the NAACP was fighting the establishment of such bogus law schools since they were clearly designed simply to satisfy the *Plessy* test. Thus, the St. Louis consultant advised Tennessee officials to continue awarding scholarships to out-of-state schools and to increase them slightly rather than establishing an in-state school. A&I granted its first master's degree in June 1944 and began to build an engineering program. The white director of Negro education in Tennessee, however, doubted that anyone "would hire a Negro engineer in America."

[*]

Through 1941 Jim Crow legislation, the State of Tennessee began making arrangements with Meharry Medical College to educate Negro citizens who wished to become doctors, nurses, and dentists. The white officials at Meharry signed the April 18, 1945, agreement, though the seventy-five dollars per student originally proposed was unacceptable to them. The fee was increased to a hundred dollars per quarter in 1946, and the legislature later authorized an increase to $166.66 per quarter per student plus a differential between the cost at UT and Meharry. Under this arrangement, the student had to be a citizen of Tennessee who had been accepted at Meharry and who had applied for the scholarship. In addition to providing $166.66 per student, the state agreed to pay the difference in the cost of attending Meharry, a private school with higher tuition, and that which the student would have paid at UT, had he or she been allowed to attend the publicly funded institution.

In order for the South to respond in a more concerted voice to the NAACP threat, Tennessee officials took a leadership role in organizing the Southern Regional Education Board (SREB), which was founded in 1948. The SREB contracted with various graduate and professional schools, especially those in the medical and health fields, to accept their Negro citizens who qualified for such programs. The states paid a set cost per student to the institutions. In this way, the SREB member states tried to meet the "separate but equal" requirements of *Plessy*.

In his January 1949 legislative message, Governor James Nance McCord said, "This [SREB] compact was not intended as a subterfuge designed to perpetuate segregation, or to avoid the civil obligations of the states in the field of education as the professional leaders of the NAACP whom [sic] reside in the North would have you believe. As it is related to Meharry it was, and now is, an honest and sincere effort to preserve for the Negro boy and girl, both in the South and elsewhere, their only real opportunity for an education in medicine, dentistry, and nursing." McCord warned the southern states that they had better participate in the SREB compact, because they "could not afford to let the federal government take over this domain [of higher education in the South]." But Negro columnist Robert Churchwell, writing in the *Nashville Commentator*, offered this opinion: "The plan to make Meharry a regional school will enable southern governments to put off democratizing . . . and is designed to hold back the wheels of progress [for Negroes]."

In 1951–52, the SREB contract included graduate social work at Clark College, Atlanta, and by the time *Brown* arrived in 1954, the SREB, headquartered in Atlanta, involved nineteen institutions and 1,069 students. Hollis Price, the first Negro president of LeMoyne College, served on the SREB board beginning in 1952. In a 1960 report, Will E. Turner, the white director of Negro education in the Tennessee Department of Education, said, "The program for Negroes simply has continued because UT does not admit qualified Negro students to the nursing program in Memphis [UT Health Sciences Center]. But the state appropriations are not in any sense scholarships." In this last statement, he was referring to the fact that the grants were based on race and not on academic requirements. In 1959–60, years after *Brown* ordered desegregation, Tennessee spent $54,500 on out-of-state scholarships and a total of $1,086,585.71 spent since 1937.

In 1952, Meharry hired its first Negro president, Dr. Harold D. West, who served through 1965, followed by an interim administrative committee from 1966 to 1968, when Dr. Lloyd C. Elam became president. Under Elam, a Ph.D. program in the sciences, new buildings, and an allied health school were added. There was another interim head for 1981–82, after which Dr. David Satcher became the third African American to head the school, serving until 1993. He was followed by Dr. John Maupin (1993–present). Meharry continued to be essential to the supply of African American doctors, dentists, and doctorates in biological sciences across the state. Avon N. Williams Jr. and other members of the Tennessee Caucus of Black State Legislators fought continuously for money for Meharry, helped to defeat bills not in the best interest of the state's only Negro medical school, and sponsored numerous bills to help fund its School of Dentistry, Preventive Medicine Program, Family Medical Practice Residency Program, and Center for Sickle Cell Anemia. Senator Williams sent copies of proposed legislation to the president of Meharry and other school officials on a periodic basis to get their opinions. On a bill to allow pharmacists to substitute drugs prescribed by doctors, Elam advised Williams to help defeat the legislation. In a letter to Williams on January 17,

1976, Elam opposed the recognition of chiropractic as a science or healthcare field because it was more akin to "traditional healer or witch doctor." When caucus members secured a $250,000 contract between Meharry and the Department of Public Health, Williams alerted Meharry that he would help the state representative from Knoxville pass a similar bill for UT's medical school as part of the deal.

Continuing racial exclusion of black citizens from medical schools made it necessary for the SREB to continue payments to Meharry. In 1973, Tennessee schools of medicine supplied 56 percent of Tennessee's 5,017 doctors, but Meharry supplied 54 percent of the primary care physicians. In 1976, Meharry claimed 96 of the 1,901 dentists practicing in Tennessee; yet, there were only 13.8 African American dentists per 100,000 black citizens, as compared to 45 white dentists per 100,000 white citizens. In 1979, 25 percent of black medical students and 40 percent of the nation's black dental students studied at Meharry and Howard University. SREB gradually increased its payments per student from $1,500 to $4,750, but by 1980, a contract with New York gave Meharry $11,000 per student. Most SREB states paid an average of $11,225 per student. Federal contributions made up the difference between the $4,750 paid by Tennessee and the actual cost of educating a student at Meharry, which had 172 student seats contracted by nine states. (Over the years, the SREB has evolved into a regional agency that handled access to educational programs regardless of race. For example, under its "Academic Common Market" program, the SREB enables a qualifying student in one member state to enroll in a degree program that is not offered in his or her own state but is offered in another SREB state—without having to pay out-of-state tuition. This allows an SREB state to reduce program duplication and avoid offering highly specialized degree programs for just a few students.)

In 1979, Governor Lamar Alexander questioned the state funding for Meharry and vetoed some appropriations for the institution. In November 1980, "A Consultant Report to Study the Relationship of Meharry to the State of Tennessee" was completed for the Tennessee Higher Education Commission (THEC); it showed that Meharry admitted more black students from Tennessee than public and private medical schools in Tennessee combined. In the following month, THEC recommended continued state funding for Meharry programs and cooperation with the public medical schools at UT and East Tennessee State University until the historically white schools began to produce more minority physicians and dentists. In 1980, the UT Center for Health Sciences in Memphis accepted only five Negroes, and three of them became enrolled. The ETSU medical school in Johnson City, meanwhile, accepted five blacks, and two of them enrolled. Meharry still enrolled as many state residents as the other two Tennessee schools combined.

Meharry's president, David Satcher, wanted the state funding to be raised from fifty-four to all the seventy-five Tennessee students at Meharry and to raise the SREB per-student rate to $20,000—the real cost per student. Tennessee paid nearly $25,000 per student at the UT medical school and would pay $42,700 per student to the recently established ETSU School of Medicine. On September 14, 1982, Satcher pointed out that 70 percent of black medical and dental school students in Tennessee studied at Meharry, and the state's current contribution of $2.4 million was only 5 percent of the Meharry budget. Senator Williams and other black caucus members were able to get additional appropriations for Meharry and increase the per-student rate to $11,000 in 1983. Yet, several southern states paid $49,000 per student in contracts with private medical schools. About 90 percent of practicing black physicians in Tennessee were Meharry graduates, and more than half of the school's family practice graduates served rural and urban populations.

[*]

In August 1951, Tennessee officials elevated Tennessee A&I State College to university status, thus finally demonstrating a commitment to *Plessy*. A&I was fully accredited in 1958, 1 of only 19 of the 105 historically black colleges and universities (HCBUs) to achieve that. But exclusion of the Negro from higher education remained a reality in Tennessee and across the nation. By 1953, some 22 southern public colleges enrolled only 453 Negro students. Blacks had received graduate degrees between 1887 and 1953 from northern institutions, including Yale, Harvard, Boston University, Columbia, Cornell, Syracuse, the University of Pennsylvania, the University of Iowa, and the University of Michigan, but these institutions refused to hire blacks as faculty members. And whites did not see this as a moral issue: by 1953, only 9 southern theological seminaries enrolled a few Negro students. Some 90 percent of nearly 100,000 Negro college students still attended the 104 HBCUs.

In Memphis there was open opposition to allowing Negro students into the city's only public university, Memphis State University (MSU). Respecting the 1909 legislative mandate, the West Tennessee State Normal School, as MSU was originally known, had been established to serve white citizens. Negro citizens were supposed to attend A&I. Nonetheless, in August 1954, in the wake of *Brown*, a group of Negro students—Elijah Noel, Joseph McGhee,

Marden Knowles, Ruth Booker, and Nellie Peoples—applied to Memphis State University only to be denied admission. "We will go all the way to the Supreme Court at Washington if necessary to achieve justice for these students," said their attorney, James F. Estes. Other Negro attorneys, including H. T. Lockard, Russell B. Sugarmon Jr., A. W. Willis Jr., and the NAACP–Legal Defense Fund's Thurgood Marshall and Constance Baker Motley, would assume the case. The federal judge in Memphis, Marion S. Boyd, refused the plaintiffs' request for a three-judge panel and supported a five-year gradualism plan. The NAACP–LDF team contested Boyd's decision in the court of appeals, which ruled on October 16, 1956, that the gradualism plan did not apply to higher education as used in *Brown*'s plans for secondary schools. Boyd's delays continued through three more college terms, from 1956 to 1959, at which point Jack Millard Smith, MSU president, finally said that anyone who could pass the entrance test and meet the requirements would be admitted to his university. After eight of ten Negro students passed the MSU admissions test, Smith asked the judge for another delay because of "fear of violence on the campus." Maxine Smith warned the MSU president, "It is completely futile to continuously oppose the edicts of the Supreme Court of our land. This only shows how important it is for us as Negroes to continuously fight until our goals have been attained, and to continue to support those organizations [i.e., the NAACP] that are bearing the brunt of the fight for us." On January 23, 1959, the appeals court ordered the federal district court to deal with the MSU case. The *Memphis Tri-State Defender*, on February 7, 1959, declared that "Jack Smith was an avowed segregationist" for barring the students after they had passed the tests. Boyd scheduled February 20 to hear the state's motion to dismiss the case.

At a federal court hearing in July 1959, the State of Tennessee finally capitulated and decided to admit the undergraduate students to Memphis State for fall 1959. Laverne Kneeland, Sammie Burnett, and Ralph Prater were among the student plaintiffs present in the courtroom. Many of the other plaintiffs involved in the long battle—including those who had originally applied at MSU in 1954—had moved on to other things, attending other schools, getting married, or going to work. "Memphis State to Admit Negro Students Next Fall," noted a *Memphis World* headline. Attorney Lockard said, "I am glad it seems to be over, and you know you really cannot earn a living with this type case."

Smith ordered MSU officials to keep the Negro students as segregated as possible until they and white students got used to each other. The Negro students were kept off the campus until classes began, and their books were delivered to their homes to prevent "them from standing in long lines and being subjected to possible harassment." As a university dean put it, "We asked them to be as inconspicuous as possible." Smith arranged for the students' classes to be stacked so that they had no idle time between classes and would leave the campus early each day. When the students protested about maltreatment, the dean of students called them "niggers" to their faces. Still, on the first day of classes, there were no other incidents—except for a car circling the campus with a sign reading "Civil Rights for Whites." By 1960–61, nearly 40 Negro students had enrolled at MSU, and they were still required to sit in certain sections at sporting events and not to use the cafeteria, where white students had thrown food on them. However, according to the *World* (June 10, 1961), complaints from the local NAACP about these "cooperative" restrictions led to their being lifted for the 1961–62 academic year. Ten years after desegregation, MSU student enrollment was 7.6 percent black, a total of 831 students.

[∗]

Desegregation of higher education in the state had proceeded slowly. Bethel College, a private school in McKenzie, Tennessee, decided to accept Negro students in the fall of 1953, although there were no applicants. School of Divinity faculty at Vanderbilt admitted the first Negro graduate student, Joseph A. Johnson, in 1953, although the university's Board of Trustees did not wish to admit Negroes "to courses of study which are already available to them in this vicinity." Maryville College decided to accept Negro students in the fall of 1954. The president reminded the press that Maryville College had been biracial until Tennessee's 1901 Jim Crow law went into effect; however, he and the faculty interpreted *Brown* as nullifying that law. Austin Peay State College in Clarksville admitted Wilbur N. Daniel, a graduate of Tennessee State, into the graduate school without fanfare in 1956. Two years later, Austin Peay began admitting black undergraduates, and would increase the black enrollment to more than 16 percent of students fifty years later. The University of the South decided to accept Negro students by 1959. By August 1955, some sixty-eight Negro graduate students were enrolled at the University of Tennessee, Knoxville. In the same year, in order to push the undergraduate admission issue, Jessie H. Turner, head of the NAACP in Memphis, personally enrolled via mail in an undergraduate course at the local evening school before UT officials recognized that he was a Negro. The dean of admissions told a reporter that the school did not admit undergraduate Negroes but quickly decided to allow Turner to remain in the course. No other Negro undergraduates were allowed to enroll until the admission of Theotis Robinson Jr., Willie May Gillespie, and Charles E. Blair in 1961. Once they were admitted, however, UT segregated the Negro students, even forcing them to eat off campus.

After admitting some Negro graduate students to summer school in 1963, the board at private University of Chattanooga (which became the University of Tennessee at Chattanooga in 1969) decided in February to admit Negro students but delayed full desegregation until the fall of 1965. Martha Galbraith, the editor of the *Echo*, the student paper, urged the school to desegregate: "The fraternities should behave themselves or get off campus." Trevecca Nazarene College admitted the first Negro student in 1964, the year Vanderbilt enrolled its first Negro undergraduates. The Civil Rights Act of 1964 forced all public and private colleges that accepted federal funds to desegregate. Violence and government confrontations were absent in the Tennessee process, unlike those in adjacent Alabama, Georgia, and particularly Mississippi, where several rioters died and many were injured.

Sports surely had an impact on decisions to desegregate higher education in Tennessee. Northern and western universities featured superior Negro athletes in triumphant national athletic contests, and southerners could not tolerate losing anything to the "Yankees." UT had been beaten on several occasions by integrated teams, and it was clear that the South could no longer remain competitive in collegiate sports by relying on a Jim Crow pool of athletes. After all, the greatest pool of Negro athletes was in the South. Southern colleges and universities turned reluctantly to the recruitment of Negroes to win contests they were otherwise likely to lose in the era of integration. In 1966, UT Knoxville accepted Albert Davis as the first black athlete at the school. Such action would be repeated many times in the South, even in Alabama, Georgia, and Mississippi. But the sudden interest in Negro athletes by America's largest universities would hurt athletic recruitment at Negro colleges that had once enjoyed a monopoly on those athletes. Tennessee State was so superior in football that the institution sent nine players to the National Football League in a single year, and TSU athletes won thirty-one medals at the Olympic Games between 1952 and 1988. Yet when TSU football tried to cut its travel expenses and boost national rankings by applying for entrance into the all-white Ohio Valley Conference, the institution was turned down three times. "No one likes to lose to a so-called black team," one TSU official said. John S. Merritt, the legendary TSU football coach, said he had a recruiting problem because coaches at integrated high schools saved the best athletes for the white universities, observing, "We have to recruit around them sometimes."

In 1966, UT Knoxville hired its first full-time black faculty member. But black academics with superior credentials avoided UT or readily left for better salaries and the opportunity to work at northern research universities where fewer racial antagonisms were present. Of 6,483 Negro students in Tennessee's public colleges that year, 5,084 of them attended Tennessee A&I State University. The UT campus at Knoxville counted 252 black undergraduates, 55 black graduate students, 4 black faculty members, and 16 part-time black students from Knoxville College. UT would develop campuses in each major city of the state and be designated the flagship university. But Tennessee had no affirmative-action program to recruit blacks to the state's white public colleges and universities, nor did it have any plans to make up for past discrimination or even make A&I equal to UT.

At Tennessee State, President Walter S. Davis was still being compelled to follow the tactic of his predecessor, W. J. Hale, who had to beg and then beg some more for adequate state funding. On November 29, 1966, in a letter to the newly elected governor, Buford Ellington, Davis wrote, "I have always loved you and have always supported you. Therefore, I look forward to the foremost productive years in the history of Tennessee . . . I want you to know our urgent needs at Tennessee A&I State University. You will make a tremendous contribution to the Negroes of Tennessee as well as to every citizen of our state. The requested expenditure is not large but most significant." Davis had sent requests to the board, asking for money to adequately fund agriculture and home economics programs, and for a name change that would delete the "A&I." In a December 6, 1966, letter, Davis pleaded with the commissioner of finance and administration for an increase in per-pupil appropriation that would be equal to the average for other black land-grant colleges or equal to that for UT. Tennessee had finally elevated A&I to full land-grant status in 1958—meaning the institution could engage in research and experimental stations, teaching, cooperative, and extension work just as UT did. In light of that, Davis pointed out that Tennessee A&I should receive $865.51 per student instead of the $700 then designated for the institution. Florida A&M State University and South Carolina State University, two other Negro land-grant schools, received $1,077.00 and $1,137.50, respectively, per student. "Since the University of Tennessee per student appropriation is based upon the averages for the white land grant universities of the Southeast, the proposal for Tennessee A&I State University seems entirely fair and justifiable," said Davis. His request was ignored. And not only that but UT also received full federal funds for agriculture and extension work while A&I received only a minimal amount.

State authorities would launch an audit (a favorite weapon against black college presidents) at Tennessee State in 1967, especially after student riots hit the black community and the campus. James Montgomery, the student government president, said that lack of support from state officials for the public Negro university was the real cause of student discontent on campus. In June 1967, Negro Citizens for a Better School, Community, State and Country sent two thousand signatures to state officials. Big decreases in student enrollment began for TSU, particularly after the General Assembly proposed a 15 percent cap on out-of-state enrollment. The commissioner of education ordered President Davis to cut out-of-state enrollment in 1967–68 even before the official state rule went into effect. Davis begged for a reprieve because recruitment for the athletic teams and the band program, which depended heavily on out-of-state students, would be devastated. This pressure, the growing unrest among the student civil rights leaders on campus, the cold attacks by Ellington and state education officials, and Davis's health problems convinced him to resign the presidency, effective September 1, 1968.

Perhaps Davis did not realize that the higher education situation in Tennessee had changed since the *Brown* decision in 1954, the push to integrate the colleges in the 1950s, the sit-in demonstrations in 1960, the Freedom Rides in 1961, and the Civil Rights Act of 1964. The majority of America's black college students increasingly attended white institutions, and by 2000, 86 percent of them would be doing so. Dozens of predominantly black colleges and universities (PBCUs) resulted when whites fled the inner cities rather than integrate. Shelby State Community College in Memphis, for example, became 72 percent black. PBCUs, mostly community colleges, would enroll more students than the HBCUs by 2003. Enrollment dropped at the HBCUs prior to 1980, and then enrollment in the HBCUs shot up dramatically, including an average of 20 percent white students by 2002. Tennessee State was not immune to these changes. If white colleges would have to desegregate, what reason was there to upgrade Tennessee A&I and other historically black colleges and universities that originated out of Jim Crow?

[*]

In 1966, black leaders quickly saw the handwriting on the wall, and they soon confronted the authorities over the public HBCU survival issue. In this developing racial milieu, the *Geier v. Tennessee* higher education desegregation case of 1968–2000, argued in the Federal District Court of Middle Tennessee, would have complex and profound implications. Since it was considered the flagship public institution and land-grant university, the University of Tennessee had a statewide mission, and in March 1968, the General Assembly approved a UT campus in Chattanooga. Thus the Nashville Chamber of Commerce, which was launching a huge economic expansion plan for the city, wanted UT to expand its locally offered evening courses, started in 1947, into full-degree programs in Nashville. UT announced a multi-million-dollar construction project in downtown Nashville on Charlotte Avenue, almost adjacent to the First Colored Baptist Church. The Youth Division of the Nashville NAACP called on the commissioner of education and the president at A&I to explain why true racial integration at all Tennessee colleges two years after the 1964 Civil Rights Act was still not a reality. In a letter to the governor, Avon Williams and the Davidson County Independent Political Council made clear their view that Nashville should have just *one* public institution of higher education—"under the name of Tennessee A&I State University."

A history instructor, Rita Sanders, and other faculty members began to talk about A&I's lack of resources and the arrogant mistreatment it received from Tennessee officials, who never seemed to take any special circumstances, even past Jim Crow restraints, into account when budgeting for the school. The outraged Sanders, Ruth Robinson, and others contacted a white labor attorney, George E. Barrett, but refrained from further action for the time being. Their outrage, however, increased when news arrived on April 4, 1968, that Martin Luther King Jr. had been murdered in Memphis. When riots broke out, armed police barricades prevented Sanders from getting to her law school classes at Vanderbilt University. That made her even angrier, and many of the things that were wrong with American society began to weigh heavily on her mind. She believed that UT Nashville would become a four-year campus with first-rate facilities, while fifty-six-year-old A&I would be neglected and prevented from becoming the city's major public university. Rita Sanders was born in Memphis in 1944 to the Reverend Edwin and Jessie Sanders and grew up in that religious family with two other children. The Reverend Sanders moved his family to Nashville to pastor the Braden Methodist Church. At Fisk University, Rita was a good student and went on to complete her graduate education at the University of Chicago. In 1966, she obtained a temporary position teaching history at A&I.

On May 21, 1968, Barrett filed *Rita Sanders v. Governor Buford Ellington* in the federal district court of Middle Tennessee to stop the UT expansion. The Sanders plaintiffs formed an integrated group: Patrick J. Gilpin, a white

TSU professor; Harold Sweatt, a senior at nearby Wilson County High School
who intended to enroll at Tennessee A&I State University the next fall; and
Harold Sweatt Sr. The U.S. Department of Justice would be admitted as a
plaintiff based on the Civil Rights Act of 1964. Barrett and his clients argued
that the establishment of an all-white university would diminish A&I and
continue segregation of public higher education. UT president Andrew Holt
told local newspapers that upgrading facilities in Nashville would continue
and that "I hope that A. & I. will continue its fine service to the Nashville
area." On August 21, 1968, Frank Gray Jr., the federal district court judge,
denied an injunction to stop the construction. "Gray's [initial] decision really
took the wind out of my sails," Sanders later said. However, Gray ordered Tennessee to develop plans to dismantle dual higher education. The judge tried to
allow the defendants time to work out some kind of plan, but he implied that
having two racially separate institutions was not the logical solution. Frank
Gray Jr. (1908–1978) was born in Franklin, received his law degree at Cumberland University in 1928, practiced law in Franklin from 1928 to 1961, and
was mayor there from 1947 on 1961). He gained a recess appointment to the
federal bench on November 20, 1961, and served as a judge until his death.

The Tennessee State Alumni Association appointed an advisory committee and tried to take part in the presidential selection process to choose a
successor to Walter S. Davis, but State Board of Education members included
only themselves on the official committee. According to the fall 1968 *Alumni
Newsletter*, the alumni advisory committee delivered names of potential presidential candidates to the board, but none were contacted. The SBOE had
similarly appointed the institution's two previous presidents without Negro
input. On August 7, 1968, alumni advisory committee members Carlton H.
Petway, Inman E. Otey, and Erskin W. Lytle were summoned to the Office of
the Commissioner of Education and introduced to the designated president,
Andrew P. Torrence. A native of Little Rock, Arkansas, Torrence was vice
president of academic affairs at Tuskegee and a 1947 graduate of Tennessee
State, who had received his doctorate from the University of Wisconsin. The
Alumni Newsletter reported: "The Committee is irritated by the officials'
apparent lack of good faith in the process." Torrence was officially appointed
president on August 9, 1968. "The 47-year-old Dr. Torrence appears to be coming into a situation marked by bitterness and strife," wrote the *Nashville
Tennessean*. "The school seems to have become factionalized, and he would
have to be a diplomat, since Torrence was selected by Mr. [Howard] Warf and
the SBOE—apparently without proper consultation with a substantial portion of those concerned at A. & I." Addressing the opening convocation on

September 12, Torrence said that the school had to be tolerant of student demonstrations: "We cannot be passive about their interests and cannot condemn them for rejecting outmoded methods and ideas and for wanting to change situations for the better. Our colleges and universities must be willing to change from the old order."

On November 26, 1968, just twenty-five days after taking office, Torrence notified the campus community that a group of Tennessee legislators would visit A&I as part of their statewide tour to assess the needs of higher education. However, he asked the faculty members not to contact the legislators on an individual basis, as he planned to appoint faculty representatives to meet with the lawmakers. This disappointed some faculty members who had wanted to confront these state officials over the legislative proposals to limit out-of-state student enrollment to no more than 15 percent. On December 18, the SBOE approved the name change to Tennessee State University, and the General Assembly passed enabling legislation by May 8, 1969. At last, those nagging letters, a legacy of Jim Crow, were gone. But the out-of-state limit was financially devastating to TSU. UT endorsed the decision, and the SBOE deferred the out-of-state matter on May 16, 1969. However, the Tennessee Higher Education Commission (THEC), which was created in 1968 to coordinate higher education between the UT and the SBOE system, recommended that the 15 percent rule be put into effect for fall 1969. "One objection is that the limitation will cause a harmful drop in enrollment," THEC said, "although the enrollment projections indicate that this will not occur anywhere but at Tennessee State."

In 1969, the state proposed to establish more engineering programs at TSU, one at UT Nashville, and a third one for students who preferred to take courses at both institutions. The president of the UT system, Andrew Holt, assured all concerned that UT had no intention of expanding beyond an evening program in Nashville. On April 13, however, UT trustee minutes quoted Holt as saying: "We have considered for the past several years giving this campus the same status as that of the Knoxville, Memphis, Martin, and Chattanooga campuses." The trustees approved Holt's recommendation of Roy Nicks for the position of "Chancellor of the University of Tennessee–Nashville." The UT system reported that ten Negro undergraduates and four Negro graduate students were admitted to UT campuses for spring 1969 and that a total of thirty-six Negroes had been admitted to various departments of the UT School of Medicine since 1961, "compared to only 12 Negroes enrolled in the South's [white] medical schools for 1969." In April 1969, Torrence provided faculty access to copies of the statements submitted to the federal court in the case of *Rita Sanders et al. v. Buford Ellington* and said he would provide materials through the university library, since he, named as a defendant, could not discuss it. Holt was placing pressure on Torrence to drop some engineering programs.

The plaintiffs proposed recruiting black students and faculty members at white colleges and universities, establishing a remedial program to help under-prepared students, and merging TSU with UT Nashville. The state defendants, meanwhile, proposed a committee to mediate program allocation and avoid program duplication in Nashville; start cooperative programs and periodic faculty exchanges between TSU and UT Nashville; offer financial aid for disadvantaged students; recruit black students, faculty, and staff members at white colleges and universities; upgrade the appearance of the TSU campus; hire more white faculty members at TSU "to help improve program quality"; and award a unique academic program at TSU to attract white students. On May 12, 1969, Barrett declared the Tennessee plan "unacceptable," because "the authorities have an unwillingness to alter the structure and character of the system of higher education [in disfavor of whites], and [it] only focuses on achieving greater racial balance."

[*]

As the suit involving TSU and UT Nashville wound through the legal system, it would assume different names after the chief plaintiff, Rita Sanders, married and became Rita Sanders-Geier, and after new governors took office. Meanwhile, racial tensions surfaced at other state campuses.

In Memphis, on April 23, 1969, black students began sit-in demonstrations at Memphis State. James Mock of Wisconsin led the discussions. The students wanted money to bring U.S. Representative Adam Clayton Powell of New York to campus, but President Cecil C. Humphreys asked the demonstrators to leave because "we have work to do." After the police arrived, the students moved to the University Center. They contacted Maxine Smith, and she and the local NAACP pledged their support, because they had received a stream of complaints for eight years that charged discrimination against blacks at MSU, including prohibition of blacks from certain courses. Charles Evers, regional director for the NAACP in Mississippi, had spoken to eight hundred students in December 1968 and urged them to use nonviolent protests. The students said that they wanted black studies, additional black faculty members, at least one black dean, and less racism at MSU. On April 28, they launched another sit-in demonstration in President Humphreys's offices. More than one hundred of them were arrested and marched into waiting buses to be transported to jail. Maxine Smith and the NAACP engaged legal counsel for the students. The major newspapers supported Humphreys; five hundred students signed a petition in support of the black students; and Humphreys received twelve hundred signatures from students who supported his position. Miriam Sugarmon, a black faculty member and adviser to the Black Students Association, said that MSU should "reduce overt racism we feel is sometimes present in some classrooms." On May 13, the Shelby County grand jury indicted 109 persons on misdemeanor charges punishable by a jail term and a heavy fine. On May 20, the university issued deferred suspensions, allowing the students to attend classes and take examinations. The indictments were dropped, and the campus quieted down. By 2004, 26 percent of the university's students were black.

At Middle Tennessee State University, about thirty miles from Tennessee State University, there were no protests, but black students were not pleased with the situation there either. According to Avon Williams, Tennessee authorities had begun a contingency plan to strengthen MTSU while building up UT Nashville, but once efforts involving UT Nashville ran into trouble, state authorities increasingly saw MTSU as a residential haven for white students. After being forced to integrate with the 1964 Civil Rights Act, MTSU enrolled 151 Negro students by 1968–69. But many blacks shied away from the institution, which displayed a bust of Nathan Bedford Forrest, a Confederate general and Grand Wizard of the Ku Klux Klan during Reconstruction, and which had named its athletic teams the Raiders, after Forrest's rebel troops. MTSU would eventually remove the offensive symbols and modify the name of its sports teams. The black enrollment would grow in number, but the black percentage would remain much less than the percentage of the black population in Tennessee.

After the Freedom Rides of May 1961, the disturbances at Tennessee State in April 1967, and the black rebellion at Memphis State in April 1969—all of which happened during the administrations of Governor Buford Ellington—conservative state legislators, including Thomas Garland, pushed through several pieces of legislation from 1967 through 1969 that were clearly designed to suppress such protest activities. Following the resolutions of 1967 to denounce Stokely Carmichael's appearance in Nashville and a request that the U.S. attorney general deport Carmichael, the General Assembly passed an act "to make it a felony for any non-student to promote or participate in a riot at any school." One law made it a misdemeanor to "engage in standing, sitting, kneeling, lying down, or inclining so as to obstruct the ingress or egress of other persons in the use of said campus buildings," while another gave the governor power to declare a state of emergency in riots and to prohibit assemblies on streets, the bearing of firearms, and the use of certain streets and highways. Perhaps in response to the visit by Carmichael, another law made it a misdemeanor for any persons to trespass in a public school building and there to engage in disorderly conduct. It also became a criminal offense to urge children to stay out of school—a response, perhaps, to civil rights leaders who engaged high school students in daily civil rights marches.

[*]

On December 23, 1969, Judge Gray ordered plaintiffs and defendants in what was now called the *Geier* case to present serious desegregation plans by April 1, 1970. On February 9, 1970, Torrence wrote to Holt, contending that the UT cooperative engineering proposal was unacceptable. John Folger at THEC responded: "I was disappointed in your letter of February 9 to President Holt, because I feel that a greater effort could be made to work out a cooperative program in engineering. 'The fact is Negro students in Tennessee who desire an education in engineering have *traditionally* sought it here' does not mean this pattern should be continued in the future. This is not a rich state and we cannot afford the luxury of two public engineering programs in Nashville. Neither can we afford a weak, specialized program [at TSU] if it will not serve the need of the community." Folger urged Torrence to engage in "a little give and take." On February 24, Torrence presented the "TSU Plan for Desegregation" to the authorities. Some thirty-seven whites were enrolled in TSU's Graduate School. On May 26, Torrence made the desegregation report available to the faculty and selected the representatives to meet with him, state officials, and the state attorney general on campus to discuss the case.

The TSU faculty senate argued that establishing another public university in Nashville would deprive TSU of needed resources. They opposed "setting up a school for white students who don't want to integrate." The plaintiffs filed for relief on June 3, 1970, officially saying the state's plan was inadequate, a compromise that would allow duplicate programs at UT Nashville and Tennessee State and prevent TSU from becoming the sole public university in the state capital. While visiting the UT Nashville site on June 5, Holt again denied any intent to establish a full campus in Nashville. The TSU Alumni Association then issued a statement against expansion of UT Nashville: "Our alma mater can and will fulfill the state's needs and obligations in this area." They recommended stopping the UT Nashville project and, instead, merging its programs with TSU. The *Tennessean* (June 14, 1970) reported that the UT Alumni Association was "appalled" at suggestions to merge TSU with "a quality institution" like UT. Ellington said that the state would develop a specific role and scope for both UT Nashville and TSU to avoid program duplication.

President Torrence, meanwhile, was busying himself as an advocate for TSU on several fronts. On July 1, 1970, he wrote to Folger about the university's need to receive additional funding to compensate for the percentage of enrolled low-income students who required more remedial preparation for college work. Folger, in his July 10 response, rejected such extra funding, saying, "Many students from poor families do not have learning disabilities." Such thinking was typical of Tennessee officials who pretended to ignore Jim Crow's lingering and debilitating effects on black citizens. Torrence sent another letter to Folger on August 11, this time attaching a list of references and recent scholarship that backed up his position. In his September 9 reply, however, Folger remained recalcitrant.

At the same time, Torrence was urging alumni and faculty to involve themselves in addressing TSU's problems. On July 8, he sent a four-page letter to alumni, asking them to write to state legislators about increasing faculty salaries, reducing teaching loads, initiating new programs, increasing library holdings to accreditation standards, and purchasing needed equipment and general supplies. "The formula on which the state appropriation is based works to the relative disadvantage of Tennessee State University," Torrence said, adding, "During the past year, Tennessee State . . . received only 1.1 percent of the $4.5 million dollars of federal funds which were allocated to [two] land-grant colleges in Tennessee." On July 13, Torrence sent a copy of this letter to alumni, suggesting that they, too, might wish to write letters to state legislators.

And, of course, the competition from UT Nashville remained a pressing concern for Torrence. On November 27, he wrote to Holt: "Dear Andy: I indicated in the meeting on November 25, the joint committee report is disappointing. In a period when our resources are inadequate to take care of existing needs, we cannot afford to develop two largely independent, uncoordinated academic programs a mile apart in Nashville. Campus status for UTN is incidental to the resolution of this problem. From an academic point of view, UT has had a complete program here for several years, and campus status will simply recognize a *de facto* situation. We should avoid duplication and wastefully small programs."

The University of Tennessee, however, had no intention of retreating from Nashville. In April 1969, Roy S. Nicks had taken over the UT Nashville campus. The black faculty increased at UT Nashville by only 0.9 percent, while white faculty members increased at TSU from 6.7 percent to 13 percent by 1970. Torrence adopted a position that TSU and UT Nashville could jointly operate a "Nashville Center for Evening Studies," but this position would not set well with UT or the TSU alumni and faculty. UT and others, including the editors of the *Tennessean* and *Banner,* who knew well the lingering effects of the 107-year-old, white-imposed Jim Crow system, apparently found it unacceptable to have TSU in charge of local public higher education in the city and instead envisioned that role for UT. In a December 3, 1970, letter, Torrence told Folger that cooperative programs would not "dismantle the dual system." On December 9, Torrence attached a five-page "Position Paper," giving the viewpoint of the TSU administration and faculty on the desegregation plans. They argued that TSU did offer quality academic programs and should not serve only a local mission. They added that TSU was a member of the Southern Association of Colleges and Schools and other accrediting associations just as UT was, had personnel and faculty to expand service to more than its traditional black clientele, had enrolled more than forty-four hundred students from seventy-five counties in Tennessee and from across the nation, and was not willing to give up its statewide mandate and well-established programs.

On December 14, THEC approved campus status for UT Nashville. The newspapers said that Folger believed no good would be accomplished by a merger with TSU. On February 4, 1971, Torrence was called to an executive session of the State Board of Education at about 4:30 P.M. He took two administrators with him to the meeting, which was supposed to have addressed a mistake in locating a parcel of university land. After twenty minutes, however, the commissioners turned abruptly to questions about the *Geier* case and Torrence's dealings with J. K. Folger and the Tennessee Higher Education Commission. They surprised Torrence by saying that they had not been informed by Folger of the UT proposals. They intended to inform THEC and UT that the SBOE was disappointed about how the situation had been handled.

On March 9, 1971, some 250 students from TSU marched on the state capitol to protest the proposed granting of campus status to UT Nashville. That evening, Avon Williams addressed the Political Science Club at TSU, where he said that UT was shown favoritism in the General Assembly and received more money than any other public colleges and universities combined. According to the *Tennessean,* Williams said, "Blacks must realize the white man has used government and money to completely enslave not only the black man but also the poor white man. We must get at these two seats of power to change the [powerless] situation we are in today. You students represent the most important people today: blacks and poor people. Black students must participate in movements today to show the white community an example of togetherness. Blacks will never attain equality as long as they are spoon-fed by whites." TSU students, joined by President Torrence, helped pack the senate chamber. Williams failed to remove the bill that would establish UT Nashville's campus status off the senate calendar.

University of Tennessee officials began to center their argument on education for working-class people. Nicks, the UT Nashville chancellor, said, "Tennessee State . . . can't attract white students in competition with UT-Nashville." He implied that TSU would die as black students went increasingly to integrated white colleges and universities. Torrence publicly assailed Nicks's inflammatory statements. UT supporters flooded the newspapers with the UT "Desegregation Report" on June 14, 1971. UT claimed 5.2 percent black students and 1.2 percent black faculty members.

Judge Gray continued the push toward an effective plan to desegregate higher education in Tennessee, basing his rulings on precedent-setting cases: *Missouri ex rel. Gaines v. Canada* (1938), *McLaurin v. Oklahoma State Regents* (1950), and *Swann v. Charlotte-Mecklenburg Board of Education* (1971), which gave the federal courts equity power in handling desegregation of education cases to a satisfactory end. Gray prodded the parties toward "the feasibility or non-feasibility of a merger or consolidation of Tennessee State and UT-Nashville into a single institution, possibly with two campuses, under the aegis and control of the SBOE, the Board of Trustees of UT, or a combination of the two."

Torrence urged TSU alumni to help with *Geier*. On October 23, 1971, the Alumni Association charged the "State of Tennessee has conspired to destroy Tennessee A. & I. State College by subverting it either to the control of the erstwhile Jim Crow, University of Tennessee . . . or reducing the status and function of Tennessee A. & I. State College." Yet, they said, this Negro college should be praised for providing education to the deprived classes and for development of "leadership and citizenship [skills] for the survival of those classes systematically deprived by the society, even resulting from official acts of government."

Defendants in the case propounded white supremacy: TSU needed more of a "white presence." It was suspected that the attorney for the plaintiffs, George Barrett, agreed. Defendants presented data to the court showing that TSU's student body was 99.7 percent black, while its faculty was 81 percent black. In response, Torrence said that he had no problem with recruiting more

whites but that TSU needed the proper resources to mount an effective recruitment campaign. On May 26, 1972, Tennessee approved twelve-hundred-
dollar scholarships for white students to attend TSU. Again, it was predicted
that TSU would die in seven years unless it discarded its image "as a black
university." Torrence said that inadequate financing, competition from UT,
and detrimental statements uttered by Nicks would kill TSU. Torrence denied
that students and alumni wanted to keep TSU black; instead, they wished for
TSU to become the comprehensive state university for all of Middle Tennessee. On February 3, 1972, Judge Gray ordered an increased "white presence" at
TSU while suggesting consideration for *one* public university. The defendants
and UT had turned the racial argument against the blacks.

On March 27, 1972, the defendants reported back to the court to suggest
that all faculty vacancies at TSU be reserved for whites and again to propose
an exchange of faculty members between UT Nashville and TSU, more financial aid to attract whites to TSU, improvement of the physical appearance
of the TSU campus, and an agreement to transfer the UT social work program to the TSU campus but to keep it under UT administration. THEC
approved a measure that all teacher education programs in Nashville be given
to TSU, which would increase white enrollment by 150 students. The defendants also presented data to the court indicating the numbers of students from
Nashville–Davidson County who were enrolled at various public universities:
1,223 at UT Knoxville; 2,203 at MTSU; 2,287 at UT Nashville; and 1,966 at
TSU. These figures were intended to show that white students from Davidson
County preferred not to attend TSU. "If TSU is to be substantially desegregated, white students must *choose* TSU," the defendants' brief said. UT was
prepared "to enhance TSU" with the loan of twenty-six white faculty members, cooperative programs, and placing the graduate program in social work
on the TSU campus. But, the March 1972 brief added, "The attitude of the
TSU faculty is not conducive to cooperation."

The militant TSU faculty senate had rejected UT's concept of white
supremacy on April 19 when they endorsed a merger that would place UT
Nashville *under* TSU. On May 30, Torrence addressed the TSU faculty in a
letter. Noting the university's "awkward position" with regard to the court's
"mandate to dismantle the dual educational system in the State of Tennessee,"
he said, "Our University faces a tremendous challenge in this matter, and we
need the input of all concerned members of the Tennessee State University
community. I am sure we shall, together, plan the wise course for the future of
our University. We have to do *something*." In June, two key TSU faculty leaders, Raymond Richardson and Sterlin N. Adams, said that a black university

indeed could serve and educate blacks and whites without losing its historical identity. They believed that an institution could be one of quality regardless of race. State officials did not feel the same way, even though they had said in 1943 to "make Tennessee A. & I. State College for Negroes equivalent to UT for white students." The TSU faculty senate repeated its earlier contention: "The merger of UTN into the TSU program is feasible as a means of dismantling the dual system of higher education in the State of Tennessee."

In July 1972, Governor Winfield Dunn approved the request by Torrence to allow TSU to submit a position statement. But he reminded Torrence that the Tennessee Board of Regents (TBR)—created that same year by the General Assembly to govern TSU, the other five universities not in the UT system, community colleges (which had been proliferating since 1965), and state technical institutes—was in its infancy and had not had time to develop a policy. The TSU statement was the result of a questionnaire administered by the graduate school, which found that most respondents believed that "the dual system of higher education should be eliminated and a merger made feasible, with UTN brought under the control, management, and administration of Tennessee State University."

Adams and Richardson did not believe that George Barrett and his plaintiffs could truly envision a merger of UT Nashville under TSU, a historically black university. Some blacks felt that many white liberals (and some blacks, too) often based their support for black causes upon white guilt, paternalistic feelings, and a racially prejudiced belief in Negro inferiority. Avon Williams dared to say that Barrett, a white attorney, was only doing what he deemed "best for black people." Moreover, with the original plaintiffs, including Rita Sanders-Geier, now living outside Tennessee, black residents really had no say in the *Geier* case. Except for hearing objections from the TSU community and the faculty senate, white defendants and the judge were talking to another white, Barrett, and perhaps, as Williams speculated, Barrett thought he knew what was best for black people in the *Geier* case. And by that, Williams suspected, he may have meant what was best for *white* people in Nashville.

In light of all this, TSU faculty leaders Adams and Richardson met with Williams, a black attorney and legislator with decades of civil rights experience. On July 31, 1972, they prepared a plaintiffs-intervener petition, which was signed by Adams, and delivered to the federal district court in downtown Nashville on Broad Street. The impressive petition involved more than a hundred black Tennesseans, including Maxine and Vasco Smith, Carl E. Johnson, Kathryn Bowers, Ezekiel Bell, Minerva J. Johnican, and "infants by their parents" in Memphis. Williams, who far outdistanced Barrett in legal skills in civil rights cases, asked the court to allow new plaintiff interveners based on the Thirteenth and Fourteenth Amendments. The Adams-Richardson petition partly read as follows:

> Permanent injunction to restrain and enjoin the defendants from continuing to operate the public institutions of higher education of the State of Tennessee on a racially dual and discriminatory basis. . . . The class action suit is on behalf of the intervening plaintiffs and all others similarly situated in Tennessee, including black minor children that will attend public institutions of higher education in Tennessee. . . . The defendants' proposals are purportedly only intended as possible temporary steps to deal with what defendants see as the problem: Tennessee State University (rather than the entire racially oriented higher education system). Their implementation will in fact largely determine the content and direction of any further steps, which defendants might propose in accordance with the order of this Court, and they almost inevitably foreshadow an unwarranted attempt to abolish Tennessee State University as a Tennessee institution by assimilation into the campus of the University of Tennessee.

Other NACCP-LDF attorneys who joined the case included Carl A. Cowan, Jack Greenberg, Lou Lucas, and Bill Caldwell.

The new plaintiffs were a brilliant bunch. They knew that the issues of class (which UT Nashville had argued) *and* race must also include local community colleges, which fed the four-year colleges. The two-year colleges could enhance (or impede) higher education opportunities for poor Tennesseans, who made up 20 percent of the state's white population and nearly a third of its black citizens. Therefore, the plaintiffs asked the court to declare "a single non-segregated campus rather than segregated units that shall be established for the Shelby County Community College in Shelby County." Jessie H. Turner and Maxine Smith represented the Memphis Branch NAACP in testimony against the attempt of authorities to split the predominantly black Shelby State into two sites, which likely would prevent the institution from ever achieving full integration. The plaintiffs argued that state officials had purchased land for the Shelby County project and likely would attempt to establish a community college also in Davidson County to further deter integration and hinder black citizens' access to quality education. The plaintiffs requested the court to enjoin the state from instituting a plan to move Shelby State Community College from downtown Memphis to east Shelby County, where the white population had shifted. State authorities intended to build a new campus there, but this would force blacks to commute rather than cause whites to travel downtown. Black citizens argued that to move the community college to predominantly white east Shelby County would also perhaps limit the number of Negro junior college students eligible to enroll at MSU, which, if its student body were to be a true reflection of the local population and its high school graduation rates, should be 42 percent black. In June 1973, the plaintiffs gained a federal court injunction to halt the plans. The battle would continue for twenty-seven years until white leaders wore the black leaders down, affecting "a merger" of Shelby State Community College and Memphis Technical State Institute into the Southwest Tennessee Community College, with two main campuses, one downtown and one in east Memphis. Students had freedom of choice to attend either campus.

Meanwhile, Maxine Smith reported that the local NAACP's education committee had met with the MSU president and department heads to help them move faster toward increasing the number of black professionals at the university. In the March 3–April 6, 1971, report, she wrote, "The NAACP group was not impressed with the university's willingness or intention to comply with this request." The institution had retained more than its share of racial conservatives on the faculty and staff, and they were opposed to increasing a black presence at MSU, period. In the local NAACP report for 1977, the executive secretary reported, "A goodly number of complaints against Memphis State University, charging discrimination in admissions, grading, and general treatment of black students." The following year's Memphis Branch NAACP report also noted that "Discriminatory practices and racist attitudes still plague students at Memphis State University." The institution only had thirty Negro professionals working there.

[*]

Now that they intended to take *Geier* out of Barrett's hands, Adams and Richardson used a cooperative leadership structure that had been effective in the Nashville Student Movement. They organized Tennesseans for Justice in Higher Education (TJHE), recruited leaders in Memphis and Knoxville, and united black educators, parents, public school children, college students, and civic leaders in the three grand regions of the state. Similar to what had been done for *Brown*, the new *Geier* plaintiffs prepared some convincing reports on higher education. A professional journalist, Reginald Stuart, with monetary support from the John Hay Whitney Foundation, published *Black Perspectives on State-Controlled Higher Education: The Tennessee Report* in November 1973. Stuart, a graduate of TSU, wrote, "The state is dragging its feet on desegregation of its institutions. Black enrollment in proportion to white enrollment declined from 1970 to 1972." William B. Vaughn, the president of the Tennessee NAACP, wrote in the foreword: "I firmly believe that the information and statistics presented in this document are evidence that state officials of Tennessee are far behind in their responsibilities and commitments to the citizenry, especially blacks." The State of Tennessee, he declared, was dragging its feet "in carrying out the court's order to dismantle the dual system of higher education, without placing a disproportionate burden on black citizens or institutions, and in insuring equality of opportunity and successful results for black participants in public higher education." According to the state's *1973 Desegregation Report*, 38 black faculty members (0.9 percent) worked at white public colleges in 1969, and only 108 (1.9 percent) worked in such institutions by 1973. The percentage of black faculty at TSU decreased to 70 percent. Nationally, 2.7 percent of doctorates awarded in 1973 went to blacks, and 2.2 percent of America's faculty members were blacks.

Judge Gray allowed the Adams-Richardson plaintiffs to present their plan. TSU president Andrew Torrence, however, was confused, frustrated, and worried. He even tried to hire counsel to represent him and the institution, since UT and others already had lawyers representing them. Avon Williams's group met quietly with Torrence and assured him that "although we were not representing the institution [TSU] in name, we were actually representing it in substance and effectively doing so." In late 1973, Torrence was stunned again when a black state legislator, Harold E. Ford of Memphis, called for the president and all other administrators at TSU to be fired for failing to maintain quality programs. "Tennessee State means too much to Tennessee and the nation to allow it to die," Ford said. The president of the TSU Alumni Association chapter in Memphis said that college presidents had to stay clear of politics and added, "If you compare the progress of TSU from 1912 to 1973, it would be likened unto a man taking brass and making gold out of it." He declared the alumni's support for Torrence and the merger of UT Nashville under Tennessee State University. State Senator J. O. Patterson of Memphis blasted Ford for his hasty remarks and pledged the support of the legislative black caucus for TSU. Perhaps because of his intent to run for Congress, Ford patched up his differences with TSU alumni, students, and fellow politicians over his unfortunate criticisms of the Torrence administration, and he even introduced an $8.5 million appropriations bill for Tennessee State University in 1974.

On April 4, 1974, during the lunch hour, Torrence called a hasty meeting in the Administration Building auditorium and announced his resignation, effective October 1, 1974. The astonished audience wondered what had happened behind the scenes to make the president resign. Some speculated that "white people at the Board of Regents and in the governor's office either threatened or had asked Dr. Torrence to do something he just could not do to his people." Avon Williams said, "We felt that Dr. Torrence, an able man, simply grew tired of the continuing conflict involved in the struggle by the state to maintain UTN as a four year degree granting institution in competition with and at the door step of TSU." For his part, Torrence explained:

> The agreement when I accepted the presidency of Tennessee
> State was that we would have autonomy equal to that of any
> other public institution of higher education under the State Board
> of Education, which was our governing board at that time. . . .
> Through the years, Tennessee State University's financial prob-
> lems have been enormous. Although there have been some
> improvements, we are still plagued in this area. In the largest
> measure our plight is due to the historical neglect suffered by the
> university—disproportionate state and federal funds, compared
> with other public higher education institutions and land-grant
> colleges, have hampered efforts to maintain a sound financial
> under girding for our programs.

The TSU faculty had declined from 333 to 280 since 1968, and the out-of-state rule diminished the enrollment and thus the budget. Torrence said that the university had excellent audits, more grants and gifts, and better programs. "The university stands poised to render expanded services to people of all races who accept its invitation to 'Enter to Learn and Go Forth to Serve'. . . . I want to return to research, contemplation, and writing," he said.

On April 12, 1974, the *Tennessean* reported, "Defendant (UT) believes that Tennessee State University must address the questions of its own academic standards and the quality of its programs before it can attract any substantial number of white students from the Nashville commuting area either for day or night classes." UT Nashville claimed 10 percent black students, and MTSU enrolled more students [whites] from Davidson County–Nashville than did TSU. In fact, since the Jim Crow normal school days, MTSU had enrolled the white students from Davidson County. In September 1976, when court arguments were heard, hundreds of TSU students marched on the U.S. Courthouse, chanting, "Save TSU." A UT Nashville student group also showed up with a similar petition to save their downtown campus. Torrence boldly testified that the only way to transfer programs from UT Nashville to TSU was for the judge to so order it; he said that the same national and regional associations that accredited programs at UT's Knoxville campus had accredited the TSU programs. Torrence also told the court that UT officials refused to discuss program allocations unless he agreed to retract the TSU faculty position that called for a merger. Avon Williams, however, was not so gentle with the defendants. He argued that Tennessee had been pouring money into MTSU to create a safe haven for white students, while neglecting TSU's needs, and he said that UT had pursued a "thinly veiled effort to disguise racial prejudice." At that point, Folger and Williams got into a heated argument, but Judge Gray quieted things down.

On May 20, 1974, Adams and Richardson published an open letter to the state's citizens: "For more than two years Tennesseans for Justice in Higher Education has been consistent in efforts to promote equity in opportunity for blacks in public higher education. . . . We have analyzed figures and presented data, which show that inequity exists in all phases of higher education activity in the state. Our involvement to alleviate the unfairness in the system has occurred on many fronts." The letter, which was circulated on the TSU campus, mentioned initiating legislation, lobbying for other acts, becoming plaintiff-interveners in the *Geier v. Dunn* case, coordinating more than fifty citizens from across Tennessee, securing legal representation to gain entry to other cases, and organizing clinics and workshops in communities across Tennessee. Enclosed with the letter was Stuart's *Black Perspectives*. In a July 24 letter to the chancellor for the Board of Regents, Torrence openly expressed his opposition to the idea of TSU being placed under the UT Board of Trustees. He again called for TSU to be open to all people who wanted to attend the institution.

Andrew Torrence had exhibited great courage when he dared to remind Tennessee officials that he had inherited a Jim Crow institution that was operating under heavy debts and constantly trying to make ends meet. With the reactionary legislation that placed a limit on out-of-state student enrollment, state lawmakers had undermined the efforts of the presidents. Torrence made public the ways in which his predecessor, President Davis, had made Herculean efforts to make A&I for Negroes "equivalent to UT for white students." The debt service at TSU was $215 per student compared to $142 at white universities under the Tennessee Board of Regents. The interest rate on TSU dormitories was an overbearing 6 percent, while TSU owed $11.59 million on the dormitories. To raise the student dormitory fees, however, would lower the occupancy rates, negatively affect enrollment, and jeopardize the budget.

Curtailment of out-of-state enrollment caused the percentage of out-of-state students to decline from 41.4 percent to 20.8 percent in five years, and it took away the real bread-and-butter revenues. The university's full-time enrollment reached 5,458 students in 1966–67 but would not reach the projected 7,400 students by 1969. Rising tuition costs deterred black college enrollment, as Negro families had a per capita income lower than that for whites. By 1970, some 60 percent of Tennessee State's students had family incomes below five thousand dollars, as compared to 18.7 percent at Austin Peay, 26 percent at Tennessee Tech, 22.4 percent at East Tennessee State, 19.6 percent at Middle Tennessee State, and 18.9 percent at Memphis State. The out-of-state restrictions caused TSU to limit its recruitment efforts to more middle-class families from large urban areas of the North and South—families that could afford to pay out-of-state fees.

TSU could not profit from reserve funds, because state agencies controlled the institution's business operations. After finding that Hale had advanced the institution through a secret reserve fund, state officials sent in auditors, took over the finances, fired President Hale, and confiscated reserve funds of $317,000—which they never returned to the institution. In 1967, Tennessee officials again sent in auditors, confiscated the financial operations, and placed their own man in that critical business position. Even a THEC report of May 14, 1970, seemed appalled that "TSU was perhaps the only public institution in Tennessee that did not and could not profit from the use of its reserve funds." When A&I regained control of its business operations on July 1, 1969, the reserves and auxiliary income, totaling $621,892, had to support general operations. Although the federal government sent grant-in-aid funds to Tennessee, state officials made sure the federal monies disproportionately benefited the predominantly white University of Tennessee and left blacks at an educational disadvantage as had occurred under Jim Crow practices. In 1969–70, TSU began receiving $19,500 a year in research funds directly from the U.S. Department of Agriculture. Under Richard Nixon's administration, this amount would increase to $747,861. In Tennessee, where the Democrats held on to Jim Crow, this was still just 15 percent of what the white land-grant university received. No government officials in Tennessee ever redressed this eighty-four-year-old grievance through affirmative action, a reparation program, or a simple apology.

In August 1974, the Tennessee Board of Regents appointed Charles B. Fancher, the TSU dean of faculty, as acting president. Officials asked Fancher for reports on the quality of TSU's programs. He pointed out that TSU had been approved by the regional agency (SACS) since 1946, had recently achieved reaccreditation of its teacher education program, and had gained first-time accreditation of most of its engineering programs in 1972. The institution would achieve accreditation of the nursing program, the home economics program, and reaffirmation of accreditation of the undergraduate social work program by 1975. Fancher acknowledged the need to accredit chemistry, and he was proceeding to expand TSU programs to include a higher degree in education and an evening program with a director. (Interestingly, at this time, Charles W. Smith, a future head of UT Nashville, was working on his doctorate at UT and soliciting input for his dissertation, "Transfer Influencing Factors," which questioned why white students did not want to attend TSU.)

As black leaders dug deeper into the awful history of Jim Crow higher education in Tennessee, they became angrier; state officials and local business leaders, on the other hand, seemed to have historical amnesia. To blacks it was as though whites were saying, "The Jim Crow past is dead, and although we did these awful, debilitating things to you, your children, and their future, now we must move on toward the so-called integrated society where you blacks still must play by our rules." On August 1, 1974, Tennesseans for Justice in Higher Education rejected all ideas for merger except for merger of UT Nashville under TSU. The group demanded the appointment of a black person to head the University of Tennessee Board of Trustees or the Tennessee Board of Regents, as well as a black president, vice president of academic affairs, vice president of student affairs, and vice president of financial affairs at the merged institution; after all, no blacks held such positions at any of Tennessee's white public institutions. The TJHE also wanted to see black students, faculty, and staff members in the UT system at a level of 16.3 percent. The organization also wanted certain programs to be assigned exclusively to TSU. On October 23, 1974, the TSU Alumni Association reprinted its position paper, in which Tennessee State was cited for developing higher education for the "deprived classes of citizens and developing leadership and citizenship [skills] for the survival of those classes systematically deprived by the society, even resulting from official acts of [Tennessee] government. The State of Tennessee has conspired to destroy TSU by subverting it either to the control of the erstwhile Jim Crow, the UT, or reducing the status and function of TSU." TSU alumni called on all citizens to resist any further "covert moves by state government."

TJHE outlined a plan to merge UT Nashville into TSU and prevent the displacement of the black administration. They formed an advisory committee consisting of notable figures in black higher education: Elias Blake, Norman Francis (president of Xavier University), John Griffin (of the Southern Education Foundation in Atlanta), Vivian Henderson (president of Clark College in Atlanta), and Herman Long (president of Talladega College). A faculty member at Fort Valley State College in Georgia and a technical expert from Fisk University were hired to prepare the final draft of the plan. As Avon Williams observed, whites viewed this plan with horror; he believed that the Nashville Chamber of Commerce and the editors of the city's two daily newspapers were using their power and influence on the side of UT. In a countermove, Adams published *Tennessee Planning for Desegregation in Public Higher Education and Black Citizen Reaction and Interaction: A Critical Review of Geier v. Blanton From a Black Perspective* (1975), whose data and analysis made state officials appear untruthful.

By a vote of 7–4, a split Board of Regents selected a new president for TSU: Frederick S. Humphries, a Ph.D. in chemistry who headed a national educational agency in Washington, D.C. Physically, he towered over most other men and had his hair styled into a large Afro as Sterlin Adams and many young blacks did during the 1970s. After coming aboard in January 1975, Humphries selected Sterlin Adams as the presidential assistant. Adams helped the newcomer build a strong relationship with the legislative black caucus, because he certainly would need it. On April 1, 1975, Humphries sent a letter to caucus members Harper Brewer, Dedrick Withers, and John Ford: "Additional expansion of the UT-Nashville, whether it be in the area of responsibility for programs and services or physical plant will duly complicate the desegregation of higher education in Nashville. Therefore, we urge you to work against the funding of any such [UT Nashville] request. We feel that representatives of Tennessee State University should be allowed to make known its view for the Finance Ways and Means Committee of both houses." Adams frequently sent Senator Williams written materials to enlist the black caucus to pressure state officials. Marcus Lucas, president of the Student Government Association, and his officers also sent a letter to Senator Williams on May 6, 1975, saying, "As students of the university, we are the recipients of the discomforts, inconveniences, limitations on programming, and constraints on future potential and success." Williams demanded a detailed TBR funding report on higher education facilities.

On cross-examination in federal court, President Humphries agreed that Tennessee had imposed a disparate burden of desegregation on TSU while denying it the financial and logistical resources needed for the job. It was difficult to attract white students to a rundown physical plant and to an institution that always suffered from a lack of resources. Richardson established in his testimony a clear discrimination in faculty salaries and resources that in effect denied black people opportunities for post-graduate education. Adams, Edward Isibor (the TSU dean of engineering), and Elias Blake gave more ammunition to use against the defendants.

In 1975, Roy Nicks was promoted from chancellor at UT Nashville to chancellor of the Tennessee Board of Regents. The TBR, THEC, and the UT Board of Trustees—the state's three higher education governing boards—were all singing the same tune, and the other "defendant," Humphries, was expected to sing that tune, too. However, in January 1975, Edward Boling, president of UT, complained to the new governor, Ray Blanton, that one official [Humphries] was "calling for a merger [which] makes our job more difficult." This "did not allow defendants to make a united front," said Boling. At a Tennessee Board of Regents meeting, Avon Williams recalled that Governor Blanton and other officials took Humphries into a restroom "and lashed him like a slave" with their rebuke of his position.

Cecille E. Crump, president of the faculty senate, wrote to the chairman of the black caucus on February 10, 1976: "For the past eight years during the [Geier] court litigation, we have been struggling against innumerable odds to maintain and develop further an institution of higher education for all people. Our deterrent has been the competition engendered by another publicly funded institution in the city. The UTN position is that they are in need of additional physical facilities for their evening-time operation. Their request strengthens the need for the state to merge the two institutions under Tennessee State University."

State authorities gave UT Nashville new, high-demand programs: a master's in business administration and a bachelor's in nursing. A joint master's degree in public administration would be established, but all courses would be given at UT Nashville. TSU began offering graduate courses in public administration in the fall of 1976, but no formal action had been taken to create the proposed joint MPA degree program. The two institutions had students enrolled in duplicate programs, although TSU had seventy-three degree programs and UT Nashville had nine. The B.A. and B.S. degree programs in arts and sciences at UT Nashville provided twenty-four areas of concentration for students but really did not allow a student to earn a degree in, say, computer science, mathematics, and other majors as at the larger TSU. The UT Nashville faculty cleverly gave the students many concentrations under a "general degree in arts and sciences"—a scheme of duplicating TSU offerings without acknowledging it outright. Class attendance and grading was slack, and even students who only had a high school certificate (GED) were admitted to UT Nashville. A U.S. Department of Justice brief noted, "The state-imposed identification of TSU as a black institution and of UTN as a white institution is the major reason that whites attend UTN."

A twenty-day evidentiary hearing in the Geier trial was held from September through October 1976. At the Geier table was Barrett's young assistant,

Aletha Arthur, who today serves on the Federal District Court of Middle Tennessee. Franz Marshall represented the U.S. Department of Justice against Tennessee, and Drew Days represented the NAACP's interest. Among those at the defendants' table were William Joe Haynes, an African American who now serves on the Federal District Court of Middle Tennessee; he represented the Tennessee Attorney General's office, and was joined by Thomas Wardlaw Steele, special counsel for UT, and Beauchamps Brogan, house counsel for UT. When the plaintiffs showed that UT Nashville had been established with the collaboration of the Nashville Chamber of Commerce, Eddie Jones, head of the Nashville Chamber, had no real defense about not supporting the enhancement and integration of TSU. Jones, however, did fire a shot at Avon Williams by saying that the chamber was not prejudiced: it had Negro members, "including Avon N. Williams Jr." Williams coolly responded that he had resigned his membership to protest the lack of input by Negroes into chamber policy-making. The plaintiffs pointed out that authorities had recently prevented UT from widening its programs in Memphis and thereby competing with Memphis State University. Outside the federal courthouse, TSU students demonstrated with signs reading, "UTN No TSU Yes" and "UTN + TSU = TSU." They were insisting that Tennessee State become Davidson County's only public university.

The court's comprehensive opinion found that the dual race system had *not* been dismantled, that "egregious" constitutional violations had *not* been remedied, that the defendants' approach to desegregation had *not* worked and had no prospect of working, that the defendants had impeded the dismantling of the dual system, and that a merger was the only effective and constitutionally permissible remedy. On January 21, 1977, Judge Gray ruled for a merger of UT Nashville into TSU.

CHAPTER 11

AFTER *GEIER* AND THE MERGER

DESEGREGATION OF HIGHER EDUCATION
IN TENNESSEE CONTINUES

On Saturday, February 12, 1977, Chancellor Charles E. Smith of UT Nashville told the University of Tennessee Board of Trustees: "Judge Gray's [*Geier*] decision has produced a chilling effect on our campus." On February 22, because of how the news media had interpreted his remarks, implying that he would simply comply with the court order, Smith sent a letter to the Tennessee Board of Regents to clear up any misunderstandings. He also sent a message from his faculty, saying, "I must tell you in all candor that reports from the Board of Regents meeting Thursday did nothing to allay the concerns expressed in the [UT Nashville] council's statement and the uncertainties which have resulted from the court's decision. As a matter of fact, the piecemeal approach to dismantling UTN which was approved in the regents' merger implementation plan has had the opposite effect on our campus and is being interpreted by those who have read the plan as a takeover rather than a merger." On February 22, 1977, UT Nashville faculty members filed a motion to be admitted as plaintiffs. On February 28, Gray denied the motion as untimely "since merger of the two institutions has been a proposal before the court for several years."

The U.S. Department of Justice and the NAACP agreed with Gray's ruling, but they pointed out, "Black faculty members were paid substantially less than similarly situated whites, on the average between $208 and $960 more per year than blacks [and] in 1901 Tennessee became the first state to pass criminal statutes requiring racial segregation in all public and private colleges." In April 1977, the University of Tennessee, the State of Tennessee, and the Tennessee Higher Education Commission appealed the Gray judgment. Thomas Wardlaw Steele, the UT special counsel, argued, "It is certainly no constitutional violation for UTN to expand its program; the court has not suggested to the contrary. Secondly, the existence of UTN is not necessarily unconstitutional solely because it has a racially disproportionate impact, but rather, to be unconstitutional, must ultimately be traced to a racially discriminatory purpose." Nevertheless, on May 11, the TBR filed "A Plan for the Merger of Tennessee State University and the University of Tennessee–Nashville." Students who had enrolled in a degree program at UT Nashville prior to February 29 would be given the option of earning a degree from TSU after transfer of the program to TSU, or of earning a degree from UT, subject to the approval of the Board of Trustees. Tenure, rank, salary, seniority, and job security went to UT Nashville faculty members.

On June 13, 1977, Richardson and Adams came to Williams's office at 1414 Parkway Towers to sign the certificate for the motions stating their objection to the TBR's merger plan because it was no more than a set of committees that "establishes a framework for the TSU administration to be taken over by white administrators." The plan guaranteed continued employment for UT Nashville faculty and staff but did not explicitly do the same for TSU faculty and provided no protection for the TSU president. On June 22, 1977, Williams filed objections of the plaintiff-interveners, which stated, "The plan was generated by the current Chancellor [Nicks] of said TBR who has a blatant conflict of interest in his former relationships with UT and UTN. [He] has been inimical towards the legitimate interests of TSU in all his actions during the history and trial of this case, including his testimony. [His] adversary position is clearly reflected in the composition of said entire proposal which he prepared and submitted to the TBR for its approval and submission to this Court." NAACP-LDF lawyers supported the appeal and the motion for further relief. They invited Williams and his associates to New York to hear a dry run of the argument in a law class at Columbia University.

Chancellor Smith shared court documents with all UT Nashville faculty and staff, and the dean of arts and sciences included a status report on the agenda for the faculty meeting. "Because the merger was to take place by July 1, 1979," Smith said, "if the district court's order was reversed by the 6th Circuit, or even the Supreme Court, UT defendants would find themselves in

373

the unenviable position of having a clear right to operate UTN for which it has no available faculty, no funding, no property, no students, no administrators, and no hope of unscrambling an accomplished merger." On May 30, 1977, he shared with UT Nashville faculty members and administrators the lengthy transcript of the recent discussion of a state appeal filed by THEC on April 4. At their meeting in Johnson City, seven THEC members voted for appeal, and two members voted no. On June 21, Smith sent a memorandum to faculty and staff: "The last filing to the court made by Senator Avon Williams in the desegregation litigation has been distributed; if you would like to review that material, please check with your dean or director." The next day Smith sent another copy of "the desegregation litigation by Williams, along with a copy of Gray's response, to UTN members."

Despite the various appeals, Judge Gray refused to stay the July 1, 1979, merger. Roy Nicks sent a memorandum to Smith, notifying him to deliver a list of merger committee appointments by July 7, 1977. On the advice of UT counsel, Smith declined to send any merger committee appointments. Instead, UT Nashville officials prepared a statement to be read to telephone callers, indicating their opposition to the court-ordered merger. UT Nashville faculty gathered in little groups to hear any news about the appeals. The assistant to Governor Blanton, Eddie Sisk, wrote an executive memorandum indicating that he had spoken with UT officials to reaffirm their support against the merger. Sisk said that the UT president and chancellor had made it clear that they intended to fight all the way to the United States Supreme Court. Sisk also said, according to President Boling, "One of our greatest allies is John Seigenthaler [then editor of the *Tennessean*] who realized that the only way TSU can be upgraded is to become a part of the University of Tennessee and the UT system." Sisk told Blanton that UT was going to make some moves to shore up its chances with the Supreme Court. "As a first step, UT would like to add a member of the Board of Trustees from Davidson County and request that the governor appoint a black girl to that position," said Sisk. Apparently Blanton agreed, because a black female graduate of UT Nashville was appointed to the UT board. THEC and the TBR also had black members.

Rumors circulated that the governor intended to fire President Humphries outright. Adams, Richardson, black caucus members, and others organized a caravan of cars and citizens to attend the next TBR meeting. Instead, the regents and Governor Blanton (the ex officio chairman of TBR) placed Humphries on probation for fiscal mismanagement and "unsolved problems" at TSU. Blacks remembered the white officials' fiscal and audit moves in 1942 and 1967, which had led to the resignations of presidents Hale and Davis. A dispirited Humphries reportedly called his circle of friends in Atlanta and Washington, D.C., to say he would resign. They told him to stay put and to let them handle the situation. E. Harper Johnson, president of local chapter of Alpha Phi Alpha Fraternity, Inc., of which Humphries was a member, sent Blanton a letter on July 8, saying, "I would like to point out that the revelation of Dr. Humphries' administrative difficulties became public following the court decision for the merger of UTN and Tennessee State University. The timing of the incidents raised some suspicions in the black community that one thing provoked another." Johnson asked that Humphries not be held accountable for errors of previous administrators: "We also believe that Dr. Humphries received some bad advice on his arrival [in Nashville] as a new person from outside the State. But we believe, after talking to him, Humphries will become a great administrator. We are asking you and the Board of Regents to consider an extension of time for him to do the job." Johnson reminded Blanton that four of the state legislators and Congressman Ford belonged to the Alpha Phi Alpha fraternity. Governor Blanton answered Johnson on July 21: "The Board has asked Dr. Humphries to identify the problems of the university to the Board to demonstrate that he can work toward solving the problems. The nine-month period given by the board for this purpose seems adequate under these circumstances. I know there is not a move to replace black leadership at Tennessee State with white leadership. I am personally committed to having strong black educators in our state system and I know that Dr. Nicks and the board are equally committed." In mid-August 1977, Gordon W. Sweet at the Southern Association for Colleges and Schools asked for a "report on news reports that the Tennessee Board of Regents had passed a June 24, 1977 Resolution, relative to the effectiveness or ineffectiveness of Dr. Frederick Humphries as president of Tennessee State University." From Atlanta, Sweet sent copies of his letter to Humphries, THEC, Nicks, and others. This startled Blanton, and after conferring with higher education officials, the governor responded within five days that the problems at TSU were related to matters in admission and records and business affairs and that it was not a resolution but a motion by the vice chairman of the Board of Regents: "The board did not place Dr. Humphries on probation but advised him of their concern and their expectations." Humphries survived the one-year "probation," but Nicks sent him letter after letter, forcing the TSU president to spend an inordinate amount of time responding to inquiries, petty complaints, and reports. On a visit to TSU on November 8, 2001, years after his tenure as president, Humphries recalled, "There were times that I went home to the president's house and just lay across the bed, and let the heat and the stress flow from my body. Hardly a day passed when Roy Nicks did not write me a letter, and every letter I answered, promptly. Those were hard years for Tennessee State and me."

On August 23, 1977, Chancellor Charles Smith announced, "Judge Gray has denied the University of Tennessee's motion for a stay in the implementation of the merger plan." On September 13, Smith sent his faculty a copy of the UT motion to the Sixth Circuit Court of Appeals. A two-page "Notice to UTN Students" read in part: "The University will continue to make every effort to have the merger decision reversed. It does feel that it is important for students to be aware of the possibilities." Classes at UT Nashville began at 5:00 P.M. and lasted into the night, and few students handled a normal load of credits (fourteen credits or more) as did the traditional college students at Tennessee State and Vanderbilt University. Faculty members at UT Nashville, who feared loss of student enrollment, reportedly used their classrooms as a soapbox and poisoned many students' minds against the idea of attending TSU.

On November 16, the UT Nashville faculty senate convened. Smith, the vice presidents, and deans also were present. An ad hoc committee continued to tinker with a faculty exchange program with TSU, as if this gesture would save UT Nashville. One faculty member reported that the school's full-time-equivalent enrollment had declined from 2,586 in the fall of 1976 to 2,562 for 1977, even though the head count rose. UT Nashville had reached a point of "flat" enrollment. The faculty member pointed out that the proportion of blacks remained steady, between 14 and 15 percent, although the area's black population was nearly 25 percent. Approximately 68.9 percent of TSU's faculty was black, but 95.9 percent of UT Nashville's faculty was white. TSU had 6,138 actual head-count students in 1976, and 7 percent of the students taking courses on the TSU campus were whites, not including adult students taking courses at its off-campus centers. In 1972, UT Nashville had reported 3,500 students (including an 11 percent black enrollment), an estimate of a 9,000-student enrollment eight years later, and a projection that TSU would stagnate at 6,150 students by the next decade.

During this period, racism remained an issue at UT's main campus in Knoxville. On October 23, 1978, UT students belonging to the Afro-American Liberation Force met with university counsel and President Ed Boling to discuss the university's investments in companies doing business with South African firms. During the meeting, the general counsel for the Board of Trustees reportedly told the black students, "If you are so concerned about South Africa, why don't you go over there?" The students regarded the statement as insensitive and indicative of the racist climate on the campus. According to its 1978 report, the legislative black caucus was informed of these concerns by several UT Knoxville faculty members at its annual retreat, which met that year at Fairfield Glades on November 26–28. The following year Dr. Luther Kindall, chairman of the Commission for Blacks at UT Knoxville, sent a letter to the faculty senate on October 29, asking why "Coach Don DeVoe had hired no black assistant coaches or trainers." Kindall persuaded the senate to investigate the athletic department, and he also got the body to agree to do a study of black faculty positions and racial representation in the senate. The chancellor agreed to place the athletic department under the Office of Affirmative Action.

[*]

After Ned Blanton left the governor's office in January 1979, the *Geier* case became *Geier v. Governor Lamar Alexander.* Winfred W. Jenkins, the SGA president at TSU, sent the new governor a letter, asking about his position on the ongoing case: "Be assured we do not wish, nor intend at this time, to question the integrity of any officials having oversight authority for our University though we will remain vigilant." Blacks were concerned that state officials would continue to try to replace Humphries in an effort to "kill TSU." Humphries, meanwhile, was holding late-night meetings with supporters in the president's home to inform them of problems with his superiors and to instigate their intervention to answer the threats. In a paper written a few years earlier, Humphries had said, "The white system of higher education cannot be entrusted with the complete education of Black Americans. . . . The sooner the nation begins to express this view that there is an expectation of black colleges to participate in higher education in the future without special contingencies, the sooner this nation can begin to cast aside the last vestiges of segregation and racism."

Avon Williams continued to complain about lack of progress in affording equal access of black students, faculty, and staff personnel to the historically white institutions. The Justice Department still wanted the case to be sent back to the district court for further findings on statewide faculty discrimination. The U.S. Appeals Court agreed and remanded the *Geier* case to the district court, saying that it had "unquestioned power to redress or prevent retaliation against President Humphries." However, there was no specific order for Judge Gray to hold new hearings.

The TSU–UT Nashville, merger took effect on July 1, 1979. The merged *General Catalog, Tennessee State University* (revised 1979–81), was designed to ease the tensions between the two faculty groups:

> The present-day Tennessee State University exists as a result of
> the merger on July 1, 1979 of the former Tennessee State Univer-
> sity and the University of Tennessee at Nashville. The General
> Assembly sanctioned the UTN as a bona fide campus of the UT
> in 1971, and the new university occupied its quarters in the then
> recently completed building at the corner of Tenth and Charlotte.
> It was the erection of the above-mentioned building which gave
> rise to a decade-long litigation to "dismantle the dual system" of
> higher education in Tennessee which culminated in the court
> ordered merger by Judge Frank Gray in February, 1977. The mis-
> sions of the two universities were highly compatible due to their
> historic backgrounds or connection to a land-grant institution.

TSU was required to continue to use the former UT Nashville campus as "the downtown campus" for evening studies and other functions. Former UT Nash-ville administrators were placed over the School of Business and School of Education, and TSU administrators retained dean positions in the other five schools. Care was taken to achieve racial balance in lower administrative positions. By 1981, TSU had 51 percent black faculty compared to 71.6 per-cent in 1975, meaning that 49 percent of the remaining faculty represented other races. At that time, no other public university in Tennessee had minor-ity faculty members at a level higher than 6.9 percent. In 1981, only 2.4 per-cent of the UT Knoxville faculty members were black, compared to 2.7 per-cent in 1975, and those numbers would not budge for the next generation. Memphis State University had 3.5 percent black faculty in 1981, compared to 3.2 percent in 1975. TBR Chancellor Nicks said in 1981 that the rural loca-tion of some institutions was a barrier to recruiting black faculty, but added, "I am not satisfied with the progress we have made in faculty recruitment."

Many UT Nashville faculty members left for other jobs. Those who re-mained petitioned unsuccessfully for jobs on other UT campuses. A core group of former UT Nashville members believed that their only hope was to form a dissident movement to discredit the black administration and develop a case for a greater white presence. TSU was too black, they believed, and until it was predominantly white, few whites in racially divided America would consider it a quality institution. The turmoil, the negative daily press, and rumors contributed to a gradual decline in white student enrollment, from about 37 percent to 27 percent; thus, while the anticipated total enrollment from the merger was to have been nearly nine thousand, it actually numbered less than sixty-six hundred students within six years of the merger, causing severe budget cuts and the release of 20 percent of TSU staff members.

The TSU campus needed renovation, an adequate budget for maintenance of buildings and grounds, and expanded facilities to handle a larger and more diverse student body. In February 1979, Senator Avon Williams worked with President Humphries and Mayor Richard Fulton to have streetlights and sidewalks placed on the major streets crossing the TSU campus. However, Governor Alexander cut the TSU budget from $16,432,300 to $15,877,300 in January 1980, while leaving money "that satisfies the stipulation of the court-ordered merger." In March 1980, Humphries held a luncheon and tour of the campus for Williams and other caucus members, pointing out the needs for repair, maintenance, and improvements in campus facilities. As president of the Tennessee Voters Council, Williams sent a letter on June 16, 1981, to TBR Chancellor Nicks, saying that TVC fully supported TSU and its "black administration and faculty, and that full and substantial support be afforded to provide the highest quality of education at said institution, notwithstanding its predominantly black staff." On March 13, 1982, Nicks said that TSU was being treated equally and would receive a $13.7 million budget based on a formula of 6,350 full-time-equivalent (FTE) students. But the FTE formula worked against TSU because of the greater need for remedial and developmental programs meant to augment inadequate high school education received by many minority students.

After state authorities denied certain programs for TSU, the chairman of the black caucus, State Representative C. B. Robinson, said, "It may be that they do not know what we consider racism. They may be sincere in what they are doing, but they are passing up the best opportunity to contribute to integration efforts in Nashville I have seen yet." Senator Williams requested sensitive data from Nicks and had it sent to Adams, who re-edited a series of papers entitled "Tennessee Planning for Desegregation in Public Higher Education and Black Citizen Reaction and Interaction: A Critical Review of *Geier vs. Blanton* from a Black Perspective" (1982) and presented them at the black caucus's Statewide Leadership Conference. It appeared that black citizens might sue in court again.

Some black students were resisting the *Geier* defendants' idea of whites being TSU's "minority." When the university was pressured to merge the School of Business into the equivalent department on the former UT Nashville campus to attract more white students and the downtown business community, black students marched on the president's office, demanding that the School of Business not be moved from the north Nashville campus. Georgette Peek, the SGA president, said that the students saw the move as another attempt to take over TSU. "Clearly, we cannot be a black institution solely any longer," Humphries responded. But the students felt that moving the business school downtown would force them to be bused for the convenience of racially prejudiced whites who shunned black north Nashville.

On December 7, 1983, the desegregation monitoring committee, which included two blacks as well representatives from THEC, TBR, and the UT system, met in Knoxville. One committee member expressed concern about the small number of blacks who received doctoral degrees in Tennessee, noting that most Ph.D. programs at the public institutions were at the University of Tennessee or Memphis State University. The monitoring committee directed MSU and UT to develop proposals to alleviate the problems. New proposals included minority fellowships to be funded through THEC, but there were no safeguards to prevent institutions from replacing their own funds with desegregation funds. Therefore, there would be no rapid increase in minority doctoral graduates and faculty members. Black administrators represented a mere 5.3 percent of the total 1,190 administrators in Tennessee's public institutions of higher education, excluding TSU, where 80 percent of them were employed. Although blacks represented 16 percent of the state's population, they made up just 3.5 percent of the 5,755 faculty members in public colleges and universities. Even the governing boards, which, incidentally, were in charge of desegregation plans, had a mere 5.9 percent blacks on staff. The total of black graduates at all levels combined declined in 1982–83 compared to 1981–82. The 1984 Tennessee Desegregation Monitoring Report showed that Tennessee State University had 32.5 percent white administrators, 10.48 percent faculty of other races, and 39.6 percent white faculty members. About 37 percent of TSU's students would be non-blacks before suffering steady declines in white undergraduate student enrollment, but whites continued to outnumber blacks in the Graduate School (mostly in education) at TSU. These commuters had a more tolerable racial situation because they did not live in dormitories or have to take part in social and extracurricular activities with blacks outside the classroom. TSU was becoming more racially diverse, but historically white colleges and universities continued to avoid what they saw as "integration."

[*]

In 1978, the new judge who inherited the *Geier* case from retiring judge Frank Gray was Thomas A. Wiseman. When gubernatorial candidate Wiseman had appeared before the TVC to solicit black support in 1974, Avon Williams and others asked him point-blank whether he would protect Tennessee State University if elected governor. Wiseman said yes but later told the *Nashville Banner* (July 10, 1974) this did not mean he would "fly a black flag over UTN." In 1983–84, rumors circulated on the campus that some dissidents had met at the judge's house to pressure him to come down hard on TSU. There were rumors that some of them, as social science teachers at UT Nashville, had aided Wiseman in his political campaigns. At any rate, new plaintiffs entered the *Geier* case, and one of them, former UT Nashville faculty member Coleman McGinnis, claimed that the merged TSU had reverted to a "black institution" with a predominantly black administration and mostly black students and was not a quality university. These plaintiffs asked the court to set quotas that would make Tennessee State predominantly white or at least 50 percent white.

Wiseman encouraged the various sides to develop a Stipulation of Settlement that would get the defendants and all sets of plaintiffs to agree on measures to further desegregate higher education in Tennessee and, especially, to reduce the blackness of TSU. However, in July 1984, many blacks believed the settlement disfavored TSU. One cause for concern was a recommendation that the Tennessee Board of Regents "will within 180 days develop at TSU an Institute of Government, funded through the normal budgetary process." Such an institute would be open only to public administration faculty; certain faculty dissidents had previously operated a public administration program at UT Nashville, and since July 1979, they had been a contentious presence in the merged Department of Government and Public Affairs at TSU. Almost everyone assumed that the dissidents had written this part of the settlement to specifically exclude black political science teachers from joining the new department, because the only persons on campus with degrees related to public administration were the three whites from the former UT Nashville. Reviewing the document, the U.S. attorney general's representative observed:

> Item K, the establishment of an Institute of Government relates
> itself to none of the five objectives and should be eliminated.
> Further, it would have the effect of weakening a department,
> which needs to be strengthened; namely, Government and Public
> Affairs—the department to be designated as the home of the Ph.D.
> program in Public Administration and a projected Ph.D. program

in Political Science. This item is simply out of place in a document, which aims to correct segregation woes in the entire state by pinpointing one program in one institution, TSU. There is no such Institute for MTSU, Memphis State, UT, or any of the white institutions. The true test of the validity of the remedies proposed is whether they fit or are related to the purposes and objectives.

The Department of Justice also said that "it was an abuse of discretion for the district court to approve the consent decree without conducting an evidentiary hearing on the Department of Justice's objections." The Justice Department's "Perspective on the Stipulation of Settlement" further said that Tennessee should focus on ensuring equal educational opportunity, eliminating the remaining vestiges of the state-imposed dual system of higher education, increasing racial diversity at all state colleges, and ensuring equitable distribution of blacks and whites in all institutions. The Justice Department representative said that the settlement "erroneously assumes that Tennessee State University (TSU) has lower admission standards than does Middle Tennessee State University (MTSU)." Actually, in some programs, TSU's admissions standards exceeded those at MTSU, and TSU was a more comprehensive university than MTSU. One of the dissidents obtained a copy of the settlement and sent it to selected persons on campus. "Colleagues—I thought you might be interested in this," he noted across the top.

It seemed that higher education officials were trying to stop Humphries's efforts to expand academic programs, while promoting Austin Peay State University (APSU) and Middle Tennessee State University. On July 26, 1984, Humphries wrote to Senator Williams, explaining that THEC had not approved the TSU proposal for a master's degree in nursing. Wayne Brown, director of THEC, said that there was no evidence that another nursing degree program in Middle Tennessee was needed because Vanderbilt University (a high-tuition private school) had such a degree program. On August 8, members of the deans' council at TSU sent a letter and petition to Nathaniel Douglass, attorney for plaintiffs, U.S. Department of Justice, Civil Rights Division. They objected to the Stipulation of Settlement's quotas for TSU and the implication of inferior academic admission standards. Indeed, TSU had a national and international reputation, as reflected by its student body, whereas MTSU was merely a large, local school. The deans resented the placement of TSU's administrative appointments under the domain of the TBR and argued against the implication that TSU was segregated. By contrast, only 9 of the 450 full-time faculty members at MTSU were minorities, and only 859 of its

11,369 students were blacks. TSU had a white enrollment of 34 percent. The deans also said that the proposal that TSU cooperate with MTSU and APSU to eliminate program duplication was hypocritical when THEC had allowed these institutions to compete against TSU. And they argued that the Stipulation of Settlement "allows selfish, personal interests to be rewarded by providing for a specific program to be established at TSU that is the design of a particular group of plaintiff-interveners who stand to personally benefit from the establishment of such an autonomous unit [i.e., the proposed Institute of Government]." The deans further objected that the settlement "omits reference to the poor desegregation record of other state institutions of higher education in Tennessee such as MSU, which is located in a service area that exceeds forty percent African American population." The letter asked, "Why is it that the proposed settlement places the burden of desegregation on TSU and overshadows the progress TSU has made in regard to desegregation?"

On August 24, the Interdenominational Ministerial Fellowship of Nashville, Concerned TSU Staff and Students, and Concerned Citizens of the Greater Nashville Community jointly declared, "A historically black institution cannot be dismantled in order to foster desegregation." They wrote:

> Whereas Geier v. Alexander was originally filed in 1968 to halt the continued expansion of the former University of Tennessee at Nashville at the expense of Tennessee State University, and which later accomplished the merger of the former UTN with Tennessee State University in 1977, and was intended to make the expanded Tennessee State University more accessible to all students in Middle Tennessee, it was never the goal of the earlier court actions to open the door for the eventual dismantling of Tennessee State University. However, much to our shock and disappointment, the door has been opened wide for the dismantling of TSU. The proposition before Judge Wiseman's court that TSU has become re-segregated is both false and ridiculous. The proposed Stipulation of Settlement now being considered by the court makes TSU the victim of segregation, a scapegoat in order to draw the attention of the general public away from the real issue in higher education in the State of Tennessee: the hypocritical and token nature of desegregation that has taken place at the State's historically white institutions. As a community, we say, "stop picking on TSU," and put the spotlight on the historically white institutions that continue to move at a snail's pace toward desegregation.

Nevertheless, Judge Wiseman approved the Stipulation of Settlement as a response to "motions for further injunctive relief to effectuate statewide desegregation of all Tennessee institutions of public higher education." The settlement noted, "It is the purpose of this order to achieve a unitary desegregated system and not to achieve a merger of existing systems of higher education in Tennessee [i.e., Tennessee Board of Regents schools and the UT system]."

The settlement also called for a new committee to establish a procedure for monitoring the progress of desegregation at all pubic institutions of higher education and to report back to the court, as well as to develop five-year plans with benchmark goals to be achieved by the end of each year. The settlement stated that the Tennessee Board of Regents "shall immediately establish a 1993 interim objective for Tennessee State University (TSU) of 50 percent white full-time equivalent enrollment." TSU was to have 50 percent white recruiters, and the white institutions had to "utilize a black for recruiting other-race [black] students." The Stipulation of Settlement also said, "All other institutions shall increase their efforts to attract and employ other-race faculty and administrators and accomplish their objectives for other-race employment by utilizing the provisions herein." The state's public schools of veterinary medicine, dentistry, pharmacy, and medicine, were to pre-enroll "75 black sophomore students who are Tennessee residents." The U.S. Justice Department objected to this provision because the size of the quota was quite modest considering the effects of Jim Crow. The settlement also allowed the Institute of Government proposal to remain.

In announcing the *Geier* settlement on September 26, 1984, the conservative *Nashville Banner* quoted President Humphries as saying that TSU would raise its admission standards and improve the quality of its programs to attract a greater number of both white and black Nashville-area students and that if the agreement created more opportunities in higher education for minority faculty and administrators, he would support it. Humphries cautioned that the state's other colleges and universities needed to increase the participation of black faculty and students and that TSU should not be singled out as the sole instrument for desegregation. There the reporter had it: President Humphries had been forced to publicly admit the need to improve educational quality at predominantly black TSU. The *Banner* said, "TSU goals set higher than other [state] schools. Under a settlement approved Tuesday by . . . Tom Wiseman, TSU's goal is to have a 50 percent white student body by 1993. The agreement also specifies that half of TSU's faculty and administration is white by 1989."

On September 25, Wiseman tried to correct this white perception by saying, "The ultimate goal is not any ideal ratio of mix of black and white students or faculty. The goal is a system of higher education in Tennessee tax-supported colleges and universities in which race is irrelevant, in which equal protection and equal application of the law is a reality." But, he added, "The heart of the problem is traditionally black TSU." TBR Chancellor Nicks announced Wiseman's approval of the Stipulation of Settlement and noted, "Each president will continue to be held accountable for progress, or the lack thereof, toward achievement of all desegregation goals." Nicks sent a letter to Humphries and ordered him to begin immediately to implement the stipulations as they applied to TSU. The university was to receive monies for upgrading its facilities, but when Nicks's staff made its report on January 29, 1985, he and the regents' general legal counsel, a black attorney, claimed that many of TSU's facilities were "equal or better than those at many of the white universities." They recommended $4 million. In reality, at least $122 million was needed.

In the spring of 1985, Humphries announced his intent to accept the presidency of his alma mater, Florida A&M State University, beginning that fall. Sterlin Adams would become his executive presidential assistant in Florida. Humphries's TSU tenure ended on June 30, 1985. He later said, "I went down [to Nashville] with the notion, hell, I want to have an opportunity to build a great institution. We never got judged on what we did, we got judged on what we took in [black students]." He added, "Racial tensions in America will not abate until black institutions and culture are respected and viewed as valuable by the general society."

On April 18, 1985, a former UT Nashville faculty member held a "Caucus for Excellence and Integrity in Higher Education" meeting whose real intent seemed to be discrediting the merged TSU and complaining about its quality as an institution. The president-elect of the Student Government Association, Augusto Macedo, wrote the man on April 22, 1985: "I was nominated to serve on your executive committee, which I declined. I was deeply disturbed and highly dissatisfied with your organization, which is composed of Neo-Nazis. Your only goals are to condemn [TSU] and return society to the 'Good Old Days' of white supremacy. I submit to you that, we the students of Tennessee State University will not allow your organization [caucus] of educated Klansmen to direct or distort the future of Black Americans." The man attached Macedo's letter to his own letter (dated April 25, 1985) and sent the documents to Chancellor Nicks, saying, "May I suggest that this letter makes Mr. Macedo's participation in selecting TSU's next president of dubious value."

The "Caucus for Excellence and Academic Integrity in Higher Education" then submitted a "Position Paper" filled with generalities: "There is an enrollment crisis; there is a budget crisis; there is a crisis in the classroom; there is a crisis in university management." What was needed, it said, was "an interim chief executive with a mandate, moral soundness, and academic integrity."

Tennessee officials hired a black higher education official from Kentucky, Roy C. Peterson, as interim president. He arrived on campus amid rumors that the governors of the two states had agreed to exchange Peterson for some political favors. Immediately, members of the student body and the surrounding community pressured Peterson about his positions on the TSU–UT Nashville merger, and he was quoted as saying, "I don't believe that any institution that's historically black can look to a future when it will [continue to] be predominately black." When speaking at the National Hook-Up of Black Women at a meeting at First Baptist Church, Capitol Hill, Peterson was questioned about student dissatisfaction at the university. He blurted out, "They are whispering lies, half-truths and unfounded rumors." At a September 26, 1985, meeting with the Student Government Association, the acting president allegedly called the student leaders "a bunch of silly children" and made threats against them. Tina L. Fox, a student more inclined to compromise, said, "We at Tennessee State University are having too many conflicts with each other. The interim president, Dr. Roy Peterson, the Student Government Association, and the student body seem to be working against one another. Why? We are having too many problems dealing with the desegregation act and the choosing of the upcoming president to be fighting against each other. We need to work together as a family first, so we can fight for what we believe is right as one." Macedo published a letter in the *Meter* on October 10, 1985, calling for a war against Peterson. David C. Mills, chairman of "The Committee to Save Tennessee State University," circulated a letter on November 17, 1985, with this quotation: "If a man has not found something he will die for he is not fit to live—Martin Luther, King Jr." Mills was a history major with an activist nature who had transferred from UT Knoxville after becoming frustrated with the lack of social change on that campus. TSU's enrollment had dropped from 7,651 students to only 6,866, a far cry from Peterson's vision of "11,000 students by 1993." The students called for Peterson's resignation, and many faculty and community leaders withdrew their support of him.

Avon Williams, meanwhile, believed that Arliss Roaden, the head of THEC, was trying to make TSU look bad. Each institution under THEC was to report on ways of further desegregating the campuses in compliance with the Stipulation of Settlement in *Geier*. On April 17, 1986, Senator Williams wrote to Roaden, saying, "I appreciate your gracious boilerplate invitation to contact you if you can be of further assistance. Although your assistance thus far has not been notable, I look forward to continue calling upon you as a paid state official and employee, upon matters within the scope of your employment and legal responsibility." The letter was copied to officers of the General Assembly, Tennessee Board of Regents, Peterson, and black caucus members. The fight became nastier when Peterson was accused of joining with state officials to divert TSU construction contracts from minority firms to construction companies connected to state officials. To have a basis for comparison with expenditures at TSU, Williams sought information on capital projects undertaken at other state-funded schools, including UT.

On April 29, 1986, a mortified Peterson arrived unannounced at Senator Williams's house near Fisk University. He protested that Williams's letter of April 24 was inaccurate about Peterson's offering the black firm of McKissack and Thompson Architects less than a "young white firm" for construction work at TSU. The McKissack firm had built many buildings at TSU since the 1940s; now, however, some believed that Nashville's racist power brokers were trying to punish the black firm, as many white southerners were strongly opposed to blacks amassing wealth. Others felt that white authorities had conspired to set up dummy companies designed to skim off money meant for TSU.

Williams replied by letter on April 30 to Peterson's visit:

> In view of your impending 30 June 1986 separation as President, you still get the "intended point of my letter": I am for, and have fought for, racial integration. However, black people, having endured so long the rigors and inequality of human slavery and segregation at the hands of white America, should not and must not be required, at the hands of either black or white people, to suffer greater losses or bear more onerous burdens than white people in the desegregation process. It is more difficult to continue fighting racial discrimination by white people against black people when black persons [like you] in positions of power and authority not only fail to show awareness of the fight in their behalf, but also participate in and/or encourage such discrimination.

Senator Williams told Peterson, "Perhaps you did not believe a black man could grant your [TSU capital funds] request." Williams copied the letter to Leatrice McKissack, the Tennessee Board of Regents, members of the State Building Commission, the Student Government Association president at TSU, black caucus members, and the TSU faculty senate president. Peterson tried to placate McKissack-Thompson by saying that they would get other contracts at $500,000 or so. The firm was awarded some jobs on the campus but not the high-dollar jobs white firms walked away with, often doing inferior work. Dormitory renovations at TSU handled by the young white firms had to be redone almost immediately. The University of Tennessee, meanwhile, submitted the requested capital report to Williams. The response came on June 17, 1986, from Charles E. Smith, vice president for administration at UT, whose report showed that the UT system had $139,815,252 in state-financed construction, repair, and maintenance projects and another $116,618,427 in "university-financed" projects for 1976–86. The report astounded Williams and other civil rights leaders because TSU had received less than $20 million.

On June 30, Tennessee authorities hustled the controversial Roy Peterson back to Kentucky, saying that an interim appointee could not be a candidate for the permanent job. Under the leadership of Levi Jones of the sociology department, Raymond Richardson, and others, a group of key black TSU faculty met in various places to plan strategies to defeat attempts by state officials to fix the presidential search process. As their colleagues had done in 1974, this faculty group contacted unbeatable and highly qualified candidates from across the nation, but some of the better-informed and most-qualified candidates had heard that the TBR staff was under instructions to bring in their choice as interim for a couple of years, and then, after things had quieted down, appoint that person as permanent president. Few of the potential outstanding candidates thus chose to participate in what they believed was a meaningless and corrupt search process that would leave them looking like losers. The Board of Regents announced that Otis F. Floyd, the sole black vice president at nearby MTSU, had been selected as interim president at TSU. He had previously served as assistant to the commissioner of education, Sam Ingram, and followed him to his appointment as president of MTSU.

[*]

After the U.S. Court of Appeals heard appeals of the *Geier* Stipulation of Settlement on July 17, 1986, the court made a decision on September 5, 1986:

> A consent decree is primarily a means by which parties settle
> their disputes without having to bear the financial and other costs
> of litigating. It has never been supposed that one party—whether
> an original party, a party that was joined later, or an intervener—
> could preclude other parties from settling their own disputes and

thereby withdrawing from litigation. The use of "racial quotas" to prefer minority students, as provided in the consent decree to aid in eliminating residual effects of de jure segregation in Tennessee's higher education system did not deprive non-minority students of equal protection.

The decision continued:

> This Court rejects the position of the Justice Department that an evidentiary record must be compiled to prove that the black youth of Tennessee are victims of discrimination and that remedial programs will benefit them specifically and exclusively. In dealing with the broad and paramount issue of public education, this Court takes judicial notice of the long history of social, economic and political oppression of blacks in Tennessee—a history marked by years of slavery followed by years of Jim Crow laws. It is the past and present state of Tennessee's universities that the Court identifies as the specific instance of racial discrimination; its effects are pervasive throughout the black community, affecting practically all black men, women, and children in the state.

Thus the appeals court vindicated Wiseman and the settlement.

[*]

One of the first things Otis Floyd did as interim TSU president was to approve the name of the former UTN building for Avon N. Williams Jr. at a ceremony on September 26, 1986. On October 21, Williams sent a thank you note: "I hope [my speech] will be put permanently some place where all students, faculty and staff, present and future, are likely to read it. However, I shall not feel truly honored unless and until all State officials, staff, faculty and students understand and always remember the historic tragedy of racial discrimination and the lessons it teaches us. 'Whites' will never get it, until they learn that white persons can and sometimes must play a subordinate or minority role in our multi-racial society, as they must play in the future of a multi-racial world."

In his January 29, 1988, report, THEC director Arliss Roaden devoted four paragraphs to "Black Participation in Education." He said that $5 million had been devoted to desegregation efforts in 1987–88, and TSU had received a total of $15 million for capital projects. Tennessee's graduate deans had met to make plans to "increase Black [sic] presence" in the public graduate schools and "increase the supply of black teachers." On February 3, 1988, Williams sent another letter to the THEC director: "One of the major problems we face at TSU is enrollment stunting both operations and development because of formula-generated financing. The UTN-TSU merger experience seems to indicate a clear relation between said under enrollment and racial prejudice. If the foregoing is true, it seems to me that we ought to be partially addressing the problems by direct education at all levels designed to reduce or eliminate racial prejudice. The director's recent report did not show that you are doing so at any level."

Meanwhile, at the University of Tennessee, the recently appointed Task Force on Race Relations issued a report on February 26, 1988, with twenty-two recommendations. It noted, for instance, that students on "fraternity row" at UT Knoxville reportedly were allowed to demonstrate white supremacy by shouting "nigger" and other hostile racial epithets at passing minority students, including the black athletes who had helped the university win football games. There was no mention in the presidential reports of any serious punishment for such abusive white behavior. The task force did recommend "a University Civil Rights Commission" to deal with complaints and civil rights violations.

On March 29, 1988, the legislative black caucus invited Roaden to meet with them and give a "Desegregation Progress Report," which drew a negative response from caucus members. Black citizens were concerned that state officials had not compiled with the Stipulation of Settlement in the *Geier* case, except to pressure TSU to give more jobs to whites while other public institutions stayed strictly under white control. On April 4, Senator Williams opposed attempts to amend a black caucus resolution in the senate, which requested the institutions to hire more blacks. Some legislators attempted to amend the resolution and soften the word "request" to "urge" or "attempt." Williams said, "To set an *attempt* as a goal is to send a signal to public officials that we are not really serious about the [desegregation] matter." He called for a roll call vote to place the members on record, and the effort to weaken the resolution failed.

On April 13, Roaden sent a copy of the "Desegregation Monitoring Report of Tennessee" (1988) to caucus members. They remained dissatisfied with the results. At the urging of Williams, on April 27, 1988, Lieutenant Governor John Wilder wrote to Roaden to express concern about the decline of enrollment of black male college students. "I hope that all of us will do everything we can to turn this trend around," Wilder said. Otis Floyd soon adopted this concern. On September 7, Williams wrote Roaden "to urge that TSU and Meharry receive the full amount of their appropriation requests." Roaden responded that "every consideration will be given" to these institutions.

Williams scribbled a note on Roaden's letter: "Send to Otis Floyd and [Meharry president] Dr. David Satcher." In the 1988–89 State Appropriation Recommendations for Higher Education, the THEC full-time equivalent enrollment formula gave TSU only a 1.1 percent increase in funding whereas most other universities received 2.5 to 4.7 percent increases.

Because caucus members needed precise data to confront the authorities about the *Geier* settlement and the racial maltreatment of Tennessee State University, Michael T. Nettles, an African American native of Memphis, a senior statistical research scientist then at the Educational Testing Service in Princeton, New Jersey, and formerly an administrator at UT Knoxville, was commissioned to analyze the *Geier* Stipulation of Settlement and the statistical mechanisms used by the Tennessee Desegregation Monitoring Committee (DMC). Entitled "A Critique of the Methodology for Calculating Long-Range Objectives for Desegregating the Enrollments of Tennessee's Public Colleges and Universities," the Nettles report (1988) concluded that the defendants were failing to comply with the Stipulation of Settlement and that the methodology used by Tennessee meant that "the long term interests of black citizens of the State of Tennessee are not well represented." The DMC had first used the percentage of citizens by race in a given area to assign quotas and goals to the public colleges and universities; then, the committee changed the method to reflect the actual percentage of high school graduates by race in a given area to assign such desegregation quotas and goals. The latter method gave other institutions lower goals and quotas, while maintaining higher goals and quotas for TSU. In other words, if the mere percentage of citizens by race were used, TSU would be 75 percent white, but some officials foresaw a worse scenario: Memphis State would be 45 percent black, which was way beyond the "tipping point" at which neighborhoods suffered "white flight" and urban colleges became predominantly black institutions. According to Nettles, white colleges increased their admission standards without weighing the impact on desegregating higher education in Tennessee, and he added, "The suggestion that a reduction of black students at TSU will result in higher black enrollments at other state universities is a hypothesis for which no data have been advanced to support."

On March 7, 1989, the attorney for *McGinnis* plaintiffs notified the defendants' legal counsel in the Attorney General's Office that "Judge Wiseman has made it clear that our focus should be on Tennessee State University." *McGinnis* plaintiffs argued that TSU should be "a non-racially identifiable institution," without suggesting that we "are satisfied with the progress of other [white] public institutions of higher education in Tennessee in eliminating the residual effects of de jure segregation." The letter questioned the hiring of "blacks and the use of black language" in TSU publications, including the student newspaper. These plaintiffs objected to TSU's hosting of the National Council for Black Studies in April 1989 and to faculty members' claims that TSU was a historically black university. The plaintiffs in the case accused the black administration of not being serious about recruiting white students.

On June 20, a mysterious newspaper called the *Radical* was distributed in black north Nashville and bore this claim: "This paper is dedicated to the liberation of Tennessee State University." The paper charged that Ron L. Dickson, who was in charge of TSU's business and financial affairs, had a cozy relationship with members of the State Comptroller's Office and was secretly investing the university's money for their private gain. Responding to the concerns of campus activists, the Nashville branch NAACP joined with certain TSU alumni and the Clarksville branch NAACP to send a letter to state authorities that attacked the *Geier* stipulation and addressed the reports about Dickson's behavior at TSU. "The division of business and financial affairs of Tennessee State University under the leadership of Mr. Ron L. Dickson is practicing racial discrimination against black employees," the letter stated, pointing out that four state auditors assigned to TSU were selected in suspicious ways and outside EEO/AA guidelines and that despite the audit exceptions found under Dickson, the state authorities said nothing publicly. Dickson had given white employees higher salaries than the black employees, and he had selectively placed whites in the strategic administrative positions in finance and computer services, the blacks claimed. Dickson left TSU for a job in another part of the state.

When Thomas Garland indicated his intent to retire in 1989, Senator Williams wrote a letter to Governor McWherter: "It is rumored that you plan to appoint Dr. Arliss Roaden as Tennessee Board of Regents Chancellor to fill the Tom Garland vacancy. I hope you will not do so. I believe that Dr. Roaden is racially prejudiced and disposed to discriminate against black people. That belief is based upon the sworn EEOC complaint of a black woman faculty member whom I represented when he was President of TTU [Tennessee Technological University], and his lukewarm treatment of black issues as Executive Director of THEC." Williams urged McWherter to appoint a minority person to "render impregnable your already strong political support among black citizens across Tennessee." And, indeed, Roaden would be passed over.

[*]

On February 23, 1990, students occupied the administration building at Tennessee State. Among the leaders was Jeff Carr, president of the Student

Government Association. The demonstrations would continue for fourteen days, including nine days of fasting. Over three hundred TSU students demanded the resignation of three of Floyd's administrators, better treatment of students and faculty, improved maintenance of campus facilities, and a black studies degree program. Roscoe Dixon, chairman of the black caucus, told the press that the legislative organization was acting as "a bridge between the student government and the administration." State Representative Lois DeBerry held talks between the students and the TSU administration in her legislative office, and Senator John Ford urged President Floyd to grant the students amnesty so that the situation could end peacefully. Caucus members were concerned about any upheaval at TSU at a time when the merged institution was still under attack by the faculty dissidents and caucus members were working to get more state funds to rehabilitate the campus. The Floyd administration agreed to plan a program in Africana Studies and bring no charges against the student demonstrators. In the spring of 1990, a community paper observed, "The Dean of the College of Arts and Sciences is about to be named [at TSU]. The . . . pathetic racists that initiate every anti-black stance on campus have threatened to go to court if a white person is not named to the position." The interim dean, Wendolyn Y. Bell, an African American, won the appointment, despite an attempt by the Board of Regents chancellor, Tom Garland, to persuade him not to accept the TSU position but instead to take a position at a white university. The new dean accepted the TSU position anyway and served until August 21, 2000.

In the meantime, TSU gained approval for a master plan that would be funded by the state at more than $122 million to renovate or replace every building on the campus within a ten-year period. Senator Williams and other black caucus members, along with the student leaders, helped to persuade Governor McWherter to include $24,481,000 in his 1990–91 budget as an installment. Then, McWherter stunned almost everyone by appointing Otis F. Floyd as chancellor of the Tennessee Board of Regents—the first black citizen to hold the position. To deal more directly with the lack of minorities at the UT Health Science Center in Memphis, local members of the black caucus met with the governor and the center's head to discuss the matter. In February 1991, faculty members of the School of Business at TSU sent a resolution to the TBR, protesting plans to convert Nashville Technical Institute into a community college. Such a conversion, they argued, would hurt TSU's ability to attract local high school students.

In early April 1991, James A. Hefner, president at Jackson State University in Mississippi, became TSU's sixth president. A native of North Carolina,

Hefner was an economist who had formerly worked at Tuskegee University and the Atlanta University complex. TBR Chancellor Floyd next secured the appointment of the first African American president at Middle Tennessee State University. However, when Floyd returned to the TSU campus in 1993 for dedication of the new Otis Floyd–Joseph A. Payne Campus Center, student leaders objected to having his name on the building, claiming that Floyd had been too soft on desegregation issues and too cozy with state officials. In 1993, Floyd would die suddenly after undergoing a knee operation. Charles E. Smith became the new chancellor of the Tennessee Board of Regents.

The essential character of TSU remained a point of contention among TSU students. In April 1991, after President Hefner arrived on the campus, student leaders pressured him about rumors that TSU would be taken over by whites. Two years later, on May 3, the *Meter* reported that Hefner believed the cultural heritage of TSU must be maintained in the midst of diversity. But then, a year after that, on April 15, the *Meter* quoted Rahssan Robinson, about his concerns over the effects of the *Geier* settlement: "The fact that African Americans at a predominantly African American university cannot receive justice from their own people is appalling. From . . . faculty who are denied positions in favor of less qualified white candidates, to the screening out of black students via financial aid cuts, to miserable dorm conditions, to academic racism in the classroom—they originate from the same common strand of racism and evil that permeates our society." A significant number of TSU's students came from inner-city schools where resegregation had left a void of whites, and some of them had had no whites as classmates and neighbors. Thus, many of these students were hostile to whites and openly opposed to any preferential treatment for them on campus. After all, TSU, especially as compared to other Tennessee public universities, had a diverse student body that originated from eighty-five of the state's ninety-five counties, more than forty-two states, and fifty or more countries. One-third of the white students were on race-based scholarships and grants. But white student flight from TSU had set in during the years of militant student activity: minority enrollment dropped to 22 percent from a high of 37 percent. Hefner formed a committee on race relations and held diversity workshops.

On May 11, 1994, the Desegregation Monitoring Committee met in the THEC boardroom. Present as part of the committee were Joe Johnson, the UT system president; Arliss Roaden of THEC; and Charles E. Smith of TBR. A. C. Wharton, a Memphis attorney and TSU graduate, and F. Oliver Hardy, a physician, were the African American members. The Eighteenth Annual Report of Progress on desegregation began with a glowing introduction:

Our progress toward the goals established in 1991 has generally been steady and positive. And in some cases, particularly in the administrative and faculty employment areas, there is some vacillation of percentages, but the number of African-American employees has, in fact, gone up. The trend in the African-American student enrollment is up. With the overall percentage now mirroring very closely the representation of the Tennessee population that percentage increased very positively just this past fall again. Both the numbers and percentages of African-American professionals employed in education have increased and we are pleased with the progress last year in degrees earned by African-American students.

Wharton questioned the decrease of black undergraduates at UT Knoxville. "I do not have anything to say about undergraduates," Johnson said, "but there is good news when you look at progression and retention rates at Knoxville—they are up for the African American students, we are proud of that." Wharton asked that the next year's report include more specifics rather than simply whole numbers for African American students. It was a critical point, and it caught the white officials off guard. But a THEC staff member quickly responded, "We will do that." Hardy supported Wharton in questioning the effectiveness of the Tennessee Pre-Professional Program (TPP), which was designed to prepare seventy-five African American students per year to enter the state's professional schools as part of the 1985 Stipulation of Settlement. Hardy pointed out that East Tennessee State University's medical school was doing a better job of attracting and graduating black students than UT was doing at its medical center in Memphis, where the population was 50 percent black. In the area around ETSU, barely 10 percent of the population was African American. The UT official shifted the discussion to law students, where UT seemed to be doing a better job. Wharton said, "The question still remains related to TPP and what it is really doing." Wharton made a "standing objection" in particular related to the committee's goals for "the Tennessee State situation." In response to a question about any new developments in the *Geier* case, the state attorney said, "There are no developments except that the *McGinnis* plaintiffs have requested a conference, and we will be talking a little bit to the judge about the status of the case. Well, the *McGinnis* interveners represent a group of predominately white faculty members at TSU. And I expect that they are going to voice their dissatisfaction with the progress at TSU. And the State is still looking at its options at this point." Wharton interjected a stunning question: "What are they dissatisfied about?" There was no response to this question.

[*]

On November 5, 1998, the Black Faculty and Staff Association at the University of Tennessee, Knoxville, called a press conference in the Taylor Law School to present a position paper on desegregation, or the lack thereof, at the university. This press conference celebrated the thirty-year anniversary of the *Geier* case and the tenth anniversary of the UT Task Force Commission Report on Race Relations. The blacks asked the members of the Tennessee black caucus, which would be holding its annual retreat at nearby Pigeon Forge–Gatlinburg, to visit the UT campus to "investigate claims contained within the position paper, bring the issues to the attention of the General Assembly, and review allocations to the UT in terms of diversity and equity, vis-à-vis compliance with the Title VI mandates of the 1964 Civil Rights Act." The signers of the position paper indicated the "urgent need to address racist practices, marginalization, denial of opportunity, and structured patterns of rejection visited upon African American faculty and staff at the UT, Knoxville." After the representative from Knoxville hurriedly left the retreat to attend the Saturday afternoon UT football game, the caucus did not attempt to do anything about the petition. In his "University of Tennessee Highlights of Campus and Institute Five-Year Plans, FY 95–FY 99," President Joe Johnson merely said that there was an "increase in the quality and diversity of the student bodies."

On November 18–21, 1999, the black caucus's Annual Legislative Retreat and Training Conference at the Sheraton Hotel in Nashville received a report from its Higher Education Task Force that by 1995 only 32 percent of African American students had graduated from four-year colleges in Tennessee. And only 12.9 percent of them had graduated at the two-year college level. In July 2000, the *Tennessean* reported that mediation in "the TSU suit" was apparently continuing past the deadline of June 30, 2000. The white press had changed the title of *Geier* to "the TSU suit," perhaps ignoring the case's implications for all higher education in Tennessee. A black faculty member at UT observed, "There are still areas [of race relations], relatively speaking, no different than it was in the 1960s."

After Tennessee approached the district federal court, asking for a motion to dismiss *Geier*, the *McGinnis* plaintiffs argued that Tennessee had failed to live up to its obligations under the Stipulation of Settlement and that there was still the image of TSU as a "black institution." However, the state attorney general advanced the position that the law had changed since the U.S. Supreme Court had decided in *U.S. v. Fordice* (1993) to reduce the State of Mississippi's burden to dismantle a dual system of higher education in terms of specific ratios and numbers. But *McGinnis* plaintiffs argued that *Fordice* also said, "Our decisions establish that a state does not discharge its constitutional obligations until it eradicates policies and practices traceable to its prior *de jure* dual system that continue to foster segregation." Yet, some black TSU constituents sided with the attorney general, because they wanted to remove the "50 percent" goal from TSU as set in the *Geier* settlement. On the other hand, some blacks believed that dismissal of the case would allow Tennessee to stop affirmative action to enforce desegregation.

In December 2000, the plaintiffs and the State of Tennessee had reached an agreement in the *Geier* case. The 50 percent quota on TSU was removed, and all schools were given mandates, not goals or quotas, to become "racially non-identifiable." TSU would receive more resources to improve the quality of its programs, institute unique graduate programs, and launch a public campaign to improve its local image in order to attract more whites. The other public universities would be compelled to attract more minority students and faculty. In a way, however, state authorities would continue to try to control the hiring process in favor of white candidates at TSU. This led the president of the TSU National Alumni Association to say, "We believe in diversity, but we do not believe that everything has to be predominantly white to be good." George E. Barrett, Ray Richardson, and other plaintiffs believed somehow that the new settlement would achieve total desegregation of Tennessee's higher education system.

The settlement mildly criticized UT for failure to achieve desegregation goals. The new UT president, J. Wade Gilley, declared:

> The University of Tennessee, while not meeting every numerical objective set by a federal court in the statewide desegregation case known as the *Geier* case, has an exceptional record of commitment to minorities in the state of Tennessee. The *Geier* case has recently taken a new direction with the announced mediated agreement. Recent newspaper articles and editorials have dwelt on the inability of the university [UT] to meet certain court-ordered desegregation goals. And it is true that the university has fallen short in several of its numerical goals. However, what has not been reported is a record of remarkable achievement by the

university in meeting many of its *Geier* goals, its commitment to equity and diversity broadly speaking and its national leadership in minority enrollments in essential academic programs. UT-Memphis had 22 percent minority professional staff, exceeding the 10.4 percent goal. The University of Tennessee is firmly committed to a sustained proactive effort of equity and diversity as a matter of good educational policy in a world that is increasingly global and multicultural.

Judge Wiseman approved "with great pleasure and with great hopes" the settlement of the thirty-two-year-old *Geier* higher education desegregation lawsuit. The *Tennessean* carried a photograph of Rita Sanders-Geier, flanked in the background by George Barrett and the Tennessee attorney general. Plaintiff interveners, including Richardson and the U.S. Justice Department, signed off on the agreement. TSU was targeted to receive millions of dollars to endow merit-based scholarships, develop a law school, create a new school in public affairs, and market the university's offerings. In reference to deletion of the quotas, Richard Dinkins, who inherited the case from his partner, Avon Williams, who had died in 1994, said, "The reality is that people, unfortunately, make racial choices. But we feel this is the best this court and these parties are able to do to make sure those choices are not a product of inadequate resources [at TSU]." Many speculated about what Williams would have done. Governor Don Sundquist said that he was glad *Geier v. Sundquist* had ended, and he promised that Tennessee would be fully committed to funding the *Geier* budget.

Rita Sanders-Geier, who had traveled from her home in Washington, D.C., to attend the hearing, said that Wiseman "has given us all we need to go forward." As the speaker at a May 2, 2001, forum at TSU, she recalled:

> The whole motivation for this was the fact that if UT-Nashville had come in with a major expansion in the Nashville community, and Tennessee State was not going to become a world-class university. TSU was not going to become a center of education in this community, as it should be. That was outrageous to me at the time because it was clearly racist. I really wanted to make a contribution, make a change. We felt the time was right to move in higher education. We wanted to make TSU a more competitive institution. We decided to seek injunction against UTN construction. . . . Thirty-two years of anybody's life represents a lot of change, but we learned a lot over 32 years.

Sanders-Geier returned to speak at TSU's 2002 Black History Month. In the faculty senate meeting on September 12 of that year, one member expressed disgruntlement at the outcome of the case, noting that the lawyers were asking for "$10 million in attorney fees" and asserting, "The case abolished affirmative action in Tennessee higher education, and the attorneys did not win the lawsuit but simply abandoned and settled the case."

Hefner would have a difficult, if not impossible, task in trying to convince the Nashville School of Law to merge with TSU, as the *Geier* decree assumed. This night law school, which was operated by local attorneys and judges, had rejected Negro applicants long after *Brown*. A black law school was opened on September 17, 1957, by a local group of progressive black and white lawyers and leaders, including Neill S. Brown, Coyness Ennix, Charles Galbreath, C. Allen High, Ramsey Leathers, William C. McIntyre, and Donald L. Washburn. Brown acted as dean and trustee, along with Z. A. Looby, Henry Allen Boyd, and M. J. Davies. This law school soon closed, however. After the 1964 Civil Rights Act forced the white YMCA Law School (which became the Nashville School of Law) to desegregate, the school appeared to minimize the number of blacks that it accepted and graduated. The school's alumni had working-class backgrounds and often rejected social and economic competition from blacks. Some of them balked at President Hefner's offer to assume the night law school outright. The law school merger talks ended fruitlessly by 2003.

The court-appointed master in charge of the *Geier* consent decree seemed to be of no help. Perhaps, judging by certain comments he made to the *Tennessean*, he agreed with whites who used the old anti-integration tactic of attacking the quality of education at a predominantly black institution. Some believed that the court had intentionally appointed a conservative master. At any rate, some professors at TSU breathed a sigh of relief, arguing that Tennessee did not need another publicly supported law school. They believed that TSU needed to direct its resources to existing academic programs and noted that the United States already had the highest number of lawyers per capita in the world.

In 2003, TSU and its president came under attack once again. George E. Barrett seemed to speak loudest for white leaders by calling for Hefner to resign. President Hefner was vulnerable to criticism because he had lied about accepting some Super Bowl football tickets from a vendor. The Attorney General's Office absolved Hefner of any criminal liability, but the TSU Foundation was cited for a $2.5 million deficit due to overruns in scholarships awards. White critics claimed that Hefner gave too many scholarships to black students who should not have received the awards. The Tennessee Board of Regents jumped at the opportunity to say that it would appoint an outside administrator "to help Dr. Hefner operate the campus," an echo of what had happened in 1942 and 1967. The TBR backed away from this idea in the face of black community meetings and protests. The real cause of the attack was that as far as many whites (perhaps including attorney Barrett) were concerned, TSU was still "too black"; certainly, in this view, it was not white enough to be accepted by the local white majority and the business community as a quality institution that could represent Nashville as its urban university. The white enrollment percentage at TSU had fallen during Hefner's tenure. Despite black community support, President Hefner announced his retirement in May 2004, effective at the end of the 2004–05 academic year; the TBR accepted his decision at its June meeting in Cookeville. This left some resentment in the African American community against Barrett, because some of them believed he was paternalistic and was trying to take credit for the result of Geier, which in fact was the work of Judge Gray, Avon N. Williams, Sterlin N. Adams, Raymond Richardson, and Tennesseans for Justice in Higher Education.

[*]

Geier was like a writ of mandamus that forced nostalgic officials to give up the Jim Crow ghost and allow Tennessee to move from a dark, evil racial past to a brighter future. For education, the state budgeted $2.066 billion by 2000. Tennessee ranked sixteenth in population with 5,689,283 people in the 2000 census; 20.2 percent of its citizens had some college education; and 21 percent had college degrees, compared to 25–30 percent in the northeastern states. During the civil rights movement, the percentage of college graduates had also risen in other southern states, including Georgia (23 percent), Mississippi (19 percent), North Carolina (22 percent), and South Carolina (23 percent). Blacks comprised high percentages of the population in these same southern states: Georgia with 29 percent, Mississippi with 36.3 percent, North Carolina with 22 percent, and South Carolina with 29.5 percent. Among the selected states, only Tennessee and North Carolina achieved racial parity in college degree rates. Blacks comprised 41,142 students (or 16.3 percent) of the 252,915 enrolled college students in Tennessee, matching their population percentage (16.4). Tennessee had 21 percent overall minority enrollments at its four-year public and private colleges and universities and 18.4 percent minority enrollment at its two-year colleges. There was expected to be an 11 percent increase in black high school graduates by 2012. With a dismal graduation rate at the two-year community colleges, where increasing numbers of black high school students were being directed, Tennessee needed to develop a triadic affirmative-action program: higher rates of recruitment, retention, and graduation of African American students.

A THEC progress report in 2000 placed TSU within seven points of the state average graduation rate of 45 percent; this rate had been 21 percent in the 1980s. Among eighty-four public and private colleges and universities, selected graduation rates were as follows: Austin Peay State University, 32 percent; University of Memphis, 32 percent; Middle Tennessee State University, 34 percent; Tennessee State University, 38 percent; UT Chattanooga, 41 percent; Tennessee Technological University, 43 percent; Belmont University, 53 percent; UT Knoxville, 57 percent; and Vanderbilt University, 81 percent. Not only did TSU outperform several institutions in graduation rates, but it ranked third—behind Vanderbilt and UT Knoxville—in total research and training grant dollars received (more than $42 million). TSU research scientists discovered a star around a distant star, making national news. TSU became the fifth largest among Tennessee's nine public universities. It remained a historically black university, but it was Tennessee's most racially diversified urban, comprehensive, land-grant, doctoral-level institution.

However, the effects of *Brown* and the desegregation of higher education were changing TSU and other HBCUs for better and worse. In 1997, TSU's faculty was 45.1 percent African American, 44.2 percent white and 10.7 percent other race-people (mostly Asian, Asian Indian, and Hispanic non-white); this would change to 43.5 percent African American, 45.3 percent white, and 11.2 percent other-race people by fall 1999. Indeed, as the era of integration advanced—without, unfortunately, a fast-enough increase in the number of African American Ph.D. recipients—the percentage of white faculty at the historically black colleges and universities increased overall to nearly 30 percent, and at least nine HBCUs had a majority white faculty. Also, ironically, the African American faculty pool increased by 5 percent in the country to 14 percent of all college faculty members, a slight increase since 1997. But historically white colleges and universities also attracted black faculty members through better salaries, lighter teaching loads, and easier working conditions. At predominantly white colleges and universities, black professors were tolerated at best by students and fellow faculty members. It seemed that black faculty had to forever prove their competence. Students expected them to be entertaining teachers but not real scholars.

America's blacks received only 5.9 percent of all earned doctoral degrees, 12.4 percent of those in the field of education but only 2.8 percent in the physical sciences. The majority of black doctorates were in the field of education instead of in the critical content areas of engineering, computer science, social sciences (history, sociology, etc.), humanities, science, business, and the performing arts. The newspaper that served HBCUs, the *University Faculty Voice* editorialized in April 2002:

> Unless the HBCUs are willing and able to compete in providing these incentives [higher salaries, lower teaching loads, and more time for research for faculty hires], we can forget about their continued existence. We need individuals with competence and dedication, not simply credentials, to fill the teaching positions at the HBCUs, if we are to maintain our relevancy and refuse to stand witness to the destruction, from within, of our institutions as the bastions of black higher education, culture, leadership, and socioeconomic development. The task is daunting, it is not impossible.

Desegregation of higher education made more progress in Tennessee than in the rest of the South. Of nineteen states that once operated segregated higher education systems, seven of them were still being monitored by the U.S. Department of Education, and four were engaged in settlement plans by 2002. There was no bloody battle when UT was integrated in 1951, compared to the lives unnecessarily lost at Ole Miss in 1962. The thirty-two-year-old *Geier* case was unprecedented in the nation's legal history, even though its results were not duplicated anywhere else in America. The merger of UT Nashville into Tennessee State University set a precedent for a white institution to be absorbed into a black one and for the merged institution to be left in the hands of a predominantly black administration. "In many states," one writer concluded, "negotiators did not have the political will to seek greater integration by taking controversial steps [like *Geier*], such as merging nearby historically black and predominantly white institutions, the experts say." The settlements of 1985 and 2000, perhaps the judge, and many local white leaders did not totally accept this concept. Yet, TSU became Tennessee's most integrated university. Still, as the *Tennessean* reported on November 17, 2004, legislator Bill Dunn of Knoxville was seeking an investigation into why TSU was not as diversified as it should be after millions of dollars had been spent in the *Geier* settlements.

CHAPTER 12

DON'T YOU WISH YOU WERE WHITE?
THE CONCLUSION

A half-century after *Brown*, some of the old civil rights leaders were still around, and they dared to keep this history, memory, and hope alive—lest they offend the memory of the late Frederick Douglass, who had warned against "historical amnesia." On August 27, 2000, Harry Belafonte spoke about prostate cancer and preventive measures to an audience at Meharry Medical College. But the discussion turned to civil rights. "Yes," Belafonte said, "the civil rights movement made things better; but the civil rights movement did not go far enough." Belafonte, a victim of Jim Crow as well as cancer and yet a beneficiary of civil rights efforts, could not help but use such engagements to keep the fire burning for an unfinished movement. He, like many other aging civil rights leaders, did not know what kinds of tactics to use and against what and whom to launch another phase of the movement, but he could talk about it and keep the fires burning for freedom. Although there were groups (perhaps well-meaning) rushing to bottle up the civil rights movement and put it in museums, galleries, holidays, and memorabilia, it would be a mistake to think that the movement belonged to the realm of settled opinion. At the "Civil Rights Legacy" program hosted by the Nashville Public Library on February 14–15, 2004, James Lawson, Diane Nash, John Lewis, James Bevel, and Bernard Lafayette agreed that the movement had to continue until Americans had achieved "the beloved community."

Hard, addictive work had taken its toll on civil rights leaders in Tennessee. Avon N. Williams Jr., the foremost of Tennessee's civil rights lawyers, suffered a muscle disease by 1983 that gradually rendered him physically impaired and confined to a wheelchair. "Avon Williams Still Fighting for Rights," proclaimed an article in the *Nashville Tennessean* on February 16, 1986. But just a few years later, on November 1, 1990, Williams announced his retirement: "I have decided to retire from the public forum at the end of my current term, as I retired from active law practice five years ago. I hope to devote the remainder of any years, as God may give them, to loving my wife, family and friends, looking after my affairs, and completing my autobiography." On August 29, 1994, upon the passing of Avon Williams, TSU's *Blue Notes* said, "Many people remember this lawyer and civil rights leader for his great contributions to law, politics, and the university. Tennessee State University's downtown campus bears his name." The TSU choir performed the Negro National Anthem at the memorial services. Congressman John Lewis said, "He believed in the power of the law. He was brilliant, aggressive, outspoken and sharp. He was dedicated and committed to change. More than 34 years ago, when we were arrested during the student sit-ins, he was there to defend us. He saw nonviolent protests as an extralegal instrument to increase the pace of change."

Z. A. Looby, meanwhile, had ended up in a wheelchair, disabled, and without much money when he retired in 1972 and then quickly passed away. A. W. Willis Jr., Carl Cowan, and C. B. Robinson died many years later. Maxine and Vasco Smith retired in the mid-1990s. Others slipped quietly into their jobs, careers, businesses, and personal lives when there were no longer mass meetings, the sound of marching feet in the streets, a TVC through which to organize black political power, crises, and opportunities to take their protests into the jails. A few of the principal civil rights leaders hit the lecture circuit, with their gray hair glistening under the lights and their idealism still impressing audiences. But the war against European American racism, discrimination, and economic exclusion of African Americans raged on ever so quietly.

The "whites" resigned themselves to treating non-whites as *constitutional* equals. But they became accustomed (as the Jacksonians had done) to refusing to accept them as socioeconomic partners. The U.S. Constitution, which had been drastically changed since 1865, guaranteed *equality* of civil rights, but it did not say that Americans privileged to be whites had to treat people of color *fairly*. In the projected American population for 2050, blacks are estimated to increase by 71.3 percent, Asians by 212.9 percent, Hispanics by 187.9 percent, all other races (excluding whites) by 217.1 percent, and whites by only 32.4 percent. Those designating themselves as "whites" are projected to drop to less than 51 percent of America's population by 2050. U.S. Census Bureau projections that whites could one day be America's minority have caused government authorities to begin changing policies and regulations, altering the Constitution's meaning, even attempting new amendments, increasing the imprisonment of minorities, and restricting immigration. As the late novelist and activist James Baldwin once told a group of white liberals, "As long as you think you are white, you force me to be black." Indeed, African Americans were subtly reminded of the anti–civil rights picket signs of the 1960s: "Nigger, don't you wish you were white?"

For sure, *Brown* and the civil rights movement by the turn of the twenty-first century had not cured America of racism. The NAACP called for the Fifth Daisy Bates Education Summit (held in Atlanta, May 16–19, 2002) in continuing its efforts to end racial disparities in the nation's public schools and institutions of higher education. Maxine Smith of Memphis, an NAACP board member and chair of its education committee, was scheduled as one of the keynote speakers. Not until January 2003 was an agreement struck with the State of Connecticut in the fourteen-year-old *Sheff v. O'Neill* school desegregation case. The new agreement allowed minority students to attend predominantly white suburban schools and provided greater resources and magnet schools for the inner-city schools in Hartford, where, by 1996, the schools had resegregated to 90 percent black and Hispanic. Social problems in America's suburban schools, 80 percent or more white, really were no less than those in inner-city schools. According to Derrick Bell, a noted civil rights lawyer and legal scholar, the fact that blacks were not calling for desegregation or integration through *Brown* but, rather, simply seeking equal-quality education was lost in the fight to end segregation in public schools. Bell insisted that this lost ideal is likely to be revisited by African Americans in the twenty-first century. *Brown*, Bell said, teaches that advocates of racial justice should rely less on judicial decision and more on tactics, actions, and even attitudes that challenge continuing assumptions of white dominance. But *Brown* positively affected the growth of tolerance of whites toward blacks and minorities, although many schools had resegregated.

News reports of recent years have noted a rise in legal action against workplace discrimination. In November 2000, a group of black employees forced Coca-Cola to settle a discrimination suit for $192.5 million. The United States Equal Employment Opportunity Commission, meanwhile, filed a lawsuit against Target Corporation, alleging discrimination in refusing to hire blacks for entry-level management positions in parts of Wisconsin. EEOC records have shown more complaints against racial discrimination than against age, sex, gender, and handicap discrimination. Since the 1980s, racial-harassment charges filed with the EEOC had increased from ten thousand to fifty thousand claims. Affirmative-action programs, particularly on the economic level, suffered attack in many states. "The debate [over discrimination] is intensifying," *USA Today* reported, "because the legal arena is fast becoming a new civil-rights battleground for business-related claims."

In Tennessee, at least, it was precisely economic disparities that continued to keep society segregated and African Americans making up the greatest percentage of the poor. Yet, the key to overcoming this disparity, as proposed by President Johnson's Great Society program, Martin Luther King Jr.'s "Poor Peoples' March," and President Nixon's affirmative-action economic programs, was to bring African Americans into the mainstream of American business, industry, and technology, not only as workers but as owners, employers, and producers. African Americans in Tennessee needed (1) to increase their presence in firms and businesses with substantial numbers of employees, and (2) to expand their presence in agriculture, manufacturing, wholesale trade, and the lucrative fields of finance, insurance, and real estate. And while striving to advance in the economic arena, African Americans have had to continue their civil rights movement by fighting against other forms of racial oppression in Tennessee and across America. As James M. Lawson Jr. noted in 2004: "[R]acism is more pervasive today than ever before. Some two million people of color are in American prisons for things that two million white people are *not* in jail for. It is one example of how white supremacy continues to dominate our American society. . . . It [America] is flirting with disaster." Indeed, the United States has reached a point where it holds 25 percent of the world's imprisoned people.

For those Americans still preoccupied with distinguishing who is "white" and who is "black"—a mental process that takes up most of their twenty-four-hour day—the revelation of an "American becoming" is worrisome. Al Gore and the Democrats received the majority of the total individual votes cast in the 2000 presidential election, but only 36 percent of those votes were from whites. The 2000 census concluded that California was one of three states *without* a racial majority, and it concluded that Hispanics had made the largest ethnic gain—from 22 million to 35 million, or an increase of 57.9 percent in ten years—and that they would soon represent 14 percent of the total American population. George Ramos, when discussing his book *No Borders: a Journalist's Search for Home* (2004), predicted that Hispanics would outnumber European whites in America in several generations. African Americans grew as much as 21.5 percent compared to only 5.9 percent for the white category in the 2000 Census. Among Indian/Native Americans, there was 26.4 percent growth to nearly 4.1 million people. Asian Americans were expected to be the fastest-growing major population category over the next half-century, tripling to 33 million in 2050.

Patrick Buchanan, a leader of the ultra-conservative wing of the Republican Party and author of *The Death of the West* (2002), told *Southern Partisan* magazine (Mar.-Apr. 2002) that recent political and racial changes in America would cause the vanishing of the European race and "the death of our culture and our civilization." Buchanan was only repeating what Madison Grant had said in *The Passing of the Great Race* (1916). Buchanan believed that western European culture was under attack in American schools and colleges and that whites could not "depend on millions of immigrants [who chose to *designate* themselves as whites, i.e., Hispanic whites] to save Western culture and civilization, if they don't come from that culture and civilization." He believed that the two major political parties had become "monoliths" and so "dependent on the same sources of corporate money in enormous volumes" that the nation was being governed by elites unwilling to hold the line. In Buchanan's view, even the Republican Party—still the best choice for the South—was "headed in the wrong direction. It is attempting to pander to the Hispanic vote [which eventually might vote Democratic]." A thoughtful Buchanan also believed that the Supreme Court had taken the legislative franchise of social policy from Congress and that few Republican leaders dared stand up and condemn "political correctness, moral relativism and multiculturalism." Buchanan blamed—of all people—the late President Nixon for furthering the liberal cause: "Where I fault him is that Nixon was not a conservative. Basically, Lyndon Johnson laid the foundations of the Great Society, and Nixon built the skyscraper. If you take a look at all those social programs of the Great Society, they were all funded and financed under Nixon."

Perhaps, however, Buchanan's alarm, which truly was a candid discussion and a fearless intellectualizing of the issues, was too late. Blacks were the majority in many American cities, and they had 480 city mayors compared to 314 in 1990 and only 81 in 1970. Hispanics or white Cubans pretty much controlled Miami's politics. Half of the minority mayors were in southern states, the heart of Republican country. From 1980 to 2000, some 130,000 young blacks moved into Georgia, and Hispanics and other minorities were rushing into the Sunbelt seeking jobs and opportunities. In an *Atlantic Monthly* article, Gregory Rodriguez wrote:

CONCLUSION

A study by the Population Research Center . . . projects that the
black intermarriage rate will climb dramatically in this century,
to a point at which 37 percent of African Americans will claim
mixed ancestry by 2100. By then, more than 40 percent of Asian
Americans will be mixed. Most remarkable, however, by century's
end the number of Latinos claiming mixed ancestry will be more
than two times the number claiming a single background. . . .
Unlike the advances of the civil rights movement, the future of
racial identity in America is unlikely to be determined by politics
or the courts or public policy. Indeed, at this point, perhaps, the
best thing the government can do is to acknowledge changes in
the meaning of race in America and then get out of the way.

In his 1996 book, *The Coming Race War in America: A Wake-Up Call,*
Tennessee native Carl T. Rowan observed, "The so-called American melting
pot has become a tinderbox that seems ready to explode. Before the end of the
century, this country seems destined to look more like South Africa of a
decade ago than any dream of racial and ethnic tranquility. That is, unless
brave and wise people move boldly and quickly to halt the spread of racial
polarization and violent bigotry in every nook and cranny of this land. . . . But
in one more moment of candor, let me say that I am not optimistic that this
society is up to the challenge before it." Letters addressed to Fisk University
and Meharry Medical College expressed this ethnic meanness: "Eventually,
we'll get rid of you. The year 2000, the war escalates—we promise."

President Bill Clinton responded to the growing racial threat to American democracy by appointing a national race relations study commission.
John Hope Franklin, a Fisk University graduate, the prolific author of history
books, and a retired professor at Duke University, chaired the commission.
The President's Race Initiative was launched in June 1997 in the belief that no
challenge facing the nation as it entered the new century was as critical and
daunting as the challenge of color and race. Christopher Edley Jr., a writer for
the final study, *America Becoming* (2002), said, "The growth of America's
diversity is breath taking. However, unless we in the United States do better
to confront and bind our racial and ethnic divisions, the powerful legacy of
racial caste will shackle our progress and rend our communities. . . . Demographic changes have moved America beyond Black and White into a complex multiethnic environment that we still do not understand." The decreas-
ing number of Americans claiming to be either black, white, Asian, Indian, or
Hispanic indicated that the idea of "race" was perhaps losing its significance.
However, in his article in *America Becoming,* "The Changing Meaning of

Race," Michael A. Omi pointed out that even though "race may have no bio-logical meaning, as used in reference to human differences, it has an extremely important and highly contested *social* one." The idea of race retains popular acceptance as an important organizing principle of individual identity and collective consciousness. Omi noted, "My general point is that the meaning of race in the U.S. has been and probably always will be fluid and subject to multiple determinations." One day, perhaps, race may not matter in America any more than it does in Brazil; however, even Brazil is a country that still shows signs of de facto racism practiced by European-Brazilians.

Finally, the civil rights movement and its continuation have been good for all Americans and for all Tennesseans. Racists, segregationists, racial supremacists, conservatives, liberals, southern nationalists, Nordic advocates in the North, the increasing population of minorities, African Americans and their civil rights leaders, judges, jurists, legislative and other political leaders, protesters against human injustice, the Negro press, African American law-yers, the spectators, and even racially biased daily newspapers in Chattanooga, Knoxville, Memphis, and Nashville—all of them, consciously or uncon-sciously, voluntarily or involuntarily, physically or metaphysically, on one side or the other, engaged in a protracted fight that has bettered American democ-racy and the U.S. Constitution, bringing the nation much closer to being truly "a beacon of light upon a hill." The civil rights movement, unlike con-servative movements, has *not* been a threat to democracy but an attempt to save and extend it for and to all Americans.

AFRICAN AMERICANS AND THE CIVIL RIGHTS MOVEMENT IN TENNESSEE

A CHRONOLOGY AND SYNOPSIS

In his foreword to the first volume of *America Becoming: Racial Trends and Their Consequences* (ed. Neil J. Smelser, William Julius Wilson, and Faith Mitchell, 2 vols. [Washington, D.C.: National Academy Press, 2001]), Christopher Edley Jr. wrote, "Race is not rocket science; it is harder than rocket science. Race demands an intellectual investment equal to the task. It also demands relentlessness in research and teaching that will overwhelm the human tendency to let our differences trigger the worst in our natures." These words apply not only to the problem of color and race in America at large but also to the situation in Tennessee.

In every historical movement, there are residual good and bad results. The civil rights movement left younger European Americans with more moderate racial attitudes—although they often remained under the influence of many older people whose ethnocentric minds were still infected with the disease of racial supremacy. Even by the year 2002, many Tennesseans would not accept social integration with blacks, but they had given up the ghost of the Old South and moved forward into the future, allowing race matters to settle within the context of time. In *Black, White, and Southern: Race Relations and Southern Culture, 1940 to the Present* (Baton Rouge: Louisiana State Univ. Press, 1990), David R. Goldfield observed:

> Blacks have become too much of a political and an economic
> force in the South for a retreat from racial progress to advance
> very far. There is nothing in a recrudescence of racial animosity
> that the white economic elite would find beneficial, especially
> since black political leaders have demonstrated a keen interest in
> and talent for economic development. . . . The advances of the
> civil rights movement have become too ingrained in regional life
> to be threatened from outside or from within. An encouraging

sign, aside from the shrines and commemorations, is that southern whites continue to expiate past sins and expose and eliminate new ones. . . . Indeed, as race relations become rountinized in more positive ways, the greatest legacy of the civil rights movement may be its preservation of southern culture. . . . For the crusade against economic injustice, southern blacks and whites are likely to be partners. (272–78)

Indeed, the civil rights movement in Tennessee was not a threat to "democracy" but was an attempt to save it and extend its benefits to all Americans.

African Americans (descendants of American slaves) have struggled for complete freedom as American citizens and full dignity and respect as human beings since arriving in America in 1619. They always had a civil rights movement in Tennessee, beginning with (1) attempts to escape slavery; (2) daily resistance to bondage; (3) the Underground Railroad; (4) the abolitionist movement; and (5) fighting as Union soldiers in the Civil War (1861–65).

Since Emancipation (1865), African Americans have continued that civil rights movement into modern times, although it rose and waned in three phases.

THE FIRST ORGANIZED CIVIL RIGHTS MOVEMENT, 1863–1880

The first civil rights movement took place from 1863 through 1880 with the objectives of (1) abolishing slavery; (2) gaining citizenship and the right to vote and hold public office; and (3) obtaining equal rights and protection through the laws.

CHRONOLOGY OF THE FIRST
CIVIL RIGHTS MOVEMENT

1863

President Lincoln's Emancipation Proclamation goes into effect on January 1, but does not affect loyal Tennessee. Some 20,133 United States Colored Troops serve the Union cause in Tennessee.

1864

Negroes in Nashville hold a rally for their rights at summer picnic at Fort Gillem (today's Fisk University); they send delegates to the National Colored Men's Convention in Syracuse, New York in August 1864; upon the delegates' return, they hold a torchlight parade to petition for their rights. In October 1864, Military Governor Andrew Johnson declares that slavery has ended in Tennessee.

NOVEMBER, THANKSGIVING DAY, 1864

Negro leaders in Nashville organize the Tennessee chapter of the National Equal Rights League. This organization was formed at the 1864 National Colored Men's Convention, held in Syracuse, New York, where Frederick Douglass, John Mercer Langston, and other nationally known Negro leaders, including delegates from Tennessee, decided to form an organization to lobby Congress and the states for a constitutional end to slavery and all citizenship rights for the freedmen (former slaves).

MARCH 1865

The Tennessee General Assembly—and then the voters—abolish slavery.

AUGUST 1865

Tennessee Negroes hold their first State Colored Men's Convention (Nashville, St. John AME Church) to discuss freedmen's problems and to petition the governments.

DECEMBER 18, 1865

The Thirteenth Amendment to the Constitution abolishes slavery throughout the United States.

1866

After race riots stun Memphis (May 1-2, 1866), Tennessee grants limited rights to freedmen. Congress passes the Civil Rights Act of 1866, giving freedmen citizenship, equal protection of laws, and due process of laws.

1867

In February, the Tennessee General Assembly grants Negroes the right to vote and hold public office.

1868

The states ratify the Fourteenth Amendment, embodying the 1866 Civil Rights Bill.

1870

States ratify the Fifteenth Amendment, guaranteeing suffrage to all citizens born in the United States, including former slaves. In Tennessee, former Confederate officers, Democrats, and Conservative Party candidates regain control of the state government, rewrite the state's constitution (including a poll tax), and allow domestic terror against the freedmen.

1871

Congress passes Force Acts and Ku Klux Klan Acts to fight radical white terrorism in the South.

1875

Congress passes the Civil Rights Act of 1875 to forbid discrimination in public accommodations based on race and previous conditions of servitude, but the bill excludes the ban against segregated schools. In March, Nashville Negroes test the public accommodations act.

THE SECOND CIVIL RIGHTS MOVEMENT, 1881-1934

The second civil rights movement occurred from 1881 to the 1930s, and included the objectives of (1) abolishing the new Jim Crow laws; (2) gaining economic parity; (3) combating racial lynching and widespread racial discrimination in American society; and (4) regaining political rights recently lost.

CHRONOLOGY OF THE SECOND CIVIL RIGHTS MOVEMENT

1881

Tennessee passes the South's first Jim Crow railroad law. Negroes in Nashville stage a freedom ride protest at the train station.

1883

The U.S. Supreme Court nullifies the 1875 Civil Rights Bill.

1884

Ida B. Wells, a schoolteacher in Memphis, sues a railroad company for racial discrimination, but the Tennessee Supreme Court upholds the 1881 Jim Crow law in an 1887 appeal by the railroad company.

1890

The Tennessee General Assembly passes a stronger poll tax to stop Negro voters. Negroes had been elected to the General Assembly since 1871, but the last of them is defeated in 1892.

1890

Congress passes the Morrill Land Grant Amendment, allowing states to use federal land grant funds to establish more state colleges that include Negro students, or to establish separate land grant colleges for Negroes—the nation's first post–Civil War Jim Crow bill.

1896

The U.S. Supreme Court affirms legality of Jim Crow laws through the *Plessy v. Ferguson* decision, which states that "separate but equal" is permissible in public accommodations.

1906

The U.S. Supreme Court approves Tennessee's Jim Crow law (1901) to force private colleges to observe segregation in *Maryville College v. Tennessee*; in 1908, the court in *Berea College v. Kentucky* says it is permissible to segregate the races under *Plessy v. Ferguson*, even in private colleges.

1909

The General Assembly authorizes a Jim Crow college for Negroes: Tennessee A&I State Normal School, which will open in June 1912 and eventually become today's Tennessee State University.

1916

Robert R. Church Jr. and others form the Memphis chapter of the NAACP, Tennessee's first.

1919

James C. Napier and others form Nashville's chapter of the NAACP and march on the governor's office to protest widespread racial lynching in Tennessee. White moderates form a biracial organization, the Commission on Interracial Cooperation (CIC); the Tennessee Interracial League is declared a CIC chapter.

THE THIRD CIVIL RIGHTS MOVEMENT, 1935–PRESENT

The election of Franklin D. Roosevelt in November 1932 and the advent of his New Deal in 1933–39 helped promote the Negro's third civil rights movement. Extending to the present, the objectives have included (1) abolishing Jim Crow; (2) desegregating schools and public places; (3) ridding the nation of a corrupt and racially discriminating law and criminal justice system; (4) removing widespread racial and gender discrimination in the nation's employment systems; and (5) gaining economic parity for African Americans and other minorities.

The third, or modern, civil rights movement reached its most dramatic heights with (1) the *Brown v. Board of Education* (1954) decision by the U.S.

Supreme Court; (2) the sit-in demonstrations in the early 1960s; and (3) the passage of the Civil Rights Acts of 1964, 1965, and 1968.

However, this movement began in 1935, when the NAACP hired Charles Hamilton Houston, dean of the law school at Howard University and a law graduate of Harvard University, to develop a legal strategy to attack Jim Crow. With his former student Thurgood Marshall, Houston masterminded the NAACP strategy that would develop the third civil rights movement using the following tactics: (1) attacking Jim Crow higher education; (2) suing in federal court against discrimination in pay between white and Negro teachers (who were paid 25 percent less even with the same college degrees); (3) assist Negro citizens in fighting discrimination in the criminal justice system; and finally, (4) filing suits against Jim Crow in secondary schools.

In the area of employment, A. Philip Randolph and his Brotherhood of Sleeping Car Porters (BSCP) fought to get the Negro union recognized and gain equal pay by 1939. Randolph and the BSCP became partners with the NAACP in leading the civil rights movement. The Negro porters agreed to donate an hour's pay to help the NAACP file the lawsuits against Jim Crow.

CHRONOLOGY OF THE THIRD CIVIL RIGHTS MOVEMENT

1935

The National Negro Congress is founded, with Randolph as president. The NAACP and Donald Murray win *Murray v. Maryland* to begin desegregation of higher education.

1936

The Southern Youth Conference is founded. Tennessee begins out-of-state-scholarships for Negro citizens to prevent the NAACP from forcing the desegregation of graduate and professional programs at the University of Tennessee.

1937

Redmond v. Tennessee is filed in an unsuccessful attempt to desegregate UT graduate program.

1938

The Southern Conference for Human Welfare (SCHW) is founded to fight Southern poll taxes and Jim Crow.

1939

Marian Anderson, Negro contralto, sings at the Lincoln Memorial in Washington, D.C.

1940

The SCHW moves to Chattanooga, Tennessee for its second biennial meeting; an NAACP chapter is organized in Chattanooga by Perry A. Stephens and others.

1941

Alexander Looby, Thurgood Marshall, and other NAACP lawyers file *Harold E. Thomas v. Nashville Schools* and *C. B. Robinson v. Chattanooga Schools*, forcing equal pay for Negro and white teachers.

1942

The court case of *Joseph Michael v. Tennessee* convinces Tennessee to begin building graduate programs at Tennessee A&I. SCHW moves from Chattanooga to Nashville. Tennessee opens a graduate school at Tennessee A&I to prevent enrollment of Negroes at the University of Tennessee. Randolph threatens a March on Washington (MOW); President Roosevelt issues Executive Order No. 8802, forbidding discrimination in employment.

1943

The CIC dies; the Southern Regional Council founded in Atlanta; A&I's new president, W. S. Davis, is told to make the school comparable "to UT for white students."

1944

In June, Tennessee A&I State College graduates its first master's degree student.

1947

Tennessee and other southern states form the Southern Regional Education Board (SREB) to contract with Meharry Medical College and other universities to provide medical, dental, and professional education to Negro citizens, thus preventing the desegregation of white universities in the South, including UT.

1948

President Harry S. Truman issues Executive Order No. 9981, prohibiting segregation and discrimination in the American military; Truman also orders no discrimination in housing and federal housing loans; he wins the 1948 election even though Strom Thurmond of South Carolina and other southerners form the Dixiecrat Party in an attempt to defeat him because of his support for the civil rights movement.

1949

Ada Spuel v. Oklahoma Law School is won by the NAACP; an NAACP case also forces Texas to desegregate its professional schools.

1950

NAACP lawyers file secondary school desegregation cases in South Carolina, Maryland, Kansas, Tennessee, Virginia, and Washington, D.C. Civil rights attorney Avon N. Williams Jr. files J. McSwain v. Anderson County, Tennessee, and Gray v. University of Tennessee.

1951

UT is forced to accept six Negro graduate students rather than fight the Gray case. Tennessee A&I State College is upgraded to Tennessee A&I State University to help fight off Jim Crow lawsuits.

1952

Federal Judge Robert Taylor of Knoxville delays the McSwain v. Anderson County school desegregation case in anticipation that the U.S. Supreme Court will soon rule on all school desegregation cases.

1953

Scarritt College and Vanderbilt University admit the first Negro graduate students in divinity.

1954

On May 17, in Brown v. Board of Education, the U.S. Supreme Court orders school desegregation in five states and lays the groundwork for national desegregation. An African American is elected to the Oak Ridge Town Council.

1955

On May 31, the U.S. Supreme Court issues Brown II, which urges school desegregation "with all deliberate speed." The case Robert W. Kelly et al. v. Board of Education of Nashville, Tennessee, is filed. A group of southern congressman issues the Southern Manifesto opposing the Brown decision; Tennessee congressmen Albert Gore, Estes Kefauver, and J. Percy Priest refuse to sign it. Nashville's Catholic schools voluntarily desegregate. In August, Oak Ridge schools desegregate voluntarily. In December, the Montgomery bus boycott begins. Memphis Negro leaders begin a political civil rights movement.

1956

On August 23, Clinton High School in Anderson County, Tennessee, desegregates under a court order, and eleven Negro students are enrolled there. On October 5, the Tennessee Supreme Court says that *Brown* nullifies Tennessee's school segregation law. The U.S. Supreme Court orders Montgomery buses to desegregate in *Gayle et al. v. Browser*. In December, the Southern Christian Leadership Conference (SCLC) is founded by Martin Luther King Jr. and others to fight Jim Crow in the South. Memphis Negroes challenge Jim Crow buses.

1957

The Civil Rights Act of 1957 is passed by Congress to shore up Negro voting rights. In May, Bobby L. Cain becomes first Negro to graduate from Clinton High School. On September 9, Nashville city schools desegregate under federal court order; that same month, radicals bomb the Hattie Cotton Public School in Nashville.

1958

In January, the Nashville Christian Leadership Council (NCLC) is founded by Kelly Miller Smith and other civil rights leaders; James M. Lawson Jr. moves to Tennessee and begins nonviolence workshops in March. Buses in Nashville desegregate.

1959

In October, the Nashville Student Movement is organized by local college students; in November, the NCLC, K. M. Smith, James M. Lawson Jr., and local college students begin precise training for nonviolence tactics to desegregate downtown Nashville. A federal court orders Smyrna, Tennessee, schools to desegregate. Negroes begin a drive to register and vote in Fayette and Haywood counties. Governor Buford Ellington and state officials attack Highlander Folk School, which promotes unionism, anti-poverty programs, and civil rights.

1960

On February 13, students launch the first sit-in demonstrations in Nashville; on March 4, Nashville police invade First Colored Baptist Church and arrest James M. Lawson; that same month, students begin sit-in demonstrations in Chattanooga, Knoxville, and Memphis. The Nashville movement spreads across the South as the model to follow. In March, LeMoyne College students and others begin sit-in demonstrations in Memphis. In April, Negro college students found the Student Nonviolent Coordinating Committee (SNCC). On May 10, Nashville begins voluntary desegregation of downtown stores;

that same month, citizens in Memphis file *Watson v. Memphis* to force desegregation of all city facilities and parks. In August, Chattanooga begins desegregation of downtown stores. In September, *Goss v. Knoxville* is filed to force desegregation of local schools. In December, "tent cities" begin in Hayward and Fayette counties as farmers evict Negro sharecropper families for daring to register and vote. By December, Memphis desegregates buses and libraries but not swimming pools and other public facilities.

1961

On January 20, President John F. Kennedy, a Democrat, is inaugurated. On May 14, CORE and SNCC launch the Freedom Ride tests. On May 17, the anniversary of *Brown*, students in Nashville, under Diane Nash and SNCC, take control of Freedom Rides; NCLC helps finance these demonstrations. That summer, the NAACP and the SCLC adopt the students' nonviolent public demonstration tactics; SNCC begins to register Negro voters in Mississippi. Landowners and county governments in Fayette and Haywood counties, Tennessee, are forced to allow Negroes to register and vote. Schools begin court-ordered desegregation in Chattanooga, rural Davidson County, Knoxville, and Memphis (*Northcross v. Memphis*). UT admits two Negro undergraduates under the threat of a lawsuit, while court-ordered desegregation begins at Memphis State University. On September 21, the Interstate Commerce Commission outlaws segregation on buses, trains, etc.

1962

On March 26, *J. H. Turner v. Memphis et al.* forces desegregation of restaurants at the Memphis airport. In July, a civil rights bill is introduced in Congress. In the *Baker v. Carr* (1962) case, the U.S. *Supreme* Court orders Tennessee to draw legislative districts fairly and according to the "one-man-one-vote" concept. In August, *Mapp v. Chattanooga* (1960) forces desegregation of Chattanooga–Hamilton County schools.

1963

Memphis, Knoxville, Chattanooga, and Nashville further desegregate downtown and city facilities and businesses. In *Watson v. Memphis*, the U.S. Supreme Court case sets the precedent that municipalities cannot enforce Jim Crow rules in public buildings and recreational facilities, including parks, playgrounds, and swimming pools. On July 1, Governor Frank G. Clement creates the Tennessee Commission on Human Relations, later named the Commission on Human Rights and the Tennessee Civil Rights Commission. On August 27, W. E. B. DuBois dies in his new home, Ghana, Africa. On August 28, the March on Washington, organized by A. Philip Randolph, Roy Wilkins, and others, is held to pressure Congress to pass a new civil rights bill. On September 15, domestic terrorists bomb a Birmingham church, killing four little Negro girls in Sunday school. On November 22, President Kennedy is murdered in Dallas, Texas, and Vice President Lyndon B. Johnson succeeds him.

1964

A comprehensive Civil Rights Act is passed. Also, the Twenty-fourth Amendment to the Constitution is ratified by the states to abolish poll taxes; legislation nullifies literacy tests. All schools, colleges, and universities in Tennessee must desegregate. Archie W. Willis Jr. of Memphis, a civil rights attorney, is elected to the Tennessee General Assembly—the first African American since Reconstruction to win a legislative seat. In November, Martin Luther King Jr. receives the Nobel Peace Prize in Sweden.

1965

In February, the civil rights leader Malcolm X is murdered. The Voting Rights Act is passed by Congress, providing punitive measures against persons discriminating against another citizen's voting rights. More Negroes are elected to the Tennessee General Assembly, including Russell B. Sugarmon. Congress holds hearings on the KKK and white terrorism.

1966

Tennessee begins to redraw legislative districts according to *Baker v. Carr*, allowing more Negroes and urban dwellers to be elected to public offices. Edward K. Brooke of Massachusetts becomes the first African American elected to the U.S. Senate since the 1880s.

1967

The U.S. Supreme Court orders busing to further desegregate schools. The number of black congressmen increases to forty seats. The NAACP and other civil rights organizations begin to sue corporations for discrimination and biased employment practices. On May 17, Tennessee makes permanent its Human Rights Commission, today's Tennessee Civil Rights Commission. In November, J. O. Patterson becomes the first Negro elected to State Senate.

1968

A garbage strike begins in Memphis; Martin Luther King Jr. is murdered there on April 4; riots erupt across the nation. Congress passes the Open Housing Act. In May, Rita Sanders (later Geier), a history instructor at Tennessee State University, and other plaintiffs file the *Rita Sanders (Geier) v. Governor Buford Ellington* suit to desegregate higher education in Tennessee.

1974

Eleven members of the General Assembly form the Tennessee Caucus of Black State Legislators. Raymond Richardson, Sterlin N. Adams (both professors at TSU), and others form Tennesseans for Justice in Higher Education to enter the *Geier* case as plaintiffs; they call for the merger of UT Nashville into TSU.

1977

In January, federal judge Frank Gray Jr. orders the merger of TSU and UT Nashville, which will occur on July 1, 1979; Tennessee begins plans to desegregate all higher education in the state.

1983

Martin Luther King Day is passed by Congress and signed by President Ronald Reagan in November.

1985

Tennessee adopts Martin Luther King Day.

1992

Congress passes more Civil Rights amendments, including women's rights. Willie Herenton becomes the first African American to be elected mayor of Memphis.

1996

Nashville appoints its first African American police chief.

2001

The 1968 *Geier* case is settled.

2002

African American professionals begin instituting class-action suits against discrimination by American companies. The first African American is elected vice mayor of Nashville.

2003

Governor Phil Bredesen, a Democrat, appoints additional African American judges to state courts.

This "Synopsis and Chronology of the Civil Rights Movement" may be used by teachers and students in schools and college classrooms, either as transparencies or as an audiovisual presentation.

BIBLIOGRAPHICAL ESSAY

In addition to the citations below, the reader will note that throughout the narrative itself, quotations from newspaper accounts often mention the publications and the dates of articles.

INTRODUCTION. THE HISTORICAL BACKGROUND

For information about African Americans in Tennessee history, I consulted Anita S. Goodstein, *Nashville 1780–1860: From Frontier to City* (Gainesville: Univ. of Florida Press, 1989), which has a chapter on Negroes; Loren Schweninger, *From Tennessee Slave to St. Louis Entrepreneur: The Autobiography of James P. Thomas* (Columbia: Univ. of Missouri Press, 1984); U.S. Census reports and manuscripts, 1790–1860; John V. Cimprich Jr., "Military Governor Johnson and Tennessee Blacks, 1862–65," *Tennessee Historical Quarterly* 39 (1980): 459–70; two books by Lester C. Lamon, *Black Tennesseans, 1900–1930* (Knoxville: Univ. of Tennessee Press, 1977) and *Blacks in Tennessee, 1791–1970* (Knoxville: Univ. of Tennessee Press, 1981); Alrutheus A. Taylor, *The Negro in Tennessee, 1860–1880* (Washington, D.C.: Associated Negro Publishers, 1941); Robert A. Hill, ed., *The Marcus Garvey and Universal Improvement Association Papers*, vol 6 (Berkeley: Univ. of California Press, 1983, 1989), xxxix, 3, 4, 578–79, 80–82, 583, 584–87; and the *Nashville Colored Tennessean* newspaper, 1865–1866.

Also useful were William Still, *The Underground Railroad* (1872; repr. New York: Arno Press, 1968) and John Hope Franklin and Loren Schweninger, *Runaway Slaves: Rebels on the Plantation* (New York: Oxford Univ. Press, 1999), which document rebellious slave cases, including some in Tennessee; Nat Love, *The Life and Adventures of Nat Love* (1907; repr. New York: Arno Press, 1968); and Willard B. Gatewood Jr., ed., *Slave and Freeman: The Autobiography of George L. Knox* (Lexington: Univ. Press of Kentucky, 1979). For my discussion of Nat D. Williams, R. Q. Venson, and race relations in Memphis, I consulted these issues of the *Memphis World*: Sept. 16, 20, 1931; Feb. 12, 23, Mar. 1, Apr. 1, May 3, 10, 31, June 17, 1932.

For more general information about Tennessee and its cities, the following were particularly helpful: Sam B. Smith, ed., *Tennessee History: A Bibliography* (Knoxville: Univ. of Tennessee Press, 1974); Paul H. Bergeron, Stephen V. Ash, and Jeanette Keith, *Tennesseans and Their History* (Knoxville: Univ. of Tennessee Press, 1999); David M. Tucker, *Memphis since Crump: Bossism, Blacks, and Civic Reformers* (Knoxville: Univ. of Tennessee Press, 1980); John E. Harkins, *Metropolis of the Nile: Memphis and Shelby County, An Illustrated History* (Oxford, MS: The Guild Bindery Press, 1982); and Robert A. Sigafoos,

Cotton Row to Beale Street: A Business History (Memphis: Memphis State University Press, 1979), 332–36.

Other books and articles I consulted for the introduction included John Hope Franklin and Alfred A. Moss Jr., *From Slavery to Freedom: A History of Negro Americans* (New York: Knopf, 1947, 1988); T. Lynn Smith, "The Redistribution of the Negro Population in the United States, 1910–1960," *Journal of Negro History* 51 (1966): 155–73; Carter G. Woodson, *The Education of the Negro Prior to 1861* (Washington, D.C.: Association for Study of Negro Life and History, 1919); Robert Weisbrot, *Freedom Bound: A History of America's Civil Rights Movement* (New York: Penguin Books, 1991); two books by Taylor Branch, *Parting the Waters: America in the King Years, 1954–63* (New York: Simon and Schuster, 1988) and *Pillar of Fire: America in the King Years, 1963–65* (New York: Simon and Schuster, 1998); and Thomas C. Holt and Elsa B. Brown, eds., *Major Problems in African-American History*, vol. 2 (New York: Houghton Mifflin Co., 2000), 256–57, 259, 292, 316.

CHAPTER 1. THE EARLY CIVIL RIGHTS MOVEMENT IN TENNESSEE

Of the many books on the New Deal, John H. Kirby, *Black Americans in the Roosevelt Era: Liberalism and Race* (Knoxville: Univ. of Tennessee Press, 1980) is especially relevant to the concerns of this volume. See also Kevin A. McMahon, *Reconsidering Roosevelt on Race: How the Presidency Paved the Road to Brown* (Chicago: Univ. of Chicago Press, 2003).

My account of Thurgood Marshall's life and work is indebted to Mark V. Tushnet, *Making Civil Rights Law: Thurgood Marshall and the Supreme Court, 1926–1961* (New York: Oxford Univ. Press, 1994) and Juan Williams, *Thurgood Marshall: American Revolutionary* (New York: Random House, 1998); see Williams especially for details on NAACP actions, Houston's comments, the Columbia riot, and Tennessee cases (96, 131, 132, 139–41, 247). Also see Genna R. McNeil, *Groundwork: Charles Hamilton Houston and the Struggle for Civil Rights* (Philadelphia: Univ. of Pennsylvania Press, 1985) for details on the life and work of Marshall's mentor at Howard University. Information accessible at the NAACP–Legal Defense Fund Web site was also helpful: http://www.naacpldf.org.

On the early life of Avon N. Williams Jr. and his family, I consulted the biographical sketch in the Avon N. Williams Papers, Special Collections, Tennessee State University Library; editions of the *Knoxville City Directory*, 1920–1953, provided other details.

Charles H. Houston's policy statements on discrimination in education (now contained in the Papers of the NAACP) were excerpted in Holt and Brown, eds., *Major Problems in African-American History*, vol. 2, 256–57. Information about R. B. Redmond and his case were drawn from the aforementioned Williams, *Thurgood Marshall*, and from Redmond's profile in *In Black and White: Special Centennial Edition* (Franklin, TN: Williamson County Historical Society, 2000); Mark V. Tushnet, *The NAACP's Legal Strategy against Segregated Education, 1925–1950* (Chapel Hill: Univ. of North Carolina, 1987), 54–55; documents on the UT-Redmond case in the NAACP Papers, Box I-D-96, 97, Series II-B, University Cases, Library of Congress; Redmond's personal legal file in the Williams archives at the old downtown Nashville office at 203 Second Avenue, North; Papers of C. H. Houston, Mooreland-Spingarn Research Center, Howard University; and NAACP Legal Defense Fund, *Thirty Years of Building American Justice* (New

York: W. W. Norton, 1975). For Houston's comments on the Redmond case's significance in history, see *Buffalo Courier Express*, Mar. 23, 1937.

Information on Z. A. Looby and his law school, as well as his role in teacher pay issues, was drawn from various documents in the Z. A. Looby Papers, Special Collections, Fisk University. The quoted passage about the law school was from the *Nashville World*, Sept. 1, 1933.

My account of Tennessee school and higher education cases and laws pertaining to the NAACP cases was derived from documents in Record Group 92 and Record Group 273, Tennessee State Library and Archives (TSLA), Nashville. Information on the early efforts of Tennessee A&I State College to establish graduate education came from the same source, especially letters and reports between the president and state commissioner of education.

For the quoted passages from Tennessee statutes, I consulted the appropriate bound volumes of *Public Acts of State of Tennessee* (Nashville: Secretary of State, 1900–present), which are arranged chronologically at the TSLA. For 1901, see Chap. 7, Sec. 1; for 1937, see Chap. 256, Sec. 1; and for 1941, see Chap. 43, Sec. 2.

I based my account of the Southern Conference on Human Welfare and its relationship to the New Deal on John Egerton, *Speak Now Against the Day: The Generation before the Civil Rights Movement* (1994; repr., Chapel Hill: Univ. of North Carolina Press, 1995), 95, 148; Thomas A. Krueger, *And Promises to Keep: The Southern Conference on Human Welfare, 1938–1948* (Nashville: Vanderbilt Univ. Press, 1967); Tushnet, *NAACP's Legal Strategy*, 50–79; James T. Baker, *Eleanor Roosevelt: First Lady* (Fort Worth: Harcourt Brace, 1999); William Whitman, *David Lilienthal: Public Servant in a Power Age* (New York: Henry Holt Publishers, 1948); and Roy Tolbert Jr., "Arthur E. Morgan's Social Philosophy and the Tennessee Valley Authority," *East Tennessee Historical Society Papers* 41 (1969): 86–99. For Hastie's comments, see "William H. Hastie Foreshadows a Shift in the NAACP," in *Negro Protest Thought in the Twentieth Century*, ed. Francis L. Broderick and August Meier (Indianapolis: Bobbs-Merrill, 1965), 189–96. And on C. B. Robinson and his political activities, see various documents in the Clarence B. Robinson Papers, Special Collections, TSU Library.

Information on certain federal cases and biographical details about federal judges in this and other chapters were found at the Federal Judicial Center Web site (http://www.fjc.gov/) and related links. See also Franklin and Moss, *From Slavery to Freedom*, 274, 349, 387, 393, 415, for information on Hastie, A. Philip Randolph, and the general racial climate of the time. Hastie's description of a desirable plaintiff came from Tushnet, *NAACP's Legal Strategy*, 37, and *Crisis* magazine, Sept. 1939. "The Story of Vivien Thomas and Dr. Alfred Blalock," *Tennessee Tribune*, Jan. 30–Feb. 5, 2002, 1C–3C, outlines the life of Harold Thomas; I also spoke by telephone to his widow, Lillian Dunn Thomas of Nashville, on Feb. 2, 2003.

For Randolph's march on Washington and other information on Randolph, see P. F. Pfeffer, *A. Philip Randolph, Pioneer of the Civil Rights Movement* (Baton Rouge: Louisiana State Univ. Press, 1990), esp. chap. 2, "Let the Masses March," 45–88.

For rating systems on teacher pay, see Donald G. Nieman, *Promises to Keep: African-Americans and the Constitutional Order, 1776 to the Present* (New York: Oxford Univ. Press, 1991). For the Chattanooga case specifics, see the C. B. Robinson Papers and the *Chattanooga Times*, May 13, 1942. *Note:* Teacher pay equity by race and gender gradually improved over the years, but by 1953 Tennessee's white male teachers still made a little more than white and black female teachers, while white teachers overall made a little more than black teachers, depending on the location of the school system. Inequities in teacher pay by gender and race were less visible in Tennessee's four major urban areas. Negro teachers on average in rural Shelby County, for example, got $63.31 a year less than white teachers, and in Memphis black teachers received an average of $37.90 less than white teachers. Also, according to the 1953 State Department of Education report, which was abstracted in the *Nashville Globe* (Oct. 30, 1953), some 77 percent of white teachers and 75 percent of Negro teachers had college degrees. In Nashville, 92 percent of Negro teachers and 83 percent of white teachers had college degrees; yet, white teachers still received on average a few more dollars per year than the Negro teachers at that time.

Gunnar Myrdal's comments on American racial problems were taken from *An American Dilemma: The Negro Problem and Modern Democracy* (New York: Harper, 1944); see esp. 438, 550, 907. For information on Charles S. Johnson, the Institutes of Race Relations, and Johnson's publications, see Richard Robbins, *Charles S. Johnson and the Struggle for Civil Rights* (Jackson: Univ. Press of Mississippi, 1996), 103–7, 122–24, 169–70, 175–84.

On the ways in which southerners linked the civil rights movement to an international Communist conspiracy, see Jeff Woods, *Black Struggle, Red Scare: Segregation and Anti-Communism in the South, 1948–1968* (Baton Rouge: Louisiana State Univ. Press, 2004); Mary L. Dudziak, *Cold War Civil Rights: Race and the Image of American Democracy* (Princeton, NJ: Princeton Univ. Press, 2000); and Matthew F. Jacobson, *Whiteness of a Different Color: European Immigrants and the Alchemy of Race* (Cambridge, MA: Harvard Univ. Press, 1998), 157. For more information on SCHW activities and James Dombrowski, see Frank T. Adams, *James A. Dombrowski: An American Heretic, 1897–1983* (Knoxville: Univ. of Tennessee Press, 1992); and James Dombrowski, "The Southern Conference for Human Welfare," *Common Ground* 6 (Summer 1946): 14–26. On W. E. B. DuBois, I consulted David Leavering Lewis, *W. E. B. DuBois*, 2 vols. (New York: Henry Holt, 1993–2000); and the FBI files on DuBois, now available on microfilm (Wilmington, DE: Scholarly Resources, 2002).

Looby's account of the handcuffed boys is from a letter dated Feb. 27, 1945, Z. Alexander Looby Papers, Special Collections, Fisk Univ., Nashville.

For details on the Columbia riot and its aftermath, I consulted many newspaper accounts, especially from the *Nashville Globe* (Feb. 1946–Feb. 1947); issues of the *National Baptist Union Review*, the *Columbia Daily Herald*, and *Lewisburg Tribune* provided additional details. Helpful, too, were the following articles and books: Kenneth R. Janken, "The Politics of Walter White," *The Crisis* (Jan./Feb. 2003): 48–52; Dorothy Beeler, "Race Riot in Columbia, Tennessee: February 25–27, 1946," *Tennessee Historical Quarterly* 39 (Spring 1980): 49–61; Robert W. Ickard, *No More Social Lynchings* (Franklin, TN: Hillsboro Press, 1997); and Gail W. O'Brien, *The Color of the Law: Race, Violence, and Justice in the Post–World War II South* (Chapel Hill: Univ. of North Carolina Press, 1999). Henry Harlan's comments appeared in Carl T. Rowan, *South of Freedom* (New York: Knopf, 1952), 50. Details of Marshall's movements in Columbia appear in Williams, *Thurgood Marshall*, 131–38. And for reference to the abilities of Looby and Cowan as civil rights lawyers, see Jack Greenberg, *Crusaders in the Court: How a Dedicated Band of Lawyers Fought for the Civil Rights Revolution* (New York: HarperCollins,

1994); Greenberg, it should be noted, succeeded Marshall as head of the LDF. *Note:* The Ickard book, *No More Social Lynchings,* includes appendixes that detail what happened to key figures in the Columbia episode in later years: James Stephenson moved to Detroit. Leon Ransom resigned from Howard University in 1946, entered private practice, and died in 1954. Julius Blair ran for the Columbia City Council in 1953 and died in 1962 at age ninety-two. Maurice Weaver drew many white clients and enjoyed a thriving law practice in Chattanooga until alcoholism forced his disbarment in 1968; he died at age seventy-two in 1983.

For information about the conferences and activities of 1946 and 1947, see the *Nashville Globe,* Apr. 26, 1946; and the *National Baptist Union-Review,* June 15, 1946, May 10, 1947. Excerpts from the 1947 report "To Secure These Rights" are included in Steven F. Lawson and Charles Payne, *Debating the Civil Rights Movement, 1945–1968* (New York: Rowman and Littlefield, 1998), 45–53.

Looby's comments on Houston's legacy are from an interview that appeared in the *Nashville Tennessean,* Apr. 23, 1971; see also McNeil, *Groundwork.* Most of the details of the *Gray* case are from 1949 issues of the *Nashville Sun.*

For information on the black press, I am indebted to Karen F. Brown, "An Historical Study of the Black Press in Tennessee," M.A. thesis, Tennessee State Univ., 1976.

CHAPTER 2. *BROWN* AND JIM CROW SCHOOLS IN TENNESSEE

See Chase C. Mooney, *Slavery in Tennessee* (Bloomington: Indiana Univ. Press, 1957); and Annual Report of the Superintendent of Education, Tennessee Board of Education Records, 1913–1970, Record Group 92, TSLA, for, respectively, statistics on land ownership and literacy levels in Tennessee.

The bound volumes of *Public Acts of State of Tennessee,* 1867–69 and the *House and Senate Journal for the State of Tennessee,* 1866–70 (both housed at the TSLA) were consulted for the racial statutes that defined persons of color. For analysis of racial definitions, see Grace E. Hale, *Making Whiteness: The Culture of Segregation in the South, 1890–1940* (New York: Pantheon, 1998); Mia Bay, *The White Image in the Black Mind: African-American Ideas about White People, 1830–1925* (New York: Oxford Univ. Press, 2000); and Matthew Frye Jacobson, *Whiteness of a Different Color: European Immigrants and the Alchemy of Race* (Cambridge: Harvard Univ. Press, 1998). Jacobson notes, "Race itself no longer retained any salient distinctions among Madison Grant's Nordics, Alpines, and Mediterranean—much less the 36 European races enumerated by the Dillingham Commission—but rather referred to the longstanding, simpler black-white dyad of the Jim Crow South" (117).

For details on William Edmondson, see Bobby L. Lovett, "From Plantation to City: William Edmondson and the African-American Community," in *The Art of William Edmondson* (Jackson: Mississippi Univ. Press, 2000), a museum exhibition catalog comprising essays by various authors on Edmondson's life and work.

See Franklin and Moss, *From Slavery to Freedom,* 242, for comments on northern views about southern education.

Reports for the Rosenwald Fund and Robert E. Clay's reports on Negro schools in Tennessee may be found in the State Board of Education records, TSLA. The bulk of the Rosenwald papers are stored at Fisk University, Special Collections.

See *Tennessee Laws*, 1925, and State Department of Education Records and Minutes, 1874–1984, RG 273, TSLA, for comparative information about education for blacks and whites in Tennessee. The quotation ("Many white Tennesseans . . .") is from Bergeron, Ash, and Keith, *Tennesseans and Their History*, 222.

My sources for information on the inferiority of Tennessee schools for Negroes from the 1930s through the 1950s included appropriate volumes of *Tennessee Laws*; *Nashville Globe*, Oct. 19, 1945; the C. B. Robinson Papers; and a 1989 interview with Helen Work, former historian for First Baptist Church, Capitol Hill, Nashville. The quotation ("On the first day of school . . .") from Haynes's *Scars of Segregation: An Auto-biography* (New York: Vantage Press, 1974) appears on p. 112.

My account in this chapter of school desegregation lawsuits drew on numerous newspaper stories and some original texts available through the Federal Judicial Center's Web site and related links. Precise comments and details on the participation by Looby and Williams, among other civil rights lawyers, were taken from their papers as well as from some NAACP reports (i.e., the Memphis case). School board records from the various districts involved were also helpful. I am indebted as well to David J. Brittain, "A Case Study of the Problems of Racial Integration in the Clinton, Tennessee, High School," Ed.D. dissertation, New York Univ., 1959, 23–30, 41–44, 80–120 (copy at Nashville Public Library, downtown branch).

My account of the *Brown* decision announcement was based on Lerone Bennett Jr., "The Day Race Relations Changed Forever," *Ebony*, May 1985; and James T. Patterson, *Brown v. Board of Education: a Civil Rights Milestone and its Troubled Legacy* (New York: Oxford Univ. Press, 2001), 222. Reactions to the decision were drawn from various Tennessee newspaper reports, including those mentioned in the text and the *Nashville Tennessean*. The Burch quotation ("The country is still shaken . . .") is from a micro-filmed copy of his diary in the TSLA's manuscript division. My summary of the response to *Brown* by the NAACP and other civil rights groups and the reaction of Georgia governor Griffin ("No matter what . . .") drew on articles in the Nashville daily papers and the *Clarksville Leaf-Chronicle* appearing in May 18–25, 1954. For Charles S. Johnson's reaction ("most important national mandate"), see his article "Some Significant Social and Educational Implications of the U.S. Supreme Court's Decision," *Journal of Negro Education* (Summer 1954): 23–29. Additional details, particularly on Marshall's response, came from Tushnet, *Making Civil Rights Law*, 269–70.

For the quotation from Carl T. Rowan's *Go South to Sorrow* (New York: Random House, 1957), see p. 7.

For details on the white resistance to *Brown*, I relied on articles in both Negro and white newspapers, as well as the TFCG pamphlet and similar documents on school desegregation archived in the Tennessee Department of Education Records, 1872–1972, RG 92, TSLA. Also helpful were issues of *Southern School News*, which was initiated after *Brown* to "report the facts on school desegregation."

My reconstruction of the Oak Ridge case and the early stages of the Clinton case drew especially on issues of the *Oak Ridger*, the *Clinton Courier News*, as well as the Knoxville, Chattanooga, and Memphis dailies. I also consulted the report by Clinton principal David J. Brittain, *A Case Study of the Problems of Racial Integration in the Clinton, Tennessee High School* (Ann Arbor, MI: University Microfilms, 1959).

Information on the January 1955 meeting at the Race Relations Institute came from the Looby Papers. The Eisenhower statement ("We [Republicans] believe in the dignity . . .") was reported in the *Oak Ridger*, Aug. 10, 1955.

BIBLIOGRAPHIC ESSAY

For details on the *Kelly* case, see the *Nashville Globe*, Oct. 14, 1955, and other *Globe* issues, Oct. 1955–Jan. 1956. The *Globe* (Feb. 3, 1956) also provided information about the desegregation of Nashville parks and golf courses. However, this paper's coverage of civil rights cases and that of another Negro paper, the *Nashville Commentator*, were not as thorough as that of the *Memphis World* and *Memphis Tri-State Defender*.

Governor Clement's letters on school desegregation are located in the Department of Education Papers, RG 92, TSLA.

For understanding the neo-Confederate movement and Southern nationalists, see *Southern Partisan* magazine (Second Quarter 2000). For the comments of the *Clinton Courier-News* on John Kasper, see its issue of Nov. 1, 1956. For the views of the *East Tennessee Reporter*, see its Nov. 7, 1957, issue. See also Wali R. Kharif, "School Desegregation in Clinton and Cookeville, Tennessee," in *Tennessee: State of the Nation*, ed. Larry H. Whiteaker and W.C. Dickinson (New York: American Heritage, 1995), 25–35; "Background of Segregation," five-part series, *Life* (Sept. 3, 10, 17, 24, and Oct. 1, 1956); and *Nashville Globe*, Feb. 10, 1956.

Additional details and analysis of the Clinton case (including Horace Wells's comments) came from June N. Adamson, "Few Black Voices Heard: The Black Community and the 1956 Desegregation Crisis in Clinton," in *Trial and Triumph: Essays in Tennessee's African American History*, ed. Carroll Van West (Knoxville: Univ. of Tennessee Press, 2002), 334–49; this article originally appeared in the *Tennessee Historical Quarterly* (Spring 1994). See also the *Knoxville Journal*, Sept. 2, 1956, for coverage of Clement's response to the crisis. Dramatic photos from Clinton ran in the Sept. 17, 1956, issue of *Life* to accompany its article "The Halting and Fitful Battle for Integration." For details of the violence, I relied on the *Life* article, on the *Clinton Courier-News* (Nov. 8, 1956), and on coverage in the Knoxville and Memphis dailies. Brittain, *A Case Study*, provided further information, including details of the events' aftermath, as did Robert E. Corlew, *Tennessee: A Short History*, 2nd ed. (Knoxville: Univ. of Tennessee Press, 1981), 530. Segregationists' letters to Governor Clement in the wake of the Clinton crisis were found in the Department of Education Papers, RG 92, TSLA. For passages from Clement's 1957 address, I consulted the *House and Senate Journal*. Also useful was Margaret Anderson, *The Children of the South* (New York: Farrar, Strauss and Giroux, 1958); this author was a teacher at CHS during the crisis.

On southern efforts to limit desegregation, see Harvard Sitkoff, *The Struggle for Black Equality, 1954–1980* (New York: Hill and Wang, 1981), 27; C. Vann Woodward, *The Strange Career of Jim Crow* (New York: Oxford Univ. Press, 1966), 160–62; and J. Harvie Wilkinson, *From Brown to Bakke: The Supreme Court and School Integration: 1954–1978* (New York: Oxford Univ. Press, 1976), 1–157. For Georgia and Tennessee responses, see *Columbia Daily Herald*, Feb. 26, 1957; and Gilbert E. Govan and James W. Livingood, *The Chattanooga Country, 1540–1976*, rev. ed. (Chapel Hill: Univ. of North Carolina Press, 1963), 409.

Details on the graduation of Bobby Cain and other Negro CHS students came from local newspaper coverage, as well as my interview with Cain, Apr. 19, 2002, Nashville. See also Adamson, "Few Black Voices Heard," 348.

On Kasper's 1957 activities, I consulted the following papers: *Knoxville Journal*, June 2, 1957; *Nashville Globe*, June 14, 28, Aug. 30, 1957; *Oak Ridger*, Sept. 11, 1957; and *Maryville-Alcoa Daily Times*, Oct. 6, 1958.

For the desegregation of Nashville schools, I relied on various journalistic accounts, including the *Nashville Globe*, Nov. 3, 1957, and the *Nashville Banner*, Sept. 10, 1957. The Reverend Smith was interviewed frequently by local reporters, and many of the interviews, including one with Alice Smith (July 26, 1993), are preserved in the K. M. Smith Papers, Special Collections, Vanderbilt Univ. I also conversed with Mrs. Smith about the 1957 events.

Historical background on Blount County came from Inez E. Burns, "Settlement and Early History of the Coves of Blount County, Tennessee," *East Tennessee Historical Society Papers* 24 (1952): 44–67.

Coverage of the Little Rock crisis that was particularly helpful included articles by L. A. Wilson in the *Memphis Tri-State Defender*. I also drew on Daisy Bates, *The Long Shadow of Little Rock* (1962; repr., Fayetteville: Univ. of Arkansas Press, 1986); Elizabeth Jacoway and C. F. Williams, *Understanding the Little Rock Crisis: An Exercise in Remembrance and Reconciliation* (Fayetteville: Univ. of Arkansas Press, 1999); and Graeme Cope, "Honest White People of the Middle and Lower Classes? A Profile of the Capitol Citizens' Council during the Little Rock Crisis of 1957," *Arkansas Historical Quarterly* 41 (2002): 37–58.

For events in Rutherford County, see *Rutherford County Courier*, Sept. 11, 1959; and Laura C. Jarmon, *Arbors to Bricks: A Hundred Years of African American Education in Rutherford County, Tennessee, 1865–1965* (Murfreesboro: Middle Tennessee State Univ., 1994).

The Knoxville case was covered not only in local papers but also in the *Memphis Press-Scimitar*, Sept. 1, 1960. A detailed account is provided by Ruby J. Anderson Hassan, "Desegregation in Knoxville Tennessee: A Case Study," Ed.D. diss., Univ. of Tennessee, 1999, v–vi, 70–219.

My reconstruction of events in Memphis during the late 1950s was derived largely from the branch NAACP quarterly and annual reports, Maxine Smith Papers, Memphis-Shelby County Room, Memphis Public Library. I also drew on reportage from the period in various Memphis papers: *Commercial Appeal*, *Press-Scimitar*, *World*, and *Tri-State Defender*.

The historical background of Chattanooga schools came from "Ordinances Pertaining to the Public Schools of Chattanooga, Tennessee," *Report of the Board of Education of the City of Chattanooga, Tennessee, 1892–1893* (1893), which are in my possession. For more recent events, I relied on Govan and Livingood, *The Chattanooga Country*, 502; and articles in the *Chattanooga Times*–see esp. Nov. 14, 1955; Jan. 10, 1956; Feb. 14 and March 28, 1961; Sept. 10, 24, and 25, 1963; and Jan. 1 and 29, 1964. See also *Chattanooga News–Free Press*, Sept. 3, 1961; Sept. 10, 1962; and Sept. 3, 1963. An interview I conducted with James Mapp (Mar. 21, 2003, Chattanooga) was valuable, as were details from his résumé. On Judge Darr, I drew on information from the Federal Judiciary Center's Web site.

For details of the rural Davidson County episode (including Williams's comments), see *Nashville Tennessean*, Sept. 12, 1960.

My conclusion for this chapter was based on Numan V. Bartley, *The Rise of Massive Resistance: Race and Politics in the South During the 1950s* (Baton Rouge: Louisiana State Univ. Press, 1997); see pp. 79–80, 82–83, 99–100, 131, 133, 137, 143, 144, 203, 214, 219, 275, for information on Tennessee. See also *Southern School News*, Sept.–Oct. 1956; and various articles on school desegregation in the *Race Relations Law Reporter*, 1958–1959, published by Vanderbilt Univ. School of Law. Also helpful were Neil McMillen, *The Citizens' Council: Organized Resistance to the Second Reconstruction, 1954–64* (Urbana: Univ. of Illinois Press, 1971); David L. Chappel, *Inside Agitators: White Southerners in the Civil Rights Movement* (Baltimore: Johns Hopkins Univ. Press, 1994); and "Bills to authorize BOE to assign pupils to designated schools," *Tennessee Senate Journal, 79th General Assembly* (Nashville: Rich Printing Co., 1955), 1683.

CHAPTER 3. CONTINUING SCHOOL DESEGREGATION IN TENNESSEE

On the subject of continued racial separatism into the 1960s, Cope's article "Honest White People of the Middle and Lower Classes?" was instructive.

Various accounts from Tennessee newspapers of the period provided facts, figures, and comments on the ongoing school integration process. The 1972 annual report of the Memphis branch NAACP (Maxine Smith Papers) was useful on the subjects of transfer plans and busing.

For information on the Cookeville case and the Darwin school, I consulted Wali R. Kharif, "Darwin School and Black Public Education: Cookeville in the Decade of the *Brown* Decision," in *Trial and Triumph*, ed. West, 351–65, an article that originally appeared in the spring 1997 issue of the *Tennessee Historical Quarterly*.

On desegregation in Fayette County, I used documents in the Williams Papers and Frankie C. Hunt, "A History of Desegregation of the Fayette County School System: Fayette County, Tennessee, 1954–1980," Ed.D. diss., Univ. of Mississippi, 1981, 50–60, 69, 77. Also, issues of the *Fayette County Falcon* were useful, as was a report, *Fear Runs Deep: Open Meeting, March 17–18, 1971, Somerville, Tennessee* (1971), which the Tennessee Advisory Committee for the U.S. Commission on Civil Rights published after holding a public hearing on the situation in Somerville. The committee recommended government investigations.

See Carl T. Rowan, *Dream Makers, Dream Breakers: The World of Thurgood Marshall* (Boston: Little, Brown, 1993), 255, for the quotation about Wallace's "ugly lessons."

For Jackson, Tennessee, I consulted the Williams Papers and accounts from the *Jackson Sun* and other Tennessee newspapers.

The Sept./Oct. 1999 issue of *Crisis*, the NAACP magazine, provided information about anti-civil rights organizations, infiltration of civil rights groups, and planted editorials. The information about Goldwater appeared in the *Jackson Sun*, Sept. 9, 17, 1964.

My account of desegregation difficulties in Franklin County drew on my conversation with Milton Kennerly (June 3, 2002, Nashville); on Arthur C. Hill's doctoral dissertation at the University of Minnesota, *The History of the Black People of Franklin County, Tennessee* (Ann Arbor, MI: Xerox Microfilm, 1981); and on my conversation with Ophelia Miller, a former Anderson County teacher now living in Shelbyville (Aug. 18, 2001). See also Ely Green, *Too Black, Too White* (Amherst: Univ. of Massachusetts Press, 1970).

Margaret R. Wolfe's comments are from *Kingsport, Tennessee: A Planned American City* (Lexington: Univ. Press of Kentucky, 1987), 187–90. I also consulted various issues of the *Kingsport Times*, including Sept. 6, 1961, Sept. 9, 1964, and May 2, 1969. For

Shelbyville and Bedford County, a key source (in addition to newspaper accounts) was *Educating Generations: History of Black Schools in 1880s to 2001*, published by the Gilliland Historical Resource Center in Shelbyville. For information on Pulaski and Giles County, I consulted *History of Black Education in Giles County, 1920–1970* (Giles County: African American History Committee, 1986), 55, as well as issues of the *Pulaski Citizen*, including Aug. 4 and 11, 1965. On Obion County, I drew on issues of the *Union City Daily Messenger*.

My account of 1967 activities in Memphis came from that year's branch NAACP reports (Maxine Smith Papers).

On the evolution of school desegregation cases, see Alfred H. Kelly and W. A. Harbison, *The American Constitution: Its Origins and Development* (New York: W. W. Norton, 1970); Richard A. Pride and J. D. Woodard, *The Burden of Busing: The Politics of Desegregation in Nashville, Tennessee* (Knoxville: Univ. of Tennessee Press, 1985); and Harold Spaeth, *The Warren Court: Cases and Commentary* (San Francisco: Chandler Publishing Co., 1966).

News articles in local papers provided details about the changing character of the Whitehaven neighborhood in Memphis, the incident involving Cameron and Stratford high schools in Nashville, and the disturbances in Chattanooga. For the outcome of the *Monroe* case in Jackson, I consulted the Williams Papers.

To reconstruct the *Mapp* case in Chattanooga and its various ramifications, I drew not only on the Chattanooga dailies (including issues of the *Chattanooga Times* for Feb. 28, 1967; June 6, 25, 1969; Nov. 11, 1969; and Jan. 1, 1998) but also on an interview with James Mapp in March 2003 in Chattanooga. Helpful, too, was a collection of clippings, "Civil Rights File, 1978–1989," at the downtown branch of the Chattanooga Public Library, Special Collections. Information on judges came from the Federal Judicial Center Web site and related links.

On "black flight" in Franklin County, see Hill, *The History of Black People in Franklin County*.

The branch NAACP's quarterly reports in the Maxine Smith Papers were invaluable in helping me detail the Black Monday protest and other school desegregation activities in Memphis. See also 1970 issues of the *Tri-State Defender*. Memphis's current mayor, Willie Herenton, a school principal at the time, was one of only a few who stayed out on the Black Mondays.

The Mays quotation ("Every scheme . . .") was from a speech published in the *Tri-State Defender*, Aug. 1, 1970.

Information on the teacher dismissals and the lawsuits they caused came from the Williams Papers; the *Nashville Tennessean*, Oct. 31, 1970; and from the government publication *The Federal Civil Rights Enforcement Effort: One Year Later* (Washington, DC: Government Printing Office, 1971), 101.

Various letters in the "desegregation file" in the Governor Buford Ellington Papers, TSLA, provided details on Ellington's dealings with other southern politicians and his positions on desegregation.

See the annual reports of the Memphis branch NAACP for 1971, 1972, 1973, 1974, 1977, and 1978, Maxine Smith Papers, for the quotations and other details about NAACP positions during these years. Smith expressed her feelings freely in these reports. Additional details came from the *Memphis Tri-State Defender*, Feb. 23, and

Mar. 9, 1974, and from *Tennessee Report Card* (Nashville: State Dept. of Education, 2001), available online via http://www.tennessee.gov/.

My account of white flight into Williamson County was based on Julian S. Carter, "From Claiborne's Institute to Natchez High School: The History of African American Education in Williamson County, Tennessee, 1890-1967," Ed.D. diss., George Peabody College, Vanderbilt Univ., 1998; Richard Warwick, *Black and White, Williamson County* (Franklin: Williamson County Historical Society, 2000); *Nashville Tennessean*, Nov. 9, 2003; and *Tennessee Schools: 2003 Report Card* (Nashville: State Department of Education, 2003), available via http://www.tennessee.gov/. The Nashville desegregation schools case drew on the Avon Williams Papers, local newspapers, the author's personal copies of public school board papers, State Board of Education documents, and Faye H. Hood, "An Historical Study of Court-Ordered Integration in Metropolitan Nashville-Davidson County Public Schools," Ed.D. diss., Tennessee State Univ., 1985.

On the busing controversy in Nashville and elsewhere, see Pride and Woodard, *The Burden of Busing,* 282; news clippings in the Williams Papers; *Nashville Ebony Gazette,* Oct. 9, 1975; and "Education Gap: In Virginia, School Lockout Still Reverberates," *Wall Street Journal,* May 17, 2004, A13. Today, the district buses its twenty-seven hundred students to a campus on the edge of Farmville. With just one public elementary, junior high, and senior high, there is no chance of resegregation. Legislators created a fund to help those locked out to get an education. Blacks now sit on the City Council and the County Board of Commissioners.

The hearing process on Nashville's "unitary school plan" generated a mountain of documents, which I retained after serving on the panel. I based my account of the hearings on these papers, as well as on issues of the *Community Key,* the Metro Nashville education newsletter, and regular coverage in the Nashville press during this period from late 1979 through early 1980.

Documents from the Williams papers informed my account of the SBOE antibusing resolution, the response of black legislators, and the legal actions involving the Metro School Board desegregation plan. For Metro School statistics on black and white enrollment, see *Nashville Banner,* Dec. 20, 1989. Note: Despite all his hard work in the school desegregation case, Avon Williams had to face the indignity of discrimination when it came time to pay him. Under the Civil Rights Attorney's Fees Awards Act (1976), the Board of Education would owe him and other NAACP lawyers $1.45 million. Although white attorneys would typically receive $150-$200 an hour for their work in such cases, city officials did not want to compensate black lawyers equally. White lawyers testified in Judge Wiseman's courtroom about the appropriateness of Williams's request for $200 per hour in fees. Williams was compelled to call white witnesses and ask about their fees and about his ranking among the Nashville bar. They all ranked Williams in the top tier. But Wiseman had the last say under existing federal court rules, and he dismissed most of the requested fees. See *Nashville Tennessean,* Dec. 12, 1982.

For data on the impact of white flight on the Nashville-Davidson County schools in recent years, the *2001 Report Card on Public Schools,* issued by a citizens' panel under the auspices of the Chamber of Commerce, Nashville, was useful.

Information about the situation in Knoxville was drawn from Hassan, *Desegregation in Knoxville,* and from the *Knoxville News-Sentinel,* May 24, 1979, and Dec. 16, 1989.

The recent statistics on black student populations came from *Tennessee Report Card: 2003*. In addition to the Tatum book mentioned in the text, another source on the resegregation issue was C. Lee, "Re-segregation Grows in Public Schools: Separate Is Unequal," *Focus* (Mar./Apr. 2003): 1, 11; this is a publication of the Joint Center of Political and Economic Studies.

For statistics on Tennessee's education expenditures, see Bergeron, Ash, and Keith, *Tennesseans and Their History*, 332; on recent appropriations and dropout rates, see *Nashville Tennessean*, Nov. 16, 2001.

Finally, an additional note about Nashville's First Baptist Church, Capitol Hill, of which I am a member and unofficial historian: In February 2004, the church hosted a busload of U.S. senators and representatives, including Senator Bill Frist of Tennessee and Representative John Lewis of Georgia, who stopped in Nashville during a southern pilgrimage to visit sacred places that marked the nation's civil rights movement. A section of the seating was reserved for the visitors, and Senator Frist and Representative Lewis gave remarks. James M. Lawson Jr. was the guest preacher for the occasion. He, along with Diane Nash and other veterans of the Nashville sit-ins, were in town for a civil rights forum sponsored by the Civil Rights Collection of the Nashville Public Library. Church members prepared a special after-service meal for the visitors in the Martin Luther King Jr. Banquet Room, related some history of First Baptist's involvement in the civil rights movement, heard their remarks, and sent them on their way to the next stop, the downtown public library, for a reception.

CHAPTER 4. SIT-IN DEMONSTRATIONS AND DESEGREGATION OF PUBLIC FACILITIES

Boss Crump was quoted ("You have a bunch . . .") in Roger Biles, "Robert R. Church, Jr., of Memphis: Black Republican Leader in the Age of Democratic Ascendancy, 1928–1940," *Tennessee Historical Quarterly* 17 (Winter 1983): 372. Other useful works on Memphis included D. M. Tucker, *Black Pastors and Leaders, Memphis 1819–1972* (Memphis: Memphis State Univ. Press, 1975), 19; and Sigafoos, *Cotton Row to Beale Street*.

For details of the segregated bus episode, see *Memphis Tri-State Defender*, Jan. 2 and 16, 1954.

David Goldfield, *Region, Race, and the Cities: Interpreting the Urban South* (Baton Rouge: Louisiana State Univ. Press, 1997), 255, 258, provided helpful information about the jobs picture for Negroes in Memphis during the New Deal era. For statistics on the African American population in Memphis in the 1940s, I drew on the following publications of the Negro Chamber of Commerce: *A Directory of the Colored People of Memphis and Shelby County* (1941), *Negro Year Book and Directory of Memphis* (1943), and *Negro Classified Directory, Memphis, Tennessee* (1952). The Negro chamber was founded by J. E. Walker in 1934; copies of its directories are available at the Memphis/Shelby County Room, Memphis Public Library. These volumes and those for other years proved invaluable throughout this chapter in constructing my profiles of local Negro leaders.

For data on Negro unemployment and underemployment, I consulted U.S. Census statistics for Tennessee, 1940–90, as well as the Negro Chamber of Commerce directories cited above. Advertisements in Memphis newspapers from 1954–56 provided information on costs of groceries and other products.

The account of life in a Memphis neighborhood drew largely on my personal recollections of living on Walnut Street, working as a paperboy for the *Press-Scimitar* and as a delivery boy for Robinson's Supermarket, and attending Porter Junior High School and Booker T. Washington High School. Also helpful was Gloria B. Melton's doctoral dissertation at Washington State University, *Blacks in Memphis, Tennessee, 1920–1955: A Historical Study* (Ann Arbor, MI: University Microfilms, 1982).

Details of Boss Crump's death and burial in October 1954—and the response to it within the Memphis black community—were reconstructed from issues of the *Memphis World, Tri-State Defender, Press-Scimitar, Commercial Appeal*, and other local papers, as well as from my own memories, the Melton dissertation, and a more recent article, "Racism killed school that survived Red Scare," *Nashville Tennessean*, Mar. 7, 2004.

The recollection of Miriam DeCosta-Willis ("Keep Memphis . . .") came from the *Commercial Appeal*, Jan. 25, 2004. My own memories of Memphis's Negro elite include Dr. P. W. Bailey, who maintained his offices upstairs at 781 Ioka Avenue not far from our house on Walnut Street; he had practiced medicine since 1938, treating my grandmother, mother, and me. He delivered my baby brother one early morning in our bedroom.

My reconstruction of the Memphis bus case involving O. Z. Evers drew on issues of various local papers. In addition, the following books have informed this and other chapters dealing with federal and U.S. Supreme Court cases: Kelly and Harbison, *The American Constitution*; Spaeth, *The Warren Court*; Jay A. Sigler, *The Courts and Public Policy: Cases and Essays* (Georgetown, Ontario: The Dorsey Press, 1970); and Charles Warren, *The Supreme Court in United States History*, 2 vols. (Boston: Little, Brown and Co., 1926). The matter of Judge Boyd's possible appointment to the Sixth Circuit Court of Appeals and the NAACP's response was detailed in Maxine Smith's report of Mar. 7–Apr. 3, 1962 (Maxine Smith Papers).

For background on Jessie Turner, who sued the City of Memphis over his ejection from the library, see issues of the *Annual Directory*, Negro Chamber of Commerce, G. W. Lee Collection, Memphis Room, Memphis Public Library.

The harassment of the Negro family in Glenview was reported in the *Memphis Press-Scimitar*, July 7 and Oct. 13, 1958.

The 1911 decision allowing Negro youngsters into the city zoo was reported in the *Memphis Commercial Appeal*, June 1 and 2, 1911. At that time, Memphis had twenty-three schools for whites with 246 rooms and a seating capacity of 10,536 and seven Negro schools with 86 rooms with a seating capacity of 4,240. About 54,000 school age children lived in the city area.

For the events of early 1959 in Memphis, I drew on local newspaper accounts. See esp. *Memphis World*, Jan. 3, 7, 1959, for details of the Matthews case; *Memphis World*, May 9, 1959, for Diggs's remarks; and *Memphis Tri-State Defender*, May 23, 1959, for information on bus station segregation. Local press coverage also provided the basis for my discussion of Memphis police brutality and black leaders' response to it.

My portrait of Maxine Smith is indebted to Anita Houk's article in the *Memphis Commercial Appeal*, Dec. 2, 1984. And here, as at various other points throughout this book, Smith's own annual and quarterly reports for the Memphis branch NAACP (contained in her papers at the Memphis Public Library) have been invaluable.

For information on Daisy Bates's visit to Nashville, I relied on letters, news clippings, and other documents provided to me in March 2002 by Harriet H. Davidson. See also Bates, *The Long Shadow of Little Rock*, 164–69; and Jacoway and Williams, *Understanding the Little Rock Crisis*, 112, 118, 127.

Information on the Reverend K. M. Smith and the NCLC was drawn from his papers at Vanderbilt University, where he served as assistant dean of the Divinity School several years after the activist movement ended. NCLC Records are contained there; see boxes 78-89. Some of Smith's papers also remain in the FCBC archives. See also B. L. Lovett, "An Afro Journey in Faith: History of First Baptist Church, Capitol Hill," *The Torch* (Nov. 2001), in the church's archives, 900 James Robertson Parkway, Nashville; Kelly Miller Smith, *Social Crisis Preaching* (Macon: Mercer Univ. Press, 1984); and Clayborne Carson, senior ed., *The Papers of Martin Luther King, Jr.*, vol. 4, *Symbol of the Movement: January 1957–December 1958* (Berkeley: Univ. of California Press, 2000), 132-33.

I consulted "Purpose, motives, and objectives of the NCLC," NCLC minutes, Apr. 4 and 28, 1958, K. M. Smith Papers, Special Collections, Vanderbilt Univ., for information on the founding and early goals of the NCLC.

The quotations from King's *Stride Toward Freedom: The Montgomery Story* (New York: Harper & Brothers, 1958), 101-7, also appear within an excerpt, "Nonviolent Resistance to Evil," in *Negro Protest Thought*, ed. Broderick and Meier, 263-69.

My discussion of the Nashville Student Movement and its leaders drew on local newspaper coverage of the period (*Nashville Globe, Banner, News-Star,* and *Tennessean; Memphis World* and *Tri-State Defender*), as well as the following sources: David Halberstam, *The Children* (1998; repr., Fawcett Books, 1999); James M. Lawson, "We Are Trying to Raise the Moral Issue," in *Negro Protest Thought*, ed. Broderick and Meier, 274-81; John Lewis, *Walking with the Wind: A Memoir of the Movement* (New York: Simon & Schuster, 1989); "The Lawson Affair, 1960: A Conversation," in *Vanderbilt Divinity School: Education, Contest, and Change*, ed. Dale A. Johnson (Nashville: Vanderbilt Univ. Press, 2001), 131-77; David E. Summer, "The Local Press and the Nashville Student Movement," Ph.D. diss., Univ. of Tennessee, 1960; and Paul K. Conkin, *Gone with the Ivy: A Biography of Vanderbilt University* (Knoxville: Univ. of Tennessee Press, 1985), esp. chap. 20, "The Unwanted," 539-80. Among other sources, a five-page account, "The Nashville Sit-in Story," and various minutes of the NCLC were consulted in the K. M. Smith Papers; I also found relevant documents in the Looby and Williams papers, particularly with regard to jailings and legal issues. See also the article "Sit-ins, Nashville" and the profiles of James Lawson, Diane Nash, and K. M. Smith in *The Tennessee Encyclopedia of History and Culture*, ed. Carroll Van West (Nashville: Rutledge Hill Press, 1998). An article on Nash also appears in *Notable Black American Women*, ed. Jessie C. Smith (Detroit: Gale Research, Inc., 1992), 796-800. See also Michele M. Viera, "A Summary of the Contributions of Four Key African American Female Figures of the Civil Rights Movement," master's thesis, Western Michigan Univ., 1994, 57-74. For information on the involvement of Tennessee State students, I consulted various issues of the campus publications the *Bulletin* and the *Meter*, which are filed by year in Special Collections, TSU Library.

A collection of civil rights songs used by the marchers are contained in the K. M. Smith Papers. Folkways Records of New York issued an album of these songs entitled *Sit-In Nashville* (FH 5590) in 1960. The album packaging includes a short essay with photographs of the students (African American and white) singing the songs, participating in demonstrations, and appearing in court.

Nashville Banner photographs of the demonstrations are filed in the Metropolitan Nashville–Davidson County Archives on Hillsboro Road and in the "Banner Room" of the Nashville downtown public library on Church Street. For information on *Banner* publisher James Stahlman during this period, I drew on correspondence in the James G. Stahlman Papers, Special Collections, Vanderbilt Univ. This collection includes a transcript of Stahlman's conversation with the *New York Herald Tribune* reporter on May 12, 1960. See also Egerton, *Speak Now Against the Day*, 246, 449, 461, 565, for further information on Stahlman.

The Fred Hobson quotation on Will Campbell ("Sociologically speaking . . .") is from *But Now I See: The White Southern Racial Conversion Narrative* (Baton Rouge: Louisiana Univ. Press, 1999), 74–79. For Campbell's own quotation ("The civil rights movement may be . . ."), see *Forty Acres and a Goat* (Atlanta: Peachtree Publishers, 1986), 270.

On the Highlander School, see Donna Langston, "The Women of Highlander," in *Women in the Civil Rights Movement: Trailblazers and Torchbearers, 1941–1965*, ed. Vicki L. Crawford, Jacqueline Anne Rouse, and Barbara Woods (Brooklyn, NY: Carlson, 1990), 145–68; Grace McFadden, *Septima P. Clark: The Struggle for Human Rights* (Bloomington: Indiana Univ. Press, 1990); Septima Clark, *Echo in My Soul* (New York: E. P. Dutton, 1960); John M. Glen, *Highlander: No Ordinary School*, 2nd. ed. (Knoxville: Univ. of Tennessee Press, 1996); Frank Adams and Myles Horton, *Unearthing Seeds of Fire : The Idea of Highlander* (Winston-Salem, NC: John F. Blair, 1975), 89–98; and the FBI file on Highlander (available on microfilm, Wilmington, DE: Scholarly Resources, Inc., 2002). For more details on the 1959 police raid on Highlander, see Myles Horton, *The Long Haul: An Autobiography* (New York: Doubleday, 1990), 64, 109, 188–91, 192. Also see Viera, "A Summary," 57–74, and K. M. Smith Papers on court efforts to close Highlander. For Clark's announcement on continuing workshops, see *Chattanooga News–Free Press*, Feb. 20, 1960.

For data on Nashville's declining African American population, I consulted U.S. Bureau of the Census, *We, the Black Americans* (Washington, D.C.: Government Printing Office, 1981), and *Census 2000 Summary*, file-4, available online through links at http://www.census.gov/. The census Web site also provided figures on effects of the Great Migration in Tennessee for 1890, 1960, and 1970. The Henderson report was described in the *Nashville News-Star, April 1960*. My discussion of the Nashville Chamber of Commerce's relations with the local black community drew on the Minutes of the Board of Governors of the Nashville Chamber of Commerce, TSLA.

For Septima Clark's contact with Ella Baker concerning the student movement and the subsequent Raleigh meeting that led to the creation of the Student Nonviolent Coordinating Committee, I drew on Viera, "A Summary," 71–78, 93–95, and documents in the K. M. Smith Papers. See also Clayborne Carson, *In Struggle: SNCC and the Black Awakening of the 1960s* (Cambridge: Harvard Univ. Press, 1981), 19–43, for perhaps the best account of SNCC's origins. Helpful as well were Lewis, *Walking with the Wind*, 135–74; and Robert Weisbort, *Freedom Bound: A History of America's Civil Rights Movement* (1990; repr., Penguin Books, 1991), 34–35. The FBI maintained a file on SNCC (available on microfilm from Scholarly Re-sources, Inc.), but it appears to contain little information about SNCC activities in Nashville.

My account of the NAACP response to and interaction with SNCC was based on Roy Wilkins, *Standing Fast: The Autobiography of Roy Wilkins* (New York: Viking Press, 1982), 241–44; Wilkins, "For 'Shock Troops' and 'Solid Legal Moves'" (remarks at a mass meeting of the Jackson, Mississippi, NAACP branch); and Lawson, "We Are Trying to Raise a Moral Issue." These last two pieces are both included in *Negro Protest Thought*, ed. Broderick and Meier; see 281–87 and 274–81, respectively.

For the events surrounding the bombing of Looby's house, see *Shelbyville Times-Gazette*, Apr. 19, 1960; and various letters in the Looby Papers. Diane Nash's remarks were quoted in the *Tennessean*, Apr. 25, 1960. Looby's remarks in Atlanta were reported by the *Memphis World*, May 28, 1960; see also Stephen G. N. Tuck, *Beyond Atlanta: The Struggle for Racial Equality in Georgia, 1940–1980* (Athens: Univ. of Georgia Press, 2003).

On efforts to draw the movement together throughout the state and on continuing protests in Nashville, I consulted NCLC minutes, Sept. 1 and Nov. 3, 1960, Jan. 17 and 28, and April 5, 1961. See Looby Papers on legal efforts to have the sit-in cases dismissed. See also Cynthia G. Fleming, "We Shall Overcome: Tennessee and the Civil Rights Movement," in *Tennessee History: The Land, the People, and the Culture*, ed. Carroll Van West (Knoxville: Univ. of Tennessee Press, 1998), 436–55.

Events in Knoxville were reconstructed from coverage in the *Knoxville News-Sentinel* and *Knoxville Journal*. Also helpful was Robert J. Booker, *Two Hundred Years of Black Culture in Knoxville, Tennessee, 1791–1991* (Knoxville: Donning Co., 1993). The Reverend Crutcher's remarks were reported in the *Nashville News-Star*, Aug. 14, 1960. See also Merrill Proudfoot, *Diary of a Sit-In* (Urbana: Univ. of Illinois Press, 1990).

For developments in Chattanooga, I drew chiefly on reports and documents in the C. B. Robinson Papers; documents in the Walter Caldwell Robinson Papers, Special Collections, TSU Library; and coverage throughout 1960 in the *Chattanooga Observer* and *Chattanooga Times*. C. B. Robinson's comments ("Whites were aware . . .") came from his participation in the Oral History Project of Chattanooga–Hamilton County, C. B. Robinson Papers.

Coverage in 1960-62 issues of the *Morristown Citizen-Tribune* and the *Johnson City Tribune* provided details of civil rights developments in those East Tennessee communities. I gleaned information about the Jackson movement from area newspapers. The *Jackson Sun* (www.jacksonsun.com) has developed an excellent feature on its Web site entitled "The Untold Story of Jackson's Civil Rights Movement"; it is filled with articles and photographs and even includes classroom lesson plans.

For the response to the Nashville Student Movement by Martin Luther King Jr., Eleanor Roosevelt, and others, see *Nashville News-Star*, Aug. 14, 1960.

For more recent assessments of the Nashville protests and their legacy, see Branch, *Pillar of Fire*, 53–54, 76, 122, 238, 353, 559; Robert Cook, *Sweet Land of Liberty: The African-American Struggle for Civil Rights in the Twentieth Century* (London: Longman, 1998); Andrew Young, *An Easy Burden: The Civil Rights Movement and the Transformation of America* (New York: HarperCollins, 1996), 126; and Weisbrot, *Freedom Bound*, 20.

The Lawson quotation ("The Nashville movement did . . .") came from "The Lawson Affair," in *Vanderbilt Divinity School*, ed. Johnson, 168–69.

CHAPTER 5. SIT-INS AND PUBLIC DEMONSTRATIONS CONTINUE TO SPREAD

The K. M. Smith Papers include documents on the 1960 meeting that completed the chapter organization of the SCLC in Tennessee. The K. M. Smith Papers also covered the desegregation efforts of Cordell Sloan and others in Lebanon; reports in the *Nashville Examiner* and *Tennessean* provided additional details, as did Patricia W. Lockett and Mattie McHollin, *In Their Voices: An Account of the Presence of African Americans in Wilson County* (Lebanon, TN: Self-published, 1999), 290–94. The Avon Williams Papers also contain documents on the Lebanon case.

My account of the Freedom Rides and their repercussions was based in large part on articles in state newspapers (*Tennessean, Banner, Tri-State Defender, Memphis Press-Scimitar, Nashville Commentator,* and others) from May 1961 through early 1962 and on NCLC minutes (K. M. Smith Papers) for meetings during that same period. The NCLC documents include a "Freedom Rides" folder. These sources were especially useful in detailing the responses of Tennesseans, black and white, to the episode. John Lewis's memoir, *Walking with the Wind,* provided details of his involvement; see pp. 158 and 185 for his quoted remarks. Kenneth O'Reilly, *"Racial Matters": The FBI's Secret File on Black America, 1960–1972* (New York: The Free Press, 1989), 90–91, 92, 93, was also useful for understanding the FBI's stance as events unfolded. For the involvement of Shuttlesworth, see Andrew Manis, *A Fire You Can't Put Out: The Civil Rights Life of Birmingham's Reverend Fred Shuttlesworth* (Tuscaloosa: Univ. of Alabama Press, 1999), 252, 253, 262–80, 287, 303, 320, 336. The Papers of Gov. Buford Ellington (TSLA) contained the letters from segregationist politicians I have quoted. Much of Ellington's correspondence is missing from those files for the 1960–61 period, but the desegregation files in the Dept. of Education and Commissioner of Education Records and Minutes (RG 92, RG 273, TSLA) enabled me to detail problems with the Freedom Riders. In fact, one of those files is labeled "The Freedom Riders"; it contains many letters from Tennesseans and others who either denounced or supported the participants. See also Jim Peck, *Freedom Ride* (New York: Simon and Schuster, 1962). For Rollins's comments, see interview transcripts about John Lewis and Archie E. Allen, 1968, Nashville Public Library. On the involvement of King, Abernathy, and the SCLC in the Freedom Rides, I drew on the Manis book cited above and on David J. Garrow, *Bearing the Cross: Martin Luther King, Jr., and the Southern Christian Leadership Conference* (New York: William Morrow, 1986), 161, 166–67.

My account of Kwame Lillard's rescue of the stranded demonstrators drew on interviews (Sept. 23, 2002, Mar. 4, 2003, Jan. 17, 2005, Nashville) I conducted with him; in the last interview, Lillard said, "The Tennessee State students are not recognized in most books about the Freedom Rides as the real 'foot soldiers' of the movement in Nashville." Indeed, he was right. For Diane Nash's perspective, I relied in part on notes I took during her presentation at the Tennessee State Museum's "Workshop for Teachers: The Civil Rights Movement," Oct. 3–4, 2003; she was greeted with a packed room for both this session and a luncheon she addressed the next day. These events are also discussed in Halberstam, *The Children,* 290–98; Manis, *A Fire You Can't Put Out,* 272–75; and Branch, *Parting the Waters,* 430–39.

For the Southern Baptist Convention's response to the rides at its St. Louis meeting, I consulted *Annual of the Southern Baptist Convention, May 1961,* SBC Historical Commission. On tensions between the NAACP and the student movement, see Halberstam, *The Children,* 72, 229, 230, 388; and Lewis, *Walking with the Wind,* 208, 209. My account of the May 2001 commemorations of the Freedom Rides drew on programs and articles I preserved from those meetings.

For the ongoing demonstrations in Nashville during 1962–63, I consulted various NCLC minutes and local newspaper coverage. Copies of the NCLC newsletter, *The Voice,* were also helpful. Kelly Miller Smith's negotiations with restaurant owner L. D. Langford were reconstructed from documents in Smith's papers, including a letter from Smith to Langford dated June 20, 1963. See the *Capitol Hill Defender,* June 20, 1963, for Lewis's comments on the need "to desegregate all public places in Nashville."

I referred to Malcolm X and James Farmer, "Separation or Integration: A Debate," *Dialogue Magazine* (May 1962): 14–18, for their differing views on the movement. Will Campbell's remarks ("The heart of the racial problem . . .") were quoted in the *Nashville Tennessean*, July 21, 1963.

For events in Chattanooga in 1963, see documents and clippings in the C. B. Robinson Papers and articles in the *Chattanooga Times*, Aug. 22, 1963, and *Chattanooga Free Press*, Jan. 6, 1963. Documents from the Williams Papers detailed the Washington meeting with JFK and Lillard's comments on public marches.

My account of the March on Washington and the response to it was based on Paula F. Pfeffer, *A. Phillip Randolph: Pioneer of the Civil Rights Movement* (Baton Rouge: Louisiana Univ. Press, 1990), esp. chap. 7, "The March on Washington," 240–80; for Malcolm's remarks, see pp. 263–64 of that account. Other sources were Jervis Anderson, *A. Phillip Randolph: A Biographical Portrait* (Berkeley: Univ. of California Press, 1972); Jervis Anderson, *Bayard Rustin: Troubles I've Seen; A Biography* (New York: HarperCollins, 1997); conversations with Delores Wilkinson, Dec. 2, 2002, and June 8, 2004, Nashville; and Malcolm X, "Blacks Can Never Be Part of the American Dream," in *African Americans: Opposing Viewpoints*, ed. William F. Dudley, American History Series (San Diego: Greenhaven Press, 1997), 239–51. In the last piece, Malcolm said, "Not only does America have a very serious problem, but our people have a very serious problem. America's problem is us." For Randolph's and Lewis's comments after the march, see Lewis, *Walking with the Wind*, 227. See also Branch, *Parting the Waters*, and its sequel, *Pillar of Fire* (1998); and David J. Garrow, *The FBI and Martin Luther King, Jr.* (New York: Penguin Books, 1983).

See Manis, *A Fire You Can't Put Out*, 403, 411, for details on the Birmingham bombings, including Shuttlesworth's comments. I also consulted news coverage in Nashville and Memphis and, for details on the family fund, the NCLC minutes, Oct. 31, 1963.

It should be noted that during this period the FBI focused heavily on the Negro's civil rights movement, keeping files on almost all the organizations, including the SCLC, SNCC, Highlander Folk School, and the NAACP, as well as files on their leaders. Scholarly Resources, Inc., has made many of these files, now residing in the Library of Congress and National Archives, available on microfilm. The microfilms and their identification numbers include the following: A. Philip Randolph (S3202); Roy Wilkins (S3201); W. E. B. DuBois (S3345); Malcolm X (S3341); Paul Robeson (S3040); Jessie Jackson (S3158); Martin Luther King Jr., FBI Assassination File (S1757); Black Panther Party, North Carolina (S3039); and Communist Infiltration of SCLC (S1754).

Nashville newspaper accounts and the NCLC minutes, Mar. 14, 1964, provided details of the NCLC's efforts to find a new direction for the movement.

On the THCR, I consulted the commission's annual reports archived at the TSLA, as well as Avon Williams's file on the THCR, now included among his papers. On the proposed anti-discrimination ordinance for Nashville, see the *Tennessean*, May 17, 1964.

For Andrew White's leadership of the NCLC during its final year, I consulted the NCLC minutes, June 24, 1964, and various pieces of White's correspondence (to ministers, fraternities and sororities, students, and others) from late 1963 through 1964, including letters he received from Martin Luther King Jr. on Nov. 22 and Dec. 20, 1963. These are all part of the K. M. Smith Papers. Articles in the *Banner* and *Tennessean*, April 1967, also mention that White was leading the NCLC.

My account of civil rights activities in Memphis during the early 1960s was based on various articles from *Memphis World, Tri-State Defender, Commercial Appeal, Press-Scimitar*, and the *Shelbyville Times-Gazette*. Maxine Smith's quarterly and annual reports for the local NAACP were, as ever, an invaluable source. On the Jewish community in Memphis, see Selma S. Lewis, *A Biblical People in the Bible Belt: The Jewish Community of Memphis, Tennessee: 1840s–1960s* (Macon, GA: Mercer Univ. Press, 1998), 252, 255; the Selma S. Lewis Papers, Memphis–Shelby County Room, Memphis Public Library; and Clive Webb, *Fight Against Fear: Southern Jews and Black Civil Rights* (Athens: Univ. of Georgia Press, 2004). Other sources included James Haskins, *Distinguished African Americans and Governmental Leaders* (Phoenix: Onyx Press, 1999), 7–8, 181–182, for details on Constance Motley; the Federal Judicial Center Web site for details on the *Watson* case; Kelly and Harbison, *The American Constitution*, 941, for comments on that case; and the Southern Regional Council's *The Report on Memphis* (Atlanta: SRC, 1964), 22–23, on efforts in the city to improve race relations.

CHAPTER 6. THE MOVEMENT TURNS VIOLENT IN TENNESSEE

On the passage of the 1964 Civil Rights Bill, see William A. Degregorio, *The Complete Book of U.S. Presidents*, 2nd. ed. (New York: Barricade Books, 1989), 563–79. On its provisions, see Franklin and Moss, *From Slavery to Freedom: a History of Negro Americans*, 449–50.

For conditions in Memphis during the mid-1960s, I consulted Maxine Smith's reports for the local NAACP, Maxine Smith Papers. For the Congressional report on KKK activities, I consulted a copy in Special Collections, Tennessee State Univ. Library.

See John S. Butler and C. C. Moskos, "Labor Force Trends: The Military as Data," in *America Becoming: Racial Trends and Their Consequences*, vol. 2, ed. Neil J. Smelser, William Julius Wilson, and Faith Mitchell (Washington, D.C.: National Academies Press, 2001) for statistics and analysis regarding blacks in the military.

Diane Nash's recollections of the Vietnam years came from her presentation at the 2003 "Workshop for Teachers: The Civil Rights Movement," Nashville. On the increasing militancy of SNCC, I drew on several flyers I found in the Avon Williams Papers. Williams apparently kept this material because he considered it an obstacle to the civil rights movement. For Tennessee State and Fisk protests and Lawson's comments ("What I expect . . ."), see *Nashville Tennessean*, Sept. 23, 1966. See also *Transcripts of Proceedings, Meetings of U.S. Commission on Civil Rights*, Dec. 9, 1966 (Washington, D.C.: Hart and Harkins, 1966).

For Governor Clement's remarks ("And as I bow out . . ."), see *Tennessee Senate Journal* (1967).

On Stokely Carmichael's appearance at Vanderbilt, I drew on a campus publication, *Hustler*, Apr. 11, 1967, and reports in the local dailies. Local news coverage also informed my account of the subsequent riots, along with, more specifically, the *Meter* (TSU newspaper), May 9, 1967; clippings in the Williams Papers; John Lewis, "A Trend Toward Aggressive Nonviolent Action," in *Negro Protest Thought*, ed. Broderick and Meier, 313–. 21 (originally published as "An Interview with John Lewis: The Chairman of SNCC Discusses the Negro Revolt; Its Problems and Prospects," *Dialogue Magazine* IV 2

[Spring 1964]: 7–9); and *Nashville Tennessean*, Apr. 7, 1967. For the John Birch Society response, see *Nashville Magazine* (July 1967): 4–6, 32.

For the involvement of Jamye C. and McDonald Williams, I interviewed the couple at their Nashville home, Mar. 10, 2001.

On the aftermath of the riots, I relied on local news coverage, and Inman Otey, an administrator at Tennessee State University, confirmed some incidents to me in various personal conversations. My account of the honorarium check controversy drew on May–June 1967 memorandums in the Stahlman Papers. For Ellington's response and the repercussions at TSU, I found some relevant documents in the W. S. Davis Papers, Special Collections, TSU. Although documents on the critical civil rights years are missing from the Ellington Papers, documents in Record Groups 92 and 273 reveal much about his actions and involvement in the shake-up at Tennessee State. For the student quotation ("I think the administration . . ."), see *Nashville Tennessean*, May 10, 1967. Carson, *In Struggle*, 244–48, also contains details on the Nashville riot.

Documents in the Davis Papers and letters and reports from Davis to the commissioner of education in RG 92, TSLA, provided information on the student expulsions. During this period, an issue of *Nashville Magazine* (July 1967) carried an article that criticized Ellington and state officials for curtailing freedom of speech.

On the Vanderbilt radicals, see correspondence, Nov. 3, 1967, in the Stahlman Papers.

The Clayborne Carson quotation ("SNCC workers failed . . .") is from *In Struggle*, 300.

The Williams Papers contain documents that informed my account of the I-40 lawsuit and controversy. For Nelson Andrews's comments, see *Nashville Tennessean*, Aug. 5, 2001.

For the story of the Memphis garbage strike, I relied largely on coverage in the local papers as well as on Joan T. Beifus, *At the River I Stand* (Memphis: St. Luke's Press, 1985); J. E. Stanfield, *In Memphis: More Than a Garbage Strike* (Atlanta: Southern Regional Council, 1968); and Michael K. Honey, *Southern Labor and Black Civil Rights* (Urbana: Univ. of Illinois Press, 1993). Some of the details about life in Memphis are drawn from my personal recollections. The National Advisory Commission on Civil Disorders quotation ("Our nation is moving . . .") is from Alex Poinsett, *Walking with Presidents: Louis Martin and the Rise of Black Political Power* (New York: Rowman and Littlefield, 1997), 172.

For the March 1968 demonstration that resulted in jailings, see *Memphis World*, Mar. 16, 1968. For James Lawson's involvement, see *Memphis Tri-State Defender*, Aug. 3, 1963. The account of King's first visit during the strike drew in part on Young, *An Easy Burden*, 201, 316, 329–32, 431–32, 448–63. For the rock-throwing incident in Knoxville, see *Morristown Citizen Tribune*, Apr. 2, 1968, and for the involvement of the National Guard, see *Milan Exchange*, April 3, 1968. Information about the proposed newspaper ad featuring King at Highlander came from the *Memphis Commercial Appeal*, Apr. 2, 1968.

Again, local newspapers were mostly used to detail King's final days in Memphis; see also Beifus, *At the River I Stand*, for press accounts and interviews. William F. Pepper, *Orders to Kill: The Truth behind the Murder of Martin Luther King, Jr.* (New York: Carroll & Graff, 1995), was useful as well. For the Mason Temple speech, see Beifus, *At the River I Stand*, 364–68. Benjamin Hooks's recollections of King's appearance at Mason Temple came from a speech he gave at the National Baptist Sunday School and

Baptist Training Union Congress in Phoenix, Arizona, June 13, 2002; I was in the audience taking notes. I also visited Mason Temple in May 2004 with my camera to gain a better sense of what King's speaking to the crowd there must have been like.

I consulted the Frank Holloman Papers, Memphis–Shelby County Room, Memphis Public Library, Popular Avenue, for information on the King assassination, but found little of value about what really happened that day. Holloman was a former FBI agent and a graduate of the University of Mississippi who had moved to Whitehaven ten years earlier. For his part, Mayor Loeb never entertained interviews about the King assassination. He died on September 9, 1992, after moving to Arkansas; see Mantri Sivandnda, "Henry Loeb's Retirement and Last Days, 1972-1992," *West Tennessee Historical Society Papers* 56 (2002): 94-110.

The letter from Governor Ellington to Coretta Scott King (Apr. 1968) is in the Ellington Papers. The Williams Papers and Nashville newspapers were used to recount the repercussions of the King murder in the Tennessee capital. For the aftermath in Memphis, see Maxine Smith's April 3–May 14, 1968, NAACP report, as well as John A. Williams, *The King God Didn't Save: Reflections on the Life and Death of Martin Luther King, Jr.* (New York: Coward-McCann, 1970), 217-18.

Ralph Abernathy's recollections of King's desire to leave Memphis, his comments on King's murder, and accounts of preparations for the 1969 King memorial and ongoing plans for the Poor People's Campaign were reported in the *Tri-State Defender*, Mar. 20, Apr. 5, 12, 26, 1968.

Lawson's comments ("The plantation theory . . .") were from his article "The Man Who Escaped the Cross," *Fellowship* 25 (Nov. 1959): 10-12. For Carmichael's remarks ("When white America . . ."), see Lewis, *Walking with the Wind*, 389. See *An Easy Burden*, 452-68, for Andrew Young's assessment. The *Nashville Ebony Gazette*, Jan. 1, 22, 1976, also included references to Young and to Clarence Kelly's comments on the King files.

Information on FBI wiretaps of King came from the *New York Times*, May 25, 1968. And for further information on the FBI's targeting of King and other black leaders, I consulted Wilson Record, *Race and Radicalism: The NAACP and the Communist Party in Conflict* (New York: Cornell Univ. Press, 1964); Williams, *The King God Didn't Save*, 211-13, 209-21; Branch, *Pillar of Fire*, 536; Athan Theoharis, *J. Edgar Hoover, Sex, and Crime* (New York: Rowman and Littlefield, 2002); Julian Bond, *A Time to Speak, a Time to Act: The Movement in Politics* (New York: Simon and Schuster, 1972), 137; and Garrow, *The FBI and Martin Luther King, Jr.*, 121-50.

My account of Joseph H. Jackson and the National Baptist Convention drew upon Bobby L. Lovett, *A Black Man's Dream: The First One Hundred Years, The Story of R. H. Boyd and the National Baptist Publishing Board* (Nashville: Mega Co., 1993), 71, 122, 125, 182-83; Joseph H. Jackson, *A Story of Activism: The History of the National Baptist Convention, U.S.A., Inc.* (Nashville: Sunday School Publishing Board, 1980), 227, 237, 283, 285, 360, 431-35, 440, 448, 491; Richard Robbins, *Sidelines Activist: Charles S. Johnson and the Struggle for Civil Rights* (Jackson: Mississippi Univ. Press, 1996), 145, 147-48, 156-57; and Smith, *Social Crisis Preaching*, 88-125. For Charles Johnson's 1956 letter to Jackson ("To me . . ."), see Charles S. Johnson Papers, Special Collections, Fisk Univ.

For the relationship between the civil rights movement and white churches, particularly the Southern Baptist Convention, see Hobson, *But Now I See*; James F. Findlay, *Church People in the Struggle: The National Council of Churches and the Black Freedom Movement, 1950-1970* (New York: Oxford Univ. Press, 1993), 212-13; and issues of the

Annual of the SBC for 1958 through 2000 (Nashville: Southern Baptist Convention Historical Commission).

My concluding paragraphs on events in Memphis in autumn 1968 drew on Maxine Smith's Memphis branch NAACP report for that year. For Lewis's assessment, see *Walking with the Wind*, 405, 406; and for the Williams quotation, see *The King God Didn't Save*, 217.

CHAPTER 7. THE BLACK REPUBLICANS

For the general background of Tennessee politics, see Bobby L. Lovett, *The African American History of Nashville, 1780–1930* (Fayetteville: Univ. of Arkansas Press, 1999), esp. chap. 9, "Politics and Civil Rights: The Black Republicans," 198–233; and Alrutheus A. Taylor, *The Negro in Tennessee, 1865–1880* (Washington, D.C.: Associated Universities Press, 1941). See Robert M. McBride, ed., The *Biographical Directory of the Tennessee General Assembly*, 6 vols. (Nashville: Tennessee State Library and Archives, 1975–1991), for biographies of Negro legislators; also, the introduction to each volume contains a good summary of political history in Tennessee. *Messages of the Governors of Tennessee*, 11 vols. (Nashville: Tennessee Historical Commission, 1952–1998) also contains valuable political histories as well as the speeches and messages of the state's chief executives.

Other important published sources for the opening of this chapter included Paul H. Bergeron, *Antebellum Politics in Tennessee* (Lexington: Univ. Press of Kentucky, 1981); Raleigh A. Wilson, "The Negro in Tennessee Politics from 1865 to the Present," *The Broadcaster* (March 1944): 42–44; Mingo Scott Jr., *The Negro in Tennessee Politics and Governmental Affairs, 1865–1965* (Nashville: Rich Printing Co., 1965); J. H. Cartwright, *The Triumph of Jim Crow: Tennessee Race Relations in the 1880s* (Knoxville: Univ. of Tennessee Press, 1976); David L. Carlton and Peter A. Coclanis, *Confronting Southern Poverty in the Great Depression* (New York: St. Martin's Press, 1996); John A. Salmond, *"My Mind Set on Freedom": A History of the Civil Rights Movement, 1954–1968* (Chicago: Ivan R. Dee, 1997); Jennings Perry, *Democracy Begins at Home: The Tennessee Fight on the Poll Tax* (Baton Rouge: Louisiana State Univ. Press, 1944); and Holt and Brown, *Major Problems in African-American History*, vol. 2, esp. 128–54, 222–23, which are part of the chapter "Rural Exodus and the Growth of New Urban Communities."

For Webster L. Porter's statement of purpose for his newspaper, see *East Tennessee News*, Mar. 26, 1936. For the activities of Walter C. Robinson, see his papers archived in Special Collections, Tennessee State Univ. Library; these papers contain some issues of Robinson's *Chattanooga Observer* newspaper, his biography, and documents on his political positions. For activities of black Republicans, I also consulted various documents, particularly newspaper clippings, in the George W. Lee Collection, Memphis–Shelby County Room, Memphis Public Library.

My account of Boss Crump and the workings of his machine drew on the G. W. Lee Papers and photo files in the Memphis–Shelby County Room, Memphis Public Library, and on William Miller, *Mr. Crump of Memphis* (Baton Rouge: Louisiana State Univ. Press, 1964). See also G. Wayne Dowdy, "A Business Government by a Business Man: E. H. Crump as a Progressive Mayor, 1910–1915," *Tennessee Historical Quarterly* 60 (Fall 2001): 162–75. For Crump's dealings with black voters, see David M. Tucker, "Black Politics in Memphis, 1865–75," *West Tennessee Historical Society Papers* 26 (1972): 13–19;

J. Street, "Mista Crump Keeps Rollin' Along," *Collier's Magazine*, Apr. 9, 1938, 16; news coverage in the *Memphis World*, esp. Dec. 2 and 20, 1932, and Jan. 1938 issues; and G. Wayne Dowdy, "Expansion of the Crump Machine: Politics in Shelby County, 1928-1936," *West Tennessee Historical Society Papers* 56 (2002): 17-39.

For the effects of the New Deal on the Negro community in Memphis and elsewhere in Tennessee, see Melton, *Blacks in Memphis*, 191-95, 220-27, 355-58; T. H. Coode, "The Presidential Election of 1940 as Reflected in the Tennessee Metropolitan Press," *East Tennessee Historical Society Papers* 40 (1968): 83-100; James D. Bennett II, "Roosevelt, Willkie, and the TVA," *Tennessee Historical Quarterly* 28 (Winter 1969): 388-96; and James R. McCarthy, "The New Deal in Tennessee," *Sewanee Review* 42 (1934): 408-14.

For the account of Church's falling-out with Crump, see the *Memphis Press-Scimitar*, Jan. 9, 1941. The *Memphis Commercial-Appeal*, Nov. 16, 1941, carried pictures of the fire consuming the Church mansion. Also helpful on Church and his role in Memphis politics was Biles, "Robert R. Church, Jr., of Memphis."

A Directory of the Colored People of Memphis and Shelby County (Memphis: Negro Chamber of Commerce, 1941) provided valuable details on Joseph H. Walker, Blair T. Hunt, Alonzo Locke, and other local black leaders. David M. Tucker, *Black Pastors and Leaders: Memphis, 1819-1972* (Memphis: Memphis State Univ. Press, 1975) was also helpful on the Reverend George Albert Long.

On Hastie's and Randolph's activities in 1943, see the *Memphis World*, Feb. 9 and July 16, 1943, and the *Bulletin* (Tennessee A&I publication), June 1943. For Randolph's controversial visit to Memphis in November of that year, I drew on articles in the *Memphis World* and *Press-Scimitar*. D. H. Grubbs, *Cry from the Cotton: The Southern Tenant Farmers' Union and the New Deal* (Chapel Hill: Univ. of North Carolina Press, 1971) provided useful information about one of the groups Randolph addressed. For Randolph's remarks before the local Brotherhood of Sleeping Car Porters ("If the American soldiers . . ."), see *Memphis World*, Nov. 9, 1943.

An essential source for Church's activities was the Robert R. Church Family Papers, Mississippi Valley Collection, Memphis State Univ. Library. See Box 6 for Lee's letter to Church about Randolph's return visit.

On Randolph's return to Memphis and Crump's reaction, see the *Memphis World*, Apr. 4, 1944. The *Chicago Defender*, Apr. 8, 1944, also reported on Randolph's visit. The sheriff's response ("This is white man's country . . .") was reported in the *Nashville Globe*, Apr. 14, 1944. Also helpful were Miller, *Mr. Crump of Memphis*, 293; and issues of the *Memphis Labor Review* (Mar.-April, 1944). In the Church Family Papers, see G. W. Lee to R. Church Jr., 1944, carton 7, folder 37, and other references to the 1944 Randolph-Crump controversy in carton 9. Clarence Kelly, "Robert Church, a Negro Tennessean in Republican State and National Politics from 1912 to 1932," M.A. thesis, Tennessee A&I State Univ., 1954, was useful as well.

On police intimidation of black leaders, Melton, *Blacks in Memphis*, 194-227, was helpful, as was the *Memphis Press-Scimitar*, Apr. 3, 1944.

My account of activities surrounding the 1944 presidential election was based on the *Memphis World*, Dec. 3, 1944, and Feb. 2, 1945; and the *Nashville Globe*, Jan. 26, 1945. I also consulted various issues of the *World*, Jan.-Dec. 1945 and June-July 1946, for my summary of Nat D. Williams's columns.

The *Memphis Commercial-Appeal*, July 9, 1946, carried a photograph of the Negro parade for Crump. For the anti-Crump sentiment among certain whites, see the *Nashville Banner*, July 9, 1946, and Aug. 27, 1946; and the *Maryville Times*, Aug. 6, 1946.

On NAACP activities, Randolph's 1947 return to Memphis, and Crump's continuing attempts to manipulate opinion on race relations, see 1947 issues of the *Memphis World* for Feb. 4, Aug. 5, and Sept. 19. On the Reverend Long's departure from Memphis, see the *National Baptist Union-Review*, Apr. 12, 1947, and Feb. 16, 1960.

The statistics on population and migration trends drew on U.S. Census figures for 1860, 1890, 1940, 1950, and 1960; see also Marcus E. Jones, *Black Migration in the United States with Emphasis on Selected Central Cities* (Saratoga, CA: Century 21 Publishing, 1980). On Elma Stuckey, see her book *The Big Gate* (Chicago: Precedent Publishers, 1976), in which her poems and stories blend northern and southern backgrounds; and David Roediger, "An Interview with Elma Stuckey," *Black American Literature Forum* 11 (1977): 151-53.

See Melton, *Blacks in Memphis*, 194-227, on the blind people's fund and Bell's departure.

On the poll tax committee and efforts to influence Truman, see *Chattanooga Observer*, July 18, 1947, and Mar. 26, 1948; *Chattanooga Labor World*, Jan. 1, 1947; and *Nashville Globe*, Apr. 13, 1944. For excerpts from "To Secure These Rights," see *Debating the Civil Rights Movement*, ed. Lawson and Payne, 45-53.

For details on Crump and the 1948 elections, I consulted news coverage in the Memphis and Nashville papers, as well as L. C. Bledsoe, "The Crump Machine, Estes Kefauver, and the Senatorial Election of 1948" (M.S. thesis, Tennessee State Univ., 1965); Joseph Bruce Gorman, *Kefauver: A Political Biography* (New York: Oxford Univ. Press, 1977); and C. Edmondson, "How Kefauver Beat Crump: the Story of a Southern Victory," *Harper's Magazine*, Jan. 1949, 78-84.

Information on the Reverend Kyle's political activities came from an interview I conducted (Apr. 21, 2001) with his wife, Grace, who spoke for her elderly husband by telephone from Los Angeles. See also the *Memphis World*, Oct. 1, 12, and 18, 1948, for details of the 1948 elections.

My account of Truman's victory and general developments in postwar America was based on Carol Berkin, C. L. Miller, R. W. Cherny, and J. L. Gormly, *Making America: A History of the United States* (Boston: Houghton Mifflin Co., 1995); see esp. A-34, 854, 859-60, 886-90.

Information on the Solid Block Party came from issues of the *Solid Block Bulletin*, available on microfilm at the TSLA; the criticisms of Browning I have quoted were contained in the January 1950 issue. See also Mae M. Bronaugh, "Gordon Browning and Tennessee Politics, 1949-1953," *Tennessee Historical Quarterly* 28 (Summer 1969): 166-18.

On the efforts of Lee and others to maintain a vital black presence within the Republican Party, see the *Memphis Press-Scimitar*, Feb. 6, 1952, and clippings and correspondence in the George W. Lee Collection.

For Church's appearance at the state and national Republican conventions and his attempt to re-enter Tennessee politics, see Melton, "Blacks in Memphis," 194-227, and a letter from Church to Lee, Aug. 21, 1951, Lee Papers. The Stahlman Papers contain a rare photograph of Church, which was likely taken at a state Republican meeting. On

Church's death, see *Memphis Commercial Appeal*, Apr. 18, 1952. Other sources on black Republican activities included various newspaper clippings in the Lee Collection; the *Memphis Negro Classified Business Directory* (1952); and Beverly G. Bond, "Roberta Church: Race and the Republican Party in the 1950s," in *Portraits of African American Life After 1865*, ed. Nina Mjagkij (Wilmington, DE: Scholarly Resources, 2003), 181–97. Walker's letter to Robinson ("I am sure men . . ."), Apr. 17, 1956, is contained in the W. C. Robinson Papers, TSU Library. The letters of April 20 and October 16 are found in Lee's papers. And see Melton, "Blacks in Memphis," for a thorough discussion of Church and Lee.

On Lee's support for Eisenhower in 1956 and his subsequent decline as a political force, see letters and clippings from the middle to late 1950s in the G. W. Lee Collection. *Note:* While Lee's papers are especially helpful regarding Memphis politics after 1952, they reveal almost nothing about the pre-1954 relations between Crump and Lee.

On the launching and goals of the "Volunteer Ticket," see local news coverage, including the *Memphis World*, July 4 and Aug. 15, 1959; and *Tri-State Defender*, July 18, 1959. On the ticket's defeat and its aftermath, see *Memphis Press-Scimitar*, Aug. 22, 1959; *Washington Post*, Sept. 26, 1959; and *Tri-State Defender*, Aug. 29, 1959, Mar. 12 and 19, 1960. The quotation from Williams ("Things are happening . . .") appeared in a front-page commentary entitled "Dark Shadows" in the *Defender* (Mar. 12, 1960); he was no longer writing a column for the *World* at this time. Williams's columns in the 1960s were sometimes criticized by local NAACP leaders for being too cynical about racial progress in Memphis; the NAACP believed that it was doing all it could at the time to speed up the desegregation process.

CHAPTER 8. THE BLACK DEMOCRATS

My portrayal of political culture in the Memphis Negro community in 1960 was based on the *Memphis Tri-State Defender*, Mar. 19, 1960; *Memphis World*, July 13 and 23, and Aug. 5, 1960; and *Memphis Commercial Appeal*, Aug. 6, 1960.

My account of the situation in Haywood County, including the Willie Jones case, was based on an extensive review of news coverage in various papers, including articles in the following issues: *Nashville Globe*, Jan. 12, 1960; *Memphis World*, Sept. 14, 1960; *Chicago Defender*, July 6, 1950; and *Brownsville States-Graphic*, Nov. 8, 1940, Sept. 5, 1958, July 19 and 31, and Oct. 23, 1959. For details about events in 1940–42, including the lynching of Elbert Williams, see Raye Springfield, *The Legacy of Tamar: Courage and Faith in an African American Family* (Knoxville: Univ. of Tennessee Press, 2000), and Richard A. Couto, *Lifting the Veil: A Political History of Struggles for Emancipation* (Knoxville: Univ. of Tennessee Press, 1993), both of which deal with the African American history of Haywood County. On land ownership, see Leo McGee and Robert Boone, eds., *The Black Rural Landowner–Endangered Species: Social, Political, and Economic Implications* (Westport, CT: Greenwood Press, 1979), 129.

Issues of the *Christian Index* (available on microfilm at TSLA) provided information on the CME Church, which is headquartered in Jackson, Tennessee, where its publishing center and the CME-supported Lane College are also located. Issues of the *Hebrew*

Watchman (also on microfilm, TSLA) informed my discussion of the Memphis Jewish community and its concerns.

Regarding continuing civil rights activities in Haywood County in 1960, I consulted the *Nashville New- Star,* June 26 and Aug. 14, 1960; *Brownsville States-Graphic,* July 22, Sept. 16, and Nov. 11, 1960; *Memphis World,* July 16, 1960; and *Memphis Commercial-Appeal,* Sept. 15, 1960.

My account of the campaign against black farmers in Fayette County relied heavily on 1959-61 coverage in the *Fayette Falcon,* including these specific issues: Apr. 23 and Dec. 23, 1959; Apr. 28, Aug. 4 and 18, Dec. 8, 1960; and Jan. 5 and 19, and Mar. 16, 1961. Issues of the *Memphis World* (including Feb. 20, Mar. 5, and June 1, 1960) were also helpful, as were issues of the *Tri-State Defender* from Sept. 1961 through July 1962. For information on legislators Rivers and Gooden, see *The Biographical Directory of the Tennessee General Assembly,* vol 2, *1861-1901.* On John McFerrin, see the section on him in Robert Hamburger, *Our Portion of Hell: An Oral History of the Struggle for Civil Rights* (New York: Links Books, 1973), 7-24, 86-88, 213-14; see also *Nashville News-Star,* Aug. 14, 1960, for his assessment of Somerville and Fayette County ("The people of the Tennessee town . . ."). Information for this chapter on John S. Wilder came in part from an Aug. 8, 1988, letter I received from him, in which he said, "I am against racism, I am against hate. I am for love." See also *Biographical Directory of the Tennessee General Assembly,* vol. 5, *1951-1971,* 471-72. The NAACP's role was detailed in Memphis branch NAACP report, Nov. 8-Dec. 5, 1961, Maxine Smith Papers. The AFL-CIO issued a publication on the episode, *Tent City, "Home of the Brave"* (Washington, D.C.: AFL-CIO Industrial Union Dept., 1961), which included Reuther's remarks. For the involvement of Joseph H. Jackson and the NBCI, see Jackson, *A Story of Activism,* and the *Nashville Commentator,* Mar. 11, 1961.

For profiles of Negro legislators (Cassels, Evans, Fields, Howard, and Norris), see the *Biographical Directory of the Tennessee General Assembly,* vol. 2, *1861-1901.*

For the visits of Nixon and Jackie Robinson to Memphis, see *Memphis World,* Oct. 1, 1960. Also valuable on Robinson's role in politics and civil rights during this period were John Vernon, "A Citizen's View of Presidential Responsibility: Jackie Robinson and Dwight D. Eisenhower; Jackie Robinson and School Integration," *Negro History Bulletin* (Dec. 1999): 18-19; and Gerald Early, "American Integration, Black Heroism, and the Meaning of Jackie Robinson," *Chronicle of Higher Education,* May 23, 1997, B-4.

For data on the November 1960 presidential election, particularly in Memphis–Shelby County, I relied on coverage in the *Memphis Press-Scimitar, World, Tri-State Defender,* and *Commercial Appeal.* The *World* (Nov. 16, 1960) was the source of the Wilkins quotation ("Negro citizens will expect . . .").

For my discussion of the Tennessee Voters Council, I drew on the records, minutes, and correspondence in the TVC Papers, Special Collections, Tennessee State Univ. Library. The Avon Williams Papers also contain files on the TVC.

Details on *Baker v. Carr* came from the Federal Judicial Center Web site. See also Richard C. Cortner, *The Apportionment Cases* (Knoxville: Univ. of Tennessee Press, 1970); and Spaeth, *The Warren Court,* 74-101.

Report of the Civil Rights Commission (Washington, D.C.: Government Printing Office, 1963), 38-40, provided data on civil rights activities and voter registration in

1961–63. Information on the Fayette County Economic Development Commission came from some papers on Leander Palmer, who directed the commission; these were given to me by Dwayne Palmer, a cousin of Leander, in September 2001. For the Memphis NAACP's involvement in voter registration efforts, see records in the Maxine Smith's branch NAACP reports for Feb. 7–Mar. 6, Mar. 7–Apr. 3, and Aug. 8–Sept. 4, 1962. I consulted the C. B. Robinson Papers for information on his efforts to encourage voter participation in 1963.

Throughout my reconstruction here of various efforts to get out the Negro vote, Mingo Scott Jr.'s *The Negro in Tennessee Politics* was a valuable source. Scott identified the years 1964 and 1965 as the true "coming-out" period for Negroes in Tennessee politics. Other important sources were my conversation with Jamye and McDonald Williams (Mar. 10, 2002, Nashville) and clippings and documents in the Avon Williams Papers and the G. W. Lee Papers. For Lee's frustration with the GOP in 1964, see the *Memphis Commercial Appeal*, July 2 and Aug. 3, 1964.

See Lewis L. Laska, "A Legal and Constitutional History of Tennessee, 1772–1972," *Memphis State University Law Review* (1976): 563–672, for details regarding Tennessee's compliance with *Baker v. Carr.*

On the 1964 Voting Rights Act and 1965 Voting Rights Act, see Berkin, Miller, Cherny, and Gormly, *Making America*, 921.

Profiles of black legislators Willis, Brown, Blakemore, Sugarmon, Booker, King, Love, Murphy, and Taylor were drawn from *Biographical Directory of the Tennessee General Assembly*, vol. 5, *1951–1971.*

On the 1967 Memphis elections, see *Memphis World*, Oct. 14, 1967, and *Tri-State Defender*, Sept. 30, 1967. On Mayor Loeb's attitudes, see Harkins, *Metropolis of the American Nile*, 114–38.

On James Brown's efforts in Giles County, see letters and notes in the Williams Papers, which were also the source for Edwin Mitchell's résumé and the newsletters Williams sent to his constituents. On Fayette County, see Couto, *Lifting the Veil*, 217, 223, 224, 333; and Springfield, *Legacy of Tamar*, 157, 163.

For the particulars of the legislative redistricting that led to the election of Avon Williams and J. O. Patterson Jr., I consulted the *Tennessean* (May 11, 1967).

A good discussion of Nixon's 1968 victory as it related to race is found in Jeremy D. Mayer, "Nixon Rides the Backlash to Victory: Racial Politics in the 1968 Presidential Campaign," *The Historian* 64 (Winter 2002): 351–65. On Nixon's positions and policies on civil rights, see Tamar Jacoby, "A Surprise, but Not a Success," *The Atlantic Monthly* (May 2002): 111–14, a review of Dean J. Kotlowski, *Nixon's Civil Rights: Politics, Principle, and Policy* (Cambridge: Harvard Univ. Press, 2002).

I used the *Tennessee Blue Book, 1967–1968* (Nashville: Secretary of State, 1968) and subsequent annual editions for details about black Tennessee legislators.

On voter registration in Mississippi, see John F. McClymer, *Mississippi Freedom Summer* (Belmont, CA: Wadsworth/Thomson Learning, 2004).

For Nat Williams's comments on black voter turnout ("It is a bad commentary . . ."), see *Memphis Tri-State Defender*, Aug. 1, 1970.

On the last years of Lieutenant Lee's career and his death in 1976, see *Nashville Tennessean*, Aug. 7, 1968; *Memphis Commercial Appeal*, Sept. 12, 1966; and the *Memphis Press-Scimitar*, Aug. 1, 1976.

CHAPTER 9. CIVIL RIGHTS AND AFRICAN AMERICAN POLITICS IN TENNESSEE

See U.S. Census for 1970 and subsequent years (http://www.census.gov/) for details on the changing demographics of the South.

Throughout this chapter, in detailing the TVC's endorsement of candidates and its internal debates over strategy, I consulted various copies of the organization's minutes (archived in the TSU Library) for the 1970–74 period.

I consulted the Looby Papers at Fisk for information on his 1971 retirement. On the 1972 Democratic convention and the Tennessee delegation, see the Williams Papers, and a letter, J. R. Smith to Looby, Aug. 30, 1972, Looby Papers.

The Kenneth O'Reilly quotation ("What he did . . .") is from his book *Nixon's Piano: Presidents and Racial Politics from Washington to Clinton* (New York: The Free Press, 1995), 329, which includes a discussion of FBI investigations and harassment of black leaders. On black voting trends in the 1972 election, see *Pittsburgh Courier*, Nov. 18, 1972.

My summary of C. B. Robinson's contacts with Williams and the TVC is based on letters in the Robinson Papers.

For Williams's various activities detailed in this chapter, I consulted his papers, which contain, among other items, all his *Legislative Report* newsletters, his correspondence, various statistics that he dutifully recorded, campaign literature, and his own election results, often compiled in comparative-chart form.

For Williams's comments on the racial climate of 1974 ("the attitudes of white hate"), see the *Nashville Tennessean*, Sept. 23, 1974.

Harold E. Ford's 1974 congressional race against Dan Kuykendall was widely reported in the Memphis newspapers, which formed the basis of my account here. For some key samplings, see 1974 issues of the following: *Tri-State Defender*, Jan. 19, 21, and 26, Sept. 28, Nov. 3 and 30; *Press-Scimitar*, Nov. 6, 7, and 13; and *Commercial-Appeal*, Nov. 13. For biographical details on Ford, see *Biographical Directory of the Tennessee General Assembly*, vol. 6, *1971–1991*.

For information on the National Association of Black Elected Officials, clippings in the Williams Papers were helpful. The Williams Papers also contained various clippings and documents related to police harassment and brutality. The Edward Davis quotation ("If there is a consensus . . .") appeared in the *Tennessean*, Mar. 10, 1983.

For information on the annual retreats of the Tennessee Caucus of Black State Legislators throughout this chapter and elsewhere, I consulted its yearly reports (*Report of Findings of the Annual Retreat*) and related documents held at the Office of Minority Affairs, Tennessee General Assembly, Legislative Plaza, Nashville. I retained my own copies of the reports after working as a TSU researcher and retreat task force member for nearly twenty years. The Williams Papers also contain caucus reports and related letters.

For details on Robert E. Lillard, see *Profiles of African Americans in Tennessee*, ed. Bobby L. Lovett and Linda T. Wynn (Nashville: Conference on Afro American Culture and History, 1996), 75–77. On Adolpho Augustus Birch Jr., see *Nashville Tennessean*, May 12, 1996. For lists and profiles of elected Tennessee officials, see the annual editions of *Tennessee Bluebook* (Nashville: Secretary of State).

The O'Reilly quotation ("Whereas Stevenson . . .") is from *Nixon's Piano*, 343. Statistical details on the 1976 election were reported in the *Nashville Banner*, Jan. 1, 1977.

The Nashville dailies and the Lamar Alexander Papers (TSLA) contained information on the Blanton pardons.

Details on Governor Alexander's feelings about the TVC came from both his papers and the Williams Papers. The Williams Papers include a copy of Francis Guess's résumé, which I consulted for facts about this Alexander appointee.

Biographical details on various black legislators (Pruitt, DeBerry, and others) came from the *Biographical Directory of the Tennessee General Assembly*, vol. 6, *1971-1991*. For DeBerry's comments on the apparent demotion of a black administrator in November 1979, see the Williams Papers.

See the Williams Papers as well for correspondence between him and Harold Ford.

Information on black participation in the 1980 presidential election came from NAACP reports and correspondence in the Williams Papers and from TVC minutes.

For the O'Reilly quotation ("If Reagan's spoken promise . . ."), see *Nixon's Piano*, 366. On Reagan's coded messages to white conservatives, see Earl Black and Merle Black, *The Rise of Southern Republicans* (Cambridge, MA: Harvard Univ. Press, 2002), 205, 251.

The J. H. Turner report on the 1982 election in Shelby County is included in the Maxine Smith Papers, Memphis Public Library.

For Alexander's conflicts with black legislators, see correspondence between Williams and the governor in the Williams Papers; see also *Nashville Banner*, June 8, 1984. On the Tennessee Human Rights Commission's request that the legislature reconsider its vote on the King holiday, see the THRC minutes and newsletters, Mar. 23, 1984, TSLA.

For the April–May 1984 correspondence between Williams and Alexander, I consulted the Alexander Papers. The Williams Papers also contains copies of some letters. For Alexander's 1986 greetings to the NAACP ("I am proud . . ."), see the Alexander Papers.

A note on Avon Rollins, who compiled data on the TVA for the annual retreat: After retiring from TVA in 2003, he headed the Beck African American Cultural Center in Knoxville through 2004.

For Reagan's insinuations about Martin Luther King Jr. upon agreeing to sign the holiday bill, see O'Reilly, *Nixon's Piano*, 361.

Declines in black family income under Reagan were reported in *Chattanooga North Star* (formerly the *Chattanooga Chronicle*), July 31, 1982. For the NAACP's views on Reagan, see the Williams Papers. See also David W. Southern, *Gunnar Myrdal and Black-White Relations: Use and Abuse of An American Dilemma, 1944–1969* (Baton Rouge: Louisiana State Univ. Press, 1987), 302, 310.

For developments in Haywood County in the 1970s and '80s, see Couto, "Freedom's Expression, 1965–1990," chap. 7 of *Lifting the Veil*, 217-52. Clippings on Jean Carney's bid for office in Haywood County were also found in the Williams Papers.

My account of the *Lockert* court case and the racial gerrymandering of legislative districts was based on legal documents and attachments in the Williams Papers. *Note:* In November 2004, through a gracious gift of Avon N. Williams Jr.'s daughter Wendy Williams, the civil rights case files in her late father's law office were transferred to Tennessee State University.

The comments of Lindsey and Coe on labor and social conditions in Memphis were taken from Michael K. Honey, *Black Workers Remember: An Oral History of Segregation, Unionism and the Freedom Struggle* (Berkeley: Univ. of California Press, 1999), 261, 369.

Issues of the *TCHD Newsletter* from December 1967 through August 1974 informed my account of the Tennessee Commission on Human Development's activities, goals, and handling of discrimination complaints. I also consulted the commission's annual reports (available at the TSLA) through 2001.

For the involvement of the Tennessee chapter of the American Civil Liberties Union in housing cases, I consulted issues of its newsletter at the TSLA.

On the racial symbolism in George H. W. Bush's 1988 campaign, see O'Reilly, *Nixon's Piano*, 364, 392. See also Lanie Guinier, "Keeping the Faith: Black Voters in the Post-Reagan Era," *Harvard Civil Rights–Civil Liberties Review* 24 (Winter 1989): 393–435.

My account of the Clarence Thomas Supreme Court nomination drew on the following: Williams, *Thurgood Marshal*, 394; O'Reilly, *Nixon's Piano*, 395–99, 400, 405, 420; Jane Mayer and Doyle McManus, *Landslide: The Unmaking of the President, 1984–1988* (Boston: Houghton Mifflin, 1988); Kathleen Hall Jamieson, *Dirty Politics: Deception, Distraction, and Democracy* (New York: Oxford Univ. Press, 1992); and Steven A. Shull, *A Kinder, Gentler Racism? The Reagan-Bush Civil Rights Legacy* (Armonk, NY: M.E. Sharpe, 1993). For Berry's remarks, see *Black Issues in Higher Education* (Mar. 10, 1994): 12–16.

On events surrounding the Clinton inauguration (Jan. 1992), I relied on various newspaper accounts (*U.S.A. Today, Wall Street Journal, New York Times,* and *Nashville Tennessean*) as well as O'Reilly, *Nixon's Piano*, 401–23.

Biographical details on legislators in the 1990s were from editions of the *Tennessee Bluebook*.

For details on the Tennessee Supreme Court's efforts to combat racial discrimination, see Adolpho A. Birch, "Final Report of the Tennessee Supreme Court Commission on Racial and Ethnic Fairness" (Feb. 1997), which I accessed through links at the State of Tennessee Web site: http://www.Tennessee.gov/.

The NAACP conclusions on national trends are taken from *The Defender* (Spring 2003), 1–4. This is the newsletter of the NAACP Legal Defense and Educational Fund, Inc.

National figures on per capita income for 2000 came from the U.S. Census Bureau reports *Money Income in the U.S.: 2000* and *Poverty in the United States: 2000* (Washington, D.C.: Government Printing Office, 2001). For Tennessee, I consulted *An Economic Report to the Governor of the State of Tennessee on the State's Economic Outlook* (Nashville: State of Tennessee, 2002); and *Tennessee Statistical Abstract, 1996–1997* (Knoxville: Univ. of Tennessee, 1996).

For information on Harold Ford Jr., Michael Hooks, and Janet Perry Hooks, see *Accent* (Nov.–Dec. 2000), a TSU publication.

Vasco Smith's perspective was drawn from clippings about him on file in the Memphis–Shelby County Room, Memphis Public Library; my conversation with him in Memphis, Mar. 6, 2002; and the *Memphis Commercial-Appeal*, Feb. 8 and Mar. 7, 1994, and Dec. 26, 2001.

My summary of politics and demographics in Nashville during the 1990s drew on local news coverage, including the *Tennessean* and the *Tennessee Tribune*; on U.S. Census figures for 2000; and the 2000 *Nashville City Directory*.

Finally, a personal note about Mayor Herenton of Memphis: When I saw him speaking on *Brown* on May 27, 2004, at the National Civil Rights Museum in Memphis, he seemed as strong as ever. Although I am sure that criticism from his own people has hurt him, he did not appear to allow that to deter his dreams and goals in life and politics.

CHAPTER 10. DESEGREGATION OF HIGHER EDUCATION

On the background of higher education for Negroes in Tennessee during the nineteenth and early twentieth centuries, see Lovett, *African-American History of Nashville*, 144-73.

See Josephine McCann Posey, *Against Great Odds: The History of Alcorn State University* (Jackson: Univ. Press of Mississippi, 1994), 1-29; and Samuel H. Shannon, "Agricultural and Industrial Education at Tennessee State University During the Normal Years, 1912-1922," Ph.D. dissertation, George Peabody Teachers College, 1974, 1-49, for information on the Morrill Act and the schools it helped to create. The latter source was especially helpful for information on Tennessee.

The creation of Tennessee State Agricultural and Industrial College is discussed at length in Lovett, *African-American History of Nashville*, 167-70. Issues of the *Globe* (1909-13) and documents of the Tennessee Department of Education, 1874-94, RG 272, TSLA, were also helpful.

For the comments of the county magistrate ("the old slaves"), see *Nashville Banner*, Apr. 5, 1910.

The *Annual Report of the State Superintendent for Instruction* (1912) and *Senate Journal of Tennessee* (Nashville: State of Tennessee, 1913) provided information on appropriations to Tennessee schools.

J. C. Napier's December 1911 letter to President Taft is in his papers, held in Special Collections, Fisk Univ. For information about Tennessee A&I's initial receipt of philanthropic funds, I consulted records of the Commissioner of the Board of Education records, RG 92, TSLA. which also provided many other details about A&I and its presidents, as well as desegregation of public colleges and universities. Invaluable for information throughout this chapter were the State Board of Education records and minutes, RG 92 (boxes 148 and 150), RG 51 (Series XI, boxes 93-111, for Division of Negro Education), and RG 273 (boxes 131, 135, 136, 147, and 148), TSLA.

For information on the Southern Regional Education Board and Governor McCord's involvement with it, see McCord Papers, Governors' Papers, TSLA; and *Messages of the Governors* (Nashville: Tennessee Historical Society). For Churchwell's response, see *Nashville Commentator*, Jan. 1, 1949. The Williams Papers also contained various documents on which I based my account of the SREB arrangement and Meharry Medical College. For information and files on Will E. Turner, Robert E. Clay, and the Division of Negro Education, see SBOE records, RG 273 (boxes 26, 29, 101, 111, 136, 138-45, 147, 148, 150-152, 160, 167).

On the elevation of Tennessee A&I to university status in 1951 and on national trends in higher education for Negroes, see Antoine Garibaldi, *Black Colleges and Universities: Challenges for the Future* (Westport, CT: Praeger Publishers, 1984), 55; Julian B. Roebuck and Komanduri S. Murty, *Historically Black Colleges and Universities: Their Place in Higher Education* (Westport, CT: Praeger Publishers, 1993), 32-40; Henry N. Drewry and Humphrey Doermann, *Stand and Prosper: Private Black Colleges and Their Students*

(Princeton, NJ: Princeton Univ. Press, 2001), 1–123; and Joe M. Richardson, *A History of Fisk University, 1865–1946* (University: Univ. of Alabama Press, 1980), 134.

Articles in the Memphis papers and especially the *Oak Ridger* (Aug. 13, 1954) provided information on attempts by five Negro students to enroll at Memphis State University. On the resolution of the case that led to MSU's admission of Negroes, see *Memphis World*, July 15, 1959, and *Memphis Tri-State Defender*, July18, 1959. On how the students were treated after admission, see the *Tri-State Defender*, Sept. 19, 1959.

See Johnson, *Vanderbilt Divinity School*, 83, for details about Vanderbilt's admission of its first Negro graduate student. Details on desegregation of other schools were assembled from various accounts in Memphis and Knoxville newspapers, 1961–62, as well as documents in the State Board of Education records in the TSLA (see RG 273, box 148, files 22–24). Additional information came from West, *Tennessee Encyclopedia*, which contains brief histories of colleges and universities in the state. For the University of Chattanooga case, see the *Chattanooga Times*, Feb. 28, 1964.

Special Collections at the TSU Library contains documents on John S. Merritt and other coaches, including track coach E. S. Temple, who dealt with Jim Crow. See also Dwight Lewis and Susan Thomas, *A Will To Win* (Mt. Juliet, TN: Cumberland Press, 1983).

The Report on Integration of Higher Education at the University of Tennessee-Knoxville (Knoxville: Univ. of Tennessee/Tennessee Higher Education Commission, November 25, 1968) provided useful statistics for the mid-1960s.

For information on Walter S. Davis's efforts to increase appropriations for A&I, see the W. S. Davis file, 1943–68, Special Collections, TSU Library; RG 92 and RG 273, TSLA (for his correspondence with the State Board of Education); and RG 273, boxes 1–30, TSLA (for correspondence with Ellington). The Ellington Papers, 1959–63, and the Minutes of the Nashville Chamber of Commerce, both at TSLA, were also helpful. See also *Nashville Banner*, May 10 and 27, 1967, and *Nashville Tennessean*, May 10, June 9 and 10, 1967, for information on the audit and the response of the black community.

The developments that set the stage for the *Geier* case were reported in the *Nashville Banner*, Mar. 4, 1966, and *Nashville Tennessean*, Sept.13, 1966. My reconstruction of this case and the mounting controversy it generated relied on an extensive review of local news coverage and archival documents. The Desegregation Papers held in Special Collections, TSU Library, include various papers and documents on the case, and the papers of the specific TSU presidents (Davis, Torrence, Humphries, and Floyd) contain letters, court documents, and university responses to the *Geier* developments. I collected and filed *Geier* documents, including two boxes of files left behind by the UT Nashville administration at TSU's downtown campus. Moreover, the case and its developments were well reported in the *Tennessean* and the *Banner*, as well as local African American newspapers throughout the 1970s. Some of the information on Rita Sanders-Geier came from notes I took at her appearance at a TSU forum in 2001. Further background was reported in the *Nashville Tennessean*, Jan. 10, 2001, and issues of *Accent* for 2001 and 2002. The Federal Judicial Center Web site provided legal specifics and background on the judges; in addition, I consulted *Geier* briefs contained in the Desegregation Papers mentioned above, as well as *Geier* legal documents and correspondence in the Williams Papers. Correspondence on the case between THEC and the State Board of Education was found in RG 273, TSLA; the papers of Tennessee governors (particularly Ellington and Blanton), TSLA, were also reviewed. And as a TSU faculty member hired in 1973, I was present at Andrew Torrence's noonday speech in April 1974 when he announced his resignation from the TSU presidency.

Information on laws passed in Tennessee following the various campus protests came from annual volumes of *Public Acts of State of Tennessee*; see Chapter No. 223, May 8, 1969; Chapter No. 257, May 14, 1969; Chapter No. 479, Mar. 27, 1968; Chapter No. 2, Apr. 4, 1968; and Chapter No. 568, Apr. 4, 1968.

For parallel developments in Memphis involving Memphis State University and Shelby State Community College, Maxine Smith's branch NAACP reports from 1969 through 1977 were most useful. See also William Sorrells, *The Exciting Years: The Cecil C. Humphreys Presidency of Memphis State University, 1960–1972* (Memphis: MSU Press, 1987); and "University of Memphis," in *Tennessee Encyclopedia of History and Culture*, ed. West, 1009–10.

CHAPTER 11. DESEGREGATION OF HIGHER EDUCATION IN TENNESSEE CONTINUES

Much of the material for my continuing discussion of the *Geier* case came from two boxes of records and correspondence left at the former UT Nashville. Key letters and memoranda from that collection included the following: Peter Jordan to Faculty Senators, Dec. 15, 1977; R. S. Nicks to F. S. Humphries, Dec. 12, 1977; C. E. Smith to the Faculty and Staff, May 10, 1977; "Notice to UTN Students"; "Statement Which Can Be Read to Callers," Smith to Faculty, Staff, and Student Council, Oct. 10, 1977; and "Tentative Agenda for Desegregation Monitoring Committee," May 10, 1978.

For the legal specifics, I drew on court case documents such as *Rita Sanders-Geier, et al. v. Ray Blanton, et al.* and *University of Tennessee, et al., Peter Jordan et al.–Applicants for Intervention*, as well as reporting in the *Banner*, *Tennessean*, the *Meter*, and *Nashville Globe*. For particulars of Avon Williams's involvement in the case, I relied on numerous letters and legal documents contained in his papers. The Humphries Papers, TSU, and the L. R. Blanton Papers and Lamar Alexander Papers, both part of the Governors' Papers, TSLA, aided me in reconstructing the positions of the TSU president and the Tennessee governors, respectively.

For Clarence B. Robinson's remarks on behalf of the black caucus ("It may be that they do not know . . ."), I consulted his correspondence, C. B. Robinson Papers. The studies that Sterlin Adams edited at Williams's behest ("Tennessee Planning for Desegregation") are contained in the Williams Papers. Copies of the *Tennessee Desegregation Monitoring Report*, 1982, and other reports and correspondence by THEC and the Desegregation Monitoring Committee further informed my account and may be found in the Williams Papers and Humphries Papers.

The Desegregation Papers archived at TSU (Special Collections) were particularly helpful in understanding the positions of various advocates for Tennessee State University throughout the case, such as the deans' objections to the proposed Institute of Government and their comments on the poor desegregation records of other Tennessee schools. The statement by various concerned groups that a "historically black institution cannot be dismantled" was also found among these papers.

Humphries's remarks looking back on his tenure at TSU ("I went down . . .") are from "Reflections," in *Leadership and Learning: An Interpretive History of Historically Black*

Land-Grant Colleges and Universities (Washington, D.C.: Association of Land Grant Colleges and Universities, 1990): 115–20. This piece includes information about the Augusto Macedo letter and the ensuing controversy, including the "Caucus for Excellence" position paper. Macedo's letter is in the Humphries Papers. *Note:* Macedo graduated from TSU, earned a master's degree in the East, and completed law school before entering law practice in the District of Columbia area.

Much of the information about the furor surrounding Peterson's appointment came from reporting in the *Meter* and, especially, correspondence in the Williams Papers. *Note:* David Mills went to work for the legislative black caucus's Office of Minority Affairs and later ran for Congress.

A personal note regarding the McKissack architectural firm: I graduated from Booker T. Washington High School in Memphis with Harold Thompson, a principal partner in McKissack and Thompson Architects, and had many conversations with him during construction projects at Tennessee State University in the 1980s and 1990s. Thompson would join another group of architects, and the almost one-hundred-year-old McKissack firm would shut down its Nashville operations by century's end.

Correspondence and documents in the Williams Papers provided much of the basis for my account of what happened at TSU following Peterson's departure and Otis Floyd's interim appointment. A note on Michael Nettles, who wrote the report analyzing the *Geier* Stipulation of Settlement: He returned to the Educational Testing Service, Princeton, New Jersey, as head of a research unit in late 2003, and I was fortunate to meet and chat with him there.

For information on the 1990 student protests at TSU, see the *Nashville Tennessean*, Feb. 28, 1990. Jeff G. Carr revisited the 1990s protests in a speech for the Martin Luther King Day young people's rally in Nashville on January 19, 2005. I attended the Jefferson Street gathering and took notes on Carr's exceptional speech, in which he said, "We were forced to live on a campus that looked like a ghetto simply because of the color of our skin. What you see today is the result of the action [that students and others took to bring about radical change]."

The Desegregation Papers provided many of the documents on which I based my account of developments at TSU through the 1990s, including the *Eighteenth Annual Report of Progress* and efforts of the legislative black caucus. The caucus's annual retreat reports for 1990 and 1999 (available through the Office of Minority Affairs) were also valuable, as were *Geier* court case documents.

For details of the 2000 settlement (including UT President Wade Gilley's comments) and events afterward, see the *Nashville Tennessean*, see Dec. 23 and 24, 2000; Jan. 2 and 4, 2001; and Jan. 5, 2002. See also Faculty Senate Minutes, Sept. 19, 2002, TSU; and *Accent*, which published President James Hefner's outline of the final *Geier* settlement. In addition, I drew on notes I took at Rita Sanders-Geier's appearance at a TSU forum in 2001.

For details on the black law school that opened in 1957 (and soon closed its doors), see the *Nashville Globe*, July 5, 1957.

The Tennessee budgetary figures and college enrollment statistics I provide came from *Tennessee Fiscal Year, 2000–2001, Budget* (Nashville: State Government, Jan. 31, 2000); and *Chronicle of Higher Education*, Aug. 31, 2000, and Nov. 30, 2000. The information about TSU scientists came from 2000 issues of *Accent*.

The statistics on HCBUs came from the U.S. Department of Education via links at its Web site (http://www.ed.gov/).

For the editorial I quote, see "Where Have all the Black Professors Gone?" *University Faculty Voice* (April 2002); an article, "HBCUs Losing Black Faculty," appears in the same issue. For other facts and perspectives, see *The State of the Black Economy, 21st Annual Legislative Retreat and Training Conference, Moving Forward with Determination and Dedication, November 16–19, 1995, Gatlinburg* (Chattanooga: Tennessee Valley Authority, Economic Development Office; Legislative Office of Minority Affairs, 1995); *Higher Education Uniting to Serve Tennesseans: A Strategic Master Plan for 1996–2000* (Nashville: Tennessee Higher Education Commission, 2000); and "The Deleterious Impact of Dr. Hoppe's Administration at APSU on African-American Faculty, Administrators and Staff," *Tennessee Tribune*, June 11–17, 2002.

For the quotation near the end of this chapter ("In many states, negotiators . . ."), see Sara Hebel, "Desegregation Lawsuits Wind Down, but to What Effect?" *The Chronicle of Higher Education* (April 12, 2002): A28.

CHAPTER 12. THE CONCLUSION

I attended—and took notes on—both Harry Belafonte's appearance at Meharry Medical College in 2000 and the "Civil Rights Legacy" program at the Nashville Public Library in 2004. I also watched the taped telecast of the latter program on Nashville's Community Access Channel 3.

John Lewis's remarks on the passing of Avon Williams were reported in the *Nashville Tennessean*, Aug. 30, 1994.

For projected changes in the makeup of the U.S. population, I relied on U.S. Census Bureau 2000 reports and projections (available on the internet at http://www.census.gov/), esp. Table 1b, "Projected Population Change in the U.S. by Race and Hispanic Origin: 2000 to 2050"; see also specific Tennessee statistics. In the eyes of the U.S. Census Bureau, one must remember, "blacks" includes any persons of African origins and not just descendants of former American slaves. Hispanics seemed to be the largest minority by 2003, but Hispanics denoted a variety of ethnic groups of various skin colors, national origins, and cultural backgrounds grouped under the Spanish-language category. Indeed, since the 1890 census, white Census Bureau workers have been trying to conceptualize "race" and who really was "white," and whatever all that meant.

James Baldwin's comment about race ("As long as you think . . .") appeared in a 2004 Public Broadcasting System television special about his life.

Regarding the NAACP's efforts to combat racism into the twenty-first century and the continuing legacy of Brown, see *The Defender* (published by the LDF), Winter 2003, Spring 2003; *Crisis*, Jan./Feb. 2003; and "Brown v. Board of Education: The Contested Legacy of a Landmark Decision," *Chronicle of Higher Education*, Apr. 2, 2004, A-10.

For *USA Today* quotation, see Jan. 10, 2001 issue.

The quotation from James M. Lawson Jr. ("[R]acism is more . . .") was from a forum at the Civil Rights Collection, downtown Nashville Public Library, Sunday, February 15, 2004. I attended the session and took notes. Lafayette, Bevel, and Nash were also present at the forum.

For discussions of ethnic percentages relating to the 2000 elections, I consulted the *Wall Street Journal*, Mar. 3, 2001, and the *Nashville Tennessean*, May 1, 2004.

Black Enterprise Magazine, July 2001, provided information about the number of black mayors in American cities and about the rising black population in Georgia.

For the Gregory Rodriguez quotation ("A study by . . ."), see his article "Mongrel America," *The Atlantic Monthly* (Jan./Feb. 2003): 95–97.

The Carl T. Rowan quotation ("The so-called American melting pot . . .") is from *The Coming Race War in America: A Wake-Up Call* (Boston: Little, Brown, 1996), ix. The vicious letters received at Fisk and Meharry were reported in the *Nashville Tennessean*, Jan. 6, 2000.

The essays by Edley ("Foreword") and Omi ("The Changing Meaning of Race") appear in *America Becoming: Racial Trends and Their Consequences*, vol. 1, ed. Neil J. Smelser, William Julius Wilson, and Faith Mitchell (Washington, DC: National Academies Press, 2001). Available online at http://www.nap.edu/books/030906838X/html/.

SELECTED BIBLIOGRAPHY

BOOKS, DISSERTATIONS, ARTICLES, REPORTS, MICROFILM DOCUMENTS, AND ONLINE SOURCES

Adams, Frank, and Myles Horton. *Unearthing Seeds of Fire: The Idea of Highlander.* Charlotte, NC: John F. Blair, 1975.

Adams, Frank T. *James A. Dombrowski: An American Heretic, 1897–1983.* Knoxville: Univ. of Tennessee Press, 1992.

AFL-CIO. *Tent City: "Home of the Brave."* New York: AFL-CIO Industrial Union Dept., 1961.

Anderson, Jervis. *A. Philip Randolph: A Biographical Portrait.* Berkeley: Univ. of California Press, 1972.

———. *Bayard Rustin: Troubles I've Seen; A Biography.* New York: Harper Collins Publishers, 1997.

Anderson, Margaret. *The Children of the South.* New York: Farrar, Straus and Giroux, 1966.

Beifus, Joan Turner. *At the River I Stand.* Memphis: St. Luke's Press, 1986.

Beeler, Dorothy. "Race Riot in Columbia, Tennessee: February 25-27, 1946." *Tennessee Historical Quarterly* 39 (Spring 1980): 49–61.

Bergeron, Paul H., Stephen V. Ash, and Jeanette Keith. *Tennesseans and Their History.* Knoxville: Univ. of Tennessee Press, 1999.

Berman, William C. *The Politics of Civil Rights in the Truman Administration.* Columbus: Ohio State Univ. Press, 1970.

Biles, Roger. "Robert R. Church, Jr., of Memphis: Black Republican Leader in the Age of Democratic Ascendancy, 1928-1940." *Tennessee Historical Quarterly* 42 (Winter 1983): 378-82.

Blaustein, Albert P., and Robert L. Zangrando, eds. *Civil Rights and the Black American: A Documentary History.* New York: Simon and Schuster, 1968.

Branch, Taylor. *Parting the Waters: America in the King Years, 1954–63.* New York: Simon and Schuster, 1988.

———. *Pillar of Fire: America in the King Years, 1963–65.* New York: Simon and Schuster, 1998.

Brauer, Carl M. *John F. Kennedy and the Second Reconstruction.* New York: Columbia Univ. Press, 1977.

Brittain, David J. *A Case Study of the Problems of Racial Integration in the Clinton, Tennessee High School.* Ann Arbor, MI: University Microfilms, 1959.

Burke, Robert F. *The Eisenhower Administration and Black Civil Rights.* Knoxville: Univ. of Tennessee Press, 1984.

Campbell, Will D. *Forty Acres and a Goat: A Memoir.* Atlanta: Peachtree Publishers, 1986.

Carson, Clayborne. *In Struggle: SNCC and the Black Awakening of the 1960s.* Cambridge, MA: Harvard Univ. Press, 1981.

Cartwright, Joseph H. *The Triumph of Jim Crow: Tennessee Race Relations in the 1880s.* Knoxville: Univ. of Tennessee Press, 1976.

Conkin, Paul K. *Gone with the Ivy: A Biography of Vanderbilt University.* Knoxville: Univ. of Tennessee Press, 1985.

Corlew, Robert E. *Tennessee: A Short History.* 2nd edition. Knoxville: Univ. of Tennessee Press, 1981.

Cortner, Richard C. *The Apportionment Cases.* Knoxville: Univ. of Tennessee Press, 1970.

Couto, Richard A. *Lifting the Veil: A Political History of Struggles for Emancipation.* Knoxville: Univ. of Tennessee Press, 1993.

DeCosta-Willis, Mariam. *The Memphis Diary of Ida B. Wells: An Intimate Portrait of the Activist as a Young Woman.* Boston: Beacon Press, 1995.

Delaney, David. *Race, Place, and the Law, 1836–1948.* Austin: Univ. of Texas Press, 1998.

Dowdy, G. Wayne. "A Business Government by a Business Man: E. H. Crump as a Progressive Mayor," *Tennessee Historical Quarterly* 60 (Fall 2001): 162–75.

———. "E. H. Crump and the Mayors of Memphis," *West Tennessee Historical Society Papers* 53 (1999): 78–99.

———. "Expansion of the Crump Machine in Shelby County, 1928–1936," *West Tennessee Historical Society Papers* 56 (2002): 17–39.

Doyle, Don H. *Nashville Since the 1920s.* Knoxville: Univ. of Tennessee Press, 1985.

Doyle, William. *An American Insurrection: The Battle of Oxford, Mississippi, 1962.* New York: Doubleday Books, 2001.

Dudziak, Mary L. *Cold War Civil Rights: Race and the Image of American Democracy.* Princeton, NJ: Princeton Univ. Press, 2000.

Duster, Alfreda M., ed. *Crusader for Justice: The Autobiography of Ida B. Wells.* Chicago: Univ. of Chicago Press, 1970.

Egerton, John. *Speak Now Against the Day: The Generation before the Civil Rights Movement in the South.* 1994. Reprint, Chapel Hill: Univ. of North Carolina Press, 1995.

FBI Files on Thurgood Marshall, Roy Wilkins, A. Philip Randolph, Highlander Folk School, NAACP, W. E. B. DuBois, Paul Robeson, SNCC, and Martin Luther King Assassination. Wilmington, DE: Scholarly Resources, 2002. Microfilm.

Federal Judiciary Center Web site. http://www.fjc.gov/. This source provided profiles of the federal judges in this book, as well as actual texts of landmark civil rights cases.

Findlay, James F., Jr. *Church People in the Struggle: The National Council of Churches and the Black Freedom Movement, 1950–1970.* New York: Oxford Univ. Press, 1993.

Fleming, Cynthia G. "White Lunch Counters and Black Consciousness: The Story of the Knoxville Sit-Ins." *Tennessee Historical Quarterly* 49 (Spring 1990): 40–52.

Franklin, John Hope, and A. A. Moss Jr. *From Slavery to Freedom: A History of Negro Americans.* 6th edition. New York: Alfred A. Knopf, 1988.

Garrow, David J. *The FBI and Martin Luther King, Jr.* New York: Penguin Books, 1983.

Glen, John M. *Highlander: No Ordinary School.* 2nd edition. Knoxville: Univ. of Tennessee Press, 1996.

Govan, Gilbert E., and J. W. Livingood. *Chattanooga Country, 1540–1976.* Knoxville: Univ. of Tennessee Press, 1977.

Green, Ely. *Too Black, Too White.* Amherst: Univ. of Massachusetts Press, 1970.

Green, Laurie B. *Battling the Plantation Mentality: Consciousness, Culture, and the Politics of Race, Class and Gender in Memphis, 1940–1968.* Ann Arbor, MI: Xerox Microfilms, Inc., 1999.

Greenberg, Jack. *Crusaders in the Court: How a Dedicated Band of Lawyers Fought for the Civil Rights Revolution.* New York: HarperCollins, 1994.

Guterl, Matthew P. *The Color of Race in America, 1900–1940.* Cambridge, MA: Harvard Univ. Press, 2002. An informed discussion of race and the categorizing of people into two large groups: "black" and "white."

Halberstam, David. *The Children.* New York: Random House, 1998.

Hale, Grace E. *Making Whiteness: The Culture of Segregation in the South, 1890–1940.* New York: Pantheon, 1998.

Hamburger, Robert. *Our Portion of Hell, Fayette County, Tennessee: An Oral History of the Struggle for Civil Rights.* New York: Links Books, 1973.

Hassan, Ruby J. A. *Desegregation in Knoxville, Tennessee: A Case Study.* Ed.D. dissertation, Univ. of Tennessee, 1999. Ann Arbor: MI: University Microfilm, Inc.

Haynes, Arthur V. *Scars of Segregation: An Autobiography.* New York: Vantage Press, 1974.

Hill, Arthur C. "The History of Black People in Franklin County, Tennessee." Ph.D. dissertation, Univ. of Minnesota, 1981.

Hill, Robert A., ed. *Marcus Garvey and the Universal Improvement Association Papers.* 8 vols. Berkeley: Univ. of California Press, 1983–95. See especially volume 4, which includes Tennessee.

Hobson, Fred. *But Now I See: The White Southern Racial Conversion Narrative.* Baton Rouge: Louisiana State Univ. Press, 1999.

Honey, Michael K. *Southern Labor and Black Civil Rights: Organizing Memphis Workers.* Urbana: Univ. of Illinois Press, 1993.

——. *Black Workers Remember: An Oral History of Segregation, Unionism, and the Freedom Struggle.* Los Angeles: Univ. of California Press, 1999.

Horace, Sanders, L. Kent, and W. Ivan Mitchell. "Killing Jim Crow in 90 Days: The Nashville Sit-Ins." Unpublished graduate research presentation, Tennessee State Univ., 1998. Special Collections, TSU Library.

Horton, Aimee I. *The Highlander Folk School: A History of Its Major Programs, 1932–1961.* New York: Carlson Publishing, Inc., 1989.

Huebner, Timothy S., and Benjamin Houston. "Campus Community and Civil Rights: Remembering Memphis and Southwestern in 1968," *Tennessee Historical Quarterly* 58 (Spring 1999): 70–87.

Hughes, Langston. *Fight for Freedom: The Story of the NAACP.* New York: W. W. Norton, 1962.

Hunt, Frankie C. *A History of Desegregation of the Fayette County School System: Fayette County, Tennessee, 1954–1980.* Ed.D. dissertation, Univ. of Mississippi, 1981. Ann Arbor, MI: University Microfilm, Inc.

Hutchins, Fred L. *What Happened in Memphis.* Memphis: Privately published, 1965.

Jakoubek, Robert E. *Walter White and the Power of Organized Protest.* Brookfield, CT.: Millbrook Press, 1994.

Jarmon, Laura C. *Arbors to Bricks: A Hundred Years of African American Education in Rutherford County, Tennessee, 1865–1965.* Murfreesboro, TN: Middle Tennessee State Univ. Division of Continuing Studies, 1994.

Johnson, Dale A., ed. *Vanderbilt Divinity School: Education, Contest, and Change.* Nashville: Vanderbilt Univ. Press, 2001. See chapter on the "James Lawson Affair."

Judges of the United States. Published under the auspices of the Bicentennial Committee of the Judicial Conference of the United States. 2nd ed. Washington, D.C.: Government Printing Office, 1983.

Kelly, Alfred H., and Winfred A. Harbison. *The American Constitution: Its Origins and Development.* New York: W.W. Norton & Company, 1970.

Kotlowski, Dean J. *Nixon's Civil Rights: Politics, Principle, and Policy.* Cambridge: Harvard Univ. Press, 2001.

Kirby, John B. *Black Americans in the Roosevelt Era: Liberalism and Race.* Knoxville: Univ. of Tennessee Press, 1981.

Krueger, Thomas A. *And Promises to Keep: The Southern Conference For Human Welfare, 1938–1948.* Nashville: Vanderbilt Univ. Press, 1967.

Lamon, Lester C. *Black Tennesseans, 1900–1930.* Knoxville: Univ. of Tennessee Press, 1977. A brief summary of African American history in Tennessee for the average reader.

Lawson, Steven F. *Black Ballots: Voting Rights in the South, 1944–1969.* New York: Columbia Univ. Press, 1976.

Lawson, Steven F., and C. Payne. *Debating the Civil Rights Movement, 1945–1968.* New York: Rowman and Littlefield, 1998. See this volume for various documents: "Excerpt from *To Secure These Rights*" (1947); "Declaration of Constitutional Principles: The Southern Manifesto" (1956); "Excerpts from Hearings before the United States Commission on Civil Rights" (1958); "The FBI and Martin Luther King, Jr." (1963); and messages by Presidents Kennedy and Johnson.

Lewis, John. *Walking with the Wind: A Memoir of the Movement.* New York: Simon and Schuster, 1989.

Lovett, Bobby L. *The African American History of Nashville, Tennessee, 1780–1930: Elites and Dilemmas.* Fayetteville: Univ. of Arkansas Press, 1999. All of the background information about early Afro-Nashville was taken from this book.

Manis, Andrew M. *A Fire You Can't Put Out: The Civil Rights Life of Birmingham's Reverend Fred Shuttlesworth.* Tuscaloosa, AL: Univ. of Alabama Press, 1999. This book was used to reconstruct the sections on Reverend Shuttlesworth and Birmingham.

Meier, August, and Elliott Rudwick. *CORE: A Study in the Civil Rights Movement, 1942–1968.* New York: Oxford Univ. Press, 1973.

Melton, Gloria. "Blacks in Memphis, 1920–1955: A Historical Study." Ph.D. dissertation, Washington State Univ., 1982.

Miller, William D. *Mr. Crump of Memphis.* Baton Rouge: Louisiana State Univ. Press, 1964.

Mooney, Chase C. *Slavery in Tennessee.* Bloomington: Indiana Univ. Press, 1957.

Morton, Dorothy R. *Fayette County.* Memphis: Memphis State Univ. Press, 1989.

Muse, Benjamin. *Memphis: Report for the Southern Regional Council.* Atlanta: Southern Regional Council, 1964.

Murray, Pauli, ed. *States' Laws on Race and Color.* Cincinnati: The Methodist Church, 1952.

Newman, Mark. *Getting Right with God: Southern Baptists and Desegregation, 1945–1995.* Tuscaloosa: Univ. of Alabama Press, 2001.

Nieman, Donald G. *Promises to Keep: African Americans and the Constitutional Order, 1776–Present.* New York: Oxford Univ. Press, 1991. This study was used to outline some of the most important civil rights cases.

Obion County Historical Society. *Obion County History.* Dallas, TX: Taylor Publishing Company, 1985. See chronology of events, including school desegregation.

Osborne, Willie P., Clara L. Osborne, and Luie Hargraves. *Contributions of Blacks to Hamblen County, 1796 to 1996.* Morristown, TN.: Progressive Business Association, 1995.

Patterson, James T. *Brown v. Board of Education: A Civil Rights Milestone and Its Troubled Legacy.* New York: Oxford Univ. Press, 2001.

Pfeffer, Paula F. *A. Philip Randolph, Pioneer of the Civil Rights Movement.* Baton Rouge: Louisiana State Univ. Press, 1990. This book was used to reconstruct Randolph's involvement in the general civil rights movement and activities in Tennessee.

Poinsett, Alex. *Walking with Presidents: Louis Martin and the Rise of Black Political Power.* New York: Rowman and Littlefield, 2000.

Pride, Richard A., and J. David Woodard. *The Burden of Busing: The Politics of Desegregation in Nashville, Tennessee.* Knoxville: Univ. of Tennessee, 1985.

Record, Wilson. *Race and Radicalism: The NAACP and the Communist Party in Conflict.* Ithaca, NY: Cornell Univ. Press, 1964.

Robbins, Richard. *Sidelines Activist: Charles S. Johnson and the Struggle for Civil Rights.* Jackson: Univ. Press of Mississippi, 1996. This study was used to reconstruct the involvement of Johnson in the civil rights movement, particularly chapter 2.

Savage, Carter J. "Cultural Capital and African American Agency: The Economic Struggle for Effective Education for African Americans in Franklin, Tennessee, 1890–1967." *Journal of African American History* 87 (2002): 206–35.

Savage, M. Jordan, and Committee. *History of Black Education in Giles County, 1920–1970.* Pulaski, TN: Giles County Society for Homecoming '86 Celebration, 1986.

Sarvis, Will. "Leaders in the Court and Community: Z. Alexander Looby, Avon N. Williams, Jr., and the Legal Fight for Civil Rights in Tennessee, 1940–1970." *Journal of African American History* 88 (2003): 42–58.

Sit-In Nashville. New York: Folkways Records, 1960. A long-playing album of freedom songs by the students in the Nashville civil rights movement; includes an extensive essay.

Smelser, Neil J., William Julius Wilson, and Faith Mitchell, eds. *America Becoming: Racial Trends and Their Consequences.* 2 vols. Washington: National Academy Press, 2001. This study of the Commission on Behavioral and Social Sciences and Education of the National Research Council was supported by funding from the National Academy of Sciences and the National Science Foundation.

Sorrells, William. *The Exciting Years: The Cecil C. Humphreys Presidency of Memphis State University, 1960–1972.* Memphis: Memphis State Univ. Press, 1987.

Sosna, Morton. *In Search of the Silent South: Southern Liberals and the Race Issue.* New York: Columbia Univ. Press, 1977.

Spaeth, Harold J. *The Warren Court: Cases and Commentary.* San Francisco: Chandler Publishing, Co., 1966. This book precisely defines the civil rights cases.

Stanfield, J. Edwin. *In Memphis: More Than a Garbage Strike.* Memphis: Southern Regional Council, 1968.

Stuart, Reginald. *Black Perspectives on State-Controlled Higher Education: The Tennessee Report.* New York: John Hay Whitney Foundation, 1973.

Sumner, David E. "The Local Press and the Nashville Student Movement, 1960," Ph.D. dissertation, Univ. of Tennessee, 1960.

Taylor, Alrutheus A. *The Negro in Tennessee, 1865–1880.* 1941. Reprint, Spartanburg, SC: Reprint Company, Publishers, 1974.

Theoharis, J. Althan. *J. Edgar Hoover, Sex, and Crime.* New York: Rowman and Littlefield, 2002.

Tucker, David. *Memphis Since Crump: Bossism, Blacks, and Civil Reformers, 1948–1968.* Knoxville: Univ. of Tennessee Press, 1980. This book was quite helpful on the subject.

Tushnet, Mark V. *Making Civil Rights Law: Thurgood Marshall and the Supreme Court, 1936–1961.* New York: Oxford Univ. Press, 1994.

U.S. Commission on Civil Rights. *Hearings Before the United States Commission on Civil Rights, Memphis, Tennessee, June 25–26, 1962.* Washington: Government Printing Office, 1963.

U.S. Commission on Civil Rights. *Fear Runs Deep: Open Meeting, March 17–18, 1971, Somerville, Tennessee.* Washington: Government Printing Office, 1971.

Waller, Robert L. "Equality or Inequality: A Comparative Study of Segregated Public Education in Memphis, Tennessee, 1862 to 1954." Ph.D. dissertation, Western Colorado Univ., 1974.

Weisbrot, Robert. *Freedom Bound: A History of America's Civil Rights Movement.* New York: Penguin Books, 1991.

Wickham, DeWayne. *Bill Clinton and Black America.* New York: Ballantine Books, 2002.

Wilkins, Roy. *Standing Fast: The Autobiography of Roy Wilkins.* New York: Viking Press, 1982.

Williams, John A. *The King God Didn't Save: Reflections on the Life and Death of Martin Luther King, Jr.* New York: Coward-McCann, Inc., 1970.

Wilson, John B. *Chattanooga's Story.* Chattanooga: J. B. Wilson, 1980. See small section on school integration.

Wright, William E. *Memphis Politics: A Study in Racial Bloc Voting.* New York: McGraw-Hill, 1962.

Wynn, Linda T. "The Dawning of the Day: The Nashville Sit-Ins, February 13–May 10, 1960," *Tennessee Historical Quarterly* 50 (Spring 1991): 42–54.

——. "Toward A Perfect Democracy: The Struggle of African Americans in Fayette County, Tennessee, to fulfill the Unfulfilled Right of the Franchise," *Tennessee Historical Quarterly* 55 (Fall 1996): 202–23.

Young, Andrew. *An Easy Burden: The Civil Rights Movement and the Transformation of America*. New York: HarperCollins Publishers, 1996.

Zagumny, Lisa L. "Sit-Ins in Knoxville, Tennessee: A Case Study of Political Rhetoric." *Journal of Negro History* 86 (Winter 2002): 45-54.

CONVERSATIONS WITH THE AUTHOR

The interviews have not been transcribed and remain as the author's rough notes, which are stored in his papers at Tennessee State University.

Julian Blackshear, Nashville, Tennessee, March 27, 2002.

Calvin Calhoun, Nashville, Tennessee, March 29, 2001.

Bobby Lynn Cain, Nashville, Tennessee, April 19, 2002.

Harriet H. Davidson, Nashville, Tennessee, March 22, 2001.

Wayne Dowdy, Memphis, May 28, 2004.

John Harris, LeMoyne College, Memphis, March 5, 2002.

Renard Hirsch and Joyce Simms, Nashville, Tennessee, July 31, 2002.

Milton Kennerly, Nashville, Tennessee, March 8, 2001.

Grace Kyle (speaking for Rev. Dwight Kyle), Los Angeles, California, via telephone, March 22, 2001.

Kwame Lillard, Nashville, Tennessee, September 24, 2002.

Vasco Smith, Memphis, Tennessee, March 2002.

Jamye C. and McDonald Williams, Nashville, Tennessee, March 10, 2001.

SPECIAL COLLECTIONS, MANUSCRIPTS, AND PAPERS

First Baptist Church Capitol Hill, 900 James Robertson Parkway, Nashville
Records and Minutes. The most valuable document in this collection is the telephone logbook for the Freedom Rides. Public access is not normally granted except through the archivist.

Fisk University, Special Collections, Nashville
Z. Alexander Looby Papers. Includes a few boxes of letters, memorabilia, and news clippings.

Charles S. Johnson Papers. I used information in these papers mainly in reference to J. C. Napier and William Edmondson, and to gain additional insight into Johnson's positions on the movement.

James C. Napier Papers. These papers are not extensive but do provide basic information and correspondence.

Library of Congress, Washington, D.C.
The NAACP Papers. Consisting of 8,114 manuscript containers and approximately 5,000,000 items (minutes, affidavits, and other materials), the papers of the National Association for the Advancement of Colored People (1909-2000) constitute perhaps the largest collection in the Library of Congress. Important documents are also held at the NAACP headquarters, Baltimore, Maryland.

Memphis Public Library, Poplar Avenue, Memphis–Shelby County Room
George W. Lee Collection. Includes pictures, letters, papers, newspaper clippings, and memorabilia. Boxes 1, 3, and 6 were useful for information on W. C.

Handy, Robert R. Church, Richard M. Nixon, Jackie Robinson, and newspaper articles.

Selma S. Lewis Papers. Contains notes and draft manuscripts of *A Biblical People in the Bible Belt: The Jewish Community of Memphis, Tennessee, 1890s–1960s*, published by Mercer University Press, 1999.

Maxine A. Smith Collection. Contains branch NAACP reports, awards, and photographs (e.g., Smith, Lawson, Middlebrook, and others in the March 1962 downtown march). This collection also includes a file on Vasco Smith.

Metropolitan Nashville–Davidson County Archives

The *Banner* Room at the archives in Green Hills contains many photographs. Also, specific clipping folders saved me from having to go through numerous reels of microfilm. Often the clippings are filed under the specific name of a Nashville mayor.

Metropolitan Public Schools, Nashville–Davidson County.

I collected many documents while serving on the task force to develop the 1979–82 desegregation plan. Other documents were collected from the various committees I served on for local public education, 1979–present.

Tennessee State Library and Archives, Nashville

Lucius E. Burch Diaries and Papers, 1921–1959. These documents were useful in reconstructing the views of a white liberal in Memphis.

Nashville Chamber of Commerce, Minutes of the Board of Governors, microfilm.

Papers of the Governors: James Nance McCord, Gordon Browning, Frank G. Clement, Buford Ellington, Ray Blanton and Lamar Alexander. As noted elsewhere, the missing 1959–62 files for Ellington are most puzzling.

Tennessee Commissioner of the Board of Education Records, 1913–1970, RG 92; Tennessee Department of Education Records, 1873–1978, RG 51; State Board of Education Records and Minutes 1874–1984, RG 273. These sets of records were especially used to detail the sit-in demonstrations and the *Geier* story related to Tennessee State University. Record Group 92 contains the most extensive files, including "Plans for Desegregation—Special Files" and the "Governor on Desegregation" (microfilm).

Senate and House Journals, Tennessee General Assembly. These large bound volumes were used to check legislation and other political matters. In particular, during the early years, 1909–1920, each state department included detailed annual reports in these volumes including, for instance, the reports for Tennessee State Normal School.

Tennessee State University, Brown Daniels Library, Special Collections, Nashville

Desegregation Files. These files, along with related documents in the TSLA and published reports by state agencies and the legislative black caucus, provided much of the detail for the chapters on the *Geier* case.

Papers of the Presidents: W. J. Hale, W. S. Davis, A. P. Torrence, and F. S. Humphries.

Clarence B. Robinson Papers. These papers contain letters, documents, photographs, legislative reports, fraternity reports, and a wealth of information about Robinson as a politician and a civic leader.

Walter C. Robinson Papers. These papers contain letters, documents, and some copies of Robinson's *Chattanooga Observer*.

Avon N. Williams Jr. Papers. Consisting of letters, documents, brochures, clippings, awards, and other items, these papers were particularly useful in my chapters dealing with politics because the late senator saved all bills, correspondence between himself and the governors and other leaders, newsletters, and black caucus materials. He also gave me access to a copy of his typescript memoirs, thinking that I might write more about his life's story. I abandoned that idea after discussing the matter with one of his children, who might, one day, write such a biography.

University of Memphis, Brister Library

Robert R. Church Papers. The register for these papers aided me in putting together the Memphis story (especially as it related to E. H. Crump) with greater accuracy than secondary sources provided. In particular, the work on Church convinced me to bring some detail to the account of the Negro's pre-*Brown* struggle in Memphis.

Vanderbilt Univ. Library, Special Collections, Nashville

Kelly Miller Smith Papers. The register is quite helpful, and some boxes contain the minutes of the Nashville Christian Leadership Council, the NCLC's few published newsletters, and a file on the Freedom Rides.

James G. Stahlman Papers. These papers contain much correspondence. Box V-19, file 22, on "The Lawson Affair" and boxes IV-9, IV-25 and V-3, were especially useful.

NEWSPAPERS

Newspapers for Tennessee are available in the extensive collection of the Tennessee State Library and Archives in Nashville. The papers are filed by city name and include available African American newspapers. The Tennessee State University library contains issues of the student newspaper, the *Meter* (1951–present), and a more recent official university publication called *Accent*. TSU Special Collections also has the copies of the *Broadcaster* (1927–1965), the official publication of the Tennessee Negro Teachers Association, and copies of the *Bulletin* (1912–1950), the university's early newsletter. Below is a list of state newspapers I consulted.

Brownsville States-Graphic
Capitol Hill Defender
Chattanooga Free Press
Chattanooga Labor World
Chattanooga News–Free Press
Chattanooga North Star
Chattanooga Observer
Chattanooga Times

Clinton Courier-News
Columbia Daily Herald
East Tennessee News
Ebony Gazette
Fayette County Falcon
Jackson Sun
Johnson City Tribune
Kingsport Times
Knoxville Journal
Knoxville News-Sentinel
Lewisburg Tribune
Maryville-Alcoa Daily Times
Memphis Commercial Appeal
Memphis Press-Scimitar
Memphis Tri-State Defender
Memphis World
Morristown Citizen-Tribune
Nashville Banner
Nashville Defender
Nashville Commentator
Nashville Globe
Nashville News-Star
Nashville Sun
Nashville Tennessean
Nashville World
National Baptist Union Review
Oak Ridger
Pulaski Citizen
Shelbyville Times-Gazette
Tennessee Tribune
Union City Daily Messenger

INDEX

(1963), 69; *McSwain v. Anderson* (1950), 32; *Memphis v. et al. v. Greene* (1981), 323-24; *Michaels et al. v. Witham et al.* (UT) 1942), 340; *Monell v. New York City* (1978), 303; *Monroe v. City of Jackson* (1968), 81, 314; *Morgan v. Virginia* (1946), 159; *Nashville I-40 Steering Committee v. Ellington* (1967), 214; *Northcross v. Memphis* (1962), 93; *Peterson v. Greenville* (1963), 180; *Plessy v. Ferguson* (1896), 333, 336, 337, 341; *Redmond v. O. W. Human* (UT) (1937), 3-4; *Robinson v. Chattanooga* (1941), 9-11, 417; *Sheff v. O'Neill* (2003), 405; *Shelley v. Kraemer* (1948), 23; *Sloan v. Wilson County* (1961, 158); *Swann v. Charlotte M.* (1971), 90; *Tennessee v. Highlander* (1959), 135-36; *U.S. v. Fordice* (1993), 396; *Watson v. Memphis* (1963), 191, 198; *Williams v. Mississippi* (1898), 234
Sweatt, Ephraim, 158
Sweatt, Harold, 351
Swinger, L. O., xxv
Sykes, Thomas, 232

T

Taft, William H., 235, 239, 453
Talladega College, 367
Tate, John C., 31
Taylor, James I., 293, 449
Taylor, Preston, 338
Taylor, Robert L., 9, 32, 42-43, 45, 48-49, 54-55, 60-61, 103, 418
Taylor, Truly Mae, 3, 17
Teachers Association, 9, 11, 22, 57, 98, 244, 371, 373
Tennesseans for Justice in Higher Education (THJE), 315, 362, 365, 367, 421
Tennessee Commission Human Relations (TCHR), 211, 307, 321, 323
Tennessee Federation for Constitutional Government (TFCG), 38, 41, 153, 305
Tennessee Higher Education Commission (THEC), 88, 313, 343, 349, 352, 357, 372, 398, 454, 457

Tennessee League of Women Voters, 7, 13, 469
Tennessee National Guards, 46, 158, 226
Tennessee Society to Maintain Segregation, 65
Tennessee State University, ix, xi, xii, xiv, 40, 54, 76, 98, 100, 101, 119, 122, 125-27; Freedom Rides; 134, 157, 161-62, 172, 174, 179, 203-11, 228; Geier, 335-402; 415, 421, 441, 442, 444, 447, 448, 453, 455, 456, 461, 465
Tennessee Valley Authority (TVA), 7-8, 15, 236, 445
Tennessee Voters Council, 295-96, 305-6, 289
Terrell, Mary Church, xxi
Thomas, Clarence, 326-27, 333, 452
Thomas, Darrell, 190
Thomas, Henry, 160
Thomas, Harold E., 12, 13, 417, 425
Thornton, James B., 170
Thornton, Matthew, Sr., 257, 280
Tipton County, 232
Tobey, Frank, 113
Torrence, Andrew P., vii, 351-53, 355-60, 363-65, 454-55, 466
Totten, Ezra, 6
Totten, Audrey L., 22
Towles, Shepherd, 277
Towns, Joe, 328, 331
Thurman, Howard, 120
Thurmond, Strom, 205, 222, 252-54, 256, 418
Traughber, C. M., 306
Trevecca College, 347
Truitt, Dorothy, 190
Truman, Harry S., 21, 23-24, 25, 39, 47, 48, 248, 251-54, 333, 417, 446, 459
Turner, Georgia Mae, 278
Turner, Jessie H., Sr., viii, 62-63, 80, 85, 115, 188, 189, 191-97, 216, 265, 279-80, 287, 300, 312, 346-47, 361, 420, 435, 451; Turner Jr., 312
Turner, Larry, 308, 309, 310, 331
Turner, Maynard P., 164
Turner, Paul, 47-50